Religion

and the

Antebellum Debate

over Slavery

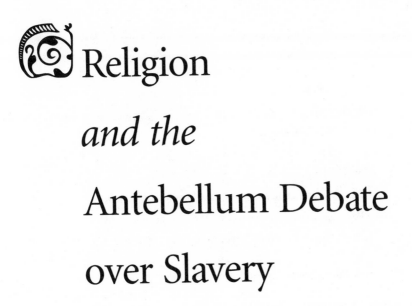

Religion

and the

Antebellum Debate

over Slavery

Edited by John R. McKivigan & Mitchell Snay

The University of Georgia Press · Athens and London

© 1998 by the University of Georgia Press

Athens, Georgia 30602

All rights reserved

Designed by Kathi Morgan

Set in Minion by G & S Typesetters

Printed and bound by Maple-Vail

The paper in this book meets the guidelines for permanence
and durability of the Committee on Production Guidelines
for Book Longevity of the Council on Library Resources.

Printed in the United States of America

02 01 00 99 98 C 5 4 3 2 1

02 01 00 99 98 P 5 4 3 2 1

Library of Congress Cataloging in Publication Data

Religion and the antebellum debate over slavery / edited by John R.
   McKivigan & Mitchell Snay.
        p.   cm.
   Includes bibliographical references and index.
      ISBN 0-8203-1972-4 (alk. paper). — ISBN 0-8203-2076-5 (pbk. :
   alk. paper)
      1. Slavery and the church—United States—History—19th century.
   2. Slavery—United States—History—19th century.   I. McKivigan,
   John R., 1949– .   II. Snay, Mitchell.
   E449.R35   1998
   261.8′34567′0973—dc21   98-21073

British Library Cataloging in Publication Data available

For our sons,

Jeb Barnes-McKivigan and Elliott Abraham Snay

CONTENTS

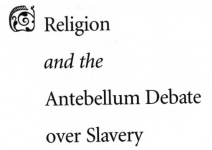 Religion

and the

Antebellum Debate

over Slavery

Religion and the Problem of Slavery

in Antebellum America

JOHN R. McKIVIGAN AND MITCHELL SNAY

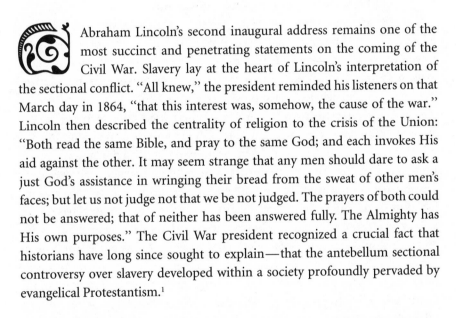

Abraham Lincoln's second inaugural address remains one of the most succinct and penetrating statements on the coming of the Civil War. Slavery lay at the heart of Lincoln's interpretation of the sectional conflict. "All knew," the president reminded his listeners on that March day in 1864, "that this interest was, somehow, the cause of the war." Lincoln then described the centrality of religion to the crisis of the Union: "Both read the same Bible, and pray to the same God; and each invokes His aid against the other. It may seem strange that any men should dare to ask a just God's assistance in wringing their bread from the sweat of other men's faces; but let us not judge not that we be not judged. The prayers of both could not be answered; that of neither has been answered fully. The Almighty has His own purposes." The Civil War president recognized a crucial fact that historians have long since sought to explain—that the antebellum sectional controversy over slavery developed within a society profoundly pervaded by evangelical Protestantism.[1]

Participants in the debate over slavery were keenly aware of the complicity of the church in promoting sectional tensions. Southern churchmen maintained that the antislavery movement was given vital support by northern ministers and their congregations. In 1836, the Methodist *Virginia Conference Sentinel* declared that abolitionism "derives its whole strength from the religious influence of the North." After Lincoln's election, the Presbyterian clergyman R. K. Porter of Waynesboro, Georgia, confirmed that northern ministers have "contributed so largely to bringing about the melancholy condition in which our country . . . is now placed." Northern abolitionists similarly recognized the close connection between religion and the slavery controversy. James Gillespie Birney, former slaveholder and the 1840 presidential candidate for the antislavery Liberty Party, compiled *American Churches the Bulwarks of American Slavery,* a fully documented demonstration of the proslavery stance of the southern churches. Radical abolitionist Stephen S. Foster was even more virulent in his denunciation of the church, both in the North and in the South. He boldly stated that ecclesiastical institutions were "the apologists and supporters of the most atrocious system of oppression and wrong, beneath which humanity has ever groaned," and he accused southern clergymen of "perpetuating slavery for the purpose of supplying themselves with concubines from among its hapless victims." Anticipating future historians, adversaries in the slavery controversy thus recognized the power of religion in inflaming sectional passions.[2]

The importance of religion in the slavery controversy was also acknowledged by the first historians of the Civil War. As the victors, northerners portrayed the war as a higher moral struggle against the evils of slavery. Henry Wilson, former Radical Republican senator from Massachusetts, popularized the image of a malevolent slave power in *Rise and Fall of the Slave Power in America.* He directed his wrath at the southern clergy for their support of slavery: "With few exceptions, they failed as religious teachers of educating the people up to the standard of a scriptural morality, shirked the duties imposed upon them by the claims of patriotism, humanity, and religion, betrayed their sacred trust, and proved recreant alike to the claims of benevolence and the Word of God." Historians from the South, on the other hand, played down slavery as a cause of the war. Though largely a legal defense of states' rights and secession, Alexander H. Stephens's *Constitutional View of the War between the States* (1870) defended the morality of slavery on religious grounds. In a brief review of the biblical defense of slavery, the former vice president of the Confederacy insisted that by the standards of the Old and New Testaments, "the relation of master and slave, even in a much more abject condition than existed with us, is not founded in sin." In these first histories of the Civil War, persisting sectional passions shaped the presentation of the role of religion in the slavery controversy.[3]

The Nationalist historians writing at the end of the nineteenth century followed the general lines of interpretation set forth by northern apologists for the Civil War. James Ford Rhodes, in his multivolume *History of the United States from the Compromise of 1850,* placed the issue of slavery at the center of his explanation of the coming of the war. Though he tried to avoid placing personal and sectional blame, Rhodes firmly believed that the South was morally wrong in fighting for slavery. He was therefore critical of southern religious defenders of slavery. For Rhodes, there was "no question" that northern critics of slavery "had altogether the better of the argument" on the question of the biblical sanction of slavery. Closely echoing the sentiments of northern reformers themselves, Rhodes was confident that the spirit of Christianity was antislavery.[4]

After the turn of the century, the idea of an "irrepressible conflict" dominated the historical writing on the sectional conflict. Reflecting the Progressive emphasis on such impersonal factors as economic systems and social institutions as agents of historical change, Charles A. Beard argued that the Civil War arose from an irreconcilable conflict between two economic interests—an agrarian South and an industrializing North. The moral debate over slavery concerned Beard very little, and he therefore dismissed religion as a source of sectional strife. He did acknowledge that "most of the men and women prominent in the anti-slavery agitation were deeply religious and made constant use of the teachings of Jesus in their appeals for support." Nonetheless, he revealed his materialist historical understanding by hinting that antislavery was strongest where the material interests in slavery were weakest.[5]

In the 1930s and 1940s, revisionist historians challenged Beard's interpretation. Rejecting the notion that fundamental differences between the sections caused the Civil War, they argued instead that it was a "needless" context for which a blundering generation of irresponsible agitators in the North and in the South was responsible. Avery O. Craven, for example, blamed both abolitionists and southern fire-eaters for agitating the slavery issue and recklessly driving the nation down the road to disunion. In assuming the avoidability of the Civil War, these scholars presumed that the morality of slavery was simply not a sufficient cause for which to fight. While Craven conceded that religion animated early abolitionism, he underestimated the power of religion as sentiment in his general denunciation of sectional agitation.[6]

After World War II and especially during the 1960s, slavery reemerged as the central issue in Civil War historiography. The generation that had defeated Nazism and fascism saw in the American Civil War a righteous moral crusade to end the evil of slavery, a point that Arthur Schlesinger Jr. made explicit. Those historians who came of age in an era of civil rights agitation understandably were more sensitive to the significance of race in U.S. history and looked with more sympathy on the abolitionists' struggle for black freedom and equality. With this shift toward the centrality of slavery came a renewed interest in the ideological controversy over slavery and a new appreciation of the role of religion in that conflict. In recent decades, the centrality of evangelicalism in the coming of the Civil War has been elevated through three broadly defined yet distinct themes in U.S. historical writing.[7]

First, religion has received increased emphasis in the current scholarly attention to political culture. This began with what is known as the "ethnocultural" interpretation of nineteenth-century political history. Challenging the older Progressive emphasis on class conflict, a group of historians in the 1960s and 1970s argued that religious, ethnic, and cultural conflicts were the principal sources of political division in the antebellum United States.[8] Although it downplayed the importance of such national political issues as slavery in determining party affiliation, ethnocultural political histories nonetheless served to elevate the importance of religion in shaping the coming of the Civil War. Religious issues are now seen as paramount in the political realignment of the 1850s. Early in the decade, the growing antislavery sentiment among northern Whigs was a potent force in splitting the party along sectional lines. Around the same time, a new political party—the Know-Nothings—appeared. They owed their astonishingly rapid rise to the growing nativism that accompanied the influx of non-Protestant immigrants into the United States. When the Republican Party was forming between 1854 and 1856, party leaders actively courted the Know-Nothings. They skillfully, if uneasily, blended antislavery and nativism into a campaign rhetoric that railed against the twin evils of slavery and popery.[9]

While the findings and even existence of an ethnocultural interpretation have been challenged, the idea that deeply rooted conflicts over morality and religion generated the second party system has persisted among American historians. With allowance for significant regional and local variations, the general consensus seems to be that Whigs drew support from evangelical Protestants eager to enlist the power of the state in achieving their moral visions while their Democratic opponents were inclined to oppose state sponsored moral enterprises. Historians speak increasingly of an antebellum political universe sharply divided between conflicting moral world views. Daniel Walker Howe, for example, termed this dichotomous division a conflict between "ecumenicism" and "confessionalism," while Curtis D. Johnson separated white Protestants into "formalists" and "antiformalists." Indeed, historians seem even more willing to ascribe to evangelicalism a powerfully determinative role in creating and giving definition to the structure and culture of Jacksonian politics. In his comprehensive study of evangelicals and antebellum politics, Richard Carwardine argues that "evangelical Protestants were amongst the principal shapers of American political culture in the middle years of the nineteenth century." Carwardine and others show, for example, how the methods of revivalist preachers were borrowed by politicians in a new style of political campaigning. Renewed importance has also been given the Sabbatarian campaign of the 1820s. The efforts of evangelicals to stop the delivery of mail on Sundays helped democratize political culture and hence served as a "prelude" to the second party system.[10]

Beyond contributing an adversarial and moral cast to antebellum political culture, evangelical religion recast the social and cultural landscape of pre–Civil War America. The attempts by religious historians to understand the impact of religion on the larger social and cultural development of the United States has been a second avenue through which religion has informed our understanding of the coming of the Civil War. In particular, historians of antebellum America searched for links between the Second Great Awakening and the pattern of social change in the North before the Civil War. In his seminal study of revivalism in upstate New York, *The Burned-Over District* (1950), Whitney Cross showed how the interaction between evangelical religion and economic change initiated a series of reform movements designed to perfect U.S. society for the coming millennium. More recently, Paul Johnson and Mary Ryan have demonstrated the ways in which evangelical religion legitimated the new social relations of free-labor capitalism and helped cast the structure and gender conventions of the middle-class family. By demonstrating how evangelical Protestantism created a distinctive social order and set of values in the antebellum North, these and other studies have been crucial in explaining why the antislavery message had such a powerful resonance in the free states before the Civil War.[11]

Historians of the South have similarly argued that religion was instrumental in creating a distinctive sectional social order before the Civil War. Donald G. Mathews, in *Religion in the Old South* (1977), argued that evangelicalism "became in the view of many Christian theorists one of the distinguishing marks of what it meant to be a Southerner." Mathews was also one of the first historians to suggest that the reformist impulse inherent in evangelical religion did not lead inexorably to an opposition to slavery. Rather, he suggests how the tenets of evangelicalism, in a different social and cultural context, could be channeled into a slaveholding ethic for masters. Eugene D. Genovese and Elizabeth Fox-Genovese have argued more recently that religion helped to legitimate an organic and hierarchical conception of the social order and a particularistic approach to human relations that could justify the subordination of women and lower-class whites as well as slaves. Finally, historians of slavery have noted the power of religion in the lives of the millions of enslaved African Americans in the South. Appreciating the pertinence of biblical history to their own hopes of freedom, slaves chose those biblical themes that emphasized God's promised redemption of his chosen but enslaved people from bondage.[12]

Finally, religion's importance in the coming of the Civil War has been made strikingly manifest through studies of abolitionism. The important link between evangelical Protestantism and abolitionism was popularized most forcefully in Gilbert Barnes's *The Antislavery Impulse, 1830–1844* (1933). Barnes argued that evangelical religion in western New York was the initial impulse behind the emergence of abolitionism. Accordingly, Barnes shifted the historical spotlight from William Lloyd Garrison to Theodore Dwight Weld, whose embrace of abolitionism closely followed his conversion to evangelicalism. By charting the spread of antislavery sentiment in the Midwest, Barnes noted the importance of religion in bringing about the Civil War: "a religious impulse which began in the West of 1830, was translated for a time into antislavery organization, and then broadened into a sectional crusade against the South." Beginning in the 1960s, historians have helped to clarify the often complex and subtle intellectual affinities between evangelical religion and abolitionism. Armed with their belief that revelation was superior to reason and that all human beings were capable of salvation, evangelical abolitionists saw slavery as a sin that required immediate abolition. From the outset, they thus insured that the antebellum controversy over slavery would be debated in religious and moral terms.[13] As a powerful determinant of antebellum society and political culture and a defining element in the ideological controversy over slavery, religion remains an important element for any explanation of the coming of the Civil War. Our inquiry into the various ways in which religion shaped the sectional conflict must begin with explaining how, at a certain point in time, slavery became a compelling moral and religious problem that engaged the hearts and minds of the laity—both men and women—and clergymen of the North.

At the time of the rise of the modern abolitionist movement in the early 1830s, northern churches had just completed a significant recovery in strength and prestige. For a few years after the Revolution, the moral authority of the clergy and churches seemed seriously weakened by the social disruption caused by that conflict and by the popularity of the deistic beliefs of many of the Founding Fathers. Around the turn of the century, however, the revivalistic enthusiasm of the Second Great Awakening had restored waning church attendance and support for religion. During the period from 1800 to 1830, Methodist membership increased sevenfold, Baptist membership tripled, and Congregationalist membership doubled. In 1850, approximately one out of every seven or eight Americans was an official member of a denomination, and two or three times that number attended church with some regularity. According to the testimony of both contemporary observers and historians, the revitalized churches exerted significant influences over the individual, social, and even political and economic behavior of millions of Americans.[14]

Another important feature of mid–nineteenth century northern religion was its diversity. During these years, the impact of immigration and conflicting theological trends, such as evangelicalism and "liberal" rationalism, had made the United States into what one contemporary observer described as "a motley sampler of all church history."[15] Among other things, U.S. denominations differed on doctrinal questions concerning free will and individual conscience, on the amount of lay versus ecclesiastical control in church government, and in their ethnic and regional distributions of membership.[16]

Despite these considerable differences in theology, polity, and demographic makeup, northern churches shared a proslavery heritage. With the exception of only a few pietistic sects, such as the Society of Friends or the Quakers, northern churches in the colonial era had displayed a high degree of toleration toward the institution in both the North and the South.[17] In the aftermath of the Revolution, however, the wide acceptance of Enlightenment concepts regarding natural rights and human liberty led several denominations to incorporate condemnations of slaveholding in their disciplines. But this early burst of antislavery vigor in the churches barely lasted out the century, and few denominations actually enforced disciplinary actions against slave-owning members. What remained of church antislavery sentiment concentrated instead on such ameliorative programs as missionary work among the slaves and advocacy of colonization.[18]

The immediate emancipation movement therefore came into direct conflict with the toleration of slavery by the vast majority of churches. At the root of this confrontation were fundamental disagreements about the morality of slavery and the churches' proper role in the face of this institution. Heavily influenced by contemporary evangelical trends, immediate abolitionists considered slaveholding a sin from which true repentance required instant voluntary renunciation. Because they regarded slave-owning sinful, the abolitionists argued that the churches must subject the practice to the same disciplinary action as intemperance, adultery, theft, and other immoral practices. Opponents of slavery hoped that the slaveholders' consciences might be reached if threatened with the mortal odium of ejection from the religious community.[19] The abolitionists sought to persuade the churches to take an unqualified stand against slavery. Their opponents held contrary views in varying degrees that formed a kind of continuum.

An unabashedly proslavery faction defended slavery on scriptural grounds, claiming that both revealed and natural religion sanctioned slavery. In denominations in which evangelicalism's impact was weak, there was usually a conservative element that declared slavery a secular matter toward which religious bodies should remain neutral. Almost as conservative were northern church members who had personal objections to slavery but felt that the denominations should defer to southern churchgoers on this issue. Perhaps the largest group of northern churchgoers could be classified as antislavery moderates. This faction acknowledged slavery as an evil institution and believed that the churches should support gradualistic programs, such as colonization, and later, nonextensionism, to end it. These moderates, however, objected to the abolitionists' blanket attacks on the character of slaveholders and to their efforts to expel southerners from the churches.[20]

Both defenders of slavery and abolitionists believed it essential to prove that their cause was fully compatible with the basic sources of Christian faith, especially the Bible. But no matter how common their original ground, there was no reconciling their different ends. A striking number of prominent northern divines—including Nathan Lord, president of Dartmouth College, Moses Stuart, a professor at Andover Seminary, and John Henry Hopkins, Episcopal bishop of Vermont—joined southerners in finding slavery sanctioned by biblical teaching. The defenders of slavery relied particularly heavily on a literal interpretation of the Scriptures. These biblical scholars argued that Old Testament patriarchs practiced a system of servitude much akin to U.S. slavery. These friends of the South also pointed out that nowhere in the New Testament did Christ condemn the slavery of his era.[21]

Many church leaders who dismissed claims of divine sanction for slavery nevertheless rejected the abolitionists' contention that slaveholding was intrinsically sinful. One commonly expressed objection to the abolitionists' position held that slavery was a morally neutral institution that had to be judged according to the circumstances surrounding each individual case. This viewpoint conceded that the Bible contained no express condemnation of slavery but, at the same time, affirmed that slaveholding was bound by the same scriptural regulations that governed all relationships between people. Conservative church leaders acknowledged that slaveholding was often a source of sinful abuses, but they laid the blame to erring individuals, not to the system. These conservatives feared that if the church expelled slaveholders as sinners it would release them from all moral restraints and ameliorative influences.[22]

Even moderate antislavery church leaders dissented from the abolitionist description of slaveholding as an unqualified sin. These antislavery moderates contended that some slave owners could not be held morally accountable for their actions. One expression of this viewpoint acknowledged grounds on which slaveholders could escape the guilt attached to their position. For example, if an individual became an owner of slaves involuntarily, perhaps through inheritance, and found himself legally prohibited from manumitting them, he was not to be adjudged a sinner. Antislavery moderates sometimes claimed that a master who recognized the evil of slavery would be morally correct to delay freeing his slaves if circumstances made such an action detrimental to their welfare.[23]

Another subject of debate was the reformer's demand that the religious institutions cease all practices that lent moral forbearance to slavery. In particular, most denominational leaders rejected abolitionist proposals to bar slaveholders from church membership regardless of the Christian piety they evinced. Liturgical denominations, such as Roman Catholic and Episcopalian, refused to deny fellowship to slaveholders because the idea that individuals could be held responsible for the sins of other church members was contrary to their established doctrines. In many denominations, sweeping guidelines on acceptable moral behavior were opposed as infringements upon the local autonomy of lower judicatories. Even moderate antislavery church members argued that the slaveholders' consciences could be enlightened better inside the religious bodies than outside them.[24]

Other objections to the abolitionists' religious principles and goals related to more worldly considerations. Many church leaders hesitated to endorse any position on slavery that might drive away southern members. Such caution is attributable both to feelings of denominational pride and to fears that divisive public quarrels would jeopardize confidence in the church's moral leadership. Both popular revivalists and local ministers complained that preaching against slavery would interfere with their missionary and other purely religious work.[25]

A final major obstacle faced by abolitionists in the churches was the strong support given by their moderate rivals to more gradualistic antislavery programs. When abolitionism and proslaveryism began making their disruptive appeals, antislavery moderates deprecated both views as "ultraism" and professed to maintain the scripturally grounded, traditional position of the churches toward slavery.[26] Antislavery moderates placed greater confidence than did abolitionists in the reasonableness and Christian character of the slaveholder. Church leaders opposed to abolitionism rejected calls for immediate emancipation and favored more gradual programs, including compensation for masters, colonization, and apprenticeship periods to prepare slaves for the responsibilities of freedom.[27]

Analysis of the northern churches' response to this debate over slavery reveals that a number of sociocultural and institutional factors interacted with theological issues to erect complex barriers against the success of abolitionist efforts.[28] To a large extent, the acceptance of abolitionism by a particular religious body seems to be correlated with its position on certain broader theological issues. The degree to which evangelical doctrines affected a denomination generally determined its receptivity to abolitionist arguments. For example, the liturgical churches, such as those of Catholics and those of Episcopalians, and liberal churches, such as the Unitarians, all objected to one or more aspects of abolitionists' evangelically inspired claim that slaveholders were inherently sinners and that the churches had a moral obligation to purify their communions by expelling them.[29] But even a strong evangelical orientation was no guarantee of denominational adoption of abolitionist principles. The evangelical doctrine of human perfectionism popular in some denominations encouraged involvement in benevolent and reform movements, but in other denominations, including Methodism, it caused a more inward-directed striving for holiness.[30]

Theological attitudes governing the composition of church membership also seemed to correlate with a predisposition to move toward or away from abolitionism. The liturgical denominations with considerable tolerance for human imperfection generally rejected the abolitionist condemnation of the slaveholder as sinner. At the other extreme, religious bodies with a desire for a scrupulously purified communion of believers generally rejected abolitionist principles that would add new, nontheological tests of fitness from membership. Abolitionists fared best among denominations that struck a balance between a near-universal and a highly exclusive membership standard.

A denomination's tradition with regard to social activism had a discernable impact on its response to abolitionism. Episcopalians, New England Congregationalists, and Unitarians, with their status as established churches, were slow to shed their defensive attitude toward the existing social order. These denominations were cautious about taking any position on controversial issues that might jeopardize their links to the social and economic elites. Another category of churches disinclined toward social activism were small sects with pietistic traditions, such as the Quakers. These sects not only preferred to withdraw from worldly corruption but also discouraged their members from associating with nonmembers in any projects with religious overtones.[31]

Ecclesiastical structure also played an important role in the progress abolitionists made in different denominations. The decentralized structure of denominations, such as the Baptists, Congregationalists, and Unitarians, delegated to local jurisdictions the authority to determine standards for membership.[32] As a result, abolitionists were able to attract numerous converts on those churches but remained powerless to establish uniform antislavery practices in them. At the other extreme, Episcopalian, Roman Catholic, and other denominations where the clergy possessed all or nearly all authority, provided abolitionists no direct means to influence church practices. It was in denominations with a federated structure (e.g., the Presbyterians and Methodists) that the abolitionists were able to make greatest headway because once in control of a few local judicatories they could dispatch delegates and address petitions to higher authorities to demand the establishment of strict antislavery rules.[33]

Another aspect of church government that affected the abolitionists' campaign was the power of a denominational hierarchy to suppress antislavery debate within church councils. Roman Catholic and Episcopalian bishops forbade their clergy to participate in organized abolitionist activities. Methodist bishops lacked the same sweeping authority but persuaded local conferences to discipline or expel persistent antislavery agitators from the ranks of their preachers and lay moderators. Through its control over all editorial appointments, the Methodist General Conference also was able to keep abolitionist articles out of its large network of newspapers and periodicals. Even in denominations with substantial local independence, conservatives found means to discourage abolitionist agitation. In New England, Congregational ministerial associations tried but failed to bar itinerant abolitionist speakers from their pulpits. Among Baptists, abolitionist influence was curtailed by a systematic purging of antislavery agitators from all positions of influence in the denominational missionary and in publication societies.[34]

Southern influence likewise proved a conservative force in many churches. In denominational and interdenominational benevolent organizations, such as missionary or Bible societies, there was a reluctance even to consider abolitionist arguments because southerners were major financial patrons of those organizations. In addition, many northern clergymen had been educated with slave owners in colleges and seminaries and had taught or preached in the slave states at some point in their careers, and, as a result, they were disinclined to agree with blanket condemnations of their intimate acquaintances.[35]

The dedication of many northern church leaders to the existing political status quo caused them to resist abolitionism in religious councils. Bishop Beverly Waugh warned New England Methodists that the abolitionist agitation risked "the destruction of our beautiful and excellent form of civil and polit- ical government, after it has cost the labor, treasure, and blood of our fathers to establish it."[36] Antiabolitionist northern Baptists rejected condemnations of slaveholding because such a course could enflame political as well as reli- gious sectionalism; they argued that "as patriots, we must cherish religious union, as one of the strongest . . . of the bonds that hold together the Union of these States."[37]

Finally, southern influence was felt through the great economic power that slavery exerted over the entire nation. Many northern merchants, bankers, and cotton-mill investors had large financial interests in slavery. As major contributors to religious and benevolent institutions, these men used their influence to promote the status quo where slavery was concerned and thus to operate against antislavery programs that would reflect negatively on the character of their enterprises. The power of these prosouthern forces proved to be a major obstacle to antislavery advances in churches in urban, com- mercial, and manufacturing centers across the entire North.[38]

The strength and determination of the antiabolitionist opposition in the northern churches produced great friction in the abolitionist ranks and con- tributed to that movement's schism over tactics in 1840. While followers of William Lloyd Garrison denounced the churches as hopelessly corrupted by slavery and turned to more exclusively secular tactics, many other abolition- ists continued the campaign to reform northern religious institutions. This second abolitionist faction worked with well-organized denominational anti- slavery movements. Methodist, Baptist, and Presbyterian abolitionists lobbied their denominations to expel slaveholders. These movements had an impor- tant impact in fomenting the sectional schisms of the Methodist and Baptist churches in the mid-1840s and the New School Presbyterians in 1857. Even following those divisions, however, abolitionists complained that the northern church branches still tolerated slavery. As evidence, abolitionists noted that none of these denominations condemned slaveholding as sinful and that each retained thousands of border state slave owners in their fellowship.[39]

Besides campaigning inside the churches, abolitionists attempted to spread their antislavery principles through lobbying the nation's network of inter- denominational missionary and religious publication societies, including the American Bible Society, the American Tract Society, the American Sunday School Society, the American Board of Commissioners for Foreign Missions, and the American Home Missionary Society. Conservatives in these societies contended that benevolent institutions should remain neutral on any question not directly related to their evangelical mission. The abolitionists, however, argued that these societies helped to sustain slavery by accepting slaveholders as contributors, missionaries, agents, and officers. After a decade or more of fruitless petitioning these societies to refuse all association with slave owners, abolitionists, sometimes in the company of antislavery moderates, seceded and created their own religious benevolent institutions. Despite these efforts, most interdenominational religious bodies remained hospitable to slaveholders until the Civil War.[40]

Political antislavery activities beginning in the 1840s also had important influence on the abolitionist campaign in the churches. The men who founded the first abolitionist political vehicle, the Liberty Party, believed antislavery efforts in the political and religious spheres to be linked inseparably. The earliest antislavery politicians condemned slave-owning as a sin and endorsed nonfellowship with slaveholders. Even the moderate antislavery arguments of the later Free Soil and Republican Parties for nonextension encouraged northerners to view slavery as a morally unacceptable institution. As a result of their close connection, the political and ecclesiastical antislavery movements reinforced each other's growth in the 1840s and 1850s.[41]

Although most northern denominations still stopped short of adopting abolitionist principles and practices, there was evidence that abolitionist pressure increased antislavery sentiment in the northern churches during the 1840s and 1850s. Only the traditionally antislavery denominations (including the Quakers and Freewill Baptists and a few new "comeouter" sects founded by abolitionists) condemned all slaveholders as sinners and refused to share religious fellowship with them before the beginning of the Civil War.[42] The secession of southern members from the New School Presbyterian and Methodist Episcopal churches in the immediate prewar years effectively ended the fellowship of slaveholders, but these major churches still refrained from making any formal endorsement of abolitionism.[43] Although many Unitarians, Baptists, and Congregationalists strengthened their testimony against the evils of slavery, none of these denominations came up to abolitionist standards by severing all ties with slaveholders.[44] The liturgical denominations remained firm in their long-standing position that slavery was a morally neutral and exclusively secular question.[45] Despite considerable antislavery progress in many denominations, abolitionism remained a minority viewpoint in the northern church in 1860.

The coming of the Civil War broke down much of the northern churches' resistance to taking aggressive antislavery actions. The secession of the southern states led many denominations to acknowledge the moral corruption inherent in a slaveholding society. Wartime antisouthern sentiment even led the Methodist Episcopal Church to adopt a discipline barring slave owners from membership. After initial hesitation, most denominations responded to abolitionist entreaties to endorse emancipation. With the exception of liturgical denominations, northern churches lobbied the president and Congress during the war to put an end to slavery. Before the war's end, many northern church leaders also enlisted in abolitionist efforts to reinforce emancipation with freedmen's aid and anti–racial discrimination programs.[46]

Shortcomings in the churches' belated concern for the blacks became apparent within a decade of the Civil War's end. Many denominations had launched freedmen's aid efforts during the war. The strong desire for reunion with southern white church members, however, led these sectarian education and missionary projects to acquiesce in local segregation practices by the mid-1870s. Northern denominations similarly failed to follow up on wartime attempts to abolish their own racially discriminatory practices. Although the northern churches had contributed significantly to encouraging the federal government to emancipate the slaves, they proved greatly remiss in helping the blacks obtain the fullest measure of freedom.[47]

The northern churches' unwillingness to stand by the freedmen exposes the abolitionists' failure to convert the religious bodies into antislavery vehicles. Despite more than three decades of abolitionist lobbying, few denominations ever accepted the principles of the inherent sinfulness of slave owning and the equality of all races. While antislavery moderates gained control of many denominations, initiative for the strongest actions against slavery came from other sources. Several northern church groups ceased fellowship with slaveholders not by erecting strong antislavery disciplines but through the secession of southern proslavery militants. The northern churches' delay in endorsing emancipation until the start of the Civil War revealed more the acceptance of wartime antisouthern passions than of moral arguments for immediate abolition. Expediency rather than antislavery principles produced decisive action against slavery by the church leaders, just as it did by the politicians. Because of these fragile origins, the churches' commitment to the welfare of blacks proved no better able to weather the storms of Reconstruction than that of other northern institutions. Although the antislavery movement failed to make the northern churches into firm friends of the blacks, the ultimate responsibility for that failure rested with the churches and the northern public and not with the abolitionists.

When the abolitionists charged that slaveholding was a sin, they unwittingly drew southern ministers and churches into the sectional conflict. At each stage in the escalation of the sectional crisis between 1820 and 1860, religion played an instrumental role in the defense of slavery and in the growth of sectionalism in the antebellum South. Southern ministers endowed slavery with biblical sanction, legitimized the southern social order, exacerbated the growing estrangement between North and South, and finally sanctified secession. By the spring of 1861, Thomas R. R. Cobb of Georgia could legitimately state that the revolution for southern independence had "been accomplished mainly by the churches."[48]

Before the 1820s, southerner's religious attitudes toward their peculiar institution might best be characterized as ambivalent. Human bondage was an accepted form of coerced labor in the developing plantation societies of the colonial South. Religious opposition to slavery had first surfaced in the eighteenth century, though it was largely confined to the Quakers in Virginia, Maryland, and North Carolina. The "contagion of liberty" unleashed by the republican ideology of the American Revolution shattered the peace of mind of such southern intellectuals as Thomas Jefferson and led others in the upper South to manumit their slaves. By the early decades of the nineteenth century, colonization had become an accepted outlet for the continuing antislavery sentiment in the South. Yet coexisting with a questioning of slavery were significant statements and actions by the southern church in defense of slavery. Ministers of all denominations quickly learned that denominational acceptance and growth in the South would require acquiescence to slavery. Although antislavery sentiment lingered in selected pockets of the South, the religious turn toward proslavery was clearly evident by the 1820s. In the wake of the Denmark Vesey slave conspiracy in 1822, two Charleston clergymen wrote pamphlets that defended slavery as a positive good.[49]

It was in response to the rise of immediate abolitionism in the 1830s that an elaborate scriptural defense of slavery was fully articulated. The abolitionist contention that slaveholding was a sin forced southern clergymen to defend the morality of slavery. Based on the assumption that the Bible was God's word revealed and the sole standard of moral authority, proslavery ministers constructed an elaborate justification of slavery. From the Old Testament, they cited the passage from Genesis in which Noah cursed Ham, the father of Canaan, to show that God had inaugurated slavery. They further argued that God sanctioned slavery in the Mosaic law of the ancient Israelites and that the Old Testament prophets, such as Abraham, held slaves. Southern ministers also searched the New Testament for scriptural defenses of slavery. They insisted that nowhere had Christ or his disciples condemned the holding of slaves, and they pointed out that the apostles had received slaveholders into the church and spoke on the relative duties of master and slave. In the moral debate with northern abolitionists, the logic of proslavery Christianity seemed impregnable. "If the Divine Author sanctioned slavery," concluded a prominent Methodist journal, "it cannot be an absolute and universal evil—a moral wrong, per se." The biblical defense of slavery would remain a mainstay of the southern proslavery argument throughout the antebellum sectional conflict.[50]

Having established the rectitude of slavery, southern clergymen sought to further sanctify slavery. First, they created a slaveholding ethic to guide the conduct of masters toward their slaves. They reminded southern slaveholders that they were morally responsible for the physical and spiritual welfare of their bondmen and bondwomen. Secondly, they helped launch an evangelical crusade to bring the Gospel to the slave quarters. Though joined by Baptists and Presbyterians, the Methodists in the South were particularly active in establishing missions to the slaves. In 1829, Methodists in Mississippi began to explore the possibility of religious instruction to the slaves, while the Rev. William Capers helped found the Methodist Missionary Society in South Carolina. It is estimated that by the time of the Civil War, Methodist missionaries had brought the Gospel to more than twenty thousand slaves across the antebellum South.[51]

The sanctification of slavery was the religious contribution to the sectional conflict in the 1830s. Through the biblical justification of human bondage, the slaveholding ethic, and the religious mission to the slaves, southern clergymen had provided a firm moral foundation to the South's peculiar institution. During the 1840s, southern religion had entered the sectional controversy in a new and potentially more lethal way. During this decade of increasing sectional strife, the moral debate over slavery seeped into the institutional foundation of the U.S. church and fractured the leading national denominations along sectional lines.

Religious schism occurred first among the Presbyterians. Conflicts over theology, church constitutional law, and ecclesiastical policy had divided Presbyterians into Old School and New School factions. In a series of exscinding acts in 1837 and 1838, the orthodox Old School leaders had driven their more liberal New School brethren out of the Presbyterian General Assembly. Although this schism was primarily theological and ecclesiastical, slavery played an important role in the division of the Presbyterian church. To obtain the support of Old Schoolmen in the South, northern conservatives agreed to oppose any General Assembly action against slavery. The close association between New School theology and abolitionism strengthened the ties of southerners to the Old School faction. The separation of the Methodist church in 1844 was more clearly a sectional schism over slavery. The growing influence of abolitionism among northern Methodists led to a confrontation over slavery at the general conference of 1844. When Bishop James O. Andrew of Georgia was barred from the episcopacy because he was a slaveholder, outraged southern Methodists seceded from the general conference and in May 1845 established the Methodist Episcopal Church, South. That same year the Baptists also divided over slavery. Though the Baptists lacked the centralized church structure of the Methodists, they were united nationally through the Triennial Convention composed of the Foreign Mission Board and the American Baptist Home Missionary Society. When the mission boards refused to sanction slaveholders, southern Baptists gathered in Augusta, Georgia, to create the Southern Baptist Convention. By 1850 then, southern Baptists and Methodists—who constituted over two thirds of the churchgoing population—were worshiping in separate sectional churches.[52]

To observing southerners, the denominational schisms had ominous political ramifications. "Let the three great religious denominations," warned an Alabama Baptist, "the Presbyterians, the Methodist and the Baptist, declare off from union of effort to do good, North and South, and our glorious union of States will be greatly weakened, if not sundered entirely." A number of southern ministers and politicians insisted that the churches were a strong bond of national unity and that an ecclesiastical division could dangerously weaken the political bonds between the North and South. Against the backdrop of the debates over the annexation of Texas and the Wilmot Proviso in the 1840s, the denominational schisms took on increasing political significance. Southerners noted the parallels between exclusion from national denominational bodies and the threatened deprivation of their constitutional rights to take slaves into the western territories. In both the church and Congress, antislavery northerners had trampled on constitutional rights and insulted southern honor by insinuating the inherent inferiority of slaveholders.[53]

The 1850s was the critical decade in the transformation of southern sectionalism into southern nationalism. From the Compromise of 1850 to the Democratic convention of 1860, southerners grew increasingly aggressive in their defense of slavery and southern rights. Important economic and social changes in the late antebellum South associated with modernization aggravated sectional tensions. Increased prosperity from the rise in cotton production, commercial expansion, and an expanding state activism exacerbated political and class conflict among southern whites. In several vital ways, religion reflected this transformation of southern society and the growth of separatism and contributed toward the final dissolution of the Union.[54]

Proslavery thought was brought to full fruition in the heated crucible of the 1850s as southerners sought to expand and perpetuate slavery. There was agitation for the reopening of the African slave trade. Expansionists and filibusters sought additional slave territory in Cuba and Central America. Some proslavery writers—George Fitzhugh, for instance—dwelled on the evils of free labor society and celebrated slavery as a model for social relations. Southern churchmen in the 1850s shared this intensified commitment to the South's peculiar institution. The *Central Presbyterian* of Richmond, Virginia, for example, venerated slavery as "the most blessed and beautiful form of social government known; the only one that solves the problem, how rich and poor may dwell together; a beneficent patriarchate."[55]

The 1850s also witnessed a rise in cultural separatism in southern religion. The denominational schisms had made clear to southern churchmen that separate sectional institutions would be necessary in order to keep the South safe for slavery. In 1856, southern Methodists organized an "educational institute" for the purpose of providing textbooks that would inculcate southern values. The attempts to establish a distinctively sectional version of moral philosophy were another manifestation of the drive toward separatism. For decades, the standard textbook in college courses in both the North and South had been Francis Wayland's *Elements of Moral Science* (1835). Yet Wayland's antislavery leanings—however modest and cautious—and the general moral debate over slavery prompted southern clergymen to create an essentially proslavery version of moral philosophy. In 1859, R. H. Rivers of Alabama published his *Elements of Moral Philosophy,* which became a required text for aspiring Methodist ministers. Like other southern authors on the subject, Rivers vindicated slavery and espoused related sectional values.[56]

Religion was also instrumental in the political realignment of the 1850s that led to the coming of the Civil War. The growing antislavery and antisouthern sentiment among northern Whigs had essentially destroyed the Whig Party in the South by 1854. Throughout the nation, the Know-Nothings had quickly materialized as the political adversary of the Democratic Party. Though there was a small number of foreign immigrants in the antebellum South, the Know-Nothings were strong enough to mount campaigns against the Demo-

crats in every slave state in 1855. Linking Free Soilism to popery, they portrayed themselves as defenders of both Protestantism and southern rights.
Though the Know-Nothings declined as quickly as they rose, they left an in-
delible mark on the party politics of the 1850s and provide additional testimony to the shaping influence of religion in the sectional conflict.[57]

The election of the Republican Abraham Lincoln in 1860 triggered the secession of the seven states of the lower South and brought the antebellum
sectional crisis to its fateful climax. The southern church played a prominent
role in the secession crisis. Clergymen from various denominations proffered
their open and enthusiastic support for disunion. The pastor of the Christian
church in Jackson, Mississippi, traveled throughout the state with the state's
attorney general whipping up support for secession. Some clergymen, such as
James C. Furman and John Gill Landrum of South Carolina, served in their
state conventions that were called to debate secession. Denominational groups
and religious newspapers throughout the lower South joined in endorsing secession. On the several fast days held in the South during the winter of 1860 –
61, southern clergymen offered scriptural sanctification of secession. Skillfully
blending language and concepts from the Bible, evangelicalism, and U.S. civil
religion, they explained and justified separation from a decaying and corrupt
union. The result of these sermons was the articulation of a religious nationalism that would become more manifest in the Confederate South during the
Civil War.[58]

The essays in this collection have been arranged topically in four
separate sections. Part 1 examines the origins of the antebellum religious debate over slavery in the changing social and intellectual environment of late
eighteenth- and early nineteenth-century United States. Douglas Ambrose
argues that proslavery sentiment was fostered by the reaction of Virginia ministers to the social and political changes unleashed by the American Revolution. Seeking to counteract the egalitarian tendencies of both evangelical religion and republican politics, a majority of Virginia ministers endorsed an
organic and hierarchical social order that confirmed and legitimated paternalistic relations between white masters and black slaves. Robert Forbes traces
the ideological roots of religious antislavery in what he terms a transatlantic
"Evangelical Enlightenment." He suggests that Scottish Common Sense philosophy, diffused through the evolving academic discipline of moral philosophy, provided northerners with a powerful intellectual tool to demand that
their churches more stringently enforce the professions of antislavery that already existed.

The essays in part 2 emphasize the intrasectional divisions within both northern and southern religious communities. Christopher Owen uncovers an ambivalence toward slavery among Georgia Methodist ministers that challenges the traditional account of a militantly proslavery southern church. Their official policy of neutrality was both a principled and an expedient position that allowed these ministers to maintain their appeal to both nonslaveholding whites and slaves as well as to retain credentials with their Wesleyan brethren across the world. The lack of unity among northern clerics is manifest in Laura Mitchell's careful analysis of the most influential books, pamphlets, and sermons produced by northern ministers on both sides in the debate over the Fugitive Slave Law of 1850. Behind the use of biblical texts and principles, she argues, were conflicting assumptions about "community" and Christians' duties to their neighbors. Those ministers who supported the return of escaped slaves argued that the Constitution established a race-based community in which northerners possessed a religious as well as a civil obligation to return the property of their southern white neighbors. Antirendition ministers, in contrast, viewed the black fugitives as their immediate neighbors whom they were instructed by the Bible to love as oneself.

Part 3 attests to the difficulty of the "center" within the church as abolition and slavery became increasingly identified as religious issues. Elizabeth Varon shows how the moderate antislavery position of women colonizationists in Virginia became increasingly less popular after the Nat Turner Rebellion and the rise of immediate abolitionism. Assaulted by both opponents and defenders of slavery, colonization lost much of its credibility as a vehicle for women's religious benevolence. Deborah Van Broeckhoven explains how Francis Wayland struggled to reconcile the Baptists' historic pro-forma criticism of slavery's morality with the careful neutrality of many northern conservatives toward the institution and the increasing proslavery militancy of some of his southern brethren. Although Wayland retained fraternal ties with clergymen in the South and called for sectional reconciliation in the church, he could never endorse the proslavery arguments of such southern Baptists as James Fuller. Hugh Davis focuses on another non-abolitionist northern church leader, the New Haven clergymen Leonard Bacon. Bacon believed that the abolitionists were wrongheaded in their sweeping moral condemnations of all slaveholders and insisted instead that close cooperation with evangelical southerners in spreading the gospel would influence the latter to accept a voluntary incremental program of emancipation. Bacon's position helped mediate between conservatives, moderates, and abolitionists within the Congregational denomination. He actively countered the agitation of the immediatists while effectively checking conservative efforts to reject all discussion of slavery in the churches as a purely "political" question.

The collection's final section examines the causes and consequences of the denominational schisms. Chris Padgett argues that the fight over abolitionism was the solvent that unglued the Plan of Union between Congregationalists and Presbyterians on the Western Reserve of Ohio. Abolitionists in the region, encouraged by the Presbyterian schism of 1837 and the founding of reform-minded Oberlin College, helped push a growing number of Western Reserve congregations to sever their ties with the New School Presbyterians. Randy Sparks locates the sectional division of the Methodist and Baptist churches within disputes in Mississippi between evangelical traditionalists and modernists over the creation of church institutions (such as missionary societies) and the relative authority of laity and ministry. According to Sparks, the modernists emerged victorious from that struggle with a proslavery ideology that strengthened their ties with planters. By the end of the antebellum period, the strong identification of the modernists with the defense of slavery had enabled them to gain dominance in southern evangelical churches over their traditionalist rivals. Beth Barton Schweiger seeks to show how the denominational schisms resulted in a significant strengthening of religious bureaucracy and clerical participation in political life in late antebellum Virginia. Within more centralized and stronger denominational structures, Baptist and Methodist ministers identified more closely with denominational projects and committees and less with their local congregations. The image of the minister subtly shifted from local pastor to that of administrator and fundraiser on behalf of denominational causes.

The final two essays in part 4 examine the sectional consequences of the denominational schisms. Edward Crowther documents the growing sectionalization in the southern churches after the schisms. In the intensified climate of moral recrimination after 1845, for example, southern churchgoers rapidly lost their ability to distinguish between abolitionists and the more conservative northern majority. By 1860, the majority of southern church leaders, rather than tolerate the federal government passing into morally suspect hands, were prepared to let the nation's political bonds go the way of ecclesiastical ones. John McKivigan reassesses the traditional interpretation of the denominational schisms as harbingers of disunion by looking at the reaction of immediate abolitionists. Since the Baptists and Methodists in the 1830s had already rejected the abolitionist contention that slaveholding should be a bar to church membership, the debates that led directly to the schisms were between northern church leaders, at best cautiously antislavery, and southern radicals who sought uncompromising endorsements of the morality of slave-owning from the churches. Fearing further abolitionist defections from their congregations and societies, the northern antislavery moderates at last drew the line and rejected the southern demands.

Along with the topical arrangement of these four sections, the essays in this collection are also tied together by several connecting themes. First among these is the effort to "contextualize" the religious debates over slavery—to place the traditional issues of antislavery, proslavery, and church schism within broader patterns of religious, social, and cultural development. Sparks, for instance, locates the denominational schisms in the larger process of evangelical transformation from sect to denomination in Mississippi. Padgett insists that the controversy over abolitionist doctrines in the Western Reserve was part of a larger clash between two conflicting ecclesiastical cultures. Ambrose and Forbes look closely at the ways in which the problem of slavery was framed within the intellectual and social contours of an evolving evangelicalism in the early Republic. Varon offers the crucial paradigm of gender roles and relations as a context for understanding the fate of colonization in Virginia.

An emphasis on the "middle ground," a center of moderation within U.S. religious institutions in the debate over slavery, is a second unifying theme of this collection. The essays by Van Broekhoven and Davis examine how individual nonabolitionist church leaders in the North sought to mediate between abolitionist and conservative factions within their denominations. Owen shows that in the discussion over slavery among Georgia Methodists, "moderates," rather than proslavery extremists, prevailed. The notion of community described by Mitchell that underlay the response of prorendition ministers in the fugitive slave crisis was similar in tone and content to that of moderates North and South. Several of the essays highlight the problems of moderation in an age of extremism. Varon shows how Virginia evangelical women struggled to keep colonization a viable option as the sectional conflict became more polarized. McKivigan and Crowther offer compelling evidence on the demise of a middle ground of moderation and the polarization of opinion within northern and southern religious communities as the Civil War approached. The parallels between the fate of the religious moderates and the politics of sectionalism between 1846 and 1861 merit further investigation.

Finally, several essays in this vein confirm the significance of chronology in understanding the religious controversy over slavery. In several ways, they attest to the importance of the 1850s as a decade of change. The intensity of the debate over northern compliance with the fugitive slave law as depicted by

Mitchell testifies to the narrowing political straits of the 1850s. Van Broeck-hoven suggests that political events in this decade of impending crisis moved Wayland to become more actively antislavery. Particular nonsectional developments in the 1850s were also important for the religious response to the conflict over slavery. In northeastern Ohio, Padgett finds that doctrinally more orthodox Congregational associations were created in the 1850s that accelerated the trend toward division between Congregationalists and abolitionism. Schweiger points to the institutional growth and maturation of religious denominations in Virginia during the 1850s and explains the impact of the denominational schisms and the changing role of ministers in this chronological context.

From a variety of angles then, the essays collected here address the general problem of religion's role in the slavery controversy. Yet not all aspects of the story have been covered. The response to the sectional conflict by the nation's liturgical denominations, its many small, pietistic sects, or the non-Christian faiths has not been examined. More noteworthy, none of the essays directly address the question of religion and antislavery among African Americans in the North. The church contributed significantly to the efforts of black abolitionists. The African Methodist Episcopal Church barred slaveholders in 1816. Black ministers, such as Samuel D. Cornish, Henry Highland Garnet, and Samuel Ringgold Ward, were prominent leaders in the abolitionist crusade. Black churches across the North undermined slavery by shielding fugitive slaves from capture. Black Christians drew inspiration from the biblical story of the redemption of the children of Israel from the bonds of slavery. Indeed, the points of intersection between the institutional church, theology, and abolition within the African American community merits further investigation. Despite these omissions from this collection, the essays presented here nonetheless provide an unprecedentedly broad and nuanced analysis of the complex relationships of religion, slavery, and sectionalism. The often traumatic response of the nation's churches to the problem of slavery provides a valuable mirror in which scholars may observe the growing sectional crisis that led to secession and Civil War.[59]

NOTES

1. Don Fehrenbacher, ed., *Abraham Lincoln: A Documentary Portrait through His Speeches and Writings* (Stanford, Calif.: Stanford University Press, 1964), 277–78. For a brief description of the inauguration, see James G. Randall and Richard Current, *Lincoln the President: Last Full*

Measure (New York: Dodd, Mead, 1956), 341–44. The best essay on Lincoln's spirituality remains Edmund Wilson, *Patriotic Gore: Studies in the Literature of the American Civil War* (New York: Oxford University Press, 1962), chap. 3.

2. Quoted in Mitchell Snay, *Gospel of Disunion: Religion and Separatism in the Antebellum South* (New York: Cambridge University Press, 1993), 32, 157; James G. Birney, *American Churches the Bulwark of Slavery* (1842; reprint, New York: Arno Press, 1969); Stephen S. Foster, *The Brotherhood of Thieves* (1886; reprint, New York: Arno Press, 1969), 7, 9. See also William Goodell, *Slavery and Anti-Slavery; A History of the Great Struggle in Both Hemispheres; with a View of the Slavery Question in the United States* (New York: William Harned, 1852), especially 143–219.

3. Henry Wilson, *The History of the Rise and Fall of the Slave Power in America* (Boston: Houghton Mifflin, 1872), v, 63; Alexander H. Stephens, *A Constitutional View of the Late War between the States* (Philadelpha: National Publishing Company; Chicago: Zeigler, McCurdy, 1868–1870), 80. For other polemical histories by participants, see John A. Logan, *The Great Conspiracy: Its Origin and History* (New York: A. R. Hart, 1886) and Robert L. Dabney, *A Defence of Virginia, [And Through Her, of the South,] in Recent and Pending Contests against the Sectional Party* (1867; reprint, New York: Greenwood Press, 1969).

4. Thomas J. Pressly, *Americans Interpret Their Civil War* (Princeton: Princeton University Press, 1954), 173; James Ford Rhodes, *A History of the United States since the Compromise of 1850, vol. 1: 1850–1854* (New York: Harper & Brothers, 1896), 371–72.

5. Charles A. Beard, *The Rise of American Civilization* (New York: Macmillan, 1927), 699. His discussion of the antislavery movement can be found on pp. 693–703. Beard does acknowledge the use of religion in the proslavery argument on pp. 705–6. Richard Hofstader, in his classic study of Beard, briefly discusses his interpretation of the Civil War. See *The Progressive Historians: Turner, Beard, Parrington* (New York: Alfred A. Knopf, 1968), 302–4. See also Pressly, *Americans Interpret Their Civil War*, 238–49.

6. In general, see Avery O. Craven, *The Coming of the Civil War* (1942; 2d ed., Chicago: University of Chicago Press, 1957), 117–75; Gilbert Hobbs Barnes, *The Antislavery Impulse, 1830–1844* (1933; New York: Hartcourt, Brace, & World, 1964), xxiii.

7. See John S. Rosenberg, "Towards a New Civil War Revisionism," *American Scholar* 38 (spring 1969): 250–72, for an interesting discussion of post–World War II historiography. For a more recent statement of the centrality of religion in the Civil War era, see Eric Foner, ed., *The New American History* (Philadelphia: Temple University Press, 1990), 78.

8. Robert W. Fogel, *The Quest for the Moral Problem of Slavery: An Historiographic Odyssey*, 33d Annual Robert Fortenbaugh Memorial Lecture (Gettysburg, Pa.: Gettysburg College, 1994), 25; Eric Foner, *Politics and Ideology in the Age of the Civil War* (New York: Oxford University Press, 1980), 17. The early and important works in the ethnocultural school include Lee Benson, *The Concept of Jacksonian Democracy: New York as a Test Case* (Princeton: Princeton University Press, 1961); Ronald P. Formisano, *The Birth of Mass Political Parties: Michigan, 1827–1852* (Princeton: Princeton University Press, 1971); Michael F. Holt, *Forging a Majority: The Formation of the Republican Party in Pittsburgh, 1848–1860* (New Haven: Yale University Press, 1969).

For an interesting recent discussion, see Ronald Formisano, "The Invention of the Ethnocultural Interpretation," *American Historical Review* 99 (April 1994): 453–77.

9. This political realignment of the 1850s is conveniently summarized in Fogel, *The Quest for the Moral Problem of Slavery,* 27. Major interpretations include Michael F. Holt, *The Political Crisis of the 1850s* (New York: W. W. Norton, 1978), and William Gienapp, *The Origins of the Republican Party, 1852–1856* (New York: Oxford University Press, 1987). On nativism, see Ray Billington, *The Protestant Crusade, 1800–1860: A Study of the Origins of American Nativism* (1938; reprint, Chicago: Quadrangle Books, 1964), Michael Holt, "The Politics of Impatience: The Origins of Know Nothingism," *Journal of American History* 55 (September 1973): 309–31, and "The Antimasonic and Know-Nothing Parties," in Arthur M. Schlesinger Jr., ed., *History of U.S. Political Parties,* vol. 1 (New York: Chelsea House, 1973), and Tyler Anbinder, *Nativism and Slavery: The Northern Know-Nothings and the Politics of the 1850s* (New York: Oxford University Press, 1992).

10. See Daniel Walker Howe, "The Evangelical Movement and Political Culture in the North during the Second Party System," *Journal of American History* 77 (March 1991): 1216–39, and Curtis D. Johnson, *Redeeming America: Evangelicals and the Coming of the Civil War* (Chicago: Ivan R. Dee, 1993), ix; Richard R. John, "Taking Sabbatarianism Seriously: The Postal System, the Sabbath, and the Transformation of American Political Culture," *Journal of the Early Republic* 10 (winter 1990): 567. See also Bertram Wyatt-Brown, "Prelude to Abolitionism: Sabbatarian Politics and the Rise of the Second Party System," *Journal of American History* 58 (September 1971): 316–41.

11. Robert Fogel, *The Quest for the Moral Problem of Slavery,* 24; Whitney Cross, *The Burned-Over District: The Social and Intellectual History of Enthusiastic Religion in Western New York, 1800–1850* (Ithaca: Cornell University Press, 1950); Paul Johnson, *A Shopkeeper's Millennium: Society and Revivals in Rochester, New York, 1815–1837* (New York: Hill and Wang, 1978); Mary P. Ryan, *The Cradle of the Middle Class: The Family in Oneida County, New York, 1790–1865* (New York: Cambridge University Press, 1981). See also Nancy F. Cott, *The Bonds of Womanhood: "Women's Sphere" in New England, 1780–1835* (New Haven: Yale University Press, 1977), and William G. McLoughlin, *Revivals, Awakenings, and Reform: An Essay on Religion and Social Change in America, 1607–1977* (Chicago: University of Chicago Press, 1978).

12. Donald G. Mathews, *Religion in the Old South* (Chicago: University of Chicago Press, 1977), 246, Eugene D. Genovese and Elizabeth Fox-Genovese, "The Divine Sanction of Social Order: Religious Foundations of the Southern Slaveholders' World View," *Journal of the American Academy of Religion* 55 (summer 1987): 211–34, and "The Religious Ideals of Southern Slave Society," *Georgia Historical Quarterly* 70 (spring 1986): 2–16. For similar interpretations, see Stephanie McCurry, "The Twin Faces of Republicanism: Gender and Proslavery Politics in Antebellum South Carolina," *Journal of American History* 78 (March 1992): 1245–64, and Rachel N. Klein, *Unification of a Slave State: The Rise of the Planter Class in the South Carolina Backcountry, 1760–1808* (Chapel Hill: Published for the Institute of Early American History and Culture, Williamsburg, by the University of North Carolina Press, 1990), chap. 9, and Randy J. Sparks, *On Jordan's Stormy Bank: Evangelicalism in Mississippi, 1776–1877* (Athens: University of Geor-

gia Press, 1994). For further studies of religion and southern society, see Snay, *Gospel of Disunion,* 3, n5. On slave religion, see Albert J. Raboteau, *Slave Religion: The "Invisible Institution" in the Antebellum South* (New York: Oxford University Press, 1978).

13. Barnes, *The Antislavery Impulse, 1830–1844,* viii and xxxiii; Fogel, *The Quest for the Moral Problem of Slavery,* 9. Early but important articles include Anne C. Loveland, "Evangelicalism and 'Immediate Emancipation' in American Antislavery Thought," *Journal of Southern History* 32 (May 1966): 172–88, and David Brion Davis, "The Emergence of Immediatism in British and American Antislavery Thought," *Mississippi Valley Historical Review* 49 (September 1962): 209–30. Two books by David Brion Davis, *The Problem of Slavery in Western Culture* (Ithaca: Cornell University Press, 1966) and *The Problem of Slavery in the Age of Revolution* (Ithaca: Cornell University Press, 1975), were seminal in delineating the religious contours of the debate over slavery. Biographies demonstrating the religious impulse behind evangelicalism include Bertram Wyatt-Brown, *Lewis Tappan and the Evangelical War against Slavery* (Cleveland: Press of Case Western Reserve University, 1969), Robert Abzug, *Passionate Liberator: Theodore Dwight Weld and the Dilemma of Reform* (New York: Oxford University Press, 1980), and Hugh Davis, *Joshua Leavitt: Evangelical Abolitionist* (Baton Rouge: Louisiana State University Press, 1990). The most current conceptualization of the origins of abolitionism revolves around the problem of the simultaneous emergence of abolitionism and capitalism. See Thomas Bender, ed., *The Antislavery Debate: Capitalism and Abolitionism as a Problem in Historical Interpretation* (Berkeley: University of California Press, 1992).

14. Russell B. Nye, *The Cultural Life of the New Nation, 1776–1830* (New York: Harper & Row, 1960), 219; Edwin S. Gaustad, *Dissent in American Religion* (Chicago: University of Chicago Press, 1973), 152–53; Timothy L. Smith, *Revivalism and Social Reform: American Protestantism on the Eve of the Civil War* (New York: Harper & Row, 1965), 196–97; C. C. Goen, *Broken Churches, Broken Nation: Denominational Schisms and the Coming of the Civil War* (Macon, Ga.: Mercer University Press, 1985), 22–27, 48–57; Ralph A. Keller, "Northern Protestant Churches and the Fugitive Slave Law of 1850" (Ph.D. diss., University of Wisconsin, 1969), 33.

15. Philip Schaff, *America: A Study of Its Political, Social, and Religious Character* (1855; reprint, Cambridge, Mass.: Harvard University Press, Belknap Press, 1961), 80.

16. Smith, *Revivalism and Social Reform,* 188–91; Keller, "Churches and the Fugitive Slave Law," 113; Milton B. Powell, "The Abolitionist Controversy in the Methodist Episcopal Church, 1840–1864" (Ph.D. diss., University of Iowa, 1963), 95–97; Conrad J. Engelder, "The Churches and Slavery: A Study of the Attitudes toward Slavery of the Major Protestant Denominations" (Ph.D. diss., University of Michigan, 1964), 285–87.

17. David B. Davis, "Slavery and Sin: The Cultural Background," in *The Antislavery Vanguard: New Essays on the Abolitionists,* ed. Martin Duberman (Princeton, N.J.: Princeton University Press, 1965), 30–31; Lester B. Scherer, *Slavery and the Churches in Early America, 1619–1819* (Grand Rapids, Mich.: William B. Eerdmans, 1975), 155–56.

18. Carleton Mabee, *Black Freedom: The Nonviolent Abolitionists from 1830 through the Civil War* (London: Macmillan, 1970), 217–18; Merton L. Dillon, *The Abolitionists: The Growth of a Dissenting Minority* (DeKalb, Ill.: Northern Illinois University Press, 1974), 9–10; Cushing Strout, *The New Heavens and New Earth: Political Religion in America* (New York: Harper &

Row, 1974), 148; Hilary A. Herbert, *The Abolition Crusade and Its Consequences: Four Periods of American History* (New York: Scribner, 1912), 176; Goen, *Broken Churches, Broken Nation*, 79; Adelaide A. Lyons, "Religious Defense of Slavery in the North," *Trinity College Historical Society Papers* 13 (1919): 5; Engelder, "Churches and Slavery," 4, 11.

19. David B. Davis, "The Emergence of Immediatism in British and American Antislavery Thought," *Mississippi Valley Historical Review* 49 (September 1962): 224–28; Sydney E. Alstrom, *A Religious History of the American People* (New Haven, Conn.: Yale University Press, 1972), 145.

20. Hugh Davis, "At the Crossroads: Leonard Bacon, Antislavery Colonization, and the Abolitionists in the 1830s," in *The Moment of Decision: Biographical Essays on American Character and Regional Identity,* Randall M. Miller and John R. Miller, eds. (Westport, Conn.: Greenwood Press, 1994), 136–37; Clifton H. Johnson, "The American Missionary Association, 1846–1861: A Study of Christian Abolitionism" (Ph.D. diss., University of North Carolina, 1958), 11–12, 25–26, has influenced my thinking on these categories of attitudes toward slavery among members of the antebellum northern churches.

21. Nathan Lord, *A Letter of Inquiry to Ministers of the Gospel of All Denominations, on Slavery, By a Northern Presbyter,* 4th ed. (Hanover, N.H.: Dartmouth Press, 1860), 7; also Lord, *A Northern Presbyterian's Second Letter to Ministers of the Gospel of All Denominations on Slavery* (New York: D. Appleton, 1855), 37, 53–61; John H. Hopkins, *A Scriptural, Ecclesiastical, and Historical View of Slavery from the Days of the Patriarch Abraham to the Nineteenth Century* (New York: W. I. Pooley, 1864), 12–13; Richard M. Cameron, *Methodism and Society in Historical Perspective* (New York: Abingdon Press, 1961), 143; Arthur C. Cole, *The Irrepressible Conflict, 1850–1865* (New York: Macmillan, 1934), 256; Arthur Y. Lloyd, *The Slavery Controversy, 1831–1860* (Chapel Hill: University of North Carolina Press, 1939), 190–92; Donald G. Mathews, *Slavery and Methodism: A Chapter in American Morality, 1780–1845* (Princeton, N.J.: Princeton University Press, 1965), 228–29; Davis, *Problem of Slavery in the Age of Revolution,* 532; Larry Edward Tise, "The Interregional Appeal of Proslavery Thought: An Ideological Profile of the Antebellum American Clergy," *Plantation Society in the Americas* 1 (February 1979): 63–72; Lyons, "Religious Defense of Slavery," 17; Engelder, "Churches and Slavery," 30–32.

22. Joseph C. Stiles, *Speech of the Slavery Resolutions, Delivered in the General Assembly Which met in Detroit in May Last* (Washington, D.C.: Jonathan T. Towers, 1850), 7–10, 30–33; Thomas J. Taylor, *Essay on Slavery as Connected with the Moral and Providential Government of God and as an Element of Church Organization* (New York: privately printed, 1851), 268; George W. Blagden, *Remarks and a Discourse on Slavery* (Boston: Ticknor, Reed & Fields, 1854), 16; John Robinson, *The Testimony and Practice of the Presbyterian Church in Reference to American Slavery* (Cincinnati: John D. Thorpe, 1852), 86–87, 100–107; Cortlandt Van Rensselaer, *Presbyterian Views on Slaveholding: Letters and Rejoinders to George D. Armstrong* (Philadelphia: M. J. Milson, 1858), 6.

23. Charles Elliott, *Sinfulness of American Slavery,* 2 vols. (Cincinnati: L. Swormstedt and A. Poe, 1851), 1:21–22; A. C. Baldwin, "Friendly Letters to a Christian Slaveholder," and R. B. Thurston, "The Error and the Duty in Regard to Slavery," in *Liberty or Slavery,* 25–26 and 51–52, respectively.

24. Blagden, *Remarks . . . on Slavery,* 21–23; Robinson, *Testimony and Practice,* 173–74, 197,

214–15; James S. Lamar, *Memoirs of Isaac Errett,* 2 vols. (Cincinnati: Standard, 1893), 1:86–87, 217–18; Whitney R. Cross, *The Burned-Over District: The Social and Intellectual History of Enthusiastic Religion in Western New York* (New York: Harper & Row, 1950), 258–59; Johnson, "American Missionary Association," 12.

25. Sidney E. Morse, *The Bible and Slavery* (New York: n.p., 1855), 2; A. C. Dickerson, *Anti-Slavery Agitation in the Church Not Authorized* (Philadelphia: King and Baird, 1857), 61; Joshua R. Balme, *American States, Churches, and Slavery* (London: Hamilton, Adams, 1863), 259–61; David D. Addison, *The Clergy in American Life and Letters* (New York: Macmillan, 1900), 32–33; Arthur S. Hoyt, *The Pulpit and American Life* (New York: Macmillan, 1921), 255–56; John R. Bodo, *The Protestant Clergy and Public Issues, 1812–1848* (Princeton, N.J.: Princeton University Press, 1954), 138–39; Jane H. Pease and William H. Pease, *Bound with Them in Chains: A Biographical History of the Antislavery Movement* (Westport, Conn.: Greenwood Press, 1972), 12–13; Martin E. Marty, *Righteous Empire: The Protestant Experience in America* (New York: Dial Press, 1970), 58; James H. Moorhead, "Social Reform and the Divided Conscience of Antebellum Protestantism," *Church History* 48 (December 1979): 424–25; Keller, "Churches and the Fugitive Slave Law," 13–15; Powell, "Abolitionist Controversy," 72–73.

26. Robert Baird, *Religion in America; or, An Account of the Origin, Relation to the State, and Present Condition of the Evangelical Churches in the United States* (New York: Harper, 1845), 40–41, 337; also Van Rensselear, *Presbyterian Views,* 43; Taylor, *Essay on Slavery,* 268; Baldwin, "Friendly Letters," 73–74; Mathews, *Slavery and Methodism,* 228–29.

27. Jarius Burt, *The Law of Christian Rebuke: A Plea for Slave-Holders* (Hartford, Conn.: N. W. Goodrich, 1843), 16–17; George Duffield, *A Sermon on American Slavery: Its Nature and the Duties of Christians in Relation to It* (Detroit: J. S. & S. A. Bragg, 1840), 30; Nathan Bangs, *Emancipation: Its Necessity and Means of Accomplishment Calmly Submitted to the Citizens of the United States* (New York: Lane & Scott, 1849), 65–66; Williston, "American Slavery," 123–24; Thurston, "Error and Duty in Regard to Slavery," 30–33; Morse, *Bible and Slavery,* 1; Bangs, *Emancipation,* 14–17; Van Rensselear, *Presbyterian Views,* 18; Baldwin, "Friendly Letters," 94–97; Philip J. Staudenraus, *The African Colonization Movement, 1816–1865* (New York: Columbia University Press, 1961), 48–58; Friedman, *Gregarious Saints,* 14–25; Marsden, *Evangelical Mind,* 92; Engelder, "Churches and Slavery," 63–64.

28. Although the works cited above are of value in explaining the reaction of specific denominations toward abolitionist appeals, only a few studies have aimed at a comprehensive explanation of the patterns of response along the spectrum of northern religious bodies. Some of these exceptions are: Smith, *Revivalism and Social Reform,* 188–98; Engelder, "Churches and Slavery," 280–88; Evans, "Abolitionism in Illinois Churches," 120–33; and Friedman, "Historical Topics Sometimes Run Dry," 188–91.

29. Willis D. Weatherford, *American Churches and the Negro: An Historical Study from Early Days to the Present* (Boston: Christopher, 1957), 154–55, 163; Douglas C. Stange, *Patterns of Antislavery among American Unitarians, 1831–1860* (Rutherford, N.J.: Fairleigh Dickinson University Press, 1977), 177–79, 189–90; Engelder, "Churches and Slavery," 260–65.

30. Mathews, *Slavery and Methodism,* 129–30; Cameron, *Methodism and Society,* 161.

31. Thomas Drake, *Quakers and Slavery in America* (New Haven, Conn.: Yale University

Press, 1950), 171–72; Dwight L. Dumond, *Antislavery: The Crusade for Freedom in America* (Ann Arbor, Mich.: University of Michigan Press, 1961), 350–52; Robert W. Doherty, *The Hicksite Separation: A Sociological Analysis of Religious Schism in Early Nineteenth Century America* (New Brunswick, N.J.: Rutgers University Press, 1967), 28–29.

32. Goodell, *Slavery and Anti-Slavery*, 183; Engelder, "Churches and Slavery," 57–61.

33. Goen, *Broken Churches, Broken Nation*, 135.

34. *Anti-Slavery Record* 1 (January 1836): 6–7; New York *Emancipator*, January 19, 1837; American Anti-Slavery Society, *Fourth Annual Report . . . 1837* (New York, 1837), 64; Goen, *Broken Churches, Broken Nation*, 80–81; Cameron, *Methodism and Society*, 160–63; Mathews, *Slavery and Methodism*, 137; Henry H. Simms, "A Critical Analysis of Abolition Literature, 1830–40," *Journal of Southern History* 6 (August 1940): 376; Davis, "At the Crossroads," 145–46; Robert C. Senior, "New England Congregationalists and the Anti-Slavery Movement" (Ph.D. diss., Yale University, 1954), 89–94, 140, 289.

35. Griffin, *Their Brothers' Keepers*, 162–63, 177–80; Davis, "At the Crossroads," 138–39, 144–45.

36. Quoted in Goen, *Broken Churches, Broken Nation*, 80–81.

37. Ibid., 93; also Leonard L. Richards, *"Gentlemen of Property and Standing": Anti-Abolition Mobs in Jacksonian America* (New York: Oxford University Press, 1970), 145–49.

38. Goddell, *Slavery and Anti-Slavery*, 402–7; Richard, *"Gentlemen of Property and Standing,"* 136, 139, 141, 149, 151; Davis, "At the Crossroads," 141.

39. Boston *Liberator*, May 17, 1844, August 15, 1845; New York *True Wesleyan*, June 29, 1844; Foster, *Brotherhood of Thieves*, 52.

40. Clifford S. Griffin, "The Abolitionists and the Benevolent Societies, 1831–1861," *Journal of Negro History* 44 (May 1959): 195–216; Robert T. Lewit, "Indian Missions and Antislavery Sentiment: A Conflict of Evangelical and Humanitarian Ideals," *Mississippi Valley Historical Review* 50 (June 1963): 39–55; Davis, "At the Crossroads," 148; Johnson, "American Missionary Association," 41–42, 59–63, 74–96.

41. David B. Cheesebrough, *"No Sorrow like Our Sorrow": Northern Protestant Ministers and the Assassination of Lincoln* (Kent, Ohio: Kent State University Press, 1994), 92–93; James B. Stewart, *Holy Warriors: The Abolitionists and American Slavery* (New York: Hill & Wang, 1976), 97, 104–5; Richard H. Sewell, *Ballots for Freedom: Antislavery Politics in the United States, 1837–1860* (New York: Oxford University Press, 1976), 81–82, 95–96; Dillon, *The Abolitionists*, 141–44; Howard, *Religion and the Radical Republican Movement*, 3–21.

42. John R. McKivigan, "The Antislavery Comeouter Sects: An Overlooked Abolitionist Strategy," *Civil War History* 26 (June 1980): 142–61.

43. *American Missionary Magazine* 1 (October 1857): 222–23; Lucius C. Matlack, *The Antislavery Struggle and Triumph in the Methodist Episcopal Church* (New York: Phillips & Hunt, 1881), 310–22; William Gravely, *Gilbert Haven, American Abolitionist: A Study in Race, Religion, and Reform, 1850–1880* (Nashville, Tenn.: Abingdon Press, 1973), 57–59; Engelder, "Churches and Slavery," 154–62, 224–33.

44. American and Foreign Anti-Slavery Society, *Thirteenth Annual Report . . . 1853* (New York, 1853), 105–6; American Anti-Slavery Society, *Annual Report . . . 1859–60* (New York, 1860),

282–84; Samuel Joseph May, *Some Recollections of Our Anti-Slavery Conflict* (Boston: Fields, Osgood, 1869), 367–69; Chester F. Dunham, *The Attitude of the Northern Clergy toward the South, 1860–1865* (Toledo, Ohio: Gray, 1942), 33; Bertram Wyatt-Brown. *Lewis Tappan and the Evangelical War against Slavery* (Cleveland: Press of Case Western Reserve University, 1969), 319; Stange, *Patterns of Antislavery*, 137–41; Senior, "New England Congregationalists," 405–10.

45. Friedman, "Historical Topics Sometimes Run Dry," 188–89; Engelder, "Churches and Slavery," 260–63, 268–70; Robert Fortenbaugh, "American Lutheran Synods and Slavery, 1830–1860," *Journal of Religion* 13 (January 1933): 73–77, 86–91.

46. Boston *Liberator*, June 17, 1864; Chesebrough, *"No Sorrow like Our Sorrow,"* 95–101; Ralph Morrow, *Northern Methodism and Reconstruction* (East Lansing, Mich.: Michigan State University Press, 1956), 14–15; Moorhead, *American Apocalypse*, 97, 101–2, 180–81; Engelder, "Churches and Slavery," 87–88, 114–15, 234–35, 256, 274–76.

47. James M. McPherson, *The Abolitionist Legacy: From Reconstruction to the NAACP* (Princeton, N.J.: Princeton University Press, 1975), 143–60; Jones, *Sectional Crisis and Northern Methodism*, 285–90, 313; Murray, *Presbyterians and the Negro*, 170–77. For a contrary assessment of the northern clergy's role in aiding the freedmen during Reconstruction, see Howard, *Religion and the Radical Republican Movement*, 125–214.

48. Quoted in Snay, *Gospel of Disunion*, 152. Older but still valuable surveys of the South and the sectional conflict are Charles S. Sydnor, *The Development of Southern Sectionalism, 1819–1848* (Baton Rouge: Louisiana State University Press, 1934) and Avery O. Craven, *The Growth of Southern Nationalism, 1848–1861* (Baton Rouge: Louisiana State University Press, 1953). Important recent statements by William W. Freehling are *The Road to Disunion, vol. 1: Secessionists at Bay, 1776–1854* (New York: Oxford University Press, 1990) and *The Reintegration of American History: Slavery and the Civil War* (New York: Oxford University Press, 1994).

49. On sentiments for and against slavery before 1820, see Snay, *Gospel of Disunion*, 20–28. David Brion Davis, *The Problem of Slavery in Western Culture* and *The Problem of Slavery in an Age of Revolution* remain essential to understanding the intellectual origins of the slavery controversy. On the question of slavery during the Revolutionary era, see Bernard Bailyn, *The Ideological Origins of the American Revolution* (Cambridge: Harvard University Press, Belknap Press, 1965), 232–46 and Winthrop Jordan, *White over Black: American Attitudes Toward the Negro, 1550–1812* (1968; New York: W. W. Norton, 1977), and Sylvia Frey, *Water from the Rock: Black Resistance in a Revolutionary Age* (Princeton: Princeton University Press, 1991).

50. Snay, *Gospel of Disunion*, 54–59. Good examples of religious defenses of slavery include Richard Furman, *Rev. Dr. Richard Furman's Exposition of the Views of the Baptists, Relative to the Coloured Population in the United States in a Communication to the Governor of South Carolina* (1822; reprint, Charleston, S.C.: A. E. Miller, 1833), Samuel Dunwody, *A Sermon Upon the Subject of Slavery* (Columbia, S.C.: S. Weir, 1837), and S. Taylor, *Relation of Master and Servant, As Exhibited in the New Testament* (Richmond, Va.: T. W. White, 1836). Good summaries of the proslavery argument remain William Sumner Jenkins, *Proslavery Thought in the Old South* (Chapel Hill: University of North Carolina Press, 1935) and H. Shelton Smith, *In His Image, But . . . Racism in Southern Religion, 1790–1910* (Durham, N.C.: Duke University Press, 1972).

Important analyses include Eugene D. Genovese, *"Slavery Ordained of God": The Southern Slaveholders' View of Biblical History and Modern Politics* (Gettysburg, Pa.: Gettysburg College 24th Annual Robert Fortenbaugh Memorial Lecture, 1985), and Jack P. Maddex Jr., "'The Southern Apostacy' Revisited: The Significance of Proslavery Christianity," *Marxist Perspectives* 2 (fall 1979): 132–42.

51. Snay, *Gospel of Disunion*, 78–99. Perhaps the clearest and most learned expression of the slaveholding ethic is James H. Thornwell, "The Christian Doctrine of Slavery," in *The Collected Writings of James Henley Thornwell, D.D. L.L.D.*, John B. Adger and John L. Girardeau, eds. (Richmond, Va.: Presbyterian Committee of Publication, 1873), though see also H. N. McTyeire, C. F. Sturgis, and A. T. Holmes, *Duties of Masters and Servants: Three Premium Essays* (1851; reprint, Freeport, N.Y.: Books for Libraries Press, 1971). On the mission to the slaves, see especially Mathews, *Religion in the Old South* and Anne C. Loveland, *Southern Evangelicals and the Social Order, 1800–1860* (Baton Rouge: Louisiana State University Press, 1980).

52. For the most recent general discussions of the denominational schisms, see Goen, *Broken Churches, Broken Nation*, Carwardine, *Evangelicals and Politics in Antebellum America*, chap. 5, and Snay, *Gospel of Disunion*, chap. 4.

53. The political implications of the schisms are discussed in Snay, *Gospel of Disunion*, 138–50. Freehling, *The Road to Disunion*, provides the most recent and trenchant discussion of sectional politics in the 1840s.

54. On the modernization of the South in the 1850s, see J. Mills Thornton, *Power and Politics in a Slave Society: Alabama, 1800–1860* (Baton Rouge: Louisiana State University Press, 1978), Joseph P. Reidy, *From Slavery to Agrarian Capitalism in the Cotton Plantation South: Central Georgia, 1800–1880* (Chapel Hill: University of North Carolina Press, 1992), Steven Hahn, *The Roots of Southern Populism: The Transformation of the Georgia Upcountry, 1850–1880* (New York: Oxford University Press, 1983), and Stephanie McCurry, *Masters of Small Worlds: Yeoman Households, Gender Relations, and the Political Culture of the Antebellum South Carolina Low Country* (New York: Oxford University Press, 1995). For the politics of the 1850s, see Holt, *The Political Crisis of the 1850s*, Freehling, *Road to Disunion*, and the older treatment by Craven, *The Growth of Southern Nationalism, 1848–1861*.

55. *Central Presbyterian*, March 22, 1856, quoted in Snay, *Gospel of Disunion*, 74. For an aggressive defense of slavery, see Iveson L. Brookes, *A Defense of the South Against the Reproaches of and Incroachments of the North: In Which Slavery is Shown to be an Institution of God intended to form the basis of the best social state and the only safeguard to the permanence of a Republican Government* (Hamburg, S.C.: Republican Office, 1850). For instances of heightened southern consciousness in the 1850s, see Ronald Takiki, *A Proslavery Crusade: The Attempt to Reopen the African Slave Trade* (New York: Free Press, 1971), Robert E. May, *The Southern Dream of a Caribbean Empire, 1854–1861* (Baton Rouge: Louisiana State University Press, 1973), and Charles A. Brown, *Agents of Manifest Destiny: The Lives and Times of the Filibusters* (Chapel Hill: University of North Carolina Press, 1980). On the general shift in proslavery thinking, see John M. McCardell, *The Idea of a Southern Nation: Southern Nationalists and Southern Nationalism, 1830–1860* (New York: W. W. Norton, 1979), 49–91.

56. McCardell, *Idea of a Southern Nation*, 202; Mitchell Snay, "American Thought and Southern Distinctiveness: The Southern Clergy and the Sanctification of Slavery," *Civil War History* 35 (December 1989): 327–28; E. Brooks Holifield, *The Gentlemen Theologians: American Theology in Southern Culture, 1790–1860* (Durham, N.C.: Duke University Press, 1978), 136.

57. William J. Cooper and Thomas E. Terrill, *The American South: A History* (New York: McGraw Hill, 1991), 315–16; Carwardine, *Evangelicals and Politics in Antebellum America*, 269–72. On the Know-Nothings in the South, see W. Darrell Overdyke, *The Know-Nothing Party in the South* (Baton Rouge: Louisiana State University Press, 1950), Jean H. Baker, *Ambivalent Americans: The Know-Nothing Party in Maryland* (Baltimore: Johns Hopkins University Press, 1977), James H. Broussard, "Some Determinants of Know-Nothing Electoral Strength in the South, 1856," *Louisiana History* 7 (winter 1966): 5–20, and Anthony G. Carey, "Too Southern to be American: Proslavery Politics and the Failure of the Know-Nothing Party in Georgia, 1854–1856," *Civil War History* 41 (March 1995): 22–40.

58. Snay, *Gospel of Disunion*, 151–75. For a good example of secessionist sermons, see Benjamin Palmer, "Slavery a Divine Trust: Duty of the South to Preserve and Perpetuate It," in *Fast Day Sermons; or The Pulpit on the State of the Country* (New York: Rudd & Carlton, 1861) and William C. Dana, *A Sermon delivered in the Central Presbyterian Church, Charleston, S.C., November 21st, 1860, being the Day appointed by State Authority for Fasting, Humiliation, and Prayer* (Charleston, S.C.: Steam Power Presses of Evans and Cogswell, 1860). On religious nationalism in the Confederacy, see Drew Gilpin Faust, *The Creation of Confederate Nationalism: Ideology and Identity in the Civil War South* (Baton Rouge: Louisiana State University Press, 1988).

59. James Oliver Horton and Lois E. Horton, *In Hope of Liberty: Culture, Community, and Protest Among Northern Free Blacks, 1700–1860* (New York: Oxford University Press, 1977), 135; Stewart, *Holy Warriors*, 138–39.

PART ONE

Religion and the Origins

of the Slavery Debate

Of Stations and Relations

Proslavery Christianity in

Early National Virginia

DOUGLAS AMBROSE

 In January 1798, Francis Asbury, the first bishop of the Methodist Episcopal Church in America, acknowledged in his journal a fear he had probably long recognized but had been reluctant to admit. "I am brought to conclude," he wrote, "that slavery will exist in Virginia perhaps for ages. . . ." Asbury believed he knew the reason why slavery would persist. "[T]here is not a sufficient sense of religion nor of liberty to destroy it." Asbury located the cause of this deficiency among the very people he had hoped would have provided "a sufficient sense of religion": "Methodists, Baptists, Presbyterians," he lamented, "in the highest flights of rapturous piety, still maintain and defend it."[1] Asbury's conclusion proved prophetic, and his criticism of Baptists, Presbyterians, and his fellow Methodists was all too accurate. Asbury and others had labored for years, even decades, to develop an antislavery Christianity in Virginia. What he and others continually confronted, however, was an entrenched commitment to slavery among both ministers and laity that not only represented a defense of valuable property but an equally powerful conviction that slavery was a divinely sanctioned relation.

Asbury's observations would have surprised few contemporaries, although modern historians have often underestimated the extent and depth of proslavery sentiment in Virginia in the generation following the Revolution.[2] What Asbury's comments and additional evidence from Baptist, Methodist, Presbyterian, and Episcopalian sources suggest is that early national Virginia witnessed the articulation not of a formal defense of slavery but rather of an understanding of slavery as a domestic relation that closely resembled those other domestic relations that comprised Virginia households. The relation between master and slave, Virginia ministers and laymen pointed out, shared much with relations between husband and wife and parent and child. By placing slavery within the realm of household relations, Virginia's ministers and churches limited the egalitarian tendencies of both evangelical religion and republican politics. By 1810 all Virginia's major denominations had reached an informal consensus on slavery that effectively silenced, even if it did not totally eliminate, antislavery sentiments and focused on infusing relations between masters and slaves with Christian notions of duty, obedience, and order. The paternalistic, proslavery Christianity that prevailed in Virginia, and elsewhere in the South, by 1810 remained one of the most consistent elements of proslavery thought up to the Civil War. In many ways, ideas and beliefs that divided southern Christians from their northern counterparts during the era of denominational schisms existed among Virginian Methodists, Baptists, and Presbyterians decades earlier. Proslavery Christianity did not develop because of attacks by northern abolitionists, the spread of cotton cultivation, or the cynical capitulation of antislavery ministers to the reality of southern life. Proslavery Christianity instead developed organically out of and remained grounded in a system of relations that prevailed in the households of Virginians, slaveholders and nonslaveholders alike.[3]

The political as well as the religious history of Virginia after the Revolution has focused naturally on the concerted efforts of dissenters and their secular allies to disestablish the Episcopalian church and enshrine religious liberty.[4] Historian Rhys Isaac has also examined the ways in which revolutionary idealism and religious liberty helped to "transform" Virginia from a deferential, hierarchical, and "patriarchal" culture into an increasingly competitive, individualistic, and contractual one.[5] Yet while Isaac is undoubtedly correct that the Virginia of 1800 differed markedly from the Virginia of 1760, the character of the transformation that the Revolution, disestablishment, and the triumph of religious liberty brought to Virginia deserves further examination. For if the structures, attitudes, and practices that characterized the public realm had been transformed by the turn of the century, the structures, attitudes, and practices of the private realm remained remarkably intact. Isaac may well have overemphasized the influence of revolutionary republicanism on the domestic lives of Virginians. Although in large measure public authority in postrevolutionary Virginia "was based on the mutual contract of the individuals who composed society," white male Virginians never extended this notion of a "contract" between equal "individuals" to the household.[6] Far from it. In the household—understood to mean both the home and the farm or plantation—the values of hierarchy, interdependence, and obedience held firm against the egalitarianism, individualism, and autonomy that informed the rhetoric and, to a considerable extent, the reality of the polity. The triumph of proslavery Christianity over an indigenous antislavery can best be understood by recognizing the distinction Virginians observed between the values and relations of the household and the values and relations of the larger polity. This distinction did not eliminate the inevitable conflicts that arose as Virginians balanced themselves between two seemingly contradictory worlds; but the distinction did allow for and was encouraged by an evangelical Christianity that taught the fulfillment of duties that flowed from one's earthly station even as it proclaimed the equality of souls.[7]

Virginia in 1790 was the most populous state in the union. It also contained the largest number of slaves. But its importance to the study of slavery and religion in the early republic transcends sheer numbers. Virginia demands scholarly attention because it struggled with slavery more openly and more intensely than any other southern state in the era after the Revolution. Thomas Jefferson's tortuous meditations on slavery are well known.[8] Virginia's manumission law of 1782 was the most liberal one south of the Mason-Dixon line. It allowed masters to free thousands of slaves, and as a result, Virginia's free black population rose dramatically from three thousand in 1780 to thirty thousand in 1810.[9] St. George Tucker's famous 1796 pamphlet, *A Dissertation on Slavery with a Proposal for the Gradual Abolition of It in the State of Virginia*, passionately attacked slavery as contrary to natural law.[10] In each of these examples, however, the limits of antislavery sentiment and action baldly stand out. Jefferson freed but a handful of his own slaves and did little to end slavery in Virginia.[11] While numerous Virginians did free slaves under the 1782 manumission law, these individual manumissions did not affect slavery on the whole; Virginia's slave population rose even more dramatically than did its free black population, from 250,000 in 1780 to 400,000 in 1810.[12] The Virginia House of Delegates would not even discuss Tucker's plan.[13] Virginia's religious denominations, like its political culture, did indeed contain the seeds of genuine antislavery sentiment. But those denominations, like the wider culture, were less than fertile grounds for the growth of antislavery ideology; they proved to be considerably more hospitable to far more broadly planted and deeply rooted proslavery beliefs.

Discussions of antislavery sentiment in postrevolutionary Virginia rightly focus primarily on the Methodists. As a church, they most clearly announced an antislavery position and many individual members bravely pronounced their antislavery beliefs. But these Methodists were not alone in their opposition to slavery. Some Baptist and Presbyterian ministers also attacked slavery.

The statewide Baptist organization, the Baptist General Committee, and some of the regional Baptist associations publicly denounced slaveholding. Yet each denomination encountered intense and ultimately irresistible popular opposition to antislavery activity. The dialectical process of antislavery action and popular response reveals both the limited breadth of antislavery sentiment and the depth of proslavery commitment among Virginia evangelicals.

The most famous episode of antislavery activity among the evangelical denominations occurred in 1784 when the Methodists demanded in the form of a rule that all slaveholders manumit their slaves within one year (two years for Virginians) or be expelled from the church. Equally famous is the church's suspension of this rule six months later "on account of the great opposition that had been given it. . . ."[14] Methodist Jesse Lee, although opposed to slavery, recognized that the "spirit of the people would be roused by pressing the subject too closely."[15] But the popular opposition to the 1784 antislavery rule was but one example of a persistent pattern of opposition encountered by antislavery Methodists. Thomas Coke—John Wesley's personal emissary to America and along with Asbury the leader of the American church—adamantly attacked slavery in his sermons. A 1785 sermon, as Coke related, "provoked many of the unawakened to retire out of the barn, and to combine together to flog me. . . ." A justice of the peace helped save Coke from the lash.[16] Methodist itinerant preacher James Meacham encountered less violent but similar opposition to his antislavery views. In October 1791 Meacham chastised a Methodist woman's cruelty toward her slaves. Unrepentant, the woman "persisted in her own way and testified she would still do the same if they would not work." When Meacham warned her that if she did "she might not expect to continue in communion with us," the woman defiantly retorted that "she could serve the lord out as well as in."[17] The difficulties with fellow members experienced by Coke and Meacham were shared by antislavery supporters in all Virginia's evangelical denominations.[18]

A number of Virginia Baptists viewed slavery as critically as did antislavery Methodists.[19] In 1785, the same year the Methodists backed down from their attempt to rid the church of slaveholders, the Baptist General Committee declared "hereditary slavery to be contrary to the word of God. . . ."[20] Little resulted from this declaration, and in 1790 the committee again agreed to consider the "equity of hereditary slavery." After the initial committee of four persons "could not agree in their opinions on the subject," it chose Rev. John Leland to draw up a resolution. Leland, originally from Massachusetts, penned a stark condemnation of slavery: The committee "[r]esolved, that slavery, is a violent deprivation of the rights of nature, and is inconsistent with a republican government; and therefore recommend it to our brethren to make use of every legal measure, to extirpate the horrid evil from the land. . . ."[21] After the 1791 and 1792 general committees referred the resolution to the district associations, the 1793 Baptist General Committee finally resolved "that the matter respecting hereditary slavery be taken up. . . ." Those present "voted by a large majority . . . that the subject be dismissed from the committee, as it belongs to the legislative body."[22]

The general committee's decision to dismiss the subject can only be understood as a reaction to popular discontent. Historian James Essig has pointed out that, in part, this popular resistance represented a fear of ecclesiastical centralization.[23] For instance, in 1792 the Strawberry District Association considered the Baptist General Committee's resolution respecting slavery. "We advise them," the Strawberry association wrote, "not to Interfere in it."[24] But the Roanoke District Association's 1790 response to the general committee's resolution demonstrates that some in the association questioned whether indeed slavery was incompatible with the word of God. The association "unanimously agreed to remonstrate, as Christians, against oppression as we discover the same, and that we are heartily disposed to be under the influence of the spirit of humanity, yet nevertheless," they continued, "we believe it would be a very great violation thereof (very little short of driving our children from us in a state of non age) to emancipate our slaves promiscuously without means of visible prospects of their support."[25] In the Roanoke association's view, emancipation, not slavery, would violate "the spirit of humanity" under which they, as Christians, sought to be. The likening of slaves to children is but a brief reference to a leitmotif that can be seen throughout early national evangelical discussions of slavery.

The Roanoke association did not confine its critique of the general committee to what it saw as, at best, a premature call for emancipation. The association further stated that "tho' we are not unanimously clear in our minds whether the God of nature ever intended, that one part of the human species should be held in an abject state of slavery to another part of the same species," they nonetheless believed that "the subject with us is very abstruse and such a set of complex circumstances attending the same, that we suppose [neither] the general committee nor any other Religious Society whatever has the least right to concern [illegible] As a society. . . ." While in this passage the association objected to the committee's interference in a subject outside its jurisdiction, the association continued by demonstrating its understanding of how good Baptists ought to relate to slavery. Rather than the committee telling

Baptists what to do, the association advocated leaving "every individual to act at discresion [*sic*] In order to keep a good conscience before God as far as the laws of our [land] will admit. . . ." A good Christian thus had to decide how best to act within the civil order; slavery did not prevent one from being a good Baptist. For the Roanoke association, slavery placed an individual responsibility on the slaveholder; the sin of slavery lay not in the holding of slaves per se, but in the misconduct one might exercise in the holding. "[I]t is the indispensable duty of masters to forbear and suppress cruelty, and do that which is Just and equal to their servants." [26]

The Roanoke association's 1790 response to the antislavery resolution of the Baptist General Committee, like the general response to the Methodist attack on slavery, demonstrates the popular resistance in Virginia to antislavery attitudes. The inability of the leadership of both churches to place their congregations on clear and forceful antislavery ground testifies to the strength of the laity. As historian Donald Mathews has pointed out, "Methodism was a people's movement, and the people either wanted slavery or feared emancipation." [27] Yet many episodes of popular proslavery—such as those that Jesse Lee, Thomas Coke, and the Strawberry District Association describe—reveal little about the beliefs of those who defended slavery, other than the desire to own slaves. The Roanoke association revealed more than the others: that Baptists, like Methodists, opposed antislavery and believed, like the woman who defied James Meacham, that slaveholders could be good Christians. The association suggests that those who opposed antislavery understood slavery. Some ministers did, however, talk about slavery; they presented it to their congregations; and they attempted to explain its relation to evangelical Christianity. Their words reveal a defense of slavery that rested on Christian principles of order and duty. While narrow self-interest played its part in the defense of slavery, the efforts of evangelical Virginians to reconcile their Christianity with their slaveholding help explain why their commitment to slavery constituted much more than the protection of an investment. In a very real sense, evangelical Virginians understood slavery as a familial relation between unequal members of a hierarchically structured and divinely ordained household. As the Roanoke association pointed out, such a relation, like all relations, carried with it duties and obligations that flowed from God. Ministers continually reminded their flocks that how well individuals fulfilled or failed to fulfill those duties and obligations would bear heavily on the fate of their immortal souls.

Discussions of slavery within Virginia's churches in the early national period only rarely focused explicitly or exclusively on slavery itself. [28] Ministers did not usually single slavery out as a "peculiar" relation requiring special justifi-cation—quite the contrary. Much more frequently, slavery arose within dis-cussions of related topics, particularly "family religion." Ministers of all de-nominations spoke of slavery as one relation among a series of relations that comprised well-ordered Christian families, households, and societies. Central to this understanding was the notion that inequality and difference character-ized the parties to those relations. Instead of equal relations between individu-als, unequal relations between complementary parts of an organic whole pro-vided the basis for Christian order.

Perhaps no minister so forcefully articulated the nature of these relations and the intimate connection between them as Devereux Jarratt. An evangelical Anglican who strongly supported the Methodist movement before it broke away from the Anglican church, Jarratt expressed in his sermons and personal letters a worldview that epitomized the widespread ministerial understanding of human relations.[29] To live a Christian life, Jarratt posited in one sermon, "implies a punctual discharge of, or a going through all the duties we owe to God—our neighbors and ourselves, in whatever state of life it hath pleased Providence to place us. . . ." The "state" in which God "placed" individuals was both categorical and relational. Obligations, duties, and responsibilities flowed from one's position, but that position only had meaning because of its relation to others' positions. "[W]hether ministers or people," Jarratt main-tained, "magistrates or subjects—husbands or wives—parents or children—masters or servants. In all of these stations and relations, a line of conduct, a straight path of duty is marked out, in the word of God, for Christians to observe and go in."[30] Jarratt, in effect, drew no distinction between station and relation. He held the firm conviction that only within relations, not as autonomous individuals, could one lead a proper Christian life. What was owed to one's neighbor, was owed because of God's command. Human rela-tions, including slavery, were divinely ordained.

Jarratt elaborated upon his conception of the organic and reciprocal nature of human relations in one sermon in which he used the church as a reflection of society. Commenting on the different abilities and duties of individuals within society, Jarratt argued that "the members [of the church] differ in this, that all are not equally useful, nor have they all the same office." God had ordered the church, like all human institutions, according to his own design. "Upon the whole, God hath set the members in the body, every one as it hath pleased him, and in such order and subserviency one to another, that the *eye cannot say unto the hand, I have no need of thee, nor the head to the feet, I have no need of you.*"[31] While countless ministers throughout America employed the metaphor of the body, Jarratt's use of it represented more than mere convention. Jarratt's specific views of slavery and the context in which he preached his sermons suggest that when he asserted that God had placed humans "in such order and subserviency one to another," more than the simple interdependency of humanity was at stake. Jarratt was helping to establish among his parishioners a religiously grounded defense of inequality and hierarchy. In the slave society of postrevolutionary Virginia and particularly in that society's households, his words, and similar ones from ministers of all denominations, strengthened the view that slavery in no way contradicted true religion but was, in fact, a necessary part of it.

Unlike most ministers in early national Virginia, Jarratt on several occasions spoke explicitly about slavery. This resulted in part from Jarratt's intimate yet problematic relations with the Methodists. Although Jarratt's acrimonious break with the Methodists was centered in the question of Methodist separation from the mother church, Methodist leaders (notably Thomas Coke) singled out Jarratt's slaveholding as evidence of his sinful character.[32] The Methodist charge hit Jarratt hard, and he responded in a manner that clearly illustrates that his view of slaveholding as a legitimate relation was firmly rooted in his larger theological and social thought.

Jarratt most clearly responded to the Methodists in a 1788 letter to Edward Dromgoole, a Methodist preacher who remained friendly with Jarratt.[33] Jarratt attacked the ways in which some Methodists characterized not only him but all slaveholders. "I think they [slaveholders] ought not to be put upon a level, (as they now are) with horsethieves and hogstealers and knaves, etc.; nor to be insulted at every turn with the odious name of oppressors, rogues, and men destitute of even heathen honesty, etc." Jarratt's criticism of these Methodist "insults" rested firmly on Scripture, as would subsequent defenses against abolitionist attacks.[34] Slaveholders should not be condemned, Jarratt argued, for "they suppose they are warranted in their practice by the example of Abraham, Isaac and all the ancient people of God; and not only those, but by the writings of the apostles, whose directions and exhortations to bond and free incline them to believe that *such stations and relations* were to exist under the Gospel, otherwise thirty or forty verses might as well be blotted out of the New Testament as being of no practical use" (my italics).[35] The "stations and relations" of free and bond, like those of husband and wife and parent and child, were biblically sanctioned; for any Christian to argue otherwise meant contradicting God's word.

Jarratt returned to the biblical defense of slavery in a 1790 letter. In one sense, this letter reflects the still-muted character of proslavery in the early republic. Rather than praise slavery as a positive good, Jarratt began his comments with a mild wish that slavery might someday be ended. But in so doing Jarratt revealed his belief that God has created slaves and freemen and that the end of slavery would only come when it accorded with both God's wishes and social expediency. "As God has numbered me among the *Free,* I wish it may be consistent with the deep and wise schemes of his Providence to open a way for the freedom of the whole human race; and especially that the Africans in the United States of America may see an end of their bondage, as soon as it may be consistent with public and private utility." Jarratt even admitted that "[s]lavery, as thousands of the slaves are treated, is indeed *shocking to humanity.*" But he then pointed out that inhuman conduct does not condemn an institution or a social relation as unchristian. "But whether slavery in itself, *be inconsistent with the dictates of reason and religion,* is what I have not as yet, after most impartial examination been able to discover."[36] Jarratt's distinction between the sinfulness of slaveholders and slavery itself was one that southerners continually made.[37] As fallen and corrupt beings, humans could not avoid sin.[38] Human institutions thus would always be imperfect. The task of the Christian was not to eliminate sin—a virtual impossibility—but to limit it by living according to God's word. Antislavery advocates who ascribed sin to institutions, Jarratt and others argued, failed to recognize that all institutions necessarily exhibited evil. For Jarratt, human conduct within an institution or relation, not the institution or relation itself, determined the level of sin. Jarratt would have agreed heartily with William Harper of South Carolina who in 1837 wrote "the condition of our whole existence is but to struggle with evils—to compare them—to choose between them, and so far as we can, to mitigate them. To say there is evil in any institution, is only to say that it is human."[39]

Jarratt's distinguishing of slavery from slaveholding allowed him to immediately demonstrate why the dilemma of whether slavery contradicted "reason and religion," was actually no dilemma at all. "I dare not say it [slavery] is inconsistent with *these* [reason and religion]. I say, I dare not pronounce it inconsistent, lest I should reproach my Maker, who as you know blessed his friend Abraham with abundance of that property, and tolerated the same among the Jews." Far from being inconsistent with religion, slavery, Jarratt argued, had always received divine approval and thus could not be inherently sinful. Noting that "[s]ome have pretended to point out a distinction between the different dispensations, and from thence infer, that what was allowed as consistent with the dictates of reason and religion in the Jewish, is not so under the Christian oeconomy: but I never could see the propriety of such reasoning. The dictates of reason and religion . . . do not fluctuate." Reiterating his belief that "slavery, as it is practiced in general is most abhorrent to my mind," Jarratt nonetheless concluded his letter with a clear summation of the proper Christian position vis-à-vis slavery. "I doubt not, but my indispensable duty is to preach the duties incumbent on all stations and relations in life, as I find them marked in holy writ."[40] Thus, because holy writ consistently and explicitly sanctioned the "stations and relations" of master and slave, Jarratt's duty, and the duty of all true Christians, was clear. It was the practice, not the principle, of slavery that was "abhorrent" and needed correction.

In a sermon on the "Cure and Conversion of Naaman," Jarratt demonstrated how he fulfilled his "indispensable duty." He also demonstrated how the relation of master and slave, if informed by the proper attitudes and behavior, could be the basis for a stable and moral social order. Jarratt noted that Naaman's slave was of such an "excellent spirit" that "so far from being embittered against the family she served, that she appears more solicitous for her master's health, than her own liberty." For Jarratt, this episode revealed two of the most fundamental principles of Christian relations: benevolence and obedience. Speaking of the slave Jarratt exclaimed, "Mark this, my hearers: what a noble, disinterested benevolence is here displayed." Singling out the slaves in the typically biracial audience, Jarratt implored them, "Take heed to this my black brethren. The condition of this sweet tempered, good little maid was, then, similar to yours now. Let her example provoke you to imitation." Jarratt concluded his message to the slaves: "this injunction stands upon record, in the New Testament—servants, be subject to your masters,—and please them in all things:—not purloining, but showing all good fidelity from the heart." Jarratt quickly followed this plea to the slaves in his audience with a corresponding message to masters. "It appears," he stated, "that Naaman was blessed with good servants in general. . . . From hence it is reasonable to infer, that he was good and gentle, mild and benevolent to all his domestics." For Jarratt, Naaman's relations with his "domestics" provided a clear lesson. "Mutual benevolence," he asserted, "is the sure bond and cement of domestic peace and happiness: where the affections of master and servants are reciprocal, we may expect happiness in such families. . . ."[41] What made slavery "abhorrent" to Jarratt's mind was "the way it [was] practiced in general." By urging slaves and, more important, masters to fulfill their divine duty and practice "mutual benevolence," Jarratt hoped to reduce slavery's abhorrence and bring "domestic peace and happiness" to Virginia's households.

Jarratt may have been among the most outspoken commentators on and defenders of slavery among Virginia ministers, but he was hardly alone. Indeed, the sources indicate that ministers from every denomination echoed Jar-ratt's basic points regarding the sanctity of slavery and its similarity to other domestic relations. Just as the Roanoke Baptist Association in 1790 conceived of slavery as a domestic relation when it likened slave emancipation to "driv-ing our children from us in a state of non age," so too did other Baptists share the association's understanding that, in essential respects, relations with slaves constituted a fundamental part of "family religion."

The Dover Baptist Association's 1796 circular letter "on the subject of family discipline, and the instruction of children" well illustrates how minis-ters' attention turned to slavery primarily when they focused on family or domestic affairs generally, and not as a subject unto itself. "The inferior part of the families of our country," the letter stated, "may be taken notice of under two heads, viz. our children, and servants. . . ." While similar in their being inferior, children and slaves nonetheless required different instruction because such instruction "ought to be adapted to the capacities, and understandings of the persons for whom it is intended."[42] Families, the letter thus implied, consisted of distinct elements with particular needs; the proper Christian par-ent had to recognize those distinctions and needs if he was to fulfill his duties to his dependents. As the Portsmouth Baptist Association stated in an 1800 circular letter, the "faithful servants of God have been, and still are to be dis-tinguished by their pious household government. . . . And if we possess reli-gion ourselves, what can be more desireable [*sic*] than to communicate the knowledge thereof to our fellow creatures! and especially those of our own House."[43] Children and slaves, both "inferior parts" of "our own House" re-quired Christian instruction from "faithful servants of God." From such cir-cular letters as these, Virginia Baptists learned that what made a "pious house-hold" was the way in which its different and unequal members related to each other and how well they fulfilled the various, differing duties that flowed from those relations.

Christopher Collins, a Baptist minister from Berkeley County, Virginia, held slaves throughout the 1790s, and by 1806 he owned thirty.[44] In a funeral sermon preached in 1804, Collins confirmed that what mattered in life was not what station one occupied, but whether one satisfied the duties that arose from that station and its concomitant relations. Choosing Ecclesiastes 7:1 ("A good name is better than precious ointment") as the text for his sermon, Collins argued that such names "as Magistrate, Subjects—Father—Child—Master—Servants," meant nothing in and of themselves. Respect and divine favor only resulted from how well individuals met the obligations that those names placed on them. "Those who possess any of these names, & discharge their duties well—they are good names—and those who bear them, even if servants, are very respectable. . . ."[45] Clearly, Collins hoped, as did many preachers in early national Virginia, to render slaves more content with their lot by linking earthly obedience with heavenly reward. But Collins's words, like those of Jarratt and others, were not mere propaganda for slaves, who may have listened but did not necessarily hear. All these ministers who spoke of duties and relations contributed to the conviction among most white Virginians that slaveholding, like child rearing, was a Christian responsibility. The proper fulfillment of that responsibility not only made for social peace, but, more important, it also ensured divine blessing. Masters and masters-to-be need not fear that slaveholding was sinful; if they "discharged their duties well," they would be, in God's eyes and their own, "very respectable."

Methodists, too, emphasized that slavery, like other human relations, rested on Christian benevolence and obedience to God's design. While some Virginia Methodist ministers remained committed to antislavery, others embraced the same basic acceptance of slaveholding that we have seen among other evangelicals.[46] Together with the clear evidence of Methodist lay opposition to antislavery, the scattered statements of ministerial proslavery individuals suggest that, in Virginia at least, most Methodists had joined the emerging proslavery consensus by 1810. No doubt some Methodists, especially those residing west of the Blue Ridge, continued to harbor antislavery sympathies. But east of the Blue Ridge, where most Virginians—white as well as black—lived, Methodist expressions of antislavery diminished to insignificance. Antislavery, primarily in its political form in western Virginia, continued to be a presence through the famous debate over slavery in the Virginia legislature in 1831–32. But the idea of slaveholding as a sin, as an immoral, unjustifiable act, never swept up Virginians, west or east of the Blue Ridge.[47]

Stith Mead, a Methodist minister, traveled through a number of Piedmont and western Virginia counties in the 1780s and 1790s. His letter book of 1792–95 tells of a devout young man who occasionally expressed acute displeasure over his father's lack of saving grace and membership among the Masons. But while Mead criticized his father, and the unsaved generally, he remained in principle committed to the belief that domestic relations imposed duties and obligations that one neglected at his peril. In a 1794 epistle to "the Botetourteans and the Greenbrireans," which Mead partially recorded in his letter book, he urged his audience to "[b]ear ye one another's burdens, and so fulfill the law of Christ." But for Mead, as for other evangelicals, this "law" required some to obey and some to exercise benevolent authority. "Wives, submit yourselves unto your own Husbands, & Husbands love your wives. Children obey your parents in the Lord for this is right & yet Fathers provoke not your children to wrath, Servants be obedient to them who are your masters; and ye masters do the same things unto them who are your servants forbearing threatening knowing there is one who is your Master in Heaven."[48] Mead thus located slavery among the familiar, and unequal, domestic relations and understood those relations between obedient slaves and benevolent masters, like those between submissive wives and loving husbands, as "fulfilling the law of Christ."

John Early, a Methodist itinerant minister who preached throughout Virginia and North Carolina in the early nineteenth century, demonstrates how individual Methodists could harbor deep reservations about slaveholding and yet still present it to their flocks as a legitimate domestic relation. In an entry in his diary of January 4, 1813, Early related that he "was most distressed and dreaded to engage in the business of my [recently deceased] father's estate but necessity prompted me to engage in disagreeable things." Chief among those "disagreeable things" was inheriting slaves. "I had now become a slaveholder, oh degrading appelation [sic] and unhappy situation."[49] Unhappy as the situation might have been, Early could not seem to free himself of his new station. A year later, on January 23, 1814, after his overseer quit, Early wrote, "Now I was left at that unseasonable time to look for another man to oversee my business without knowing where to look. Nevertheless I tried to make things easy at home and was brought to abhor slavery more than ever."[50]

Early clearly did abhor slavery, even if "necessity prompted" him to remain a slaveholder. But in a sermon preached on January 8, 1809, Early gave no indication either of his personal abhorrence of slavery or of its inherent sinfulness. On that Sunday, Early recollected, "I preached at eleven oclock [sic] on the commandments of God to rulers, parents, children, husbands, wives, masters and servants and at the same time on the duty of ministers. Some were displeased and some delighted but none of these things moved me."[51] Early did not elaborate about what may have displeased or delighted his listeners, but his brief summation leaves little doubt about the message he meant to convey. "Commandments" and duties informed all relations; slavery existed along the continuum of these relations, all of which involved different stations and obligations. While Early himself found slaveholding "degrading," he told his audience that it was as natural and as divinely sanctioned as marriage and parenting. The message preached by Early, the Methodist critic of slavery, differed little, if at all, from the messages that Jarratt, the evangelical

Episcopalian defender of slavery, and Collins, the Baptist slaveholder, urged upon their congregations. Virginia Presbyterians conformed as well to this evangelical consensus.

The Rev. William Graham, the Presbyterian rector and instructor of Moral Philosophy at Liberty Hall Academy (now Washington and Lee University), shared much with his fellow Virginia evangelicals. Graham taught a course at Liberty Hall on "Human Nature" beginning in the late 1780s through 1796. The basis of the course was a series of "Lectures on Moral Philosophy." Graham's "Lecture 25," entitled "Of the Relation of Man to Man," clearly distinguished between the relations of the household and those of the polity. "We now come to speak of the relations of man to man, which may be divided into two great branches, domestic and civil." In this lecture Graham left no doubt as to the domestic nature of slavery. "His [man's] domestic relations may be comprehended under the following particulars; 1. Husband and wife. 2. Parent and child. 3. Master and servant."[52] Although here Graham did not elaborate upon his views of slavery, he did return to them in a subsequent lecture that directly confronted the question of slavery's relation to Christianity.

"Lecture 30th. An Important Question Answered," Graham's lecture on slavery, stands as one of the clearest defenses of slavery from the early republic, as historian David Robson has pointed out.[53] But Robson seriously errs when he claims that Graham was "the first late eighteenth-century Virginia clergyman to defend slavery."[54] For while Graham did differ from other defenders of slavery in making slavery the primary focus of his lecture, his defense displays a remarkable consistency with what can be observed in the writings and activities of other postrevolutionary Virginia evangelicals. Most important, Graham viewed slavery as but one of an intimately connected series of divinely sanctioned familial relations.

In his lecture Graham criticized those "zealous declaimers" who sought "universal emancipation," and he objected in particular to those who employed Christianity in their attacks. "Christianity," he insisted, "was never designed to alter the political or civil state of men. . . ." Rather, its purpose was "only to bring them to the love of God and inculcate the performance of the duties of their several stations, whether magistrate or people, husband or wife, parent or child, master or servant." Graham proceeded to demonstrate that the Bible "does not point out any mode of their [slaves'] emancipation nor ever suggest the propriety of it but only directs them diligently and faithfully to perform the duties of their station as doing the Lord's service and therefore performing his will."[55] The wife, child, and slave shared much in God's plan;

Christianity required that they perform "the duties of their several stations . . . diligently and faithfully." Far from representing an exceptional defense of slaveholding, Graham's lecture reiterated principles and even the very terms that Virginians of all denominations heard throughout the decades following the Revolution.

Graham was not the only Presbyterian who expressed the widespread understanding of slavery as a Christian relation with particular duties and responsibilities. Rev. William Hill, who in 1790 wrote that "it is both a duty and a happiness to be content in whatever situation it shall please God to place us," considered the faithful discharge of one's duties as deserving of the highest praise.[56] In a funeral sermon preached for Gen. Daniel Morgan in 1802, Hill eulogized Morgan as "the affectionate Husband, the tender and indulgent Parent, the humane Master, the steady Friend. . . ."[57] The Rev. James Blythe's 1804 sermon commemorating the Rev. John Brown, the recently deceased pastor of the New Providence, Virginia, church, similarly focused on Brown's fulfillment of his relational responsibilities. "As the husband, parent, master and friend, he was exceeded by none, and equalled by few." Blythe noted that Brown not only met the obligations his station in life demanded of him, but also that he preached that meeting such obligations constituted the essence of a Christian life. "It was a favorite opinion, with him," Blythe stated, "that much of our holy religion consisted in the punctual and faithful discharge of the relative duties of life."[58]

"A Prayer for Family," which appeared in an 1805 edition of the Presbyterian *Virginia Religious Magazine,* reinforced the importance that "the punctual and faithful discharge of the relative duties of life" played in Christian living. "We beseech thee to bless us as a family; whether we preside over it, or belong to it as children, sojourners, or servants, may we all be found in faithful discharge of our duty to thee, and to each other!"[59] To discharge one's duties to God and to each other required both the recognition of the divine basis of inequality within families and of the need to conduct one's relations with other family members in a Christian manner. While Presbyterians and all evangelicals implored all household members to conduct themselves according to the demands of their particular "stations," they spoke most frequently and forcefully to masters. As evangelicals developed an increasingly consensual defense of the divine sanction of slavery, they continually insisted that southern slavery would only be acceptable to God if masters, in particular, fulfilled their duties. In their admonitions and instructions to masters, Virginia evangelicals promoted and cultivated the paternalist ideal with which the antebellum South would identify so strongly. Ministers, through these efforts, asserted their cultural and moral authority by shaping both the behavior and beliefs of white southerners and black southerners in general and of slaveholders in particular.[60]

The evangelicals' repeated references to the familial character of slavery naturally included calls for fathers-masters to meet their specific responsibilities. But as heads of households fathers had particularly weighty responsibilities—most notably to ensure that Christianity informed the entire household. If the father-master failed in his obligations, the household—and by extension the society—faced ruin and damnation. Masters would not be judged only by their own individual actions but also by the actions of those whom God had placed under their authority. In an 1807 address to its congregations, the Presbytery of Hanover warned its slaveholding members to "[r]emember that [slaves] have immortal souls; that they are under your authority and direction; that all sins which they commit through your neglect, all the ruin which is brought upon their souls on account of their ignorance of those truths in which you ought to have instructed them, will be charged upon you." Such neglect would bring both spiritual and temporal punishment. "Fearful indeed," the address continued, "will be the account which you will have to render unto God, if these things are slighted; and fearful, it is probable, will be the judgements, which heaven will bring upon you, even in this world, on account of the great neglect in training up servants in the knowledge of the way of salvation."[61]

Ministers demonstrated concern not only about the Christian instruction of slaves but also about their physical treatment. Evangelicals recognized that slaves, while integral parts of Virginia households, nonetheless differed from wives and children. Ministers suggested that unlike the "natural" bonds of affection that informed husband-wife and parent-child relations, the bonds between master and slave remained far more open to abuse. These bonds, ministers thus argued, had to be understood as familial ones, different from, yet in essential respects similar to, relations between "natural" family members. Christian masters, according to the 1796 Dover Baptist Association, thus had to "instruct their servants in the most important and essential doctrines of the gospel," and in order "to give this the greater impression, they ought to take every opportunity to shew them acts of humanity and tenderness, and to adapt as mild a discipline as possible, to shew a forgiveness of faults and by no means to exercise wrath nor cruelty in chastisement."[62] The attention ministers devoted to inculcating Christian paternalism within masters testifies to their perceived need to convince masters that slavery was, indeed, a domestic relation and that God would, in fact, judge masters according to the ways in which they fulfilled the duties that the relation imposed. In the decades after 1810, the extent to which masters identified themselves as good Christians and their slave society as one that enjoyed God's blessing would reveal just how successful the ministers were in their endeavor.[63]

Devereux Jarratt, as one would expect, focused sharply on the duties of masters. In a sermon on "Family Religion," Jarratt insisted "that it is the indispensable duty of all masters and heads of families to teach those that are under them, whether children or servants, the principles of religion and the doctrines of salvation. . . ." "[P]lain precepts both in the Old and New Testament" demonstrated "that it is the will of God, that not only your children, but household should be instructed by you. . . ." Jarratt implored masters not to shirk their obligations but to do what was needed to fulfill them. God's will required that household dependents not only be instructed by masters "but commanded; intimating the authority committed to every parent and master of a family to carry his instruction into effect. . . ." Meeting one's obligations as a Christian master meant using "the means appointed, in obedience to God," means that included "correction" with "the rod of authority, as need may require." The good paternalist, Jarratt made very clear, had to chastise as well as to reward. Masters who justly punished their dependents demonstrated their "obedience to God."[64]

The Portsmouth Baptist Association's circular letter of 1800 also singled out masters in its discussion of "family religion." And it too implied that the master's duty might require the exercise of force. Emphasizing the importance of "personal religion . . . in those persons whose prerogative it is to govern the family," the letter bluntly stated that "they are the persons for whom this epistle is principally intended." If "those in inferior stations" in the household did not practice proper religion, only the master was to blame. The need for a Christian household "behoves [*sic*] him to extend his authority so far, as to make all under him submit, at least, to the form of religious worship in the family." But the Portsmouth association tempered this call for an extension of the master's authority with an appeal to his conscience. Noting that "we are continually receiving the fruits of our servants labours," the letter asked whether "it not be base ingratitude to be incessantly receiving *all their temporals,* and yet at the same time feel no disposition to communicate unto them our spirituals . . . ?" While a subtle critique of slavery can be detected here, more apparent is the elaboration of the notion of reciprocity that lay at the center of paternalism. By instructing and "governing" his slaves, the master compensated his slaves for their labor. Rather than simple exploitation, the master-slave relation provided benefits to both parties, and it spread God's word as well.

The Portsmouth association demanded that this "exchange" between master and slave be sincere; the master could not "play" the Christian paternalist, he had to *be* one: "For the best instructions will prove abortive, unless our families can be convinced they proceed out of a *pure heart, a good conscience, and faith unfeigned.*" Yet, as if to remind slaveholders, as had Jarratt, that good masters must still exercise authority and require, at times, submission, the letter continued, "We likewise wish that you not only use your influence as prophets to teach, and as priests to intercede, but also as kings to rule, govern, and provide for your families." [65] The Dover Baptist Association's circular letter of 1796 conveyed the same message, in almost the exact same language. "[I]f small things may be compared with great," the Dover association posited, "a man and his family, may be said to act in a character similar to that of Christ to his church, viz. as a prophet to teach them, as a priest to offer sacrifice in their behalf; as a Governor to rule over them. This last it is necessary he should exercise, that he may be capable rightly to perform the other two." [66]

Ministers of all denominations constantly reminded masters that although God granted them authority over their slaves, they nonetheless had to exercise that authority in a Christian manner, lest they endanger their own souls. The Portsmouth association's circular letter of 1800, cited above, concluded with a stern message to masters that reminded them of both the divine basis of their authority and the divine judgment their use of that authority would bring: "[I]f you wish to shew gratitude to the Father of all mercies, and God of all comforts for placing you at the head of families, instead of fixing you in inferior stations . . . if you desire to have good children and servants; if you wish the good of the community at large; if you are indeed what you profess to be, *good Republicans, good Patriots;* above all if you desire the declarative *glory of God,* and the credit and reputation of his cause to increase, labour by all means in your power to constitute your habitations the Temples of the Lord of Hosts, and your families his true worshippers." [67] A 1797 circular letter from the Dover Baptist Association stated that in order "to discharge that duty, which our relational characters require," masters had to remember that their authority was earthly, and thus limited. Invoking the much-quoted verse from Paul's Epistle to the Colossians, the letter entreated that "as masters we may 'render unto our servants that which is just and equal, knowing that we have a Master who is in Heaven.'" [68]

Perhaps the most forceful evangelical voice promoting paternalism in early national Virginia was the Presbyterian *Virginia Religious Magazine.* In the preface to its inaugural edition in 1804 the editors noted that "the present state of things calls aloud for the exertions of every one, according to the station in which Divine Providence has placed him." The editors followed this familiar appeal with a pointed message to masters: "In a particular manner, we would entreat parents and heads of families, seriously to consider the trust committed to them; the injuries they may do to their children and servants, by neglecting their religious instruction, the guilt they will themselves contract by omitting their duty, and the strict account they must render of their stewardship." The magazine left no doubt that it believed that the "division of mankind into families, constituting parents their head, is the plan of Infinite Wisdom and carries with it the authority of Heaven." [69] But this divine plan demanded that masters-fathers exercise Christian authority. Subsequent issues of the *Virginia Religious Magazine* reiterated and expounded upon the paramount importance of paternalistic masters to a Christian slave society.

Because of the continued persistence and expansion of slavery in Virginia after the Revolution, the magazine found that it could reprint a 1749 address by the noted evangelical Philip Doddridge of Northampton, England. While Doddridge's thoughts on family religion may had lost some of their relevance by 1805 in the North, where slavery and other forms of unfree labor had been declining for decades, his words had much meaning for southern households that still contained relations of production as well as reproduction. [70] Doddridge's "Plain and Serious Address to the Master of a Family, on the Important Subject of Family Religion," urged masters to consider "the children and servants committed to your care." Doddridge sounded much like Virginia ministers who wrote and preached decades after him when he stated, "I now consider you as a parent, and a master. *The father of a family* is a phrase that comprehends both these relations; and with great propriety, as humanity obliges us to endeavour to take a parental care of all under our roof." [71] The ideals of "family religion" that Doddridge promoted continued half a century later to resonate strongly among Virginia evangelicals interested in molding paternalistic slaveholders.

The *Religious Magazine*'s desire to promote the ideals, and obligations, of "parental care" among masters continued in the very next issue. An article entitled "Observations on the Sabbath" lamented that masters "long accustomed to opinions both erroneous and unjust . . . have become easy in the utter neglect of their duty to their servants. . . ." The present behavior of masters deviated drastically from proper Christian paternal care. "He is now a humane and benevolent master, who takes care of the body, even if he pays no respect to the soul."[72] The material treatment of slaves was no accurate measure of a true Christian household; as other evangelicals also pointed out, only the sincere interest in the spiritual life of his slaves made one a genuine Christian master.

Undoubtedly the strongest and most thorough vision of the ideal paternalistic slaveholder appeared in the May–June 1807 edition of the *Religious Magazine*. "A Sabbath Evening, at Mr. Jervas's" depicts the model paternalist, who teaches his visitor the duties and benefits of the Christian care of slaves.[73] This article brings together the several strands of paternalistic proslavery Christianity and presents a conception of southern slave society that strikingly resembles the conceptions found in the writings of proslavery ideologues of the 1850s. While other aspects of proslavery thought, such as the critique of free labor and the pseudoscientific racial argument, were only beginning to emerge in the generation after the Revolution and would not figure prominently until the 1830s, the notion of the hierarchical, paternalistic, Christian household that characterized evangelical discussions of slavery by 1810 remained a constant feature of the southern defense of the social order there.[74]

Much of the article on Jervas is in the form of a conversation in which the narrator questioned Jervas about his conduct of his household in general and of his slaves in particular. Struck by the slaves' ability to recite part of the catechism, the narrator asked Jervas, "[I]f you were not afraid, that giving them such instructions would inspire them with high notions of liberty, and make them both troublesome and dangerous?" Jervas immediately replied "not at all" and proceeded to expound upon the protection Christian instruction of slaves would provide both individual masters and the society as a whole. "The knowledge and precepts of Christianity," Jervas claimed, "and the practice of its duties will never lead men to rebellion or insurrection."[75] Perhaps responding to the uncertainty and fears prompted by Gabriel's Rebellion of 1800 and the Easter Plot of 1802, Jervas argued that only the proper Christianization of slaves could avoid further uprisings.[76] Far from encouraging rebellion among slaves, "the readiest way to incline them to act as they ought, is to train them up according to the precepts of the gospel."[77]

Jervas further contended that not only did Christianity reduce the possibility of rebellion, it also produced better workers by instilling in them more effective motivations for industriousness and obedience than fear. Maintaining that "the best and most enlightened christians, were the best servants," Jervas related a story about "an excellent old lady, who frequently observed, that the preachers who instructed her servants in the doctrines and duties of religion, were of much more advantage to her, than all the overseers she ever employed." Jervas echoed those ministers who criticized masters who abused their authority and claimed that those masters who believed and acted as if slaves "were only made to work, to be cursed, and to be beaten," were both "inhuman and impolitic." "It is inhuman, because negroes have immortal souls. . . . It is impolitic, because every servant is thus made an enemy; or to say the least, no servant has any motive but that of fear to induce him to discharge his duty."[78] Christian paternalism would strengthen slavery and reduce the potential for slave revolt by producing faithful, dutiful laborers. Jervas's primary message, like that of many other evangelicals, was that masters had to meet their obligations; God's favor depended upon the sincere fulfillment of their Christian duties. The point of being a good Christian master was not exclusively or even primarily to increase production or eliminate slave rebellion. One was a Christian master because God desired it, for his sake. A master acted as he did not for profit or earthly security but for divine glory.

Jervas succinctly conveyed the essence of the Christian paternalistic ideal in the course of the interview. "[T]he duties of masters and servants are reciprocal. It is the servant's duty to honour and obey his master, and serve him with fidelity. It is the master's duty to protect, feed, and clothe his servant, and give him such instruction as is necessary for salvation." Jervas recognized, however, that while these duties were reciprocal, the enforcement of the slave's was far easier than the master's. Thus, he argued, the master must rely on his sense of Christian duty even more so than must the slave. The master's freedom from external coercion made him depend all the more on his own internal conscience. "If the servant fails on his part," Jervas asserted, "the law allows compulsory measures; if the master fails in his duty, what can be done? Shall it be said, he has so many [slaves] that he cannot discharge the duties which he owes them? I fear that in the bar of conscience, the validity of this excuse can hardly be admitted." Jervas then returned to a familiar theme in these evangelical writings: What determined the sinfulness or sanctity of a relation was how well the parties to it fulfilled the duties it imposed upon them. "The only question here is, do the duties I have mentioned, result from the relation of master and servant? If they do, then no accidental circumstance can destroy the obligation. . . . At the day of *judgement,* it will hardly be enquired, how many servants we possessed; but how we discharged the duties we owed them." Jervas insisted that unless masters overcame "a worldly spirit," which encouraged accumulation of wealth and neglect of duties, and recognized the divine nature of their duties, "the judgements of Heaven" could not for long be averted.[79]

Jervas's "gloomy apprehensions" about the lack of proper Christian paternalism did not, however, triumph over his more optimistic expectations of a Christian slaveholding society. If, he pondered hopefully, "the time were once come, when all the slaves in Virginia were Christianized, and made acquainted with those truths which are necessary to a holy life, all nations in the earth might call us blessed." Not only would the world look favorably upon such a Virginia, but white Virginians, whose Christian behavior and instruction had brought the slaves to Christianity, would enjoy earthly peace and divine blessing. "Plots and insurrections, and all the horrid ideas, which now haunt the minds of so many misguided people, would no more be apprehended, servants would do their duty. . . ."[80] Like his fellow evangelicals throughout Virginia, Jervas believed that the master-slave relation could become, through Christianity, the basis of a society "all nations in the earth might call blessed."

By 1810, the ideas expressed by Jervas had become commonplace among Virginia evangelicals. Individual Virginians opposed to slavery no doubt continued to believe that slaveholding and Christianity were incompatible; but these individuals could not turn the denominations to which they belonged into vehicles of organized antislavery. Nowhere was the triumph of the proslavery consensus more apparent than among the Methodists, who had moved against slavery most vigorously in the years following the Revolution. The Methodist general conference, which had maintained an official antislavery position in its rules contained in the *Doctrines and Discipline,* in 1808 authorized "each annual conference to form [its] own regulations relative to buying and selling slaves."[81] This rule essentially let southerners determine for themselves how to deal with the questions of slavery and slave trading. Jesse Lee, the antislavery Methodist minister and historian, demonstrated a gift for understatement in 1810 when he wrote that "a long experience has taught us, that the various rules which have been made on this business [slavery] have not been attended with that success which was expected."[82]

Perhaps most revealing, Francis Asbury by 1809 had reconciled himself to the reality he had fearfully glimpsed in 1798. Although he remained steadfastly opposed to slavery, he now wondered, "Would not an *amelioration* in the condition and treatment of slaves have produced more practical good to the poor Africans, than any attempt at their *emancipation?*" Frustrated at the continued reluctance of slaveholders, particularly in South Carolina, to permit Methodists to preach to their slaves, Asbury worried that because "the blacks are deprived of the means of instruction; who will take the pains to lead them into the way of salvation . . . but the Methodists?" Recognizing, as did many who did not share his attitudes toward slavery, that as a Christian and a minister the spirit mattered far more than the flesh, Asbury resigned himself to asking rhetorical questions: "What is the personal liberty of the African which he may abuse, to the salvation of his soul; how may it be compared?"[83] Asbury's questions reflected not so much the reversal of southern Christian antislavery as an admission of its defeat. Faced with not only a materially powerful system of social relations but a theologically entrenched Christian proslavery sentiment, those few remaining antislavery southern Christians, like Asbury, accepted what they could not change. After 1810 the silence of the opponents of slavery merely allowed the proslavery ministers and laity more latitude to develop and refine the ideas and beliefs they had been promulgating and embracing for decades. When the showdown in the churches between northerners and southerners arrived in the 1840s, southerners drew upon more than a half century of experience to claim, without hesitation or fear of inconsistency, that "[w]e who own slaves honor God's law."[84]

NOTES

1. Elmer T. Clark, Manning J. Potts, and Jacob S. Payton, eds., *The Journal and Letters of Francis Asbury*, 3 vols. (Nashville, Tenn.: Abingdon Press, 1958), 2:151.

2. See, for instance, Arthur Dicken Thomas Jr., "The Second Great Awakening in Virginia and Slavery Reform" (Th.D. thesis, Union Theological Seminary, 1981); J. Earl Thompson Jr., "Slavery and Presbyterianism in the Revolutionary Era," *Journal of Presbyterian History* 54 (spring 1976): 121–41; John Boles, *The Great Revival, 1787–1805: The Origins of the Southern Evangelical Mind* (Lexington: University Press of Kentucky, 1972); Nathan Hatch, *The Democratization of American Christianity* (New Haven: Yale University Press, 1989); Rhys Isaac, *The Transformation of Virginia, 1740–1790* (Chapel Hill: University of North Carolina Press, 1982); and Gerald Mullin, *Flight and Rebellion: Slave Resistance in Eighteenth-Century Virginia* (New York: Oxford University Press, 1972). Notable exceptions to this tendency include Robert McColley, *Slavery and Jeffersonian Virginia*, 2d ed.(Urbana: University of Illinois Press, 1973); Peter Joseph Albert, "The Protean Institution: The Geography, Economy, and Ideology of Slavery in Post-Revolutionary Virginia" (Ph.D. diss., University of Maryland, 1976); Allan Kulikoff, *Tobacco and Slaves: The Development of Southern Cultures in the Chesapeake, 1680–1800* (Chapel Hill: University of North Carolina Press, 1986); Fredrika Teute Schmidt and Barbara Ripel Wilhelm, "Early Proslavery Petitions in Virginia," *William and Mary Quarterly*, 3d ser., 30 (January 1973), 133–146; and most recently, Sylvia Frey, *Water from the Rock: Black Resistance in a Revolutionary Age* (Princeton: Princeton University Press, 1991).

3. The idea that proslavery Christianity developed well before the rise of the abolitionist movement in the 1830s can be found in the following works: W. Harrison Daniel, "Southern Protestantism and Slavery in the Revolutionary Generation," *Virginia Social Science Journal* 14 (November 1979): 36–43; Daniel, "The Methodist Episcopal Church and the Negro in the Early National Period," *Methodist History* 11 (January 1973): 40–53; Rachel Klein, *Unification of a*

Slave State: The Rise of the Planter Class in the South Carolina Backcountry, 1760–1808 (Chapel Hill: University of North Carolina Press, 1990), especially chap. 9; Frey, *Water from the Rock,* Richard Beeman, *The Evolution of the Southern Backcountry: A Case Study of Lunenburg County, Virginia, 1746–1832* (Philadelphia: University of Pennsylvania Press, 1984); James Essig, *The Bonds of Wickedness: American Evangelicals against Slavery, 1770–1808* (Philadelphia: Temple University Press, 1982); Donald Mathews, *Slavery and American Methodism: A Chapter in American Morality, 1780–1845* (Princeton: Princeton University Press, 1965); Essig, *Religion in the Old South* (Chicago: University of Chicago Press, 1977); David Brion Davis, *The Problem of Slavery in the Age of Revolution, 1770–1823* (Ithaca, N.Y.: Cornell University Press, 1975); and Larry E. Tise, *Proslavery: A History of the Defense of Slavery in America, 1701–1840* (Athens: University of Georgia Press, 1987).

4. See Isaac, *Transformation of Virginia;* Thomas J. Buckley, S.J., *Church and State in Revolutionary Virginia, 1776–1787* (Charlottesville: University of Virginia Press, 1977); Buckley, "Evangelicals Triumphant: The Baptists' Assault on the Virginia Glebes, 1786–1801," *William and Mary Quarterly,* 45 (January 1988): 33–69.

5. Isaac, *Transformation of Virginia,* especially chap. 13.

6. Ibid., 309.

7. Elizabeth Fox-Genovese, "Antebellum Southern Households: A New Perspective on a Familiar Question," *Review* 7, no. 2 (fall 1983): 215–253, and *Within the Plantation Household: Black and White Women of the Old South* (Chapel Hill: University of North Carolina Press, 1988), especially chap. 1, most forcefully and persuasively establishes the fundamental importance of the household in southern slave society. For other works that similarly demonstrate the southern household's persistent hierarchical character, see Stephanie McCurry, "Defence of Their World: Gender, Class, and the Yeomanry of the South Carolina Low Country, 1820–1860" (Ph.D. diss., State University of New York at Binghamton, 1989); McCurry, "The Politics of Yeoman Households in South Carolina," in *Divided Houses: Gender and the Civil War,* Catherine Clinton and Nina Silber, eds. (New York: Oxford University Press, 1992), 22–38; and Klein, *Unification of a Slave State.*

8. See, for example, Winthrop Jordan, *White over Black: American Attitudes toward the Negro, 1550–1812* (Chapel Hill: University of North Carolina Press, 1968), chap. 12; John C. Miller, *The Wolf by the Ears: Thomas Jefferson and Slavery* (New York: The Free Press, 1977); Davis, *Problem of Slavery in the Age of Revolution,* chap. 4; Lucia C. Stanton, "'Those Who Labor For My Happiness': Thomas Jefferson and His Slaves," in *Jeffersonian Legacies,* Peter Onuf, ed. (Charlottesville: University of Virginia Press, 1992), 147–80; and Paul Finkelman, "Jefferson and Slavery: 'Treason Against the Hopes of the World,'" in *Jeffersonian Legacies,* 181–221.

9. See Albert, "Protean Institution"; and Theodore Stoddard Babcock, "Manumission in Virginia, 1782–1806" (M.A. thesis, University of Virginia, 1974).

10. St. George Tucker, *A Dissertation on Slavery: With a Proposal for the Gradual Abolition of It, in the State of Virginia,* (Philadelphia: Matthew Carey, 1796).

11. See those sources listed in fn. 8 above.

12. McColley, *Slavery and Jeffersonian Virginia,* 141; Babcock, "Manumission in Virginia."

13. McColley, *Slavery and Jeffersonian Virginia,* 135. Tucker's lack of success with the Virginia

legislature led him to appeal to the wider public. He appended his pamphlet to his widely read edition of Blackstone's *Commentaries on the Laws of England.* Yet here too Tucker's plan received little response or support.

14. The quotation is from Thomas Coke, *Extracts of the Journals of the Rev. Dr. Coke's Three Visits to America* (London: Printed and sold at the New Chapel, City Road; and at the Rev. Mr. Wesley's Preaching-House, in Town and Country, 1790), 46. For another contemporary account of this episode, see Jesse Lee, *A Short History of the Methodists, . . .* (Baltimore: Magill and Clime, 1810), 88, 101–2. Most secondary studies of early Methodism discuss the brief history of the antislavery rule. Among them see especially, Robert A. Armour, "The Opposition to the Methodist Church in Eighteenth-Century Virginia" (Ph.D. diss., University of Georgia, 1968), chap. 5; Mathews, *Slavery and American Methodism,* 9–13; and W. Harrison Daniel, "The Methodist Episcopal Church and the Negro."

15. Minton Thrift, *Memoirs of the Rev. Jesse Lee with Extracts from his Journals* (New York: N. Bangs and T. Mason, 1823; reprint, New York: Arno Press, 1969), 79.

16. Coke, *Extracts of the Journals,* 35.

17. William K. Boyd, ed., "A Journal and Travel of James Meacham," pt. 2, *Historical Papers,* Trinity College Historical Society, ser. 10 (1914), 90.

18. The discussion below will focus on Baptist antislavery and the popular reaction against it. Henry Pattillo, a Presbyterian minister from Granville County, North Carolina, who occasionally preached in Virginia, spoke of similar popular opposition to antislavery in a 1799 letter to William Williamson of South Carolina. "The subject of manumission," Pattillo wrote, "will greatly injure our interest as a church. I once treated it with caution: it offended some, & pleased none; tho' I mentioned it in a very distant object." Pattillo to Williamson, December 4, 1799, Shane Collection, Presbyterian Historical Society, Philadelphia, Pa. In 1787 Pattillo wrote *The Plain Planter's Family Assistant; Containing an Address to Husbands and Wives, Children and Servants, . . .* (Wilmington, N.C.: James Adams, 1787). In it he not only did not promote manumission, he presented one of the most paternalistic views of southern slavery in the postrevolutionary South. Although Pattillo will not be discussed below, his *Plain Planter's Family Assistant* was surely read by some Virginians, and it strongly supports this essay's contention that paternalistic, proslavery Christianity was well established in the decades following the Revolution. See *Plain Planter's Family Assistant,* 21–28; 46–50.

19. For some individual Baptist critiques of slavery, see John Leland, *The Virginia Chronicle: With Judicious and Critical Remarks, Under 24 Heads* (Fredricksburg, Va.: T. Green, 1790); Leland, "Letter of Valediction, on Leaving Virginia in 1791," in *The Writings of Elder John Leland,* L. F. Greene, ed., (New York: G. Wood, 1845); David Barrow, *Circular Letter* (Norfolk, Va.: Willett & O'Connor, 1798); John Poindexter to Isaac Backus, April 3, 1797, Virginia Baptist Historical Society, Richmond, Va. (hereafter VBHS); and Benjamin Watkins to Isaac Backus, May 22, 1795, VBHS. Both Leland and Barrow left Virginia before the end of the decade, in large part because of the intransigence of the people on slavery.

20. *Minutes of the Baptist General Committee Held at Nuckol's Meeting-House in the County of Goochland; May, 1791* (Richmond, Va., 1791), typescript copy, VBHS. These minutes from 1791 contain the only reference to the 1785 resolution. See also, Essig, *Bonds of Wickedness,* 67–69.

21. *Minutes of the Baptist General Committee at Their Yearly Meeting Held in the City of Richmond, May 8th, 1790* (Richmond, Va., 1790), typescript copy, VBHS.

22. *Minutes of the Baptist General Committee, Holden at Muddy Creek Meeting-House: Powhatan County, Virginia, May, 1793* (Richmond, Va., 1793), typescript copy, VBHS. The position of the committee reflects the paradoxical stance many southern clergy and churches took vis-à-vis slavery throughout the antebellum era. The abolition of slavery, they often asserted, was essentially a political question and therefore beyond the scope of legitimate church action. But slaveholding, as a relation between human beings, necessarily involved ethical and moral elements and, thus, fell within the rightful jurisdiction of ministers and the churches generally. For more on this point, see Mitchell Snay, *Gospel of Disunion: Religion and Separatism in the Antebellum South* (New York: Cambridge University Press, 1993), 28–29, 38–39, 41.

23. Essig, *Bonds of Wickedness,* 68–69.

24. "Minutes of the Strawberry District Association, (Concord Meeting-House), May, 1792," handwritten MS copy, 45, VBHS.

25. "Minutes of the Roanoak [*sic*] District Association (Pittsylvania County), June, 1790 (Hillsborough, Va.: Printed by R. Ferguson), handwritten copy, 39, VBHS.

26. Ibid., 39–40.

27. Mathews, *Slavery and Methodism,* 23. The evidence from Virginia tends to support Nathan Hatch's argument that the period following the Revolution witnessed the emergence of "religious populism." That evidence, however, calls into question Hatch's assertion that Methodist and Baptist attacks on slavery posed a "radical challenge to the doctrines of paternalism and absolute slave obedience that Anglican evangelizers had so actively formulated." Hatch, *The Democratization of American Christianity* (New Haven: Yale University Press, 1989), 103. While some Methodists and Baptists did pose this challenge, they were hardly "popular." The popular ministers, as will be argued below, promoted paternalism and preached obedience. See also Armour, "Opposition to the Methodist Church," chap. 5.

28. The most famous instance of explicit proslavery action in early national Virginia occurred in 1784–85 when a series of proslavery petitions poured into the House of Delegates. Fearful of liberal manumission or even general emancipation bills, which some antislavery Methodists had petitioned for, some petitioners appealed to scriptural justifications of slavery as well as to other arguments based on expedience that would become familiar in the decades ahead. They argued that freed slaves would become public charges at best, dangerous "banditti" at worst; that emancipation would undermine the property rights only recently secured by the Revolution; and that the unrestrained African American might commit every crime from theft to rape to murder. These petitions clearly demonstrate the strength of proslavery sentiment at a moment when slavery itself seemed in imminent danger. Although some of the petitions did not mention religion and others used it primarily as a gloss, others, particularly that petition from Brunswick County, did invoke the divine sanction of slavery and alluded to a slaveholding ethic that delineated the duties, obligations, and values that inhered in the relation between master and slave. While the petitions, in general, basically expressed fears and appealed to expedience, some did foreshadow the proslavery Christianity that grew in the generation following the Revolution and established among many white Virginians the conviction that slavery both prevented the atroci-

ties so feared by the petitioners and, more important, constituted the fulfillment of God's commands. See the petitions from Amelia County, November 10, 1785; Brunswick County, November 10, 1785; and Halifax County, November 10, 1785 —all located in the Virginia State Library, Richmond, Va. These petitions and others have been reprinted and intelligently introduced in Schmidt and Wilhelm, "Early Proslavery Petitions in Virginia," 133 –46. On the Methodist petition for general emancipation, which the legislature unanimously rejected, see Richard K. MacMaster, "Liberty or Property? The Methodists [*sic*] Petition for Emancipation in Virginia, 1785," *Methodist History* 10, no. 1 (October 1971): 44–55, and Armour, "Opposition to the Methodist Church," chap. 5.

29. There are a number of useful studies of Jarratt, although we need a full-length study of him. See Wesley M. Gewehr, *The Great Awakening in Virginia, 1740–1790* (Durham, N.C.: Duke University Press, 1930), chap. 6; Harry G. Rabe, "The Reverend Devereaux [*sic*] Jarratt and the Virginia Social Order," *Historical Magazine of the Protestant Episcopal Church* (hereafter *HMPEC*), 33, no. 4 (December 1964): 299–306; William Warren Sweet, *Men of Zeal: The Romance of American Methodist Beginnings* (New York, 1935), chap. 1; and David L. Holmes, "Devereux Jarratt: A Letter and a Reevaluation," *HMPEC,* 47, no. 1 (March 1978): 37–49. Also see Jarratt's autobiography, *The Life of Devereux Jarratt Rector of Bath Parish, Dinwiddie County, Virginia . . .* , John Coleman, ed. (Baltimore: Warner & Hanna, 1806).

30. Jarratt, *Sermons on Various and Important Subjects, In Practical Divinity, Adapted to the Meanest Capacities and Suited to the Family and Closet. In Three Volumes* (Philadelphia: Johnston & Justice, 1793), I, 250.

31. Jarratt, *Sermons,* 2:297.

32. Coke's criticism of Jarratt can be found in his journals. On one occasion Coke mentions that he "passed by the house of Mr. Jarratt that violent asserter of the propriety and justice of Negro slavery." Coke, *Extracts of the Journals,* 39. For more on Jarratt's break with the Methodists, see Jarratt, *Life of the Reverend Devereux Jarratt,* 114, 119; Rabe, "The Reverend Devereaux [*sic*] Jarratt,"; and William Warren Sweet, "New Light on the Relation of Early American Methodism to the Anglican Clergy in Virginia and North Carolina," *HMPEC,* 22, no. 1 (March 1953): 69–90.

33. The original letter of March 22, 1788, is located in the Dromgoole Papers, Southern Historical Collection, University of North Carolina Library, Chapel Hill, N.C. The papers are available on microfilm, and several of the letters between Jarratt and Dromgoole have been reprinted in Sweet, "New Light on the Relation. . . ." Dromgoole was not alone among Methodists who continued to maintain good relations with Jarratt. In a 1790 journal entry Asbury mentioned that Jarratt "preached for us [at a conference]; friends at first are friends again at last." Asbury, *Journals* 1:642. Upon Jarratt's death in 1801 Asbury wrote, "He was a man of genius, possessed a great deal of natural oratory, was an excellent reader, and a good writer. . . . I have reason to presume that he was instrumentally successful in awakening hundreds of souls to some sense of religion, in that dark day and time [1770s and 1780s]." Asbury, *Journals* 2:289. Asbury also preached Jarratt's funeral sermon. Jesse Lee in his 1810 history of the Methodists also spoke highly of Jarratt. See Lee, *Short History,* 54, 81–82. Also see Thrift, *Memoir of Jesse Lee,* 11, 63.

34. For antebellum scriptural defenses of slavery, see, for example, Thornton Stringfellow,

"The Bible Argument: or, Slavery in the Light of Divine Revelation," in *Cotton is King and Pro-Slavery Arguments* (Augusta, Ga.: Pritchard, Abbott & Loomis, 1860), 459–546; Richard Furman, *Exposition of the Baptists in Relation to the Colored Population of the United States in a Communication to the Governor of South Carolina* (Charleston, S.C., 1823); and Frederick A. Ross, *Slavery Ordained of God* (Philadelphia: J. B. Lippincott, 1859).

35. Jarratt to Dromgoole, March 22, 1788, Dromgoole Papers, microfilm, reel 1, Virginia Historical Society, Richmond, Va. (hereafter VHS).

36. Jarratt, *Thoughts on Some Important Subjects in Divinity, in a Series of Letters to a Friend* (Baltimore: Warner & Hanna, 1806), 76. This pamphlet was included as an appendix to Jarratt's *Autobiography*. Arno Press's 1969 reprint of the *Autobiography* does not include the pamphlet.

37. Among others, Anne Loveland and Eugene Genovese and Elizabeth Fox-Genovese have made this point in their studies of antebellum southern evangelicals. See Loveland, *Southern Evangelicals and the Social Order, 1800–1860* (Baton Rouge: Louisiana State University Press, 1980), 209, and Genovese and Fox-Genovese, "The Divine Sanction of Social Order: Religious Foundations of the Southern Slaveholders' World View," *Journal of the American Academy of Religion* 55, no. 2 (June 1987): 211–33.

38. Jarratt spoke frequently about fallen humanity. "By nature indeed," he wrote in one sermon, "there is no good dwelling in man. He is altogether corrupt and abominable, and every imagination of the heart is evil continually." Jarratt, *Sermons*, 3:164. For similar comments Jarrett, 1:69; 2:22, 181–82, 270; Jarratt, *A Sermon Preached Before the Convention of the Protestant Episcopal Church in Virginia, at Richmond, May 3, 1792*, 4th ed. (Danbury, Va.: John C. Gray, 1809), iii, 12.

39. William Harper, "Memoir on Slavery," in *The Pro-Slavery Argument as Maintained by the Most Distinguished Writers of the Southern States* (Charleston, S.C.: Walker, Richards, 1852), 9.

40. Jarratt, *Thoughts on Some Important Subjects*, 76–78.

41. Jarratt, *Sermons*, 2:8–9. As this sermon makes clear, churches during this era were interracial. While separate African American meetings may have taken place, they were in addition to biracial services. Thus, slaves heard ministers implore masters to act according to Christian precepts of responsible authority, even if those slaves did not necessarily internalize all the ministers' advice regarding their own divinely ordained duties. Nonetheless, from such sermons as this, Christian slaves received instruction on how not only to conduct themselves but also on how they could judge their masters. Such instruction provided them with a model of relations that, however unjust, recognized them as human beings to whom masters owed certain obligations. While this essay focuses on the role of religion in white Virginians' evolving ideas about slavery, the evidence considered also suggests that black Virginians were taught the same principles about duties, responsibilities, and proper Christian behavior. The inculcation of these principles among all Virginians helped make paternalism the guiding ideal, if not always the reality, of master-slave relations. On paternalism, see Eugene Genovese, *Roll, Jordan, Roll: The World the Slaves Made* (New York: Pantheon, 1975), passim. On the biracial character of southern churches, see John B. Boles, introduction, *Masters and Slaves in the House of the Lord: Race and Religion in the American South 1740–1870*, Boles, ed. (Lexington: University of Kentucky Press, 1988), 1–18; Larry M. James, "Biracial Fellowship in Antebellum Baptist

Churches," in Boles, ed., *Masters and Slaves*, 37–57; and Boles, *Black Southerners, 1619–1869* (Lexington: University of Kentucky Press, 1983), 153–69.

42. *Minutes of the Baptist Dover Association . . . October, 1796* (Richmond, Va.: Thomas Nicolson, 1797), 9.

43. "Minutes of the Virginia Portsmouth Baptist Association, May 1800" (n.p., n.d.; front page of copy in VBHS missing), 7.

44. Christopher Collins, "Memorandum Book, 1796–1803," VHS.

45. Collins, "Journal, 1803–1804," VHS.

46. Perhaps the most noted Virginia Methodist opponent of slavery was James O'Kelly. O'Kelly, an elder of the church who eventually split from it in 1792 over the question of Episcopal authority, wrote the strongly antislavery *Essay on Negro Slavery* (Philadelphia: Prichard and Hall, 1789). For more on O'Kelly, see Lee, *A Short History*, 203–4, Charles Franklin Kilgore, *The James O'Kelly Schism in the Methodist Episcopal Church* (Mexico City: Casa Unida de Publicaciones, 1963), and Sweet, *Virginia Methodism*, 128–34.

47. The most complete study of the debate over slavery in antebellum Virginia is Alison Goodyear Freehling, *Drift toward Dissolution: The Virginia Slavery Debate of 1831–1832* (Baton Rouge: Louisiana State University Press, 1982). Freehling's argument that a "legacy of emancipation" existed in Virginia in the years leading up to the debate focuses rather narrowly on political leaders, such as Thomas Jefferson, and actions, such as the 1806 revision of the manumission law. She thus tends to underestimate the ways in which rank and file Virginia slaveholders continued to maintain a "legacy of slavery" that enabled them to reconcile their slaveholding with their morality. While political leaders may have continued to label slavery an "evil," they emphasized, as Freehling points out, the economic costs and physical danger of slave rebellion rather than the immorality and oppression of slaveholding. The morality of slaveholding did not become an object of debate; no antislavery Christian argument emerged in Virginia in 1831–32. Freehling's important study allows us to see how the two competing traditions of antislavery and proslavery existed within Virginia for decades following the Revolution. But by 1831 that antislavery tradition had abandoned moral, humanitarian arguments in favor of pragmatic, expedient economic and social ones. See Freehling, *Drift Toward Dissolution*, chaps. 4 and 5.

48. Stith Mead, "A General Letter My Third Epistle to the Botetourteans and the Greenbrireans," November 22, 1794, Stith Mead Letterbook, VHS, 108. One cannot help but read Mead's admonition about "fathers provoking their children to wrath" as justification for his own estrangement from his father. Mead could still preach obedience of children to fathers in good faith, of course, because his father had failed to fulfill his Christian duty. For more on Mead, see Sweet, *Virginia Methodism*, 163–64, and Robert M. Calhoon, *Evangelicals and Conservatives in the Early South, 1740–1861* (Columbia: University of South Carolina Press, 1988), 101. Mead's reference to the "Botetourteans and the Greenbrireans" suggests that while much of the evidence of proslavery Christianity comes from those regions with the highest concentration of slaves and slaveholders, the Tidewater and Piedmont counties, Christians in counties located west of the Blue Ridge, such as Botetourt, and even in counties west of the Alleghenies, such as Greenbrier, heard similar messages from their ministers.

49. John Early Diary, VHS, January 4, 1813.

50. Ibid., January 23, 1814.

51. Ibid., January 8, 1809.

52. William Graham, "Lectures on Moral Philosophy," "Lecture 25. Of the Relations of Man to Man," microfilm copy, Union Theological Seminary Library, Union Theological Seminary, Richmond, Va., 131. The material from these lectures comes from the notes taken by Joseph Glass in 1796 and hand copied in 1896. The copy is located in the Special Collections of Cyrus Hall McCormick Library, Washington and Lee University, Lexington, Va. For more on Graham, see Robert Goggin Gillespie Jr., "Reverend William Graham: Presbyterian Minister and Rector of Liberty Hall Academy" (M.A. thesis, University of Virginia, 1970), Ernest Trice Thompson, *Presbyterians in the South,* 3 vols. (Richmond: John Knox Press, 1963–1973), 1:80–82, 252–254, and David W. Robson, "'An Important Question Answered': William Graham's Defense of Slavery in Post-Revolutionary Virginia," *William and Mary Quarterly,* 3d. ser. 37, no. 4 (October 1980): 644–52. Robson's article also contains the text of one of Graham's most important lectures, "Lecture 30th. An Important Question Answered," which is discussed below.

53. Robson, "'An Important Question Answered.'"

54. Ibid., 648.

55. Graham, "Lectures on Moral Philosophy," "Lecture 30th. An Important Question Answered," 161–65. Note here Graham's interesting reasoning regarding emancipation and slaveholding, which resembles the position of the 1793 Baptist General Committee discussed in n. 22 above. Graham considered emancipation a "political or civil" action. The church had no specific role in the "civil" realm, and emancipation was thus irrelevant to Christian concerns. But because in the earlier lecture he had included slavery among the "domestic" rather than the "civil" relations of man to man, the church rightfully judged "the performance of the duties of" people according to their "several stations."

56. William Hill, "Journal and Autobiography, 1787–1792," Union Theological Seminary Library. Hill's writings have been published as *Autobiographical Sketches of Dr. William Hill, Together With His Account of the Revival of Religion in Prince Edward County and Biographical Sketches of the Life and Character of the Reverend Dr. Moses Hoge of Virginia* (Richmond, Va.: Union Theological Seminary Historical Transcripts, no. 4, 1968). For more on Hill, see W. B. Sprague, *Annals of the American Pulpit,* 9 vols. (New York: R. Carter and Brothers, 1858–1869), 3:563–70.

57. William Hill, "Funeral Sermon for General Daniel Morgan, July, 1802," VHS.

58. James Blythe, *The Death of the Good Man Precious in the Sight of God....* (Lexington, Ky.: Joseph Charles, 1804), 24.

59. "A Prayer for Family," *The Virginia Religious Magazine,* 1, no. 2 (March 1805): 111.

60. The most important discussion of paternalism in the antebellum South is Genovese, *Roll, Jordan, Roll.* Scholars have subsequently explored the "origins of paternalism" in the eighteenth century. See Alan Gallay, "The Origins of Slaveholders' Paternalism: George Whitefield, the Bryan Family, and the Great Awakening in the South," *Journal of Southern History* 53, no. 3 (August 1987): 369–94; Philip Morgan, "Three Planters and Their Slaves: Perspectives on Slavery in Virginia, South Carolina, and Jamaica, 1750–1790," in Winthrop D. Jordan and Sheila Skemp, eds., *Race and Family in the Colonial South* (Jackson: University Press of Mississippi,

1987), 37–80; and Frey, *Water from the Rock,* chap. 8. As Frey and Morgan both point out, the elaboration and acceptance of paternalism was a process that took place at an uneven rate over a long period. Nonetheless, as all these studies point out, paternalism as an ideal to be preached and practiced existed and circulated, particularly in the churches, well before the end of the eighteenth century.

61. "An Address from the Presbytery of Hanover, to the Congregations under its care," *Virginia Religious Magazine* 3, no. 3 (May–June 1807): 159.

62. *Minutes of the Baptist Dover Association . . . October, 1796,* 12.

63. For some of the secondary studies that examine the religious conviction of proslavery southerners, see William Sumner Jenkins, *Pro-Slavery Thought in the Old South* (Chapel Hill: University of North Carolina Press, 1935; reprint, Gloucester, Mass.: Peter Smith, 1960), chap. 5; Mathews, *Religion in the Old South,* especially chap. 4; McCurry, "Defense of Their World," chaps. 3–5; Genovese, *"Slavery Ordained of God";* Genovese and Fox-Genovese, "Religious Ideals of Southern Slave Society"; Genovese and Fox-Genovese, "Divine Sanction of Southern Order"; Jack P. Maddex Jr., "Proslavery Millennialism: Social Eschatology in Antebellum Southern Calvinism," *American Quarterly* 31 (spring 1979): 46–61; Maddex, "'The Southern Apostasy' Revisited: The Significance of Proslavery Christianity," *Marxist Perspectives* 7 (fall 1979): 132–41; Loveland, *Southern Evangelicals and the Social Order;* Mitchell Snay, "American Thought and Southern Distinctiveness: The Southern Clergy and the Sanctification of Slavery," *Civil War History* 35, no. 4 (September 1989): 311–28; Snay, *Gospel of Disunion,* especially chaps. 2 and 3; and James Oscar Farmer Jr., *The Metaphysical Confederacy: James Henley Thornwell and the Synthesis of Southern Values* (Macon, Ga.: Mercer University Press, 1986).

64. Jarratt, *Sermons,* 3:267–68.

65. *Minutes of the Virginia Portsmouth Baptist Association, May, 1800,* 7–9.

66. *Minutes of the Baptist Dover Association . . . October, 1796* (Richmond, Va.: Thomas Nicolson, 1797), 9.

67. *Minutes of the Virginia Portsmouth Association, May, 1800,* 7–10.

68. *Minutes of the Baptist Dover Association . . . October 14th, 1797* (Richmond, Va.: John Dixon), 8. The passage is from Colossians 4:1. The Dover Association's circular letter of 1796 cited the exact same verse. See *Minutes of the Baptist Dover Association . . . October, 1796,* 12.

69. *The Virginia Religious Magazine* 1, no. 1 (October 1804): iv.

70. On the decline of slavery and other forms of unfree labor in the North after the Revolution, see Arthur Zilversmit, *The First Emancipation: The Abolition of Slavery in the North* (Chicago: University of Chicago Press, 1967); Gary B. Nash and Jean R. Soderlund, *Freedom by Degrees: Emancipation in Pennsylvania and its Aftermath* (New York: Oxford University Press, 1991); and Shane White, *Somewhat More Independent: The End of Slavery in New York City, 1770–1810* (Athens: University of Georgia Press, 1991). On the nature of southern households, see Fox-Genovese, *Within the Plantation Household,* especially chap. 1, and McCurry, "The Politics of Yeoman Households in South Carolina."

71. P. Doddridge, "A Plain and Serious Address to the Master of a Family, on The Important Subject of Family Religion" (1749), *Virginia Religious Magazine* 1, no. 2, (March 31, 1805): 90–91. Historian Robert M. Calhoon has termed Doddridge's 1744 work, *The Rise and Progress*

of Religion in the Soul, "the most popular and effective of all the evangelical self-help books of the eighteenth century." Calhoon, *Evangelicals and Conservatives,* 17. Doddridge was intimately connected with one of the earliest efforts to Christianize Virginia slaves. The Rev. Samuel Davies, who had been deeply influenced by Doddridge and his writings, published *The Duty of Christians to Propagate Their Religion Among the Heathens, Earnestly Recommended to the Masters of Negro Slaves in Virginia; a Sermon Preached in Hanover, January 8, 1757* (London: J. Oliver, 1758). This pamphlet, like Henry Pattillo's *Plain Planter's Family Assistant* thirty years later and the advice of "Mr. Jervas" discussed below, sought both to extend Christianity to the slaves and to allay fears that such proselytizing would undermine slavery by making slaves rebellious. Davies assured Virginians that "[t]he Appointments of Providence, and the Order of the World, not only admit, but require, that there should be civil Distinctions among Mankind; that some should rule, and some be subject; that some should be Masters, and some Servants. And Christianity does not blend or destroy these Distinctions, but establishes and regulates them, and enjoins every Man to conduct himself according to them." Davies, *The Duty of Christians . . . ,* 23. Davies's pamphlet thus constituted an early effort to promote paternalism as a means of strengthening both Christianity and slavery. Nearly all the arguments proslavery evangelicals made in the decades after the Revolution can be found in Davies's sermon. On Davies's activities in Virginia, see Calhoon, *Evangelicals and Conservatives,* 13–33, and Mechal Sobel, *The World They Made Together: Black and White Values in Eighteenth-Century Virginia* (Princeton: Princeton University Press, 1987), 181–87.

72. "Observations on the Sabbath," *Virginia Religious Magazine* 1, no. 3 (May 31, 1805): 145.

73. "A Sabbath Evening, at Mr. Jervas's," *Virginia Religious Magazine* 3, no. 3 (May–June 1807).

74. Perhaps the greatest antebellum exponent of the household-based Christian slave society was James Henley Thornwell, the brilliant Presbyterian divine, editor of the influential *Southern Presbyterian Review,* and professor and president of the similarly influential South Carolina College. In 1852 Thornwell succinctly pointed out that in the Bible "[w]e find masters exhorted in the same connection with husbands, parents, magistrates; slaves exhorted in the same connection with wives, children and subjects." Thornwell, "Report on Slavery," *Southern Presbyterian Review* 5, no. 3 (January 1852): 383. Although Thornwell's writings contain some of the best examples of antebellum proslavery Christianity, dramatically similar sentiments can be found in countless other religious writings of the 1840s and 1850s. For more on Thornwell, see Farmer, *Metaphysical Confederacy.* For more on southern proslavery religion, see the writings and studies noted in nn. 34 and 63 above. On the development of the proslavery critique of free labor, see Eugene D. Genovese, *The World the Slaveholders Made: Two Essays in Interpretation* (New York: Pantheon, 1969), pt. 2; and Jenkins, *Pro-Slavery Thought in the Old South,* chap. 7. Jenkins, *Pro-Slavery Thought in the Old South,* chap. 6, William Stanton, *The Leopard's Spots: Scientific Attitudes Towards Race in America, 1815–1859* (Chicago: University of Chicago Press, 1960), and Reginald Horsman, *Josiah Nott of Mobile: Southerner, Physician, and Racial Theorist* (Baton Rouge: Louisiana State University Press, 1986) discuss the development of the racial defense of slavery. It is interesting to note that race, while not absent, figures only peripherally in the evidence of proslavery Christianity in early national Virginia.

75. "A Sabbath Evening, at Mr. Jervas's," 162–63.

76. For more on both Gabriel's Rebellion and the Easter Plot, see Douglas Egerton, *Gabriel's Rebellion: The Virginia Slave Conspiracies of 1800 and 1802* (Chapel Hill: University of North Carolina Press, 1993). The conspiracies of 1800 and 1802 elicited little explicit comment from Virginia ministers, unlike the response among politicians. From the religious sources, one could hardly grasp that any conspiracies or reactions had occurred.

77. "A Sabbath Evening, at Mr. Jervas's," 163.

78. Ibid., 163–64.

79. Ibid., 165–167.

80. Ibid., 167, 169–70.

81. *Doctrines and Discipline of the Methodist Episcopal Church,* 14th ed. (1808) (New York: John Wilson and Daniel Hitt, 1808). For more on the Methodists' rules concerning slavery, see Mathews, *Slavery and Methodism,* chaps. 1 and 2. Mathews has conveniently reproduced the rules concerning slavery in an appendix located on pages 293–303.

82. Lee, *A Short History,* 102.

83. Asbury, *Journals,* 2:591.

84. James Furman to W. E. Bailey, quoted in Mathews, *Religion in the Old South,* 136.

Slavery and the Evangelical Enlightenment

ROBERT P. FORBES

It is a truism that evangelical Christianity and Enlightenment liberalism have constituted two of the most influential movements in America. For much of the nation's history, the two forces have existed in a state of tension or outright conflict, each checking the most extreme tendencies and thwarting the ultimate goals of the other. To many participants, American history itself has seemed a struggle between these two poles—interpreted as the clash between righteousness and infidelity, in the eyes of one set of combatants; between the growth of knowledge and the persistence of ignorance and superstition, in the perception of the other.

On rare occasions, however, the goals and assumptions of the adherents of the two movements have converged to extraordinarily powerful effect. (Indeed, on one level, the American Revolution itself may be regarded as the most momentous result of such a convergence.[1]) A similar intersection took place in the second decade of the nineteenth century, when, under the tutelage of moral philosophy, evangelical Christianity accepted and broadened the universalism of the Enlightenment and endowed it with the social authority and the existential urgency of religion.[2] This development created a distinctive cultural phenomenon, which I will refer to here as the Evangelical Enlightenment: a quasi-messianic vision of social and material progress, of global renovation and reform, anticipating the advent of an age of universal liberty, equality, and prosperity within an explicitly Christian, Providential framework.

This vision encompassed many aspects, of which the overthrow of slavery was an essential part. While the separate streams of evangelicalism and moral philosophy *could* be interpreted in ways that did not fundamentally undermine slavery, the fragile supports that each lent to the institution were undermined by crucial aspects of the other. By wedding the empiricism and cosmopolitan civic vision of the Scottish philosophy to the spiritual fervor of evangelicalism, the Evangelical Enlightenment galvanized a radical northern opposition to slavery and contributed to an ideological crisis within the southern planter class that seemed for a moment in the 1830s actually to have shaken its hold.[3]

In this essay, the origins and attributes of the Evangelical Enlightenment will be discussed; an exploration will be made of the ways in which defenders of slavery sought to neutralize this momentous threat to the institution—efforts that, while they failed in their goal of preserving slavery, did succeed in restoring the hostility between liberalism and religion and redirected much of the Enlightenment project of the study of mankind to the service of racism and the justification of European supremacy. These unfortunate developments left a painful legacy that persists to the present day.

The confluence of evangelical Christianity and Enlightenment liberalism only became possible because of a rare conjunction of historical events. The most important of these was the downfall of Napoleon and the end of a quarter century of world war. Like the later conclusions of the First and Second World Wars, and the fall of the Berlin Wall, the peace of 1815 gave rise to sweeping—if short-lived—visions of global peace and cooperation. For Americans, the apparently Providential deliverance of the United States after her own disastrous second war with Britain resulted in an even more urgent sense of relief and gratitude for her unlikely deliverance. No conscientious observer could honestly claim that the nation had been saved by her own efforts. "A revolution, immense, striking, glorious, and delightful, has taken place in the affairs of our blessed country," proclaimed Mathew Carey in April of 1815, "for which we cannot be sufficiently grateful to heaven. We have not—I say emphatically we have not—merited the change."[4]

The peace secured by the Treaty of Ghent that ended the War of 1812 paved the way to an authentically American national policy for the first time. To some observers, it seemed that the true American nation was only now emerging, after a generation of revolution and political violence. "It is but four years," Frances Wright observed in 1819, "that the United States can be said to have enjoyed an acknowledged national existence."[5] Finally disentangled from the European wars of religious politics that they had been fighting by proxy, religious radicals and conservatives declared a partial truce, as the "era of good feelings" defused Republican fears of clerical despotism and freed Federalist religious conservatives to acknowledge, and in some cases to welcome, the socially radical dimension of their biblical faith.

Such phraseology may sound strange to the ears of a generation of historians nurtured on secularism and unfamiliar at firsthand with the narratives of the Bible. The near-monopoly that conservatives have had in overtly Christian political discourse in recent years, combined with the tendency of liberals to focus on individual liberties—a dimension of freedom concededly not much stressed by the Bible—has left the impression that Christianity in general and evangelicalism in particular are fundamentally conservative doctrines. This is one reason why the biblical defense of slavery has received more respectful treatment of late than its abolitionist antithesis.[6] Understandably repelled by post–Civil War northern triumphalism and historians' anachronistic moralism, modern scholars have bent over backward to do justice to the proslavery argument, discovering in it a formal consistency, integrity, and intellectual merit that few even of its champions claimed for it during its ascendancy.[7] One of the most brilliant scholars of the ideology of slavery, Eugene Genovese, has frankly asserted the decisive intellectual and theological superiority of slavery's defenders over its detractors and has even gone so far, he has claimed, as to offer his students an "A" on the spot if they could point to a single passage in the Bible that condemns slavery—he evidently is convinced of the impossibility of the feat.[8] The historian Forrest G. Wood has carried this line of argument to its logical outcome, arguing that "English North Americans embraced slavery *because* they were Christians, not in spite of it."[9] Thus slavery may not necessarily be in conflict with traditional American values, as it was once assumed: according to its most thorough recent student, the proslavery argument "was precisely one of the clearest possible indications of the nature and character of American society and its values—not merely in the Old South but throughout the nation."[10] This new scholarship thus finds the advocates of a religious defense of slavery to be consistent, sincere, and even, in the frankness of their views, in some ways more attractive than their clerical opponents who condemned slavery in the abstract but floundered and temporized in their ineffectual efforts to counter the actual workings of the institution.

Such a perception, it seems to me, is not quite fair. Few groups in American history have been more subject to what E. P. Thompson called "the enormous condescension of posterity" than those Americans who agonized over the complexity of the slavery question without finding an effective and consistent answer—a condescension the more inexplicable in that the spectacular bloodbath that they feared might accompany the end of slavery actually did come to pass. "We can hardly expect that reformers should have persuaded southern planters to give up their slaves," observes David Brion Davis. "Even in times of crisis, no other group of planters accepted emancipation except when coerced by a central government or the slaves themselves."[11] The failure of Christian principles to effect the peaceful end of slavery should hardly be taken as proof that Christianity sanctioned slavery.

To address the issue directly, then: did evangelical Christianity sanction slavery or condemn it? Clearly, as Lincoln suggested in his second inaugural address, in practice it could and did do both.[12] Taken by itself, the question perhaps cannot be answered and may indeed be considered a more appropriate subject for theologians than for historians. Evangelicalism does not exist in a cultural vacuum, however; it must be studied in the context of the society in which it manifests itself. Here, fortunately, we are on much more solid ground.

To the contemporary reader, the Bible's position on slavery is ambiguous and contradictory. On the one hand, a host of passages paint the institution in a negative light and impose stiff sanctions on certain practices related to it. Most notably on the antislavery side of the ledger, the book of Exodus provides a classic paradigm of the passage from slavery to freedom.[13] Deuteronomy 24:7 condemns "man-stealing" as a capital offense, and another passage forbids the Israelites to return an escaped slave to his master (23:15-16). On the proslavery side, however, both the Hebrew Scriptures and the New Testament portray societies not only tolerant of, but economically dependent upon slave labor; the institution is never condemned outright, even by Jesus, while Paul explicitly enjoins slaves' obedience. In a pitched battle of exegesis, as generations of controversy would prove, pro- and antislavery controversialists could generally match each other verse for verse and interpretation for interpretation.

This fact has often led historians to the reductionist conclusion that the Bible served the purposes of both sides equally well—an assumption that is often accompanied by reproachful observations about the misuse of scripture by "both sides" to grind their own "secular" axes.[14] But such an interpretation is patently unhistorical in the context of the late eighteenth and early nineteenth centuries, a period when it was still impossible to make a sharp division between "secular" and "religious" aspects of life. While there are clearly many alternative ways of reading Scripture, we can be much more specific about how Americans of the early republic, particularly those who actively identified themselves as Christians, interpreted it, and about aspects upon which they agreed. Although scriptural precedents for slavery continued into the nineteenth century to pose "a problem for orthodox Biblicists," we need not assume that the existence of slavery in biblical times meant that genuine and consistent Bible-believing Christians therefore had to concede that slavery possessed divine sanction, as later defenders of slavery insisted.[15]

It is fair to say that none of the disputants considered the point at issue to be the simple textual question of whether the Bible "sanctioned" or "condemned" slavery. There has never been an objective biblical literalism, nor can there be because the Bible is such a sprawling, dynamic, multifaceted work—certainly more narrative than prescriptive. Encompassing a historical period of almost fourteen centuries, it has always and in every age demanded interpretation; indeed, this is undoubtedly the key to its resiliency. The search for the "plain truth of Scripture" is confounded as early as the second chapter of Genesis, which presents an alternative account of the creation of Adam and Eve to the one given in the first chapter. Thus the question of "what the Bible teaches" on a given subject must always be determined by reference to a set of values at least partially rooted *outside* the text—in society. The "truth" of the Bible inevitably reflects the assumptions, understandings, and aspirations of the culture interpreting it.

Most of the "approved" interpretations of the Bible in the Anglo-American world in the late eighteenth and early nineteenth century were composed by clerics in England, Scotland, and the northern United States who had little or no personal stake in, and often little knowledge of, domestic slavery in the Americas. It is hardly surprising that they produced few scriptural defenses of the institution. Indeed, in most cases, they historicized it, as they did polygamy, concubinage, and divorce, as a practice permitted to the Jews on account of the "hardness of their hearts," but contrary to the spirit of the Gospel.[16] Local clergy were free to adopt different interpretations, of course (as were laymen, for that matter); but their jurisdiction and authority would be limited. Moreover, it was not uncommon for clerics and laypeople who were slaveholders themselves, such as Arthur Lee of Virginia or Philadelphia's Benjamin Rush, to affirm that the Bible did not support slavery.[17]

In the context of the times, it could hardly be otherwise. Americans had just fought a Revolution on the principle that "all men are created equal" and endowed with inalienable rights to "life, liberty, and the pursuit of happiness." The author of these famous phrases asserted later that his purpose was simply "to place before mankind the common sense of the subject."[18] Garry Wills argues convincingly that Jefferson used the expression "common sense" as a technical term, representing the systematic science of man elucidated by Reid, Kames, Ferguson, Hutcheson, and the other philosophers of the Scottish Enlightenment whose thought reigned supreme in America.[19] As Henry May explained, "Americans wanted to believe at once in social and even scientific progress and in unchanging moral principles. Thus the only completely acceptable European teachers, for the early builders of nineteenth-century American official culture, were the Common Sense philosophers of Scotland."[20]

A radical opposition to slavery had been implicit in the Scottish philosophy from the start, although significantly, it was hardly a libertarian objection. From Francis Hutcheson on, texts of moral philosophy examined the three-fold principle of one's duty to God, to oneself, and to others. All three relationships presupposed a condition of liberty and were rendered impossible by slavery. Thus slavery not only constituted an infringement of the enslaved person's inalienable rights; perhaps even more urgently, it rendered him or her incapable of discharging solemn responsibilities to man and to God that could neither be revoked nor delegated.[21]

James Beattie went considerably further in his *Elements of Moral Science* (1793). "It is impossible for the considerate and unprejudiced mind to think of slavery without horror," Beattie asserted flatly; he added: "If this be equitable, or excusable, or pardonable, it is vain to talk any longer of the eternal distinctions of right and wrong, truth and falsehood, good and evil." Beattie clearly saw nothing radical or controversial in his pronouncement. Indeed, "[i]n arguing against slavery," he remarked, "it may perhaps be thought that I dispute without an opponent."[22]

Yet Scottish antislavery sentiment in the eighteenth century largely remained in the realm of abstract theory and failed to engage the concrete issues of British involvement in the slave trade and in slavery in the West Indies. Discussing the enormous upsurge in theoretical antislavery thought in eighteenth-century Scotland, C. Duncan Rice noted, "The most striking thing about this ferment of criticism is that it had no material effect."[23] The point may be applied with still greater force to the Americans, whose "free" republic rested on the foundation of liberty and equality. If slavery was condemned by Scripture, by natural law, and by the unimpeachable authority of the Scottish Philosophy, why did they not move against it? From the American Revolution on, observers were struck by the inconsistency of a people aggressively asserting their inalienable right to liberty while denying it to an enslaved population in their midst. "How is it," marveled Dr. Johnson, "that we hear the loudest *yelps* for liberty among the drivers of negroes?" The Scottish philosopher John Millar agreed; speaking of the incongruity of Americans asserting the right to impose their own taxes as an "unalienable right," while depriving "a great proportion of their fellow-creatures" of "almost every species of right," Millar concluded, "Fortune perhaps never produced a situation more calculated to ridicule a liberal hypothesis, or to show how little the conduct of men is at the bottom directed by any philosophical principles."[24]

What seemed to Dr. Johnson like the rankest hypocrisy and to Millar a lesson in human folly appeared in 1763 to the dean of the Scottish Enlightenment, Millar's mentor Adam Smith, as a practical illustration of a basic principle of political science. "In a republican government," Smith asserted, "it will scarcely ever happen that [slavery] should be abolished. The persons who make all the laws in that country are persons who have slaves themselves. These will never make any laws mitigating their usage; whatever laws are made with regard to slaves are intended to strengthen the authority of the masters and reduce the slaves to a more absolute subjection. . . . The authority of the masters over the slaves is therefore unbounded in all republican governments."[25] Prefiguring Jefferson's famous condemnation of slavery in his *Notes on the State of Virginia,* Smith asserted that "the love of domination and tyrannizing" among slaveholding legislators would make it "impossible for the slaves in a free country ever to recover their liberty."[26] In a "monarchicall and absolute government," Smith asserted, slavery would be at once less rigorous and easier to remove than in a republic: "the monarch [t]here being the sole judge and ruler, and not being affected by the easing of the condition of the slaves, may probably incline to mitigate their condition; and this we see has been done in all arbitrary governments in a considerable degree."

The slaves' greatest ally, for political as well as theological reasons, Smith argued, was the church. In ancient Rome, slaves had been regarded as profane, deprived not only of social relations with other men and women such as marriage, but entirely excluded from religion: "we may justly say they had . . . no god."[27] Their exclusion from Roman religion was the reason that the monotheistic faiths, "which taught the being of one supreme and universall god, who presided over all," were "so greedily receivd by this order of men." The masses of slaves who flocked to Christianity thus became the church's most powerful constituency in the power struggles between nobles and kings. "The great power of the clergy thus concurring with that of the king set the slaves at liberty. But it was absolutely necessary both that the authority of the king and of the clergy should be great." Such was the case in "Scotland, England, . . . France, Spain, etc.," where villeinage was abolished by the end of the Middle Ages. Where the authority of the government was weak, however, as in the cases of the elective monarchies of Poland or Bohemia, or the elective Habsburg empire, slavery continued; and it was likewise where the state decisively overshadowed even a strong church, as in Russia. Nor was Christianity necessarily hostile to slavery, Smith added: "The masters in our colonies are Christians, and yet slavery is allowed amongst them." It appeared that only under special circumstances, where the influence of both the state and the church were great, could the power of slaveholders be thwarted.[28]

It is instructive to apply Smith's observation on the intractability of slavery in a republic to the case of the United States. Whether or not we should attribute to it the force of an iron law of political economy, it can be illuminating in several ways. First, it can be helpful in dispelling scholars' unrealistic estimations both of the power of moral suasion and of the feebleness of the institution of slavery. Too often, discussions of the failure of antislavery movements embrace the perfectionist notion that the United States should have been able to shuck off the burden of slavery by a sheer effort of good will, without having to resort to some form of coercion. The profound institutional obstacles to antislavery in America frequently go unexplored, and a fundamental question is rarely posed: *Could antislavery beliefs alone have ended slavery in the United States without coercion?* Experience suggests they could not. While such an outcome is impossible to rule out in principle, there is no historical evidence to support it.[29]

Second, this provisional understanding that slavery was not going to go away except by coercion can help us to pursue an inquiry into Americans' *beliefs* about slavery which is not unfairly tied to *outcomes.*[30] Doing so allows us to reconcile Americans' professed hostility toward slavery with the nation's manifest and growing involvement in it without having to construct retrospectively out of a few scattered texts, a hitherto-undiscovered "genuine" strain of proslavery ideology percolating through the late eighteenth and early nineteenth centuries.[31] Republican slaveholders were far less troubled by the problem of ideological inconsistency than historians seem to be. In the Kentucky constitutional convention of 1790, for example, advocates of slavery saw no need to employ appeals to natural rights philosophy or proslavery interpretations of the Bible; instead, they "blatantly announced their selfish intention to hold on to all of their worldly possessions and trusted in universal acknowledgement of property rights to make their position appear one of principle rather than naked self-interest. . . . there was little need in frontier America for a sophisticated defense of the right to turn men into chattel."[32]

It also seems perfectly plausible, in light of Adam Smith's analysis of the intractability of slavery in a republic, that many thoughtful slaveholders believed that the cost of removing the institution—were it possible at all—was simply higher than any society would willingly pay. If the alternatives to slavery appeared to be either civil war or bloody slave insurrection on the Haitian model, it is hard to fault conscientious slaveholders for an unwillingness to choose between them, particularly considering the way in which events actually turned out.

Similarly, Smith's analysis suggests that the failure of the churches to counter successfully the institution need not be viewed as evidence of their acceptance or even promotion of it.[33] Such a view once again confuses *outcomes* with *beliefs*. It ignores or downplays the valiant efforts of evangelicals in the last decades of the eighteenth century to combat slavery with the weapons of moral suasion alone, a campaign effectively countered by social pressure, physical violence, and intellectual attacks, and undergirded by the overwhelming political force of massive institutional resistance.[34] Significantly, moreover, this successful effort to quash antislavery evangelicalism did not involve, at least at the denominational level, a formal acknowledgment of a scriptural sanction for slavery; under pressure from slaveholding laymen and clergy, denominational bodies simply gave up. The report of the Methodist General Conference of 1816 is remarkable chiefly for its candor:

> The committee . . . are of the opinion that, under the present circumstances in relation to slavery, little can be done to abolish a practice so contrary to the principles of moral justice. They are sorry to say that the evil appears to be past remedy. . . . [I]n the South and West the civil authorities render emancipation impracticable, and . . . to bring about such a change in the civil code as would favour the cause of liberty is not in the power of the General Conference.[35]

Even the celebrated "proslavery" arguments from Scripture offered by the South Carolina clerics Richard Furman and Frederick Dalcho in the wake of the Denmark Vesey slave conspiracy of 1822 do not in fact represent defenses of slavery—it needed no defense in that state—but defenses of *Christianity*, which many planters had come to regard as a dangerous luxury in a slave society. "To pious minds," wrote Furman, "it has given pain to hear men . . . sometimes say, that holding slaves is indeed indefensible, but that to us it is necessary, and must be supported." These authors therefore sought to prove that South Carolina did not have to choose between Christianity and slavery.[36] A realistic assessment of the status of the churches within southern slave society suggests that ultimately the only options open to them regarding slavery were acquiescence or exile. The Quakers, alone among denominations in the South, chose the latter course, although many thousands of members of other sects did so as individuals.[37] It is undoubtedly true, as historian Henry May has asserted, that "[t]he collapse of evangelical antislavery is the most melancholy fact in American religious history"; but the blame for that collapse cannot be assigned solely, or even principally, to the moral failings of the church leadership.[38]

Finally, Adam Smith's analysis of the nature of the threat to slavery may provide us with a key to understanding the strategies employed by its defenders in the United States. It is not necessary to postulate that American slaveholders were familiar with Smith's theories directly.[39] The content conveyed in them, however, is implicit in much of Scottish and continental political philosophy (including Montesquieu), and it is entirely consistent with Smith's *Theory of Moral Sentiments* and *Wealth of Nations*, works well known in the southern states. From their actions and their words, it is clear that many slaveholders accepted the principle that the chief danger to slavery was a strong federal state bolstered by the moral authority of religion, and they took steps to avert it.

If belief alone could not threaten slavery, as we have asserted, why did slaveholders fear the union of evangelicalism and moral philosophy? Not principally because it might undermine the internal solidarity of slave society, although this was a serious concern; but more fundamentally because of its potential to mobilize the citizens of the free states to take the reins of the one institution that had a realistic chance of crushing slavery: the federal government. "We have abolition-colonizing bible and peace societies," North Carolina's senator Nathaniel Macon warned, "and if the general government shall continue to stretch their powers, these societies will undoubtedly push them to try the question of emancipation." [40]

Slaveholders were unanimous in viewing the strong federal government created by the Constitution as the principal potential threat to slavery. By sharing sovereignty with states with no direct investment in the institution, the southern states were linking their destinies with potentially hostile societies that might, in time, choose to strike at it. This had been the chief argument of the southern antifederalists against ratification; and though, like Macon, most antifederalists had since become strict constructionists, fulsomely praising the wisdom—when narrowly interpreted—of the document they had unsuccessfully opposed, they still eyed the Constitution and the extended republic it created with suspicion.[41]

Until the second decade of the nineteenth century, however, the threat remained entirely hypothetical. A pervasive and perennial localism helped to check the growth of dangerous national sentiment. Besides, the document itself provided essential supports to slavery, such as the fugitive slave clause and the protection of a national militia, as well as critical safeguards against federal interference with slavery, particularly the requirement of a supermajority for amendments and a twenty-year protection for the slave trade.[42] An inviolable guarantee of equal senate representation ("the strong and strongest Federal feature") ensured a southern veto over legislation for many years after the population growth in the free states secured a vast northern majority in the House of Representatives.[43]

Moreover, the American political style, itself inherited in good measure from the Scottish philosophy, eschewed the "factious" coalition-building and arm-twisting that would have been necessary to create a unified antislavery voting bloc, in favor of an elevated but thoroughly ineffectual discourse of appeals to reason and the higher good. In the debate over the Quaker slave trade petitions of 1790, for example, abolitionists "stressed individual conscience over interest and practicality and harmony over faction," framing their petitions as "supplications to do justice instead of requests loaded with arguments that would appeal to a congressman's practical interests. . . . This view of politics made it difficult for abolitionists to organize their activity in a politically effective way."[44] At the same time, the overriding interest of slavery provided slaveholders with precisely the kind of clarity of purpose and organizational focus that northerners lacked, almost without having to say a word. The slave trade debate of 1790 showed how thoroughly this interest transcended politics or ideology: the two most unbridled opponents of the Quaker petitions were William Loughton Smith, perhaps South Carolina's most prominent Federalist, and Aedanus Burke, one of Georgia's most zealous Republicans—men on opposite sides of every party question.

Despite these institutional and cultural safeguards, the lack of a practicable proslavery ideology posed a serious problem for slaveholders locked in a federal union with nonslaveholding states. It is not necessary to postulate a wellspring of southern "guilt" over slaveholding to recognize the extent of this difficulty.[45] Domestically, it is hard to see where such guilt would have come from. Within their own homes, plantations, warehouses, auction houses, commercial exchanges, and courts, slaveholders found all the lineaments of a functioning, well-arranged, prosperous society with its own traditions, folkways, and mores.[46] "[M]an is an imitative animal," observed Thomas Jefferson. "From his cradle to grave he is learning to do what he sees others do." Inside the socially constructed reality of the individual communities that made up southern society, there was no element intrinsically so alien to human experience as to cause the southerner to call into question the legitimacy of "the manners of his own nation, familiarized to him by habit."[47] The problem for southern slaveholders was not one of *absolute* social mores, however, but of *relative* ones. The world *outside* their plantations—the Anglo-American cultural world of which they considered themselves an integral part—increasingly rejected slavery and slaveholding as incompatible with its fundamental norms.

For our purposes, it is unimportant whether such condemnations of slavery were valid and sincere or self-serving and hypocritical; whether they were authentic expressions of humanitarian concern or smokescreens for the expansion of industrial capitalism.[48] What is important is that the attack on slavery was widespread and virtually uncontested, except on the relatively narrow grounds of national mercantile interest.[49] Southern slaveholders in the Revolutionary era themselves marveled at the incongruous position in which they found themselves and scorned to construct excuses: "Would anyone believe," wrote a rueful Patrick Henry, "that I am master of Slave[s] of my own purchase: I am drawn along by the general inconveniency of living without them, I will not, I cannot justify it."[50] He could not do so because his identity as a leader of the American Revolution and as an international symbol of liberty were as essential to his identity as his slaveholding—but perhaps not more so. Instead of justifying it, Henry's generation of Virginians turned their talents to developing institutional safeguards for slavery that would not compromise their place in history as heroic champions of freedom.

In his unremitting hostility to the centralized power of religion and the state, Patrick Henry's own career after the Revolution may be taken as a case in point. In 1785, as governor of Virginia, he successfully shepherded Thomas Jefferson's historic "Act for Establishing Freedom of Religion" to passage; two years later, he strenuously opposed ratification of the federal constitution.[51] Henry's actions before the adoption of the Constitution were unflaggingly devoted to preventing the establishment of a state religion, both in Virginia and in the nation, and to opposing a strong central government—in other words, to preventing the conditions that Adam Smith had argued were essential to the removal of slavery. In his legendary speech against ratification of the Constitution in the Virginia Convention, where he again stressed the danger of established religion, Henry appealed explicitly to slaveholders to emphasize the acute danger the new government would pose to their interest.[52] After the document's adoption, Henry promised to submit to it peacefully and devoted his efforts to securing a Bill of Rights that barred any religious establishment, guaranteed the right of property, and secured all unenumerated rights to the people, or to the states. While all these amendments can be seen as boons to freedom, they were also important safeguards to slavery. Henry's later years were devoted to preventing a clash between the federal power and his state—a battle, he was convinced, that Virginia could not win.

The historian of Puritanism, Harry S. Stout, has pointed to the other side
of the coin in Henry's anticlerical struggle. "Significantly," Stout observes, the
Congregational ministers of New England "were defeated both in their efforts
to avoid disestablishment and in their campaign to eradicate slavery. And
herein lies a clue," Stout continues, to the "most radical and far-reaching
transformation" produced by the Revolution: "the weakening of deference
and the theory of fixed hierarchy on which it rested." In New England, with
its relatively equal distribution of wealth and purely economic power, the
breakdown of "centers of authority," such as the established church and the
traditional ruling gentry elite, led to the relocation of sovereignty "among
the people." [53] In Virginia, the same Revolutionary rhetoric and the disestablishment of the far weaker Episcopal church led not to a redistribution of
sovereignty "among the people," as historian Thomas Buckley has recently
shown, but to the removal of an important check to the "raw power of a
multitude of diverse, contending interests," among which the predominant
economic and social force of the major slaveholders inexorably prevailed.
Slaveholding Virginia legislators stripped clergymen of the right to hold office,
deprived religious groups of the right to receive bequests and hold property,
and even confiscated church lands in the manner of the French Revolution.
"Rather than ensuring complete religious freedom and separating church and
state as autonomous entities," Buckley demonstrates, "Virginia's antebellum
leaders used the statute [of religious freedom] to subordinate the churches and
their corporate activities to legislative direction," guaranteeing to the conservative antebellum planter class "the same privileged position over church and
state that their colonial forebears had enjoyed." [54] While Buckley views this
outcome as ironic and inadvertent, it seems likely that Thomas Jefferson and
Patrick Henry knew precisely what they were doing and were as interested in
preserving freedom from clerical coercion as they were in protecting freedom
of conscience.

Slaveholders in the generation after the Revolution did not have to believe
in or act upon the doctrines that slavery was fundamentally wrong, and that
all men, including Africans, were created equal. But they could not reject these
principles categorically and retain their "enlightened" status as full participants in what John Stuart Mill called "the Spirit of the Age." [55] Many southern
planters, Virginians in particular, desired deeply to have it both ways: they
longed to participate in the great revolution in moral and material advancement sweeping the western world, which they and their fathers had done so
much to launch, while at the same time retaining the high social status and
standard of living secured to them by slavery. [56] Typically, "enlightened" slave-

holders vociferously declared, especially to nonsoutherners, that the days of slavery were numbered. Jefferson was hardly unique in his assertion that "[n]othing is more certainly written in the book of fate than that these people are to be free." His sentiment was a commonplace, even among South Carolinians—the Americans most dedicated to preserving the institution.[57] If the end of slavery was not a matter of *if* but of *when* and *how*, such "enlightened" planters believed they could remain on the side of progress and benevolence by offering lip service to emancipation on every relevant occasion, cherishing it as a goal, proclaiming its inevitability, and asserting its divine sanction, while scrupulously doing nothing to alleviate the insurmountable difficulties entailed in determining "when" and "how" it would take place.[58]

This "high-minded" approach was not without its dangers, as tidewater planters living in districts with substantial slave majorities were quick to point out. As long as slaveholders sought to stay on the side of progress by refraining from mounting a coherent defense of slavery, and even endorsing the abstract goal of emancipation, they weakened the intellectual cohesion of the planter class, which would then have to depend upon pure class interest, naked of any sophisticated ideological support for slavery.[59] First, the tactic opened the door to desertions, particularly among the young—a prime concern of Jefferson's.[60] Second, it relied too heavily upon purely institutional safeguards for slavery, trusting to the dispersed nature of federal power, as well as on the localism (and the apathy) of the citizens of nonslaveholding states to keep them from adopting emancipation as a national goal.

What made this high-risk southern strategy work was its ability to stigmatize the essential elements of any effective challenge to slavery—a powerful central government in concert with a strong religious authority—as mortal threats to republican liberty.[61] The explosion of party conflict in the early 1790s proved to be an unparalleled boon to the "high-minded" defense of slavery. Southern Republicans' defense of the French Revolution, in alliance with northern artisans, farmers, and mechanics, secured for them gilt-edged radical credentials at little obvious cost to the security of their dominant position in a slave society.[62] For their part, the Federalist coalition of conservative politicians and orthodox clergymen could not have more perfectly played the role of dictatorial "monarchists" and inquisitorial priests had their scripts been written for them by Jefferson himself. The Federalist agenda, particularly in the last years of the century, seemed to represent a genuine threat to basic American freedoms, perhaps even to independence itself. The jailing of Republican editors under the Sedition Act created martyrs to liberty whose names would be a rallying cry against oppression for a generation, while the

Virginia and Kentucky Resolves of 1798–99, which were designed to preserve constitutional liberty, would serve as the template for nullification and secession. The memory of the infamous Hartford Convention, at which New England Federalists reputedly plotted treason during the War of 1812, would be invoked to fan the flames of Republican outrage and rally the faithful to the polls for decades, exactly as the "waving of the bloody shirt" did in the years after the Civil War.[63] The High Federalists were genuine reactionaries; hence Republicans, arraying themselves against all that the Federalists stood for, successfully portrayed themselves as progressives, in spite of holding slaves.

Jeffersonian Republicans were so successful in shaping the interpretation of the events of this critical period that their version of the Jeffersonian-Federalist struggle still remains the dominant paradigm of American history for many historians, as well as for the public at large.[64] As long as such southern Republicans as Jefferson continued to proclaim their hatred of slavery and their determination to eradicate it as soon as practicable, most of their political allies in the free states were willing to give them the benefit of the doubt and leave emancipation in the hands of those who, presumably, knew best how to accomplish it and allowed it to be undertaken when the more pressing danger of Federalism had been defeated. It failed to occur to most of them that in dismantling the detested apparatus of the Federalist state and replacing it with the hands-off Jeffersonian government, the Revolution of 1800 had neutralized the one institution in the United States capable of implementing effective measures against slavery.

The ongoing tendency of American historians to view the events of the early republic from a Jeffersonian-Jacksonian perspective has perhaps nowhere led to more confusion than in the study of the slavery issue. The fundamental historiographic theme of the early republic has been the triumph of democracy and egalitarianism; the fact that the period also saw the federalization of the defense of slavery, the flowering of the "positive good" argument, and the formalization of racism has engendered such profound cognitive dissonance that, for years, scholars generally either skirted the issue or allowed it to drop from their histories entirely. "Slavery was the most accusing, the most tragic, and the most dangerous of all questions," wrote Arthur Schlesinger Jr., who testified eloquently to its danger by all but omitting it from his celebrated study of the Jacksonian age.[65] Even where slavery is the focus, the picture presented is distorted frequently through a Jeffersonian lens. In his *Proslavery*, for example, Larry Tise portrays an exaggerated portrait of New England Federalism after 1800 as the progenitor of an implicitly proslavery "conservative counterrevolution" against a presumably antislavery "Jeffersonian Democracy." [66]

Such interpretations are in keeping with a secularist teleology that views religion in general, and evangelicalism in particular, as inherently reactionary and inimical to liberty. A classic work in this genre is Ford K. Brown's *Fathers of the Victorians,* a study—or rather an exposé—of William Wilberforce and the evangelical Clapham Sect of which he was the spiritual father; the book astonishingly managed almost completely to ignore the antislavery work that contemporaries and most later admirers almost universally regarded as the sect's central mission.[67] Forrest Wood's *Arrogance of Faith,* discussed previously in this chapter, is a more extreme example of this powerful antipathy toward religion in general and Christianity in particular. I am indifferent here to any possible theological or psychological explanations for these scholars' antireligious animus. My concern is rather that their interpretations are demonstrably ahistorical as a result of it.

An earlier historical tradition offered a very different interpretation of the significance of Anglo-American religious developments during the early nineteenth century. Historians from John Bach McMaster to Gilbert Hobbs Barnes viewed the rise of evangelicalism as an important element in the development both of antislavery and of democratization.[68] According to the Russian political scientist Mosei Ostrogorski, writing in the early twentieth century, the British campaign against West Indian slavery, inspired and directed by evangelicals, helped to transform the very nature of the political process by calling forth an unprecedented outpouring of popular participation in national affairs: "A new character—the fellow-creature, the 'man'—was ushered from the [speaking] platform into the social and political world of aristocratic England, and was destined to remain there." In addition to awakening a sense of fellow-feeling, the religious revival had prompted an expanded conception of duty that extended not only to personal morality but to responsibility for society as a whole.[69] Hundreds of thousands of men, women, and minors engaged in petition campaigns, antislavery fairs, monster meetings, and other forms of collective action that radically expanded the boundaries of political participation and reflected a changed sense of the relationship of the individual to the state.[70] The ramifications in in the United States of these British developments were important but limited. In the early years of the American Republic, educators brought a relatively theoretical and passionless doctrine of antislavery to congregations possessing few or no slaves. By the end of the century, however, both of these factors had changed. Sensitized by Granville

Sharp's legal battle to abolish slavery in Britain proper and by the massive public struggle of the campaign to end the British slave trade (which finally triumphed in 1808), authors of texts on moral philosophy infused their anti-slavery arguments with a new urgency. At the same time, the explosive spread of cotton cultivation, made possible by Eli Whitney's cotton gin, was drastically expanding the demand for slaves and opening the ranks of slaveholding to a much wider class of Americans. Ironically, then, even as slaveholding became increasingly common and accepted in America, textbook opinions on slavery, still heavily influenced by British norms, increasingly portrayed the institution as outdated and immoral.

The standard discussion of the morality of slavery could be found in William Paley's textbook of practical ethics, *Moral and Political Philosophy* (1784). Perhaps the most influential, and certainly the most widely read work on moral science, Paley's text formed a major part of the senior-year curriculum at Yale, Harvard, and most other American colleges. Although Lawrence Cremin describes Paley's work as "bland" and "utilitarian," his denunciation of slavery was uncharacteristically scathing and uncompromising.[71] Slavery, in Paley's definition, consisted of "an obligation to labour for the benefit of the master, without the contract or consent of the servant." Following traditional formulations, Paley argued that such obligation can only legitimately arise, "consistently with the state of nature," from crimes, from captivity, or from debt. "The slave-trade upon the coast of Africa is not excused by these principles," Paley observed. "When slaves in that country are brought to market, no questions, I believe, are asked about the origin or justice of the vender's title." Paley's picture of the slave trade constituted a veritable catalogue of crimes and violations of natural right: "The natives are excited to war and mutual depredation. . . . The slaves, torn away from parents, wives, children . . . are transported to the European settlements in America, with no other accommodation on shipboard than what is provided for brutes. . . . the miserable exiles are [then] placed . . . in subjection to a dominion and system of laws, the most merciless and tyrannical, that ever were tolerated upon the face of the earth. . . ." With uncharacteristic sarcasm, Paley dispensed with the claim of the "necessity" of slavery to cultivate America: "It is said that [the land] could not be cultivated with quite the same conveniency and cheapness, as by the labour of slaves; by which means, a pound of sugar, which the planter now sells for sixpence, could not be afforded under sixpence-halfpenny;—and this is the *necessity*."[72]

Prof. John Daniel Gross of Columbia College in New York, author of *Natural Principles of Rectitude for the Conduct of Man* (1795), went even further than Paley in denouncing the malevolent influence of slavery, which had "already so far advanced in our free country, that even the children of the farmer refuse the most necessary work, such as is essential to the management of a farm, under the foolish notion, that it is degrading to a freeman, and an occupation only fit for slaves."[73] A generation later, John L. Parkhurst of New Hampshire appended an inflammatory codicil to a discussion of slavery taken otherwise verbatim from Paley: "That the blacks, by the system of slavery, suffer more than the whites gain, is a proposition so evident, that he who disputes it, hardly deserves to be refuted,—unless it were by being chained, and subjected to the lash of a task-master. Therefore, as human happiness is diminished by the system of slavery, it is unlawful and ought to be abolished."[74] Finally, in 1835, Paley was decisively superseded by Francis Wayland's *Elements of Moral Science,* one of the best-selling books of the century, which argued ingeniously and unequivocally that slavery was forbidden by the Gospel, whose principles, "having gained a lodgment in every part of the known world," had instigated a "universal moral revolution" in order "to effect the universal abolition of slavery."[75]

To what degree did such radical antislavery pronouncements in establishment-sanctioned educational texts reflect popular attitudes? In Britain, it appears likely that public opinion against slavery outstripped the moral philosophers, who merely strove in their works to constrain antislavery within acceptable theoretical bounds. Armed with the religious imprimatur provided by the evangelical wing of the Anglican church and aided by the centralized institutional framework of the British state, antislavery activists were able to translate moral fervor into concrete political results in remarkably short order. From the end of the Napoleonic Wars, "a universal outburst of public opinion" against the slave trade shocked politicians into taking a much stronger position than they had intended. "The nation is bent upon this object," wrote a bemused Lord Castlereagh in 1814. "I believe there is hardly a village that has not met and petitioned upon it . . . and the ministers must make it their policy."[76] In the United States six years later, the movement to restrict slavery in Missouri sparked a similar popular outpouring of activism. Almost immediately, however, an unbreachable wall of southern intransigence deadlocked Congress and stopped the campaign dead in its tracks.[77] Thus, as I have suggested, it is not necessary to point to any philosophical or theological change to explain the withering away of antislavery activity in the United States after the Revolution. The increasing economic power of the institution as well as the political intractability of the federal system (specifically designed to thwart the kind of sweeping social and economic changes imposed by the general government that legislated antislavery would represent) provide all the explanation that is needed. While Britain and the United States possessed many remarkably similar antecedent cultural conditions, the political and economic exigencies of slaveholding in the United States substantially checked the moral response to arguments that galvanized thousands in Britain.

Thus we are able to observe a widening split between Anglo-American moral theory and American practice regarding the institution of slavery. Paralleling this division we may trace a growing cleavage within American society itself—one not without considerable irony. While Anglophilia continued to be the abiding trait of most socially conservative Americans (New Englanders in particular), the aristocratic English society from which they took their cues was undergoing major changes. British social thought, unencumbered by the presence of slavery in the metropolis and influenced and educated by the outcome of the American Revolution, developed along increasingly egalitarian lines, frequently carrying imitative Americans along with it. Practiced by patrician Clapham Sect abolitionists, such as Wilberforce and Hannah More, evangelical religion acquired a following among Anglophilic northeasterners that Cane Ridge–style frontier revivalism would never have gained for it.

Viewed in this Anglo-American context, the turn away from Jeffersonian liberalism to evangelicalism can only be described as a "conservative counter-revolution" by a severe twisting of terms. Even Jeffersonian Republicans had turned away from the extremism of the French Revolution and the violence and megalomania of the dictator who commandeered it. The upheavals caused by Napoleon's conquests and the international coalition raised to defeat him had together increased the interdependence of the world community, inspiring visions of cooperation and reform on a global scale. The end of the wars immediately sparked a rebirth of shipping and commerce, of which the United States was the greatest beneficiary, turning a new generation of provincial New England farm boys into seasoned world travelers and bringing an assortment of seamen from all over the world to American ports. At the same time, a fervent atmosphere of evangelical revival provided Americans with a psychological, as well as a theological, basis for regarding all the dizzyingly varied inhabitants of the globe as members of one community. The period of the Congress of Vienna has been regarded, with some justice, as an era of retrenchment and reaction, but this is only part of its legacy: to many contemporaries it appeared to be an age of limitless potential and Providentially directed progress. After the defeat of the Napoleonic "Antichrist," anything seemed possible—even the prospect of the American nation living out the true meaning of its creed.

Yet the openings and opportunities of the second decade of the 1800s had the further effect of generating an increasingly powerful backlash. Slavery was too important an institution, both economically and socially, for slave society to in effect commit suicide by instructing its youth in demonstrably dangerous views. "Reforming" education—reshaping the beliefs of the next generation—became a chief priority of southern intellectuals. As early as 1779, Thomas Jefferson, as a visitor to the College of William and Mary, had replaced the professorship of divinity with one of "Law and Police."[78] Intriguingly, Jefferson, who had once bemoaned the "unhappy influence on the manners of our people" caused by the "influence of slavery among us," now became the first major advocate of "home education at the South."[79] Before 1820, Jefferson began to spread the alarm of the dangers of northern schooling. "We are now trusting to those who are against us in position and principle," he warned, "to fashion in their own form the minds and affections of our youth. . . . [who are] imbibing opinions and principles in discord with our own country. This canker is eating out the vitals of our existence, and if not arrested at once, will be beyond remedy."[80] No contemporary Virginian could have had any doubt that slavery was the institution of "our own country" that Jefferson considered to be under attack.

Jefferson's solution was to create a state university in Virginia, where moral philosophy would never be taught, to forestall the need to send the state's youths to the North, where they would be turned into "fanatics & tories."[81] Jefferson's tireless campaign to build the University of Virginia has understandably been regarded as one of his greatest achievements, as he himself regarded it. But the reactionary dimension of Jefferson's project is demonstrated most glaringly in his quixotic efforts to put the University of Virginia under the direction of Thomas Cooper, an immigrant British physician and political economist and future pioneering formal racist and secessionist. Self-exiled from England at the time of the treason trials of 1794, Cooper settled in Philadelphia, where he practiced medicine, engaged in Republican politics, and displayed a hostility toward the clergy and religion perhaps more extreme than any other man in American public life. Thomas Jefferson's impassioned campaign to install Cooper at the helm of the university tells us volumes about the kind of "opinions and principles" Jefferson considered appropriate for Virginia's youth.

In one of his earliest letters on the subject, Jefferson wrote in 1800 to Cooper's mentor and father-in-law, the English scientist and theologian Joseph Priestley, that he intended to establish a "broad and liberal and *modern*" university in which "some branches of science formerly esteemed, may now be omitted. . . ."[82] Fourteen years later, he broached with Cooper his plan to establish a university to teach "all the branches of science useful *to us,* and *at this day,*" hinting that Cooper might be the man to lead it.[83] In 1819, after Cooper had been asked to step down from a teaching position at the University of Pennsylvania, Jefferson not only invited Cooper to accept a professorship at the still-unfunded university, but he actually committed the school to a long-term contract with Cooper and advanced him fifteen hundred dollars—an action that nearly destroyed the institution before its birth.[84]

Jefferson told Joseph C. Cabell, the university's chief supporter in the Virginia senate, that he considered Cooper to be "the greatest man in America, in the powers of mind, and in acquired information."[85] Nonetheless, Cabell frankly informed Jefferson that "the enlightened part of society" found "that either in point of manners, habits, or character, [Cooper] is defective."[86] The controversy exploded publicly in 1820, when a member of the university's board of visitors, John Holt Rice, a moderate Presbyterian clergyman, printed in his *Virginia Evangelical and Literary Magazine* a damning selection of frankly irreligious quotations from Cooper's appendix to Priestley's *Memoirs,* published in 1806.

In the appendix, Cooper blasted away at the central tenets of the Christian faith. "[T]he time seems to have arrived," Cooper exulted, "when the separate existence of the human soul, the freedom of the will, and the eternal duration of future punishment, like the doctrines of the Trinity, and Transubstantiation, may be regarded as no longer entitled to public discussion." The doctrine of the soul, Cooper asserted, "originated in ignorance" and was "supported by imposture." As for Jefferson's beloved Scottish Common Sense philosophy, Cooper averred that he "paid no attention to the hypothesis of the Scotch Doctors, Reid[,] Beattie and Oswald," derisively asserting that "the utter insufficiency of such young gentlemen and lady's philosophy as they have adopted, has secured them from further animadversion," and plunged them "into merited obscurity." Later in the book, exploring the possibility that a particular series of experiments investigating the theory of spontaneous generation might tend toward atheism, Cooper opined, "But if it do lead to Atheism, what then? . . . I [cannot] see how the belief of no God can be more detrimental to society or render a man less fit as a citizen than the belief of the thirty thousand Gods of the Pagans, or the equal absurdities of trinitarian orthodoxy."[87]

Unsurprisingly, Rice reacted to these remarkable passages with indignation and fury. It was not enough for Cooper to describe such basic Christian doctrines as the immateriality and immortality of the soul and of future retribution as "pernicious error"; he scornfully rejected the arguments in support of them of the Scottish school of Common Sense, which Rice considered "the most cherished sentiments of the wisest and best men that the world has ever seen!" as "feeble and sophistical—mere lady's philosophy." On top of this, Cooper likened the fundamental tenet of orthodox Christianity, the doctrine of the Trinity, to the "exploded" doctrine of transubstantiation—the litmus test of popery—and sneeringly branded Trinitarians as polytheists. Finally, Rice took up Cooper's dismissive rhetorical question about the implications of doubtful scientific experiments:

> "*But if it do lead to Atheism, what then? . . .* " What then? Why *then*, farewel to the dearest hopes and best consolations of man!—*then*, let the apostles be rejected with scorn, and the martyrs be branded with folly—*then*, the magnificent conceptions of immortality, and the anticipated joys of heaven are a dream—*then*, let us eat and drink, for to-morrow we die—*we die forever*—*then* all that is grand and goodly, in creation; all that is noble in man; all that is magnificent in eternity, is but the *ignis fatuus* which for a while tantalizes and misleads the weary traveller in a stormy night, and then leaves him hopeless of home and helpless, to sink in despair.[88]

Although Jefferson had expected that such Presbyterians as Rice would oppose Cooper, he had thought that Episcopalians, Baptists, and Methodists would fall into line behind the choice. Instead, the nearly unanimous outcry against the appointment forced Cooper to withdraw, and the legislature converted his fifteen hundred dollar salary advance into a severance payment. This was not the end of the issue, however. As the editor of Jefferson's letters on the university observed with dry understatement, "the having been thus traversed in a favorite measure, seems to have somewhat disturbed the usual philosophic serenity of the venerable rector." [89] In fact, Jefferson was apoplectic, denouncing Rice, the visitors, and the entire Presbyterian church; attacking their religious opinions and accusing them of seeking to be established by law and to monopolize the whole system of education in the state.[90] These absurd charges, against a sect that included many steadfast Republicans and long-time personal allies, did much to tarnish Jefferson's reputation among his fellow citizens in his later years.

Why was Jefferson willing to threaten his beloved "bantling," the University of Virginia, over this controversial appointment? Why would Jefferson, who paraphrased Reid and Hutcheson in the Declaration of Independence and believed that Edinburgh was the best university in the world, want to place a man who scoffed at the Scottish Common Sense school as "lady's philosophy" in charge of education of Virginia's youth? Why did Jefferson insist that

Cooper, a versatile but superficial thinker, possessed "more science in his single head than all the colleges of New England, New Jersey, and . . . Virginia, put together?"[91]

Jefferson did not say, and his admiration for Cooper constituted a problem that perplexed many of his closest friends.[92] We may find some hints, I believe, however, in his letters. In a well-known 1786 letter to Maria Cosway, known as the "Dialogue of the Head and the Heart," Jefferson's "two halves" debate whether he should see Maria again and expose himself to emotional harm, or whether he should avoid the entanglement and the potential emotional bruising it portended. "The art of life is the art of avoiding pain," says the head. This assertion Jefferson repeated years later in his "syllabus to the doctrines of Epictetus," which he annexed to an invitation to visit the University of Virginia in a letter to William Short:

> *Moral.*—Happiness the aim of life.
> Virtue the foundation of happiness.
> Utility the test of virtue.
> Pleasure active and In-do-lent.
> In-do-lence is the absence of pain, the true felicity . . . .
> The *summum bonum* is not to be pained in body, nor troubled in mind.[93]

This is the doctrine of the head in the Cosway letter. It is precisely the materialist doctrine taught by Thomas Cooper, the man whose "head" contained more "science" than all the colleges in America. The response of the heart, however, is that "[m]orals were too essentiall to the happiness of man to be risked on the incertain combinations of the head. She laid their foundation therefore in sentiment, not in science." "That this represents Jefferson's own belief," states Douglas L. Wilson, "is as certain as our knowledge of its source—Scottish common-sense philosophy."[94]

Yet Wilson, along with several earlier commentators, mistakenly believed that the head stood for duty; the heart for the self-indulgent "philosophy of following wherever one's emotions lead." This is an anachronistic interpretation, at least as far as Jefferson is concerned. "To reach such conclusions," argues Garry Wills, one must "ignore the fact that all the arguments for duty and virtue come from the Heart; that the Head speaks only for a narrow, selfish interest. . . ."[95] For the slaveholding author of the Declaration of Independence, the demands of the heart—that is, the demands of one's conscience, one's "common sense"—were painful indeed.

This was just as it should be, asserted John Holt Rice in his discussion of Cooper's philosophy. "Many a man knows what is for his good, who does not pursue it. . . . The heart must be imbued with sound principles, and right affections cultivated, and good habits formed, or man will continue to be a wretched wanderer from the path of happiness, his superior cultivation only serving to make self condemnation and remorse more pungent."[96] In the appointment of Cooper, Rice thought he detected an effort by the "Monticello-men" to inculcate "atheistical opinions" in the youth of the Old Dominion. "But let the faith of a nation be undermined," Rice admonished:

> . . . let the whole community be without the fear of God before their eyes, and a
> storm is raised compared with which the uproar of the elements, the desolations
> of the tornado and the earthquake, are a mere "civil game." Unhappily many of
> our youth are brought up without religious principle. . . . They are allowed to live
> as they list, and their passions, unaccustomed to restraint, are particularly violent.
> We *may* reap the bitter fruit of this folly. Should the bonds which now unite us as
> a people be disseevered, and civil war arise—Which may God in his great mercy
> forbid—we believe that the contest would be marked by deeds of ferocity, and
> works of desolation, of which the world has exhibited few examples.[97]

Jefferson himself had once written: "Can the liberties of a nation be thought secure when we have removed their only firm basis, a conviction in the minds of the people that these liberties are the gift of God? That they are not to be violated but with his wrath?" Now he proposed to instruct the children of Virginia that such fears as "the eternal duration of future punishment" were mere "ignorance, . . . no longer entitled to public discussion." But Jefferson could never, of course, teach such a doctrine himself, without ceasing to be Jefferson; nor could he even bring himself to hold it in his heart. Thus he had recourse to Cooper. Ironically, Douglas Wilson concluded that the message of Jefferson's letter to Maria Cosway was "that the Heart, while not wanting in warmth, is obliged to occupy the same person as the Head." In actuality, Jefferson found it impossible to hold both sides of his personality within himself, and he deputized Cooper to pursue the "narrow, selfish interest" of the head.

It is to just such an interest that Thomas Cooper devoted himself when, as the second president of South Carolina College, he served the slaveholding class of that state with unparalleled zealousness for more than a decade. The historian Michael Sugrue has recounted the thoroughness and deliberation with which Cooper, the ostentatious champion of free speech, literally catechized the youth of the planter class in the principles of disunion, while inculcating a uniquely virulent and uncompromising proslavery ideology, founded on a formal assertion of the separate creation and inferiority of Africans—thus bringing to fruition the suggestions that Jefferson advanced in the *Notes on Virginia* "as a suspicion only."[98] In South Carolina, Cooper carried out to the letter Jefferson's hope for a university which would prevent the propagation of "opinions and principles in discord with our own country."[99] To prevent the spread of such principles, Cooper found it necessary to dispense with the troublesome notion of "self-evident truths" in the Declaration of Independence, declaring that "he knew of no sense in which it ever was, or would, or could be true that men are 'born free, equal and independent,'" and that there was no validity to the doctrine of "unalienable and indefeasible rights." "Rights," Cooper taught, "are what society acknowledges and sanctions, and they are nothing else."[100]

This socially determined definition of rights enabled Cooper to transmute the prejudice under which African Americans suffered into a fundamental principle of black subordination: "People of colour are, in every part of the United States, considered, not merely by the populace, but by the law, as a permanently degraded people; not participating as by right, of the civil privileges belonging to every white man, but enjoying what civil privileges they possess, as a right and grant, as a matter of favour conceded by the law, and revocable by the law."[101] As Cooper's (and Jefferson's) biographer Dumas Malone recognized, this was the doctrine that Roger B. Taney would later adopt in his Dred Scott decision—though it would not be until the 1850s that Taney and others would make the fearful leap to viewing such a doctrine not as *invalidating* the Declaration of Independence but as *implicit* in it.[102]

Most defenders of the slaveholding status quo were unwilling innovators, for obvious reasons. The strongest defense of a conservative social order was an appeal to tradition—a fact so plain that modern historians have often assumed that that is what defenders of slavery were making. Despite their incontrovertible social conservatism, however, such a strategy was denied because the most "approved" authorities disapproved of slavery. Proslavery writers, such as John Fletcher of Louisiana, were placed on the uncomfortable ground of opposing "the eloquent and magical pens of Dr. Johnson, Dr. Paley, Dr. Channing, Dr. Wayland, Mr. Barnes, and others," including Hutcheson and Reid—in other words, it was Fletcher of Louisiana versus the entire establishment of moral philosophy.[103] Against these bastions of authority, slavery's defenders could offer a few quotations from "Grotius or Huber," some passages of biblical commentary by Michaelis, and unnamed "numerous and elaborate treatises" from France that, while "learned, acute, and industriously compiled," were "impregnated, of course, with the poison of fanatical prejudices," and "colored with the peculiar sentiments and sociological reveries of their authors"—in other words, they were hardly tailor-made to the purpose at hand.[104] It is scarcely surprising, then, that even though southern states-men urged the "practical necessity" of developing an effective proslavery ide-ology, southern thinkers turned resolutely to the task, and southern educators showed a willingness to promote their efforts, southern *parents* for the most part ignored their novel efforts, preferring still to send their sons to northern schools or insisting that southern colleges continue to teach Paley and Way-land (despite their strictures against slavery) instead of such anodyne treatises as Jasper Adams's *Elements of Moral Philosophy* or John Fletcher's "*Easy Les-sons*" on slavery.[105]

More conservative slaveholders simply refused to play the game of search-ing for philosophical justifications for slavery. Charleston's Hugh S. Legaré dis-missed the practice of justifying or condemning slavery on principles of natu-ral law as "a very good thesis for young casuists to discuss in the college moot-club," but he asserted that "[w]e shall not undertake it, for we have no taste for abstractions." The true justification of slavery was historical: slavery, like war, had always existed and had always been "as lawful as any other ar-rangement of civil society." Perhaps the opinion of the world was changing; "but *we* must be allowed to hold on to the old logic a little longer."[106]

The younger generation of slaveholding intellectuals, with South Carolini-ans trained by Thomas Cooper in the vanguard, considered this approach foolhardy if not suicidal. How could their addled elders have sat in silent acquiescence, the proslavery evangelist J. D. B. De Bow wondered, while the abolitionists indicted them on the basis of wooly-headed "unascertained premises"? "The abolitionists proceeded in their indictment of slave-holders like honest Dogberry: 'Masters, it is proved already that you are little better than false knaves; and it will go near to be thought so shortly. . . .' Unfortu-nately, the issue was at once accepted in this blundering form by the defen-dants, and the earliest replies amounted to nothing more than a plea of con-fession and avoidance." De Bow's revised "line of defence" sounded less like the friendly debates of the "college moot-club" and more like intellectual commando warfare: "Opposition is vain, unless we seize the hostile battery, and turn against our adversary the same guns which have been making havoc in our ranks. The strength of our convictions, the soundness of our reason-ings, the ingenuity and cogency of our speculative combinations, will prove utterly futile, unless we first conquer the facts which barricade and protect the hostile position."[107]

The most effective tactic for capturing the heavy artillery of antislavery thought was also the most fearsome—and the most strongly resisted. It was a flanking attack on the most obstinate of accepted "facts"—the authority of the Bible itself. The Bible's assertion of the common descent of all people, interpreted in light of the meaning of equality in the republican United States, proved to be a serious obstacle to the development of an effective rationale for African slavery. To the pioneering racist and proslavery advocate Josiah Nott— a devoted student of Thomas Cooper—it was essential to destroy the belief, handed down from Genesis, that blacks and whites had descended from the same set of parents. "Just get the dam'd stupid crowd safely around Moses," as Nott pungently put it, "and the difficulty is at an end." [108]

A majority of southerners always refused to countenance such a move, ruling it out on grounds of propriety as well as theology. But perhaps as few slaveholders fully took to heart the more far-fetched attempts to sweeten the pill of slavery with the sugar coating of religion. Such efforts were, more often than not, northern imports, as Harriet Beecher Stowe's Augustine St. Claire asserted (almost 150 years before Larry Tise made the same point): " . . . To this day, I have no patience with the unutterable trash that some of you patronizing Northerners have made up, as in their zeal to apologize for our sins. We all know better. . . ." "I had often supposed," said Miss Ophelia, "that you, all of you, approved of these things, and thought them *right*,—according to Scripture."

"Humbug! We are not quite reduced to that yet." [109]

The effort to reconstruct American ethics to defend slavery against the onslaught of the Evangelical Enlightenment ultimately failed. But it came close enough to succeeding to redraw the picture of traditional attitudes from a consensus that the institution was an evil—necessary or otherwise—to a debate, presumably more or less evenly matched, between "antislavery" and "proslavery" arguments. Yet it is essential that these arguments should not be abstracted from each other, from slavery itself, and from the larger complex of events that helped to shape their content and that they in turn helped to bring about.[110] Appropriately, Abraham Lincoln rightly admonished his countrymen not to sit in judgment on a people who believed that religion sanctified slavery: "It may seem strange that any men should dare to ask a just God's assistance in wringing their bread from the sweat of other men's faces; but let us judge not that we not be judged." But this by no means implied that he felt that no judgment could be made; it simply meant that humans, with all their imperfections, were in no position to act as judge. The Civil War, however, Lincoln did consider a decisive and terrible verdict against slavery: "as was said three thousand years ago, so still it must be said: 'the judgments of the Lord, are true and righteous altogether.'" [111]

NOTES

1. See, for example, Douglas Sloan, *The Scottish Enlightenment and the American College Ideal* (New York: Teachers College Press, 1971), 129.

2. The conjunction of evangelical religion and moral philosophy in the early nineteenth century rarely has been examined in detail. Useful, but incomplete, are Sidney Ahsltrom, "The Scottish Philosophy and American Theology," *Church History* 24 (September 1955), 257–72; Henry F. May, *The Enlightenment in America* (New York: Oxford University Press, 1976), 337–57, and David Brion Davis, *Slavery and Human Progress* (New York: Oxford University Press, 1984), 116–41. Daniel Walker Howe's *The Unitarian Conscience: Harvard Moral Philosophy, 1805–1861* (Cambridge, Mass.: Harvard University Press, 1970) is more useful than Donald H. Meyer, *The Instructed Conscience: The Shaping of the American National Ethic* (Philadelphia: University of Pennsylvania Press, 1972), but the value of the former work is somewhat diminished by its narrow focus. Mitchell Snay, in *Gospel of Disunion: Religion and Separatism in the Antebellum South* (New York: Cambridge University Press, 1993), 82–89, examines the conjunction at a later period, arguing that moral philosophy was particularly "useful" and "attractive" to southern clergymen in developing their defenses of slavery (82). Rather, I would argue that the discipline was ubiquitous and unavoidable, thus demanding of proslavery advocates reformulations that substantively turned its doctrines of "rights, duties and relations" on their head.

3. On the relationship of evangelicalism to antislavery, see Robert H. Abzug, *Cosmos Crumbling: American Reform and the Religious Imagination* (New York: Oxford University Press, 1994), Anne C. Loveland, "Evangelicalism and 'Immediate Emancipation' in American Antislavery Thought," *Journal of Southern History* 32 (May 1966): 172–88, and Donald M. Scott, "Abolitionism as a Sacred Vocation," in *Antislavery Reconsidered: New Perspectives on the Abolitionists,* Lewis Perry and Michael Fellman, eds. (Baton Rouge: Louisiana State University Press, 1979), 51–74. Still invaluable as well is Gilbert Hobbs Barnes, *The Antislavery Impulse 1830–1844* (1933; reprint, New York: Harcourt, Brace & World, 1964), 3–50. On the impact of evangelical antislavery on slaveholders, see Charles Henry Ambler, *Sectionalism in Virginia from 1776 to 1861* (Chicago: University of Chicago Press, 1910), 185–218, esp. 190–97; also see William Campbell Preston, "Speech on the Abolition Question," March 1, 1836, in E. L. Magoon, ed., *Living Orators in America* (New York: Baker and Scribner, 1850), 349–62.

4. M. Carey, "Preface to the Fourth Edition," *The Olive Branch: or, Faults on Both Sides, Federal and Democratic. A Serious Appeal on the Necessity of Mutual Forgiveness and Harmony* (Freeport, N.Y.: Books for Libraries Press, 1969), 22.

5. [Frances Wright Darusmont,] *Views of Society and Manners in America; in a Series of Letters from that Country to a Friend in England, during the Years 1818, 1819, and 1820* (London: Longman, Hurst, Rees, Orme, and Brown, 1821), 313–14. See also Robert Wiebe, *The Opening of American Society from the Adoption of the Constitution to the Eve of Disunion* (New York: Random House, 1984), chap. 4, "The Politics of Independence," 67–89.

6. Important recent works in this vein include E. Brooks Holifield, *The Gentlemen Theologians: American Theology in Southern Culture, 1795–1860* (Durham, N.C.: Duke University Press,

1978); Anne C. Loveland, *Southern Evangelicals and the Social Order, 1800–1860* (Baton Rouge: Louisiana State University Press, 1980); Eugene Genovese, *"Slavery Ordained by God": The Southern Slaveholders' View of Biblical History and Modern Politics* (Gettysburg, Pa.: Gettysburg College, 24th Annual Robert Fortenbaugh Memorial Lecture, 1985); James Oscar Farmer, *The Metaphysical Confederacy: James Henley Thornwell and the Synthesis of Southern Values* (Macon, Ga.: Mercer University Press, 1986), and Snay, *Gospel of Disunion.* Works reflecting the more traditional, critical view of proslavery religion include William Sumner Jenkins, *Proslavery Thought in the Old South* (Chapel Hill: University of North Carolina Press, 1937); Donald G. Mathews, *Slavery and Methodism: A Chapter in American Morality, 1780–1845* (Princeton, N.J.: Princeton University Press, 1965); H. Shelton Smith, *In His Image, But . . . : Racism in Southern Religion, 1780–1910* (Durham, N.C.: Duke University Press, 1972), and John Lee Eighmy, *Churches in Cultural Captivity: A History of the Social Attitudes of Southern Baptists* (Knoxville: University of Tennessee Press, 1972).

7. For example, the proslavery spokesman Josiah Nott wrote to former South Carolina governor James Henry Hammond that Nott's lectures on black inferiority, which he described as his "Nigger hallucinations," were written "with as little care as I write you, save the main points of the discussion," adding, "I want a reputation which will pay—that *Almighty dollar* is the thing at last" (Reginald Horsman, *Josiah Nott of Mobile: Southerner, Physician, and Racial Theorist* (Baton Rouge: Louisiana State University Press, 1987), 92, 101.

8. See esp. *"Slavery Ordained of God"* and "The Logical Outcome of the Slaveholders' Philosophy: An Exposition, Interpretation, and Critique of the Social Thought of George Fitzhugh of Port Royal, Virginia," in Eugene Genovese, *The World the Slaveholders Made: Two Essays in Interpretation* (New York: Vintage Books, 1969), 118–244; and Genovese, *The Slaveholders' Dilemma: Freedom and Progress in Southern Conservative Thought, 1820–1860* (Columbia: University of South Carolina Press, 1992). Genovese made the comment about awarding an "A" at the 1993 meeting of the Society for Historians of the Early Republic, Chapel Hill, North Carolina.

9. Forrest G. Wood, *The Arrogance of Faith: Christianity and Race in America from the Colonial Era to the Twentieth Century* (New York: Alfred A. Knopf, 1990), 38. For a devastating refutation of Wood, see the review by Eugene Genovese in *The New Republic* 203 (August 1990): 33.

10. Larry E. Tise, *Proslavery: A History of the Defense of Slavery in America, 1701–1840* (Athens: University of Georgia Press, 1987), xiv.

11. E. P. Thompson, *The Making of the English Working Class* (New York: Vintage Books, 1996), 12; David Brion Davis, *The Problem of Slavery in the Age of Revolution* (Ithaca, N.Y.: Cornell University Press, 1975), 256.

12. See the introduction to this volume, p. 1.

13. See, for example, Michael Walzer, *Exodus and Revolution* (New York: Basic Books, 1985).

14. See, for example, Nathan O. Hatch and Mark O. Noll, eds., *The Bible in America: Essays in Cultural History* (New York: Oxford University Press, 1982), 39–58.

15. Davis, *Slavery and Human Progress,* 111; for proslavery literalism, see John Fletcher, *Studies on Slavery, in Easy Lessons, Compiled into Eight Studies, and Subdivided into Short Lessons for the Convenience of Readers* (Natchez, 1852); Albert Taylor Bledsoe, *An Essay on Liberty and Slav-*

ery (Philadelphia: J. B. Lippincott, 1856), and Howell Cobb, *A Scriptural Examination of Slavery in the United States; with its Objects and Purposes* (Perry, Ga.: privately printed, 1856).

16. *Methodist General Discipline on Slavery* (1796), quoted in Lucius C. Matlack, *The History of American Slavery and Methodism, from 1780 to 1849* (New York, 1849), 21; see Matthew 19: 3–12.

17. Nash, *Race and Revolution*, 31–33, 91–94.

18. Paul Leicester Ford, ed., *The Writings of Thomas Jefferson*, 12 vols. (New York: G. P. Putnam's Sons, 1905), 10:343.

19. Garry Wills, *Inventing America: Jefferson's Declaration of Independence* (New York: Doubleday, 1980), 175–80. Also see Terence Martin, *The Instructed Vision: Scottish Common Sense Philosophy and the Origins of American Fiction* (Bloomington: Indiana University Press, 1961), and Gilman M. Ostrander, "Jefferson and Scottish Culture," *Historical Reflections* 2 (1975): 233–48; but see Ronald Hamowy, "Jefferson and the Scottish Enlightenment," *William and Mary Quarterly*, 3d ser., 36 (October 1979): 502–23.

20. May, *The Enlightenment in America*, 342.

21. This principle helps to explain why British social and religious conservatives, otherwise so friendly toward paternalism, rejected slavery so vehemently, even in its most benign and paternalistic forms: the master presumed to accept responsibilities for another created being that were not his or hers to transfer.

22. James Beattie, *Elements of Moral Science* (London, 1793), 26.

23. C. Duncan Rice, "Controversies Over Slavery in Eighteenth- and Nineteenth-Century Scotland," in *Antislavery Reconsidered: New Perspectives on the Abolitionists*, Lewis Perry and Michael Fellman, eds. (Baton Rouge: Louisiana State University Press, 1979), 30.

24. John Millar, *The Origin of the Distinction of Ranks; Or, an Inquiry into the Circumstances which Give Rise to Influence and Authority in the Different Members of Society* (Basle, Switzerland, 1793), 282–83.

25. Adam Smith, *Lectures on Jurisprudence*, ed. R. L. Meek, D. D. Raphael, and P. G. Stein (Oxford: Clarendon Press, 1976), 185. To Smith, then, the fact that the historian Edmund Morgan called the "central paradox of American history," that "[t]he rise of liberty and equality in America had been accompanied by the rise of slavery," was not a paradox at all but a logical outcome of republicanism in a slave society. See Morgan, *American Slavery, American Freedom: The Ordeal of Colonial Virginia* (New York: W. W. Norton, 1976), 4, 375–76.

26. Thomas Jefferson, *Notes on the State of Virginia*, William Peden, ed. (Chapel Hill: University of North Carolina Press, 1955), 162–63.

27. Ibid., 179.

28. Smith, *Lectures on Jurisprudence*, 189, 191.

29. For an excellent theoretical discussion that points to this conclusion and explains its origins in the relationship of liberty and slavery, see Orlando Patterson, *Slavery and Social Death: A Comparative Study* (Cambridge, Mass.: Harvard University Press, 1982). Important discussions of the American context include Edmund Morgan, *American Slavery, American Freedom: The Ordeal of Colonial Virginia* (New York: W. W. Norton, 1976); Robert Fogel, *Without Consent or Contract: The Rise and Fall of American Slavery* (New York: W. W. Norton, 1989); Sylvia Frey,

Water from the Rock: Black Resistance in a Revolutionary Age (Princeton, N.J.: Princeton University Press, 1991), 234–42. Gary Nash's provocative and influential *Race and Revolution* comes closest to suggesting that slavery could have been ended peacefully at the time of the Revolution; although his later study with Jean R. Soderlund of the painfully drawn-out experience of emancipation in Pennsylvania, *Freedom By Degrees: Emancipation in Pennsylvania and its Aftermath* (New York: Oxford University Press, 1991), seems to cast doubt on such sanguine expectations and indeed bears out Adam Smith's theoretical point. In any case, it is likely that any form of emancipation envisioned by Nash during the era of the founding would have entailed federal coercion, sweetened with financial compensation (*Race and Revolution,* 36–38). Betty Fladeland demonstrates convincingly that compensated emancipation, far from being a neglected alternative, had been categorically rejected by slaveholders early and often in American history; Fladeland, "Compensated Emancipation: A Rejected Alternative," *Journal of Southern History* 42 (May 1976): 169–86. The well-known thesis of Charles W. Ramsdell that slavery had approached its "natural limits" by 1860 has been refuted convincingly by Alfred H. Conrad and John Meyer in "The Economics of Slavery in the Ante-Bellum South," *Journal of Political Economy* 66 (April 1958): 95–130; Harry V. Jaffa, *Crisis of the House Divided: An Interpretation of the Issues in the Lincoln-Douglas Debates* (Garden City, N.Y.: Doubleday, 1959), 387–404, and Robert William Fogel and Stanley L. Engerman, *Time on the Cross: The Economics of American Negro Slavery* (Boston: Little, Brown, 1974), 62–64, 86–106. Historians have yet to propose a convincing alternative, then, to the view that slavery in the United States could have been ended only by coercion.

30. Robert W. Fogel, in *Without Consent or Contract,* has demonstrated that this linkage naturally stems from the long-standing but inaccurate American conviction that any economic practice that is morally wrong must intrinsically be unprofitable as well; or, in theological terms, "the proposition that divine Providence rewarded virtue and punished evil" (410). Thus George Washington, in his inaugural address: "[T]here is no truth more thoroughly established than that there exists in the economy and course of nature an indissoluble union between virtue and happiness" and "between duty and advantage" (U.S. Congress, *Inaugural Addresses of the Presidents of the United States from George Washington 1789 to George Bush 1989* [Washington, D.C.: General Printing Office, 1989], 3). In other words, if slavery were contrary to virtue, it must also be opposed to advantage.

A more typical assumption among modern scholars is that every practice engaged in by society on a wide scale *must* be buttressed by a convincing ideological justification, no matter how obscure. Thus Robert E. Shalhope, in his otherwise brilliant dissection of Thomas Jefferson's essential role in the development of southern secessionist ideas, chooses on the last page of his essay to postulate Jefferson's adherence to a hitherto-undiscussed ideology of "pastoral republicanism," which presumably reconciles all Jefferson's conflicts and avoids the unforgivable offense of "a historical bifurcation." It is apparently impossible that such southerners as Jefferson could have been deeply wedded to slavery if they did not have an ideological justification for it—that they could have chosen to pursue a way of life they did *not* "believe to be well and good" (556). For an impressive theoretical rebuttal of the view that racism is based on a consistent philosopical foundation, see Lewis R. Gordon, *Bad Faith and Antiblack Racism* (Atlantic Highlands, N.J.: Humanities Press, 1995).

31. It is remarkable that, at a time when the hoary Lovejoyan paradigm of the history of a pure idea, abstracted from its social and cultural milieu, has long since fallen into disfavor, the peculiarly Platonic conception of a disembodied, transhistorical "proslavery ideology"—an unchangeable domain of concepts and ideas, accessible to partisans in every age irrespective of differing social, political, or economic conditions—has obtained remarkable currency among historians otherwise conspicuous for their hardheaded materialism. The great exemplar of the old school of the history of ideas is Arthur O. Lovejoy, *The Great Chain of Being: A Study of the History of an Idea* (1936; New York: Harper and Row, 1960). The most striking application of the Lovejoyan model to the idea of proslavery is Larry Tise's influential *Proslavery;* see esp. p. 14.

32. Jeffrey Brooke Allen, "The Debate over Slavery and Race in Ante-Bellum Kentucky: 1792–1850" (Ph.D. diss., Northwestern University, 1973), 30. Similarly, David T. Bailey describes the "silence of the proslavery forces" as "perhaps the great puzzle in the history of slavery and southwestern religion," and asks, "How, then, did this opposition so effectively thwart the goals of a highly organized antislavery movement, and how did it avoid taking a public stand in favor of the peculiar institution?"; *Shadow on the Church: Southwestern Evangelical Religion and the Issue of Slavery* (Ithaca, N.Y.: Cornell University Press, 1985), 112. Actually, these are hardly "great puzzles"; the West India lobby successfully employed silence—in combination with cash and other forms of influence—as its chief tactic in more than four decades of struggle with the eloquent British abolition movement. In each of these cases, silence perhaps merely demonstrated the absence of better arguments.

33. See, for example, E. Brooks Holifield, *The Gentlemen Theologians: American Theology in Southern Culture, 1795–1860* (Durham, N.C.: Duke University Press, 1978); Snay, *Gospel of Disunion* (esp. chap. 2); and Tise, *Proslavery.*

34. The tragic story is well told in James Essig, *The Bonds of Wickedness: American Evangelicals Against Slavery, 1770–1808* (Philadelphia: Temple University Press, 1982). See also Anne C. Loveland, *Southern Evangelicals and the Social Order, 1800–1860* (Baton Rouge: Louisiana State University Press, 1980), chap. 7, and Rhys Isaac, *The Transformation of Virginia, 1740–1790* (Chapel Hill: University of North Carolina Press, 1982), chap. 8. For a passionate and scholarly account of the churches' travails that, however, fails to acknowledge the institutional obstacles to antislavery, see H. Shelton Smith, *In His Image, But . . .*, chap. 1. For an alternative view, see Douglas Ambrose, "Of Stations and Relations: Proslavery Christianity in Early National Virginia," in this volume.

35. *Journals of the General Conference of the Methodist Episcopal Church*, 1:169–70, cited in Smith, *In His Image, But . . .*, 45; see also Lucius P. Matlack, *The History of American Slavery and Methodism from 1780 to 1849 . . .* (New York, 1849), chap. 1; Eighmy, *Churches in Cultural Captivity*, ch. 1; Ernest T. Thompson, *Presbyterians in the South*, 3 vols. (Richmond, Va.: John Knox Press, 1963–73), vol. 1; Walter B. Posey, "The Slavery Question in the Presbyterian Church in the Old Southwest," *Journal of Southern History* 15 (August 1949): 311–24, and John W. Christie and Dwight L. Dumond, *George Bourne and "The Book and Slavery Irreconcilable"* (Wil-

mington and Philadelphia: Historical Society of Delaware and Presbyterian Historical Society, 1969), 15–65.

36. Richard Furman, *Exposition of the Views of the Baptists Relative to the Coloured Population of the United States in a Communication to the Governor of South Carolina* (Charleston, 1823), reprinted in James A. Rogers, *Richard Furman: Life and Legacy* ([Macon, Ga.]: Mercer University Press, 1985), 284. The elaborate and tortuous efforts of Furman and Dalcho to justify slavery by means of Scripture testify clearly to the novelty of the project. Dalcho, for example, concludes his painfully complicated attempt to link the biblical curse against Canaan to the Africans, whom he recognizes are not Canaan's descendents, with the highly antifundamentalist suggestion that "if we were to correct the text, as we should any classic author in a like case, the whole, perhaps, might be made easier and plainer"; [Frederick Dalcho], *Practical Considerations Founded on the Scriptures, Relative to the Slave Population of South–Carolina* (Charleston: A. E. Miller, 1823), 16. Furman's and Dalcho's deference to the authority of the "benevolent Wilberforce" and other "highly respectable" religious and political writers against slavery underscores the difficulty faced by relatively cultivated southern clergymen in attempting to defend the institution. See Furman, *Exposition,* 280, 285, and Dalcho, *Practical Considerations,* 6; see also Randy J. Sparks, "'To Rend the Body of Christ': Proslavery Ideology and Religious Schism from a Mississippi Perspective," in this volume.

37. See Stephen B. Weeks, *Southern Quakers and Slavery: A Study in Institutional History,* Johns Hopkins University Studies in Historical and Political Science, extra vol. 15 (Baltimore: Johns Hopkins Press, 1896).

38. May, *Enlightenment in America,* 328.

39. This is highly unlikely because the notes from Smith's lectures were not published until 1896. It is quite plausible, however, that some southerners may have studied under students of Smith or even attended his lectures at Glasgow.

40. Noble E. Cunningham Jr., "Nathaniel Macon and the Southern Protest against National Consolidation," *North Carolina Historical Review* 32, no. 3 (July 1955): 380.

41. See, for example, R. Kent Newmyer, "John Marshall and the Southern Constitutional Tradition," in *An Uncertain Tradition: Constitutionalism and the History of the South,* Kermit L. Hall and James W. Ely Jr., eds. (Athens: University of Georgia Press, 1989), 105–23; Edwin Mood Wilson, "The Congressional Career of Nathaniel Macon," James Sprunt Historical Monographs, No. 2 (Chapel Hill: University of North Carolina Press, 1900), 48–49, 72–73, 76–78, and Norman K. Risjord, *The Old Republicans: Southern Conservatives in the Age of Jefferson* (New York: Columbia University Press, 1965), 175–79. Orlando Patterson's observations with regard to the relationship of Roman slaveholders to the central government is relevant here:

> The slave latifundists needed the strong centralized state, because without it they were at the mercy of their slaves. But rural slavery irrevocably led to the localization of power. That, I feel confident in claiming, is a virtual law of large-scale slave society. Absolute power, which is what the latifundist had on his slave villa, did not necessarily corrupt the individual absolutely, as Lord Acton so famously imagined. What absolute power on the local and individual level did corrupt absolutely was the state and any sense of loyalty to it.

Orlando Patterson, *Freedom, vol. 1: Freedom in the Making of Western Culture* (New York: Basic Books, 1991), 347.

42. U.S. Constitution, art. 4, sec. 2; art 1, sec. 8, respectively.

43. U. S. Constitution, art. 1, sec. 9; art. 5. The quote is from a letter by Willie P. Mangum to Bartlett Yancey, 15 January 1826, in Edwin Mood Wilson, "The Congressional Career of Nathaniel Macon," *James Sprunt Historical Monographs, No. 2* (Chapel Hill: University of North Carolina Press, 1900), 108. See Paul Finkelman, "Slavery and the Constitutional Convention: Making a Covenant with Death," in *Beyond Confederation: Origins of the Constitution and American National Identity,* Richard Beeman, Stephen Botein, and Edward C. Carter II, eds. (Chapel Hill: University of North Carolina Press, 1987).

44. Howard Ohline, "Slavery, Economics, and Congressional Politics, 1790," *Journal of Southern History* 46, no. 3 (August 1980): 358.

45. See Gaines M. Foster, "Guilt Over Slavery: A Historiographical Analysis," *Journal of Southern History* 56, no. 4 (November 1990): 665–94.

46. Elizabeth Fox-Genovese has rightly directed attention to the "objective constraints" within which the "subjective dimensions" of community life must be evaluated. *Within the Plantation Household: Black and White Women of the Old South* (Chapel Hill: University of North Carolina Press, 1988), 68–70. See also Eugene Genovese, *The Political Economy of Slavery: Studies in the Economy and Society of the Slave South* (New York: Pantheon Books, 1965).

47. Thomas Jefferson, *Notes on the State of Virginia,* 162. Indeed, from the standpoint of most of human experience throughout history, and even in comparison with most of the rest of the contemporary world, living conditions on southern plantations, even for slaves, were likely far better than those endured by a majority of the world's population, just as southerners asserted. See George Fitzhugh, *Sociology for the South, or the Failure of Free Society* (Richmond, Va.: A Morris, 1854), chap. 4; and Fogel and Engerman, *Time on the Cross,* 116, 249.

48. For a thorough examination of these issues, see Thomas Bender, ed., *The Antislavery Debate: Capitalism and Abolitionism as a Problem in Historical Interpretation* (Berkeley: University of California Press, 1992).

49. Thus George Fitzhugh: "All books in the whole range of moral science, if not written by Southern authors, within the last twenty or thirty years, inculcate abolition either directly or indirectly. If written before that time, even by Southern authors, they are likely to be as absurd and dangerous as the Declaration of Independence, or the Virginia Bill of Rights." "Southern Thought," *De Bow's Review* 23 (1857): 341. See also the observation of Eric Williams: "It is almost pathetic to have to deal today with the writers who opposed [Adam] Smith and [Thomas] Clarkson. None of the defenders of slavery have any merit or international significance today. If one had to mention a political economist who was opposed to Adam Smith, one could think only of Malachi Postlethwayt. Who has ever heard of Postlethwayt?"; *British Historians and the West Indies* (New York: Charles Scribner's Sons, 1966), 25. Williams exaggerates for effect, but not greatly.

50. Roger Bruns, ed., *Am I Not a Man and a Brother* (New York: Chelsea House, 1977), 221.

51. Isaac, *Transformation of Virginia,* 284–85; Forrest McDonald, *E Pluribus Unum: The Formation of the American Republic, 1776–1790* (Boston: Houghton Mifflin, 1965), 356–58.

52. Merrill Jensen, et al., eds., *The Documentary History of the Ratification of the Constitution* (Madison, Wis.: State Historical Society of Wisconsin, 1976–), 10:1209ff.

53. Harry F. Stout, *The New England Soul: Preaching and Religious Culture in Colonial New England* (New York: Oxford University Press, 1986), 315.

54. Thomas E. Buckley, "After Disestablishment: Thomas Jefferson's Wall of Separation in Antebellum Virginia," *Journal of Southern History* 61 (August 1995): 448. See also Isaac, *Transformation of Virginia,* 278–95.

55. John Stuart Mill, *The Spirit of the Age* (1831; reprint Chicago: University of Chicago Press, 1942), 91.

56. On white southerners' dual image of blacks as men and property, see Richard Bruce Erno, "Dominant Images of the Negro in the Ante-Bellum South" (Ph.D. diss., University of Minnesota, 1961), chap. 1.

57. Jefferson, *Autobiography* (1821), in Paul Leicester Ford, ed., *The Writings of Thomas Jefferson,* 10 vols. (New York: G. P. Putnam's Sons, 1892–99), 1:77. On Jefferson's ambiguous antislavery commitment, see Davis, *Problem of Slavery in the Age of Revolution,* 182–85, and Paul Finkelman, "Thomas Jefferson and Antislavery: The Myth Goes On," *Virginia Magazine of History and Biography* 102 (April 1994): 193–228; on the representativeness of Jefferson's attitudes, see Winthrop D. Jordan, *White over Black: American Attitudes toward the Negro, 1550– 1812* (1968; reprint, Baltimore: Pelican Books, 1969), 429–40, 455–56; Robert McColley, *Slavery and Jeffersonian Virginia* (Urbana: University of Illinois Press, 1964), and Robert E. Shalhope, "Thomas Jefferson's Republicanism and Antebellum Southern Thought," *Journal of Southern History* 42 (November 1976): 529–56. Unfortunately, this essay was written too early to benefit from Conor Cruse O'Brien's powerful article, "Thomas Jefferson: Radical and Racist," *Atlantic Monthly* 278 (October 1996): 53–66.

58. See Paul Finkelman, "Jefferson and Slavery: 'Treason against the Hopes of the World,'" in *Jeffersonian Legacies,* Peter S. Onuf, ed. (Charlottesville: University of Virginia Press, 1994), 207– 10. On the class identity of southern planters, see Jack P. Maddex Jr., "'The Southern Apostasy' Revisited: The Significance of Proslavery Christianity," *Marxist Perspectives* 2 (fall 1979): 132– 41. Unfortunately, Maddex falls into the error I have discussed above of assuming that southern planters necessarily possessed an ideology to complement their class identity from an early date.

59. I am here using the expanded understanding of the slaveholding class offered by Davis, *The Problem of Slavery in the Age of Revolution,* 182–83.

60. The most celebrated such desertion was Edward Coles, a protégé of both Jefferson and Madison, who freed his slaves and left Virginia for Illinois in 1819. See Ralph L. Ketcham, "The Dictates of Conscience: Edward Coles and Slavery," *Virginia Quarterly Review* 36 (winter 1960): 46–62, and Drew R. McCoy, *The Last of the Fathers: James Madison and the Republican Legacy* (Cambridge: Cambridge University Press, 1989), 308–22.

61. See Shalhope, "Thomas Jefferson's Republicanism," 540–41, 553.

62. For an examination of a narrowly averted catastrophe brought on in part by the slaveholders' embrace of republicanism, see Douglas R. Egerton, *Gabriel's Rebellion: The Virginia Slave Conspiracies of 1800 and 1802* (Chapel Hill: University of North Carolina Press, 1993).

63. See Theodore Dwight, *History of the Hartford Convention* (1833; reprint, New York: Da Capo Press, 1970).

64. The historian Paul Finkelman has quoted a recent observation of Gordon S. Wood to this effect: "Most Americans think of Jefferson much as our first professional biographer James Parton did. 'If Jefferson was wrong,' wrote Parton in 1874, 'America is wrong. If America is right, Jefferson is right.'" Thus, Finkelman observes, "The historian who questions Jefferson, it would seem, implicitly questions America." Finkelman, "Thomas Jefferson and Antislavery," 194–95.

65. Arthur Schlesinger Jr., *The Age of Jackson* (Boston: Houghton Mifflin, 1945), 424. Schlesinger refers to the subject only three times in discussion of events before 1845. The classic critiques of Jacksonianism have likewise virtually ignored the question of slavery. Leonard D. White's *The Jacksonians: A Study in Administrative History, 1829–1861* (New York: McMillan, 1954) is so artfully circumscribed as to exclude the issue entirely, except for the author's condemnation of northern citizens' "unlawful and tumultuous" opposition to the enforcement of the Fugitive Slave Law (526). Marvin Meyers's *The Jacksonian Persuasion: Politics and Belief* (Stanford, Calif.: Stanford University Press, 1957) similarly ignores the slavery question (the index contains not a single reference to the topic). Lee Benson, like the 1844 Whig platform, "maintained eloquent silence" on the significance of slavery in antebellum American politics in his important study *The Concept of Jacksonian Democracy: New York as a Test Case* (1961; reprint, New York: Atheneum, 1964), 238. See also Joel H. Silbey, *The Partisan Imperative: The Dynamics of American Politics Before the Civil War* (New York: Oxford University Press, 1985), for a summary of its author's lengthy efforts to exorcise the issue of slavery from the antebellum period.

66. Tise, *Proslavery*, chaps. 8 and 9.

67. Ford K. Brown, *Fathers of the Victorians: The Age of Wilberforce* (Cambridge: Cambridge University Press, 1961). Wilberforce's Oxford Movement sons performed an equally remarkable act of omission in their five-volume biography of their father by almost completely excluding references to his evangelicalism. See Robert Isaac and Samuel Wilberforce, *The Life of William Wilberforce*, 5 vols. (London, 1838). Paul I. Johnson's *A Shopkeeper's Millennium: Society and Revivals in Rochester, 1815–1837* (New York: Hill and Wang, 1978) is perhaps the best-known American exemplar of the genre.

68. See John Bach McMaster, *A History of the People of the United States from the Revolution to the Civil War*, 8 vols. (New York: D. Appleton, 1883–1913), and Gilbert Hobbs Barnes, *The Antislavery Impulse, 1830–1844* (1933; reprint, New York: Harbinger, 1964).

69. M. Ostrogorski, *Democracy and the Organization of Political Parties, Volume 1: England*, Seymour Martin Lipset, ed. (Garden City, N.Y.: Anchor Books, 1964), 18–20. Ostrogorski's impression of the links between antislavery and democratization in Britain was widely shared by historians before the early twentieth century; it has been substantiated recently by the works of Seymour Drescher and James Walvin. See Drescher, *Econocide: British Slavery in the Era of Abolition* (Pittsburgh: University of Pittsburgh Press, 1977), and *Capitalism and Antislavery: British Mobilization in Comparative Perspective* (New York: Oxford University Press, 1986), and Walvin, "The Public Campaign in England against Slavery," in *The Abolition of the Atlantic Slave Trade*, David Eltis and James Walvin, ed. (Madison: University of Wisconsin Press, 1981), 63–89. The

story of the virtual expulsion of the British antislavery campaign from historical memory is a fascinating and important one that has yet to be told in full.

70. Linda Colley, *Britons: Forging the Nation, 1707–1837* (New Haven: Yale University Press, 1992), 354–60; Elie Halévy, *A History of the English People in 1815* (London: Ark, 1987), 400–401.

71. Lawrence A. Cremin, *American Education: The National Experience, 1783–1876* (New York: Harper & Row, 1980), 27.

72. William Paley, *Moral and Political Philosophy* (1784; reprint, New York, 1824), 145–47.

73. Johan Daniel Gross, *Natural Principles of Rectitude for the Conduct of Man in all States and Situations of Life Demonstrated and Explained in a Systematic Treatise on Moral Philosophy Comprehending the Law of Nature—Ethics—Natural Jurisprudence—General Economics—Politics—and the Law of Nations* (New York, 1795), 338.

74. John L. Parkhurst, *Elements of Moral Philosophy: Comprising the Theory of Morals and Practical Ethics* (Concord, N.H.: J. B. Moore and J. W. Shepard, 1825), 124.

75. Francis Wayland, *Elements of Moral Science* (New York: Cooke, 1835), 214. For Wayland's ambiguous stance regarding slavery, see Deborah Van Broekhoven, "Suffering with Slaveholders: The Limits of Francis Wayland's Antislavery Witness," in this volume.

76. Halévy, *History of the English People*, 400–401.

77. See Robert P. Forbes, "Slavery and the Meaning of America, 1819–1833" (Ph.D. diss., Yale University, 1994), chaps. 4 and 5.

78. William T. Foster, *Administration of the College Curriculum* (Boston: Houghton Mifflin, 1911), 16. Jefferson's revisions of 1779 also added the Law of Nature and of Nations and the Fine Arts to the duties of the professor of Moral Philosophy.

79. Jefferson, *Notes on Virginia*, 162. The expression is from the title of an article in *De Bow's Review* 10 (1851): 362, and refers of course to educating southern youth in southern schools, not to home schooling.

80. Jefferson to Gen. James Breckinridge, 15 February 1821, quoted in John S. Ezell, "A Southern Education for Southrons," *Journal of Southern History* 17 (August 1951): 303.

81. Ford, ed., *The Writings of Thomas Jefferson*, 12:154–56.

82. Nathaniel Francis Cabell, ed., *Early History of the University of Virginia, as Contained in the Letters of Thomas Jefferson and Joseph C. Cabell . . .* (Richmond, Va.: J. W. Randolph, 1856), xx. The emphasis here and in the following quotations is Jefferson's.

83. Ibid., xxi.

84. Ibid., 164–65; Alf J. Mapp Jr., *Thomas Jefferson, Passionate Pilgrim: The Presidency, the Founding of the University, and the Private Battle* (Madison, Wisc.: Madison Books, 1991), 308.

85. Cabell, *Early History of the University of Virginia*, 169.

86. Ibid., 165.

87. Cited in "Review," *The Virginia Evangelical and Literary Magazine* 3 (1820): 69, 71.

88. Ibid., 72–73.

89. Cabell, *Early History*, 234.

90. Ibid., 234–35.

91. Wills, *Inventing America*, pt. 3; Foster, *Administration of the College Curriculum*, 42n.; Mapp, *Passionate Pilgrim*, 308; see also May, *Enlightenment in America*, 333.

92. See John Adams to Thomas Jefferson, 14 September 1813, in *The Adams-Jefferson Letters: The Complete Correspondence between Thomas Jefferson and Abigail and John Adams,* Leslie J. Capon, ed. (Chapel Hill: University of North Carolina Press, 1987), 373; Joseph C. Cabell to Thomas Jefferson, February 22 and March 8, 1819, in Cabell, *Early History,* 165–66, 171–72.

93. Ford, ed., *Writings,* 12:143–45.

94. Douglas L. Wilson, "Jefferson and the Republic of Letters," in *Jeffersonian Legacies,* Onuf, ed., 70.

95. Wilson, ibid.; Wills, *Inventing America,* 276.

96. Rice, "Review," 70.

97. May, *Enlightenment in America,* 333; Rice, "Review," 74.

98. Michael Sugrue, "'We Desired our Future Rulers to be Educated Men': South Carolina College, the Defense of Slavery, and the Development of Secessionist Politics," *Higher Education Annual* 14 (1994): 39–71. Thus Paul Finkelman is correct in arguing that "Jefferson was the intellectual godfather of the racist pseudo-science of the American school of anthropology"; but his patronage of Cooper, whose students spread and elaborated his racist proslavery arguments throughout the antebellum South, may have been as influential, if not more so, than his speculations in the *Notes on Virginia.* Finkelman, "Jefferson and Slavery," 186.

99. See Michael Sugrue, "'We Desired Our Future Rulers to be Educated Men,'" 39–71; and see also Sugrue, "South Carolina College: The Education of an Antebellum Elite" (Ph.D. diss., Columbia University, 1992).

100. Dumas Malone, *The Public Life of Thomas Cooper, 1783–1839* (New Haven: Yale University Press, 1926), 290.

101. Cooper, "Coloured Marriages," (1823), cited in Malone, ibid., 285.

102. William M. Wiecek, sounding suspiciously like Roger B. Taney, argued that the lines of the Declaration of Independence, "properly read in the light of American social conditions in 1776, contain the word 'white' before the word 'men'" (*The Sources of Antislavery Constitutionalism in America, 1760–1848* (Ithaca, N.Y.: Cornell University Press, 1977), 51. This contradicts the emphatic assertion of Abraham Lincoln in 1858 that "the entire records of the world from the date of the Declaration of Independence up to within three years ago, may be searched in vain for one single declaration from one single man, that the negro was not included in the Declaration of Independence." According to Lincoln, no man "ever said so until the necessities of the Democratic party had to invent that declaration." Harold Holzer, ed., *The Lincoln-Douglas Debates: The First Complete, Unexpurgated Text* (New York: Harper Perennial, 1993), 252.

103. John Fletcher, *Studies on Slavery, in Easy Lessons* (1852; reprint, Miami: Mnemosyne, 1969), iv. Typically, Fletcher's defense of slavery is posited on scriptural grounds, but he calls into question his pose of pious orthodoxy in an unguarded observation: "[For] [m]ost men . . . , [t]he wonderful works of nature create no wonder. A mine of sea-shells on the Andes excites no surprise" (p. 17). Fletcher's reference to this geological anomaly shows his familarity with a favorite argument used in "parson skinning"—the efforts of anticlerical proslavery polygenists, such as Josiah Nott, to undermine the biblical doctrine of human unity by calling into question the chronology of Scripture. See J. C. Nott, "Ancient and Scripture Chronology," *Southern Quarterly Review* 2 (1850): 385–426, and William Stanton, *The Leopard's Spots: Scientific Attitudes toward Race in America, 1815–59* (Chicago: University of Chicago Press, 1959).

104. Michael O'Brien, *A Character of Hugh Legaré* (Knoxville: University of Tennessee Press, 1985), 164; "Ancient Slavery," *De Bow's Review* 19 (1855): 561. John Perkins Jr. in the same volume of *De Bow's,* also cites "French works on the organization of labor . . . which should be particularly pressed upon our attention at this time," although he does not name them. "Southern Education for Southern Youth," ibid., 463.

105. John Hope Franklin, *A Southern Odyssey* (Baton Rouge: University of Louisiana Press, 1976), 71–80; Ezell, "Southern Education for Southrons," *passim.*

106. O'Brien, *A Character of Hugh Legaré,* 164.

107. "Ancient Slavery," *De Bow's Review* 19 (1855): 560, 562.

108. Reginald Horsman, *Josiah Nott of Mobile: Southerner, Physician, and Racial Theorist* (Baton Rouge: Louisiana State University Press, 1987), 100.

109. Harriet Beecher Stowe, *Uncle Tom's Cabin: or, Life Among the Lowly* (Boston: John P. Jewett, 1851), 88.

110. On the importance of reconnecting the study of abolitionism with the concrete institution of slavery, see James L. Huston, "The Experiential Basis of the Northern Antislavery Impulse," *Journal of Southern History* 56 (November 1990): 609–40.

111. Roy P. Basler, ed., *The Collected Works of Abraham Lincoln,* 9 vols. (New Brunswick, N.J.: Rutgers University Press, 1953–1955), 8:333.

PART TWO

 Conflict within the Ranks

"To Keep the Way Open for Methodism"

Georgia Wesleyan Neutrality

toward Slavery, 1844–1861

CHRISTOPHER H. OWEN

On a steamy July day in 1844 Lewis Myers of Effingham County, Georgia, sat down and meditated upon the sectional disintegration of his beloved Methodist Episcopal Church (MEC). Myers had helped establish Methodism in Georgia, preaching there as early as 1803. Illness forced him to retire in 1825, but Myers had carved out a position of respect in church circles. He continued to influence Georgia Wesleyans and frequently urged fellow ministers to hold closely to early Methodist principles. The disaster of the 1844 split within the church, Myers decided, took place because a self-righteous "Northern Conscience" made it almost impossible for southern Wesleyans to cooperate with their free-state counterparts. But southern Methodists shared the blame. With "more *humility, and self-abasement* . . . among the *whole of us*," he lamented, Methodists could have remained united, "conquering Slavery, and the world without Shedding one drop of blood."[1]

In detesting abolition while hoping to "conquer" slavery, Myers displayed ambivalence toward human bondage. Similar doubts sometimes plagued younger churchmen, but among Georgia Methodists such ideas were chiefly the intellectual baggage of an older generation nostalgic for the antislavery ideals of early Methodism. Most southern Wesleyans had long ago decided to play down antislavery principles. As evangelicals they wanted desperately, in the words of one historian, to spread "vital Christianity through all ranks of society." Achieving this task, as the experience of southern Quakers showed, was not compatible with open antislavery. By 1815, then, Methodists in Georgia and most other southern states had decided to coexist with slavery.[2] Yet even fifty years after this decision, they would not officially adopt an unambiguously proslavery position.

Instead, they would promulgate a position of official neutrality toward the peculiar institution and advocate (with less consistency) withdrawal, as a church, from politics. Like many southern Baptists and Presbyterians, Georgia Wesleyans repeatedly maintained that slavery was a civil institution outside the purview of the church. Genuine Christianity, they argued, could exist (and had existed) either with slavery or without it; hence, religious bodies, whose chief goal should be saving souls, had no business "intermeddling" with an essentially secular institution. It was up to the government, not the church, to decide whether to maintain or to dismantle slavery. All three major southern denominations—Presbyterian, Baptist, and Methodist—officially subscribed to this position and decried ecclesiastical involvement in politics. Presbyterians pioneered the doctrine, which is usually known as the "spirituality of the church."[3]

Despite the frequency with which this position was reiterated, scholars have repeatedly refused to accept the doctrine at face value. Many historians, for example, have maintained that southern believers, Methodists included, were zeal-filled crusaders for the "Southern way of life." Ensnared in "cultural captivity," southern evangelicals, in this view, put defense of slavery above all else. According to these historians, the spirituality of the church was a smoke screen to disguise a proslavery political agenda and wholehearted endorsement of human bondage.[4] Meanwhile, another group of scholars sees evangelical theology as intensely, though covertly, "antislavery." In this view, slavery violated basic evangelical commitments to brotherhood and equality and burdened southern church folk with a heavy load of guilt. Insofar as evangelicals failed to attack slavery, they refrained, according to these scholars, out of fear and not out of conviction. When given the chance (during the Civil War), the southern faithful moved aggressively to dismantle the institution.[5] For Georgia Wesleyans the first school of thought has the better argument. The state's Methodists provided far more support for slavery than opposition to it. Many of them held slaves, almost none actively opposed the institution, and most fiercely opposed abolition. Nonetheless, the theoretical position of their church was neither "proslavery" nor "antislavery" but neutrality.[6]

Such neutrality may have involved expediency rather than heartfelt belief, but its ramifications were more useful and more important for southern evangelicals than most scholars have realized. The doctrine, for example, helped salve troubled consciences of older Wesleyans ambivalent about the institution. By taking a neutral stance toward slavery based mainly on the New Testament, Georgia Methodists also tried (with mixed success) to maintain their evangelical credentials in the Protestant world. To yeoman whites and to slaves, Wesleyan ministers used neutrality to make themselves appear as something more than stooges of the planter class. Most important, neutrality on this issue protected Methodists from the charge of abolitionism while it allowed them to push forward many other aspects of Wesleyan ideology. From conviction and necessity, Georgia Wesleyans would accept slavery, but many of them, including planters, retained a large dose of reformist evangelical activism. Furthermore, Georgia Wesleyan support for the spirituality of the church and for neutrality toward slavery did *not* exist simply to provide cover for rabidly secessionist political views. Georgia Wesleyans split their votes between the parties and divided deeply on the wisdom of political separatism. Perhaps southern evangelicals helped "sanctify" a society based on bondage, and even provided the "warp" that held its class system together.[7] But, at least for Georgia Wesleyans, a stance of theoretical neutrality toward the peculiar institution and an effort to keep slavery-related politics at arm's length helped give the church its strength.

Georgia Methodism provides a useful (though not necessarily representative) vehicle by which to examine southern evangelical views toward slavery. Georgia was large and populous. Its churches were numerous and prosperous and its religious leaders deeply involved in church debates on the institution of slavery. Focusing on Wesleyans has advantages over melding all denominations into an indistinct lump. Methodist theology, church structure, and denominational history conditioned Wesleyan religious and social attitudes. In many ways, their attitudes mirrored those of other evangelicals, but at times their opinions diverged from those of other southern churches. More than some groups, for example, Georgia Wesleyans favored measures that would remake society in an evangelical image by creating colleges, publishing newspapers, financing missions, and distributing tracts. Adopting a relatively hands-off approach to slavery, then, probably came less easily to them than to Baptists, who had a historic wariness of government involvement and ecumenical cooperation. The following look at the roots and nature of Georgia Wesleyan neutrality toward slavery and at the consequences of this doctrine for the church and its place in society can, therefore, deepen our understanding of the nature and the variety of southern evangelicalism.[8]

Slavery was *the* reason Georgia Methodists severed connection with their northern coreligionists. Before 1844 the Georgia Methodist Conference had demonstrated no special regard for maintaining the bishops' powers (a question some scholars see behind the split). On the other hand, the conference had regularly expressed opposition to abolitionism and had remonstrated frequently against strengthening Methodist antislavery rules. In 1838, for example, a Georgia conference resolution argued that slavery was legally recognized and permitted by the Bible and that it was therefore not "proper to the exercise of church authority."[9]

Indeed, Georgia Methodist connections to the institution—Bishop James O. Andrew's acquisition of slaves through marriage—provided the catalyst for MEC disintegration. Elected bishop as a nonslaveholder, Andrew deeded the slaves back to his wife in an unsuccessful effort to placate northern antislavery sentiment. Urged on by delegates from Georgia and other southern states, however, Andrew refused to resign his position. This decision led to his suspension as bishop and to the dismemberment of the Methodist Episcopal Church, but Georgia Wesleyans, lay and clerical, supported Andrew's course and applauded the actions of their delegation. Andrew's conduct, said one young minister, boosted "him still Hyer in the Estimation of the Ga. Conference." In later years, Georgians led efforts to expunge "the obnoxious section on slavery" from the *Discipline* of the new southern church. Considerable opposition to these changes existed in other conferences, but there was relatively little in Georgia. In 1857, for example, the conference voted 154–0 to delete all antislavery references from the *Discipline*.[10]

If Methodism anywhere became genuinely proslavery, it was in Georgia. Hysteria on slavery gripped the state, and any person who publicly advocated abolition risked life and limb. In 1844, for example, when Rev. Daniel Curry upheld antislavery views from the Methodist pulpit in Columbus, he was forced to flee the state in fear of his life. Violent threats later drove Rev. George W. Craven, an antislavery Canadian Methodist, out of Georgia. "No man is condemned for his opinions of slavery," said Georgia minister James B. Payne in 1844, but "brethren who cannot abide southern institutions" ought to "seek a new home where they might live in peace, and not war on the church and country here." Even mild calls for better treatment of slaves caused controversy. A Georgia minister, said Rev. James O. A. Clark, must be "prudent & cautious," for "a single false step" would "greatly endanger" his "usefulness." Only preachers "well known & long resident" in the region might admonish masters for "neglect to their slaves." Bishop George F. Pierce could condemn "intemperate" treatment of slaves from his Sparta pulpit. But even Josiah Lewis, Georgia native and presiding elder, received threats when he demanded "reform" from masters who failed to clothe their slaves adequately.[11]

And yet, in general, Georgia Methodist views of slavery stuck to neutral principles associated with the spirituality of the church. Furthermore, in comparison to the well-wrought theories of South Carolina Presbyterian James H.

Thornwell or Virginia Baptist Thornton Stringfellow, their efforts on the subject were sporadic and undisciplined. In the 1840s, Augustus Baldwin Longstreet, well-known author, Methodist minister, and college educator, published two short books on slavery, but he considered the quality of his writings on this subject to be "the weakest" of his literary life. Only one other Georgia Methodist, Rev. Howell Cobb (a local preacher and judge, not the statesman) produced a full-length book defending slavery: *A Scriptural Examination of the Institution of Slavery* published in 1856. Yet Georgia Wesleyans crafted (mostly in newspaper articles and official church documents) a coherent and fairly consistent set of beliefs about slavery.

The essential elements of the Georgia Methodist position were present in the 1840s in Longstreet's *Letters on the Epistle of Paul to Philemon* (1845) and his *Voice From the South* (1847), and those elements changed little thereafter. In general, Georgia Methodist defenses of slavery were directed more against abolitionists than in favor of slavery per se. These defenses argued for church noninvolvement in politics; relied on biblical arguments over all others and favored literal reading of scripture; were based on New Testament ideas of individual repentance and conversion more than on a patriarchal, Old Testament social vision; and argued that the Bible *allowed*, not that it commended, slavery.

In the mid-1840s feelings of betrayal and antiabolitionist outrage stood in the forefront. Georgia Wesleyans believed that the suspension of Andrew, if unanswered, would stigmatize even the most devout slaveholder as unchristian. And, as the 1846 General Conference of the Methodist Episcopal Church, South (MECS) argued, such antislavery action reversed "the solemn and explicit assurances of two successive General Conferences" to tolerate slave owning by clergymen whose states did not allow manumission. Augustus Longstreet seethed with anger toward northern Methodists for abandoning moderation on the issue of slavery. He wrote several newspaper articles in 1844, which the next year were collected and printed as *Philemon*. Through exegesis of the New Testament epistle Longstreet tried to put slavery "to the test of full dispassionate argument upon scriptural principles!" "A slaveholder," he argued, "may be a good Christian," for Philemon was both minister and master. The letters were hardly dispassionate, for the author kept recent events in mind. In the final letter, he asked: "If Paul and his colleagues thus esteemed Philemon, how can you and your colleagues reconcile it to your consciences to treat Bishop Andrew as you have treated him, and as you are still treating him?" [12]

Philemon was part of the rancorous dispute between Georgia Wesleyans and their northern coreligionists. Like many similar treatises, it was addressed to northern and southern audiences. Anti-abolitionist outrage permeates Georgia Methodist writings on slavery. Georgia Methodists felt betrayed by northern "ultraism," which, they thought, had undercut their own attempts to ameliorate the institution by converting masters and slaves. They believed such "interference" had disastrously hardened southern attitudes toward any modification of slavery. Both Longstreet and Cobb, for example, decried abolitionist attacks on what they saw as the sober-minded efforts of colonizationists.[13]

Georgia Methodists continually criticized northern Christians for combining religion and politics, for carrying "a Bible in one hand and a torch in the other." "Methodist preachers instead of spending their time on politico-religious lecturing," said Bishop Andrew in 1844, "ought to do the one work of preaching the gospel of the grace of God." Georgia Wesleyans could not and did not want to isolate themselves completely from world events. The MECS never forbade members, or even ministers, from expressing political preferences, but it frowned on *ex cathedra* political statements. As Bishop William Capers (who had held several Georgia ministerial posts), said in 1847, Methodism "is neither for Cesar nor Pompey, North nor South, but for Jesus Christ." The only reason for establishing an independent southern church, proclaimed Capers, was "to keep the way open for Methodism to spread scriptural holiness over these lands."[14]

Like Protestants everywhere, most Georgia Methodists accepted, at least in theory, the finality of biblical authority. By relying on arguments from "the Word of God," Georgia Methodists spoke in the voice of global evangelicalism. But the slavery debate led them to give greater emphasis to a literalistic reading of the Bible and to define their viewpoint in contradistinction to northern Protestants, whom, they argued, had strayed from scriptural paths. "When the Bible speaks," wrote Rev. Howell Cobb, "there is an end to controversy and discussion: our duty then becomes very simple; it is—to be silent—to listen—to understand—to obey: for this authority no man may question or disregard." Georgia Methodists believed they had taken purely biblical ground, uncorrupted even by American or Wesleyan ideas. Longstreet, for example, asked northern Methodists to meet his Biblical justifications for slavery squarely rather than retreat "behind the Declaration of Independence." Similarly, he argued that if John Wesley and the Bible were in conflict, then sincere Christians must follow the latter. In 1845 Kentucky Methodist Henry B. Bascom, echoing sentiments already voiced by Old School Presbyterians, criticized abolitionists for making nonslaveholding a condition for church membership, a requirement not even Christ had made.

Georgia Methodists often repeated Bascom's argument, even his words, in defining their position toward slavery.[15]

Among Georgia Methodists, biblical arguments predominated over other justifications of slavery. Belief that the plain meaning of scripture was easily discernible derived in part from Scottish Common Sense theories of knowledge. But Georgia Methodists concentrated on the biblical arguments themselves and only occasionally discussed the philosophical and natural law underpinnings of their arguments. Believing that they adhered more strictly to gospel-based religion than did their northern counterparts, they felt little need to move beyond Scripture. Georgia Wesleyans continually denounced the "higher-law conscience" of northern Methodists. Abolitionists, they argued, derived antislavery principles from certain passages (like the golden rule) that did not deal specifically with slavery but rejected the literal meaning of more directly pertinent verses. This abolitionist repudiation of scriptural literalism allowed southern churchmen to launch telling attacks on antislavery forces. Lovick Pierce, an influential Georgia Methodist leader, argued, for example, that abolitionists had grafted humanistic, "modern innovations" onto the Bible. Many northern Christians, added Longstreet, "perverted the Word of God, and made it speak a language its author never meant to speak." In 1850 the editor of the *Southern Christian Advocate* (published in Charleston as the official voice of Georgia and South Carolina Methodism) argued that Methodist reunion was impossible because of the extrabiblical notions of the MEC.[16]

Georgia Wesleyans, along with other southern evangelicals, occasionally argued that slavery provided southern society with the benefits of a hierarchical society like that of the Old Testament. At times this seemed a natural comparison. In a planter-dominated society church officers in Vienna, Georgia, could argue that slavery was a "patriarchal" system like that of "ancient fathers and their servants in olden times." On similar grounds, William J. Sasnett, an Emory College professor, defended slavery as positively beneficial to southern society. Sasnett believed slavery was an integral and permanent part of building God's kingdom on earth and tried to demonstrate the advantages of a hierarchical, nondemocratic society. Preservation of the peculiar institution demanded a stable social order, he said, and discouraged the radical experimentation in church and state that characterized the North.[17]

Nonetheless, an antidemocratic, Old Testament outlook did not dominate Georgia Methodism. In 1859, for example, James R. Thomas, president of Emory College, berated Sasnett for the antidemocratic aspects of his theories. Four years later, when a Jeffersonville planter vowed to rule his "own roost," plain-folk preacher James L. Fowler bristled back, "understand, you won't rule me." Georgia Methodist worship remained centered on individual repentance, emotional conversion, and personal rectitude. New Testament themes predominated in their defenses of slavery, as well as in their sermons, publications, and theology. In 1859, for example, Rev. James V. M. Morris took 56 percent of his sermons from New Testament texts, with the remainder divided between Old Testament and Wesleyan themes. Of hundreds of sermons that Rev. John W. Talley delivered from 1844 to 1851, less than 20 percent were based on Old Testament passages. Georgia Wesleyans proclaimed their message to everyone—masters, slaves, factory workers, housewives, and plain-folk farmers—and exalted a relatively simple, "born-again" creed. "To know God, to love him and to trust him," said Bishop Andrew in 1851, "constitute the sum total of the principles of the religion of Jesus Christ." Any person, he believed, could find eternal salvation. Next to this achievement, one's social position, skin "complexion," and even society itself, faded to insignificance. Longstreet made this argument in *Philemon,* and it often reappeared in Georgia Methodist treatments of slavery.[18]

Georgia Wesleyans were reluctant to abandon neutrality in favor of positive good theories of slavery. Some Methodists, especially such older ones as Lewis Myers, harbored misgivings about the morality of slavery. In 1848, for example, Bishop Andrew asserted that "large numbers of our own people in every one of the Southern Conferences" regarded the antislavery principles of the MECS *Discipline* as "plain and palpable truth." In 1846, 1850, and 1854, delegates to the General Conference defeated attempts to repeal antislavery principles from the MECS *Discipline.* These votes went against the expressed wishes of the Georgia Conference, whose delegates supported repeal. Georgia Methodist leaders, such as Isaac Boring, consistently maintained that slavery was "a civil institution" and "not a proper subject of ecclesiastical legislation." In 1858 the MECS finally purged antislavery principles from its creed, but this did not entail positive endorsement of human bondage. Georgia Bishop George F. Pierce, for example, argued that the deletion was consistent with church neutrality toward slavery. He stressed obedience to the law and to the Bible, neither of which proscribed slavery, and vehemently opposed reopening the African slave trade. By the 1850s many ordinary Methodists probably thought slavery beneficent, but the official MECS position, in Georgia and elsewhere, expressed neither approval nor disapproval of the institution. Even Longstreet argued that slavery was a necessary evil allowed by the Bible, not that it was divinely sanctioned as a positive good.[19]

No one element of their proslavery position was peculiar to Georgia Methodists. But taken together the justifications for the peculiar institution represented an evangelical theology that had made peace with slavery. To justify slavery Georgia Methodists did not need to adopt a Calvinistic theology of the unredeemable depravity of most of humanity. Occasionally they made reference to themselves as a chosen people, the "sons of Japeth," destined to rule the accursed black "sons of Ham."[20] But this belief was *not* central to their outlook. Rather, on grounds accepted by evangelicals worldwide, the primacy of the Bible and the importance of individual salvation, they argued that slavery was not sinful per se. One's social position had little importance to God; therefore, slavery, in religious terms, offered as good a social system as any other. In intent and effect, this position safeguarded slavery. But it allowed Georgia Methodists to maintain some distance from the institution. Georgia Wesleyans never found it necessary to make a hierarchical society based on slavery the centerpiece of their outlook. First and foremost, they regarded themselves as orthodox, evangelical Christians, not as proslavery protagonists.

At times, Georgia Methodists pictured the South as a besieged bastion of the true faith. In 1846, for instance, the Evangelical Alliance of American and British Churches criticized southern Christians for supporting slavery. The *Southern Christian Advocate* replied that the alliance, "in mixing up political and civil relations with religious and ecclesiastical questions," had forsaken "the true Protestant ground." Real Protestantism, the newspaper argued, should embody the "great principle, that there is no authority to be found on earth to bind the conscience but the word of God: that there is no other standard of genuine morality than that same word of God." The editor felt the purpose of the alliance was "to unite . . . Protestant Christendom against the churches and the professors of religion in the Southern states of this Republic." A letter writer from Clinton, Georgia even suggested that southern churches "form a Christian Union of their own, suited to their peculiar circumstances."[21]

An actual merger of southern denominations was never a realistic possibility. Nonetheless, according to many scholars, a de facto uniformity existed in southern religion. These scholars were convinced that a certain style of evangelicalism, which stressed individual conversion and ignored large social questions, long dominated southern religion. Beginning in the early nineteenth century, this conservative evangelical hegemony has reigned supreme in the region very nearly until the present.[22] If taken out of context, Georgia Methodist views on slavery tend to confirm this theory. For on this important subject, Georgia Wesleyans adopted a doctrine—the spirituality of the church—that was clearly asocial and nonpolitical in nature. Meanwhile, their southern

Baptist and Presbyterian counterparts, faced with similar sectional pressures, adopted an essentially identical view.

But, for Methodists, ecclesiastical neutrality toward slavery did not translate easily into inaction on other issues. In many ways an otherworldly theology fit poorly with Wesleyan traditions and ideology. Methodists were the most unambiguously evangelical of major church groups in the region and supported many philanthropic measures designed to produce positive social change. Georgia Wesleyans, like Methodists outside the region, conceived of their denomination as an "aggressive" force for world betterment. They thought church-sponsored efforts could transform society by infusing it with Christian principles and were confident that their activist church vision would prevail in the South and around the globe. Since the 1820s they had supported many "benevolent institutions" and continued to do so throughout the antebellum era. Per white member, in fact, Georgia Methodist financial contributions to church causes equaled or surpassed the contributions of their northern coreligionists. The state's Methodists put great store in identity as bona fide Wesleyans and engaged in frequent controversies with Baptists, Presbyterians, and Episcopalians. "Calvinistic Establishments are giving way," Reddick Pierce crowed to his brother Lovick in 1849, and Wesleyanism soon "will be the prevailing Doctrine of Christendom." Even northern Methodists sometimes acknowledged that southern Wesleyans held "tenaciously to the leading parts of pure and original Methodism." As Charles H. Elliot, MEC stalwart and Ohio newspaper editor, said in 1855, southern Methodists were "attached to all the fundamentals and peculiarities of Methodism, the instance of slavery excepted." [23]

In fact, Georgia Methodists believed that they followed Wesleyan principles better than their northern counterparts did. On slavery, as we have seen, Georgia Wesleyans ignored their founder and appealed to a higher court—the Bible. By adopting neutral principles of the spirituality of the church, however, Georgia Methodists actually modified their founder's views on the subject as little as was consistent with their survival as a significant force in the state. Given the state's frenzied political climate, Methodism could not have endured in Georgia if it attacked slavery. To safeguard "the interests of Christ's kingdom," Methodists knew that neutrality on this subject was the bare minimum that "public opinion" demanded.[24] Knowledge of Wesley's views, however, restrained Georgia Methodists. Without them they could more easily have adopted an outright, positive, and good theory of slavery.

In several ways, however, neutrality actually served Georgia Methodists better than a full-fledged proslavery position would have. Aware that the eyes of their northern and English brethren were on them, neutrality allowed them to keep their Wesleyan credentials in good order, at least in as good of order as was possible given southern social constraints. Even more important, neutrality strengthened the ability of the state's Methodists to appeal to social groups outside the planter class. A faith narrowly centered on defending the peculiar institution would have bored many Georgia listeners and repelled others.

Neutrality, on the other hand, allowed Methodism to span Georgia's social and geographic divisions. Wesleyan believers comprised a rough cross section of Georgia society, for Methodist congregations and members were spread evenly throughout the state. The denomination was equally strong in plain-folk and plantation areas. Proslavery preaching was not normally repugnant to plain-folk believers, but it was largely irrelevant. And focusing on this aspect of church belief had the potential for negative consequences, for southern yeomen were reluctant to receive dictates from distant authorities. Fearing the "tyranny" of bishops, several thousand Georgia believers, mainly in plain-folk regions, had already abandoned Episcopal Wesleyanism for the Methodist Protestant and Congregational Methodist churches. Like Antimission Baptists, such groups vowed to defend local liberties against centralized encroachment.

In general, however, the MECS met the spiritual needs of plain-folk churchgoers. Religious life in such areas continued, with denominational acquiescence, to operate much as it had during the Great Revival of 1801–5. Methodism in plain-folk areas remained austere, emotional, revivalistic, and conversion-centered. Churchgoers were suspicious of organized philanthropy, gave almost nothing to denominational causes, and worshiped in poorly built, "barn-like" edifices. New members tended to join the church during emotional summer camp meetings. Circuit riders in yeoman areas were often simple and semiliterate men, and if a Sunday school existed, it met irregularly. Most plain-folk members did not feel a heavy hand of religious tyranny, and few left the MECS. In 1860, for example, only 6 percent of Methodist members in the state belonged to splinter groups. Indeed, the greatest strength of the MECS, relative to other denominations, lay in the infertile and thinly populated Wiregrass region. If the MECS had defended slavery too vigorously or focused on it too exclusively, yeomen may have perceived the church as a tool of the planter class. A few up-country farmers (like the Fowler family of Dekalb County) came to this conclusion anyway. In general, however, neutrality toward slavery allowed Georgia Wesleyans to avoid this possible pitfall.[25]

Official neutrality toward the institution also proved serendipitous in winning slave converts. Any excess emphasis on proslavery strictures risked alienating slave audiences, and, in their spiritual lives, slaves usually had choices. They might be required to attend church, but no one forced them to respond to an altar call, and they could turn a deaf ear to objectionable teachings. Georgia Methodists retained the belief in spiritual equality and potential salvation for all human beings that lay at the core of Wesleyan theology. They acutely desired to share their message with African Americans. Bondsmen, Bishop Andrew reminded Methodist masters, "are men like yourselves" with immortal souls. "We may be town preachers or circuit preachers, or president of a college, or editor of a paper, or bishop," said Georgia layman J. C. Postell in 1846, "but I believe that the negro preacher has as honourable a station, as happy a time and as good a chance for heaven as any other man." Georgia Wesleyans worked hard and rather successfully to convert slaves. They focused enough on the spiritual aspects of Christian life (rather than solely on defending slavery) to make the message acceptable to a captive audience. Between 1844 and 1861, for example, the membership of Georgia MECS slave missions grew from three thousand to eleven thousand. In 1861 thirty-one thousand blacks belonged to Georgia Wesleyan churches and comprised an increasing percentage (one third) of overall Methodist membership.[26]

Georgia Methodists even made sporadic stabs at slavery reform, seeking to ameliorate the harshness of state laws and to improve the material conditions of bondage. In rejecting abolitionist charges, said James O. Andrew, southerners were in "danger of overlooking the evils which really exist among us." In the 1840s and 1850s, Georgia Methodists gingerly proposed to put "slavery on a scriptural basis." They urged masters to provide sufficient food and decent clothing for their servants. Georgia Methodists also argued that slave marriages deserved legal recognition and that laws against teaching slaves to read should be repealed (so bondsmen could read the Bible). It was a "great shame and sin," they thought, that slave marriages lacked legal sanction. The Georgia Conference advised Methodists to make sure, if "the owners do not object," to have an ordained minister preside at slave marriages. Methodists also flouted state law by teaching their slaves to read. But with North and South at odds over slavery, calls even for modest reforms were muted and infrequent.[27]

Methodists won slave converts because of proselytizing zeal and humanitarian concern, but only by linking their enthusiasm with neutrality toward slavery were they able to gain access to slave "souls." The 1844 divorce from northern "radicalism" made Methodist preaching more palatable to planters. By 1860 Methodists no longer had to beg suspicious slave owners (as they had in the 1820s) to allow evangelization of their charges. Once convinced that missionaries were not crypto-abolitionists, slave owners often welcomed establishment of plantation preaching places.[28] The spirituality of the church, then, was extremely useful to Georgia Wesleyans. It allowed them to attract yeomen and slaves in large numbers, for the doctrine was at least minimally acceptable to each of these groups. But the same doctrine also kept Wesleyanism on good terms with planter families who were Georgia's wealthiest, best-educated, and most philanthropic citizens.

It is tempting to ascribe the emotional and asocial evangelicalism (that some scholars see as typical of southern evangelicalism) to suspicions that associated philanthropy with abolitionism. But if slavery *caused* southern religious conservatism, one would expect slaveholders to be the most conservative and penurious of Methodists. In fact the opposite was true. Wesleyan asceticism survived best in plain-folk areas where slavery had the least impact. In yeoman-dominated regions, plain folk, wary of market involvement, often practiced household-based, "safety-first" agriculture and, though fairly prosperous, had little cash for denominational donations. On the other hand, Sabbath schools, ornate churches, charitable giving, and women's missionary societies increasingly characterized Methodism in cities and wealthy plantation districts. "Rich Methodists" of the Black Belt, egged on by MECS clergymen, even subsidized construction of churches in less affluent areas.[29]

Benevolent giving by Georgia Methodists increased remarkably from 1845 to 1860. Prosperous members, mainly from towns and plantation districts, donated considerable sums of money for denominational purposes. Georgia Methodists gave financial support to many charitable enterprises, including the "Bible Cause," publishing, schools, missions, and a fund for "worn-out" preachers and the widows of itinerants. The conference frequently urged itinerants to secure financial support for ecclesiastical projects and "admonished" preachers who failed to make sufficient exertions to collect funds. Often, collections did not meet proposed goals, but this was not because of lack of ministerial effort. In 1855, for example, when dedicating a new, fancifully-pilastered church in Bainbridge, Rev. Simon P. Richardson told the congregation that to prosper financially but give nothing to the church was "robbery" because all earthly goods belonged to God. As president of Emory College, George F. Pierce was known by friends as "the most accomplished beggar in Georgia." Regular fast days were held to benefit Methodist missions and schools. From 1850 to 1860 Georgia Conference collections for missions more than doubled while donations to other denominational causes grew equivalently.[30]

Clergymen and prosperous lay members voiced frequent support for measures aimed at social improvement. "The spirit of Christianity," said George Pierce, "is benevolence embodied and alive, full of plans for the benefit of the world, and actively at work to make them effective." William J. Sasnett's *Progress Considered* (1856) exemplified Georgia Wesleyan ambivalence toward progress. Sasnett argued that unchanging Bible principles must undergird the church, but he favored reforms designed to encourage ecclesiastical "usefulness." If subordinated "to thought and virtue," said Sasnett, "progress is the glory of the age—conservative, yet independent and expansive." On the other hand, without authority and tradition, progress became "revolutionary and fearful." Sasnett went on to argue for huge increases in church philanthropy, including a system of church schools at all grade levels. Sasnett exemplified the view in extreme form, but faith in progressive change, if circumscribed by biblical and ministerial authority, prevailed among Georgia Methodists, at least in towns and plantation districts (where most church leaders lived).[31]

Like their northern counterparts, Georgia Wesleyans were troubled by social "sinfulness." In resolutions, letters, and editorials, they often denounced "dancing frolics," smoking, "low groceries," and "irreligious amusements." Many hoped to excise such blemishes from the body politic. Individual Wesleyans were in the forefront of the state temperance movement and supported various prohibitionist groups. Many joined such fraternal societies as the Sons of Temperance. Rather than view their efforts as tainted by association with northern Protestants, many Methodists argued that Georgia should not fall behind other regions in promulgating worthy reforms. But their efforts achieved little. In 1855, for example, Basil H. Overby, Atlanta lawyer and Methodist local preacher, ran as a prohibition candidate for governor but garnered only six thousand votes.[32] Georgia Methodists, then, did not focus entirely on personal conversion but engaged fairly often in politics and social reform.

Several historians, however, have asserted that southern church leaders were ardent secessionists and "Calhounites in their political philosophy."[33] For Georgia Methodists this statement is demonstrably untrue. Most prominent Georgia Wesleyans, far from being part of a separatist political conspiracy, hoped that the church split would not widen sectional political differences. Rev. Joshua Payne argued that church separation implied no need for a corresponding political move. In early 1844 Bishop Andrew desired "continued union of the [MEC] . . . mainly in view of the perpetuity of our political union." In 1852 George F. Pierce expressed hope that "the sectionalism which threatens the unity of the Republic will hide its Gorgon head, and its Babel tongue and be heard no more in the councils of the nation."[34]

Nor were Wesleyans closely tied to the Democrats, the party that pushed through secession. In fact, according to Georgia congressman James Jackson, "Methodism was the very citadel of the Whig doctrines of 1840." Bishop Andrew, Bishop Pierce, Lovick Pierce, and most other clerics who recorded their political preferences, were in the Whig camp. One should not overstate the case, for many Georgia Wesleyans were separatists and Democrats. Augustus Longstreet was a follower of Calhoun and a secessionist, as were many ordinary church members. But Georgia Methodist clergymen (as well as prosperous, educated laymen) often tended to be Whigs. As in the North, such individuals found Whig rhetoric friendlier to the "progressive" and benevolent measures that they favored. In Black Belt counties, for example, Democratic vote percentages in the 1856 presidential election show a slight negative correlation (-.35) with Methodist seat percentages in 1860. This figure suggests (but does not prove) that prosperous Georgia Wesleyans tended to avoid the Democratic Party. Statewide the tendency does not hold. In plain-folk areas, where Wesleyan support for benevolence was weaker, Methodists felt more at ease with the Jacksonian rhetoric of the Democratic Party. In any case, neither the Democrats nor their opponents could take Wesleyan votes for granted.[35]

By the late 1850s, Georgia Methodist leaders tended toward political conservatism and distrusted secessionist "Hotspurs." When a state convention met to consider secession in 1861, two MECS members, Benjamin H. Hill and Rev. Alexander Means, were among the six "most prominent men" opposed to severing Union ties. Some Wesleyans "remained true" to the "old whig faith" right through 1860, and many even supported the American Party (Know-Nothings). In 1855, for example, Rev. Robert F. Williamson expressed support in his diary for the Know-Nothing candidate for governor. In 1859 MECS local preacher Warren Akin, with support from many rank-and-file Wesleyans, ran for governor on the American Party ticket. In Watkinsville, a local preacher urged Rev. John W. Burke, himself a Democrat, to join the Know-Nothings because "all our people are going in." Augustus Longstreet, also a Democrat, estimated that 70 percent of southern Methodists supported the Know-Nothings.[36] Statistical correlations do not conclusively confirm this connection. But if Wesleyans supported the American Party in disproportionate numbers, it must have brought home to them their relative political impotence—for Democrats hopelessly outnumbered Know-Nothings in Georgia.

Although sectional tensions did not eliminate Methodist interest in philanthropy or politics, the spirituality of the church cast a shadow over Georgia Wesleyan actions in both spheres. Methodists embraced *only* reforms that did not challenge the region's fundamental interests. Even on issues extraneous to slavery, the spirituality of the church sometimes restrained Methodist activism. In 1839, for example, the Georgia Conference strongly supported an organized drive to restrict retailing of distilled spirits and even petitioned the state legislature on the subject. In the 1850s, when Georgia witnessed another campaign for statewide temperance laws, many Methodists still favored such reform. This time, however, the Georgia Conference maintained official silence, probably because, in the bitter dispute with northern Wesleyans, it had so often denounced ecclesiastical involvement with politics.[37]

Slavery posed a dilemma for Georgia Wesleyans, forcing them to decide what balance to strike between an otherworldly, soul-saving focus and a social reform emphasis. Sectional debates pushed them to accentuate individualistic, purely "spiritual" aspects of their faith, but never submerged their reformist urges. They compromised Wesley's views on slavery and to an extent were "cultural captives" of their region. But their dilemma and their choice were not unique. Churches everywhere made similar decisions. In Britain, for example, John Wesley and his successors could safely attack slavery, but they supported an undemocratic and repressive government. Closer to home, abolitionists (after a long struggle) finally put enough pressure on MEC authorities to enforce Wesleyan rules against slavery. But an individualistic view of ethics and salvation remained powerful in the free states, and even here abolitionists faced an uphill struggle. Only in 1864, for example, did the MEC make slaveholding an absolute bar to church membership. Furthermore, many (though not all) abolitionists simply accepted the injustices of a free market economic system.[38]

Antislavery simply was not viable in antebellum Georgia. If their church was to survive, Wesleyans could *not* take an abolitionist stand. But the denomination *could* have taken an unambiguously proslavery line. It did not have to argue that religion's appeal was more individual than social. Church leaders might, for example, have argued that the mastery of slave owners replicated God's authority and that planters, in a sense, ruled by divine right. But Wesleyans seldom made this argument. Their church had arisen among plain folk resentful of elitist pretensions, and an ethos of spiritual democracy clung to prosperous antebellum Methodists. Wesleyans would not base their religion, or even justify slavery, on the same grounds Archbishop Laud had used to defend Stuart absolutism. They believed that every person, whatever his social station, could choose to accept or to reject God. Consequently, to retain religious liberty and yet not menace the social status quo, they carefully distinguished between civil and spiritual freedom. Bishop Pierce, for example, argued that "unsanctified liberty" and "unholy longing for freedom" were "the last fellest" foes of Bible truth. Christian brotherhood was likewise understood in otherworldly terms.[39] The spirituality of the church and official neutrality toward slavery allowed Georgia Methodists to retain a theoretically egalitarian theology, without subverting the southern social system.

Although Methodists did not refrain from all political activities, a relatively strong belief in separation of church and state and distrust in the latter significantly influenced antebellum Georgia Wesleyanism. Starting around 1827 elite Georgians (including politicians) had begun to join evangelical churches in large numbers, but many church people, and especially the clergy, continued to express grave distrust of politics and politicians. From Macon in 1851, for example, Bishop Capers welcomed a revival at Wesleyan Female College, but noted that the surrounding community focused on "things that perish—politics, money, and mountebanks." "We must come out from an ungodly generation," said Bishop Andrew in 1852, "reprove [its] follies and guard our own purity." "The first aim of every christian citizen," said the bishop six years later, "should be to have the country governed by the principles of Bible truth." Methodists viewed many southern politicians as drunken and immoral louts but were not quite certain how to challenge them. For, even if only partially realized, the spirituality of the church presented a barrier against "pulpit politics." In private, for example, Bishop Pierce detested the Democratic Party, but he refrained from public partisanship.[40]

Evangelicals played an important role in the antebellum South, but, even in 1860, they could not dictate to society at large. Only 11 percent of white Georgians belonged to a Methodist church in 1860. Because Methodists and Baptists, who had a roughly equal number of members, included more than 90 percent of Georgia church members, less than 25 percent of Georgia whites belonged to any church. Of course, more people attended divine services than joined any church. And churches exercised considerable clout in the lives of many Georgians.[41] But secular values, often contradictory to evangelical beliefs, continued to flourish in the state. In political and intellectual circles, romanticism and Lockean rationalism, not austere evangelicalism, continued to dominate the region. Southern politicians spoke a language of individual and state's rights. Dominant planters prided themselves on their assertiveness as masters. Alcohol and violence were endemic in a society that cherished honor and masculine aggression. Cotton was king in Georgia, and its citizens strived mightily for "a pretty little wife and a big plantation."[42] Hard-eyed politicians, obsessed with slavery and supported by public opinion, ruled this world.

It was the same world Lewis Myers hoped wistfully that Methodists could "conquer." Slavery was its defining characteristic. It is unlikely that Georgia Wesleyans, however much "humility and self-abasement" they demonstrated, could have transformed this society. From experience, they believed that an open attack on slavery would be suicidal, if not for individuals, then certainly for Methodism. Georgia Wesleyans saw abuses in slavery and hoped to correct them, but they believed the institution was compatible with Christianity. They hoped that by converting members of all social classes, Georgia society as a whole, and slavery in particular, could be made to conform more closely to Christian principles. A position of theoretical neutrality toward the institution was useful, and probably necessary, in this quest. It allowed Georgia Methodists to win converts in the big house, the slave quarters, and the yeoman's cabin alike. On such relatively minor issues as temperance, Methodists dabbled in politics. Slavery was different. Even its abuses, they believed, were not readily amenable to political solutions. Perhaps their otherworldly approach to slavery was hypocritical, even immoral. But Georgia Methodists could not bring themselves to accept what they believed to be the only other alternatives— martyrdom or exile.

NOTES

1. Lewis Myers to William Wightman, 22 July 1844, Methodist Leaders Papers, Emory University; Harold Lawrence, *Methodist Preachers in Georgia, 1783–1900* (Tignall, Ga.: Boyd Publishing, 1984), 388.

2. Even James Thornwell, the region's foremost proslavery theologian, sometimes had doubts about the institution. See William W. Freehling, "James Henley Thornwell's Mysterious Antislavery Moment," *Journal of Southern History* 57(August 1991): 383–406; David Brion Davis, *Slavery and Human Progress* (New York: Oxford University Press, 1984), 165; Thomas E. Drake, *Quakers and Slavery in America* (New Haven: Yale University Press, 1950), 150. For early antislavery efforts of southern Wesleyans, see Donald G. Mathews, *Slavery and Methodism: A Chapter in American Morality, 1785–1844* (Princeton, N.J.: Princeton University Press, 1965).

3. In 1845, for example, southern Baptists, including Georgia leaders, promised to work for "extension of the Messiah's kingdom" but "never interfere with what is *Caesar's.*" See *Milledgeville (Georgia) Southern Recorder*, 27 May 1845; Ernest T. Thompson, *Presbyterians in the South* (Richmond, Va.: Dietz Press, 1973), 2:30; James O. Farmer Jr., *The Metaphysical Confederacy: James Henley Thornwell and the Synthesis of Southern Values* (Macon, Ga.: Mercer University Press, 1986), 230–31. In 1861 Thornwell spoke for the Old School Presbyterians when he said

"in our ecclesiastical capacity, we are neither the friends nor the foes of slavery, that is to say, we have no commission either to propagate it or abolish it." See H. Shelton Smith, Robert T. Handy, and Lefferts A. Loetscher, *American Christianity: An Historical Interpretation with Representative Documents, vol. 2, 1820–1960* (New York: Charles Scribner's Sons, 1963), 206.

4. H. Shelton Smith, *In His Image, But . . . Racism in Southern Religion, 1790–1910* (Durham, N.C.: Duke University Press, 1972), 113–14; John Lee Eighmy, *Churches in Cultural Captivity: A History of the Social Attitudes of Southern Baptists*, rev. ed. (Knoxville: University of Tennessee Press, 1987), chap. 1; Mitchell Snay, *Gospel of Disunion: Religion and Separatism in the Antebellum South* (New York: Cambridge University Press, 1993), 9–11; Henry Lee Curry, *God's Rebels: Confederate Clergy in the Civil War* (Lafayette, La.: Huntington House, 1990), 1.

5. Gaines M. Foster, "Guilt over Slavery: A Historiographical Analysis," *Journal of Southern History* 56 (November 1990): 665–94; James Oakes, *The Ruling Race: A History of American Slaveholders* (New York: Vintage Books, 1983), 109; Richard E. Beringer, et al., *Why the South Lost the Civil War* (Athens: University of Georgia Press, 1986), 337–61.

6. The conclusions of these schools of thought are incompatible because neither adequately defines proslavery or antislavery. One scholar, for example, defines proslavery so broadly that it could include Abraham Lincoln. See Larry E. Tise, *Proslavery: A History of the Defense of Slavery in America, 1701–1840* (Athens: University of Georgia Press, 1987). Another scholar views "ameliorative" efforts to reform slave law as secret abolitionism. See Clarence Mohr, *On the Threshold of Freedom: Masters and Slaves in Civil War Georgia* (Athens: University of Georgia Press, 1986), chap. 8. Here "proslavery" means avowedly favoring (not merely accepting) indefinite perpetuation of bondage, "antislavery" means avowedly favoring near-term dismantling of the institution (not vaguely mooning over its shortcomings), and "neutrality" means taking a position on slavery that conforms to neither above definition.

7. Mitchell Snay, *Gospel of Disunion: Religion and Separatism in the Antebellum South* (New York: Cambridge University Press, 1993), 9–11, chap. 2; Eugene D. Genovese and Elizabeth Fox-Genovese, "The Ideals of Southern Slave Society," *Georgia Historical Quarterly* (spring 1986): 2–3. Even scholars who give credence to theoretical neutrality toward slavery have not entirely realized its important uses for southern evangelicals. See Anne C. Loveland, *Southern Evangelicals and the Social Order, 1800–1860* (Baton Rouge: Louisiana State University Press, 1980), x.

8. George G. Smith, *History of Methodism in Georgia and Florida From 1785 to 1865* (Macon, Ga., 1881), 387; P. A. Peterson, *Handbook of Southern Methodism Being a Digest of the History and Statistics of the Methodist Episcopal Church, South From 1845 to 1882* (Richmond, Va., 1883), 3–85; George G. Smith, *The Life and Times of James Osgood Andrew* (Nashville, 1882), 342–43; Lewis M. Purifoy Jr., "The Methodist Episcopal Church, South and Slavery, 1844–1865" (Ph.D. diss., University of North Carolina, 1965), 47–48. Roughly ninety-seven thousand Methodists lived in Georgia in 1860.

9. In 1837, for example, Ignatius Few induced the Georgia Conference to pass a resolution denying that American slavery was a "moral evil." See Georgia Conference, Methodist Episcopal Church, Manuscript Minutes, 1837, Pitts Theology Library, Emory University (the Georgia Conference belonged to the Methodist Episcopal Church until 1845 when it joined the Meth-

odist Episcopal Church, South); *Southern Christian Advocate* (hereafter *SCA*), 7 October 1837, 22 December 1837, 2 February 1838, 23 March, 30 March 1838.

10. *SCA,* 3 January 1845, 11 October, 22 November, 29 November, 20 December 1850, 28 February 1851, 29 October 1852, 30 July 1869; Purifoy, "Church, South," 75, 177; James O. Andrew to William Wightman, 19 August 1844, James Osgood Andrew Papers, Emory University; Charles F. Deems, ed., *Annals of Southern Methodism for 1857* (Nashville, Tenn., 1858), 79–80; Haygood S. Bowden, *History of Savannah Methodism from John Wesley to Silas Johnson* (Macon, Ga.: Burke, 1929), 91; Georgia Conference, Methodist Episcopal Church, South, Manuscript Minutes, 1845, 1846, 1857; Sidney H. Smith Diary, 15 January 1845, Georgia Department of Archives and History.

11. Frank J. Dudley, *100 Years History of St. Luke M.E. Church, South* (Columbus, Ga.: privately printed, 1929), 37; *SCA,* 2 November 1838, 10 January 1845, 2 April 1847, 31 March, 9 June 1848, 30 July 1869; *Wesleyan Christian Advocate,* 26 October 1887, 3 October 1888; Lewis Myers to William Wightman, 22 July 1844, Methodist Leaders Papers; Wesley J. Gaines, *African Methodism in the South; Or Twenty-five Years of Freedom* (1880; reprint, Chicago: Afro-Am Press, 1969), 274; J. O. A. Clark to Lake McNemar, 1859, James O. A. Clark Papers, Emory University; Richard M. Johnston to Atticus G. Haygood, 12 February 1885, Haygood Papers, Emory University; W. J. Scott, *Biographic Etchings of Ministers and Laymen of the Georgia Conference* (Atlanta, Ga., 1896), 153–54.

12. *Journals of the General Conference of the Methodist Episcopal Church, South, Held 1846 and 1850* (Louisville, Ky., 1851), 105; Augustus B. Longstreet, *Letters on the Epistle of Paul to Philemon, or the Connection of Apostolic Christianity With Slavery* (Charleston, S.C., 1845) and *A Voice from the South: Comprising Letters from Georgia to Massachusetts and to the Southern States* (Baltimore, 1847); Howell Cobb, *A Scriptural Examination of the Institution of Slavery in the United States; With Its Objects and Purposes* (Perry, Ga., 1856).

13. Lewis M. Purifoy Jr., "The Southern Methodist Church and the Proslavey Argument," *Journal of Southern History* 32 (August 1966): 329–36; *SCA,* 13 October 1843, 18 February 1853; Donald G. Mathews, *Religion in the Old South* (Chicago: University of Chicago Press, 1977), 153–56; Samuel Dunwody, *A Sermon Upon the Subject of Slavery* (1837; reprint, Marietta, Ga., 1850).

14. *SCA,* 15 November 1844, 2 April 1847; Few Debating Society Minutes, Emory College, 20 April 1857, Emory University.

15. Cobb, *Examination,* 5; Longstreet, *Philemon,* passim; Mathews, *Old South,* 157; *SCA,* 15 August 1850, 18 April 1851, 19 August 1853.

16. John R. McKivigan, *The War against Proslavery Religion: Abolitionism and the Northern Churches, 1830–1865* (Ithaca, N.Y.: Cornell University Press, 1984), 30–31; Lovick Pierce, "Paul's Commission to Preach," in *The Methodist Pulpit South,* ed. William T. Smithson (Washington, D.C., 1858), 202; Longstreet, *Voice; SCA,* 10 December 1847, 15 August 1850, 21 March 1851; Thomas Peterson, *Ham and Japeth: The Mythic World of Whites in the Antebellum South* (Metuchen, N.J.: Scarecrow, 1978), 7, 20–21; Loveland, *Evangelicals,* 144–46, 258–60; Charles F. Deems, ed., *Annals of Southern Methodism for 1855* (New York, 1856), 333; George G. Smith, *The Life and Times of George Foster Pierce* (Sparta, Ga., 1888), 153.

17. Mathews, *Old South,* 163–64; Holland N. McTyeire to Amelia Townsend McTyeire, 14 July 1859, McTyeire-Baskervill Papers, Vanderbilt University; *SCA,* 13 December 1850, 24 February, 17 March 1859; Jack P. Maddex, "Proslavery Millennialism: Social Eschatology in Antebellum Southern Calvinism," *American Quarterly* 31 (spring 1979): 51–53; Farmer, *Thornwell,* 154; William J. Sasnett, *Progress: Considered With Particular Reference to the Methodist Episcopal Church, South* (Nashville, Tenn., 1855), passim; Notes of Sasnett lecture, G. Lovick P. Wren Diary, 30 March 1858, G. Lovick P. Wren Papers, Emory University.

18. *SCA,* 22 December, 29 December 1844, 6 August 1847, 1 September 1848, 4 May 1849, 4 April, 2 May 1851, 16 July 1852, 22 April, 23 December 1853, 15 September 1854, 12 June 1856, 17 March, 7 April, 2 June 1859; Robert H. Robb, *A Biographical Sketch of Rev. James Lowry Fowler: The Hero of the Reorganization in Georgia* (Cincinnati, n.d.), 26. Yet it is in Jeffersonville that one historian sees planter dominance as complete and virtually unquestioned. See Frederick A. Bode, "The Formation of Evangelical Communities in Middle Georgia: Twiggs County, 1820–1861," *Journal of Southern History* 60 (November 1994): 713; James V. M. Morris Diary, 1859, Emory University; John Wesley Talley, Sermon Book, 1844–51, Emory University; Catherine Whitaker to George Gilman Smith Jr., 6 December 1857, 1 February 1858, 23 February 1859, Mary F. Smythe to George Gilman Smith Jr., 21 January 1858, Charles Crawford Jarrell Papers, Emory University; William B. Gravely, "Methodist Preachers, Slavery and Caste: Types of Social Concern in Antebellum America," *Duke Divinity School Review* 34 (autumn 1969): 218; Longstreet, *Philemon,* 5–10, 47; Longstreet, *Voice,* 17–22, 32.

19. Longstreet, *Philemon,* 17; Bailey, "Protestants and Afro-Americans in the Old South: Another Look," *Journal of Southern History* 41 (November 1975): 471–72; Purifoy, "Church, South," 178–80, 189; Purifoy, "Proslavery," 326–28; James O. Andrew to William Wightman, 24 March 1848, Andrew Papers; *SCA,* 13 April 1849, 29 November 1850, 6 October 1854; Bowden, *Savannah,* 91, 95; *General Conference, 1846 and 1850,* 74–76, 213; *Journal of the General Conference of the Methodist Episcopal Church, South, for 1858* (Nashville, Tenn., 1859), 460–61.

20. Wilbur J. Cash, *The Mind of the South* (New York: Vintage, 1941), 84; Peterson, *Ham,* passim; Cobb, *Examination,* chap. 1.

21. Clement Eaton, *Freedom of Thought in the Old South* (1940; reprint, New York: Peter Smith, 1951), 292–96; James O. Andrew to William Wightman, 15 June 1847, Andrew Papers; G. Clinton Prim, "Southern Methodism in the Confederacy," *Methodist History* 23 (July 1985): 240; Charles F. Deems, *Annals of Southern Methodism for 1856* (Nashville, Tenn., 1857), 307–8; *SCA,* 12 June 1846, 3 September, 10 September 1847, 22 September 1854, 15 January, 10 September 1857, 29 July 1858, 25 August 1859.

22. John B. Boles, "Evangelical Protestantism in the Old South: From Religious Dissent to Cultural Dominance," in *Religion in the South,* Charles R. Wilson, ed. (Jackson: University of Mississippi Press, 1985), 148; Samuel S. Hill, *Southern Churches in Crisis* (New York: Holt, Rinehart, and Winston, 1967), 21–22, 48; Mathews, *Old South,* 34–38; Samuel S. Hill, *The South and the North in American Religion* (Athens: University of Georgia Press, 1980); Ernest Kurtz, "The Tragedy of Southern Religion," *Georgia Historical Quarterly* 66 (June 1982): 217–23.

23. John W. Burke, *Autobiography: Chapters from the Life of A Preacher* (Macon, Ga., 1884), 90; Robert E. Chiles, *Theological Transition in American Methodism, 1790–1935* (1965; reprint,

New York: University Press of America, 1983), 53–56; *SCA,* 22 December 1843, 18 September 1846, 12 February, 5 March, 12 November 1847, 10 November 1848, 14 September 1849, 5 July, 16 August 1850, 18 August, 13 October, 27 October 1854, 24 July 1856, 2 July, 27 August 1857, 15 July, 25 November 1858, 26 May 1859; Deems, *Annals* (1855), 96; Edward H. Myers, "Reasons for Rejecting the Calvinistic Doctrine of Election," in *Methodist Pulpit South,* Smithson, ed., 1–68; Reddick Pierce to Lovick Pierce, 28 February 1849, Methodist Leaders Papers; Charles Elliot, *History of the Great Secession from the Methodist Episcopal Church* (Cincinnati, 1855), 825.

24. So argued a General Conference report adopted in 1846 at the behest of Georgia minister James E. Evans. See *General Conference, 1846 and 1850,* 70–71.

25. Sidney Smith Diary, 7 December 1851; Burke, *Autobiography,* 32–36, 48–51; Morris Diary, 1859; Methodist Protestant Church, Georgia District, Manuscript Minutes, 1856–61; S. C. McDaniel, *Origins and Early History of the Congregational Methodist Church* (Atlanta, Ga., 1881), 13–14; Bertram Wyatt–Brown, "The Anti-Mission Movement in the Jacksonian South: A Study in Regional Folk Culture," *Journal of Southern History* 36 (November 1970): 502–3, 528; Robb, *Fowler,* 9–12, 26. For low-country South Carolina, one author asserts that "male yeomen demonstrated an unequivocal commitment to hierarchical social order and to conservative Christian republicanism." See Stephanie McCurry, "The Two Faces of Republicanism: Gender and Proslavery Politics in Antebellum South Carolina," *Journal of American History* 78 (March 1992): 1258. For Georgia the situation is less clear because some yeomen (especially in the up-country) stood ready to resist religious (or political) domination by planter elites. Appeals to racial fears and denunciations of northern radicalism may have cemented their support for the planter-dominated social order and for the MECS (whose leaders were mainly slaveholders). But yeomen support for the denomination was not "unequivocal." Had their views on religion been ignored for constant proslavery harangues, more might have withdrawn from the MECS. But church leaders carefully played the neutrality card. The doctrine prevented them from identifying so closely with planter elites that they alienated nonslaveholders.

26. E. Brooks Holifield, *The Gentlemen Theologians: American Theology in Southern Culture, 1795–1860* (Durham, N.C.: Duke University Press, 1978), 140; *SCA,* 18 September 1846, 16 November, 23 November, 21 December 1849, 19 May 1854; Bailey, "Afro-Americans," 453–54; Margaret Washington Creel, *"A Peculiar People": Slave Religion and Community-Culture Among the Gullahs* (New York: New York University Press, 1988), chap. 6; Randy J. Sparks, "Religion in Amite County, Mississippi, 1800–1861," in *Masters and Slaves,* Boles, ed., 78; Raboteau, *Slave Religion,* 271; Christopher H. Owen, "Sanctity, Slavery, and Segregation: Methodists and Society in Nineteenth-Century Georgia" (Ph.D. diss., Emory University, 1991), 126, 302.

27. Bailey, "Afro-Americans," 453–55; Mathews, *Old South,* 161; Robert W. Lovett to Sallie Andrew, 14 August 1849, Robert Watkins Lovett Papers, Emory University; Atticus G. Haygood, *Our Brother in Black: His Freedom and His Future* (New York, 1881), 14, 190–91; John D. Wade, *August Baldwin Longstreet: A Study of the Development of Culture in the South* (New York: Macmillan, 1824), 272; Mathews, *Slavery and Methodism,* 69–70; *SCA,* 14 August 1846, 31 December 1847, 6 April, 13 April 1849, 30 May 1851, 20 May 1859; James O. Andrew, *Miscellanies: Comprising Letters, Essays and Addresses* (Louisville, 1854), 320–21; Andrew to Wightman, 24 March 1848, Andrew Papers. Georgia Conference Manuscript Minutes, 1849; Eaton, *Thought,* 271;

Loveland, *Evangelicals,* ix, 227; Kenneth Coleman and Charles S. Orr, eds., *Dictionary of Georgia Biography* (Athens: University of Georgia Press, 1983), 28; Purifoy, "Church, South," passim; Gaines, *African,* 253–54.

28. William P. Harrison and Anna M. Barnes, *The Gospel among the Slaves: A Short Account of Missionary Operations among the African Slaves of the Southern States* (Nashville, Tenn., 1893), 195–96, 321–25; David O. Christy, *Pulpit Politics, Or Ecclesiastical Legislation on Slavery, in it Disturbing Influences on the American Union* (1862; reprint, New York: Negro Universities Press, 1969), v, 99–254; Avery O. Craven, *Edmund Ruffin, Southerner: A Study in Secession* (Baton Rouge: Louisiana State University Press, 1932), 134; Blake Touchstone, "Planters and Slave Religion in the Deep South," in *Masters and Slaves in the House of the Lord: Race and Religion in the American South, 1740–1870,* John B. Boles, ed. (Lexington: University of Kentucky Press, 1988), 99; Taliaferro Dillard Diary, 24 September 1854, Atlanta Historical Society; L. G. Chiles to David C. Barrow, 17 February 1859, David Crenshaw Barrow Sr. Papers, University of Georgia.

29. Touchstone, "Planters," 110–11; John B. McGehee, *Autobiography of Rev. J. B. McGehee* (Buena Vista, Ga., 1915), 16–17; Ella Gertrude Clanton Thomas Diary, 19 February, 23 February 1852, Duke University; Samuel L. Akers, "Wesleyan's Early Missionaries," *Historical Highlights* 2 (December 1972): 5; *SCA,* 27 November 1846, 16 July 1847, 4 February 1848, 28 December 1849, 28 June, 23 August, 13 December 1850, 26 August 1853, 11 August 1854, 14 February 1856, 1 October 1857, 15 July 1858, 3 March, 21 April 1859; Georgia Conference Manuscript Minutes, 1860; W. J. Rorabaugh, "The Sons of Temperance in Antebellum Jasper County," *Georgia Historical Quarterly* 64 (fall 1980): 263–69.

30. Georgia Conference Manuscript Minutes, (January) 1846, (December) 1846, 1847, 1849, 1850, 1860; Thomas Diary, 20 May 1855; Burke, *Autobiography,* 66; Morris Diary, 8 February 1859; Raymond A. Cook, "Fletcher Institute, May 1848–June 1879," *Historical Highlights,* 7 (December 1977):18–19; *SCA,* 3 February 1843, 22 January, 19 February, 13 August 1847, 10 March, 17 March, 28 April 1854, 20 September 1855, 14 May, 9 July 1857, 5 August 1858, 18 August 1859; Georgia Conference Manuscript Minutes, 1851, 1862; Listings of Methodist Colleges and Schools, 1858–59, John M. Bonnell Papers, Emory University.

31. George F. Pierce, "Anniversary Address Delivered Before the Southern Central Agricultural Society at Augusta, Georgia, October 20, 1853," and "Devotedness to Christ: Sermon Preached in Memory of William Capers at McKendree Church, Nashville, April 15, 1855," George Foster Pierce Collection, Georgia Department of Archives and History; John B. Weaver, "Charles F. Deems: The Ministry as Profession in Nineteenth-Century America," *Methodist History* 21 (April 1983): 163; Sasnett, *Progress,* 7–8, 218–19; *SCA,* 7 January 1842, 11 June 1847; Harold W. Mann, *Atticus Greene Haygood: Methodist Bishop, Editor, and Educator* (Athens: University of Georgia Press, 1965), 13–16. Georgia Methodist leaders acquiesced to the lack of philanthropy in plain-folk areas but did not really approve of indifference to benevolence.

32. Dillard Diary, 26 April, 1 September 1854, 22 February, 2 May 1855; *Southern Recorder,* 14 November 1846; *SCA,* 17 June 1842, 10 July 1846, 25 February, 16 July, 24 September, 3 December 1847, 5 May, 4 August 1848, 25 May, 13 July, 17 August, 24 August, 16 November 1849, 12 July, 25 October 1850, 2 September 1853, 6 January 1854, 30 March, 28 June 1855, 21 February, 7 August, 6 November 1856, 29 October, 3 December 1857, 15 July 1858, 23 De-

cember 1858; Andrew to Wightman, 20 August 1845, Andrew Papers; Jimmy R. Scafidel, "The Letters of Augustus Baldwin Longstreet" (Ph.D. diss., University of South Carolina, 1976), 230; George G. Smith Sr. to George G. Smith Jr., 6 July 1858, 29 July 1859, Jarrell Papers; Sons of Temperance, Monticello (Ocmulgee) Division, Jasper County, 18 June, 3 July, 21 August, 23 October 1848; Sons of Temperance, Swanee Mountain Division, Cumming, Forsyth County, 6 July, 28 December 1850, 12 July 1851; Sons of Temperance, Worth Division, Upson County, 26 May 1847, Georgia Department of Archives and History; Henry A. Scomp, *King Alcohol in the Realm of King Cotton* (1888), passim; Samuel B. Clark to John W. Clark, 27 March 1851, Samuel Clark Papers, Duke University.

33. Edward R. Crowther, "Holy Honor: Sacred and Secular in the Old South," *Journal of Southern History* 58 (November 1992): 636; William W. Sweet, *Methodism in American History* (New York: Abingdon, 1953), 278; C. C. Goen, *Broken Churches, Broken Nation: Denominational Schisms and the Coming of the Civil War* (Macon, Ga.: Mercer University Press, 1985), 171; W. Harrison Daniel, *Southern Protestantism in the Confederacy* (Bedford, Va.: Print Shop, 1989), 12–14, 21.

34. Andrew to Wightman, 6 July, 19 August 1844, Andrew Papers; Diary of Robert F. Williamson, 1855, Robert F. Williamson Papers, Emory University; Purifoy, "Proslavery," 322; Oscar P. Fitzgerald, *Judge Longstreet: A Life Sketch* (Nashville, Tenn., 1886), 111–27; Pierce, "Anniversary Address;" Smith, *Methodism in Georgia and Florida,* 404; Deems, *Annals* (1858), 212.

35. *SCA,* 9 October 1840, 16 August 1871; Robert W. Lovett Jr. to Robert W. Lovett Sr. and Lucy Lovett, 1 October 1840, Lovett Papers; George W. Yarbrough, *Boyhood and Other Days in Georgia* (Nashville, Tenn., 1917), 14; Mann, *Haygood,* 4–5; Pamela Gray to Wesley Thomas, 27 August 1844, Edward Lloyd Thomas Papers, Emory University; Loveland, *Evangelicals,* 123–24; Smith, *Andrew,* 436; *Southern Recorder,* 14 November 1845; Paul E. Johnson, *A Shopkeeper's Millennium: Society and Revivals in Rochester, New York, 1815–1837* (New York: Hill and Wang, 1978), 127–29; U.S. Census Office, *Statistics of the United States in 1860* (Washington, D.C., 1865). Dr. Anthony G. Carey of Auburn University furnished me with the county-level election returns.

36. Obituary of William H. Felton, September 1909, Rebecca Latimer Felton Collection, University of Georgia; George G. Smith Sr. to George G. Smith Jr., 15 November 1853, 4 October 1857, 16 October 1860, Jarrell Papers; James O. Andrew to Thomas Meriwether, 9 August 1852, George Gilman Smith Papers, Emory University; James R. Smith to George G. Smith, Jr., 17 August 1854, James Rembert Smith Letters, University of Georgia; Percy Scott Flippin, *Herschel V. Johnson of Georgia: States Rights Unionist* (Richmond, Va.: Dietz Press, 1931), 177; Mann, *Haygood,* 4, 10–13; *Wesleyan Christian Advocate,* 30 July 1890; Scomp, *Alcohol,* 299, 510–513; Dillard Diary, September 1855; Williamson Diary, 1855; Morris Diary, 3 October 1859; Sidney Smith Diary, 7 November 1848, 26 June, 27 June, 20 October 1849; Burke, *Autobiography,* 29–30; Fitzgerald, *Longstreet,* 126; Scafidel, "Letters," 485–556.

37. Burke, *Autobiography,* 13; Charles D. Parr to E. A. Dorsey, A. M. V. Latimer, S. A. Lewis, and R. M. Latimer, 7 May 1850, Charles D. Parr Letters, University of Georgia; *SCA,* 7 January 1842, 12 April 1844, 11 June, 16 July, 24 September 1847, 11 April 1851; William Hauser to Samuel B. Clark, 1855, Samuel B. Clark Papers, Duke University; Carnesville Circuit Quarterly Conference Minutes, 4 June 1853; Georgia Conference Manuscript Minutes, 1855–56.

38. E. P. Thompson, *The Making of the English Working Class* (New York: Pantheon, 1963), 372–79; Eric Foner, *Free Soil, Free Labor, Free Men: The Ideology of the Republican Party before the Civil War* (New York: Oxford University Press, 1970), 109–10; *SCA*, 16 April 1857; Mitchell Snay, "American Thought and Southern Distinctiveness: The Southern Clergy and the Sanctification of Slavery," *Civil War History* 35 (December 1989): 311–328; Mathews, *Old South*, 157–64; Jones, *Northern Methodism*, 69–70, 147; Smith, *Image*, 114; James L. Huston, "The Experiential Basis of the Northern Antislavery Impulse," *Journal of Southern History* 56 (November 1990): 639; Mathews, *Slavery and Methodism*, chaps. 5–6; McKivigan, *War on Proslavery*, 84–87, 97–98.

39. Purifoy, "Church, South," 170–71; Dickson D. Bruce, "Religion, Society, and Culture in the Old South: A Comparative View," *American Quarterly* 27 (October 1974): 414–16; John S. Strickland, "The Prophetic Tradition in Southern Evangelicalism," paper delivered at the annual meeting of the Southern Historical Association, Lexington, Kentucky, 9 November 1989; *SCA*, 15 August 1850; Lovick Pierce, "The Fundamental Element of Church Government," *Quarterly Review (MECS)* 7 (January 1853): 15.

40. Sweet, *Methodism*, 278; *SCA*, 1 July 1842, 2 April 1847, 14 January, 31 March 1848, 16 January 1852, 11 February, 18 February 1858; Andrew to Wightman, 14 August 1844, Andrew Papers; Longstreet, *Philemon*, 7; Walter B. Posey, *Frontier Mission: A History of Religion West of the Southern Appalachians to 1861* (Lexington: University of Kentucky Press, 1966), 391; Hunter D. Farish, *The Circuit Rider Dismounts: A Social History of Southern Methodism, 1865–1900* (Richmond, Va.: Dietz Press, 1938), 20; George G. Smith Sr. to George G. Smith Jr., 16 October 1860, 23 October 1860, Jarrell Papers; Richard Johnston to Atticus Haygood, 12 February 1885, Haygood Papers; Christy, *Pulpit Politics*, passim.

41. *SCA*, 11 May, 2 August, 16 August 1855; Owen, "Methodists," 126; Wayne Mixon, "Georgia," in *Religion in the Southern States: A Historical Study*, Samuel S. Hill, ed. (Macon, Ga.: Mercer University Press, 1983), 83–84.

42. James R. Coombs, "Recollections of a Twiggs County Planter," James Rowe Coombs Papers, Duke University; John L. Baker to John H. Stephens, 3 August 1846, Alexander H. Stephens Papers, Duke University; Bertram Wyatt-Brown, *Southern Honor: Ethics and Behavior in the Old South* (New York: Oxford University Press, 1982), passim; Louis Hartz, *The Liberal Tradition in America: An Interpretation of American Political Thought since the Revolution* (New York: Harcourt, Brace, and World, 1955), chap. 6; Michael O'Brien, *Rethinking the South: Essays in Intellectual History* (Baltimore: Johns Hopkins University Press, 1988), chaps. 1–2; Mathews, *Old South*, 246; *SCA*, 12 January 1844, 25 April 1845, 16 August 1850, 12 July 1855, 1 July, 5 August, 2 September 1858; Numan V. Bartley, *The Creation of Modern Georgia* (Athens: University of Georgia Press, 1983), 15, 207. Edward Crowther sees evangelicals as part of the ruling order and entirely at ease with slavery. See "Holy Honor," 633. And no clear distinction did exist between "pristine" evangelicals and "worldly" planters, for many churchgoers, including clergymen, were planters. But, as Frederick Bode has recognized, evangelicals, slaveholders or not, spoke a language of asceticism, personal responsibility, duty, humility, peace, and otherworldliness—principles rarely associated with leading antebellum southern politicians. See "Evangelical Communities," 740–42.

"Matters of Justice between Man and Man"

Northern Divines, the Bible, and the

Fugitive Slave Act of 1850

LAURA L. MITCHELL

 ONE   In her immensely influential novel *Uncle Tom's Cabin,* Harriet Beecher Stowe described many now familiar acts of personal courage and heroism. One of the most gripping scenes that Stowe created was that of the fugitive slave Eliza dashing across the partially frozen Ohio River to save her young son from being sold to a cruel master. The river had no bridge near where Eliza stood, so she struggled across the chunks of ice floating precariously on the water. When she reached the free-soil banks of the river, she encountered the familiar face of Mr. Symmes. When she asked Symmes for help, he replied that he could do nothing for her but point her toward a home where she might receive some aid. As Eliza departed for the house, Symmes expressed two regrets: that he could not help Eliza more and that he had betrayed his friend, who was Eliza's master. Stowe described her character Symmes as a "poor, heathenish Kentuckian," who made his choice to aid Eliza in this small way because he "had not been instructed in his constitutional relations, and consequently was betrayed into acting in a sort of Christianized manner, which, if he had been better situated and more enlightened, he would not have been left to do." [1]

Symmes presents an interesting case study of a free man's response to a fugitive slave in the wake of the Fugitive Slave Act of 1850. The law was passed to honor those "constitutional relations," of which Symmes was apparently ignorant, and thereby fulfill the Constitution's guarantee that fugitives from labor would be returned to their masters. In this respect, the 1850 law was the same as earlier laws regarding fugitive slaves, but in other aspects, the new law differed markedly from previous fugitive rendition measures. First the new law dramatically increased the federal government's role in the capture and return of fugitive slaves. The law gave special commissioners the sole right to judge whether or not an alleged slave was a runaway and authorized him to make his decision based on evidence provided only by the master. The alleged fugitive could not testify on his own behalf and was denied a jury trial. The commissioner also had extensive authority to command federal marshals to apprehend fugitives and return them to slavery. Second, the law required "all good citizens" to aid marshals, when requested to serve in a posse, in the capture of alleged fugitives. Prior to 1850 northerners could walk away from a fugitive slave, but with the new law, they potentially became slave catchers themselves. In addition to these odious features, the law also aroused the North's ire because the commissioner was to be paid ten dollars for every instance that an alleged fugitive found to be the slave in question, but only five dollars for every alleged fugitive that went free. The law's defenders justified the fee differential on the grounds that the process of extraditing a fugitive took more time and effort than releasing an alleged fugitive. According to the law's many critics, this constituted little more than a bribe, especially because the master paid the commissioner's fee. Outraged over the law, the City of Chicago voted to secede from the Union in October 1850 and calls for civil disobedience permeated the North.[2]

Despite the North's anger over the law, however, most northerners acquiesced within months of its passage.[3] Most northerners decided to honor their constitutional obligations and refused to aid slaves attempting to flee to freedom. One of the most important factors in these northerners' decision to love masters as themselves was their commitment to the community of political neighbors that was the union of states. The impact of their sense of community, and the Bible's role in shaping that vision, are the focus of this essay.

TWO   The problem of emancipation in antebellum America can be seen as the problem of community, both real and imagined. Free blacks were few, and few whites interacted with them socially; to visualize large numbers of free blacks therefore required a tremendous act of creative conceptualization. The human imagination has this potential, but as the volumes analyzing the history of racism in the United States suggest, Americans have usually imagined their communities as racially homogeneous. Indeed, the assumption is not just that communities are racially homogeneous, but that they are supposed to be homogeneous, and that they are better when they are comprised of individuals with similar pigmentation.

The idea of a neighbor implies a neighborhood as well; it suggests a location, either physical or mental, which one's neighbors inhabit. The geographic neighborhood usually includes people whose faces are familiar, but the mental or imaginative neighborhood can include both people who are familiar and unfamiliar. Residents of a town, city, state, or country often feel a sense of solidarity with other citizens whom they have never met. Members of religious organizations often feel a sense of community with coreligionists around the globe. Similarly, persons sharing a profession or hobby also often have a sense of common identity and form national and international organizations to express their camaraderie. Participants in these groups are joined in a community, whether or not they ever personally interact with one another.

Each of these neighborhoods can also be seen as a location of duty. In the case of large political communities, the rules usually consist of well-developed and detailed laws that govern multiple aspects of society and help individuals identify their responsibilities to the other members of the community. In such neighborhoods, physical proximity is no indication of a neighbor's significance. A neighbor may feel and may legally owe duties to a person who lives thousands of miles away. The Constitution created such a neighborhood; northerners and southerners who never saw one another were bound together by ties of legal obligation. A neighborhood can thus provide order in people's lives through the rules that govern the community. These rules are predicated on reciprocity and respect and can be summed up in the golden rule: the principle of treating others as we would wish to be treated.

Neighborhoods, whether tangible or intangible, can also provide order in people's lives by establishing or emphasizing homogeneity. By including some individuals and excluding others, an emphasis on shared characteristics identifies the difference between the familiar and the strange and between the local and the distant. Acceptability within a community depends on being familiar and local, and strangeness and distance are often sure paths to being labeled "undesirable."[4] In 1850 northerners' tangible and imagined neighborhoods were comprised of strikingly similar individuals. Even with the antebellum period's tremendous influx of European immigrants and its increasing religious diversity, previously established communities of Anglo-Protestants, whether defined by neighborhoods or churches, were largely homogeneous. Immigration threatened this bond of similarity, but until the post–Civil War period, the North's human sameness was so thorough that it is difficult to comprehend from the vantage point of the multicultural late twentieth century, even given its current, virulent forms of prejudice.

The emancipation of even an isolated fugitive slave had the potential to undermine white northerners' existing communities in two ways. First, emancipation was the act of turning slaves, who were distant both conceptually and physically, into free men and women. Northerners often worried aloud that if the South's slaves were emancipated, they would move en masse to the North. But even if emancipated slaves remained in the South, they would still become members of the North's conceptual community the moment that they became free. The free black community in the antebellum North was minuscule, concentrated in small districts of a few cities, and its presence did not pressure white northerners to reinvent their assumptions about the color of a free community. As such, conceptualizing freedom for slaves and fugitives required a fundamental reordering of the concept of community that few were willing or able to achieve in their minds, let alone in their physical surroundings.

Second, the prospect of emancipation altered northerners' sense of community with southerners. Just as the abolition of slavery represented the transformation of the distant and unfamiliar into the local and familiar, it also represented the transformation of the southern neighbor into a stranger. Southerners were kinfolk, related to northerners by blood, marriage, and association; despite their physical distance, they were members of the same political community—the Union—and with the North they shared a common history, a common set of customs, and a common hope for a joint future. When considering the abolition of slavery, northerners had to visualize the process of chastising their familiar, white, southern equals and depriving them of what they believed was their property. Emancipation was therefore a moral reprimand to and an economic and a legal attack on their social, political, and economic peers below the Mason-Dixon line. It was an act of moral superiority that justified the use of political force and that eroded the community of equality and respect that the two regions claimed to share. The idea of emancipation therefore required white northerners simultaneously to elevate blacks to the status of neighbors and to demote white southerners to the level of political strangers or moral children. To reimagine a community that welcomed former slaves and shut the door on a large number of political peers was a tremendous task.

Some antebellum white northerners did, of course, make the mental leap required to imagine the emancipation of slaves and the denigration of slaveholders. As the vast historiography of antislavery details, a small group of American and British abolitionists revised their concept of who belonged to the community of freedom and acted on their revised perceptions. The origins of the proslavery argument, in all its manifestations, have also been masterfully explored. In particular, the historiography of both pro- and antislavery advocacy carefully describes and analyzes the impact of authoritative texts on the perceptions, values, and motivations of the men and women who were at the forefront of the debates over slavery. Historians have focused especially on the impact of pivotal political, legal, and philosophical writings over time.[5]

However, with a few important exceptions, the role of the preeminent authoritative text in antebellum America, the Bible, has received less attention than it deserves in the historiography of antislavery and proslavery thought. This lacuna is particularly unfortunate because the Bible was absolutely central to the debates over slavery. The Bible, more than any other text, shaped antebellum American minds. As the words of Abraham Lincoln demonstrate, even the virtually unchurched spoke and thought in language rich with biblical metaphor. Throughout the antebellum period, northerners heatedly debated the biblical view of slavery. By 1850 this debate was well defined and biblical texts played a pivotal role in the public debate over fugitive slaves.[6]

The vast literature on the debates over slavery also pays too little attention to those northerners who were neither abolitionists nor proslavery apologists. As is well known, slavery's public detractors and defenders were a vocal minority and are only a small part of the story. Much less studied are the attitudes of the majority of northerners who neither condoned slavery nor the abolitionists' solution to the problem. Rather, they favored a gradual emancipation, similar perhaps to that in Latin America, coupled with a plan to colonize free blacks in Africa or the Caribbean. The historian Donald Scott has called some of the Protestants in this camp "antiimmediatist evangelicals"; whatever the label, these northerners loathed slavery and feared emancipation.[7]

This chapter focuses on the attitudes of northern gradualists, paying special attention to some of the biblical arguments that shaped their response to the Fugitive Slave Law of 1850. Gradualists cared about slavery when it intruded on their daily lives or altered their relationship to the local, state, and federal governments. When slavery curtailed the right of free speech, affected the delivery of mail, or threatened violence, it became a present reality in the free states and not just a distant, moral concern. The presence of runaway slaves brought the slavery question front and center, made the plight of the millions in chains real and inescapable, and gave northerners the opportunity to secure the freedom of one individual. Just as the fictional Eliza confronted Mr. Symmes, on the northern banks of the Ohio, the real fugitive challenged northerners' visions of themselves as moral agents, committed to freedom and to loving their neighbors as themselves, and exposed the inherent contradiction of slavery in a nation claiming to be free and democratic. The fugitive slave required free northerners to reconsider the nature of their community and their duties to their neighbors. Masters' claims on their runaway property therefore had to be considered carefully.

From the moment that the fugitive slave bill was introduced in Congress, clergymen from every denomination throughout the North delivered sermons on the Christian citizen's duty toward fugitive slaves and toward southern masters. After the bill became law in September 1850, the number of sermons published on the law increased, reaching a high point in December 1850. The majority of these sermons exhorted obedience while simultaneously itemizing slavery's attendant evils in a fashion that echoed Theodore Dwight Weld's *Slavery As It Is.* The message from the North's pulpits, from nearly every denomination, was that although slavery was wrong, the reenslavement of a handful of fugitives was acceptable, necessary, and even virtuous.

Prorendition ministers rested their call to obey the fugitive slave law on several key biblical texts and as such, provided a biblical justification for ignoring the plight of the fugitive.[8] They presented the Bible as the key determinant of Christian duty and preached sermons filled with biblical references, analogies, exhortations, and commands.[9] They employed dozens of relevant references, especially Old Testament accounts of slavery and New Testament instructions to servants to obey their masters. Prorendition clergymen paid special attention to the thirteenth chapter of Paul's Epistle to the Romans, in which Paul commanded Christians to obey the secular authority on the grounds that it was ordained by God. They also turned to biblical models of rendition for guidance, employing passages from Deuteronomy, Philemon, and the Gospels. This chapter focuses exclusively on northern ministers' understanding of these models.

THREE   Soon after the contentious Senate debates in March 1850 Prof. Moses Stuart (1780–1852) of Andover Theological Seminary signed a public letter "expressing approbation of Mr. Webster's late Speech," especially of Webster's "aim and desire to cherish our Union as inviolable."[10] Within a week, Stuart began to receive letters, some full of praise and others, scorn. Still others wrote out of pious confusion. What was a Christian to think of Mr. Webster's speech? Many correspondents asked the revered professor to point out "some way of Christian politics, in which they might conscientiously proceed."[11] Stuart wrote that he was moved by the knowledge that "in a *Christian* land, there are many-many thousands, sincerely desirous to know what light can be obtained from the Bible, to aid them in discerning and performing their duty."[12] He responded quickly with *Conscience and the Constitution,* a

119-page exhortation to obey the fugitive slave act, in which he contended that the preservation of the Union, the most important community, depended on obedience to the new law.

Although Stuart never delivered any portion of the tract before a congregation, the pamphlet was a sort of sermon for the general public about the political pressures of the day. Many of his arguments were either repeated in other sermons defending the law or were attacked in sermons condemning the law. At least three pamphlets were published specifically to refute Stuart, including one from a former Andover seminarian, Rufus W. Clark, and another from the lawyer and abolitionist William Jay, son of John Jay. Stuart's shot was the first volley in what became a pulpit war over the biblical view of fugitive slaves—a battle fought to win the hearts and minds of northern Christian citizens.[13]

Stuart's commentary commanded immediate attention, for he was perhaps the most famous clergyman of his day to publish on the fugitive slave controversy. Among orthodox, Trinitarian Protestants, Stuart's credibility as a biblical exegete was unassailable. A forty-year veteran of Andover Theological Seminary, Stuart had published dozens of books and articles on biblical languages, history, and interpretation. During his tenure at Andover, he had trained more than three hundred ministers, many of whom entered the mission field as Bible translators. His pioneering work in biblical languages led his contemporary Edwards A. Park to call him "the father of Biblical philology" in America. Through philology and biblical history, Stuart introduced his students to the revolutionary impact of German scholarship that was then filtering into American higher education. Many of Stuart's colleagues at Andover associated the study of foreign scholarship with impiety, and in 1825 several members of the Andover faculty formed a committee to study the impact of Stuart's syllabus. They concluded that studying German criticism led to a decrease in piety and an increase in skepticism; Stuart, undaunted, continued to break new intellectual ground for himself and for his students.[14]

Despite his colleagues' concerns, Stuart was no skeptic. A staunch Trinitarian, he had defended that doctrine in a published reply to William Ellery Channing's Baltimore sermon, and as a professor, he used biblical scholarship to counter the claims of his Unitarian adversaries. According to Stuart's contemporary Calvin Stowe, husband of Harriet Beecher Stowe, Stuart's "vocation was to call back the Bible, the genuine, original Bible, in its true interpretation, into the Theology of the Anglo-Saxon nations." Francis Wayland, a well-known moral philosopher, author, and educator, also testified to Stuart's orthodox motives and goals and characterized him as an "awakening force for his students' minds." [15] Stuart's impeccable orthodox credentials made him the perfect scholar-soldier to combat the exegeses of abolitionist clergymen, whose attitudes and methods were often markedly latitudinarian. His opinion on the fugitive slave crisis therefore carried tremendous weight. To Princeton's leading Old School Presbyterian divine, Charles Hodge, Stuart's *Conscience and the Constitution* was simply the final word on fugitive rendition in the United States. [16]

At the time Stuart published his essay, the nation's churches were deeply divided over slavery. Each of the major denominations had split into regional organizations by 1850; these divisions in part reflected the nationwide churches' inability to settle the slavery question within their ranks. In the North slavery continued to spark controversy within denominations and churches. Numerous pastors lost pulpits because their views on slavery did not comport with their congregations' attitudes, individual churches were divided over the issue, and slavery was hotly debated. Into this fractious environment, Stuart introduced his thoughts on slavery and fugitives. [17]

Stuart couched his analysis in two assumptions. First, like most of his contemporaries, Stuart believed that the Bible was the ultimate authority for Christian citizens. The "thorough Protestant," Stuart wrote, ". . . professes to believe, that 'the Scriptures are the sufficient and only rule of faith and practice.'" [18] Second, like many of his clerical and lay contemporaries, Stuart assumed that slavery could not be considered an evil in and of itself because it had existed in the Old and New Testaments and because Christ and the apostles had never explicitly condemned bondage. This was not to say that slavery was a preferable form of human relationship, nor that it was entirely acceptable. Slavery was known to produce numerous ills, Stuart acknowledged, both for the master and for the slave. Stuart's point was that the evil and guilt of slavery lay in the masters' treatment of their slaves and in the effects of slavery, not in the institution itself. [19]

Working within these assumptions, Stuart identified two biblical models of fugitive rendition and applied them to the United States with a thoroughness befitting the esteemed scholar. The first model, recorded in Deuteronomy 23: 15–16, reads "[t]hou shalt not deliver unto his master the servant which is escaped from his master unto thee. He shall dwell with thee, even among you, in that place which he shall choose, in one of thy gates, where it liketh him best; thou shalt not oppress him." Resting his exegesis on the word "thee," Stuart contended that "thee" signified the entire nation of Israel and not an individual Israelite. Because the pronoun referred to the collective entity of Israel, the slave in question was an immigrant from a foreign nation and the property of a heathen master and not, by definition, a slave owned by a fellow Hebrew, fleeing within Israel from one tribe to another. Stuart concluded that the passage therefore provided an unequivocal defense of the fugitive slave bill, then under debate in Congress.[20]

The division between Israel and all the other nations of the world created two distinct political communities that differed from one another in their religious beliefs and practices. The important distinction in Stuart's eyes was religious not political. What made Israel special as a nation, and what made it a refuge for the fugitive slave, was its unique spiritual relationship with the God of Israel. Slaves arriving from the foreign, pagan reaches of the world were to receive a warm welcome because they fled from heathen darkness to Hebrew light. Israel was obligated to accept these refugees because to refuse them was to imperil human souls. As Stuart explained, the biblical Moses allowed the slaves of heathens to remain in Israel because "only among the Hebrews could the fugitive slave come to the knowledge and worship of the only living and true God."[21] Those fleeing Hebrew masters already enjoyed a spiritual sanctuary, had no reason to flee, and were to be returned to their masters according to relevant property laws.

The implications for the United States were straightforward. The United States, like Israel, was a single community made up of various constituent parts that enjoyed a special relationship with the Hebrew God. Southern masters were religious and political kinsmen, as were the tribal Israelites, and not foreign idolaters. "We do *not* send back the refugee from the South to a *heathen* nation or tribe," Stuart asserted, "there is many a *Christian* master there, and many too who deal with their servants as immortal beings."[22] Slaves fleeing from tribe to tribe in ancient Israel or from state to state in the United States therefore sought refuge where they were already—within the community of God's chosen people. As in ancient Israel, then, fugitive slaves in the United States were to be returned to their masters according to prevailing property laws.

The master's religious and national status was central to Stuart's interpretation and application of Deuteronomy 23. If a master were a heathen foreigner, the slave was to be welcomed, but if the master enjoyed the light of religious truth, the fugitive was to be remanded to his master. The master's religious and political identity determined the fugitives' fate in Israel, and by implication, their fate in the North. Southern masters were assumed to be Christians because they resided in a Christian country and were therefore members of the greater community. Just as the labels "foreign" and "heathen" went in tandem, so too did the assumption that someone who was "domestic" was also not heathen. In the United States, the North and the South enjoyed an essential religious and political unity that implicitly defined the master as a Christian neighbor.[23] Fugitives in the United States therefore could not be released from temporal bondage; their bodies remained only objects in a transaction between tribal neighbors within the United States.

Throughout the antebellum period, numerous biblical scholars corroborated Stuart's interpretation of Deuteronomy 23. The passage could therefore serve as a well-documented proof text for rendition. Nevertheless, Stuart was one of only a handful of northern ministers to turn to Deuteronomy 23 to defend fugitive rendition. One explanation might be that because Stuart's sermon was so well documented, ministers felt no need to discuss it any further. Stuart's thorough study was widely available to the northern public; perhaps most ministers agreed with Charles Hodge that they could add little to *Conscience and the Constitution*. Ministers may also have felt that the passage was too complicated to discuss from the pulpit. Stuart's exegesis relied on an intricate linguistic analysis of the pronoun "thee" that ministers may have deemed inaccessible or uninteresting to general audiences.[24]

More problematic than philology, though, are the ways in which Deuteronomy 23 potentially destabilized existing notions of the Union as a faithful Protestant community. Stuart's interpretation used the southerners' religious identity to remind his audience that these slaveholders were neighbors not strangers. However, the one concession that antiabolitionist evangelicals consistently made to their abolitionist peers was that slavery promoted heathenism, even if the slaveholders were not themselves pagans. As Stuart himself observed, slavery was known to promote spiritual laxity, sexual immorality, intemperance, ignorance, vanity, and laziness among both masters and slaves. Furthermore, slavery undermined the family unit by preventing marriage and by selling off family members. As such, it was not conducive to the progress of Christianity, even if the plantation was ostensibly a Christian family unit. Laws that prohibited slaves from learning how to read or from attending church alienated northerners who were committed to Bible societies and Sunday schools. The passage left open the possibility that northerners might be required to harbor a fugitive slave who arrived at their doorsteps with chilling stories of being prohibited to worship, pray, or read the Scripture and implicitly indicted southern social mores and religious practice and undermined the North's sense of similarity with the South.[25]

Ministers may have also avoided Deuteronomy 23 because comparing the United States to Israel led to several pitfalls. Every churched or Bible-reading northerner knew that the tribes of Israel had abandoned their protodemocratic government in favor of a monarchy and had split into two warring factions, one northern and one southern. By splitting into two kingdoms, the Israelites had made themselves simultaneously both neighbors and strangers, both familiar and foreign, both local and distant. Ultimately, the northern kingdom was destroyed, and the tribes of Israel were dispersed forever. With American southerners rattling sabers and threatening to form their own domain, Israel's precedents had to be applied to the Union with extreme care. Stuart articulated this difficulty when he observed that like the tribes of Israel, each of the "tribes" composing the Union was its own entity that enjoyed rights that made them simultaneously independent of and connected to one another. The states had "by solemn compact, a separate and independent jurisdiction in respect to all matters of justice between man and man, with which no stranger can on any pretence whatever intermeddle." As the modern Israel, they were kinsmen, yet in regard to "matters of justice between man and man," they were strangers with no authority to intervene in each other's affairs.[26]

The advantage to this separateness was that it absolved the North of any responsibility for slaves or slavery. As Moses Stuart put it, "Virginia may do wrong, (I fear she is so doing), but Virginia is not under our supervision or jurisdiction; nor are we, in any degree, accountable or responsible for her errors or sins!" Whatever the master's nature, Stuart explained, "we of the North are only the other tribes of the same great commonwealth" and "cannot sit in judgment on cruel masters belonging to tribes different from our own." But in absolving each region of responsibility to the other, Stuart also dissolved the bonds of community. No matter what their ties, slavery made the North and the South separate and independent, without the ability to influence one another in a matter of looming significance. Unlike a homogeneous covenanted community in which members were mutually responsible to one another, in the Union, the customs and responsibilities of the states were localized and isolated. With this depiction of the bonds of union, Stuart echoed the strains of a Puritan federal theology but abandoned the sense of collective responsibility and guilt for what he and others acknowledged was fraught with evil: slavery as it existed in the southern United States. To employ Deuteronomy 23 was therefore to raise contentious questions about southerners, their relationship to northerners, and the nature of the political union itself.[27]

In addition to undermining the North's sense of similarity with the South, Deuteronomy 23 also threatened the North's religious identity at the local level. Although Stuart's interpretation might keep fugitive slaves out, it provided a ready invitation to European Catholics to flee to the United States. Who deserved refuge in the North more than the "slaves" to Catholicism who arrived daily? As the Rev. Thomas Skinner, a professor at Union Theological Seminary, explained to a New York City congregation, Catholic immigrants could not be turned away, "[n]or should we receive them otherwise than with kindness, nor deal with them otherwise than as brethren." Of course, their fate once they arrived depended on their willingness to conform to Protestant norms. As Stuart explained, Deuteronomy 23 promised economic benefits to the fugitives who fled spiritual darkness, but receiving those benefits depended on adopting Hebrew practice. The fugitive could live where he chose, "in one of thy gates," but the fugitive was, in Stuart's words, still "the admitted denizen," who had to earn his place among the Jews through circumcision.[28]

FOUR   Stuart's second biblical model for the return of a fugitive slave was Paul's epistle to Philemon. Paul wrote the letter from Rome, where he was under house arrest, to a friend named Philemon. The subject of the letter is a man named Onesimus, then in Rome with Paul. Onesimus's identity and status are not completely clear from the text, but most biblical scholars in the mid-nineteenth century agreed that he was probably Philemon's slave for life. Onesimus's reason for being in Rome is also not identified in the text, but antebellum clergymen generally argued that Onesimus had run away from Philemon. The few who claimed that Onesimus was a freeman, not a fugitive slave, surmised that Philemon had sent Onesimus to minister to Paul during his imprisonment. While in Rome, Onesimus had apparently converted to Christianity and was now, in Paul's words, a "brother beloved" both in body and spirit. Onesimus was now about to return to Philemon with a letter from Paul in which Paul asked Philemon to receive Onesimus as a member of the family. Paul also asks Philemon to forgive Onesimus for any wrongs and offers to cover his debts. In verses 15–19, Paul tells Philemon,

> For perhaps he therefore departed for a season, that thou shouldest receive him for ever; Not now as a servant, but above a servant, a brother beloved, specially to me, but how much more unto thee, both in the flesh, and in the Lord? If thou count me therefore a partner, receive him as myself. If he hath wronged thee, or oweth thee ought, put that on mine account; I Paul have written it with mine own hand, I will repay it: albeit I do not say to thee how thou owest unto me even thine own self besides.

Reminding Philemon that he owed Paul for his own spiritual awakening, Paul seems to pressure Philemon to do as he requested.[29]

Stuart employed Paul's letter to defend fugitive rendition, interpreting the passage as a vindication of Philemon's "vested rights" in his property, Onesimus.[30] As in his interpretation of Deuteronomy 23, Stuart saw Onesimus's rendition as a transaction between two coreligionists, Paul and Philemon. Presumably, in Stuart's opinion, if Onesimus had escaped from a heathen master, Paul would not have returned him. But Philemon was a Christian; Onesimus therefore had no reason nor right to flee. In Stuart's eyes, Onesimus's own conversion was irrelevant except that his new religious commitment would make him a better laborer.[31] This, Stuart contended, was why Paul commanded Onesimus to return to his master "forever" and not for a limited amount of time. The apostle "supposed that the sense of Christian obligation, which was now entertained by Onesimus, would prevent him from ever repeating his offence." [32] Ignoring Paul's words of affection for Onesimus, Stuart used the epistle solely to highlight Paul's relationship with Philemon, and white northerners' relationship with southern slave owners. Like Paul and Philemon, northerners and southerners were members of the same religious and political family who shared a common commitment to constitutionally guaranteed property rights. The fugitive's religious faith in no way changed his earthly status as a slave; Onesimus's conversion did not earn him a membership in the community of those enjoying temporal freedom. As Stuart interpreted the text, Paul's letter offered undeniable proof that Christians were bound to return fugitives to their masters, even if the fugitives shared the Christian faith.

Like the passage from Deuteronomy, the book of Philemon was a well-known passage that was a standard part of the proslavery interpretation of the Bible. Yet in sermons about the fugitive slave act, Philemon is often alluded to but only infrequently considered in full. Ministers drawing on the epistle as a way to urge compliance with the law were probably reluctant to play the role of Paul who, according to tradition, supported and educated Onesimus for several years before returning him to his master. The expense of harboring a fugitive, let alone the risk of fines and imprisonment, would have been daunting even to those who sincerely sought the fugitive's freedom. The psychological expense of harboring a nineteenth-century Onesimus was even more overwhelming. To label a black fugitive "above a servant, a brother beloved," even while keeping him in chains, had revolutionary implications that few were willing to contemplate, let alone implement. Even though Paul sent Onesimus back to Philemon, thus providing a clear defense of fugitive rendition in the United States, Paul's description threatened northerners' assumptions about the composition of their community and their households. By making the fugitive slave an intimate neighbor and a member of the spiritual family, Paul's example blurred the distinction between master and slave and condemned the North's strict codes prohibiting mixing of the races. Paul also gently chided Philemon and demanded merciful treatment of Onesimus. Paul's example therefore both undermined the North's sense of community with the South by placing the North in a position of moral superiority over the South and called for a dramatic reordering of northerners' relationships with blacks, both free and slave. Although these tensions are not explicitly mentioned within the sermons themselves, they undoubtedly had an impact on ministers as they weighed their choices and considered the biblical examples and mandates.

Of the seventy or so sermons about the fugitive slave law published in late 1850 and early 1851, only a handful attacked the law, and only a small number of those drew on either Deuteronomy 23 or Philemon.[33] The most thorough response to Stuart's essay came from a former Andover seminarian, the Rev. Rufus W. Clark. A Yale graduate, Clark (1813–1886) attended Andover Theological Seminary and Yale Divinity School, where he likely encountered Moses Stuart and Yale's Nathaniel Taylor. Clark published his reply to Stuart's tract in 1850 while pastor of the First Church of Christ, Portsmouth, New Hampshire. Approximately a year later, he left Portsmouth, in part because the congregation disapproved of his outspoken position on slavery.[34] He moved to Boston where he became pastor of the Maverick Church, an antislavery congregation previously led by Amos A. Phelps. While at Maverick, Clark distinguished himself among Boston's well-known ministers; he drew larger Sabbath school crowds than the four pastors who had dominated Boston for the previous decade and his congregation's membership more than doubled in three years.[35] By the time Clark left the Maverick Church in 1857, he was well on his way to a national reputation as a preacher and a writer. Clark wrote more than one hundred books and authored a series of Sunday school primers, the latter which sold more than five hundred thousand copies.[36]

Clark attacked Stuart's exegesis as an insider who shared Stuart's orthodox theology and could parse Hebrew and Greek as well as Stuart himself. In fact, Stuart may well have taught Clark how to interpret the Bible while Clark was at Andover. Clark contended that Stuart had no grounds for concluding that the word "thee" in Deuteronomy 23 referred to the entire nation of Israel. Why, Clark asked, could it not mean "the individual, or family, to which the slave flees, as well as the whole Hebrew nation?" Dismissing Stuart's narrow interpretation, Clark contended that the passage described a situation in which a fugitive fled to a single Israelite and asked for help, as one neighbor to another. Clark inferred from his interpretation of Deuteronomy that the fugitive who fled from the South to the North was therefore also entitled to freedom, regardless of the master's religious beliefs and practice.

Second, Clark asserted that the whole tenor of the passage implied that the biblical Moses was, "as rapidly as possible, making Palestine a free country." As Clark saw it, the passage was an "invitation" for slaves "to escape to Palestine, as to an asylum of freedom," where heaven-ordained laws would "be extended over them for their protection." Both Israel and the North were beacons of liberty for the world's oppressed; they were open communities whose primary purpose was to bestow the blessings of political and spiritual liberty on all people.[37] Like most of his antirendition peers, Clark's understanding of fugitive rendition was of northerners interacting with fugitive slaves as persons whose rights did not depend on the religious or political status of their supposed owner. In addition to making fugitives neighbors, he unhesitatingly indicted southern slaveholders as infidels. Masters were responsible for the evils of slavery; their unwillingness to cleanse themselves of their sin made them as heathenish as any of Israel's neighbors.[38]

Like many other clerics, both pro- and antirendition, Clark omitted a discussion of Paul's epistle to Philemon. Paul's promise to assume Onesimus's debts was probably enough to make anyone think twice, even someone capable of imagining a biracial community. Abolitionists were certainly ahead of their peers in their ability to imagine former slaves as residents in their mental neighborhood, but their sense of community with blacks still had severe limitations. Even the most committed abolitionists often had trouble perceiving blacks as "beloved" brothers. Furthermore, even though the text could powerfully demonstrate Onesimus's right to freedom and equality, antirendition ministers still had to confront the part of the story where Paul returned Onesimus to Philemon. Whereas the Old Testament example had allowed for the integration of a select group of immigrants, the New Testament example sanctioned expulsion, even if it condemned slavery. What abolitionist could fathom sending a slave back to the South with a note requesting that the master treat the fugitive as a member of the family? What fugitive would consent to go? Such a scenario was unthinkable to the Rev. George Perkins, a Connecticut Congregationalist and one of the few antirendition clergymen to discuss Philemon. Perkins claimed that Onesimus was not a slave in the first place and ridiculed Stuart's exegesis by painting the comical picture of Moses Stuart and Daniel Webster preaching to fugitives in Boston, trying to convince them that like Onesimus, they ought to return to their masters. "The refugees," Perkins snickered, "I have no doubt, would listen to them with profound attention. . . . Let them persuade the slave back then, *if they can.*"[39]

For both pro- and antirendition clergymen, Deuteronomy 23 and Philemon could present insurmountable interpretive obstacles. One reason that these passages from the Old and New Testaments were so difficult to apply in the United States is that they describe specific situations whose applicability to the antebellum United States was complicated and imperfect. The passages raised many questions that could not be answered within the body of the text, even when approached with Stuart's formidable linguistic skills. A more satisfying source of guidance therefore came from a set of general, accepted, and biblically ordained principles that were a part of every day life: the golden rule and the great commandments.

FIVE   In the Christian tradition, Christ himself issues the golden rule, which is recorded in the Gospel of Matthew: "Therefore all things whatsoever ye would that men should do to you, do ye even so to them: for this is the law and the prophets." In Christian ethics, the golden rule is often linked to Christ's declaration of the "great commandments," also recorded in Matthew. In chapter 22, a Pharisee asks Christ to name the greatest commandment, to which Christ replies, "Thou shalt love the Lord thy God with all thy heart, and with all thy soul, and with all thy mind. This is the first and great commandment. And the second is like unto it, Thou shalt love thy neighbour as thyself." For antebellum Christians North and South, the golden rule and the great commandments were the foundation of Christian duty. Christians were to love God, neighbor, and self; this triad of obligation formed the basis for Christian ethics and decision making.[40]

Both the golden rule and the command to love one's neighbor as oneself are reflexive propositions that require individuals to imagine themselves as the objects of their own behavior and to think of those individuals as "neighbors." The act of imagination requires the moral agent to identify with the object and to assume the other person's perspective. The agent does not assume the identity of the object, but he or she does attempt to assume the object's perceptions. The acquisition of the neighbor's perspective presumably then influences the agent's own perspective and leads to a modification of the agent's behavior. The reflexive nature of the exchange is therefore not a simple act of mirroring one's self in another person. When acting upon these behavioral codes, agents do not treat others simply as they would treat themselves, but rather as they would wish to be treated if they were the other person. An example often used in the literature of religious ethics to illustrate this point is the parent-child relationship. When a parent loves a child as himself or herself, the parent does not treat the child as an adult and a parent. Instead, the parent assumes the child's perspective and behaves toward the child according to the child's limits, vulnerabilities, and needs.

The introduction of a third person complicates the ethical mandates of the golden rule and the great commandments. The commands to love one's neighbor as oneself and to treat others as one would wish to be treated are dyadic; they describe transactions between two individuals, oneself and one's neighbor. They do not address the situation in which the moral agent is simultaneously faced with more than one neighbor. The demands of fugitives, masters, and marshals painfully revealed this failure to specify which neighbor to love first. Individuals could choose to identify with masters, who potentially lost time, money, and property; with marshals, who captured fugitives because it was their duty under the law; or with fugitive slaves, who potentially gained or lost their freedom. The individual citizen thus faced a conflict of duty, making the choice of neighbor crucial.

The primary purpose of sermons delivered on the fugitive slave act was to identify which neighbor and neighborhood to love first. Once the neighbor was chosen, the appropriate behavior could be deduced. As the historian Donald Meyer has explained, in antebellum ethical thought, one's duties were determined by the person with whom one interacted. A person owed one set of duties to a parent, another to a spouse, another to a child, and so on. The first step in defining duty was therefore choosing a neighbor. In the wake of the Fugitive Slave Act of 1850, most northern Protestant ministers chose to love physically distant southerners rather than fugitive slaves within their city limits. That they chose to love white southerners as themselves is hardly surprising, but the way in which they defended their choice had significant implications.

Northern ministers justified the reenslavement of fugitives by establishing the Union as the most important community for Christian citizens and ultimately, the most important community in the world. Once the Union was elevated to the status of the most important and only relevant neighborhood, the Union's rule book, the Constitution, necessarily became the most important determinant of duty. The result of this logic was a virtually unchallengeable defense of fugitive rendition and an absolute demand for loyalty to the Constitution. By championing the duties of the Constitution over all other duties, prorendition clergymen made fugitive rendition acceptable and even virtuous, thus providing the moral cushioning northerners needed to make the difficult choice to turn their collective back on the fugitive slave. Their unwavering defense of the Constitution would also have important implications later in the decade, when southerners appeared to value the nation's constitutional history less than they valued its revolutionary origins.

In numerous sermons, northern Protestant ministers from nearly every denomination preached that the Union, the white citizenry's community, was divinely ordained and that the Constitution was its divinely inspired set of laws. The Constitution was to the Union what, in effect, the Ten Commandments had been to the Hebrews. As the Rev. Henry Boardman, the famous Philadelphia minister, put it, the Union with its Constitution was "another ark of the covenant to us . . . the symbol of the Divine presence with us, and the pledge of his future protection." The document, which never mentioned God by name, was to the Rev. B. R. Allen of Maine a "sacred instrument" that created "a Republic of the purest, noblest form." [41]

The neighbor and the neighborhood having been so defined, all that mattered was the appropriateness of fugitive rendition within the Constitution and the constitutionality of the Fugitive Slave Act of 1850. Prorendition ministers speedily dispensed with this issue, stating flatly that the Constitution guaranteed both slavery and the return of fugitive slaves and that the new law simply fulfilled that guarantee. These guarantees, they argued, were the glue that held the Union together. However unpleasant, Stuart reminded his readers, the Constitution "bound all States to acknowledge as property, that which any particular State, acting within its own jurisdiction has decided to be property, and of course it forbids all detaining of it, and commands deliverance of it, wherever the claim is properly made out." The most recent fugitive slave law simply fulfilled constitutional obligations to southern neighbors. The law had some unpleasant features, it was true, but those aspects could be changed through constitutionally sanctioned means: elections and repeal. In the meantime, good neighbors respected the Constitution and the property rights it secured to the owners of slaves. Just as they would not want their property confiscated, northerners ought not trample on the property rights of their southern neighbors. This was why, in Moses Stuart's opinion, Paul had returned Onesimus to Philemon. Paul, the ultimate example of Christian duty, had treated Philemon as he would want Philemon to treat him. [42]

Through the Constitution, the Union made neighbors of enfranchised northerners and southerners and precluded those of African descent from the neighborhood. The Union, the Constitution, and the sanctity of property rights thus became a surrogate for a race-based community. By limiting the neighborhood to white people joined under the Constitution's covenant, pro-rendition ministers banished fugitive slaves from their mental and physical neighborhoods; this sentiment prompted the Rev. Jonathan Stearns to open his sermon on fugitive rendition with 2 Kings 4:14, "I dwell among mine own people." Fugitive slaves from Onesimus to Ellen and William Craft could never enter the dyadic model of interaction that the golden rule provided be-cause they would never be the North's "own people." Rather than becoming moral agents or objects within the golden rule and the great commandments, they remained objects over which political and religious neighbors negotiated the meaning of loving the other as himself. Slaves and former slaves lived in the neighborhood, but they could never become fully vested members of it.[43]

Prorendition ministers failed to conceive of fugitive slaves as their primary neighbors, but they nevertheless recognized that the slaves were still human beings who deserved some consideration within the framework of the golden rule. In the concluding portion of *Conscience and the Constitution,* Moses Stu-art asserted unequivocally that slaves were fully human beings and that no slaveholder could claim honestly that slavery conformed to Christ's command to love one's neighbor as oneself. The question for Stuart was not whether slaves deserved freedom as human beings but how slavery should be abol-ished. Stuart denounced slavery strongly and made the case for emancipation convincingly, but he still concluded that emancipation in the short run was an impossibility. Having faced the golden rule squarely, Stuart quickly retreated to the safer terrain of constitutional obligation. The bottom line was that slaves could not have what they deserved because the rules governing white neigh-bors precluded that possibility.[44]

Although Stuart and other evangelical gradualists ultimately concluded that the slaves could not enjoy the rights to which they were entitled in the near future, two obligations to slaves remained: the slaves' spiritual welfare and their future political freedom. As mentioned earlier, prorendition ministers often condemned southerners for failing to promote their slaves' spiritual wel-fare and advocated religious education for slaves. While the goal of spiritual liberty could be fulfilled within the Union, securing temporal freedom for slaves required another continent: Africa. Many northern ministers endorsed the American Colonization Society's plan to send emancipated slaves to Li-beria. Colonizationists argued that the removal of free blacks would benefit both blacks and whites. The former slaves would be spared the pain of an irremediable prejudice against them and would gain an opportunity to prac-tice self-government and economic independence, using the tools they had learned in the school of American slavery. Colonization would also alleviate the United States of a permanent and inassimilable black population. Colonizationists saw a divine imprint in the symbiosis of their plan and concluded that the slaves' eventual return to Africa was a part of the Union's providential history.[45]

The goals of religious education and colonization recognized that slaves had legitimate temporal and eternal concerns but contended that only spiritual emancipation could be achieved immediately and within the physical boundaries of the white, covenanted Union. The political promise of emancipation required a separate community; it required those of African descent to be returned "home," to their own neighborhood, where they would be among their racial neighbors. One could argue that the spiritual goal was also achieved in another world: the afterlife. Spiritual conversion might take place on earth, but as Stuart's interpretation of Onesimus showed, conversion did not necessarily have an impact on the present. The blessings of spiritual liberty came with death, not life.

SIX   Antirendition ministers, in contrast, embraced fugitives as their immediate neighbors, claiming for them spiritual and political benefits within the larger white community. Stressing the fugitives' common humanity with white men and white women, antislavery ministers, such as the Rev. William Whitcomb (1820–1862), embraced slaves as members of their own families and communities. Whitcomb, pastor of the Congregational Church in Stoneham, Massachusetts, was a New Hampshire native who graduated from Gilmanton Seminary (New Hampshire) and continued his studies at Andover Theological Seminary. Throughout the 1850s he pastored several Congregationalist churches in New England. In a sermon preached in November 1850 and published soon after, Whitcomb told those assembled in Stoneham that the fugitives were "brethren," who were almost as dear to Whitcomb "as any of the people of Stoneham" or the members of his own family. The fugitives were "bone of our bone and flesh of our flesh"; they were, in effect, blood relatives. Invoking the creation imagery of Genesis, Whitcomb connected the fugitive slaves to the people of Stoneham in the same way that Eve was connected to Adam: as God's gift and creation. As members of their community in Stoneham and of the human family in general, the fugitives were more than pawns in a power struggle between the North and the South; they had rights that their white kin were obligated to protect. Without "fear of contradiction," Whitcomb preached, "I assert their perfect equality with the whole brotherhood of man, and their inherent right to liberty."[46]

In his sermon, Whitcomb figuratively stepped into the fugitive's place and imagined himself in danger from the law. He explained that under the law, not even those with fair skin were secure. Because the 1850 law denied the accused the right to make a statement in his or her defense, every northerner was at the mercy of southern testimony. "This new law is so framed . . . that none of us are entirely safe," Whitcomb warned. "At the false swearing of some one who has sold himself body and soul to work mischief," the law could arrest one of the church's "deacons and drag him in broad daylight from his pew." It could also incarcerate Whitcomb himself for aiding and abetting a fugitive slave.[47] The people of Stoneham had only one alternative: to fight for the freedom of their oppressed brethren as though they were fighting for their own freedom, even if that meant suffering and death. Invoking the image of Christ's sacrifice, Whitcomb issued a charge to his congregation: "O would it not be a glorious privilege to 'lay down our lives for the brethren'?" In little more than a decade, Whitcomb fulfilled his charge himself. In 1862 he assumed the post of U.S. Army hospital chaplain in New Bern, North Carolina, and died two years later in the coastal town of Morehead City, North Carolina.[48]

Whitcomb's exegesis reflected a vision of human community that was broad and welcoming. His depiction of the neighborhood of humanity was typical of other antirendition ministers who also painted a community that had neither physical nor racial boundaries. Few ministers expressed this image of a global, human neighborhood as well as the Rev. Thomas Stone. Stone was a prolific Unitarian who published numerous sermons and contributed to such periodicals as the *Dial* and the *Biblical Repository*. Born in Maine, he graduated from Bowdoin College in 1820 and pastored two Congregationalist churches in his home state. In 1846 he moved to Massachusetts, where he served two congregations over the next fifteen years. His published sermons covered a variety of topics, both political and theological.

In December 1851, while still a pastor at the First Unitarian Church of Salem, Stone delivered a lecture at the annual meeting of the Salem Female Anti-Slavery Society. In his address, delivered in the shadow of the trial of more than forty Pennsylvanians indicted for treason because they had allegedly helped fugitive slaves, Stone offered a vision of community that connected all human beings through bonds of mutual love and respect. To Stone, all human beings participated in God's divinity and were therefore inherently valuable. Like those who enjoyed freedom from earthly chains, the slave was a "child of the common Father, and so connected with the human race by divine and universal sympathies." Every person, including the slave, was the "image and son of the present God, the being of such immeasurable worth." Not even sin could alter humanity's divinity and value. "The very depth of his fall, suppose it ever so great," Stone explained, "does but assure us of the height at which he stands, when indeed he stands."[49] With this spiritual vision, those with an "eye lighted by divine faith" saw that all human beings were of "unspeakable worth" despite the effects of sin. These eyes also recognized the essential equality of the members of the human family regardless of race or gender. Focusing only on the divine in each individual, the Christian eye saw, "not king or subject, chieftain or vassal, priest or laic, noble or vulgar, male or female, statesman or citizen, rich or poor, master or servant," but God in all his glory. Every slave should therefore be treated as a tangible expression of "Divine Love," not as the property that "human tyranny has made him."[50]

As Stone explained, this recognition of human divinity, worth, and equality erased the barriers that separated people from one another and created a "family" of "whatever is divine in heaven or on earth." It created a common community that spread the world over and united all of creation. The energy that destroyed the barriers and sustained the global family was religious sympathy. In Stone's world, religious sympathy was "the very spirit of the Lord, in which we become all of us members one of another." Through the mutuality of religious sympathy, the world's brothers and sisters experienced each other's joys and sufferings, regardless of physical proximity. The "neighborhood" of religious sympathy had no borders, east, west, north, or south, but rather occupied "the realm which unites earth and heaven." Religious sympathy, therefore, created a community of humanity throughout the universe that transcended race and physical location.[51]

Stone illustrated the workings of religious sympathy with two contrasting examples. Some men, he explained to the gathering of women, loved their families and enjoyed the love of their families but nevertheless had little regard for others. In the shadow of revolutions in Europe and the United States's recent conflict with Mexico, Stone described how such men "could exult over the details of a battle gained by their own country" without considering those killed in their victory. They could forget "altogether the wives and children and friends to whom each death has brought as it were another death, in the sorrows, the wants, the untold sufferings, which the slain have escaped, to which the survivors are doomed."[52] This lack of sympathy reflected a spiritual myopia, an inability to see that all people were essentially the same in their human and divine attachments. To Stone, the concept of an enemy made no sense; humanity was one and ultimately could not be broken down into conflicting factions; the sufferings of the conquered were equally those of the conqueror. Within the community, independence evaporated and mutual responsibility grew, making the rendition of a fugitive slave unthinkable. To return a fugitive to slavery was to enslave oneself.

Others, such as the slave trader John Newton, were transformed by religious sympathy. At first, Stone recounted, Newton was unaware that the slaves aboard his ship were people just like himself. But over time, "the divine sympathy" grew within him, and "his heart entered the whole living heart of humanity." Through religious sympathy, Newton integrated himself into those whom he had oppressed. As a result, he abandoned the slave trade "and made himself one with the outcast and despised, whose number he had in his blindness helped to swell." Once religious sympathy held sway within him, Newton identified himself fully with the slaves and changed his behavior. He had learned to love his neighbor as himself.[53]

Stone's unbounded sense of community based on "sympathetic cooperation" challenged the dichotomy between neighbor and stranger. Rather than people being unfamiliar to one another, they were all children of God, independent of race or place. The glue in the borderless community was a spiritual force that prompted individuals to imagine themselves experiencing other peoples' joys and sorrows. All of creation, including human beings, were "united from within by mystic attractions and concords."[54] Interestingly, Stone did not posit a world of total freedom. Rather, he described a world in which surrender to an inexorable force—religious sympathy—established a benevolent, egalitarian order.

Stone's vision of a world in which all neighbors were near and beloved implied that loving one's neighbor was equivalent to loving them all, but at a practical level he did not solve the golden rule's problem of choosing a neighbor. He identified a global neighborhood that made each person a neighbor, but he did not provide any guidelines for prioritizing neighbors' claims. Other antirendition ministers addressed this difficulty by resolving all strangers into a single, familiar person: Jesus Christ. The parable often used to establish Christ as the stranger turned neighbor is found in Matthew 25:33–46. The parable describes a king, metaphorically representing Christ, who welcomes those seated at his right hand into the heavenly kingdom. The king declares that the blessed will "inherit the kingdom" because they ministered to the king when he was in need. The king explains, "For I was an hungered, and ye gave me meat: I was thirsty, and ye gave me drink: I was a stranger, and ye took me in: Naked, and ye clothed me: I was sick, and ye visited me: I was in prison, and ye came unto me." The righteous, unaware that they ever fed, clothed, or visited the king, ask when they had offered such hospitality. The king responds that they helped him when they helped others, for "[i]nasmuch as ye have done it unto one of the least of these my brethren, ye have done it unto me." The king then curses those on his left hand because they failed to feed, clothe, and visit the "least of these" in their distress. In terms of the fugitive slave question, the parable's implication was straightforward: the northerner who aided and harbored a fugitive slave also aided and harbored the king, who was Christ himself.[55]

By equating the king with the lowliest of people, the parable effectively reduced the three-part obligation to love God, neighbor, and self to a dyad, self and God-neighbor, that fit into the structure of the golden rule. The stranger and Christ were identical, and thus the stranger was transformed from a stranger into an intimate neighbor, a representative of the deity, and a potential savior. The stranger-neighbor now had more to offer than those who aided and harbored him, and those helping the stranger owed him more than just food and shelter: they owed him their eternal salvation. As such, the parable not only required Christians to love the stranger in their midst, it dictated that they love that needy stranger first, before they fulfilled the demands of their more familiar neighbors.

Antirendition ministers' use of Christ's "new commandment" further emphasized Christ's presence in the interaction with the fugitive slave. Recorded in John 13:34, the new commandment made Christ the standard for charitable giving: "A new commandment I give unto you, That ye love one another; as I have loved you, that ye also love one another." Whereas the old commandment was to love one's neighbor as oneself, the new commandment was to love one's neighbor as Christ had loved humanity. The new commandment thus dramatically raised the standard for benevolence. Human beings were no longer to act as human beings but were to do what Christ would do in any given situation. They were to superimpose divine intent upon their interactions with others, including fugitive slaves. As such, the parable in Matthew 25 and the new commandment made Christ the generic benefactor of neighborly conduct and the generic object of benevolence. The inputs for the golden rule were no longer average, imperfect people but the savior himself, whose love was "heartfelt sympathy," "helpful service," and "life-giving devotedness."[56] The savior made personal sacrifice the behavioral norm; with Christ as both the benefactor and the recipient of benevolence, charity to the slave had no limits.

This understanding of the golden rule reflected a "Christocentric" trend in nineteenth-century romantic religion. Liberal theologians increasingly focused on Christ as the revealer of human possibilities and the leader of divine and human causes. As the historian Daniel D. Williams has explained, they believed that Christ's purpose was *"to demolish the principle of selfishness,"* and to replace it with the principle of benevolence, including the abolition of slavery. As the manifestation of the ideal man, Christ was the Christian's true image and standard for behavior, not just a moral example.[57] The fact that neither Christ nor the apostles ever condemned slavery verbally was therefore irrelevant; all that mattered was Christ's tangible example of personal sacrifice. The trend toward Christocentric religion did not come to fruition in the United States until after the Civil War. Most antebellum Christian citizens did not view their neighbors as representatives of God on earth but rather saw them as fellow sinners.

Like most antebellum northerners, clergymen who opposed slavery and rendition also had limits to their sense of community with black slaves. Despite the innovative ways in which they interpreted and applied prescriptive texts, so far ahead of their fellow Americans, slavery's opponents were often unable to comprehend emancipation as a fundamental reordering of their community. Although they identified slaves as neighbors, the main result of this identification was that slaves became worthy recipients of benevolence; as such, blacks still remained in an inferior position to whites. This is in no way to denigrate the abolitionists; it is only to recognize that they, like their contemporaries and like all people, placed limits on their imagined communities.

SEVEN   In the political histories of the 1850s, the fugitive slave controversy appears as a relatively minor event, especially when compared to the Kansas-Nebraska controversy. Observing northern complicity with the fugitive slave law, historians have concluded that the fugitive rendition storm blew over relatively quickly and easily. As the quantity and tenor of these sermons show, however, the fugitive slave controversy was no small matter. The law's requirement that "all good citizens" help in the capture of fugitive slaves flouted the golden rule's requirement to treat others with kindness and evoked a heated response from the North's pulpits. The majority of northerners never directly faced the choice between a slave and a master, but the very existence of fugitives forced northerners seriously to reconsider the nature of their relationship to slaves and to masters.

These sermons also make clear that for the majority of white northerners, blacks would be accepted into established neighborhoods only with great difficulty, and in fact, most fugitives who fled to freedom were sheltered and aided by the North's free black communities, not by sympathetic whites. For most northern clergymen, a biracial community was difficult to imagine, let alone achieve. Sermons preached and published in the wake of the fugitive slave controversy provide a window onto the antebellum religious values and beliefs that justified and supported the North's racial prejudice against blacks, both slave and free.

Sermons about the Fugitive Slave Act of 1850 also show that although northerners acquiesced quickly to the law, their cooperation came at a high price, both to themselves and to southerners. Prorendition interpretations of Deuteronomy 23, Philemon, and the golden rule demanded that white northerners love white southerners as themselves, thus protecting masters' positions as neighbors, but they also implied a demand that southerners return the favor. The sermons defined neighbors' duties in a tone that would brook no future compromise: whether in the North or the South, citizens of the divinely ordained Union were obligated to protect and honor the Constitution. In the wake of the fugitive slave act, most northern clergymen preached acquiescence to the law because they valued solutions to conflicts within the Constitution. As the debate over slavery continued, they would expect southerners to seek redress to their complaints through the same divinely inspired document, not by violence or secession.

NOTES

1. Harriet Beecher Stowe, *Uncle Tom's Cabin; or Life Among the Lowly* (1852; reprint, New York: Penguin, 1986), 118-20.

2. For a brief consideration of the law's provisions, see Stanley Campbell, *The Slave Catchers: Enforcement of the Fugitive Slave Law, 1850–1860* (Chapel Hill: University of North Carolina Press, 1968), 23–25, 39–40. For a fuller discussion of the law, its impact, and its history, see Robert Cover, *Justice Accused* (New Haven: Yale University Press, 1975), 175–93, and Paul Finkelman, *An Imperfect Union: Slavery, Federalism, and Comity* (Chapel Hill: University of North Carolina Press, 1981), 175–77, 336–38.

3. Stanley Campbell provides a good overview of northern public opinion of the fugitive slave law in chapter 3 of *The Slave Catchers*. Campbell also discusses the Chicago aldermen's vote to secede (p. 54). After Stephen Douglas made a personal appearance in Chicago, the aldermen rescinded their vote. See "Speech of the Hon. Stephen A. Douglas, on the 'Measures of Adjustment,' delivered in the City Hall, Chicago, October 23, 1850," (Washington, D.C.: Gideon, 1851). According to the historian Robert Cover, the number of cases brought against those aiding and abetting fugitives multiplied tremendously after the 1850 law; see Cover *Justice Accused,* 191. Two other sources also document the impact of the law on fugitives and their friends: Samuel May, *The Fugitive Slave Law and Its Victims* (New York: American Anti-Slavery Society, 1861), and Mary G. McDougall, *Fugitive Slaves, 1619–1865* (Boston: Ginn, 1891). The Christiana riot in the fall of 1851 was one of the more well-known incidents. In the subsequent trial, more

than 40 people were indicted for treason for their role in the escape of two fugitives. For more on the Christiana riot, see Thomas P. Slaughter, *Bloody Dawn: The Christiana Riot and Racial Violence in the Antebellum North* (New York: Oxford University Press, 1991). In absolute terms, the number of northerners personally affected by the law was small. A handful of celebrated cases kept the threat of being fined and jailed for helping a fugitive at the forefront, but only a small number of northerners were personally implicated.

4. My understanding of "neighborhoods" and the nature of duty within them has been shaped by a fascinating and provocative interchange among John Ashworth, David Brion Davis, and Thomas Haskell. The discussion, with an excellent introduction by Thomas Bender, is found in *The Antislavery Debate: Capitalism and Abolitionism as a Problem in Historical Interpretation,* Thomas Bender, ed. (Berkeley: University of California Press, 1992).

5. For discussions of the development of western thought on slavery, see David Brion Davis, *The Problem of Slavery in Western Culture* (Ithaca, N.Y.: Cornell University Press, 1966) and *The Problem of Slavery in the Age of Revolution* (Ithaca, N.Y.: Cornell University Press, 1975). For a consideration of northern churches and the battle against slavery, see John R. McKivigan, *The War against Proslavery Religion* (Ithaca, N.Y.: Cornell University Press, 1984). For evaluations of southern attitudes toward slavery, see Drew Gilpin Faust, *A Sacred Circle: The Dilemma of the Intellectual in the Old South, 1840–1860* (Philadelphia: University of Pennsylvania Press, 1977); Eugene Genovese, *The Slaveholders' Dilemma: Freedom and Progress in Southern Conservative Thought, 1820–1860* (Columbia: University of South Carolina Press, 1992); Mitchell Snay, *Gospel of Disunion: Religion and Separatism in the Antebellum South* (New York: Cambridge University Press, 1993); and Larry E. Tise, *Proslavery: A History of the Defense of Slavery in America, 1701–1840* (Athens: University of Georgia Press, 1987).

6. The role of the Bible in shaping southern attitudes toward slavery has been insightfully analyzed in Elizabeth Fox-Genovese and Eugene D. Genovese, "The Divine Sanction of Social Order: Religious Foundations of the Southern Slaveholders' World View," *Journal of the American Academy of Religion* 55 (summer 1987): 211–33; Thomas V. Peterson, *Ham and Japheth: The Mythic World of Whites in the Antebellum South* (Metuchen, N.J.: American Theological Library Association, 1978); and Mitchell Snay, *Gospel of Disunion.* For abolitionists' use of the Bible, see James B. Stewart, "Abolitionists, the Bible, and the Challenge of Slavery," in *The Bible and Social Reform,* Ernest Sandeen, ed. (Philadelphia: Fortress Press, 1982). Mark Noll considers various denominations' biblical views of slavery in "The Bible and Slavery," in *Religion and the Civil War,* Harry S. Stout, Charles Regan Wilson, and Randall Miller, eds. (New York: Oxford University Press, forthcoming). For general discussions of the role of the Bible in antebellum American culture, see Nathan Hatch and Mark Noll, eds., *The Bible in America* (New York: Oxford University Press, 1982), 41–43; Peter J. Wosh, *Spreading the Word: The Bible Business in Nineteenth-Century America* (Ithaca, N.Y.: Cornell University Press, 1994); and Philip L. Barlow, *Mormons and the Bible: The Place of the Latter-day Saints in American Religion* (New York: Oxford University Press, 1991), 3–9.

7. Donald M. Scott, *From Office to Profession: The New England Ministry, 1750–1850* (Philadelphia: University of Pennsylvania Press, 1978), 106. A tremendously valuable study of northerners who fell into this group is George M. Frederickson, *The Black Image in the White Mind*

(1971; Middletown, Conn.: Wesleyan University Press, 1987). Another invaluable analysis of northern perceptions of slavery and other issues is Richard Carwardine, *Evangelicals and Politics in Antebellum America* (New Haven: Yale University Press, 1993).

8. The greater incidence of proobedience sermons appears to have been a good reflection of public opinion. Despite their initial outrage and a persisting frustration with the law, most northerners embraced the Compromise of 1850, including the fugitive slave law, as a solution to sectional conflict. For northerners' political acquiescence, see James McPherson, *Battle Cry of Freedom* (New York: Oxford University Press, 1988), 80–91. David Potter also describes their compliance with the law but characterizes the compromise as an "armistice" rather than as a solution; see Potter, *The Impending Crisis 1848–1861* (New York: Harper and Row, 1976), 113–18, 122. Religious periodicals throughout the North and Old Northwest also ultimately encouraged conciliation. See Ralph Keller, "Methodist Newspapers and the Fugitive Slave Law," *Church History* 43 (September 1974): 319–39, and L. Wesley Norton, "The Religious Press and the Compromise of 1850: A Study of the Relationship of the Methodist, Baptist, and Presbyterian Press to the Slavery Controversy, 1846–1851" (Ph.D. diss., University of Illinois, 1959).

9. Some historians have noted a decline in biblically based preaching in the antebellum period. See Mark Noll, "The Image of the United States as a Biblical Nation, 1776–1865," in *Bible in America,* Hatch and Noll, eds., 42–43; D. G. Hart, "Divided Between Heart and Mind: The Critical Period for Protestant Thought in America," *Journal of Ecclesiastical History* 33 (1987): 257. Sermons about the fugitive slave issue seem to contradict this thesis.

10. Moses Stuart, *Conscience and the Constitution, with Remarks on the Recent Speech of the Hon. Daniel Webster in the Senate of the United States on the Subject of Slavery* (Boston: Crocker and Brewster, 1850), 7.

11. Ibid., 16–17

12. Ibid., 12.

13. Rufus W. Clark, *A Review of the Rev. Moses Stuart's Pamphlet on Slavery, entitled "Conscience and the Constitution"* (Boston: Moody, 1850); William Jay, *Reply to Remarks of Rev. Moses Stuart, Lately a Professor in the Theological Seminary at Andover, on Hon. John Jay, and an Examination of his Scriptural Exegesis, contained in his Recent Pamphlet entitled, "Conscience and the Constitution"* (New York: John A. Gray, 1850); G. W. Perkins, *Prof. Stuart and Slave Catching: Remarks on Mr. Stuart's Book "Conscience and the Constitution"* (West Meriden, Conn.: Rinman's Print, 1850).

14. Edwards A. Park, *A Discourse Delivered at the Funeral of Professor Moses Stuart* (Boston: Tappan and Whittemore, 1852), 25–28. See also Anson P. Stokes, *Memorials of Eminent Yale Men* (New Haven: Yale University Press, 1914), 1:61. Stokes claimed that Stuart "did more than any American up to the middle of the nineteenth century to introduce our scholars to the best results of German studies in Biblical philology." See also letter from Calvin Stowe to William B. Sprague, in William B. Sprague, *Annals of the American Pulpit* (New York: Robert Carter and Brothers, 1859–69), 2:480. For a consideration of Stuart's pivotal role in the history of theological education, see Jerry Wayne Brown, *The Rise of Biblical Criticism in America* (Middletown, Conn.: Wesleyan University Press, 1969), and Daniel D. Williams, *The Andover Liberals* (New York: King's Crown Press, 1941).

15. Brown, *Biblical Criticism,* 110; Calvin Stowe to William Sprague in *Annals,* 2:479; Francis Wayland quoted in Stokes, *Memorials,* 1:62.

16. Charles Hodge, "Civil Government," in *The Biblical Repertory and Princeton Review* 23 (1851): 129.

17. For a discussion of the impact of slavery on the national churches, see C. C. Goen, *Broken Churches, Broken Nation: Denominational Schisms and the Coming of the Civil War* (Macon, Ga.: Mercer University Press, 1985).

18. Stuart, *Conscience and Constitution,* 23.

19. Stuart's views were similar to those of most biblical scholars of his time and throughout history. An overview of the biblical debate over slavery can be found in Willard M. Swartley, *Slavery, Sabbath, War, and Women: Case Issues in Biblical Interpretation* (Scottsdale, Pa.: Herald Press, 1983). For a more general discussion, see David Brion Davis, *The Problem of Slavery in Western Culture* (Ithaca, N.Y.: Cornell University Press, 1966), especially chap. 12 and *The Problem of Slavery in the Age of Revolution,* especially chap. 11.

20. Stuart, *Conscience and Constitution,* 30–34. Rev. J. M. Peck made a similar argument in a sermon delivered before the Illinois state legislature, published as *The Duties of American Citizens: A Discourse, Preached in the State-House, Springfield, Illinois, January 26, 1851* (St. Louis: T. W. Ustick, 1851), 19. See also Rev. G. F. Kettell, *A Sermon on the Duty of Citizens, with respect to the Fugitive Slave Law, by Rev. G. F. Kettell, of the Methodist Episcopal Society, Poughkeepsie, N. Y.* (White Plains, N.Y.: Eastern State Journal Print, 1851), 17. Unitarian minister Ezra Stiles Gannett, who succeeded William Ellery Channing at the Federal Street Meetinghouse, also referred to the states in the Union as tribes. See his *Thanksgiving for the Union: A Discourse delivered in the Federal-Street Meetinghouse in Boston, on Thanksgiving-Day, November 28, 1850* (Boston: Crosby and Nichols, 1850), 4.

21. Stuart, *Conscience and Constitution,* 31.

22. Ibid., 32.

23. Ibid., 31.

24. In addition to Hodge's commentary in the *Princeton Review,* other antebellum sources confirmed Stuart's reading of the text. For example, see the entry for Deuteronomy 23 in *The Holy Bible . . . with Explanatory Notes, Practical Observations, and Copious Marginal References. By Thomas Scott* (Philadelphia: James M. Campbell, 1844).

25. Stuart, 103–6, 109–13. Most sermons urging compliance with the law carried a blanket condemnation of slavery. In addition to Stuart, see, for example, Henry A. Boardman, *The American Union* (Philadelphia: Lippincott, Grambo, 1851), 32.

26. Stuart, *Conscience and Constitution,* 32.

27. Ibid., 56–60.

28. Ibid., 31.

29. Ibid., 60–61.

30. Ibid., 61. Other clergymen also made similar arguments. See Boardman, *American Union,* 35–36; Kettell, *Duty of Citizens,* 17–18; John M. Krebs, D.D., *The American Citizen. A Discourse on the Nature and Extent of our Religious Subjection to the Government under which we live: Including an Inquiry into the Scriptural Authority of that Provision of the Constitution of the United*

States, which requires the Surrender of Fugitive Slaves (New York: Charles Scribner, 1851), 33–37. N. S. Wheaton, D.D., *A Discourse on St. Paul's Epistle to Philemon . . . delivered in Christ Church, Hartford, Dec. 22, 1850* (Hartford, Conn.: Case, Tiffany, 1851). Wheaton was a Congregationalist pastor and founder of Trinity College in Hartford, Connecticut. Also see entry for Philemon in *Scott's Family Bible.*

31. Stuart's assumption that Onesimus's conversion had no impact on his temporal status was in keeping with the opinions of most divines for centuries. In his essay on Philemon, the twentieth-century biblical scholar John M. G. Barclay notes that the proslavery interpretation of Philemon was common through the nineteenth century. Barclay contends that an antislavery reading of the text is "peculiarly modern" and "post-abolitionist." See Barclay, "Paul, Philemon, and the Dilemma of Christian Slave-Ownership," *New Testament Studies* 37 (April 1991): 161. See also Davis, *Problem of Slavery in Western Culture,* especially chaps. 11 and 12; Davis, *Problem of Slavery in the Age of Revolution,* chaps. 10 and 11.

32. Stuart, *Conscience and Constitution,* 60.

33. The approximately seventy sermons I have found in my research include regular Sunday sermons, Thanksgiving Day sermons, Fast Day Sermons, Fourth of July orations, and other special events for which a minister delivered a sermon. A footnote to Theodore Parker's 1854 sermon entitled *The New Crime Against Humanity. A Sermon, preached at the Music Hall, in Boston, on Sunday, June 4, 1854, . . . with the lesson of the day for the previous Sunday* (Boston: Benjamin B. Mussey, 1854), 38–41, includes a nearly comprehensive list of the small number of sermons preached against the fugitive slave act between 1850 and 1854.

34. Lucius Thayer, *The Story of a Religious Democracy During Two and One-Half Centuries* (Concord, N.H.: Rumford Press, 1921), 34–36.

35. *Minutes of the General Association of Massachusetts* (Boston: Crocker and Brewster, 1838–56), see statistical appendices.

36. For biographical information on Rufus W. Clark, see *National Cyclopaedia* (New York: James T. White, 1909), 10:359; *The Obituary Record of Graduates of Yale University Deceased from June, 1880, to June, 1890* (New Haven: Tuttle, Morehouse, and Taylor, 1890), 374. The obituary record lists 1838 as the year Clark graduated from Yale College; other sources list 1836. The obituary record also indicates that he spent his first year in seminary at Andover and his second at Yale.

37. Clark, *Review,* 36–37.

38. Ibid., 41. Davis, *Problem of Slavery in the Age of Revolution,* 519–20; 534.

39. Perkins, *Prof. Stuart,* 16.

40. The golden rule is recorded in Matthew 7:12 and the great commandment can be found in Matthew 22:37–39. Donald H. Meyer insightfully discusses antebellum concepts of duty in *The Instructed Conscience* (Philadelphia: University of Pennsylvania Press, 1972). Antebellum Bible commentaries also attest to the prescriptive power of the golden rule and the great commandment. See *Scott's Family Bible* and Francis Wayland's *Elements of Moral Science,* both of which appear in several editions throughout the antebellum period. Wayland's *Elements* was the most popular moral philosophy text in use before the war. Peter B. Knupfer also provides an interesting discussion of the duty to compromise in his *The Union As It Is* (Chapel Hill: Univer-

sity of North Carolina Press, 1991), 83. For a brief consideration of the golden rule and its history, see Paul Edwards, ed., *The Encyclopedia of Philosophy* (New York: Macmillan Company and The Free Press, 1967), 3:365–66. The *Encyclopedia* notes that despite its universal significance, the golden rule has received very little scholarly attention. See also Simon Blackburn, *The Oxford Dictionary of Philosophy* (Oxford: Oxford University Press, 1994), 160; Antony Flew, ed., *A Dictionary of Philosophy*, rev. 2d ed. (New York: St. Martin's Press, 1979), 134.

41. Boardman, *American Union*, 36, 43; B. R. Allen, *The Responsibilities and Duties of American Citizens, A Sermon Preached in the Congregational Church, South Berwick, ME., Thanksgiving Day, Dec. 19, 1850* (Boston: Crocker and Brewster, 1851), 4–6, 8, 23; Gannett, *Thanksgiving for the Union*, 7–13; Henry Hopkins, *Slavery: Its Religious Sanction, Its Political Dangers, and the Best Mode of Doing It Away* (Buffalo, N.Y.: Phinney, 1851), 5; L. E. Lathrop, *A Discourse, delivered at Auburn, on the Day of the Annual Thanksgiving, Dec. 12, 1850* (Auburn, N.Y.: Derby and Miller, 1850), 9, 11.

42. Stuart, *Conscience and Constitution*, 60, 66–67, 81; Allen, *Responsibilities and Duties*, 5–6; Boardman, *American Union*, 30–35; Lathrop, *Discourse*, 11. For compromises over slavery and the formation and continuation of the union, see Cover, *Justice Accused*, 150–52; Knupfer, *Union As It Is*, especially 94–95.

43. Jonathan F. Stearns, *The Good Republican: A Discourse, delivered in the First Presbyterian Church, Newark, N.J., on Thanksgiving Day, Dec. 12, 1850* (New York: J. F. Trow, 1850), 3.

44. Stuart, *Conscience and Constitution*, 100, 112. Numerous other prorendition sermons follow this same pattern.

45. Frederickson, *The Black Image in the White Mind*, 115–16. Moses Stuart invoked Jonathan Edwards to support his argument that colonization was a part of the divine plan for Africa and North America. Stuart claimed that Edwards left a manuscript in which he defended the slave trade on the basis of Deuteronomy 23 and concluded that the trade was a part of God's plan to bring Christianity to Africa; see Stuart, *Conscience and Constitution*, 33. If the manuscript existed, it is no longer extant, according to the editors of Edwards's papers at Yale University.

46. William C. Whitcomb, *A Discourse on the Recapture of Fugitive Slaves, delivered at Stoneham Mass, Nov. 3, 1850. By William C. Whitcomb, Pastor of the Congregational Church* (Boston: Charles C. P. Moody, 1850), 19, 22.

47. Whitcomb, *Recapture of Fugitive Slaves*, 32. Others shared Whitcomb's concern for the security of white people. The *Friends' Review* of Philadelphia carried a story about alleged fugitive slaves who were visibly white. Under the headline "White Slaves," the reporter wrote ". . . this case furnishes a practical illustration of what has been sometimes regarded as a wild and extravagant supposition, the possibility of carrying white as well as coloured persons into slavery by a summary proceeding, under authority of the fugitive slave act." *Friends' Review* Twelfth Month, 7 and 21, 1850, 190, 217.

48. Ibid., 35. In exhorting his congregation, Whitcomb paraphrased 1 John 3:16: "Hereby perceive we the love of God, because he laid down his life for us: and we ought to lay down our lives for the brethren." For biographical information, see *General Catalogue of the Theological Seminary Andover, Massachusetts, 1808–1908* (Boston: Thomas Todd, 1909), 245.

49. Thomas T. Stone, *An Address before the Salem Female Anti-Slavery Society, at its Annual Meeting, December 7, 1851* (Salem, Mass.: William Ives, 1852), 5–6, 11.

50. Ibid., 7–8.

51. Ibid., 7–10.

52. Ibid., 9.

53. Ibid., 10.

54. Ibid., 10–12.

55. Whitcomb, *Recapture of Fugitive Slaves,* 18. The Rev. Isaac J. P. Collyer made the same argument in his *Review of Rev. W. W. Eell's* [sic] *Thanksgiving Sermon . . . delivered in the Methodist Episcopal Church, Newburyport, Dec. 29, 1850* (Newburyport: Charles Whipple, 1851), 13. This interpretation is interesting in terms of a recent consideration of Hegel's analysis of the master-slave relationship. As philosopher Steven B. Smith explains, Hegel's dialectic is the struggle for recognition. The person who wins recognition is the master, the person who loses is the slave. Christianity, Smith argues, "introduces the idea of universal recognition." The abolitionists' interpretation of this parable is a case in point. See Steven B. Smith, "Hegel on Slavery and Domination," *Review of Metaphysics* 46 (September 1992): 106.

56. Nathaniel Hall, *The Limits of Civil Obedience. A Sermon preached in the First Church, Dorchester, January 12, 1851* (Boston: Crosby and Nichols, 1851), 9.

57. Williams, *Andover Liberals,* 24.

PART THREE

 The Center Does Not Hold

Individuals, Institutions, and Slavery

Evangelical Womanhood and the Politics of the African Colonization Movement in Virginia

ELIZABETH R. VARON

In 1835 Presbyterian minister Ralph Gurley, secretary of the American Colonization Society (ACS), paid tribute to Virginia women. "Devout ladies" of the Old Dominion, he wrote, had long demonstrated a commendable "zeal and charity" on behalf of enslaved blacks and had by their example inspired "ministers and statesmen" to champion the cause of sending manumitted slaves and free blacks to colonize and Christianize Africa. In this passage and in the articles he penned and edited for the ACS monthly journal, the *African Repository,* Gurley made a case that was familiar to reform-minded evangelicals. He argued that colonization fell squarely into the realm of "Christian benevolence" and that the scheme counted pious white women among its strongest supporters.[1]

Gurley was one in a host of reformers, ministers, educators, and politicians who together helped to forge a "benevolent consensus" among Evangelical Protestants in the first three decades of the nineteenth century. In the aftermath of the Second Great Awakening, Evangelicals around the country organized, historian John Kuykendall has written, "for the deliberate conversion of their nation and the world into an empire under the governance of Christ." That empire took on a distinct institutional form. Northern and southern evangelicals from each of the four major denominations cooperated in supporting a series of national enterprises they deemed benevolent—the American Bible Society, the American Tract Society, the American Education Society, the American Sunday School Union, the American Home Missionary Society, the American Temperance Union, and the American Colonization Society.[2]

Each of these organizations, and their state auxiliaries, relied on and celebrated the contributions of women.[3] At the core of the benevolent consensus was a new ideology of female duty, one that historian Donald Mathews
has dubbed "Evangelical womanhood." Evangelical womanhood urged white
women to practice lives of "usefulness"—to promote piety and practice
charity not only within the domestic circle but within the social circle more
broadly defined. In the South, that social circle included slaves: Well before the emergence of an organized abolitionist movement, Mathews argues,
"Evangelical southern women had already established their peculiar and most
important act of benevolence by becoming tribunes, teachers and missionaries
to slaves."[4]

In the last three decades of the antebellum period, the benevolent consensus
gradually and inexorably disintegrated. As sectional tensions mounted, each
of the national reform societies enumerated above met with increasing an-
tagonism from southerners who feared that the benevolent empire had come
under the control of northern abolitionists. The American Colonization Society was the first casualty. In the 1830s, the colonization movement was not
only assailed by proslavery and abolitionist critics but also internally divided
into two increasingly antagonistic factions. Some supporters of the movement, motivated by sympathy for blacks, hoped that colonization would pave
the way for the gradual emancipation of the slaves; others, motivated by racism, saw colonization as a means to rid the country of free blacks and thereby
make the slave system more secure. The schism within the colonization movement did not simply pit antislavery northerners against proslavery southerners; it also turned southerners against each other. In Virginia, the setting for
this essay, proslavery colonizationists won their battle with antislavery colonizationists, but, ultimately, they lost the war for southern support. By the mid-
1850s, the colonization cause was in decline in Virginia, as in the rest of
the South.[5]

The story of how southern evangelicals came to retreat from the field of
social reform has been told in recent scholarship; it is the aim of this essay to
demonstrate that women and gender construction are integral to that story.
The leading practitioners of southern women's history have hotly debated
whether elite white women were "covert abolitionists," more inclined to antislavery sentiments than their men, or proslavery partisans, who equaled or
even surpassed men in their zeal for the peculiar institution and in their capacity for cruelty toward slaves.[6] The Virginia sources suggest that the question of whether or not women were "covert abolitionists" is the wrong one to
ask. White Virginians of both sexes resoundingly rejected abolitionism. But

that rejection did not preclude meaningful debate over slavery. Hundreds of women, through the agency of the American Colonization Society, overtly expressed their opposition to slavery. Because the slave system bred both domestic chaos and immorality, they argued, it was the duty of Christian women to work for its gradual demise.

As the colonization society came under attack, so too did the gradualist reading of evangelical womanhood. Those who embraced the "positive good" defense of slavery held that southern white women were the beneficiaries of the peculiar institution and should work not to dismantle but to defend it. The ascendancy of the latter view of woman's duty over the former was accomplished neither swiftly nor easily in Virginia. For a determined cadre of women colonizationists clung to gradual emancipation even as it lost political viability, keeping alive public anxieties about white women's loyalty to slavery. Their story serves as an important reminder that southern evangelicals argued amongst each other about the nature and fate of the slave system—and about white women's place in it—up until the eve of the Civil War.

Evangelical womanhood was first elaborated in the 1810s, in newspapers, journals, lectures, essays, sermons, and books. Prescriptive literature by Virginia authors made the case that women's domestic and religious duties included charitable activities and that such social problems as poverty and irreligion could best be solved by "benevolent" rather than "political" means. Instead of explicitly defining the benevolent and political, writers in Virginia, like those in the North, associated each sphere of activity with certain qualities. Benevolence was "disinterested" in nature, while politics involved ambition and self-aggrandizement. Benevolent reformers relied on "influence" and "suasion," while politicians, vested with the power to make laws, could practice "coercion." Benevolence involved the exercise of compassion, while politics unleashed passion and even fanaticism. Benevolence was suited to women; politics was not.[7]

Among the leading articulators of evangelical womanhood was Presbyterian clergyman John Holt Rice of Richmond, editor of the *Virginia Evangelical and Literary Magazine*. Rice's magazine studiously eschewed any mention of politics, but it endorsed a broad range of voluntary associations, from Sunday schools to tract societies to temperance societies to the American Colonization Society, lumping all them under the heading of "religious benevolence." Rice encouraged women to contribute to these enterprises, to serve as a "generous hearted missionaries" to the distressed.[8]

Rice's willingness to endorse both colonization and female benevolence located him in the mainstream of public opinion in Virginia in the 1820s. The American Colonization Society received the blessing of the religious establish-ment in the Old Dominion. Each of the four major Protestant denominations endorsed the ACS and took up collections on its behalf. Among the religious leaders who, along with Rice, actively promoted colonization were Episcopal bishop William Meade, Methodist minister John Early, and Baptist minister Robert Ryland. The religious press categorized colonization as a cause that, like Bible societies, tract and temperance societies deserved the active support of all Christian women and men. Such newspapers as the Presbyterian *Watch-man of the South,* Methodist *Christian Sentinel,* Baptist *Religious Herald,* and Episcopalian *Southern Churchman* publicized colonization. At the heart of the evangelical view of colonization was the notion that the ACS was fundamen-tally a missionary society, dedicated to the charitable work of improving the lot of a people "plunged in all the degradation of idolatry, superstition, and ignorance." A small but significant group of Afro-Virginians embraced the cause of evangelizing Africa. In 1815, black members of Richmond's First Bap-tist Church formed the Richmond African Missionary Society. In 1821, in cooperation with the ACS, the missionary society sent its charter member, preacher Lott Cary, and his wife and family to West Africa; Cary would earn a reputation as the foremost black missionary in the ACS colony of Liberia.[9]

The political establishment was no less enthusiastic than the religious in its support for the ACS. The Virginia General Assembly appropriated money for the colonization society, and male-headed auxiliaries to the ACS were established across the length and breadth of Virginia. The most prominent auxiliary, the Richmond and Manchester Society, was presided over by such political luminaries as John Marshall and James Madison. For many coloni-zationists, the ACS's mandate was not only to Christianize Africa but also to transform the American political landscape—to stake out a "middle ground" between the extremes of northern abolitionism and southern proslavery ide-ology. Political leaders, like religious ones, solicited and celebrated women's contributions to the ACS. ACS vice president Henry Clay, speaking in Ken-tucky in 1829, declared that colonization had been "countenanced and aided by that fair sex, which is ever prompt to contribute its exertions in works of charity and benevolence, because it always acts from the generous impulses of pure and uncorrupted hearts."[10]

Abundant evidence of women's zeal for colonization can be found both in ACS publications and in the private papers of Virginia women. Throughout the 1820s, scores of Virginia women donated time and money to the colonization cause. Contributions by women, which were publicized in the ACS monthly journal, the *African Repository*, took a wide variety of forms. Some women acted through their churches, typically by purchasing membership in the ACS for their pastors. Some made outright donations in their own names; some bequeathed money to the ACS, or provided for the manumission and emigration of their slaves in their wills. Beginning in 1825, a number of informal networks of women colonizationists were converted into women's auxiliaries to the ACS. These organizations proved to be highly effective at soliciting contributions for the cause. Colonization women favored a fund-raising tactic that would later be adopted by women abolitionists—raising money by selling goods at fairs. In May of 1830, for example, the women of Charlottesville raised five hundred dollars for "the benevolent objects of the American Colonization Society," by holding a colonization fair at a local hotel.[11]

A common thread running through writings by and about women adherents of the ACS is their view that colonization was a religious scheme, not a political one. Colonization women saw themselves as missionaries, drawn to the ACS out of a sense of religious duty—they would spread the Gospel among slaves in order to prepare them to promote Christianity in Africa. For Virginia's most prominent women colonizationists, the conviction that Africa should be Christianized went hand in hand with the conviction that the institution of slavery was sinful and should, on moral grounds, be gradually dismantled.

Anne Rice, wife of John Holt Rice, shared her husband's enthusiasm for reform causes and for the ACS. Rice superintended her slaves' religious education, delivering Sunday night Scripture readings for their edification. According to her niece Mary Virginia Terhune [Marion Harland], a popular novelist of the 1850s, Rice was a fervent "convert" to colonization and saw the scheme as "the practical abolition of negro slavery in America." In 1848 she manumitted her oldest slave, Anderson, and his family and sent them to Liberia; "in the fullness of time," Terhune writes, Rice arranged for the emigration of five families and "well nigh impoverished herself" in so doing.[12]

Louisa Cocke shared Rice's sentiments. A devout Presbyterian, she believed that slavery was an evil institution and that whites would have to "render an account hereafter for . . . injustice" to slaves. Mistress of a large plantation in Fluvanna County, Cocke participated in a variety of benevolent causes and presided over a Sabbath school for her slaves, teaching children the rudiments of reading and writing. In 1833, her husband, John Hartwell Cocke, manumitted Peyton Skipwith, his wife, Lydia, and their six children and sent them to Liberia; the Cockes and Skipwiths maintained an extensive and often poignant correspondence throughout the antebellum period. Like many colonizationists, Cocke practiced selective manumission. He sent fourteen other freed slaves—only a small fraction of the total number in his control—to Liberia over the course of the antebellum period.[13]

Ann R. Page, an ardent Episcopalian from Frederick County, hoped the colonization movement would break the "evil power of slavery." Page felt, her biographer asserts, that she was called by God "to a great missionary work in her own country, and at her own home." Like Louisa Cocke, she taught a Sabbath school for her slaves and tried to instill in them the moral values, such as temperance, which she believed they could disseminate in Liberia; "to see Western Africa seasoned with divine salt, from American Christians," Page confided to fellow colonizationist Mary Lee (Fitzhugh) Custis, was her fondest wish. Page lamented the effects of absolute power on the souls of masters and mistresses. In 1823 she wrote that "we are especially tempted to make the poor subservient to our own indulgence when those poor are our bond slaves and we can do as we like with them, and hush their murmurs by authority or by selling them." Debt, the proverbial nemesis of would-be emancipators, eventually compelled Page to do the very thing she decried. In order to satisfy the creditors of her late husband, Page sold more than one hundred slaves in 1826. The rest she worked zealously to prepare for freedom and for emigration to Liberia; between 1832 and 1838 she sent an estimated twenty-three manumitted slaves to the colony.[14]

The most prominent woman colonizationist in Virginia was Mary Berkeley Minor Blackford of Fredericksburg. A staunch Episcopalian, Mary had learned her devotion to the ACS at the knee of her mother, Lucy Minor, who sent nine manumitted slaves to Liberia in 1826. An excerpt from the biography of Mary's younger brother Launcelot, who served as a missionary in Liberia, conveys the tenor of life in the Minor household—as children, Mary and her brother were accustomed to depositing their savings in a joint money box, "whose contents were carefully hoarded to aid the benevolent designs of the Colonization Society." In 1825, Mary married lawyer William Blackford. William shared his wife's passion for the colonization cause but not her antislavery views: While Mary hoped that colonization would pave the way for the gradual emancipation of the slaves, William saw the scheme primarily as a means to remove the "vicious and degraded" free black population. After years of entreaties, Mary finally persuaded William to free and provide for the emigration of one of their slaves, Abram, in 1844.[15]

In 1829, Blackford founded the Fredericksburg and Falmouth Female Auxiliary to the ACS, soon to become Virginia's most active female society. The Fredericksburg auxiliary distributed ACS tracts throughout the countryside and tried to provoke the languishing men's auxiliary to good works. The work of her auxiliary, Mary Blackford wrote to ACS secretary Ralph Gurley, was carried on "in the domestic circle, around our own or the firesides of our neighbors, without the sacrifice of time or the proprieties of our sex." She and her coworkers were merely exerting their benign influence in popularly sanctioned ways—using familiar vehicles for benevolence, such as fairs and the distribution of tracts, to exhort their neighbors to good deeds. The leaders of the Richmond and Manchester Female Colonization Society had a similar view of women's activism. Their 1830 annual report declared that "as a missionary scheme," colonization commended itself to "every Christian." The auxiliary's fund-rasing efforts for the ACS were "perfectly within the sphere" that Christianity dictated for women.[16]

While men and women colonizationists alike trumpeted the religious benevolence of the cause, their claims did not insulate the ACS from criticism. By the late 1820s the ACS was meeting with considerable political opposition in Virginia from proslavery men who thought it an abolitionist front, and from states'-rights Jacksonians who saw colonization as part of an effort by such nationalists as Henry Clay and John Quincy Adams to extend the power of the federal government. Hoping to win the support of Virginians who were wary of the northern ties and nationalism of the ACS, the Richmond male auxiliary reorganized in 1828 as the Virginia Colonization Society (VCS), an independent state society that continued to remit its funds to the ACS but took over the job of publicizing the cause in Virginia. While some VCS leaders believed in gradual emancipation, they reasoned that in order to win converts and legislative support in the commonwealth, they needed to focus on the removal of free blacks rather than on encouraging manumissions.[17] The formation of the VCS was the first in a series of events that would expose the fallacy of the notion that women could work on behalf of colonization without addressing the politics of slavery. The ideology of religious benevolence could not protect the ACS from criticism—nor could evangelical womanhood protect colonization women.

On August 21, 1831, in Southampton County, Virginia, a slave preacher named Nat Turner led a revolt that sent shockwaves of fear through the white population of the Old Dominion. Moving from farmhouse to farmhouse, Turner and his band of men left some sixty whites dead and others maimed and terrified in their wake. The Virginia militia and federal troops caught up with the rebels and put down the outbreak on August 23. But they could not restore order and peace—already, furious whites had begun indiscriminately massacring dozens of innocent blacks. Martha Jefferson Randolph, Thomas Jefferson's daughter, spoke for many elite Virginians when she advanced the opinion that Nat Turner's Rebellion was the result of abolitionist agitation— particularly the distribution of David Walker's stirring booklet, *An Appeal to the Colored Citizens of the World* (1829), and William Lloyd Garrison's anti- slavery newspaper the *Liberator* (founded in 1831). The rebellion confirmed Randolph in her belief that "exportation [of the slaves] must be the conse- quence of emancipation." She lamented that raising money for colonization was a "very slow business" and that in response to Turner's rebellion, whites were rendering the conditions of the slaves "more insupportable." [18]

Virginia governor John Floyd put a distinct spin on this conspiracy theory in a letter of November 1831. The "most respectable . . . females," he opined, had paved the way for the Southampton incident by teaching blacks to read and write and by distributing northern religious tracts proclaiming the spiri- tual equality of blacks and whites. Floyd, in effect, pointed up the political implications of evangelical womanhood—the work among slaves that such women as Cocke and Blackford saw as benevolent, Floyd refigured as subver- sive. The notion that women were both unwitting dupes, especially vulnerable to northern heresies, and effective agents of political propaganda would be echoed in the coming years by proslavery Virginians who were unsure about the allegiance of Virginia women to the slave system. Floyd believed that Vir- ginia had to act immediately, during the legislative session of 1831–32, to pre- vent another uprising, and the leading politicians and editors of the common- wealth agreed. As the General Assembly began its deliberations, colonization petitions poured into the General Assembly from around the state, mostly from the Tidewater counties that had large numbers of free black inhabitants. The majority of these memorials called attention to the dangers posed by the presence of free blacks in the commonwealth. [19]

Three of the petitions intended for the legislature had a special agenda—to provide white women's perspectives on the slavery issue. The "Memorial of the Female Citizens of the County of Fluvanna" was drafted in the winter of 1831. While the petitioners did not explicitly identify themselves as coloniza- tionists, the ACS hailed the petition as an example of colonization sentiment and published it in the *African Repository*. It is likely that the authors of the petition were members of the Fluvanna County colonization auxiliary. [20]

The petitioners began by saying that they had never before "had occasion to appeal to the guardians of their country's rights for redress of any national grievance." But, they continued, "a blight now hangs over our national prospects, and a cloud dims the sunshine of domestic peace throughout our State." The "increasing evils of slavery" undermined "domestic discipline." Evoking a scenario meant to strike terror in the hearts of the legislators, the petitioners suggested that as men tended to public affairs, white women were left vulnerable to harm from the slaves. In the name of family and country, they concluded, the legislature must take steps to abolish slavery: "We now conjure you by the sacred charities of kindred, by the solemn obligations of justice, by every consideration of domestic affection and patriotic duty, to nerve every faculty of your minds to the investigation of this important subject—and let not the united voices of your mothers, wives, daughters, and kindred, have sounded in your ears in vain!!"[21] Gradual emancipation was no longer merely the business of churches and voluntary associations. It was the business, indeed the responsibility, of the state.

The "Female Citizens of Fredericksburg" could "not refrain in uniting with their sisters from Fluvanna." So wrote Mary Blackford in a second women's petition to the General Assembly on the subject of gradual emancipation. Blackford, too, reminded the legislature of women's vulnerability—their "defenseless state in the absence of our Lords, in times of apparent peace." Whereas the Fluvanna petitioners had urged the legislature to empathize with white women, Blackford also spoke of the interest of the slaves: "We would not amid a crowd of selfish considerations, forget the interests of an unfortunate people. We would supplicate for them, from your body, such an attention to their welfare and happiness."[22]

Blackford closed her petition with the secular image of women's civic duty in times of crisis. "The example too of the Females of every great people, from the virtuous wife of Coriolanus to our own Revolutionary Matrons teach us," she averred, "that in times of great interest to their Country, women may come forward, meekly and humbly, to do what they can to strengthen the hands, and inspire the hearts of their wise and brave country men." Unlike the Fluvanna petition, Blackford's never made it to the legislature. Blackford admitted that she was too "weak and timid" to circulate the petition. It rests in her family papers, with only one signature, that of her friend Lucy Gray.[23]

The Shenandoah Valley produced a third women's petition, one signed by 215 women. The January 19, 1832, memorial of the women of Augusta County begged the legislature "for the adoption of some measure for the speedy extirpation of slavery from the Commonwealth." The petitioners, many of whom were Presbyterians of Scots-Irish origins, lived in a region of the state in which large-scale plantation slavery had never taken root and reservations about slavery ran high. While the Augusta women did not specifically endorse colonization as a remedy for the slavery problem, they included in their number relatives of male officers of the Augusta colonization auxiliary. The petition was presented to the legislature by delegate John McCue, a Presbyterian minister and an avid colonizationist.[24]

Like that of the Fluvanna women, the Augusta appeal was animated by fear of, not empathy for, slaves—it bade the legislature to remember "the late slaughter of our sisters and little ones, in certain parts of our land," an event that the women suspected was part of a larger plot. The petitioners evoked the specter of their destruction at the hands of the "bloody monster" that lived at their "own hearths." They attested that they would rather do without slave labor than live with those hardships "we now endure in providing for and ruling the faithless beings who are subjected to us."[25]

In a remarkable passage, the petitioners laid out their interpretation of the relation between the private and public spheres: "We are no political economists; but our domestic employments, our engagements, in rearing up the children of our husbands & brothers, our intimate concern with the intercourse & prosperity of society; we presume, cannot but inform us of the great & elementary principles of that important science. Indeed it is impossible that that science can have any other basis than the principles that are constantly developing themselves to us in our domestic relations. What is a nation but a family upon a large scale?"[26] Rather than advancing the notion that woman's sphere operated according to rules and values all its own, the women of Augusta portrayed the domestic sphere as a microcosm of the public one. Like the Fluvanna and Fredericksburg petitions, the Augusta memorial reminded men of their patriotic duty. "We implore you," it concluded, "by our female virtues, by the patriotism which animates and grows in our bosoms . . . not to let the power with which you are invested lie dormant. . . . This we pray and in duty bound will ever pray."[27]

Taken together, the three petitions shed light on how the events of August 1831 had transformed the public discourse over slavery. While Blackford and her counterparts in Fluvanna and Augusta came at the slavery issue from different angles, the three petitions used similar language to justify political intervention by women. One of the effects of Turner's Revolt, the petitioners implied, was to politicize domestic life. The Fluvanna and Augusta women challenged the validity of the domestic metaphor for slavery—that slaves were obedient members of the patriarchal household—and argued instead that blacks and whites lived in a state of protracted domestic warfare. Without help from the legislature, the memorials suggested, women simply could not fulfill their mandate of preserving domestic harmony. Blackford's memorial, alone among the three, recognized that slaves were the true victims of domestic warfare between blacks and whites.

The Augusta and Fluvanna petitions, like other antislavery petitions, were taken into consideration by the special legislative committee charged with recommending a course of action to the General Assembly. After weeks of deliberation, the select committee on slavery decided that it was inexpedient for the legislature to take any measures to dismantle the slave system. Historian Alison Goodyear Freehling has convincingly argued that the 1831–32 slavery debate, rather than representing the triumph of proslavery forces in Virginia, was rather another chapter in the "perennial political quest for a 'middle ground' between slaveholding and non-slaveholding interests." While the legislature rejected immediate emancipation, a procolonization majority, including many conservatives, endorsed—but took no steps to implement—gradual emancipation.[28]

Freehling's contention that the 1832 legislative session did not put an end to meaningful debate over slavery in Virginia is borne out by the testimony of women. Rather than being discouraged by the legislature's pronouncements, colonization women redoubled their efforts to promote the cause. In July of 1832, sixty women in Albemarle County formed a women's auxiliary society to the ACS. Its secretary, Susan Terrell, evinced her belief that the society would soon have "every lady in the county" and boasted that its efforts had won the approval of "some of our best men." The Albemarle auxiliary raised five hundred dollars in 1832; women's societies in Louisa County, Warrenton, and Richmond likewise made healthy remittances to the ACS that year.[29]

Blackford's Fredericksburg society continued to be the best publicized women's auxiliary in the state. In order to dispel the "mists of ignorance and prejudice" surrounding the colonization cause, Blackford penned an annual report for her society and had it published as a broadside. The report, which also appeared in the Methodist *Christian Sentinel*, urged Blackford's sisters throughout the state to come forward and aid in the work of "this most important charity." Blackford conceded that some prejudices still existed against women who were active in charities, particularly in colonization saying it "divides public sentiment, and is, in some respects, a political question." But she had this to say to opponents of female activism: " . . . we would ask whether, because the scheme of Colonization involves ultimate political interests, our sex is to be forever precluded from any agency in its promotion? . . . The same course of reasoning would go to exclude female agency from the promotion of the Sunday School, the Missionary, or the Bible cause—for who will pretend to say that each of these schemes of amelioration is not pregnant with the highest consequences to the peace and prosperity of the State[?]"[30] Blackford turned the popular argument that colonization was like other benevolent enterprises, and therefore not political, on its head. Because religious benevolent societies, like the colonization society, involved "ultimate political interests," it was wrong to exclude women from either sort of enterprise.

While she worked in public to promote her auxiliary, principally by distributing literature to her neighbors, Blackford undertook, in the fall of 1832, a new project: a private journal entitled "Notes Illustrative of the Wrongs of Slavery." Her preface states that the "notes" constitute a challenge to those who maintain "that Slavery is in accordance with the will of God." The entries that follow the preface are anecdotes about the horrors of slavery—not of "isolated instances of wrong and oppression but daily occurrences so common as scarcely to excite remark." What render Blackford's observations into an analytical indictment of the system are the themes that tie them together: the notion that the necessary setting for the exercise of Christian virtue is a republic in which everyone's fundamental rights are protected by law; that slavery "hardens the heart" to human suffering; and that blacks have the same innate capacity for "tender feelings" as whites.[31]

By denying blacks the protection of the law, Blackford argued, the institution of slavery undermined the exercise of virtue by whites and blacks alike. She inveighed against the measures that prohibited blacks from holding religious assemblies or learning to read and write. To illustrate the ill effects of such laws, she described a horrible scene in which a group of slaves who attended a Baptist meeting in Hanover County were "all whipped, old and young, Men & women," by an armed patrol. Nor did she shy away from the subject of sexual abuse. Black women, she understood, were the special victims of a system in which "the conjugal tie can be broken at the will of the Master at any time." Telling the story of a "wretched Mother" who had been impregnated and then abandoned and was left destitute by a slave trader, Blackford noted that black women often became "the prey of the brutal lust of their oppressors." "Mercy is not in man when interest and power unite in drawing him from it," Blackford concluded from observing the intractable racism of her neighbors.[32]

Blackford's journal is both a unique document, without counterpart in southern antislavery literature, and an embodiment of the limitations of and contradictions in the colonization movement. With the exception of the abolitionist publications of South Carolina's exiled Grimké sisters, Blackford's

journal is the most thoroughgoing attack on slavery penned by a white southern woman in the antebellum era. First and foremost a plea for empathy, it
implores the reader to conjure the "nameless horrors" of being deprived of
one's rights as a human being. It shares a number of themes—the prevalence
of sexual exploitation, the breakup of families, the disregard of marriage ties,
the suffering of mothers and children—with slave narratives produced by
women. The narrative of Betheny Veney, who had been a slave in Virginia,
poignantly put into words a sentiment that Blackford struggled to express:
"hearts that love are much the same in bond or free, in white or black." [33]

But for all the merits of her analysis, there were distinct limits to Blackford's
powers of empathy. Like other colonizationists, she did not reckon among
blacks' rights the right to live in freedom in their native country, nor did she
imagine that blacks and whites could coexist as equals. Having been kept in
"profound ignorance" by whites, she argued, blacks were "not prepared" for
immediate emancipation and full participation in the American republic.
Only in Liberia would they be safe from prejudice and united in communities
of common interest. There, she noted in a letter to Ralph Gurley, "the delightful consciousness of freedom and equal rights may, like a sculptor's tools,
bring forth hidden qualities" in the race. Moreover, Blackford, unlike white
and black abolitionists, seemed reluctant to acknowledge white women's complicity in the brutal enforcement of the slave system. "Slaveholding ladies,"
ex-slave Austin Stewart of Prince William County, Virginia, wrote in his memoirs, not only looked on the punishment of bondspeople "with approbation"
but often used "the lash and cowhide themselves, on the backs of their own
slaves, and that too on those of their own sex!" Blackford surely must have
known of such instances, yet she reserved her harshest criticisms for white
men, slave traders in particular. Finally, like so many other southern colonizationists who saw fit to emancipate some—but not all—of their slaves,
Blackford herself relied on the labor of slaves. Believing that his chronically
infirm wife needed help tending to the couple's six children, William Blackford in 1846 bought a slave girl named Peggy to serve as a "mammy." In spite
of Mary's "abhorrence of slavery," the Blackfords kept Peggy in bondage
throughout the antebellum period; the family assumed, conveniently, that the
affection they held for "Ma'm Peggy" was mutual. [34]

Isolated in an increasingly hostile proslavery environment, Blackford remained steadfast in the belief that the American Colonization Society, while it
claimed only to "send free people of color by *their own consent* to Liberia,"
was "gradually preparing a Country for the whole unfortunate race when Slavery shall be abolished." Unfortunately for her and other like-minded coloni-

zationists, the doctrine of gradual emancipation came under withering attack in the early 1830s. In the minds of abolitionists, the antislavery credentials of such southern slaveholders as Blackford were highly suspect. William Lloyd Garrison's "Thoughts on African Colonization" (1832) and his journal the *Liberator* rejected the notion that colonization was "benevolent," and he argued instead that the ACS was a slaveholders' tool, meant to undermine support for immediate emancipation. Moreover, Garrison held that free blacks had vehemently rejected the colonization movement. He produced as evidence nineteen proclamations by free blacks in northern cities expressing opposition to the ACS.[35]

Indeed, as historian Marie Tyler-McGraw has demonstrated, the changing composition of the Liberian emigrant pool signaled free blacks' growing unwillingness to migrate: While the majority of emigrants in the 1820s were free black families, by the early 1830s the majority were manumitted slaves from large estates. Free blacks had come to believe that "colonization was less an opportunity presented to them than a judgment placed upon them." Most damaging to the cause of emigration in Virginia, Tyler-McGraw argues, were the grim reports of economic hardship, appalling death rates, and internecine warfare that black emigrants, such as Richmonders Edward and Helen Lewis, brought back from Liberia.[36]

By the mid-1830s, white women were playing a prominent role in the abolitionist critique of colonization. In 1836, the Grimké sisters launched a speaking tour of antislavery societies in New England and New York, giving women unprecedented visibility in the abolition movement. A national convention of antislavery women met in New York in 1837, initiating a petition drive to convince Congress of the need for immediate abolition. The southern press took notice of these activities, branding them as subversive and unfeminine. Angelina Grimke specifically targeted southern women in her 1836 "Appeal to the Christian Women of the South." She argued that Christian women should act as "instruments of reform" by advancing the antislavery cause as a "matter of *morals* and *religion*, not of expediency or politics." To those, like Blackford, who believed that immediate emancipation without colonization would leave blacks vulnerable to prejudice and lacking in resources, Grimke replied that "duty is ours and events are God's." To those who feared that such bold actions would alienate them from their communities, Grimke responded that women must find the moral courage to endure persecution. In later works, Grimke would call the ACS an "EXPATRIATION Society" that hid the "monster of prejudice" behind the "mantle of benevolence."[37]

Even as abolitionists attacked colonization and urged southern women to abandon it, Thomas Dew, a Virginia professor, dealt colonization a crippling blow from the other end of the political spectrum. Dew's 1832 essay, *Review of the Debate in the Virginia Legislature of 1831 and 1832*, portrayed colonization as an abolitionist plot, and a "totally impracticable" one at that. Because Liberia was a failure, Dew averred, manumitted blacks would stay in Virginia, posing a threat not only to slaveholders but to nonslaveholding whites as well. Dew devoted a section of his essay to the "influence of Slavery on the female sex." He constructed what would become a popular argument among proslavery theorists—that white women benefitted from the institution of slavery, for the labor of the slave was a substitute for that of the woman. Dew not only addressed slavery's impact on white women but also women's attitudes toward slavery. Southern women, Dew lamented, did not seem to recognize that slavery was responsible for their "elevation" in society. Instead, filled with "benevolence and philanthropy" and "fine feelings unchecked by considerations of interest or calculations of remote consequences," women were inclined "to embrace with eagerness even the wildest and most destructive schemes of emancipation." Women's influence was powerful and would be exercised either for the "weal or woe" of southern society. Southern men, Dew cautioned, should take an interest in the moral and intellectual development of "*her* in whose career we feel so deep an interest."[38]

Colonizationists were slow to join the battle against their foes. In late 1832, at Gurley's request, Jesse Burton Harrison of Lynchburg penned a response to Thomas Dew, denying that there was any connection between colonization and abolition. All over Virginia, colonizationists repudiated abolition. At its 1833 annual meeting, for example, the secretary of the Lynchburg Colonization Society proclaimed that like Bible, missionary, and education societies, the ACS was benevolent, intent on "snatching from the depths of the most cheerless and hopeless poverty a class of beings, who . . . are proverbially heedless of the future." An 1833 editorial in the *Christian Sentinel* claimed that Christians should not "engage in the political controversies which may arise out of the subject of slavery as existing in our country." But to support colonization was acceptable because "it meddles with no State policy . . . but receives all free colored persons who may offer themselves voluntarily to emigrate to Africa." Christians, the editor suggested, should resist the attempts of "designing and interested individuals" to make colonization a "political question."[39]

Unfortunately for those who sought to cloak colonization in the mantle of benevolence, the "designing individuals" who saw colonization as a "political question" included not only the movement's critics but also some of its most prominent supporters. By the mid-1830s, northern colonization societies, such as those in New York and Philadelphia, were trying to increase public support for the cause by arguing that colonization principles did indeed embrace emancipation. Southern state societies, such as the VCS, countered with bitterly sectional rhetoric in which colonization became a weapon in the South's battle against northern aggression. At the seventh annual meeting of the VCS in 1838, Henry Wise denounced the abolitionists for trying to "demolish all social relations." No longer was there room in the VCS for those who hoped colonization was a wedge to general emancipation—while abolitionists favored "Philanthropy to the SLAVE!," colonizationists favored "Friendship to the SLAVEHOLDER." [40]

On the subject of white women's part in the slavery controversy, men colonizationists in the South sent out mixed messages. The notion that women were easy prey for the abolitionists had its share of advocates. In his speech at the state society's 1838 annual meeting, VCS president John Tyler fumed that the abolitionists "seek to enlist woman—she who was placed upon the earth, as the rainbow in the heavens, as a sign that the tempest of the passions should subside. Woman is made an instrument to expel us from the paradise of union in which we dwell." [41]

What part did Virginia's white women take in the debate over colonization and abolition? Unwilling to disavow the goal of philanthropy toward the slave or to embrace immediate emancipation, Virginia's staunchest women colonizationists adopted a new tack in the mid-1830s, focusing their energy on the promotion of female education in Liberia. Such a strategy had many merits— it allowed Virginia women to build bridges to their counterparts in other states, while at the same time distancing them from the radical tactics of women abolitionists. Blackford announced in the *African Repository* in 1834 that her auxiliary was reconstituting itself as the Female African Education Society; "it would seem to us that it is peculiarly befitting our sex to be thus engaged," she noted. After searching fruitlessly for an appropriate outlet for its funds, Blackford's group began in 1837 to support a girls' academy run by Presbyterian missionaries in the Maryland colony, Cape Palmas. In its third annual report, Blackford's society reemphasized the missionary aspect of colonization: "We would make it our main object to promote the knowledge of God." [42]

The Richmond and Manchester women's auxiliary adopted a similar strategy. In order to reassure the public of the benevolence of their aims, the Richmond women changed the name of their auxiliary in 1834 to the Ladies Society for Promoting Female Education in the Colony of Liberia. The actions of the

Fredericksburg and Richmond auxiliaries reflect a national trend. Margaret Mercer, who served as a teacher at girls' academies in Essex County, Virginia, and then in Cedar Park, Maryland, devoted the proceeds of her Cedar Park Liberian Society to promoting the founding of a high school in Liberia. Female education societies were formed in such places as Louisville, Kentucky, New York City, and Philadelphia; the Richmond and Philadelphia enterprises cooperated closely. Such efforts won the hearty approbation of men leaders of the ACS, who saw in them a refutation of the abolitionist charge that colonizationists cared nothing for the fate of those who emigrated.[43]

As promising as it may have seemed however, women colonizationists' change of tack ultimately did not revive their beleaguered movement. The schools sponsored by women proved prohibitively expensive to maintain. "The Society is now in great want of funds," the Richmond society's 1837 annual report declared. "Without them our school must suffer, and our benevolent operations must remain stationary or be curtailed." Apparently these appeals fell on deaf ears—the auxiliary's 1838 annual report declared that its orphan school was "languishing." Nor ultimately could Virginia's colonization women reverse the political trends in their home state. All over the commonwealth, the fate of gradual decline befell women's auxiliaries in the 1830s. The Albemarle auxiliary, described in the *African Repository* in 1833 as a "flourishing institution," was, by 1836, in trouble. Susan Terrell, its secretary, attributed the decline in receipts to northern agitation: "Many of [the auxiliary's] members since the great Abolition stir of the North have become apparently indifferent while a portion are more zealous in the cause than ever." In the heart of the Shenandoah Valley, too, colonization sentiment among women was evaporating. The VCS mounted an unsuccessful petition drive for legislative aid in 1837. Only 35 signed a colonization petition of February 10, 1837, from the citizens of Rockingham and Augusta counties—an alarmingly small number compared to the 215 women who had signed the 1832 antislavery petition from Augusta.[44]

In what appears to have been a last ditch effort to improve the prospects of the cause, women in the Richmond area formed the Female Colonization Society of Virginia (FCS) in 1840. Its eight officers represented each of the major churches in Richmond and Manchester. The society was designed to be the medium through which Virginia women's donations were forwarded to the ACS. "[W]e hope that not only will the Ladies of every city, town and village in Virginia, form Societies auxiliary to the State Society," the managers ambitiously declared, "but that in every State of the Union, the ladies will go and do likewise." As the Richmond women's auxiliary had more than a decade earlier, the new women's society described colonization as a missionary scheme. And it passed a resolution requesting that the editors of religious newspapers publish its constitution and circular. The Female Colonization Society received brief mentions in an 1841 issue of the *African Repository* and in the 1845 ACS annual report. But after 1845, it disappears from the historical record.[45]

Whether the FCS disbanded or continued to carry out its mission in obscurity is unclear. Over the course of the 1840s, references to southern colonization auxiliaries, men's and women's, dwindled not only in ACS publications but also in the religious newspapers that had helped to promote colonization in its heyday. The declining visibility of southern colonizationists in the press reflects the southern evangelical retreat from politics in the wake of the denominational schisms in the Presbyterian, Methodist, and Baptist churches. Despite the fact that the ACS continued to have some powerful allies among Virginia's clergymen, such as Presbyterian William Henry Ruffner and Methodists William A. Smith and Charles A. Davis, donations from churches, especially Methodist and Baptist congregations, slowed to a trickle in the 1840s.[46]

Historian Mitchell Snay has demonstrated that southern clergymen perceived in abolitionism "a threat to traditional boundaries between religion and politics"; as that threat became more potent, finally culminating in the schisms, clergymen strove to define slavery as a political question, outside the bounds of religion.[47] The colonization movement defied clear categorization, for it retained its missionary element long after it became the center of political controversy. Rather than writing off colonization altogether, evangelical newspapers in Virginia adopted a narrower view of the movement than before, and reported on the progress of missions in Liberia rather than on the progress of the cause in the South. Evangelical rhetoric divorced the goal of gradual emancipation from the goal of Christianizing Africa.[48]

Popular perceptions of domestic missions to slaves underwent a concomitant shift. Once embraced by critics of slavery as a means of preparing slaves for "temporal and eternal freedom," domestic missions to slaves came to be seen in the 1840s and 1850s as means for inculcating subservience in blacks and thereby buttressing the slave system. Proslavery apologists pointed to such missions as evidence of the "positive good" slavery brought to slaves.[49]

Rather than publicizing the activities of those southern women who remained faithful to the cause of gradual emancipation, and therefore raising the thorny issue of whether colonization activism was still appropriate for women, religious newspapers opted instead to ignore women. In place of the former consensus that women should reform the slave system through their benevolent influence, a new consensus gradually emerged. Women's religious duty was to minister to the slaves—but their political duty was to defend slavery and the southern social order.

By 1850, the American Colonization Society was firmly under the control of a northern-dominated board of directors, while the Virginia Colonization Society, by contrast, was an unabashedly proslavery organization. Neither organization flourished. Unfavorable reports from Liberia discouraged emigration. An economic recovery made whites less inclined to urge emigration and more inclined to hold on to or sell valuable slave property. Most important, the rise of sectional tensions increased public hostility to any reform movement that smacked of northern "interference" in southern affairs.[50]

Mary Blackford and Anne Rice testified to the isolation of those who continued to see colonization as a middle ground between North and South. In an 1856 letter to Gurley, Blackford lamented the growth of proslavery sectionalism in Virginia. "It has become a reproach to advocate human liberty, and I hear statements so high handed and oppressive, that I can hardly believe I live in a free government," she confided. Rice, in an 1857 letter to ACS secretary Rev. William McLain, offered a critique of the radicals on either side of the slavery issue—"I think both sides go too far & are on extremes and such as I know will not receive any information but what suits their own views." By 1859, she was so sensitive about her antislavery views that she apologized even to her friend and ally Gurley. After declaring that "our good, & wise, & pious now seem to set down content, with consciences quite relieved that [slavery] is the very best state for the coloured race," she excused herself for writing so indiscreetly on the subject.[51]

Ironically, the most powerful testimony to the chilling effect sectionalism had on southern women's efforts to reform slavery comes from a woman who was an avowed defender of the institution, Margaret Douglass. Douglass, a longtime resident of South Carolina, moved to Norfolk, Virginia, in 1852. After observing women in Norfolk's Episcopalian Christ Church conducting a Sunday school for black children, Douglass established a school of her own. On May 9, 1853, eleven months after her school had opened, Douglass was arrested and charged with the crime of teaching free black children to read. In the court case that ensued, Douglass mounted her own defense, claiming that if she were guilty of a crime, so too were the women of Christ Church, whose actions she had emulated. Douglass further argued that she was no abolitionist but a loyal southerner, who thought that slaves should be instructed in religion "that they may know their duties to their master." Neither tactic worked.

Douglass was convicted and sentenced to a month in jail. After serving her term, she moved to Philadelphia and wrote a memoir of her experiences.[52]

The public response to Douglass's case reveals how the concept of Evangelical womanhood had been politicized. When Douglass claimed to "glory in works of benevolence and charity to a race down-trodden," the *Southern Argus* of Norfolk fumed that she aroused the "righteous indignation" of the community. Abolitionist papers, by contrast, hailed Douglass as a heroine. The *Liberator*, noting that a Quaker woman in Norfolk had delivered a sermon on Douglass's behalf while Douglass was in jail, went so far as to claim that "the women are a great trouble to our Norfolk neighbors. If they want peace, they must expel all Christian women . . . from the city."[53]

According to her biographers, Douglass paid the price for being an outsider in a community that was "increasingly in a panic about secret enemies." While they saw the teaching activities of the elite ladies of Christ Church as harmless, Norfolk residents saw the work of Douglass, a lower middle-class woman who made little effort to cultivate friendly relations with her white neighbors, as threatening to the social order. Douglass's own testimony only heightened the perception that she was an outside agitator—her professions of loyalty to the South were overshadowed by her critique of white southern men, whom she accused of harboring "criminal passions" for slave women.[54]

Douglass's critique of slaveholders flew in the face of the growing consensus among white Virginians that the slave system did not need reforming, let alone dismantling. Embedded in the "positive good" view of slavery was the notion that white women were the special beneficiaries, not the victims, of slavery. In the 1850s, proslavery apologists, such as George Fitzhugh and Alfred Taylor Bledsoe, systematically constructed an argument that white southern women were naturally disposed to defend, rather than oppose, slavery. Fitzhugh, for example, conceded the moral superiority of women to men—of *southern* women, that is; he averred that the "judgment of women is far superior to that of men." But in Fitzhugh's opinion, southern women's moral refinement was a product of the institution of slavery, and their superior perceptions led them to support, unequivocally, the peculiar institution.[55]

Fitzhugh's contention received support from a new generation of women authors in Virginia who took it upon themselves to prove that masters and mistresses were humane and well-meaning. Two defenders of slavery, Mary Eastman and Julia Gardiner Tyler, endorsed the missionary aspect of colonization in their writings even as they defended the morality of slaveholders and slavery. Eastman's *Aunt Phillis's Cabin; or, Southern Life As It Is* (1852) was the first—and generally considered the best—fictional proslavery response to

Harriet Beecher Stowe's *Uncle Tom's Cabin*. Eastman editorialized on behalf of the colonization cause: "Good men assist in colonizing [ex-slaves], and the Creator may thus intend to Christianize benighted Africa." But she coupled that endorsement with proslavery rhetoric typical of the time. The Bible and the historical record alike sanctioned slavery, Eastman argued, proceeding from the curse of Ham, to the historical examples of Egypt and Rome, to Jesus's tacit acceptance of the institution, to the experience of the Revolutionary forefathers and -mothers, who shed their lifeblood to defend the South's social system. In Eastman's fictional portrayal of antebellum Virginia, white slave owners were benign and genteel and slaves docile and content.[56]

Julia Gardiner Tyler, the wife of ex-president John Tyler, published her own defense of slavery, "To the Duchess of Sutherland and Ladies of England," in February of 1853. Tyler saw colonization as the most efficacious means to deal with the growing free black population. Colonizationists sought to "retribute the wrongs done by England to Africa, by returning civilization for barbarity—Christianity for idolatry." In response to English abolitionists who had embraced Harriet Beecher Stowe's view of the South, Tyler argued that southerners were trying to do right by their slaves; in her opinion, most slave owners provided for the religious instruction and the material comfort of the slaves.[57]

Ironically, Stowe herself advocated colonization in *Uncle Tom's Cabin*. But Eastman's and Tyler's endorsement of the cause had a very different meaning than Stowe's. Unlike Stowe (and Blackford, for that matter, a rare southern fan of *Uncle Tom's Cabin*), Eastman and Tyler were unwilling to concede that slavery was inherently sinful or that it engendered the widespread abuse of blacks by whites. For them, colonization represented not a catalyst to the abolition of slavery but an alternative to it.[58]

The ascendancy of the positive good justification for slavery did not, however, completely lay to rest southern anxieties about the lingering impact of women's "benevolence" on the slave system. In the late 1850s, as in the 1830s, some prominent defenders of slavery saw "secret enemies" not only in such outsiders as Margaret Douglass but in Virginia's white female population. An 1859 letter from southern nationalist Edmund Ruffin to the *South* (Richmond), a states'-rights paper, portrayed women as especially vulnerable to antislavery heresy: "The teachings and arguments of the agents & mouthpieces of the [Colonization] Society, and their efforts have mainly operated on morbidly tender consciences and weak minds of benevolent men, and women more especially, to induce them to emancipate their slaves." Roger Pryor, editor of the *South*, agreed that southern security depended on the inculcation of a *"proper sentiment"* on the slavery question among women. "If, especially, the mothers of the Southern country were all sound on the question," he suggested, "there would be less occasion for combined effort on the part of our citizens to put down the insolent schemes" of the abolitionists.[59]

Alexander H. Sands, a lawyer who later became a Baptist minister, echoed Pryor in his commencement address at the 1859 graduation ceremony of the Hollins Female Institute in Richmond. Sands called on proslavery women to educate their misinformed sisters in order "to correct a false sentiment, which I fear is already too prevalent among females, that the institution is wrong. It is not wrong . . . and our educated women ought to know it that they may imbue their children with it and educate in the truest and best method a popular sentiment in conformity to right reason and to the word of the Living God."[60]

Whether or not "false sentiment" on slavery was more prevalent among southern women than among men, we will never know with certainty. But the fact that proslavery ideologues feared, as late as 1859, that there was an affinity between white southern women and the antislavery cause is surely significant. For it serves as a potent testimony, more potent perhaps than the encomiums of Ralph Gurley, John Holt Rice, and other champions of the ACS, to the influence of such evangelical women as Mary Blackford and Anne Rice on Virginia's political culture. ACS ideology continued to resonate with them long after sectional tensions had undermined support for colonization. The ACS had defined a host of activities, from education to manumission, as philanthropy, and had defined philanthropy as the special province of women. As the benevolent consensus on slavery broke down, so too, this essay has argued, did the fragile national consensus on the meaning of evangelical womanhood. In the 1820s, evangelicals in the North and South could agree that Christian women should demonstrate their usefulness through benevolent acts. By the 1850s, they could no longer agree on what constituted benevolence and what treason.

NOTES

1. Ralph Randolph Gurley, *Life of Jehndi Ashmun, Late Colonial Agent in Liberia* (Washington, D.C.: James C. Dunn, 1835), 110.

2. John Kuykendall, *Southern Enterprize: The Work of National Evangelical Societies in the Antebellum South* (Westport, Conn.: Greenwood Press, 1982), 4–5.

3. See, for example, Anne Boylan, *Sunday School: The Formation of an American Institution 1790–1880* (New Haven: Yale University Press, 1988), 31; C. C. Pearson and J. Edwin Hendricks, *Liquor and Anti-Liquor in Virginia 1619–1919* (Durham, N.C.: Duke University Press, 1967);

Twenty-Fourth Annual Report of the Bible Society of Virginia (Richmond, Va.: Office of the Southern Churchman, 1837), 11–12; *Third Annual Report of the Virginia Tract Society, With the Proceedings of the Annual Meeting, Held in the City of Richmond, April 7, 1837* (Richmond, Va.: William MacFarlane, 1837), 20.

4. Donald Mathews, *Religion in the Old South* (Chicago: University of Chicago Press, 1977), 101–16.

5. Kuykendall's *Southern Enterprize* describes the toll sectionalism took on the American Bible Society, American Tract Society, American Education Society, American Sunday School Union, and American Home Missionary Society. See also Anne Loveland, *Southern Evangelicals and the Social Order, 1800–1860* (Baton Rouge: Louisiana State University Press, 1980), and Richard J. Carwadine, *Evangelicals and Politics in Antebellum America* (New Haven: Yale University Press, 1993). On the decline of the temperance movement in the South, see Pearson and Hendricks, *Liquor and Anti-Liquor in Virginia.* For a general history of the colonization movement, see P. J. Staunderaus, *The African Colonization Movement, 1816–1865* (New York: Columbia University Press, 1961).

6. This debate has focused on Mary Boykin Chesnut of South Carolina, who, in her extensive Civil War diary, described slavery as a "monstrous system," lamenting that it made white women and slaves alike victims of the absolute power of white men. Anne Firor Scott argued in her seminal *The Southern Lady* (1970) that Chesnut's lament was but one of many manifestations of white women's discontent with and even opposition to the system of slavery. More recently, Elizabeth Fox-Genovese has made the case that Chesnut was no abolitionist: Chesnut criticized the abuses of the system of slavery, particularly miscegenation, and not the system itself. According to Fox-Genovese, even such mild critics of slavery as Chesnut were "few and far between" in the antebellum South; the vast majority of slaveholding women understood that they were beneficiaries and not victims of slavery. Anne Firor Scott, *The Southern Lady: From Pedestal to Politics, 1830–1930* (Chicago: University of Chicago Press, 1970), 46–61; Elizabeth Fox-Genovese, *Within the Plantation Household: Black and White Women of the Old South* (Chapel Hill: University of North Carolina Press, 1988), 334–71.

7. Lori Ginzberg demonstrates that moral reformers in the North made similar distinctions between the "benevolent" and the "political." *Women and the Work of Benevolence: Morality, Politics, and Class in the Nineteenth-Century United States* (New Haven: Yale University Press, 1990), 13–15, 65–67.

8. Louis Weeks III, "John Holt Rice and the American Colonization Society," *Journal of Presbyterian History* 46 (March 1968): 26–41; John H. Rice, "Short Discourses for Families [To Young Women.]," *Virginia Evangelical and Literary Magazine* 2 (April 1819): 171–74; Rice, "Extract from Camelford's Letter No. 5," *Virginia Evangelical and Literary Magazine* 3 (February 1820): 91.

9. Douglas Egerton, "'Its Origin Is Not a Little Curious': A New Look at the American Colonization Society," *Journal of the Early Republic* 5 (Winter 1985): 463–67; *Seventh Annual Report of the American Society for Colonizing the Free People of Colour of the United States* (Washington, D.C.: James C. Dunn, 1824), 7. For colonization publicity in the religious press, see for example,

Christian Sentinel (Richmond), July 13, 1832; *Southern Churchman* (Richmond), April 15, 1836; *Religious Herald* (Richmond), December 12, 1839. On black missionaries, see William A. Poe, "Lott Cary: Man of Purchased Freedom," *Church History* 39 (March 1970): 50–56.

10. Alison Goodyear Freehling, *Drift toward Dissolution: The Virginia Slavery Debate of 1831–1832* (Baton Rouge: Louisiana State University Press, 1982), 118–21; Henry Clay, *An Address Delivered to the Colonization Society of Kentucky* (Lexington, Ky.: American Colonization Society, 1829), 18.

11. On individual bequests to the ACS, see *African Repository* 1 (December 1825): 343; *African Repository* 2 (September 1826): 220; *African Repository* 2 (December 1826): 324. On the Charlottesville society, *African Repository* 6 (May 1830): 87–88. On northern antislavery fairs, see, for example, Ginzberg, *Women and the Work of Benevolence*, 45–47.

12. Mary Virginia Terhune [Marion Harland], *Marion Harland's Autobiography* (New York: Harper & Brothers, 1910), 99–101.

13. Louis Gimelli, "Louisa Maxwell Cocke: An Evangelical Plantation Mistress in the Antebellum South," *Journal of the Early Republic* 9 (spring 1989): 39, 59–64; *African Repository* 3 (July 1827): 159; Louisa Cocke Diary, January 27, 1825, Manuscripts Department, Alderman Library, University of Virginia, Charlottesville (UVA); Bell I. Wiley, ed., *Slaves No More: Letters from Liberia, 1833–1869* (Lexington: University of Kentucky Press, 1980), 35.

14. Charles Andrews, *Memoir of Mrs. Ann R. Page* (New York: Protestant Episcopal Society for the Promotion of Evangelical Knowledge, 1856), 24–27, 36, 45–46; Ann R. Page to Mary Lee (Fitzhugh) Custis, n.d., Mary Lee (Fitzhugh) Custis Papers, Virginia Historical Society, Richmond (VHS); Wiley, *Slaves No More*, 100.

15. L. Minor Blackford, *Mine Eyes Have Seen the Glory: The Story of a Virginia Lady, Mary Berkeley Minor Blackford, 1802–1896, Who Taught Her Sons to Hate Slavery and to Love the Union* (Cambridge: Harvard University Press, 1954), 20; Mrs. E. F. Hening, *History of the African Mission of the Protestant Episcopal Church in the United States* (New York: Stanford and Swords, 1850), 123; William Blackford to Ralph Gurley, October 21, 1829, American Colonization Society (ACS) Papers, Library of Congress, Washington, D.C. (LC); Wiley, ed., *Slaves No More*, 15.

16. On the Fredericksburg auxiliary, see *African Repository* 6 (May 1830): 87–88; Mary Blackford to Ralph Gurley, May 12, 1829, ACS Papers, LC. On the Richmond auxiliary, *African Repository* 5 (February 1830): 374–75.

17. Freehling, *Drift toward Dissolution* 119–21; P. J. Staudenraus, *The African Colonization Movement, 1816–1865* (New York: Columbia University Press, 1961), 173–78.

18. Carl Degler, *The Other South: Southern Dissenters in the Nineteenth Century* (Boston: Northeastern University Press, 1982), 13; William W. Freehling, *The Road to Disunion: Secessionists at Bay, 1776–1854*, vol. 1 (New York: Oxford University Press, 1990), 178–82; Ira Berlin, *Slaves without Masters: The Free Negro in the Antebellum South* (New York: New Press, 1974), 188; Martha Jefferson Randolph to Joseph Coolidge Jr., October 27, 1831, Edgehill-Randolph Papers, UVA.

19. A. G. Freehling, *Drift toward Dissolution*, 83, 121–25.

20. On the format and functions of legislative petitions, see Robert Bailey, *Popular Influence upon Public Policy: Petitioning in Eighteenth-Century Virginia* (Westport, Conn.: Greenwood

Press, 1979), 9–19, 27–32. The Fluvanna petition is published in the *African Repository* 7 (December 1831): 310–12.

21. *African Repository* 7(December 1831): 310–12.

22. Mary Blackford, "The Memorial of the Female Citizens of Fredericksburg," c. 1831, Blackford Family Papers, Southern Historical Collection, University of North Carolina, Chapel Hill (UNC).

23. Ibid.; Suzanne Lebsock, *"A Share of Honour": Virginia Women, 1600–1945* (Richmond, Va.: Virginia Women's Cultural History Project, 1984), 77.

24. Legislative Petitions, Augusta County, January 19, 1832, LV; Tom Blair, "The Southern Dilemma: The Augusta-Rockingham Area as a Mirror to Virginia's Struggle over Slavery in the 1830s," *Augusta Historical Bulletin* 21 (fall 1985): 73–78. Women relatives of Conrad Speece, John McCue, Samuel Gilkeson and William Kinney, all Augusta auxiliary officers, were among the signatories of the petition. *African Repository* 7 (June 1831): 124; John Vogt and T. William Kethley Jr., *Augusta County Marriages, 1748–1850* (Athens, Ga.: Iberian Publishing Company, 1986).

25. Augusta Petition, January 19, 1832, LV.

26. Ibid.

27. Ibid.

28. A. G. Freehling, *Drift toward Dissolution*, 180–85.

29. Susan Terrell to Ralph Gurley, July 24, 1832, ACS Papers, LC; *African Repository* 8 (July 1832): 150; *African Repository* 8 (January 1833): 350.

30. "Report of the Board of Managers of the Fredericksburg and Falmouth Female Auxiliary Colonization Society" (broadside appended to letter), Mary Blackford to Ralph Gurley, May 1832, ACS Papers, LC; *Christian Sentinel* (Richmond, Va.), June 22, 1832; Patricia Hickin, *Antislavery in Virginia, 1832–1860* (Ann Arbor, Mich.: University Microfilms, 1979), 268–70.

31. Blackford made sporadic entries in this journal from 1832 to 1866. Blackford, "Notes Illustrative of the Wrongs of Slavery," unpublished typescript, preface, p. 1; September 2, 1832, pp. 3–4, Blackford Family Papers, UVA.

32. Blackford, "Notes," September 2, 1832, p. 3–5; 1833, p. 6; February 20, 1836, p. 15–16.

33. Blackford, "Notes," February 29, 1833, p. 10; Betheny Veney, *The Narrative of Betheny Veney: A Slave Woman* (Worcester, Mass.: Press of George H. Ellis, 1889), 19.

34. Blackford, "Notes," 1866, p. 20; Mary Blackford to Ralph Gurley, October 12, 1832, ACS Papers, LC; Austin Steward as quoted in *Don't Carry Me Back! Narratives by Former Virginia Slaves*, Maurice Duke, ed. (Richmond, Va.: Dietz Press, 1995), 37–38; L. M. Blackford, *Mine Eyes*, 48, 73.

35. Blackford, "Notes," February 22, 1833, p. 11; Marie Tyler-McGraw, "Richmond Free Blacks and African Colonization, 1816–1832," *Journal of American Studies* 21 (1987): 209; David M. Streifford, "The American Colonization Society: An Application of Republican Ideology to Early Antebellum Reform," *Journal of Southern History* 45 (February 1979): 213–14.

36. Tyler-McGraw, "Richmond Free Blacks," 210, 221–22. See also Berlin, *Slaves without Masters*, 201–4; Brenda E. Stevenson, *Life in Black and White: Family and Community in the Slave South* (New York: Oxford University Press, 1996), 282–85.

37. Sara Evans, *Born for Liberty: A History of Women in America* (New York: Free Press, 1989), 75–79; Angelina Grimké, *Appeal to the Christian Women of the South* (New York: American Anti-Slavery Society, 1836), 16–26, and *Letters to Catharine E. Beecher in Reply to An Essay on Slavery and Abolitionism* (1838; reprint, New York: Arno Press, 1969), 35–40.

38. Thomas Dew, *Review of the Debate in the Virginia Legislature of 1831 and 1832* (Richmond, Va.: T. W. White, 1832), 35–37.

39. Staudenraus, *The African Colonization Movement*, 182–87; *Christian Sentinel* (Richmond, Va.), September 6, November 15, 1833.

40. Staudenraus, *The African Colonization Movement*, 182–87; *Seventh Annual Report of the Board of Managers of the Colonization Society of Virginia* (Richmond, Va.: Office of the Southern Churchman, 1838), 24.

41. *African Repository* 14 (April 1838): 44; *African Repository* 14 (April 1838): 119.

42. Mary Blackford to Ralph Gurley, June 19, 1834, LC; *African Repository* 10 (October 18, 1834): 252–53; *African Repository* 13 (October 1837): 311–13.

43. On the Richmond society, see *African Repository* 10 (December 1834): 314–15; *African Repository* 11 (August 1835): 247. On others, *African Repository* 9 (July 1833): 149; *African Repository* 10 (July 1834): 149; *African Repository* 11 (November 1835): 340.

44. *Watchman of the South* (Richmond, Va.), January 25, 1838; *African Repository* 14 (September 1838): 272–73; *African Repository* 9 (November 1833): 280–81; Susan Terrell to Joseph Gales, January 30, 1836, ACS Papers, LC; Blair, "The Southern Dilemma," 73–78.

45. *African Repository* 16 (August 1840): 248–49; *African Repository* 16 (January 1841): 313; *Twenty-Eighth Annual Report of the American Society for Colonizing the Free People of Colour of the United States* (Washington, D.C.: James C. Dunn, 1845), 9.

46. See receipts in the *African Repository*, 1845–1850.

47. Mitchell Snay, *Gospel of Disunion: Religion and Separatism in the Antebellum South* (New York: Cambridge University Press, 1993), 34.

48. For coverage of colonization in religious papers, see, for example, the *Religious Herald*, December 5, 1844, July 2, 1846.

49. Carwadine, *Evangelicals and Politics in Antebellum America*, 156; Loveland, *Southern Evangelicals and the Social Order*, 227.

50. Staudenraus, *The African Colonization Movement*, 237; Marie Tyler-McGraw, *The American Colonization Society in Virginia, 1816–1832* (Ann Arbor, Mich.: University Microfilms, 1979), 218–20; Hickin, *Antislavery in Virginia*, 322–25, 331, 339–40.

51. Mary Blackford to Ralph Gurley, August 23, 1856, ACS Papers, LC; Anne Rice to William McLain, May 2, 1857, and Anne Rice to Ralph Gurley, April 28, 1859, ACS Papers, LC.

52. Phillip Foner and Phillip Pacheo, *Three Who Dared: Prudence Crandall, Margaret Douglass, Myrtilla Miner—Champions of Antebellum Black Education* (Westport, Conn.: Greenwood Press, 1984), 58–63; Margaret Douglass, *Educational Laws of Virginia: The Personal Narrative of Margaret Douglass* (Boston: John P. Jewett, 1854), 29–33.

53. Foner and Pacheo, *Three Who Dared*, 88, 91.

54. Foner and Pacheo, *Three Who Dared*, 68–69, 72–83; Douglass, *Educational Laws*, 68.

55. George Fitzhugh, *Sociology for the South, Or the Failure of Free Society* (1854; reprint, New

York: B. Franklin, 1965), 119, 239; Albert Taylor Bledsoe, *An Essay on Slavery and Liberty* (Philadelphia: J. B. Lippincott, 1856), 224.

56. Mary Eastman, *Aunt Phillis's Cabin; or, Southern Life As It Is* (Philadelphia: Lippincott, Grambo, 1852); Minrose Gwin, *Black and White Women of the Old South: The Peculiar Sisterhood in American Literature* (Knoxville: University of Tennessee Press, 1985), 36–39, 50–51.

57. Julia Gardiner Tyler, "To the Duchess of Sutherland and Ladies of England," *Southern Literary Messenger* 19 (February 1853): 120–26; Robert Seager II, *And Tyler Too: A Biography of John and Julia Gardiner Tyler* (New York: McGraw-Hill, 1963), 402–5.

58. Harriet Beecher Stowe, *Uncle Tom's Cabin, or Life Among the Lowly* (1852; reprint, New York: Penguin, 1986), 626; L. M. Blackford, *Mine Eyes Have Seen the Glory*, 98, 100, 104.

59. *The South* (Richmond, Va.), October 13, 22, 1857.

60. Alexander H. Sands, "Intellectual Culture of Woman," *Southern Literary Messenger* 28 (May 1859): 330–31; "Alexander Sands," *Herringshaw's Library of American Biography*, vol. 5 (Chicago: American Publishers Association, 1914), 102. Another Baptist minister, Thornton Stringfellow, directed his influential defense of slavery not only to men but to women: "Every man and woman in the United States should not only be willing, but desirous to know, what is the matter-of-fact evidence on this all-absorbing question." Thornton Stringfellow, *Scriptural and Statistical Views in Favor of Slavery* (Richmond, Va.: J. W. Randolph, 1856), 110.

Suffering with Slaveholders

The Limits of Francis Wayland's

Antislavery Witness

DEBORAH BINGHAM VAN BROEKHOVEN

In 1835, many months before the U.S. House of Representatives passed a gag on antislavery petitions, Francis Wayland banned discussion of slavery in Brown University classes. His campus rule prohibited students from mentioning slavery either in written compositions or class speeches. Initially some students evaded their president's ban by mentioning slavery while speaking on another topic. To tighten the gag, faculty eliminated student choice of topics, assigning each "subject of written composition" and requiring that every speech "be examined by the professor of Rhetoric before it could be spoken on the stage." Any line judged to touch on abolition was "expunged." Despite these precautions, one student almost eluded the ban by speaking on the topic of American philanthropy. Most of his talk was a straightforward celebration of aid offered to Poles, Greeks, and other targets of American missionary zeal. But then the student asked, "what have we done to ameliorate the condition of more than two millions of our own oppressed country men?" He got no further. Dr. Wayland "hastily arose & apparently much excited, Stamped his foot, & said *Stop! Stop!!* enough of this, I won't have this subject agitated here & drove the speaker from the stage." [1]

Wayland's agitated response to talk about slavery was not entirely new. Some months earlier he had condemned before a formal assembly the twenty college students who had signed a call for the first Rhode Island State Anti-Slavery Convention. According to one of those criticized, President Wayland "*rebuked us, ridiculed us, blackguarded us,* in short abused us in a most unchristian manner, & forbid our signing any such instrument again without his permission." This student, who left school the following year to work with an agent of the New England Anti-Slavery Society, recalled as most insulting the mocking of their youth by Wayland, who told the college assembly: "I know of no *wise, cool, & deliberate man* who knows what to do in relation to this matter (slavery): but you (spoken sneeringly) *young men,* are going to rise up & tell us what to do!!" The student judged the remarks as inappropriate, not only for their mocking tone, but also because he thought Wayland's denigration of youthful foolishness wrongfully assumed a greater age gap than actually existed between professors and students, some of whom were almost as old as Wayland (who was not yet forty). Several students responded to Wayland's humiliating attacks by leaving Brown.[2] In his opposition to the new immediatism, Wayland also tangled with other abolitionists who, prior to formal organization of new antislavery chapters in Rhode Island, had attended a local meeting of the American Colonization Society. There Wayland disavowed any knowledge of the new abolitionism, arguing that he wished to focus solely on his support for "colonization principles."[3]

This picture of a short-tempered, hostile Wayland contrasts sharply with that drawn by admirers after his death in 1865, when obituary writers stressed the Christian character, student-centered teaching, and humanitarian interests of this leading northern Baptist. Perhaps in deference to the national passion for reunion of warring sections, no mention was included of Wayland's writings about slavery, something later biographies emphasized, or of Wayland's unsuccessful efforts to prevent a schism between southern and northern Baptists.[4] The most widely read moral philosopher of his generation, Wayland was also active in Baptist ministerial circles and served as president of Brown University from 1827 to 1855. Commanding widespread respect, Wayland was in a position to shape responses of evangelicals and educators to slavery and to slaveholding Baptists, which is one reason why his statements on this subject drew scrutiny from both his contemporaries and later historians. One can readily find examples of Wayland acting both as a conservative, reluctant to condemn slaveholders, and as a reformer, ready to condemn slavery. In order to understand these apparent discrepancies as something more complicated than the hypocrisy of which Wayland was frequently accused by abolitionists, historians need to pay careful attention to the timing and context for his varied statements and actions. However concerned Wayland was to stop abolitionists from generating more controversy about slavery, Wayland in fact did maintain that American slavery should be phased out. His frequent silences and close relationships with southern leaders caused radical abolitionists to condemn him as proslavery. Wayland's behavior was ambiguous, his silences on slavery punctuated with occasional antislavery statements.

Wayland's cautious, sometimes contradictory position was rooted less in his conventional assumptions about the racial inferiority of blacks, or in his Calvinistic reluctance to act on a problem which seemed too complicated for anyone but God to solve, but largely because his position as America's foremost moral philosopher and leading Baptist made him temperamentally and institutionally eager for compromise. Much of the confusion among contemporaries and later historians about Wayland's position on slavery is based not on his changing opinions, for he remained an antislavery moderate throughout his life, but on Wayland's consistent subordination of his real concerns about slavery to the larger Baptist and evangelical mission of converting the lost. Wayland's rejection of extreme positions on slavery was clear even prior to riots aimed at, and some thought provoked by, distribution of abolitionist tracts to many towns and cities, including Charleston, South Carolina, where a mob burned mail sent by abolitionists to Charleston leaders. In assuming a moderate position, Wayland was balancing his personal aversion to slavery with his sensitivity to the feelings of Christian slaveholders, some of whom sent students to Wayland's school. Wayland never accepted the proslavery arguments of Southern Baptists, arguing in print that slavery was a sin.[5] Yet he also excused Christian slaveholders from moral guilt, condemned abolitionists for inflaming sectional tension, and suggested that ending slavery might better be left to divine intervention, a compromise position which was frustrating to abolitionists, many of whom had hoped that Wayland would lead Baptists into antislavery activism. Instead, Wayland quieted antislavery voices on campus and at denominational meetings but tolerated the proslavery pronouncements of some students and at least one faculty member, the professor of belles lettres responsible for censuring student essays.[6] Whatever he taught on this subject, Wayland seems to have kept in mind the viewpoints of leading southern Baptists, most of whom enjoyed cordial relations with him. Ironically, his concern to avoid extreme positions undermined programs that Wayland assumed his moderate voice would promote—Baptist unity and gradual emancipation.

With Wayland so careful to maintain relationships with southerners, it is not surprising that he never singled out a slaveholder or slaveholding group for criticism. One can read the anger Wayland directed at abolitionists as rooted both in his concern to maintain these southern contacts and in his resentment at the charge that his antislavery position was not genuine. Wayland's concerns here were intertwined because he also feared that the uncompromising stand of abolitionists, especially if they made inroads among his faculty and students, would endanger both college and Baptist unity. Wayland had assumed the presidency of Brown University when institutional support was declining and the college's survival was in question.[7] Wayland clearly saw denominational unity as vital if he was to resurrect the university and raise support for the benevolence societies he depicted as the logical application of true faith. Despite his textbook's labeling of slavery as evil, Wayland otherwise avoided public discussion of either emancipation plans or slaveholders' conduct, a reluctance rooted in his belief that slavery was a problem that defied human remedy. Immediate emancipation, Wayland argued, might rend the social fabric and harm both freedmen and society in general. This conviction, combined with an expedient concern to avoid controversy, resulted in Wayland's refusal to discuss slavery further or to allow students to debate slavery. He believed humans were foolish to tackle something as insolvable as slavery, especially when they might instead focus their energies on the profitable and noncontroversial task of evangelism and Christian education.

Despite this reticence to enter public debate about slavery, Wayland repeated his view that slavery was sinful in the several antebellum editions of *Elements of Moral Science,* his textbook that after 1835 became the standard in moral philosophy classes across the country, including southern schools.[8] His critique seems to have been based on a long-term aversion to slavery; a schoolmate remembered that as a student Wayland had chosen to speak "several times in succession, an extract from an oration on 'injured Africa.'"[9] This early translation of soul liberty, always a central tenet of Baptists, into broader, even political definitions of liberty meant that Wayland had long seen chattel slavery as an evil to be eradicated. In 1835, at the same time when Wayland was hushing student debate about slavery, he privately was glad to see ministers outside the radical abolitionist camp condemn slavery. As Wayland wrote to Unitarian minister William Ellery Channing, "It was high time that the subject should be fully and plainly set forth; . . . and that the spirit of the North should be awakened to the great subject of liberty. . . ." Wayland pledged to "seize every opportunity" and to "do any thing" that might influence Baptist feelings and policies on slavery.[10] Wayland never published this letter, apparently assuming that his textbook's mention of slavery, as part of a discussion detailing ways that individuals might wrongly violate the liberty of others, was his best opportunity for influencing southerners. Even when, in 1845, Wayland focused an entire book on slavery, his views were expressed in letters sent to Rev. Richard Fuller, a southern Baptist minister in Beaufort, South Carolina, whose proslavery letters also were included in the publication. Wayland repeated and elaborated on his earlier condemnation of slavery as sin, but he still rejected the idea that slaveholders were sinners and made clear that any plans to end slavery must be developed very slowly. Noting that current social conditions prevented free persons of color from obtaining a spiritual or material livelihood, Wayland concluded that these circumstances justified, and often required, Christians to continue owning slaves.

This early and repeated publication of Wayland's antislavery beliefs, no matter how mild, may have led abolitionists, particularly students at Brown, to overlook Wayland's reservations about immediate emancipation and to assume that he would encourage antislavery discussion in college classrooms. For despite his dislike of most antislavery organizations and his refusal to discuss slavery in the classroom or pulpit, Wayland did continue thinking about the issue. In his 1837 revisions of *Moral Science,* Wayland enlarged the section on slavery. Still, this ten-page section and the new paragraphs drew no public criticism, perhaps because it was buried in the middle of a long book and quite brief in comparison to the pages devoted to practical topics, such as marriage and parental responsibilities or property rights and Christian duties to the state. The new section argued that "God imposed obligations upon men which are inconsistent with the existence of domestic slavery," particularly the duties to preach the gospel and to honor marriage and familial obligations. Wayland allowed that the Bible did not directly prohibit slavery and reemphasized the dangers of immediate emancipation, but he argued that God indirectly had prohibited slavery by teaching principles about marriage and family and religious education that were incompatible with slavery.[11] The vehemence of abolitionists' later attacks on Wayland suggest that these early, relatively mild criticisms of slavery made reformers hopeful that America's leading moral philosopher might come to support their more radical position. For whatever combination of reasons, abolitionists initially refrained from comment when Wayland gagged antislavery speech and writing at Brown University.

This tactic of avoiding discussion of slavery was employed by other leading churchmen and politicians. But this avoidance may have surprised some who had experienced Wayland as an exceptional and progressive teacher, someone who promoted classroom debate and discussion as more conducive to solid intellectual development than recitation from memory.[12] Wayland earned respect through his position at Brown, through his widely read publications, and through his sermons at national meetings, which often moved young men to answer Wayland's call to join the ranks of American preachers. Wayland also promoted a variety of new philanthropic endeavors, serving as an officer for home and foreign mission societies. Most friends described Wayland as sensitive to his audience, and beginning in 1823, with the publication of his sermon, "The Moral Dignity of the Missionary Enterprise," that audience included southern ministers.[13] Wayland was especially close to the Rev. Basil Manly, president of the University of Alabama from 1837 to 1855. In 1837 Manly made a special trip north to meet the author of *Moral Science,* declaring after the meeting, "I find him a great deal more satisfactory than any man I meet [sic] on all the points about which I wish to inquire." [14] They maintained a regular correspondence, with Wayland continuing to offer advice on both student and curriculum issues, even after the official split between southern and northern Baptists in 1844-45.[15]

This kind of friendship was fairly common, for, even before the Baptist schism, denominational structure consisted mainly of national conventions that served as inspirational forums in which ministers could develop informal relationships with clergy from other regions. Some interregional meetings continued even after 1845. Informal relationships, made easier because local congregations were traditionally without close structural ties to other churches, meant Baptists in both north and south could continue to correspond, meet, and cooperate on a variety of evangelical enterprises.

Wayland must have been accustomed to avoiding the sensitive subject of slavery, not simply because he sensed the risk of abolitionists converting many of his students, but because his own friends and faculty varied in their opinions on this issue. The reality that the Brown faculty included one professor strongly in favor of slavery and others for emancipation was not a unique circumstance. Most northern communities, religious or social, included individuals with this range of opinions on slavery. Believing with many northerners that slaveholders were not invariably sinful, Wayland saw no barriers to his friendships with slaveholding ministers, and many of them had no hesitation about using and recommending his book on moral philosophy. Of course, while assigning or reading Wayland's text, southerners did not necessarily absorb his criticism of slavery. One scholar suggests that the southern professors who used Wayland's textbook well into the 1850s may simply have skipped over the section on slavery.[16]

Student essays from 1854, written most probably at the University of Virginia, refute Wayland's criticism of the Kansas-Nebraska Bill and reveal that southern professors still assigned their students Wayland's writings on slavery. The student authors referred not simply to Wayland's signing of a petition from New England clergymen opposing the extension of slavery but to passages and page numbers in *Moral Science.*[17] This year was, in fact, the first time that Wayland's antislavery convictions seriously strained his otherwise positive relationship with southern churchmen, who, until this time, seemed to have felt little concern about Wayland's mild criticism. In assuming that church divisions over slavery were complete in 1845, some scholars have overlooked the intense respect of many southern clergy for Wayland, continuing even after his political pronouncement against the extension of slavery.

Wayland's extreme care to maintain a moderate position on slavery may not have been as unusual as radical abolitionists or southern nationalist rhetoric might lead us to believe. Perhaps the factors that allowed southerners to continue their reading of Wayland might have preserved other interregional friendships after 1845 and even after 1854, even among non-Baptists. These informal relationships were quite easy for Baptists to negotiate since because there were no denominational assets to divide and the direct impact of schism was felt keenly only in certain missionary societies.

Certainly formal denominational schism did not stop southern schools, professors, and clergy from continuing to read Wayland, with some individuals, such as Richard Fuller, coming very close to affirming Wayland's position that slavery could be a problematic institution, if not a sin. Wayland pleased more southerners than Fuller when he concluded that owning slaves was not necessarily wrong if, as Wayland believed was the case, American law and social custom made it impossible for free blacks to maintain either legal or economic independence.[18]

This apparent coziness with slaveholders, together with Wayland's emphasis on merely ameliorating the conditions of slaves (presumably in preparation for some future emancipation day), exposed him to much criticism from immediatists, especially after 1838, the year in which Wayland condemned abolitionists and their organizations in his tract, *The Limits of Human Responsibility*. It was this publication that caused abolitionist leaders to query former Brown student James Blakesley for his account of how Wayland had enforced an antislavery gag rule at the college. *Limits*, the shortened title used by abolitionists to mock and by supporters to praise Wayland, expanded and published what Wayland had first told his student body—that institutional slavery was one of those problems that defied mortal wisdom and therefore remained beyond the limits of human guilt and responsibility. Wayland sharply attacked abolitionists, whose extremism he argued inflamed tensions, and he defended Christian slaveholders by showing them handling as kindly and morally as possible the slaves they had inherited. This majority of slaveholders, Wayland argued, treated their slaves well.

Wayland himself considered African Americans, whether slave or free, inferior to the white population, and his arguments for the colonization of free blacks outside the United States and for segregated schools reflected this viewpoint. On this point Wayland was not all that different from other white leaders, north and south, who felt that African Americans, whether free or slave, were part of the social and moral burden whites were obliged to shoulder.[19] Assuming the blamelessness of current slaveholders, Wayland could not fathom why abolitionists advocated withdrawing from fellowship with slaveholders, and he refuted this tactic both in print and by encouraging a young southerner Basil Manly Jr. (the son of his Alabama friend and fellow college president) to begin his ministry in Providence.[20]

But exactly what role Wayland played in shaping opinions about slavery remains murky—lost in the contradictions between hagiographers' portraits of his humanitarian sensibility and abolitionist denunciations of Wayland as proslavery. His defense of slaveholders, which to radical abolitionists and to later historians made Wayland appear a social and political conservative,[21] was in fact a widely held and moderately antislavery view in the 1840s. Wayland was not so much constructing a new position on slavery as he was voicing and amplifying the views of most northern whites in the period. Like most northern evangelicals, Wayland believed that slavery was morally wrong. But like the many Baptist ministers who looked to him for leadership, Wayland always refrained from criticizing slaveholders as an immoral group nor did he ever suggest that nonslaveholders should force their ideas of morality upon southerners. Because of this moderate position, critics could denounce him for opposite reasons, with radical reformers picturing Wayland as proslavery and *DeBow's Journal* denouncing him for teaching "ultra abolition."[22] Rather than seeing Wayland as moving away from gradual and toward immediate emancipation sometime during the 1840s, the "ultra abolition" implied by *DeBow's,* Wayland always remained a gradualist. Only in his methods of dealing with southerners on this issue did Wayland change at all. His long silences on slavery make this evolution difficult to trace, but this evolution most likely developed as Wayland, evidenced by his move into the Free Soil Party, became disillusioned with southerners, who instead of creating plans to emancipate their slaves, were increasing pressure for the extension of slavery into such northern territories as Kansas.

Abolitionists showered most of their criticism on Wayland in the early 1840s, before Wayland had accepted Free Soilers' concerns about the slave power. Their criticism is rooted in keen disappointment that he, despite early antislavery statements, both defended slaveholders and attacked abolitionist organizations. While suggesting that emancipation was a goal, Wayland frowned on the stance of Garrisonian immediatists, whose attacks on southerners he saw as multiplying the difficulties associated with ending slavery. Rather than confronting southerners, Wayland believed a conciliatory stand

204 · DEBORAH BINGHAM VAN BROEKHOVEN

the more effective means of reform, as illustrated by his published letter to Rev. Richard Fuller, which stated that if all slaveholders treated their slaves as well as Fuller did, slavery would cease to be a moral issue. Continuing to hold that the institution of slavery was a moral evil, Wayland, as a pragmatist and moderate Calvinist, concluded that corporate action by either church or state was neither necessary nor feasible. Pointing out that most slaveholders legally could not free their slaves, Wayland suggested that owners performed their Christian duty if they governed their slaves benevolently, as his friend, the Reverend Fuller, did by teaching them to read the Bible.[23]

Like other moderates, Wayland showed that he sympathized with both slave and slaveholder. The single group toward which Wayland continued to express hostility was abolitionists, whom he saw as radicals lacking sensitivity to the burdens of Christian slaveholders. He pictured abolitionists as proudly playing God, trying to stop an evil that defied human solutions. Wayland singled out abolitionists for criticism because he viewed their denunciations of slaveholders as undermining the work of evangelism and religious education, a mission he saw as requiring cordial relations with all mainstream Baptists, including southern ministers and the students that he trained at Brown. Beyond this cultivating of southern alumni, Wayland also saw his audience as the greater number of evangelicals who read and were influenced by his writings. By warning his readers that abolitionists were wrong, Wayland reassured his readers that an immediate end to slavery was neither desirable nor dictated by Christian morals.

This moderate stance did forestall southern criticism of Wayland's moral philosophy, particularly when he published a direct attack on abolitionists in 1838, *The Limits of Human Responsibility*. Wayland was hurt but unrepentant when some Baptists criticized him for defending slaveholders. His belief in "limits" to human ability did not extend to most missionary enterprises, including prison reform. Because Wayland supported these popular reforms but refused to tackle slavery, abolitionists criticized Wayland both as inconsistent and as caring more about building academic and financial support for his college than he did about correct morality.[24] These critics had a point because Wayland was very concerned to maintain peace among Baptists and other evangelicals. He asserted that the mild, compromising tone of his published comments on slavery would foster more antislavery sentiment than would demands for an immediate end to slavery. However sincere Wayland's beliefs, abolitionists were right in noting that this moderate stance made Wayland appear paralyzed by compromise, unable to act on what he admitted was a moral issue. One abolitionist joked that Wayland's Rhode Island was blighted by "your University Doctor's 'Limitations.' Unlucky Roger Williams! How much trouble and sore travel he might have saved himself, if he had only lived in our blessed day" of few responsibilities. This critic sarcastically concluded that if "human responsibility" had always been as limited as Wayland argued, then in earlier times such limitations would have left Baptist Rhode Island unsettled.[25]

In Wayland's own times, the widespread acceptance of these limitations did keep much antislavery talk out of Baptist meetings, but even Wayland's endorsement of moderation failed to unite Baptists. While he retained friendships and textbook sales in the South, by the 1840s many evangelicals in the North and in Britain had grown as disillusioned with Wayland as young abolitionist students had been earlier. Wayland first encountered this sharp criticism from coreligionists while touring England in 1840–41. Despite a warm reception from a few clerics who knew his writings, Wayland suffered greatly from the snubs that his antiabolitionist position earned him among British dissenters, many of whom endorsed the idea of immediate emancipation. In some cases he was denied the opportunity to speak, and he complained that a person who did not share the abolitionist views of British Baptists was "excommunicated from church and society."[26] If Wayland was seeking reassurance from British Baptists, his timing was unfortunate because he toured England just months after the World Anti-Slavery Convention of 1840. Sometimes, as when Wayland visited Birmingham, his visits followed by mere days the visits of popular American abolitionists and, consequently, Wayland found his hosts brimming with uncomfortable, even hostile questions about the position of American Baptists on slavery.[27]

After 1845, when controversy over slaveholding missionaries precipitated southerners' rupture with northern Baptists, Wayland continued his moderate approach, hoping that the exclusion of abolitionists from tract, missionary, and denominational meetings would make possible a reconciliation of southern and northern Baptists—a goal that eluded him throughout the 1850s.[28] Essentially Wayland's positions on slavery were varied and contradictory. He felt strongly that Baptist missionaries should not bring the "bond servants" to the mission field with them, thereby introducing slavery to a people unfamiliar with that institution. And while publicly silent on this issue, Wayland must have resented the fact that it was Alabama Baptists and his friend Basil Manly who had precipitated the 1844 church schism by appointing a slaveholding missionary. Wayland's correspondence with Manly had begun in 1835, when Manly, still pastor of the prominent First Baptist Church of Charleston, South Carolina, wrote to him asking for clarification of Wayland's position on slavery and advice about the relative merits of preaching and college teaching. In response Wayland made clear that he was open to discussing slavery, but that anything other than discussion, anything which might interfere "with our Southern Brethren, in any way, . . . I am and have been ever opposed to such interference."[29] Wayland assumed his views differed from Manly's, but noted their agreement that Christian kindness, justice, and mercy would undermine the tyranny fostered by any structural flaws in government. Even church schism, however, did not end Wayland's cautious avoidance of such topics as slavery and emancipation. After 1845, when he had published more arguments against slavery (and repeated his defense of Christian slaveholders), Wayland advised his students against even attending a local antislavery meeting, warning them that they would only hear himself abused as an "antislavery hypocrite."[30]

Wayland declared himself "no abolitionist," but he did on one occasion raise the topic privately and indirectly. In 1839 he wrote to his friend Manly, pleading with him to intervene on behalf of two black sailors from Rhode Island who had been jailed in Mobile, Alabama, on suspicion of aiding runaways. The northern ship's cook had already been hanged on this charge, but Wayland plead that the two remaining sailors should be freed because both were of good reputation and could, in fact, be innocent. Sensitive to southerners' abhorrence of meddling northerners, Wayland disingenuiously argued that the sailors' safe and speedy return home would prevent such meddling, something he implied would surely result if poor treatment of the sailors converted the Providence citizenry to abolitionism.[31] In his diplomatic approach to the topic of slavery, Wayland was in effect affirming the antiabolitionist position of Manly. Wayland urged that the black sailors be freed because, lacking proof of their guilt, a conviction would enable abolitionists to make converts and spread further what he and Manly agreed was an incorrect view—that southern slaveholders abused African Americans.

Even after formal schism, Wayland continued this mediating role between northern and southern Christians. Hoping to heal the split between northern and southern Baptist missionary organizations, Wayland continued to work with southern Baptists, many of whom after 1845 remained active in northern-based tract, Bible, and missionary organizations. He clearly understood that formal division did not mean complete separation, particularly given the limited structure of Baptist church associations. Regional missionary societies might form, and southern Baptists could and did hold their own denominational meetings. But because Baptist churches functioned as independent congregations, national meetings had never formulated or enforced uniform beliefs, policies, and practices for congregations the way Methodist or Presbyterian structures did.[32] The affiliation of Baptist churches and state conventions of Baptists with national meetings remained informal, with many congregations barely aware of these national meetings. This is why separation, when it did come, developed within the largest Baptist missionary society and focused on finances. Southerners felt that missionaries should not be judged if they happened to own slaves, while northerners, including Wayland, resisted the idea that their missionary dollars might support slaveholders, who, as part of their missionary work would be introducing slavery to a culture in which it had not been known.

When Wayland could not prevent schism, he remained committed to associations with slaveholding Baptists. Wayland further explained his views on slavery in an exchange of letters with one of these slaveholders, Rev. Richard Fuller. Perhaps continued criticism from his British friends pushed Wayland to write more about the evils of slavery. Certainly he continued to care about the issue, responding in 1845 to Fuller's positive defense of slavery with eight long letters published in the *Christian Reflector,* a Boston newspaper serving both northern and southern Baptists. Suggesting that slaveholders themselves could work out plans to free their slaves, Wayland assumed he was undermining the abolitionist position when he encouraged owners to see education of their slaves as the first step in any plan for emancipation. He rejected the idea that corporate action by either church or state was necessary to bring about gradual emancipation. Emphasizing the legal reality that many slaveholders could not free their slaves, Wayland suggested that such owners performed their Christian duty if they kept in mind the best interests of the slaves. Both Fuller and Wayland wrote their exchanges cautiously, avoiding words of condemnation and invective, and Wayland concluded by listing their agreements. The letters were published immediately as a book, *Domestic Slavery Considered As A Scriptural Institution,* demonstrating that despite Wayland's emphasis on compromise and moderation, he was not as reticent as many other church leaders, who somehow managed to ignore slavery as a moral issue for another decade.[33]

Whatever influence Wayland had on individual readers, it would have taken more than these gentle writings to introduce antislavery discussion and reform into Baptist circles. Indeed, Wayland erred in ignoring the appeal of the proslavery arguments offered by such ministers as Manly and Fuller, who both assumed that slavery was a Christian institution designed to elevate and Christianize "savages," a view that Wayland neglected to attack outright. Instead, Wayland assumed that most coreligionists in the South shared his antislavery

sentiments and that emancipation would soon come about if radical abolitionists did not polarize northern and southern Baptists. And because Wayland did not demand public action from his readers, his writings about slavery
did not introduce debate over slavery into churches, where members interested in reform heard stronger arguments for immediate emancipation as they
appeared in such newspapers as the *Liberator* or in negative reviews of Wayland's letters by Baptists with stronger antislavery concerns.

Two such reviews were printed as books in their own right. The milder
critique of Wayland was published by Rev. William Hague and endorsed by
his Albany, New York, ministerial association, the original audience for his
anti-Wayland sermons.[34] Hague was horrified that any Christian minister
might excuse slavery, and he especially deplored the popularity of Fuller's
views among southern ministers. Shocked most by Fuller's positive defense of
slavery, Hague had assumed wrongly that southern Christians saw their faith
as undermining slavery "and that in proportion as their influence in the state
was increasing, the day of emancipation was hastening on."[35] In refuting Fuller's support of slavery in the Bible, Hague used a verse often cited by radical
abolitionists, a reference to the obligation of Hebrews who had captured slaves
in wartime, that every fifty years they were to "proclaim liberty throughout
the land, unto ALL THE INHABITANTS THEREOF."[36] Hague was disap-
pointed also by the vagueness of Wayland's argument, which suggested that
the teachings of Jesus only required masters to work toward emancipation.
Wayland's critique of slaveholders was weak, Hague argued, and "falls far
short of the truth."[37] Hague also rebuked Wayland for accepting Roman law
over biblical and for neglecting passages that encouraged Christians to settle
differences outside the law.[38]

Another Baptist minister, Cyrus Grosvenor, published a stronger critique.
Having worked as an agent of the American Anti-Slavery Society in Rhode
Island, Grosvenor had earlier encountered and attacked Wayland's resistance
to immediate emancipation. As a cleric who had prior to 1845 "come out"
from mainline Baptists to form a missionary association free of any association with slaveholders, Grosvenor was less gentle than Hague in his critique,
which was published by churches affiliated with the separatist American Baptist Free Missionary Society. Citing Wayland's sweeping condemnation of abolitionists as a "party," Grosvenor felt no reservations about condemning slaveholders as a party, in quoting Thomas Jefferson's depiction of slavery as
undermining both republican and religious institutions, or in predicting that
God would soon respond to the groans and misery of poor slaves.[39]

Grosvenor's most clever and effective attack on Wayland, however, was his reprinting of Roger Williams's attack on the "Hireling Ministry," thereby labeling Wayland as a compromised "hireling," paid by the wealthy to stifle interest in emancipation. Grosvenor was aware that Williams's reputation had risen considerably since the seventeenth century, and not just among Baptists. If Grosvenor could make Williams's criticism of ministers stick to Wayland and Fuller, he knew that readers could not dismiss the radical antislavery argument as that of a "selfish politician," "headstrong mutineer against government, or a wily traitor to his country." Reprinting Roger Williams in the 1840s suggested to readers that the unpopular beliefs of abolitionists might be as correct as they now regarded Williams's once radical belief in separation of church and state. As Grosvenor pointed out about Williams, he too was unpopular in his times: "what religionist ever promulgated sentiments more novel to the times or more antagonistical to the prevailing Church policy? or what politician ever more firmly planted his foot in opposition to governmental assumption of power? or advocated principles of a true Republicanism, with a truer zeal . . . ?"[40] Grosvenor concluded his tract by asking readers what they now thought about ministers eager for titles, formal education, and larger salaries more than "calls from God." Noting that Williams himself had believed that slavery prevented slaves from proper observance of religion and marriage, Grosvenor asks readers to judge Wayland by Williams' standards: "What think you of the Northern man who *speaks* eulogiums on the character of Roger Williams, but treats with contempt the sentiments whose advocacy has made his name worthy of remembrance, and despises those brethren who are now humbly endeavoring to make those sentiments practical realities in the 'American Churches.' 'PROVE ALL THINGS: HOLD FAST THAT WHICH IS GOOD.'"[41]

In this indirect way, Wayland encouraged more discussion of slavery among Baptists. But this discussion occurred outside the major church associations through which Wayland and some southerners continued to operate.[42] With Wayland, as with most Baptist and other denominational leaders, an overriding concern for religious unity and moderation quickly subverted any antislavery agenda. Reasoning that he, and not abolitionists, kept alive some dialogue with leading southerners and knowing that his text was being used in southern schools, Wayland chose to fight abolitionists rather than his southern brethren. His tortured efforts to present a Christian position on slavery drew further criticism from abolitionists, whom most historians have followed in labeling Wayland a "conservative" on the issue of slavery.[43] Yet this character-

ization is fair only if one used the idealistic scale employed by radical abolitionists, who grew increasingly bitter that this leading churchman would not
use his great influence to aid their cause.

On a rare occasion, however, Wayland's private feelings about slavery surfaced. In 1850, for example, Wayland felt the new fugitive slave act so repulsive
that he departed from a prepared sermon text to denounce "human oppression."[44] While this public outburst against slavery was unprecedented for
Wayland, this brief denunciation, along with his refusal to join fellow clergy
who greeted the compromise by preaching the necessity for Christians to obey
the law, suggests that Wayland's continued abhorrence of slavery at this point
pushed him just a bit away from his usual conciliatory attitude toward slaveholders. Yet the public significance of this single outburst should not be exaggerated. For despite this implied criticism of southern views, Wayland never
did utter the word "slavery," and he quickly returned to his usual focus on
religious education and evangelism. *Moral Science* continued to be read in
most southern schools, Brown still attracted southern students, and Wayland
himself kept up his correspondence with moderate southerners.

In 1854, however, when northern opinion finally coalesced against any further extension of slavery, Wayland abandoned his silence. The occasion was
dramatic; Wayland denounced the Kansas-Nebraska Bill before a packed
crowd assembled in Providence's large downtown Beneficent Congregational
Church. Yet even this speech reflected Wayland's reluctance to apply his moral
philosophy to current political issues. Still, some radicals praised Wayland for
this belated stand. One abolitionist reported that Wayland's speech was good,
opposing those favoring an end to "agitation" on slavery, but not quite as
excellent as speeches by three other community leaders that were characterized "as radical Anti-Slavery as could be wished." Still Wayland did argue that
"a man had a right to himself, and not be the property of another, in order
to be an accountable being."[45] Of course what Wayland said was not a new
viewpoint, even for him, but rather his first venture into public argument,
even "agitation," on this subject.[46]

This one venture into antislavery politics does not mean that after 1854
Wayland repeatedly denounced the extension of slavery. Yet southerners could
no longer ignore this highly publicized statement by Wayland. Even Baptists
in the north were grudging in their praise of what they noted was a very late
entry into the moral debate.[47] Perhaps still hoping for reconciliation, Wayland himself continued to make other work his focus, so much so that six
months after the anti-Nebraska rally, abolitionists complained that Wayland
had raised their hopes only to disappoint them. Wayland was the most promi-

nent of the disappointing clergy in Providence, a city that *Liberator* editor William Lloyd Garrison increasingly characterized as "the stronghold of pro-slavery" sentiment. Most ministers lacked knowledge, Garrison suggested, of even "the first letters of the Anti-Slavery alphabet," and most galling, "the great First Baptist" (the church of Wayland) still would not allow a notice of antislavery meetings to be read. "And where is Dr. Wayland, after his one . . . speech last March 7th? And what ever happened to the proposed 'great New England clerical Anti-Slavery Convention' planned for last June?"[48]

Despite this criticism, Wayland had in fact accepted one abolitionist view—that some southerners were working hard to enlarge the territory in which slavery was tolerated. More important for southern Baptists, Wayland's public stand against the Nebraska act signaled his unwillingness to accept in silence continued arguments for the positive benefits of slavery, even from coreligionists. Southern schools, such as Mississippi College and Randolph-Macon College, dropped his textbook, their professors and students no longer tolerant of the few pages discussing the evils of slavery and ethical obligations of Christian slaveholders.[49] By 1857, Wayland seems to have realized that reconciliation was impossible and that more missionary activity directed at slaves and slaveholders was his Christian duty. Finally deciding that the American Tract Society should publish material describing slavery as a sin, Wayland argued (unsuccessfully to his peers) that Christians were responsible for the salvation of all groups, not just white owners or those offended by slavery discussions. Further evidence that Wayland had been modifying his opinions, even allowing discussion of slavery to creep back into the classrooms at Brown, comes from a former student's recollection that Wayland's own son pointed out in class to his father (and teacher) the contradictions between the earlier and later, more antislavery writings of Wayland: Wayland responded, "It only shows, my son, that since the learned author wrote the first book, he has learned something more."[50]

As always, Wayland's public position on slavery was rooted in tension between his Baptist affirmation of almost total separation of religious and political issues and his membership in the intellectual and political elite of his day. It was more in his role as community leader rather than as a Baptist minister that Wayland assumed that political change should be handled through present authorities. Even when Wayland denounced the extension of slavery into Nebraska territory, he still insisted that Christians must obey the law or submit to jail as the price for following one's conscience.[51] Wayland continued to find it difficult to criticize fellow evangelicals, even if they were slaveholders, particularly because he saw them as allies in the struggle against indifference to religion. Laws touching on slavery remained a concern to him, and Wayland struggled with the realization that his country was drifting away from Christian values in its public policies, especially regarding slavery. With these concerns propelling him, Wayland moved first from Whig to Free Soil Party, eventually joining the new Republican Party, willing to applaud its stand against the extension of slavery.[52]

Wayland's reluctance to deal with slavery, even as a strictly moral issue about which religious teachers could provide guidance, was increasingly overwhelmed on several fronts. Abolitionists were most vociferous in mocking Wayland's attempt to stop discussion of slavery by suggesting that only God could devise a solution to this problem. Initially, most southerners were comfortable with this approach, viewing Wayland's limited critique of slavery as a small and unobjectionable part of his popular textbook. But even Wayland's southern friends increasingly grew wary of any northerner judging slavery, even in the abstract, to be an immoral institution. The response to Wayland's 1845 letters on slavery augured poorly for his moderate attempt at compromise: Wayland was attacked both for his lack of antislavery speech and for writing too much on the subject. No longer could Wayland win over most Baptists by balancing an abstract antislavery argument with practical tolerance for Christian slaveholding. Nevertheless Wayland persisted in attempts at compromise. Yet neither silence nor mild speech satisfied most parties, partly because Wayland, at least after 1854, could no longer convince himself that many southerners shared his assumptions about the evils of slavery. Wayland was, in fact, in the same position held fifteen years earlier by an even more prominent Whig leader, Henry Clay: both were the recipients of harsh criticism from abolitionists who scorned their compromises and from southerners who rejected first Clay and then Wayland's private assumption that slavery was evil and should be phased out. Instead of emphasizing the biblical, humanitarian, and patriarchal reasons for maintaining slavery, those very reasons offered by Fuller, and which Wayland conceded were Christian reasons, southern nationalists were emphasizing harsher, racial arguments for slavery.[53]

In following Clay's strategy of compromise, Wayland was in fact avoiding these contemporary views, that slavery was justified by racial differences, and indulging in an older debate no longer of interest to the leading promoters of sectional tension. Their use of the older discourse suggests just how remote both Fuller and Wayland were from understanding the fears and ambitions of the fire-eaters who more often offered a racial and not a humanitarian defense of slavery. For all Wayland's efforts at reconciliation, he lost on two counts:

first, Baptist churches diminished and confused their evangelical outreach by sectionally dividing most operations; and second, the separated southern Baptists, rather than discussing how to end slavery, grew more attached to an institution that they had concluded was compatible with Christian values. Wayland's concern for compromise had been based on his fear that materialism, slavery, and even missions might detract from the presentation of the Gospel. But his moderate voice did not keep controversy about those matters out of Baptist meetings.

A series of shocks caused Wayland to rethink his limited position on slavery; the criticism voiced during his 1840 visit to England, the split initiated in 1844 by his Alabaman friend Basil Manly, enforcement of the Fugitive Slave Law of 1850, and, most important, the possibility in 1854 that slavery would be extended into the northern territories of Kansas and Nebraska. Wayland's anger at the Nebraska bill elicited negative reactions among his southern readers, and one southern university professor responded to Wayland's 1854 speech by assigning students to write an essay critiquing Wayland's position on slavery. Quoting many sections of *Moral Science,* these students judged harshly what they saw as Wayland's acceptance of northern materialism, something they viewed as both a biblical sin and a moral evil outlined in Wayland's textbook. Why, one author queried, did Wayland not discuss the modern application of Jesus' directive that Christians should "[l]ay not up for yourselves treasures on earth" but instead "give alms?" This same student also noted that Wayland narrowly construed the story of the Good Samaritan (Luke 10:25–27) to mean, "As we do not want our own rights to be interfered with; so we are not to interfere with the rights of others." And worse yet, from this student's viewpoint, Wayland made trivial the greatest commandment, to love God and your neighbor by assuming the only application was for southern slaveholders and not northerners.[54]

This focus on materialism and economic issues is ironic, given Wayland's Republican concern to keep western territories open to northern, "free" labor. There is little evidence about which development was the most destructive of Wayland's hopes for sectional harmony, the conflict over Kansas, the attacks on him from southerners, or the formation of the Republican Party. Not until 1856, when some southern schools began banning his books, did he pull back from efforts to foster North-South cooperation through several smaller Baptist organizations. Despite his resolve to lead, and his success as an educational reformer, the limitations of Wayland's economic and moral philosophy made him a follower rather than a leader of public opinion about slavery. In the long term, one ironic result of Wayland's conciliatory approach is the continuing sectarian division between and among northern and southern Baptists, especially in regard to social and racial issues.

NOTES

1. Manuscript letter of J[ames] M. Blakesley to Rev. Amos Phelps, April 11, 1838, Spencertown, New York, Slavery Collection, Boston Public Library Rare Book and Manuscript Room (hereafter, BPL). As late as 1908, one of Blakesley's classmates also remembered the practice of censuring student speeches mentioning slavery and noted that Professor Goddard was "in favor of slavery"; William Lawton Brown, "Memories of 1832–36" in *Memories of Brown: Traditions and Recollections Gathered from Many Sources* (Providence, R.I.: Brown Alumni Magazine Company, 1909), 59. No source mentions the exact date when Wayland began enforcing his campus gag rule, but because Blakesley left the college in 1835, the rule must have been in place no later than that year. For help in locating Wayland materials, I thank Martha Mitchell, Archivist of the Brown University Collection in the Hay Library, and for comments on the essay, Kate Burns, Wendy Harrison, Karie Kirkpatrick, Jack McKivigan, Morgan Phillips, and Bill Shade.

2. Blakesley letter.

3. Manuscript letter of Henry E. Benson to William L. Garrison and Isaac Knapp, [1834] (BPL). In his analysis of church positions on slavery, John R. McKivigan characterizes Wayland as conservative and reluctant to raise the topic of slavery, much less to condemn slaveholding as unchristian; see McKivigan, *The War against Proslavery Religion: Abolitionism and the Northern Churches, 1830–1865* (Ithaca, N.Y.: Cornell University Press, 1984), 88–89, 177.

4. "Death of Dr. Francis Wayland," *New York Times* (2 October 1865); also Francis Wayland and H. L. Wayland, *A Memoir of the Life and Labors of Francis Wayland, D.D., LL.D.,* 2 vols. (1867; reprint, New York: Arno Press, 1972), 1:173; 2:262-67, 331-33. James O. Murray, in *Francis Wayland* (Boston: Houghton, Mifflin, 1891), argued that slavery and prison reform were Wayland's best known philanthropies (263), but in recounting a sermon that Murray argues was an antislavery message, even Murray admits that Wayland never mentioned the word slavery (238-39).

5. For this condemnation, see Francis Wayland, *The Elements of Moral Science,* Joseph L. Blau, ed. (New York: Cooke, 1835; reprint, Cambridge: Harvard University Press, 1963), 188–98. McKivigan characterizes Wayland as a "moderate," not primarily for his written statements but for his 1858 stand that the American Tract Society should circulate tracts that elaborated on the Christian duties of slaveholders (122). The reluctance of Wayland and other evangelicals to endorse the most conservative social positions has been noted; for example, Mark Y. Hanley makes clear the discomfort of evangelical ministers with the materialism of American culture in *Beyond a Christian Commonwealth: The Protestant Quarrel with the American Republic, 1830–1860* (Chapel Hill: University of North Carolina Press, 1994), 30–31, 134–35. See also his unpublished paper, "Antebellum Protestants and the Process of Cultural Dissent: The Case of Francis

Wayland, 1825–1858," delivered at the Society for Historians of the Early American Republic (Chapel Hill, 1993). Because he does not focus on slavery, Hanley emphasizes more than I do the dissent and tension in Wayland's approach to American culture.

6. William Goddard, professor of moral philosophy and metaphysics (1825–34) and of belles lettres (1834–42), was identified as proslavery by William Lawton Brown, class of 1842, in *Memories of Brown,* 59. Another student recalled that when the less respected Rev. Romero Elton, professor of Latin and Greek (1825–42), was responsible for evening devotions, he regularly prayed for "the soldier, the sailor and the slave," wording that the students calculated Elton had settled on "as both comprehensive and euphonious" (65). Information about these faculty members (and also about students) is found in *The Historical Catalogue of Brown University, 1764–1934* (Providence, R.I.: Brown University, 1936), 32, 36.

7. Wayland's caution was not without basis: Congregationalists had just watched Lane Seminary in Cincinnati lose most of its student body during an extended debate initiated by abolitionist students; see Lawrence T. Lesick, *The Lane Rebels: Evangelicals and Antislavery in Antebellum America* (Metuchen, N.J.: Scarecrow Press, 1980).

8. Scholars of higher education, moral philosophy, and evangelicalism all agree that Wayland's book dominated the field for most of the century: for examples see Blau, xlii; Lawrence A. Cremin, *American Education: The National Experience, 1783–1876* (New York: Harper and Row, 1980), 27–28; Wilson Smith, *Professors and Public Ethics: Studies of Northern Moral Philosophers before the Civil War* (Ithaca, N.Y.: Cornell University Press, 1956), 128. Wayland's college audience increased after 1837, when he published an even more popular textbook, *Elements of Political Economy,* a work that generated no controversy among abolitionists or proslavery types.

9. Wayland and Wayland, 1:27–28. The classmate was Samuel B. Ruggles, whose memory of Wayland as uninterested in sports clashes with that of another youthful friend, who remembered Wayland as sharing his interest in sports; (compare Ruggles with B. P. Johnson's recollection that Wayland was "fond of athletic sports," Wayland and Wayland, *Memoir,* 33). Wayland's tenderness toward those he saw as less fortunate extended into his tenure as president of Brown University, when former students and friends remembered him providing funds for impoverished students and lawyer's fees for poor defendants he judged "innocent" (*Memoir,* 1:78–79 and 1:243n).

10. Wayland's letter to Channing, dated December 15, 1835, was published in the *Christian Register* for July 10, September 5, and September 12, 1929, with the original in scrapbook 30, p. 51, Channing Autographs, no. 68, Rhode Island Historical Society manuscripts.

11. Wayland, *Moral Science,* 193–94. This reprint edition is based on several editions, although most directly on the 1837 edition, with editor Blau marking the passages that were not part of the first edition.

12. Wayland and Wayland, *Memoir,* 230–35. Another former student, however, remembered the detailed lecture notes students took and the way in which Wayland stopped "unprofitable debate" (245–49).

13. John H. Rice of the *Richmond Literary and Evangelical Magazine* and a Deacon Crane of Baltimore praised and circulated this Wayland sermon; see Wayland and Wayland, *Memoir,* 166.

Wayland understood regional sensitivities, approving in the 1820s that money earmarked for Baptist missions be used to keep afloat the Columbian College, a new school for educating Baptist clergy and located in Washington, D.C., from where the money could more easily serve Baptists from the southern and middle states than from Brown University. At the 1826 triennial meeting of Baptists, however, Wayland successfully argued that this national association withdraw financial support from the Columbian College because the school's needs overshadowed more important missionary enterprises. That this move strengthened the position of Brown University, then also struggling financially and needing a larger portion of Baptist ministerial students, was surely not lost upon northern Baptists, who then concluded that Wayland was the right man to bring order, discipline, and academic reputation to struggling Brown University (Wayland and Wayland, *Memoir,* 176–80).

14. Basil Manly to Sarah Manly, September 30, 1837, Manly Papers, Special Collections, Perkins Library, University of North Carolina at Chapel Hill, and quoted in E. Brooks Holifield, *The Gentlemen Theologians: American Theology in Southern Culture, 1795–1860* (Durham, N.C.: Duke University Press, 1978): 134–35. Holifield argues that southerners loved Wayland for his rejection of the utilitarian moral philosophy of his predecessor, Paley, and that when southerners did write their own textbooks they copied most of Wayland's ideas, simply dropping Wayland's criticism of slavery.

15. Much of the Manly-Wayland correspondence is held in the Brown University Archives, Hay Library, Providence, Rhode Island (hereafter Hay). McKivigan points out that even after this schism, northerners and southerners cooperated in such organizations as the American and Foreign Bible Society; see John R. McKivigan, "The American Baptist Free Mission Society: Abolitionist Reaction to the 1845 Baptist Schism," *Foundations* 21 (October–December 1978): 345.

16. Smith, *Professors,* 196, n23.

17. "Slavery Justified," manuscript student essays, (1854, pieces missing), Special Collections, Perkins Library, University of North Carolina at Chapel Hill. The inference made long ago by one archivist and penciled onto the holding file is that the essays were assigned by a professor at the University of Virginia.

18. Compare, for example, Fuller's amplification of Wayland's position that immediate abolition of slavery was a cause seen as "reckless" by most ministers, who like Fuller understood that immediate emancipation would constitute a "revolution" harmful to law and order and to the slaves themselves (letter 1 to the Rev. Francis Wayland, D.D., 127–28, 136; from the 1847 edition, slightly revised from the first edition) with Wayland's benevolent conclusions about Christian slaveholders in his final letter to Fuller (226, 230, 251–52; 1847 edition); Wayland, *Domestic Slavery Considered As A Scriptural Institution: in a correspondence between the Rev. Richard Fuller, of Beaufort, S.C., and The Rev. Francis Wayland, of Providence, R.I.* (Boston and New York: Gould, Kendall, and Lincoln and Lewis Colby, 1845). For a similar view from another northerner, see Caroline Rush's *The North and South, or, Slavery and Its Contrasts* (Philadelphia: Crissy and Markley, 1852; reprint, Negro Universities Press, 1968), which is a response to *Uncle Tom's Cabin* and depicts the inferior position of free blacks in Philadelphia and the brutal treatment of "white slaves" by harsh employers as much worse than anything experienced by southern slaves.

19. The classic discussion of this view is Winthrop Jordan, *White over Black: American Atti-*

tudes toward the Negro, 1550–1812 (Chapel Hill: University of North Carolina Press, 1968). Leon Litwack describes white assumptions about racial superiority and the consequences in *North of Slavery: The Negro in the Free States, 1790–1860* (Chicago: University of Chicago Press, 1961).

20. For information on that young minister, Basil Manly Jr., see *Appleton's Cyclopaedia of American Biography*, vol. 4 (New York: Appleton, 1888), 189. It is likely that Manly's appearance in Providence was the cause of renewed attacks by abolitionists upon Wayland and Rhode Island Baptists.

21. For historians concluding that Wayland was very conservative, see for examples, D. H. Meyer, *The Instructed Conscience: The Shaping of the American National Ethic* (Philadelphia: University of Pennsylvania Press, 1972), 14–16, and Charles C. Cole, *Social Ideas of the Northern Evangelists, 1826–1860* (New York: Octagon, 1966), 211–13. Cole's conclusion that Wayland radically changed his position around 1842 is based on dubious evidence from a comment by Charles Sumner that Wayland's "views on slavery, and with regard to the South have materially changed lately" (214). This single piece of evidence could just as easily be interpreted as the wishful thinking of Sumner, who wanted to count the influential Wayland as a convert.

22. Smith, *Professors*, 196, n23.

23. Wayland, *Moral Science*, 197; Wayland, *Domestic Slavery*, 240, 252. For a well-documented example of this type of "benevolent" slaveholding, see Randall M. Miller, ed., *Dear Master: Letters of a Slave Family* (Athens: University of Georgia Press, 1990), especially 23–36. For samples of southern ministerial opinion concerning slavery, see Randy Sparks's and Ted Crowther's essays in this volume. I do think, however, that Crowther's characterization of Wayland owes more to antiabolitionist stereotypes than to Wayland's mild criticism of slavery.

24. Walter C. Bronson slips broad hints of Brown's financial difficulties into descriptions of changing curriculum and facilities and acknowledges that Wayland had to deal with deficits caused by declining enrollments; Walter C. Bronson, *The History of Brown University, 1764–1914* (Providence: Brown University, 1914): 22–25, 231–32.

25. It is probable that this editorial was by William Lloyd Garrison, *Liberator*, December 7, 1838.

26. Wayland and Wayland, *Memoir*, 2:12–14. Wayland seemed particularly pained by ministers who insisted on their personal willingness to offer a speaking opportunity but explained they could not offer their pulpits because "some doctrines in your treatise on 'The Limitations of Human Responsibility' have rendered you unpopular in England. . . ."

27. For a sense of the speaking tours of abolitionists, see Annie Heloise Abel and Frank J. Klingberg, *A Side-light on Anglo-American Relations, 1839–1858: Furnished by the Correspondence of Lewis Tappan and Others with the British and Foreign Anti-Slavery Society* (Lancaster, Penn.: Association for the Study of Negro Life, 1927), 71–77, nn37, 38.

28. Abolitionists were not forcibly excluded, but left the denomination voluntarily in much the fashion as did the proslavery southern Baptists, in order to form their own organizations. For one clear example of abolitionists separating from northern Baptists over the issue of slavery, see McKivigan, "The American Baptist Free Missionary Society."

29. Wayland to Basil Manly, Providence, December 2, 1835 (Hay). Manly's side of the correspondence is missing, but clearly another issue was Manly's concern that he could not send

ministerial students to study at Brown if Wayland taught his students that slavery was immoral. Wayland sought to reassure Manly that his position only involved discussion—the very position he was in the middle of retreating from on his own campus—and that if Manly decided he could not send students to Brown there would be no hard feelings. Most of the letter, however, concerned more generic college and church business.

30. *Memories*, 80. This memory was contributed by a Virginian, who almost certainly was in error when he recalled that Abby Folsom, a notable and unmanageable eccentric, was scheduled to speak along side Abby Kelly, Stephen Foster, and Wendell Phillips. Because her free speaking often had little to do with slavery and because she was judged "crazy" by most observers, Folsom was mocked frequently by critics as an example of reformers' excesses. Folsom was frequently carried out of meetings by reformers generally tolerant of free speech.

31. Wayland to Manly, Providence, February 14, 1839 (Hay).

32. See especially, Conrad James Engelder, "The Churches and Slavery: A Study of the Attitudes toward Slavery of the Major Protestant Denominations," (Ph.D. diss., University of Michigan, 1964), 68–75; also McKivigan, "The American Baptist Free Mission Society," 340–55.

33. Wayland, *Domestic Slavery Considered*, 43. The book was praised, especially in the north, as balanced and went through many editions. The American Antiquarian Society, where I examined several editions, has a fifth edition issued in 1847. For the reluctance of most churches and their leaders, see McKivigan, *The War Against Proslavery Religion*, chap. 9.

34. William Hague, *Christianity and Slavery: A Review of Doctors Fuller and Wayland, on Domestic Slavery* (Boston: Gould, Kendall & Lincoln, 1847).

35. Hague, *Christianity and Slavery*, 8–9. Hague was just a bit out of date in his assumptions. Donald G. Matthews, in *Religion in the Old South* (Chicago: University of Chicago Press, 1977), argues that this assumption that slavery was a temporary measure, to be eradicated with the advance of Christianity, was fast fading before 1830; see especially 136–39.

36. Hague, *Christianity and Slavery*, 12, also cites Jeremiah 34:12ff.

37. Ibid., 17, is critiquing Wayland-Fuller, 100.

38. Hague cites scripture verses, including Acts 17:26, Ephesians 6:1–3, and Christ's Sermon on the Mount; Hague, *Christianity and Slavery*, 26–27, 49–53. He argues that the American church was nearing the apocalypse about which the writer of Revelations had warned the church at Pergamos. American Christians would soon be condemned for allowing a system "devised to grind your brethren into hard bondage." If God should send a special message to Americans, Hague concluded, it would be: "I have a few things against thee, because thou hast there them that hold the doctrine of the devil, saying that this system is from *me* and that it bears the sanction of your Lord and Master. Repent, or else I will come unto thee quickly, and will fight against thee with the sword of my mouth" (53).

39. Cyrus Pitt Grosvenor, *A Review of the "Correspondence" of Messrs. Fuller and Wayland, on the subject of American Slavery. to which is added a discourse by Roger Williams, printed, London, 1652, on "The Hireling Ministry"* (Utica, N.Y.: H. H. Curtiss, Christian Contributor Office, 1847): 89, 111–12. The introduction indicates that part of this review was first published in the *Christian Contributor* and that the request for both the review and its publication came from three bodies of Baptist ministers, one meeting in the North Beriah Baptist Church, New York,

May 9, 1845 (A. L. Post and I. B. Price officers), a second group meeting in Utica, August 5, 1846 (Brother Tillinghast, moderator), and the third a meeting of the American Baptist Free Missionary Society, Albany, May 5 and 6, 1847 (1–4). Grosvenor mocks Hague's friendly criticism of Fuller's slavery as good in its root but just unfortunate in the poor fruit born: "But for the grafting, then, the fruit would always have been both delicious and salubrious; nay, the tree itself would have been pleasant to look upon, and would have spread its cooling foliage over many millions more of 'the best conditioned peasantry in the world'" (13). For more on the Free Baptist Missionary Society, see McKivigan, "The American Baptist Free Missionary Society."

40. Grosvenor continued to imply that abolitionists would eventually attain the respect Williams now claimed: "His triumph will ever stand as a great fact for the light and encouragement of reformers, who respect truth for its intrinsic beauty and value, and who fear God more than earthly dishonor; for, though he was calumniated by any of that age, his works have followed him since, diffusing a light which occasions the admiration of both the pious and the profane. God is gloried in him" (156).

41. Grosvenor, *Review,* 156. The emphasis is his.

42. See McKivigan's chapters on "Interdenominational Antislavery Endeavors" and "Vote as You Pray and Pray as You Vote" in *Proslavery Religion,* 128–60 and especially 176–78.

43. Engelder, "Churches and Slavery," 70; Charles C. Cole Jr., *The Social Ideas of Northern Evangelists, 1826–1860* (New York: Octagon, 1966), 211–13; McKivigan, *Proslavery Religion,* 88, 177. In the context of attempts to prevent schism, McKivigan characterizes Wayland's position as moderate, in contrast with that of radical abolitionists. Contemporaries also saw Wayland as "conservative" on slavery, contrasting his gradualism with the immediatism of Garrison; see *Liberator* (July 2, 1858) for a letter (E. H. H. to Mr. Garrison, Providence, June 18, 1858) reporting that recently in Providence both the YMCA and Franklin Lyceum members debated the question: "Has American society benefited more by its Conservatism than by its professed Reformers?" Scholars who have emphasized the antislavery, reformist bent in Wayland do so by stressing his promotion of other social reforms, such as temperance or better prison conditions; see, for example, Cole, who sees Wayland as progressively more radical and on very thin evidence depicts southern rejections of Wayland as common (217).

44. Cole, *Social Ideas of Northern Evangelists,* 215. Even hagiographer James O. Murray notes about Wayland's sermon digression, "there was no direct allusion" to slavery or the fugitive slave bill (238).

45. S. W. W[heeler] to Brother Garrison and printed in the *Liberator* (March 17, 1854); this newspaper also printed the text of Wayland's speech (March 24, 1854) and reported Wayland is the most prominent Rhode Islander to sign a petition from New England clergy opposing the Nebraska Act (April 14, 1854).

46. Other religious leaders in the North abandoned their silence on slavery over the Kansas-Nebraska Bill; see for example the sermon delivered at Ohio Wesleyan University by another college president, who preached his first public attack on southern proslavery policies at this time; Edward Thomson, *The Pulpit and Politics* (Cincinnati, 1854). For more on ministers' response to the Kansas-Nebraska Bill, see the essay by Laura L. Mitchell in this volume.

47. The *American Baptist* applauded Wayland's speech but chided him for timing, noting,

"Had he, and the other leaders of the conservative classes, with whom he has formerly sympathized and acted, done this at the proper time, there would have been, now, no Nebraska bill for
him or them to oppose," reprinted in the *Liberator* (April 21, 1854); for southern attacks on
Wayland (reprinted from southern newspapers), see the *Liberator* (June 9, 1854).

48. Garrison added this note to a reprinting of favorable coverage of antislavery meetings
in the *Rhode Island Freeman,* then edited by a man active in immediatist circles; the original
story was entitled, "The Providence Press on the Anti-Slavery Convention," in *Liberator* (January 26, 1855).

49. See "Dr Wayland Annihilated" for the *Liberator's* tongue-in-cheek report (copied from
the *Providence Journal*) that Mississippi College had just banned his "Moral Science" because of
its teachings on African slavery (September 18, 1857). Other schools dropped the text as late as
1860, with Albea Godbold suggesting that church-related schools were more tolerant of northern
textbooks and viewpoints than state universities; see his *Church College of the Old South* (Durham, N.C.: Duke University Press, 1944), 166.

50. Letter of F. Wayland to Rev. Joel Hawes, Rev. Ray Palmer, Providence, October 19, 1857,
in *Liberator* (November 20, 1857). The son, Heman Lincoln, was referring to differences between
Wayland's 1838 tract, "The Limitations of Human Responsibility," and his letters to Rev. Fuller,
written in 1845; James Burrill Angell, class of 1849, in *Memories,* 88.

51. Murray, *Francis Wayland,* 274.

52. Murray, *Francis Wayland,* 263–64, 274–75. For a sample of Wayland's Whiggish views
on the economy, see *An Address, delivered before the Rhode-Island Society for the Encouragement
of Domestic Industry, October 6, 1841* (Providence, R.I.: B. Cranston, 1841) in which he favors
adopting modern farming practices and promoting commercial development in the east over
expansion in the west. His sons also reported (but only after his death) that Wayland had voted
Free Soil, presumably while on his odyssey from Whig to Republican Party.

53. For a clear analysis of Clay's unpopular compromises on slavery, see William Freehling,
Road to Disunion: Secessionists at Bay, 1789–1854, vol. 1 (New York: Oxford University Press,
1990), 493–510. Wayland's conflicted position was not unique in either North or South: John
McCardell also makes this general point about the incompatibility of southern assumptions
about slavery, on the one hand as a positive good, and on the other hand, as the least evil, in *The
Idea of Southern Nation: Southern Nationalists and Southern Nationalism, 1830–1860* (New York:
Norton, 1979), see especially chap. 7.

54. "Slavery Justified."

Leonard Bacon, the Congregational Church, and Slavery, 1845–1861

HUGH DAVIS

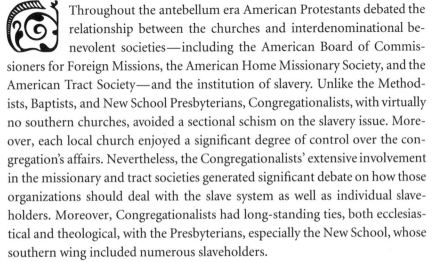 Throughout the antebellum era American Protestants debated the relationship between the churches and interdenominational benevolent societies—including the American Board of Commissioners for Foreign Missions, the American Home Missionary Society, and the American Tract Society—and the institution of slavery. Unlike the Methodists, Baptists, and New School Presbyterians, Congregationalists, with virtually no southern churches, avoided a sectional schism on the slavery issue. Moreover, each local church enjoyed a significant degree of control over the congregation's affairs. Nevertheless, the Congregationalists' extensive involvement in the missionary and tract societies generated significant debate on how those organizations should deal with the slave system as well as individual slaveholders. Moreover, Congregationalists had long-standing ties, both ecclesiastical and theological, with the Presbyterians, especially the New School, whose southern wing included numerous slaveholders.

The debate among Congregationalists on the slavery issue did not tend to divide along theological lines, for New Divinity and conservative members could be found on both sides of the question. Rather, they often coalesced along ideological, and to a lesser extent geographical, lines. The slavery issue created sustained conflict and at times cooperation between the immediatists and the antislavery moderates. These groups agreed that slavery was sinful. But the abolitionists demanded immediate emancipation, and, because they were convinced that slaveholding was in all cases sinful, they insisted that everyone who owned slaves must be denied membership in the churches. On the other hand, the antislavery moderates believed that the abolitionists' ideology and tactics exacerbated social tension and sectional strife. Valuing reconciliation and harmony, they urged incremental steps toward emancipation and looked to southern Christians, including slaveholders, to end slavery. While they acknowledged that the apostles had not sanctioned slavery, they maintained that the Bible recognized masters as believers. To expel all slave-holders from the churches, they claimed, would therefore be both unscriptual and counterproductive. These groups frequently divided along East-West lines, with western Congregationalists being more inclined than easterners to demand the disfellowship of slaveholders and an end to the benevolent soci-eties' contact with, and silence on, slavery. At the same time, abolitionists and antislavery moderates, who together constituted a large majority of Congre-gationalists, rejected the arguments of the conservatives, who considered slav-ery a political issue, not a purely religious matter, and therefore sought to subordinate the slavery question to the cause of evangelism, if not to ignore it altogether.

The debate among Congregationalists had begun in the 1830s, when Lewis Tappan, Joshua Leavitt, Amos A. Phelps, and other abolitionists accused the church's leaders, many of whom were colonizationists, of protecting slavery by failing to speak out against it. With the Baptist and Methodist schisms as well as the growing divisions within the benevolent societies on the slavery issue in the mid-1840s, the debate in the Congregational church escalated in intensity.

Historians have devoted considerable attention to the abolitionists' efforts to pressure the churches and the benevolent societies to condemn slavery and to cease fellowship with churches that included slaveholders as members.[1] But antislavery moderates, such as Leonard Bacon, Calvin Stowe, Edward and Henry Ward Beecher, Edward N. Kirk, and Joseph P. Thompson, who consti-tuted the dominant group within the Congregational church, have largely been ignored.[2]

An examination of Bacon's role in the debate on slavery provides valuable insight into the views presented by the moderate Congregationalists in their struggle with the abolitionists and the conservatives. The son of missionaries on the Michigan frontier and a graduate of Yale College and Andover Theo-logical Seminary, Bacon had served as pastor of the prestigious Center Church in New Haven since 1825. From the early 1820s until the mid-1830s, he had written and spoken widely on race and slavery, combining an outspoken criti-cism of slavery with vigorous support for colonization. He and other anti-slavery colonizationists believed that the repatriation of free blacks would en-courage slaveholders to free their slaves and colonize them in Africa. This, he maintained, would eventually end slavery. From the inception of the aboli-tionist movement, he stood forth as a leading moderate antislavery spokes-man, engaging in an often bitter debate with the immediatists. The abolitionists' agitation, he maintained, pitted North against South, stiffened southern resistance to the abolition, or even the amelioration, of slavery, and endangered the general welfare. Yet he also criticized both slaveholders and northern conservatives, who opposed debate on slavery. Although by the mid-1830s he concluded that colonization was an unrealistic and badly managed cause, he continued to attack the abolitionists.[3]

Following the collapse of the American Union for the Relief and Improvement of the Colored Race in the mid-1830s, which sought to carve out a moderate antislavery position between the abolitionists and colonizationists, Bacon wrote relatively little on the slavery issue. But when the debate on the territorial issue and on the Congregational church's relationship with slavery began in earnest in the mid-1840s, he became an active participant. Between 1845 and 1861, he spoke and wrote widely on the subject of slavery: as the pastor of Center Church in New Haven and a prominent figure in state and national Congregational meetings; as an active member of several benevolent organizations; as a frequent contributor to the *New York Evangelist,* a New School Presbyterian newspaper, and the *New Englander,* a periodical he helped to found in the early 1840s; and as senior editor from 1848 to 1861 of the *Independent,* which appealed above all to Congregationalists and was perhaps the most influential northern religious newspaper during the 1850s. In 1848 William H. Bidwell, editor of the *New York Evangelist,* informed Bacon: "I do not believe that any single pen has done as much as yours to influence public opinion aright on this important subject."[4]

Throughout the 1840s and 1850s Bacon condemned slavery as "an utter and atrocious abomination in the sight of God" that must "be abolished and forbidden by the sovereign power of the people wherever that power extends" and "at the earliest practical date."[5] Contrary to the conservatives' position, he believed that the clergy must speak out forcefully on the issue. As he stated in 1846: "To keep such a question as that of slavery out of the pulpit, in such a country as this, must be impossible, as long as the pulpit is faithful to its trust. . . ."[6]

Yet Bacon and most other Congregational antislavery moderates frequently reminded the immediatists that it was necessary to change the hearts and minds of southerners through the "Christianity of light and love. . . ."[7] Above all, he rejected the abolitionists' contention that slaveholding was a sin *per se:* "I deny that they have any right to make such a definition. The attempt to do so is a fraud upon themselves and upon the public. . . . It is the fountain-head of a perpetual stream of sophistry."[8] This issue stood at the heart of the debate within the American Board of Commissioners for Foreign Missions. Congregationalists, along with Presbyterians, Dutch Reformed, Baptists, and Methodists, had long been active in the society's operations. Because the society considered its fundamental objective to be the evangelization of the world, it exhibited little concern about its relationship with slavery in its missions to the Cherokees and Choctaws. The society's admission of slaveholders to the mission churches and its hiring of slave labor exposed it to charges that it was proslavery. Yet, while concerned by the immediatists' threats to withhold support from the board, its officers above all feared that the slavery issue would hinder efforts to convert the Native Americans.[9]

Congregationalists were the principal participants in the foreign missionary society's first full debate on its relationship with slavery, which occurred at the 1845 annual meeting. Amos A. Phelps presented the abolitionists' position, while Bacon, Edward Beecher, and Calvin Stowe defended the moderate antislavery stance. A committee of the board staked out a moderate antislavery position. Terming slavery unjust and contrary to the Gospel, the committee called for its "speedy and universal termination." Yet it also declared that the missions' primary objective was conversion, not emancipation, and that the missionaries in the field, not the board, must decide who was truly converted. It also insisted that the board could not refuse converts, even if they were slaveholders because slaveholding "is not *such* a sin as to warrant an immediate expulsion from the church."[10]

Phelps called for a categorical condemnation of slaveholding as a sin per se. He complained that, in the report, slavery was deemed an "atrocious thing, but he who is guilty of it may persist in it unrebuked, and be counted unworthy of discipline." He denied that masters were admitted to the primitive church and called upon the board to brand both slavery and slaveholding "a great moral evil" and to withdraw support from churches that included slaveholders, as it did with drunkards and gamblers. Slaveholders, he averred, must be condemned for having the power to oppress, not simply for acts of oppression.[11]

Bacon, whom David Greene, a secretary of the board, urged to attend the 1845 meeting in part because he would challenge the "ultra views on both sides," sought to occupy a middle ground on the issue. He could not accept the claims by southerners and their conservative northern allies including such Congregationalists as Nathan Lord, George W. Blagden, Leonard Woods, Gerard Hallock, and Parson Cooke, as well as Sidney E. Morse, Amasa Converse, and other Presbyterians that the slavery question should be entirely subordinated to the conversion of Native Americans and the evangelical independence of the missionaries in the field.[12] During the 1840s and 1850s, he frequently chided the conservatives for their "old habits of temporizing and compromising on any issue remotely connected with slavery" and their "chronic dread of being termed an abolitionist." He was especially disgusted by their belief that "abolitionism and not slavery is the great danger and sin in our country and the great evil above all others against which all Christian men are bound constantly to testify."[13]

Bacon, in fact, agreed with the abolitionists on several points regarding slavery and the missions to the Native Americans. He regretted that slavery had been introduced to the Cherokees and Choctaws and believed that the board's cooperation with southern churches was not desirable. He also shared their conviction that slaveholders should not be appointed as missionaries and conceded that the board had made too much of the "one great object" of converting the heathen. Finally, although he informed Phelps that "as a Congregationalist, I would stand for the independence of the churches gathered upon missionary grounds," he acknowledged that the society could rightfully insist that its missionaries preach the antislavery message in their churches—or be dismissed.[14]

But the differences between the abolitionists and Bacon were substantial. While he chided the conservatives for their fear of being termed abolitionists, he exhibited much the same concern. Indeed, following a meeting with Bacon and Edward Beecher in New Haven in 1845, George W. Perkins, a Congregational abolitionist, wrote Phelps: "They both wish, and honestly so, that the Board should take different ground from that on which they [its officers] now stand. But they are both afraid of being among the 'abolitionists' and would avoid any course which will compel them to seem to act in unison with such men as you; indeed they almost so said in express terms."[15]

Perkins may well have engaged in wishful thinking, for Bacon in fact was critical of the board's 1845 majority report for implying that slavery should be equated with slaveholding. Rather than attempting to placate abolitionist critics, he argued, it should have stated clearly that the immediatists' call for the expulsion of all slaveholders from the churches was a "miserable, paltering, juggling sophism."[16] In a series of amendments to the board's committee report, which ultimately were defeated, Bacon therefore stated categorically that a master could be a good Christian—a position that he acknowledged was less antislavery in tone than the committee's report.[17]

Throughout the antebellum era a majority of Congregationalists, as well as

Francis Wayland and many other northern Protestants, adhered to the concept of the "good slaveholder"; Bacon was perhaps its foremost proponent.[18] Unlike the immediatists, he favored "censuring and excommunicating sinners, not for having the power to be wrong, but for doing wrong, not for standing in a certain constitutional relation toward his servants, but for his conduct toward them in that relation." Only those masters who bought and sold slaves for gain, refused to recognize their marriages or to teach them the Gospel, and failed to render their slaves "dignity and worth," he asserted, should be investigated and, if found guilty of these transgressions, excommunicated. As he warned Phelps, "The power of Christianity will never be brought to bear against slavery by excommunicating slaveholders *eo nomine.*"[19]

Some Congregational moderates carried the defense of the "good slaveholder" even further. Edward Beecher, for example, contended that the sin of slavery involved the entire society in such a way as not to make an individual a sinner, provided that he was otherwise a religious and humane person. In distinguishing between organic and individual sins, Beecher declared that guilt did not belong to all masters but, rather, to those who had either created slavery or had not done what they could to free their slaves "as soon as they may be."[20]

These moderates frequently drew distinctions between sinful and innocent slaveholders, faithful and unfaithful churches, and southern state laws and the southern people. They also set forth numerous conditions that they believed absolved "good slaveholders" of guilt for participating in a sinful system— inheritance, the need to do what was necessary for the slaves' welfare under existing circumstances, the establishment of an apprenticeship leading to emancipation, and state laws that often rendered it difficult to manumit slaves.[21]

Particularly during the 1840s Bacon was sanguine concerning the presence of "good slaveholders," though both the numbers and the exact criteria were rather elusive. At various times he claimed that "the entire people of the South," "thousands of Southerners," and "the more intelligent Southerners" were "a great deal better than their laws are." At one point he implied that even those who merely taught their slaves to read the Bible were "good slaveholders." He also sought to buttress his argument by citing, as the epitome of this type, an anonymous Georgia slaveholder (probably Thomas Clay, whose plantation Bacon had visited in the early 1840s), who had inherited one hundred slaves and had chosen to care for them in bondage.[22] Bacon was not without his doubts, even in the 1840s. He confessed that he had to "try very hard" to hold on to his optimism, especially in the face of proslavery mobs and treatises. He even conceded that Clay was "a voluntary slaveholder" who probably profited from his ownership of slaves. Nevertheless, he clung tenaciously to the concept of the "good slaveholder."[23]

The refusal by most Congregationalists and other Protestants to demand the excommunication of all slaveholders not only divided the American churches but also undermined efforts to establish ecumenical ties between American and British evangelicals. The Evangelical Alliance was established in 1846 as an anti-Catholic organization, but from the beginning the slavery issue divided these groups. Most American delegates to the alliance's 1846 meeting in London—including Edward N. Kirk, John Marsh, Swan L. Pomeroy, and other Congregationalists, as well as a few slaveholders—resisted British attempts to exclude slaveholders, warning that the exclusion of those who owned slaves "from benevolent motives" would destroy the alliance. Indeed, the American and English branches of the alliance soon parted ways.[24] Bacon agreed with these Americans, terming the British action "a grand breach of decorum." And, while in England in 1851 he attended the British Evangelical Alliance meeting, where he once more denounced the British policy as a "disputed and unscriptural dogma" that millions of antislavery Americans rejected unequivocally.[25]

Bacon feared that unless "good slaveholders" acted to end slavery, violence would be the only alternative, and this would produce enormous social disorder and perhaps destroy the nation. But he was not a social conservative. Rather, he stood forth as the quintessential moderate on the slavery issue. He refused to join the abolitionist cause, but, unlike the conservatives, he was unwilling to draw back from vocal condemnation of slavery in order to maintain social stability, or for that matter, Christian unity. As he conceded in 1852, "I have always found myself in a state of 'betweenity' in relation to parties on the questions connected with slavery. . . ."[26]

Throughout the late 1840s and the 1850s, Bacon consistently held to a moderate position regarding the ABCFM's relationship with slavery. In arguing that the board should not focus its attention on attacking slavery and, at least until the late 1850s, that it should not break completely with the Native American mission churches, he stood with the society's majority in opposition to the abolitionists. Many Congregationalists—including members of the New York General Association as well as delegates to the 1847 Chicago Congregational Convention and a missionary convention held in Chicago in 1851—echoed Bacon's sentiments.[27] In response to the board's position, George Whipple, Lewis Tappan, Simeon Jocelyn, and other Congregational abolitionists, who hoped to reform the ABCFM by drawing away contributions, helped to create the rival American Missionary Association, which established missions that denied fellowship to all slaveholders. From its inception the AMA, whose annual income averaged approximately one tenth that of the ABCFM, depended heavily upon Congregationalists for support and leadership, though it attempted to remain nonsectarian.[28]

Yet, concerned that defections to the AMA would weaken the ABCFM and disturbed by the Cherokees' and Choctaws' unwillingness even to ameliorate slavery among their members, Bacon and other antislavery Congregationalists also supported and encouraged the increasingly antislavery posture of the board's secretaries, especially Selah B. Treat, against the protests of the missionaries and their conservative defenders. He particularly agreed with Treat's demand that the board's missionaries show converts the injustice of slavery, and he warned the board that, because most of its contributors were Northerners, it must be sensitive to antislavery sensibilities, or it would be bankrupted. Indeed, he conceded in 1854 that at times the board had been "backward or evasive on the slavery issue"; four years later he applauded the society's decision largely to disband the Native American missions in order to rid itself of the embarrassing problems related to slaveholding members of the mission churches.[29]

Bacon's search for the middle ground on the slavery issue elicited criticism from both abolitionists and conservatives. As he noted in the *Independent,* "where other men have had one adversary I have had two." His experience indicated, he complained, that "I must make up my mind to encounter reproach from the most opposite quarters." His gradual movement toward a more advanced antislavery position during the ABCFM debate earned him no respect from the immediatists, who denounced him and other antislavery moderates for being blind to the evils of slavery.[30] At the same time, conservatives viewed Bacon as little better than an abolitionist.[31]

While Bacon ridiculed the "overcautious and morbidly conservative northern men," he nevertheless was deeply alarmed by the abolitionists' moral intensity and their categorical condemnation of slaveholders. He preferred to focus on specific, not generic, abuses within the slave system, and he sought to move toward abolition in incremental steps, not bold leaps.[32] Bacon and the abolitionists also differed in their definitions of "free missions." To the immediatists this term meant that no slaveholders were admitted as members of the mission churches, whereas the *Independent* editors believed that there were missions "where the missionary is free to follow his own judgment as to what the Scriptures teach concerning the proper method of abolishing slavery. . . ."[33] Moreover, long after most abolitionists had abandoned hope that slaveholders could be moved to action by moral suasion, Bacon remained optimistic that once God's laws were incorporated into the slave codes (presumably by "good slaveholders") and the system's worst abuses were ameliorated, Christian masters and nonslaveholders alike would enact gradual emancipation statutes. Finally, because Bacon drew back from absolutist thinking, he, unlike the immediatists, was reluctant to draw sharp lines within the antislavery ranks. Throughout the forties and fifties, he generally emphasized the need to follow one's own path toward abolition. "When conscientious men differ conscientiously, and neither of them can convince the other," he informed Phelps, "the best thing they can do is to differ."[34]

At the same time that Bacon debated the matter of fellowship with slaveholders in mission churches, he also confronted two related matters: how to discipline those who were not deemed "good slaveholders" and what effect that would have on the Congregationalists' relations with the Presbyterians, particularly the New Schoolers, both within and outside the American Home Missionary Society. Much as he and other antislavery moderates did in the foreign missionary debate, Bacon sought to occupy the middle ground within the Congregational church and the home missionary movement.

Bacon realized that the argument on behalf of "good slaveholders" was worthless unless ecclesiastical bodies investigated the practices of masters and applied appropriate discipline. He especially had the Presbyterians in mind. Although the Old School Presbyterians had revoked the Plan of Union with the Congregationalists in the 1830s and refused to condemn slavery or to call for its abolition, they maintained official correspondence with most of the Congregational state ministerial associations.[35]

Many Congregationalists, however, were especially troubled by the New School's position on slavery, for they had long felt a close theological affinity with the New Schoolers and interacted with them in the Plan of Union and the benevolent empire. For Bacon this connection with the New School also included a stint in the mid- and late 1840s as an editorial writer and columnist for the *New York Evangelist,* the organ of the New School Presbyterian General Assembly. Yet northern New Schoolers, eager to prevent a secession by their southern colleagues, and thereby to maintain a national church in the wake of the 1837 Presbyterian schism, did little more than periodically make vague, and at times contradictory, statements regarding slaveholding in the church. They generally posited the existence of "good slaveholders" and sought to apply enough pressure to move southern New Schoolers to act against slavery but ultimately drew back from any action that might drive the southern wing from the church.[36]

Many Congregationalists, particularly in the West, became increasingly impatient with the New School's failure to take concerted action against slavery in its midst. Driven by a potent mix of egalitarianism, optimism, and initiative, Congregationalists in Illinois, Ohio, and other northwestern states were receptive to the antislavery message. Often influenced by Oberlin perfectionism, which emphasized a life of perfect holiness and freedom from sin, and having broken away from the Presbyterian church rather than defending the ecclesiastical status quo, they sought to use the antislavery appeal to draw members of the Presbygational churches into the newly established Congregational churches. These Westerners were more inclined than their eastern brethren—many of whom had formed a deep attachment to the moderate antislavery position in the 1830s in response to Garrisonian abolitionism—to convert their social leadership into aggressive activism and their independent tradition and theology of individual accountability into a righteous separation from slaveholders.[37]

Local and state Congregational associations in Illinois, Iowa, parts of Michigan, and the Western Reserve area of Ohio, as well as a meeting of western Congregationalists held in Michigan City, Indiana, in 1846, criticized Presbyterians for their refusal to condemn slavery in the church.[38] While western Congregationalists and New School Presbyterians did come together on several occasions to demand that the missionary societies break completely with slavery, in the West slavery was a major factor that served to move Congregationalists away from collaboration with the New School. At the same time, growing numbers of western New School Presbyterians, disgusted with a polity that would not stand firm on the slavery issue, defected to Congregationalism.[39]

Bacon, too, increasingly became frustrated by the New Schoolers' policy. In his *Slavery Discussed,* a collection of essays published in 1846, he complained that a "great scandal" had been developing within the Presbyterian Church for twenty years. Congregationalists, he argued, therefore should inform Presbyterians of their "unchristian neglect of discipline," and he warned that if nothing was done to rectify the situation they must end all correspondence with the Presbyterians. Bacon and a majority of the Connecticut General Association were heartened by the New School's exhortation to all slaveholders in 1846 to free their slaves.[40] But no hard evidence was forthcoming regarding discipline of slaveholders by either the Old School or the New School. Thus, in 1848 a committee of the Connecticut General Association, which included Bacon, conceded that it was "in the dark" on this matter. Other eastern Congregational ministerial associations went even further. For example, the Maine General Association threatened to cease correspondence with slaveholding Presbyterian churches, and by 1850 the general associations of Massachusetts, New York, and Rhode Island had ended fraternal relations with the New School General Assembly.[41]

Yet, much as he did in the foreign missionary society debate on slavery, Bacon ultimately was prepared to give both the Presbyterians and slaveholders the benefit of the doubt. Speaking for the majority of a committee of the Connecticut General Association in 1849, he claimed that reports of "common fame" among southern Presbyterians had been exaggerated by abolitionists intent upon "agitating the public mind" and concluded that more information was required before judgment could be rendered. He also reiterated his adherence to the "good slaveholder" view. As soon as a slaveholder took advantage of the law and compelled slaves to work, however, that person could no longer plead innocence. The minority report, on the other hand, charged that Presbyterians, especially in the Old School, were "deeply implicated in the guilt of upholding and sanctioning slavery."[42]

Growing concern among Congregationalists regarding the Presbyterians' relationship with slavery was bound to affect their interaction within the American Home Missionary Society, which depended heavily upon both groups for funding and leadership. In the 1840s Congregational associations in Illinois, Iowa, and the Western Reserve, as well as several conventions dominated by Congregationalists, asserted that the AHMS must not sanction any slaveholding churches. The society's policy, declared Jonathan Blanchard, a leading Illinois abolitionist, was "indefensible."[43]

This pressure from western Congregationalists, as well as warnings even by many warm friends of the AHMS that it must attempt to be "blameless and pure" on the slavery issue, gradually moved the society away from its position that it had no control over the churches it subsidized.[44] Fearing the loss of antislavery contributions and facing growing defections to the American Missionary Association, the society's officers urged its missionaries to expound antislavery doctrines and appointed no more slaveholders as missionaries. Yet, because it continued to accept contributions from slaveholders and to allow them to be members of the mission churches, Congregational abolitionists, such as Philo Carpenter and Jonathan Blanchard, left the AHMS by the early 1850s.[45]

The slavery issue, especially as it related to home missions, was instrumental in driving both New School Presbyterians and Congregationalists inexorably toward denominationalism. New Schoolers, offended by the Congregationalists' criticism of their policy on slavery and resentful of the growing competition from Congregationalists in the West, established a Standing Committee on Home Missions, which was charged with planting new churches "in advance of all others." At the same time, Congregationalists' concerns about their contact with New School slaveholding churches subsidized by the AHMS intensified efforts to establish Congregational churches throughout the West and accelerated the development of a self-image characterized by a belief in a free church and a free gospel for free Americans.[46]

These were the driving forces behind the National Congregational Convention held in Albany in 1852, the first general Congregational convention in approximately two hundred years. Blanchard assured western abolitionists that slavery would be the "leading and engrossing topic" at the convention. While some easterners, such as Absalom Peters, Joel Hawes, and William T. Dwight, feared that the convention might drive a permanent wedge between Congregationalists and Presbyterians, many supported the call for the convention.[47]

Bacon was uncertain about the outcome of the convention, though he favored holding it. He was concerned that any attempt by easterners to suppress free discussion of slavery might well lead to an irreparable rift between eastern and western Congregationalists. While he warned that westerners must not expect their "violent antislaveryism" to be adopted, he also informed Parson Cooke, a conservative on the slavery issue, that the convention "must not be afraid to utter in a manful and Christianlike tone, the old New England sentiment of opposition to slavery." Only in this way, he believed, could serious divisions on slavery be avoided. Searching further for an elusive middle ground, he added that, although southern Christians seemed to be "growing worse" on the slavery issue, they must not be irritated needlessly with "modern doctrines and modern applications of Christian discipline. . . ."[48]

At the Albany Convention both the majority and minority reports on slavery fell short of the abolitionists' nonfellowship position. The business committee unanimously supported the AHMS but divided 9–6 in favor of a resolution that churches that recognized slaveholders who used slaves for profit ought not to receive assistance from the society. The minority report maintained that the tendency of the Gospel was to correct all social evils and that the missionary societies must grant aid only to southern churches that attempted to preach the Gospel in such a way as to mitigate the oppressions of slavery.[49]

Bacon attempted to fine tune both the majority and minority reports. He disliked the phrase "slaveholding churches" contained in the majority report, believing that the AHMS should focus its attention on the fitness and fidelity of the missionaries, not the state of discipline in the churches the missionaries presided over. He warned that the missionaries could not preach to all listeners if the churches must first end their connection with slavery. Yet he also was not pleased with the language of the minority report, for it spoke only of the Gospel mitigating the effects of slavery, not leading to its abolition. Something "stronger and more definite" was required, he reasoned.[50] He agreed with the majority report's statement that emphasis should be placed upon discipline for those who held slaves for profit. But, because serious differences persisted among Congregationalists on the application of church discipline of slaveholders, he presented a compromise resolution that narrowed the language of the majority report by stipulating that only masters who held slaves for profit should be excommunicated but also strengthened the minority report by declaring that the Gospel would end slavery and that the AHMS must give aid only to churches that testified against slavery. With strong support from Richard S. Storrs, Absalom Peters, Henry Ward Beecher, and other antislavery moderates, a slightly amended version of Bacon's resolution was adopted by the convention.[51]

Bacon's hope that eastern and western Congregationalists would cooperate on church matters, particularly in expanding the church in the West, was largely realized, for the convention's resolution on slavery went far to placate, if not fully satisfy, most westerners. Indeed, antislavery Congregationalists generally welcomed the convention's condemnation of slavery as a "stupendous wrong" that must be abolished.[52] But Bacon's efforts did nothing to resolve the Congregationalists' differences with the New School and its slaveholding minority in relation to the AHMS. If anything, the convention's action on missions and slavery, as well as its abrogation of the Plan of Union on the grounds that under its auspices Presbyterians had treated Congregationalists unfairly, placed the home missionary society in an awkward position. While the southern churches the society subsidized were invariably Presbyterian, during the mid-1850s antislavery Congregationalists in both the East and West pressured the AHMS to declare that it would aid no churches with slaveholders unless there was evidence that they temporarily held them under the "law of love." These developments intensified the New School's concentration on its own missions and accelerated the southern churches' withdrawal from the AHMS.[53]

The missionary society's move toward firmer antislavery ground was deemed inadequate by many Congregational abolitionists, while it drove Gerard Hallock, Leonard Woods, and a number of other conservative Congregationalists into the Southern Aid Society, which subsidized slaveholding churches. Once again Bacon occupied the middle ground. He, like a majority of Congregationalists in both the East and West, remained steadfastly loyal to the AHMS, even though it still refused to cast out all slaveholders from the churches it subsidized.[54] Yet these Congregationalists also were still very troubled by the refusal of southern New School churches to discipline slaveholders or to permit the general assembly to investigate their practices. This failure to discipline masters for even the "grossest oppression," he stated in 1854, was "ever troublesome" and "growing more delicate and perplexing." During the early and mid-1850s, he and his fellow *Independent* editors therefore urged northern New Schoolers to pressure their southern brethren to explain their practices and to accept secession if no action was forthcoming. He acknowledged the difficulty that northern New Schoolers experienced in their attempts to investigate the practices of slaveholders. But when nothing happened, he chided New Schoolers for placing church unity and competition with the Old School above forceful action against "concrete enormities" within the church.[55]

Bacon also was very disturbed by what he viewed as the New School's aggressive denominationalism, especially in relation to the AHMS. He had long been critical of what he termed "sectarian propagandism" among all Protestants.[56] Yet he also believed strongly that the Congregational system of church government was superior to that of all other denominations, and during the antebellum era he worked assiduously to protect and spread Congregationalism beyond New England. Indeed, he was the driving force behind the formation of the Congregational Union in the 1850s, which monitored and reported on Congregational expansion in the nation, and he served as its president for many years. He was convinced that New School Presbyterians consciously sought to use the AHMS to establish new churches at the expense of the Congregationalists, and he frequently charged that, while Congregationalists contributed far more money to the AHMS than did Presbyterians, New Schoolers received more than half of the society's outlays.[57]

In the final analysis, Bacon chose to criticize New Schoolers above all for holding to a system of church government that encouraged "timid declarations" against slavery. Because northern New Schoolers were compelled to recognize slaveholding southerners as members in good standing—however lax their discipline regarding slavery—it was, he wrote in 1852, "every way better—more candid, more manly, more in accordance with spiritual principles of church order—to separate from the New School Presbyterian Church because it is Presbyterian, than to do so under the plea that its General Assembly has shown an unchristian reluctance to testify against the wickedness of slavery."[58] The southern New Schoolers' secession from the church in 1857 redeemed it in the eyes of most Congregationalists, but the denominational rift persisted. Northern New Schoolers continued to leave the AHMS, which eventually became a Congregational missionary society, while most Congregational ministerial associations bitterly denounced the New School's assertive denominationalism as "unfraternal" and devoid of Christian integrity.[59]

Bacon's concern about the New School's relationship with slavery was inextricably linked to the escalating political debate on the slavery issue. Between 1845 and 1861, he increasingly became alarmed by what he considered a concerted effort by the slave interests to extend slavery into the West and to force all northerners to uphold the system. Convinced that slavery was "a question for the pulpit, unless the pulpit is itself to be dishonored and enslaved," he spoke out forcefully, in sermons, journal articles, and editorials, in support of the Wilmot Proviso and the Free Soil and Republican parties and against the Fugitive Slave Law of 1850, the Kansas-Nebraska Act, and the Dred Scott decision.[60] It was, he argued in 1850, "a naked question between liberty and slavery, light and darkness, and . . . right and wrong." As he came to believe that blatant southern aggression directly threatened vital northern interests, his criticism of the southern churches became progressively harsh. He was especially angered by their defense of slavery, which, in his opinion, violated the "first principles of righteousness." He had long held that owning a slave was "*prima facie* evidence of wrong-doing" that "creates some presumption of guilt." By 1852 he concluded that at least thirty-nine of every forty slaveholders were guilty of sin. As he moved toward an ever more explicit antisouthern position, his faith in the concept of the "good slaveholder" diminished dramatically, though he and most other Congregationalists continued to reject the abolitionists' contention that all slaveholders should be excommunicated.[61]

When antislavery Congregationalists turned their attention to the effort to force the American Tract Society to publish material related to slavery, they achieved less success than they had in the missionary society debates. In this struggle the principle of no fellowship with slaveholders did not divide the antislavery forces, though the moderates tended not to push their demands as far as, and ultimately were more reluctant to leave the ATS than, the abolitionists. Yet, because of the conservatives' control of the ATS's executive and publishing committees and their refusal to publish material that might offend any evangelical Christian, the groups attempting to persuade the society to publish even mild criticism of slavery confronted nearly a hopeless task.[62]

Beginning in the early 1850s, Bacon and Joseph Thompson, in numerous *Independent* editorials as well as in Congregational ministerial meetings, led the assault by religious newspapers and antislavery activists on the tract society's policy. They, like the abolitionists, denounced the society's actions as "a disgrace to American Christianity" and accused it of caving into southern pressure out of "fear of Lynch Law and Southern mobs the dread of Southern demagogues."[63] As a powerful agent of Christianity, Bacon asserted in 1855, the society must be in the forefront of efforts to abolish slavery. In addition, he noted that evangelical Christians were less divided on the evils of the slave trade and the need to teach slaves the Bible and pay them wages than on dancing and drinking, which the society saw fit to discuss in its publications. He and Thompson especially condemned the appointment of Nehemiah Adams, a proslavery Congregational minister, and Gerard Hallock, a conservative, to prominent positions in the ATS. By 1856 Bacon was so disgusted with the society's policy that he warned its executive committee that it would be driven from power if it did not change its ways.[64]

Yet Bacon also attempted, as he had in the missionary society debates, to distance himself from the abolitionists. He urged the antislavery forces to occupy a position between "Southern apostasy" and the doctrine of abolitionist comeouterism espoused by Parker Pillsbury. In response to harsh criticism from the *New York Observer,* the *Protestant Churchman,* and other conservative newspapers, which labeled him an abolitionist, "the enemy," "a revolutionist," and "a man of no religion," he even sought to establish his conservative credentials.[65] At the 1856 tract society meeting he stated defensively: "I am not a disorganizer. I am not a radical reformer. I am a conservative man. . . . I wish to perpetuate and not to paralyze the usefulness of this great institution."[66]

Notwithstanding his impassioned plea to the conservatives, Bacon was convinced that, by refusing to publish works that pointed out the evils of slavery, they had lost sight of the very foundations of Christianity. In the mid-1850s his efforts were instrumental in forcing the tract society to agree to publish nonpolitical tracts condemning evils that slavery produced. With his confidence in the society renewed, he urged Congregationalists and other Protestants to support the society. However, members of the American Reform Tract and Book Society (formed especially by western Congregational abolitionists in 1851 to publish antislavery tracts) viewed this shift in policy as inadequate.

More important, southern protests forced the American Tract Society to suppress circulation of a tract that merely encouraged masters to treat their slaves with Christian compassion.[67] Outraged by the executive committee's reneging on its promise, Bacon termed its members "the real revolutionists." Also, in urging southerners to leave the society, he drew a clear analogy with the recent southern secession from the New School Presbyterian Church: "It has long been our opinion that all attempts at ecclesiastical union between the churches in the slaveholding states and churches in the free states, however well intended, are disadvantageous to both parties."[68]

The conservatives' intransigence, John R. McKivigan notes, had forced antislavery moderates into "uncharacteristically strong counteraction." In a rare display of cooperation, Bacon, Thompson, Henry Ward Beecher, and other moderates met with a group of abolitionists prior to the 1858 tract society meeting. The moderates continued to reject the immediatists' contention that all slaveholding was sinful, but the groups agreed that the ATS must publish works on the evils of slavery. In a powerful speech at the society's meeting, which was echoed by William Jay and other abolitionists, Bacon condemned the officers' denunciation of drinking and dancing as hypocritical because the society's leaders engaged in these very practices and refused to mention slavery in their publications.[69]

Despite the united effort by the antislavery forces, following their overwhelming defeat by those loyal to the executive committee, which successfully packed the 1858 and subsequent annual meetings with its conservative supporters, the differences between Bacon and the abolitionists persisted. Growing numbers of immediatists joined the American Reform Tract and Book Society, while many antislavery moderates now threw their support to the Boston auxiliary of the ATS, which promised to publish mildly antislavery tracts. Bacon applauded the Boston society's program and urged his Center Church congregation to cease contributing to the ATS. But he attended the American Tract Society's 1859 and 1860 meetings in a futile effort to change its policy on slavery.[70] Indeed, at the same time that abolitionists were applauding Bacon for attacking the ATS's hypocrisy, George B. Cheever used the columns of the *Independent* to accuse Bacon, Thompson, Beecher, and other antislavery moderates of being hypocrites themselves. Cheever maintained that the tract society was less culpable than the ABCFM, which they supported, because the former society, in refusing to condemn slavery as a sin, sinned by omission, while the latter, in sanctioning and supporting slavery among the Cherokee and Choctaw churches, sinned by commission.[71]

Cheever engaged in a degree of hyperbole, for by the late 1850s the ABCFM, with the support of such antislavery moderates as Bacon, had largely abandoned the Native American missions in the South. Indeed, by cautiously encouraging the missionary boards to move toward a more advanced antislavery stance, the moderates had maintained broad Congregational support for these organizations. Moreover, Bacon was instrumental in assuring unity between eastern and western Congregationalists by supporting the westerners' denominational objectives and by moving just far enough toward their views regarding the missionary societies' policies on slavery to placate many of them.

The abolitionists in the church certainly were more aggressive than Bacon and other moderates in applying pressure on these societies, but they would not have accomplished their objectives without the moderates' sustained, albeit conditional, support for antislavery action. In the debates of the 1840s and 1850s, the moderates tended to be more devoted than the immediatists to upholding the national benevolent societies, but they also were far more committed than the conservatives to employing these societies in the struggle against slavery. Yet, in the final analysis, the institution that Bacon most cherished was the Congregational church, which he was prepared to defend even at the expense of interdenominational cooperation within the missionary organizations.

The moderates, however, not only prevented the Congregational church from becoming thoroughly abolitionized; they also failed to move southern Christians toward abolition. Their insistence on conditions and distinctions regarding slaveholding was unrealistic, for the vague concept of the "good slaveholder" could not easily have been either determined precisely or enforced, even under the most propitious circumstances. Despite this reality, they clung, nearly to the end, to a concept that, as much as anything, divided the antislavery forces. Much like Abraham Lincoln, who disliked both slavery and the abolitionists, moderate antislavery Congregationalists were left with the vague hope that preventing the spread of slavery into the territories would, "in God's own good time," pressure southerners to take direct action against the system.[72]

When southern Christians and their northern conservative allies proved intransigent on the slavery issue, Bacon ultimately resorted to a reverse form of the abolitionists' comeouterism he so disliked. Rather than leaving the missionary and tract societies, he urged southern Presbyterians to leave the AHMS, the missionaries to the Choctaws to leave the ABCFM, and southern Christians generally to leave the ATS. The abolitionists failed to capture control of any of these institutions. But, while the antislavery moderates may well have formed the vital center of the Congregational church and the missionary societies (though not the ATS), on the eve of the Civil War the religious community and the benevolent empire were profoundly fragmented and sectionalized.

NOTES

1. See John R. McKivigan, *The War against Proslavery Religion: Abolitionism and the Northern Churches, 1830–1865* (Ithaca, N.Y.: Cornell University Press, 1984); Clifford S. Griffin, "The Abolitionists and the Benevolent Societies, 1831–1861," *Journal of Negro History* 44 (July 1959): 195–216; Robert T. Lewit, "Indian Missions and Anti-Slavery Sentiment: A Conflict of Evangelical and Humanitarian Ideals," *Mississippi Valley Historical Review* 50 (June 1963): 39–55; David B. Chesebrough, ed., *"God Ordained This War": Sermons on the Sectional Crisis, 1830–1865* (Columbia: University of South Carolina Press, 1991).

2. For treatments of the antislavery moderates, see Robert Cholerton Senior, "The New England Congregationalists and the Anti-Slavery Movement, 1830–1860" (Ph.D. diss., Yale University, 1954); John Harvey Gossard, "The New York City Congregational Cluster, 1848–1871: Congregationalism and Antislavery in the Careers of Henry Ward Beecher, George B. Cheever, Richard S. Storrs, and Joseph P. Thompson" (Ph.D. diss., Bowling Green State University, 1986); C. C. Goen, *Broken Churches, Broken Nation: Denominational Schisms and the Coming of the American Civil War* (Macon, Ga.: Mercer University Press, 1985); McKivigan, *The War against Proslavery Religion;* Marie Caskey, *Chariot of Fire: Religion and the Beecher Family* (New Haven, Conn.: Yale University Press, 1978). Victor B. Howard, *Conscience and Slavery: The Evangelistic Calvinist Domestic Missions, 1837–1861* (Kent, Ohio: Kent State University Press, 1990), ignores the antislavery moderates altogether, choosing instead to view the debate as one between abolitionists and conservatives. Larry E. Tise, *Proslavery: A History of the Defense of Slavery in America, 1701–1840* (Athens: University of Georgia Press, 1987), goes even further, terming proslavery as all those who, in one degree or another, opposed the abolitionists.

3. See, for example, Leonard Bacon to Ralph R. Gurley, 28 February, 22 July 1823, Records of the Society of Inquiry Respecting Missions (Andover Newton Theological Seminary); Leonard Bacon, *Plea for Africa* (New Haven, Conn.: T. G. Woodward, 1825); Bacon to Gerrit Smith, 24 October 1834, Bacon Family Papers (Yale University); *Journal of Freedom,* 8 December 1834.

4. William H. Bidwell to Bacon, 4 October 1848, Bacon Family Papers. The *Independent's* extensive circulation is discussed in Louis Filler, "Liberalism, Anti-Slavery, and the Founders of the *Independent,*" *New England Quarterly* 27 (Sepember 1954): 302–3.

5. April 4, 1854 sermon, Bacon Family Papers; New York *Evangelist,* 18 September 1845, 19 March 1846; Bacon, *Slavery Discussed in Occasional Essays, From 1833 to 1846* (New York: Baker and Scribner, 1846), 188; see also Leonard Bacon, "Thornwell on Slavery," *New Englander* 12 (February 1854): 118; "The Application of Political Economy," *New Englander* 7 (August 1849): 419–42; *Two Sermons Preached to the First Church in New Haven, On a Day of Fasting, viz., Good Friday, the 10th of April, 1857* (New Haven, Conn.: n.p., 1857), 21–22. Bacon was instrumental in passing strong antislavery resolutions in Connecticut General Association meet-

ings during the 1840s. See *Minutes of the General Association of Connecticut* (1840) 8, (1843) 8, (1844) 9, (1845) 6, 15–16, (1847) 9.

6. Bacon, *Slavery Discussed*, 191. For similar statements, see Leonard Bacon, "The Pulpit and the Crisis," *New Englander* 19 (January 1861): 142–44; *Independent*, 1 January 1852, 29 September 1853, 23 March 1854, 5 April 1855, 11 September 1856.

7. Bacon, *Slavery Discussed*, 245–46.

8. Ibid., 193, 230.

9. Clifton Jackson Phillips, *Protestant America and the Pagan World: The First Half-Century of the American Board of Commissioners for Foreign Missions, 1810–1860* (Cambridge, Mass.: Harvard University Press, 1968), 231; Lewit, "Indian Missions and Anti-Slavery Sentiment," 41–42; Deborah Van Broekhoven, "Suffering with Slaveholders: The Limits of Francis Wayland's Antislavery Witness," in this volume.

10. *Thirty-sixth Annual Report of the American Board of Commissioners for Foreign Missions* (Boston: n.p., 1845), 54–61; American Board of Commissioners for Foreign Missions, *Report of the Committee on Anti-Slavery Memorials, 1845* (Boston: T. R. Marvin, 1845), 11–13; New York *Evangelist*, 18 September 1845.

11. Bertram Wyatt-Brown, *Lewis Tappan and the Evangelical War against Slavery* (Cleveland: Press of Case Western Reserve University, 1969), 293, 313; New York *Evangelist*, 18 September 1845; Bacon, *Slavery Discussed*, 140–42; Phillips, *Protestant America and the Pagan World*, 226–31.

12. David Greene to Bacon, 14 July 1845, Bacon Family Papers; Tise, *Proslavery*, 282–83; *Independent*, 4 October 1849.

13. *Independent*, 5 October 1854, 4 October 1849; see also Bacon, *The Jugglers Detected: A Discourse, Delivered by Request, in the Chapel Street Church, New Haven, December 30, 1860* (New Haven, Conn.: n.p., 1861), 15–16.

14. Bacon to Phelps, 29 August 1845, Amos A. Phelps Papers, Boston Public Library; Amos A. Phelps, *Letters to Professor Stowe and Dr. Bacon on God's Real Method with Great Social Wrongs in Which the Bible is Vindicated from Grossly Erroneous Interpretations* (New York: William Harned, 1848), 129.

15. George W. Perkins to Phelps, 30 August 1845, Amos A. Phelps Papers.

16. Bacon, *Slavery Discussed*, 134; New York *Evangelist*, 18 September 1845.

17. Bacon, *Slavery Discussed*, 134, 145–61. A new committee, on which Bacon served, recommended adoption of the original report. Although this committee favored Bacon's resolutions, it feared that to append them to the report would appear that the board was attempting to legislate to various ecclesiastical bodies. Bacon denied that either Congregationalists or New School Presbyterians would interpret it in this way, but he joined other corporate members in adopting the committee's report. Bacon, *Slavery Discussed*, 145–61.

18. See, for example, Senior, "The New England Congregationalists and the Anti-Slavery Movement, 1830–1860," 211, 214, 229; Gossard, "The New York City Congregational Cluster, 1848–1871," 28–29; Clifford E. Clark Jr., *Henry Ward Beecher: Spokesman for a Middle-Class America* (Urbana: University of Illinois Press, 1978), 139–42; George W. Blagden, *Remarks and a Discourse on Slavery* (Boston: Ticknor, Reed, and Fields, 1854), 4–7, 12–16; Martin E. Marty,

Righteous Empire: The Protestant Experience in America (New York: Dial Press, 1970), 96, 99; William G. McLoughlin, *The Meaning of Henry Ward Beecher: An Essay on the Shifting Values of Mid-Victorian America, 1840–1870* (New York: Alfred A. Knopf, 1970), 195–97; New York *Evangelist*, 18 September 1845; Van Broekhoven, "Suffering with Slaveholders," 197–98, 199–200, 202.

19. New York *Evangelist*, 18 September 1845; Bacon to Phelps, 29 August 1845, Amos A. Phelps Papers; Bacon, *Slavery Discussed*, 243–44; also New York *Evangelist*, 26 March 1846, 8 April 1847; *Independent*, 13 September 1860; Bacon, *Two Sermons*, 30–32; Timothy J. Sehr, "Leonard Bacon and the Myth of the Good Slaveholder," *New England Quarterly* 49 (June 1976): 194–213.

20. Beecher's concept of "organic sin" helped to inspire the later social gospel movement. Caskey, *Chariot of Fire*, 134. Calvin Stowe's views were quite similar to those of Beecher. New York *Evangelist*, 18 September 1845.

21. See, for example, Senior, "New England Congregationalists and the Anti-Slavery Movement, 1830–1860," 211, 214, 219; Sehr, "Leonard Bacon and the Myth of the Good Slaveholder," 195–97; Clark, *Henry Ward Beecher*, 139–42; Caskey, *Chariot of Fire*, 134; New York *Evangelist*, 18 September 1845.

22. New York *Evangelist*, 23 October 1845, 19 March 1846, 11 February, 4 March, 8 April 1847; Bacon, "Thornwell on Slavery," 111, 123; Bacon, *Slavery Discussed*, 195–203.

23. See New York *Evangelist*, 23 October 1845, 11 February 1847; Bacon, *Slavery Discussed*, 195–201.

24. J. F. Maclear, "The Evangelical Alliance and the Antislavery Crusade," *Huntington Library Quarterly* 42 (spring 1979): 141–45, 152–53, 158–62; Ernest R. Sandeen, "The Distinctiveness of American Denominationalism: A Case Study of the 1846 Evangelical Alliance," *Church History* 45 (June 1976): 226–28; Timothy L. Smith, *Revivalism and Social Reform in Mid-Nineteenth-Century America* (New York: Abingdon Press, 1957), 42; New York *Evangelist*, 28 May 1846.

25. Maclear, "The Evangelical Alliance and the Antislavery Crusade," 149; Bacon, "Evangelical Alliance," *New Englander* 10 (May 1852): 323; *Independent*, 18 September 1851.

26. *Independent*, 21 October 1852; Bacon, *Slavery Discussed*, 233. Bacon's position was quite different from that occupied by Francis Wayland, who prohibited discussion of slavery at Brown University. Van Broekhoven, "Suffering with Slaveholders," 196–197.

27. Bacon, "The American Board and Slavery," *New Englander* 7 (May 1849): 273–88; New York *Evangelist*, 31 May 1846; *Independent*, 7 June 1849, 23 June 1854; *Report of the New York General Association on the Relation of the American Board of Commissioners for Foreign Missions, the American Home Missionary Society, the American Tract Society, the American Missionary Association, and the American Sunday School Union, to the Subject of Slavery* (New York: n.p., 1855), 1–2; Frederick Irving Kuhns, *The American Home Missionary Society in Relation to the Antislavery Controversy in the Old Northwest* (Billings, Mont.: privately printed, 1959), 29.

28. For treatments of the Congregationalists and the American Missionary Association, see Wyatt-Brown, *Lewis Tappan and the Evangelical War against Slavery*, 293, 313–14; Kuhns, *The American Home Missionary Society in Relation to the Antislavery Controversy in the Old North-*

west, 21; Calvin Montague Clark, *American Slavery and Maine Congregationalists: A Chapter in the Development of Anti-Slavery Sentiment in the Protestant Churches of the North* (Bangor, Maine: privately printed, 1940), 134–36; Rev. Dexter Clary, *History of the Churches and Ministers Connected with the Presbyterian and Congregational Convention of Wisconsin, and of the Operations of the American Home Missionary Society in the State, For the Past Ten Years* (Beloit, Wis.: privately printed, 1861), 52; Truman O. Douglass, *The Pilgrims of Iowa* (Boston: Pilgrim Press, 1911), 116; McKivigan, *The War against Proslavery Religion*, 117; Clifton H. Johnson, "The American Missionary Association, 1846–61: A Study of Christian Abolitionism" (Ph.D. diss., University of North Carolina, 1958), 273–74, 279–80, 283–85.

29. Wyatt-Brown, *Lewis Tappan and the Evangelical War against Slavery*, 292–96; Lewit, "Indian Missions and Anti-Slavery Sentiment," 42–53; McKivigan, *The War against Proslavery Religion*, 113–18; Bacon, "The American Board and Slavery," 273–88. For Bacon's views on the Board's relationship with slavery in the 1850s, see *Independent*, 12 April, 26 April, 31 May, 7 June, 26 July 1949, 23 June 1853, 16 February, 21 September 1854, 11 October 1860.

30. *Independent*, 21 October 1852; Bacon, *Slavery Discussed*, 233; George B. Cheever to Mark Hopkins, 28 October 1858, Bacon Family Papers; Donald David Housley, "The *Independent*: A Study in Religious and Social Opinion, 1848–1870" (Ph.D. diss., Pennsylvania State University, 1971), 121–23. In 1858 George B. Cheever, a columnist for the *Independent*, caustically referred to the dilemma that confronted Bacon and other moderates: "Between their anguish in the views of it [slavery] and anxiety not to cripple the Board, they know not what to do." George B. Cheever to Mark Hopkins, 28 October 1858, Bacon Family Papers. For the debate between Cheever and the editors of the *Independent* on this matter, see *Independent*, 30 September, 7 October, 21 October 1858; Robert M. York, *George B. Cheever, Religious and Social Reformer, 1807–1890* (Orono, Maine: University of Maine Press, 1955), 157–59. See also Theodore Tilton's criticism of Henry Ward Beecher's moderate antislavery position on the board's policy in *The American Board and American Slavery: Speech of Theodore Tilton, in Plymouth Church, Brooklyn, January 28, 1860* (New York: John A. Gay, 1860), 6–8, 13, 30–35, 42.

31. The New York *Observer* condemned him and his fellow *Independent* editors, Joseph P. Thompson and Richard S. Storrs, as "mouthpieces of the revolutionists" who were "unworthy of a Christian age or a Christian land." New York *Observer*, 15 April, 20 May, 27 May 1852. For similar criticism by the Philadelphia *Christian Observer*, a proslavery New School newspaper, see New York *Evangelist*, 23 October 1845.

32. Phelps, *Letters to Professor Stowe and Dr. Bacon*, 152–55; *Independent*, 18 May 1854; see also E.T. Foote to Phelps, 13 April 1846, Amos A. Phelps Papers.

33. Bacon to Dr. Pomeroy, 18 January 1855, Bacon Family Papers.

34. Phelps, *Letters to Professor Stowe and Dr. Bacon*, 131; Bacon to Phelps, 29 August 1845, Amos A. Phelps Papers.

35. Bacon to Phelps, 29 August 1845, Amos A. Phelps Papers; Linda Jeanne Evans, "Abolitionism in the Illinois Churches, 1830–1865" (Ph.D. diss., Northwestern University, 1981), 171–72; Irving S. Kull, "Presbyterian Attitudes toward Slavery," *Church History* 7 (June 1938): 101–14.

36. Hugh Davis, "The New York *Evangelist*, New School Presbyterians, and Slavery, 1837–

1857," *American Presbyterians* 68 (spring 1990): 18–19. Nearly half of all Old School Presbyterians were southerners, while only 10 percent of New Schoolers lived in the South. George M. Marsden, *The Evangelical Mind and the New School Presbyterian Experience: A Case Study of Thought and Theology in Nineteenth-Century America* (New Haven, Conn.: Yale University Press, 1970), 98, 188.

37. For an explanation of this phenomenon, see Evans, "Abolitionism in the Illinois Churches, 1830–1865"; Chris Padgett, "Evangelicals Divided: Abolition and the Plan of Union's Demise in Ohio's Western Reserve," in this volume, 249–272, passim.

38. See Kuhns, *The American Home Missionary Society in Relation to the Antislavery Controversy in the Old Northwest,* 13–14, 17–22, 25; Hermann R. Muelder, *Fighters for Freedom: The History of Anti-Slavery Activities of Men and Women Associated with Knox College* (New York: Columbia University Press, 1959), 277, 293; Howard, *Conscience and Slavery,* 48.

39. McKivigan, *The War against Proslavery Religion,* 128–37; Evans, "Abolitionism in the Illinois Churches, 1830–1865," 177–79; Kuhns, *The American Home Missionary Society in Relation to the Antislavery Controversy in the Old Northwest,* 278; Muelder, *Fighters for Freedom,* 273–74, 276–78, 284, 293.

40. Bacon, *Slavery Discussed,* 220–23; *Minutes of the General Association of Connecticut* (1845), 6, 15–16; New York *Evangelist,* 26 March 1846.

41. *Minutes of the General Association of Connecticut* (1848), 9; Clark, *American Slavery and Maine Congregationalists,* 123–28; Samuel C. Pearson Jr., "From Church to Denomination: American Congregationalism in the Nineteenth Century," *Church History* 38 (March 1969): 83–84.

42. *Minority Report of a Committee of the General Association of Connecticut, on the Sin of Slavery. Presented, June 1849, at the Meeting of the Association, at Salisbury, Conn.* (1849) 2–20; *Minutes of the General Association of Connecticut* (1849), 6.

43. Kuhns, *The American Home Missionary Society in Relation to the Antislavery Controversy in the Old Northwest,* 19, 21–22, 25; Muelder, *Fighters for Freedom,* 254, 276, 279–80; Evans, "Abolitionism in the Illinois Churches, 1830–1865," 195, 213–14; Howard, *Conscience and Slavery,* 48, 50–54, 100–107.

44. *Report on the Relations of the American Home Missionary Society to Slavery. Adopted by the General Association of Michigan, June 1853* (1853), 26; see also *Report of the New-York General Association on the Relation of the American Board of Commissioners for Foreign Missions, the American Home Missionary Society . . . to the Subject of Slavery,* 2.

45. Howard, *Conscience and Slavery,* 40–54, 65–71; Griffin, "The Abolitionists and the Benevolent Societies, 1831–1861," 205; Clifford S. Griffin, *Their Brothers' Keepers: Moral Stewardship in the United States, 1800–1865* (New Brunswick, N.J.: Rutgers University Press, 1960), 182–85; McKivigan, *The War against Proslavery Religion,* 112–13.

46. Davis, "The New York *Evangelist,* New School Presbyterians, and Slavery, 1837–1857," 20; McKivigan, *The War against Proslavery Religion,* 118; Pearson, "From Church to Denomination," 85.

47. *Proceedings of the General Convention of Congregational Ministers and Delegates in the United States, Held at Albany, New York, on the 5th, 6th, 7th and 8th of October, 1852, Together*

With the Sermon Preached on the Occasion, by Rev. Joel Hawes, D.D. (New York: S. W. Benedict, 1852), 71; Muelder, *Fighters for Freedom*, 297; H. D. Kitchell, "The Congregational Convention," *New Englander* 11 (February 1853): 90.

48. Bacon to Parson Cooke, 29 September 1852, Bacon Family Papers.

49. *Proceedings of the General Association of Congregational Ministers and Delegates*, 77–81.

50. Ibid., 83–84.

51. Ibid, 86, 90; also 77–85.

52. Jonathan Blanchard to Bacon, 7 October 1856, Bacon Family Papers; ibid., 92–93; Howard, *Conscience and Slavery*, 112; Muelder, *Fighters for Freedom*, 300.

53. Senior, "The New England Congregationalists and the Anti-Slavery Movement, 1830–1860," 293; Kuhns, *The American Home Missionary Society in Relation to the Antislavery Controversy in the Old Northwest*, 37, 39; Colin Brummitt Goodykoontz, *Home Missions on the American Frontier* (New York: Octagon Books, 1971), 292; Howard, *Conscience and Slavery*, 170–71.

54. For widespread support by Congregationalists for the AHMS, see, for example, *Minutes of the General Association of Connecticut* (1857), 7; *Report of the New-York General Association on the Relation of the American Board of Commissioners for Foreign Missions, the American Home Missionary Society . . . to the subject of Slavery*, 2–3; *Report on the Relations of the American Home Missionary Society to Slavery. Adopted by the General Association of Michigan, June 1853*, 19–27; Bacon, *The American Church. A Discourse in Behalf of the American Home Missionary Society, Preached in the Cities of New York and Brooklyn, May, 1852* (New York: Baker, Goodwin, 1852), 5–6, 15–16; Muelder, *Fighters for Freedom*, 300; Evans, "Abolitionism in the Illinois Churches, 1830–1865," 194–95. For an analysis of the Southern Aid Society, see Howard, *Conscience and Slavery*, 121–31.

55. *Independent*, 12 January 1854, 12 June 1856; also 22 December, 29 December 1853, 16 July 1857.

56. Bacon, *The Old Way: A Commemorative Discourse for the Fiftieth Anniversary of the American Home Missionary Society. Preached in the Broadway Tabernacle Church, New York, May 7, 1876* (New York: American Home Missionary Society, 1876), 23. For similar statements, see *Independent*, 19 July 1855, 6 March, 9 October 1856; Leonard Bacon, "The Relative Character and Merits of the Congregational and Presbyterian Systems," *New Englander* 3 (July 1845): 438–39.

57. Bacon, "The Relative Character and Merits of the Congregational and Presbyterian Systems," 440–49; Leonard Bacon, "Hodge on Presbyterianism," *New Englander* 14 (February 1856): 22–29; *Contributions to the Ecclesiastical History of Connecticut . . .* (New Haven, Conn.: William L. Kingsley, 1861), 63–65; Theodore Dwight Bacon, *Leonard Bacon: A Statesman in the Church*, Benjamin W. Bacon, ed. (New Haven, Conn.: Yale University Press, 1931), 363; *Independent*, 19 February 1852, 28 April 1853, 17 May, 28 June, 12 July, 26 July, 9 August, 23 August 1855, 8 May, 29 May 1856.

58. *Independent*, 16 December 1852; also 12 June 1856, 25 August 1857.

59. *Independent*, 9 June 1859, 7 June 1860; McKivigan, *The War against Proslavery Religion*, 176; *Minutes of the General Association of Connecticut* (1854), 20; Clark, *American Slavery and Maine Congregationalists*, 158; *Independent*, 12 January 1854, 19 March, 23 April 1857.

60. Bacon, *Two Sermons Preached*, 30. For Bacon's views on the territorial issue, the Fugitive Slave Law of 1850, and the deepening political conflict between the North and South, see for example, New York *Evangelist,* 4 March, 23 September, 21 October 1847; Leonard Bacon, "The War With Mexico," *New Englander* 5 (October 1847): 604–13, "Conscience and the Constitution," *New Englander* 8 (August 1850): 472–75, and "Buchanan on Kansas," *New Englander* 15 (November 1857): 682–89; *Independent,* 7 December 1848, 24 May 1849, 14 February 1850, 1 April, 15 April 1852; 16 February 1854, 12 June, 26 June, 23 October 1856, 12 March, 19 March, 26 March, 9 April, 7 May 1857, 15 March, 12 July, 30 August 1860.

61. Bacon, "The Question! Are You Ready for the Question?" *New Englander* 8 (May 1850): 293; "The Southern Apostasy," *New Englander* 12 (November 1854): 627, 637, 644–45; *Slavery Discussed,* 325; *Independent,* 23 December 1852; also 8 July 1858; Bacon, "Thornwell on Slavery," 103–4; "The Pulpit and the Crisis," *New Englander* 19 (January 1861): 151–54.

62. See Griffin, *Their Brothers' Keepers,* 191–93; McKivigan, *The War against Proslavery Religion,* 120–21; Griffin, "The Abolitionists and the Benevolent Societies, 1831–1861," 210–11.

63. *Independent,* 23 June 1853, 15 March 1855; also 5 August, 26 August 1852, 25 January, 1 February, 8 February 1855; Bacon, "The Southern Apostasy," 629, 633–34. Bacon led the way in the Connecticut General Association in calling upon the ATS to testify against slavery in order "to promote vital godliness and sound morality." *Minutes of the General Association of Connecticut* (1855), 8. For Congregational attacks on the ATS, see Elizabeth Twaddell, "The American Tract Society, 1814–1860," *Church History* 15 (June 1946): 129–32.

64. *Independent,* 8 February 1855, 24 January, 14 February, 29 March 1856.

65. *Independent,* 1 March, 20 September, 11 October, 25 October 1855, 27 March, 12 June 1856. For the conservatives' attacks on Bacon, see New York *Observer,* 22 November, 29 November 1855, 27 May, 23 July 1857, 15 April, 20 May, 27 May 1858.

66. *Independent,* 15 May 1856.

67. *Independent,* 19 June 1856, 19 February, 12 March, 14 May 1857; McKivigan, *The War against Proslavery Religion,* 120–21; Griffin, *Their Brothers' Keepers,* 194.

68. *Independent,* 9 July 1857, 29 April 1858; also 19 June 1856, 15, 22, and 29 October 1857, 18 February, 18 March, 25 March, 8 April 1858.

69. McKivigan, *The War against Proslavery Religion,* 122; *Independent,* 20 May 1858; also Griffin, *Their Brothers' Keepers,* 214–15.

70. *Independent,* 30 September, 21 October, 1858, 5, 12, 19, and 26 May 1859; diary entry for 11 May 1859, Bacon to his wife, 9 May 1860, Bacon Family Papers; Bacon, "What is the Cost of Tract-Distribution?" *New Englander* 21 (July 1862): 587–613.

71. *Independent,* 18 November 1858.

72. See Robert W. Johannsen, *Lincoln, the South, and Slavery: The Political Dimension* (Baton Rouge: Louisiana State University Press, 1991), 30–31, 39–40, 59–61, 66–67; Stephen B. Oates, *Abraham Lincoln: The Man Behind the Myths* (New York: Harper and Row, 1984), 62–65.

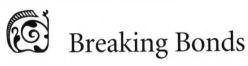

PART FOUR

Breaking Bonds

The Denominational Schisms

Evangelicals Divided

Abolition and the Plan of Union's

Demise in Ohio's Western Reserve

CHRIS PADGETT

 The Presbyterian schism of 1837 was among the most divisive sectional conflicts of the antebellum period, and historians themselves generally have disagreed about the fundamental causes of the split. Some argue that the precipitating crisis, namely, the Presbyterian general assembly's expulsion of four synods in 1837, was caused by disagreements over slavery, pitting abolitionist-minded evangelicals against more conservative nonevangelicals. Others argue that doctrinal differences, especially the rift between conservative Old School Calvinists and liberal New School Calvinists, brought about the schism. Whatever their interpretive differences, historians generally agree that the basic opposition was between doctrinaire Old School conservatives and liberal New School evangelicals.[1]

Those who hold that slavery drove the deepest wedge into the Presbyterian establishment tend to argue that New Schoolers-evangelicals were abolitionists, while Old Schoolers-nonevangelicals were not. Upon closer scrutiny, however, it seems that the supposedly liberal New School evangelicals were themselves often divided over the contentious issues of slavery and doctrine and that no easy line separated abolitionists and nonabolitionists within the Presbyterian polity. Indeed, a look at local grass roots conflict shows that evangelicals were divided over controversial issues, whether slavery or doctrine, and that no simple Old School–New School, evangelical-nonevangelical, or slavery-doctrine dichotomy sufficiently answers the basic question of church schism. Indeed, before we can understand the full story of ecclesiastical division, or even the religious appeal of antislavery, we must also understand the basis for disagreement among evangelical Christians.[2]

The story of evangelical division played out in a Presbyterian province that inspired trepidation among conservatives. By 1837 the synod of the Western

Reserve, tucked away in northeastern Ohio, was viewed by wary conservatives as a bastion of radicalism for its support of controversial reform efforts, especially abolitionism. And because the Western Reserve synod was the offspring of the Plan of Union, the Plan of Union itself was radicalized in conservative minds. First established in 1801, the plan was born of a partnership between two ecclesiastical mates: the Congregational Association of Connecticut and the General Assembly of the Presbyterian Church. These church bodies were the heavyweights of American missionary enterprise in the early nineteenth century, and their Plan of Union was an ambitious attempt to spread and preserve the Calvinist faith over the expanding boundaries of the American republic, particularly the scattered settlements of western New York and the Ohio Valley.

According to its architects, the plan was designed to "promote union and harmony" in those new settlements that were composed of Presbyterians and Congregationalists. Its four articles created a blueprint for interdenominational cooperation whereby clerics from one side could minister to congregations on the other. According to the plan, each congregation could decide its ministerial preference, and whether to affiliate with a presbytery or a Congregational association. Provisions were made for settling congregational disputes, either through the local presbyteries or associations, and in cases of further appeal, to the synod or General Assembly of the Presbyterian Church.[3]

For three and a half decades the Plan of Union served as the mechanism for interdenominational missionary cooperation throughout the northern and western United States. In matters of organization the union churches tended toward the Presbyterian governmental plan, with its convenient constitutional framework of judicatures: presbytery, synod, and general assembly. In doctrinal matters, union churches generally were beholden to a Yale-influenced, neo-Calvinist theology. This latter influence was long a point of concern for orthodox Calvinists within the Presbyterian fold, who often rejected the more liberal, revival-oriented New England Calvinism. Nevertheless, the first settlers to migrate into Plan of Union territory in western New York and Ohio's Western Reserve were typically New Englanders, as were many of the Yale- and Andover-trained missionaries who established the first union churches beyond the Appalachian mountains. For most of its career the plan generally accomplished its goal of organizing a united front of Christian missionary activity on the northwestern frontier.[4]

Over the years the Western Reserve came to be a center of evangelical Calvinism in the old northwest just as its missionary sponsors had hoped. From the time when the Plan of Union was conceived, the Connecticut Missionary

Society (CMS) had set its sights on the trans-Appalachian frontier and the Ohio Valley. A report issued by the CMS in 1802 emphasized that "furnishing the inhabitants of that territory with the best ministerial instruction" was a "matter of the first importance." The entire endeavor was designed, as one historian put it, to "transform an uncouth frontier and bring it into a pious and well-behaved Christian republic."[5]

The Western Reserve, earlier known as New Connecticut, encompassed 3.3 million acres of northeastern Ohio along the southern shore of Lake Erie. Originally claimed by Connecticut from its colonial charter, the land was sold in the 1790s to speculators who plotted its future sale and development by dividing it into a checkerboard pattern of townships and ranges. When territorial governor Arthur St. Clair incorporated the entire region as Trumbull County in July 1800, it was already a long-time hunting ground for Lake Erie Native American tribes, and such local names as Ashtabula and Cuyahoga bore mute testimony to a once strong Native American presence.[6]

When the Plan of Union was formalized in 1801 the Western Reserve hosted only a patchwork of white pioneer settlements, and there was little to substantiate the hopes of New England investors and missionaries who touted it as a "Zion in the western wilderness." Nearly all the early Plan of Union missionaries were ordained Congregationalists, and their reports typically commented on how bereft the area was of religious observance. The pioneer minister Ezekiel Chapman, for example, lamented that in too many instances "religion insensibly loses ground, and prayer in the family and closet is generally omitted. The consequences of these things are infidelity, stupidity and licentiousness."[7]

Despite their initial disappointments, Chapman and his missionary brethren working through the Plan of Union were soon rewarded as their efforts bore fruit in the fertile soil of revivalism. From 1802 to 1808 Congregational and Presbyterian missionaries led powerful revivals in the Reserve that seemed to validate the designs of the Plan of Union's sponsors. The Connecticut Missionary Society published reports in 1804 of a "very general revival" in most of the settlements and concluded with satisfaction that "the harvest there is truly great." A steady arrival of Yankee settlers along the shores of Lake Erie bolstered the efforts of church builders, and in the years following the War of 1812, as the British retreated and the focus of Native American resistance moved farther West, a spectacular population increase followed. Within a decade of the Erie Canal's completion in 1825, more than 112,000 settlers, most of them transplanted New England farmers, called the Western Reserve home.[8]

The Plan of Union encouraged a uniformity of sentiment and practice in the early Western Reserve churches. When the time arrived for such fledgling settlements as Austinburg, Richfield, Hudson, Vernon, Canfield, Vienna, and Warren to build their own local churches, they naturally adopted the same confession of faith, covenant, and articles of practice supplied by the Plan of Union missionaries. In this way, a "common bond of union" was established, just as the missionary sponsors, both Congregational and Presbyterian, had hoped. The great majority of local communicants were Connecticut Congregationalists who followed the example of their clergymen by settling into the Presbyterian framework as directed by the plan. Congregational ministers, such as Joseph Badger, regularly attended the meetings of presbyteries and synods, while Congregational laymen attended the same functions as delegates. There was little jealousy expressed toward the blurring of church boundaries. The locals who convened the Ecclesiastical Convention at Hudson in 1806, for example, were careful to thank both the Connecticut Missionary Society and the General Assembly of the Presbyterian Church for sending missionaries to the Western Reserve.[9]

The Plan of Union proved an effective strategy for marshaling religious resources on the Reserve during the period of the early republic. As the number of churches grew, the Presbyterian influence ensured that new institutional forms would arise to maintain their union. The Grand River presbytery was the first of these formed in 1814, and it was joined a few years later by the presbyteries of Hartford and Portage. In 1823 the Huron presbytery was established, and in 1825 all these bodies were brought under the purview of the newly formed synod of the Western Reserve. The coming years would see other judicatures added or otherwise realigned, including presbyteries at Cleveland, Trumbull, and Lorain.[10]

From the beginning the Western Reserve's Calvinist vanguard was vigorous in its doctrinal and institutional pursuits. A growing cadre of Union ministers and laymen worked through the presbyteries to imprint their counties and townships with the "animating spirit" of their faith. In 1826, for example, the Calvinist establishment organized a Western Reserve Domestic Missionary Society. Missionary enterprise had been integral to the planning of Western Reserve settlement and culture, and with the advancement of domestic missionary efforts nationally in the 1820s, local church and lay leaders eagerly joined the effort.[11]

The missionary movement illustrates how Calvinist church polity had grown increasingly complicated in the Jacksonian period. Reserve missionary leaders first allied themselves in 1826 with the board of missions of the Pres-

byterian church, but four years later switched to the American Home Missionary Society (AHMS). The AHMS had been organized in 1826 as a national
umbrella organization for the various Calvinist churches involved in missionary efforts. It was part of an emerging benevolent empire in the 1820s sponsored by Christian enterprisers whose evangelical zeal and millenarian faith
dedicated them to funding projects of benevolence. The voluntary associations
that they financed addressed the ills of a modernizing society, including
drunkenness, prostitution, and the violation of the Sabbath. The Calvinist
churches were particularly vigorous in their support of these reform efforts,
and they produced a new generation of ministers who plied the populace with
messages of spiritual uplift and personal reform. Toward this end, the AHMS
was organized to foster a growing home missionary movement. In less than a
decade the original 169 missionaries of the AHMS grew to more than 700.
This success reinforced the basic tenet of evangelical Calvinism that mankind,
if not perfectible, could at least be improved.[12]

Despite its straightforward missionary goals, the AHMS inspired division
among Calvinists. By the early 1830s the organization had become a lightning
rod with conservative critics for the support it enjoyed among New School
evangelicals. Conservatives who saw only heresy in New School doctrine were
wary of organizations outside of church control that were dominated by evangelicals. Because churches in western New York and the Western Reserve
tended to support such organizations, it was natural for conservatives to view
the Plan of Union itself with suspicion. As Sidney Ahlstrom put it, the Plan of
Union was perceived by them as "an open gate through which alien ideas and
practices entered the Presbyterian church. The only corrective was to establish
definitively Presbyterian agencies and to make missions a responsibility of the
church as a whole." Accordingly, Old Schoolers sought to separate themselves
from their evangelical brethren whom they collectively labeled "radicals" or
"ultraists" by insisting that all reform and missionary work be channeled
through orthodox Presbyterian associations.[13]

Further complicating matters were the subtle but stubborn divisions between evangelicals over the growing issue of slavery in the 1830s. Although
evangelical Calvinists shared common ground within missionary societies and
joined efforts to encourage revivals, they often parted company on more contentious issues, such as abolitionism. While they could agree on the moral
degeneracy of slavery, many New School moderates felt that abolitionist agitation too often proved distracting to their more essential mission of winning
converts. That not all evangelicals sanctioned abolitionism is evident from the
positions taken by such prominent New Schoolers as Lyman Beecher and

Charles Grandison Finney. Both Beecher and Finney denounced slavery, and both inspired their students to take up the abolitionist banner, but each of them stopped short of personally embracing immediate abolitionism. Finney, for example, criticized the Presbyterian church for having taken the "wrong side" on the slavery issue and for suffering "prejudice to prevail over principle." But he also lamented the "angry controversy" generated by the antislavery movement, and he condemned the "censorious" and "denunciatory" spirit found in abolitionist writing and speeches. Such conflict was particularly regrettable, he felt, because it diluted the commitment to revivals.[14]

As these and other issues found their way upward through the taproot of ecclesiastical governance, the Plan of Union was pulled directly into the ensuing conflicts. Historians generally have taken their cue from conservatives in identifying the competing interests. Conservatives, it seems, blamed church divisions on a circle of New Schoolers, revivalists, evangelical missionaries, and abolitionists and various other "ultra" influences all seemingly epitomized by the Plan of Union. That these categories did not always include the same people was not the point for conservatives, only that they represented generally the influences that undermined the "peace and purity of the Presbyterian church."

The Plan of Union symbolized in conservative minds all that was wrong with the church, and historians often have accepted the basic conservative viewpoint that the Western Reserve was uniformly liberal. When considering the record, it is hard to disagree. After all, in every instance the Western Reserve presbyteries had supported the dangerous practices outlined by the conservatives in the general assembly of 1837, including alliance with the American Home Missionary Society which that they deemed "exceedingly injurious" to the church's interest. The connection was solidified when in 1831 ministers and laymen of the Reserve's Grand River presbytery invited Charles Grandison Finney to settle in their region. When Finney accepted a position at nearby Oberlin College in 1835, it must have looked to conservatives like the Western Reserve had become the very center of New School "fanaticism and radicalism."[15]

Equally distasteful for conservatives, especially southern Presbyterians, was the growing antislavery agitation within the ranks, and its apparent support in the Western Reserve. An old friend of the Reserve, abolitionist Theodore Dwight Weld, so thoroughly canvassed the 1835 general assembly with his antislavery lectures that the following year northern conservatives, southerners, and nervous moderates voted to postpone any discussion of slavery. They denied an antislavery memorial from the Western Reserve's Portage presbytery that charged that slavery existed "even in the bosom of our beloved church," and they ignored the call for the general assembly to "raise [its] voice on the subject."[16]

The Western Reserve already had earned a general reputation for supporting the abolitionist standard. Three years before his appearance at the general assembly, Theodore Weld was welcomed by a number of churches on a speaking tour of the Western Reserve. That same year Western Reserve College in Portage County became embroiled in a noisy battle between abolitionists and local leaders of the African colonization movement. In 1834 nearby Oberlin College entered the fray by welcoming the abolitionist castoffs from Cincinnati's Lane Seminary for enrollment by and naming their faculty leader, Asa Mahan, president of the college. In subsequent months ministers and laymen organized local antislavery societies, and in 1835 the synod of the Western Reserve declared slavery "a sin against God, a high-handed trespass on the rights of man." Weeks before the fateful showdown of the 1837 general assembly, Western Reserve presbyteries busily prepared additional memorials on slavery.[17]

These were "times of high and dangerous excitability in the public mind," according to one Old School memorial, and the Western Reserve, with its heavy concentration of Congregationalists and New School Presbyterians, curried little favor with those seeking to restore orthodoxy to the Presbyterian church. The growing agitation of the slavery issue on the Western Reserve gave the Old School conservatives and their southern allies all the reason they needed in the 1837 general assembly to join in abrogating the Plan of Union and thereby exscind the Western Reserve synod from the ranks of the Presbyterian church.[18]

The church's decision to extinguish the Plan of Union ended a thirty-six-year experiment in interdenominational missionary cooperation, yet it had less effect on the church polity of the Western Reserve than is sometimes supposed. Far from being a death sentence, the general assembly's vote for abrogation did little by itself to change the ecclesiastical orientation of most churches. Local presbyteries acknowledged the action but expressed defiance rather than disappointment. Anger at the Presbyterian church rather than despair over the Plan of Union typified their attitudes. They rejected the general assembly's claim that the plan was unconstitutional and reaffirmed their commitment to interdenominational union. The Portage presbytery, for example, resolved that the Plan of Union had "been productive of peace and harmony in the churches, and of . . . good to the cause of Christ." The Lorain presbytery likewise rejected the abrogation as "unconstitutional" and declared it to be a "tyrannical invasion of the guaranteed rights of the synods of the Presbyterian Church." [19]

The spirit of independence demonstrated by the Western Reserve reflected a circling of the wagons by local presbyteries responding to outside hostility. Yet their proclamations of independence masked a lingering split between local evangelicals that had first formed almost a decade earlier. Some evangelicals, especially younger ministers inspired by the "new measures" of Charles Grandison Finney, felt that ecclesiastical dominion obstructed their efforts as moral agents of God. Older, more moderate evangelicals, however, were not so sure. The questions and concerns that divided them just as often found expression in the local political culture as they did in the minutes of the local presbyteries. Indeed, the evangelical response to the evolving political culture offers a key for understanding ecclesiastical division and the religious appeal of abolitionism.

As the deferential political culture of the colonial era gave way in the 1820s to a more participatory one, a number of evangelical concerns worked their way into the political spectrum, including the preservation of the Sabbath and the fight against Native American removal. The first to inspire an independent political party was antimasonry, and it prefigured many of the same divisions within the evangelical community that abolitionism later brought to light.

Antimasonry came to northern Ohio fresh on the heels of the infamous William Morgan case in New York. The 1826 abduction and apparent murder of Morgan, a dissident Mason who published a volume exposing the society's secrets, suggested to many that Freemasonry represented a danger to American liberties. For many evangelicals the mysterious rituals and supposedly ancient rites of the Masonic order appeared inimical to a God-fearing and democratic society, and so they undertook the politicization of antimasonic sentiment to safeguard the Christian republic.[20]

Antimasonry became the country's first third party, fitting in with neither of the traditional wings of the old Republican Party. Antimasonry's greatest support came from the burned over evangelical districts of New England, western New York, and the Western Reserve. Ohio's first antimasonic newspaper appeared in the Reserve's Ashtabula County in 1828, and within two years ten antimasonic papers appeared throughout the state. All but one were published in northeastern Ohio, four in the Western Reserve alone.[21]

Compared to the traditional style of politics that it helped replace, the political culture created by evangelicals was less deferential and less circumspect, and because it was unabashedly moral, it was perfectly suited to a crusade like antimasonry. Many Western Reserve evangelicals were attracted to antimasonry for the same reason they joined other benevolent empire crusades: It offered a single-minded attack on an institution that "has been found to cherish principles and tend to purposes, which ought not to be tolerated in this republic—principles repugnant to Christianity." Calling Freemasonry a "monstrous moral evil," one antimasonic editor denied that Masons were "positively in support of Religion and the evangelical morality of the Bible." [22]

Unlike other objects of moral reform, Freemasonry was an evil embedded in a secretive institutional framework whose members often wielded substantial political power, making it, as one antimasonic resolution put it, an *imperium in imperio.* Freemasonry posed a double threat, therefore, both moral and political, to the well being of the republic. Only an enlightened electorate acting out of Christian duty could hope to combat such a foe. Those who attended an 1830 Portage County antimasonic convention were convinced of "the necessity and propriety of using political means for counteracting political masonry." This was a millenarian politics: "[M]asonry must finally prevail and predominate, or be put down. So with antimasonry. The appeal is to the public; let every voter record his opinion in the ballot box; and whichever is thus put down, great will be the fall!" The broadening political culture of the 1820s and the evangelicals' growing confidence that they could cure society of its moral ills made antimasonic politics a logical extension of benevolent empire reform. In this way, evangelicals demonstrated an independent grass roots influence in the polity of the Western Reserve. [23]

During the 1830 elections, antimasonic candidates won solid majorities throughout the Reserve in their bids for local office. In Ashtabula County, the antimasonic ticket elected its candidates for state representative, sheriff, auditor, commissioner, assessor, and gave a 173-vote majority to congressional candidate Jonathan Sloane over incumbent Elisha Whittlesey. The result was nearly the same in neighboring Geauga County, with the only losses coming against incumbents. In Portage County, the entire antimasonic ticket was elected by an average margin of about 40 percent, and antimasons scored scattered victories in Medina and Huron Counties also. [24]

Though often seen as a monolithic evangelical crusade, both by contemporaries and modern historians, antimasonry ushered in a millenarian politics volatile enough to divide even evangelicals. In the long-standing Plan of Union stronghold of Portage County, for example, evangelicals split over antimasonic politics, creating a division that would abide throughout the abolitionist movement as well. [25]

During its first quarter century, Portage County's Hudson township typified the early republic Yankee farming community. The town's socioeconomic

profile changed relatively little as the leading property-owning families dominated the tax rolls year after year. The propertied also tended to stay in Hudson over time, comprising a steady core in an otherwise fluid population. Because township proprietor David Hudson was among the original investors
who purchased the 16,000-acre township parcel, he was able to secure order
through control over land sales. This orderliness meant that individuals like
Hudson wielded a proportionately greater share of cultural influence as well,
an influence that was mediated through control of the local church. For its
first twenty-five years, then, Hudson was the model of frontier evangelical
community envisioned by the Plan of Union's sponsors.[26]

Following the Erie Canal's completion in 1825, however, a stronger and
more varied stream of migration reached the Western Reserve. As a result,
Hudson's population of steady habits became rather less predictable during
the 1830s, as patterns of upward mobility for the propertied were overwhelmed by the increased transiency of the population and frequency of
downward mobility among newcomers. This socioeconomic turbulence was
mirrored by the shake-ups in local political culture.

Among the first cracks to appear in the reliable consensus came with the
departure of Benjamin Whedon from the Congregational church. Whedon,
an original trustee of the local Western Reserve College, resisted the growing
tide of temperance reform then popular among evangelicals and supported
Andrew Jackson in 1828. For this apostasy he was rewarded with the post-
master's job by the new administration. Whedon's sin was all the more painful,
for the man he replaced was the only man ever to fill that position in Hudson:
David Hudson.[27]

The antimasonic excitement could not have been better timed. Following
close on the heels of the 1828 political shake-up, antimasonry proved even
more unsettling to Hudson's old guard than had Andrew Jackson's election.
For those evangelicals, such as David Hudson, who came of age before the
growth of the benevolent empire and fashioned their political loyalties before
leaving New England, the aggressive political tone taken by a younger generation of antimasonic reformers was disturbing. A few of the pioneers, such as
Heman Oviatt, put aside their doubts and joined the antimasonic crusade,
while others, such as Hudson, simply could not consent to enter the fray.
David Hudson joined with others in renouncing his Masonic affiliation, but
he refused any further antimasonic overtures. He felt that Masonry was too
"loaded down with the trash of the dark ages" and that as a Christian he was
bound to "perform all those excellent things which Masonry enjoins, from

better motives and higher sanctions." Yet he disapproved of the accusatory tone of the antimasons, at one point referring to their "clamor, personal abuse, low scurrility, and base scandal." He refused to embrace antimasonry so as not to offend "a very large number of my Christian brethren" who had not renounced their membership. In other words, Hudson still clung to a deferential standard in politics.[28]

His opponents were not so circumspect. Although he labeled Hudson a "venerable citizen," Portage County antimasonic editor L. L. Rice opened his columns to a series of attacks on the older man for his criticism of antimasonry and suggested that he had become an unwitting dupe of Masonic "instigators" and their "miserable subterfuges." Up to this point, Rice claimed, he had respectfully refrained from exposing Hudson's mistakes in regard to anti-masonry, but he warned that "if men do err in spite of age and experience, we do not conceive it to be incumbent on an editor to be silent, especially in a matter that concerns the public." A striking feature of the new political culture it seems was the willingness of combatants to discard the gloves of deference.[29]

David Hudson's hometown newspaper announced in early 1830 that it would waive all discussion of antimasonry. Editor Warren Isham, newly arrived from Massachusetts, said he avoided the subject not out of sympathy for Masonry but merely to cover other subjects. He could not have known how short the respite would be, for within two years Hudson was once again shaken with the turbulence of evangelical politics as abolitionism was introduced.[30]

Like antimasonry, but even more powerfully, abolitionism led evangelicals on a course that immediately began to undermine the basis for evangelical union on the Western Reserve. Ironically, the institution that first symbolized the divisiveness of abolitionism on the Reserve in the 1830s was also the one most closely connected with the Plan of Union. From 1832 to 1833 Western Reserve College and the Hudson church establishment played nervous host to the abolitionist crusade, which rocked the area with startling force. The college was heir to the Calvinist mission spawned by the Plan of Union. Beginning with the earliest settlements in the region, leading clergy and laymen lobbied for an institution of higher learning from which sons of the Reserve might venture forth into the ministry. Their hopes materialized in 1826 with the chartering of Western Reserve College in Hudson. Because most of the vital support for its establishment came from those associated with the local pres-byteries, including influential laymen like David Hudson, Western Reserve

College was seen as a monument to the enterprise of western Calvinism. Its builder was Lemuel Porter, a member of the Hudson congregation and a church architect of some renown on the Western Reserve. Its first president was Caleb Pitkin, a Congregational minister and charter member of the Portage County presbytery. Its board of trustees included David Hudson, Heman Oviatt, Elizur Wright Sr., and Owen Brown, all long-time members of Hudson's Congregational church.[31]

The opening volley in the abolitionist crusade was launched by college mathematics professor Elizur Wright Jr., who in July 1832 commenced a series of five abolition articles for Warren Isham's *Ohio Observer*. Wright grew up in Portage County under the tutelage of his father, college trustee Elizur Wright Sr. He was of the new breed of young evangelicals, having first enlisted in moral reform causes while a student at Yale. Upon his return to west he labored as an agent of the American Tract Society, and by the late 1820s he was back in the Western Reserve, zealously lobbying the Portage presbytery on behalf of various moral reform issues. His aggressiveness paid off as the presbytery pledged to "use [their] efforts to give one tract monthly, during the year 1830, to each family in the county, willing to receive it." Yet his straightforward style apparently rubbed some members of the establishment the wrong way, for in January 1829 Wright's request to "preach the gospel with special reference to his operations as an agent" of the tract society was turned down by the presiding ministers of the presbytery. Nevertheless, the indefatigable Wright was soon appointed by Western Reserve College to be Professor of Mathematics and Natural Philosophy.[32]

Before the 1830s antislavery sentiment on the Western Reserve was primarily expressed through local colonization societies, and most reformers, including Elizur Wright, endorsed in principle African colonization as they did a host of other moral reform concerns. Fueled by outrage over the issues of Native American removal, however, northern reformers began paying closer attention to southern problems, and by the late 1820s when talk of nullification emanated from South Carolina, the likelihood of an intersectional antislavery effort seemed dubious. When news of William Lloyd Garrison's imprisonment in Baltimore for libel reached Hudson in the late spring of 1830 a sympathetic *Ohio Observer* took the abolitionist's side and later approvingly printed his prospectus for the *Liberator*. Once copies of Garrison's scathing attack on the American Colonization Society were circulated on the Western Reserve College campus, support for African colonization never again attracted the same undivided support among evangelicals on the Western Reserve.[33]

Discrediting the colonization movement was the aim of Elizur Wright's articles that appeared in the *Ohio Observer* from July to November 1832. Like antimasonry had first done a few years earlier, Wright's diatribes raised the hackles of Hudson's old guard, and within weeks a new controversy was in full bloom. The contest pitted a circle of abolitionist converts, including Wright, Western Reserve College president Charles Storrs, and Beriah Green, a professor of theology and sacred religion, against colonization society supporters, including such evangelicals as the Rev. Caleb Pitkin and Deacon David Hudson. The conflict played out in the pages of Isham's *Observer*.

Antislavery was the issue, and the division formed around the two political cultures first polarized by the antimasonic excitement. One spoke for an older, deferential political voice, while the other fronted an aggressive, millenarian, and often contentious spirit. For such conservatives as David Hudson, abolitionism epitomized the disruptive social, economic, and political influences besetting his world. Colonization was one of the last pillars of traditional local leadership, and it was now under siege from yet a new insurgency, which, of all places, had taken root in Western Reserve College. In effect, the Plan of Union establishment was estranged from its own creation, and the fight over abolition was now a contest for political and cultural leadership among evangelicals.[34]

No one understood the terms of this fight better than the upstart Wright. Having been stung once by a presbytery that spurned his benevolent empire credentials, he was eager to settle the score. Speaking of the old guard, he told Theodore Dwight Weld: "We now very clearly see what is before us . . . and we are taking in breath for a *long pull.* Here is an enormous rock to be turned over and the very first business is to shove off the lubberly Colonization Society which is, at the very best, a superimposed dead weight." Wright was certain that "if the mass of American Christians" were to have any part in ending slavery, "the American Colonization Society must be given up, or it must retire into . . . comparative insignificance." The time had come, he wrote on another occasion, "to leave the ground of operation . . . to a society which shall use a more aggressive moral influence."[35]

For their part the "persons of distinction" whom Wright targeted spoke in condescending tones about the "young men and lads" of Western Reserve College who supported abolitionism. When a campus abolitionist society was formed in late 1832 and students toured the Reserve preaching the gospel of immediate abolitionism, most of the trustees had had enough. David Hudson and Caleb Pitkin signed a letter to the *Observer* lamenting the disruption to the campus caused by abolitionism, a sentiment shared by all but one or two of the college's twelve trustees. According to Elizur Wright, they showed a "resolute disposition to *hush up* the controversy." The columns of the *Observer*, a paper owned by the college, were closed to further agitation. Editor Warren Isham, acting as the mouthpiece for more moderate evangelical reform interests, continued to preach the merits of colonization.[36]

Western Reserve College was never again the center of abolitionist thought and agitation on the Western Reserve, and instead the antislavery banner was passed to another nearby institution. Throughout 1834 the Rev. John Jay Shipherd made preparations for a new college in Lorain County. Conceived in the spiritual wake created by the new measure revivals of the early 1830s, Shipherd's Oberlin Collegiate Institute figured to serve as the counterpoint to Western Reserve College, promoting the "more aggressive moral influence" of which Elizur Wright spoke. A native of Granville, New York, John Shipherd was a product of Middlebury College in Vermont. A good friend and fellow alumnus was Beriah Green, the abolitionist professor who had recently departed Western Reserve College. A convert of Charles Grandison Finney, Shipherd traveled to the Western Reserve as pastor of the Plan of Union church at Elyria, in Lorain County, but resigned in 1832 to promote the establishment of a new missionary institution. "I can do more for His honor and the good of souls in this valley of dry bones," wrote Shipherd, "by gathering such a colony and planting it, with its literary and religious institutions, in this region."[37]

Like the evangelicals who devised the Plan of Union, Shipherd believed that the "valley of the Mississippi" could exert a moral influence "over our nation and the nations of the earth." He prevailed upon a number of the benevolent empire's leading lights for assistance: financial help from the New York benefactors the Tappan brothers, evangelical leadership from Finney, and, recently arrived from Lane Seminary in Cincinnati, a student body of ready missionaries. Moreover, he shaped Oberlin according to the most progressive evangelical ideals of the day: He instituted a regimen of manual labor for students, appointed an abolitionist as president, implemented collegiate instruction for women, and accepted students for admittance "according to character, irrespective of color." In practice as well as in spirit, then, Shipherd foresaw Oberlin residents and students manifesting the "deep-toned and elevated personal piety" characteristic of the more aggressive evangelical spirit. He intended to succeed where the old guard of Western Reserve College would not dare.[38]

Following as it did the antislavery controversy at Western Reserve College, Oberlin's rise had a reshuffling effect on the Western Reserve's evangelical establishment. The reverend-professors of Oberlin exhorted their fellow clergymen throughout the presbytery to accept the essential sinfulness of slavery and to disavow fellowship with slaveholders. It seems that most Plan of Union ministers basically were sympathetic to the moral precepts of abolitionism but resented the vituperation and anticlericalism associated with the now familiar Garrisonian abolitionism. Asa Mahan and his Oberlin colleagues sought to create, therefore, an independent antislavery path and formed a new church that soon took the lead on antislavery issues in the Western Reserve. It was this action that hastened a full blown schism in the Plan of Union establishment.[39]

Although the Oberlin church connected itself with the local presbytery, as was long the practice under the Plan of Union, changes in the Western Reserve's ecclesiastical makeup were already underway. Congregationalists meeting in Williamsfield in 1834 founded the Independent Congregational Union of the Western Reserve, and in spring 1835 the Portage presbytery was entertaining a request of dismissal from the Hudson church. This so-called seceder church had formed after the abolitionist purge at Western Reserve College and enjoyed a close relationship with the Oberlin circle. While expressing their wish to accommodate the feelings of the Hudson church, the presiding ministers of the presbytery voiced "their serious opinion, that at the present time, no organization, merely Congregational, among the churches in this County, would, on the whole be beneficial to the cause of religion, or promote the peace and harmony of the churches." The same voices that had stifled abolitionism at Western Reserve College objected that an independent Congregational association "would increase the number of agitating questions, divide some of the churches, perplex others, and turn away the minds of Christians, from greater and more important objects."[40]

Certainly the level of agitation increased later that fall when Theodore Dwight Weld visited Oberlin and delivered more than twenty lectures on slavery. Weld's visit so thoroughly abolitionized Oberlin that during winter vacation a score of Oberlin students traveled through Ohio and Pennsylvania as agents of the American Anti-Slavery Society. Within a year Oberlin president Asa Mahan and professor John Cowles were leading the Oberlin church out of the presbytery and into the new General Association of the Western Reserve.[41]

In September 1836 nine ministers and thirty-four delegates representing twenty churches attended the first meeting of the association, which was held, appropriately enough, in Oberlin. Although its constitution said nothing about slavery and spoke only in general terms about "moral law," the new body quickly affirmed its dedication to abolitionism by passing repeated resolutions denouncing slavery and declaring no communion with slaveholders.[42]

Meanwhile reports of church secessions continued to trickle in to the presbyteries. The Portage presbytery bitterly noted the "degree of ingratitude" shown by the church in Shalersville for removing itself from their connection. The members "labored under a mistake," noted the presbytery's report, "in supposing they could not enjoy the rights and privileges of a Congregational Church while in connection with this presbytery." This was a supposition shared by others, however, including former Lane seminarian James A. Thome, who led his Cleveland church from the presbytery and into the Oberlin association. By 1837 enough churches had left the fold to form the Lorain County Association, an organization to facilitate the ordination of Oberlin theology graduates.[43]

Following the general assembly's excision of the Western Reserve synod in May 1837, local presbyteries generally responded to requests for dismissal with quiet approval and a simple "request granted." In some cases, a ministerial committee was appointed to confer with seceding churches, but this generally was followed in the next meeting's records with confirmation of dismissal. Enough churches had left the Lorain presbytery by 1839 that its ministers requested a reunification with the Cleveland presbytery from which it had emerged years earlier.[44]

Estrangement between former brethren deepened by decade's end with the formulation of a distinctive Oberlin doctrine. The publication of Asa Mahan's *Christian Perfection* in 1839 brought together strands of liberal Calvinist philosophy that had circulated through New School and revivalist thought for several years. Since publication of the Oberlin *Evangelist* had begun the previous year, editor Henry Cowles, Mahan, and faculty member Charles Grandison Finney had sought to express in systematic fashion principles derived from the various elements of Yale theology, Scottish Common Sense philosophy, and Finney's own revivals. Coming together in Mahan's book, the result was a belief that humans, while not free from error, were capable of intuiting the principles of Christian righteousness and could at least choose to avoid voluntary sin.[45]

Those already irked by the Oberlin-inspired departures from the Plan of Union now seemed inclined to view the doctrines of Messrs. Mayan, Cowles, and Finney as doubly pernicious. Throughout the Reserve moderate evangelicals denounced the perfectionist doctrines as a new kind of Oberlin heresy.

The presbytery of Cleveland appointed a committee to refute them and in 1841 published an eighty-four-page pamphlet devoted solely to that purpose. The same year, the synod of Ohio called Oberlin perfectionism "exceedingly dangerous and corrupting" and advised churches not to accept Oberlin-trained ministers.[46]

Secessions from the Plan of Union continued throughout the 1840s. In 1843 Oberlin, stymied by the unwillingness of local presbyteries to give Oberlin men desirable missionary assignments, created the Western Evangelical Missionary Society.[47]

Despite the noisy defections of the Oberlin-led revolt, the Plan of Union proved more resilient than is sometimes assumed by students of church history. For years after the formal dissolution in 1837, churches clung to their union alliances in such evangelical strongholds as Ohio's Western Reserve. Even in such a staunchly Congregationalist district as the Reserve's Ashtabula County, a number of churches maintained their connection with the regional Grand River presbytery. Thirteen years after the general assembly abrogated the Plan of Union, at least ten churches were still affiliated. Not until 1850, when the Grand River Congregational Association was formed with the express purpose of uniting all local Congregationalists under one banner did the last Plan of Union connections expire. Two years later a statewide Congregational association was formed, welcoming even the Oberlin churches of the Western Reserve and thereby formally putting to rest the Plan of Union in Ohio.[48]

The story of the Plan of Union in the Western Reserve illustrates how divisions among evangelicals led to ecclesiastical schisms not entirely explained by the national rupture of the Presbyterian church. Disputes over such moral crusades as antimasonry and slavery within local church polities spilled over into the increasingly participatory political culture of the North, where the reform efforts and ideals of many, often younger, more aggressive evangelicals found expression outside the hierarchical, ecclesiastical chains of command. In turn, the organizations that they founded, including missionary societies, collegiate institutions, and especially such reform associations as abolitionist societies, came to be regarded by more moderate evangelical brethren as ecclesiastically dangerous, doctrinally unsound, and politically intemperate. Though they are often lost in the wash of larger scale ecclesiastical and sectional divisions, these more local disputes among northern evangelicals reveal as much or more about the character of the abolitionist impulse and the political and religious context in which it took root.

NOTES

1. The conflict referred to here as Old School vs. New School represented in large part a doctrinal schism within Presbyterian ranks that emerged during the Second Great Awakening of the early nineteenth century. The basic difference lay in each side's conception of man's nature. The Old School, or orthodox, interpretation held to a strict Calvinist understanding of man's essential sin and his inability to do the will of God. New School advocates, influenced by New England theologians from Jonathan Edwards to Nathaniel Taylor, on the other hand, preached the improvability of man and the importance of individual religious experience. Whereas Old Schoolers tended to distrust revivalism, with its emphasis on religious experience and conversions rather than purity of doctrine, New Schoolers generally embraced it as a key instrument in the work of winning converts to the faith. Detailed accounts of this story include George M. Marsden, *The Evangelical Mind and the New School Presbyterian Experience: A Case Study of Thought and Theology in Nineteenth-Century America* (New Haven: Yale University Press, 1970), and Sidney E. Ahlstrom, *A Religious History of the American People* (New Haven: Yale University Press, 1972), 464–66.

2. Slavery and schism have been integral to studies of antebellum church history. The three *Church History* journal articles dealing with the Presbyterian Schism of 1837 and the Plan of Union are: Edmund A. Moore, "Robert J. Breckinridge and the Slavery Aspect of the Presbyterian Schism of 1837," *Church History* 4 (December 1935): 282–94, Robert Hastings Nichols, "The Plan of Union in New York," *Church History* 5 (March 1936): 29–51, and Charles L. Zorbaugh, "The Plan of Union in Ohio," *Church History* 6 (June 1937): 145–64. These works followed Gilbert Hobbes Barnes's scholarly 1933 revision of the abolitionists in *The Antislavery Impulse, 1830–1844* (Gloucester, Mass.: Peter Smith, 1957). Barnes's analysis revolved around the twin themes of antislavery and the evangelical culture of the North. Subsequent studies that urged the importance of slavery on Presbyterian affairs are C. Bruce Staiger, "Abolitionism and the Presbyterian Schism of 1837–1838," *Mississippi Valley Historical Review* 36 (December 1949): 391–414, and Victor B. Howard, "The Anti-Slavery Movement in the Presbyterian Church, 1835–1861" (Ph.D. diss., Ohio State University, 1961). These studies should be compared to more recent works that deemphasize the antislavery character of mainstream Presbyterians: George M. Marsden, *The Evangelical Mind and the New School Presbyterian Experience* (New Haven: Yale University Press, 1970), and John R. McKivigan, *The War against Proslavery Religion: Abolitionism and the Northern Churches, 1830–1865* (Ithaca: Cornell University Press, 1984).

3. A copy of the original Plan of Union, approved June 16, 1801, is reprinted in the *Connecticut Evangelical Magazine*, September 1801.

4. Of the four synods exscinded by the Presbyterian Church in 1837, three were in New York—Genesee, Geneva, and Utica—while the other was the Western Reserve Synod of northern Ohio.

5. Report of the Connecticut Missionary Society, excerpted in the *Connecticut Evangelical Magazine*, July 1802. Ahlstrom, *A Religious History of the American People*, 457.

6. For a concise introduction to the early history of Ohio, see George W. Knepper, *Ohio and Its People* (Kent, Ohio: Kent State University Press, 1989). An overview dealing specifically with

the Western Reserve is Harlan Hatcher, *The Western Reserve: The Story of New Connecticut in Ohio* (Kent, Ohio: Kent State University Press, 1991). The Western Reserve came to comprise eight full counties, including Ashtabula, Geauga, Lake, Trumbull, Cuyahoga, Portage, Medina, and Lorain, as well as most of Summit County and about half of Mahoning.

7. The *Connecticut Evangelical Magazine,* February 1803.

8. The *Connecticut Evangelical Magazine,* March 1804. Beginning in 1807, the Connecticut Missionary Society arranged for the Synod of Pittsburgh to supply Presbyterian missionaries to the Western Reserve, initiating the first wave of Presbyterian clerics into the region. Zorbaugh, "The Plan of Union in Ohio," 148–49.

9. The bidenominational participation of ministers has sometimes been a source of confusion among students of the early Western Reserve who have assumed that Badger and other Plan of Union missionaries were Presbyterian because they attended gatherings of the Erie Presbytery or the Synod of Pittsburgh. Also, Congregational laymen who attended these meetings were designated "delegates" instead of the more Presbyterian sounding "elder." The *Connecticut Evangelical Magazine,* February 1807. In his 1935 article, Robert Nichols first revised the long held notion that congregants chafed under the Plan of Union and celebrated its demise. He argued instead for the "abiding results" brought about by the plan. Nichols, "The Plan of Union in New York," 29–30, 50. Indeed, relatively few Western Reserve churches are on record for having resisted the partnership in its formative years and most seemed to embrace the spirit of "accommodation." See, Zorbaugh, "The Plan of Union in Ohio," 153. In the decades that followed, much of the scrutiny given to the Plan of Union's demise suffered from partisan myopia. For a brief discussion of this, see Robert S. Fletcher, *A History of Oberlin College: From Its Foundation through the Civil War,* vol. 1 (Oberlin, Ohio: 1943), 220, fn39, as well as the aforementioned *Church History* articles.

10. Regular meetings of the presbytery were scheduled and presided over by local ministers and lay delegates. The duties of the presbytery included reporting on the state of religion, including the numbers of those converted and baptised. Ministers would also interview and ordain candidates for the ministry and grant licenses to preach. The presbytery also heard various requests from area churches, including appeals to resolve disputes between ministers and congregations and to distribute generally whatever resources were available to fledgling churches.

11. Fletcher, *A History of Oberlin College,* 73.

12. Charles Sellers writes of those he calls Christian businessmen, reform-minded individuals who financed the Benevolent Empire "partly because their market perspective and heightened sense of potency made them the first to feel responsible for a broader range of evil wrought or good left undone. . . ." It was their experience in "projecting, organizing, and managing large schemes to yield large results over long periods" that made the reform and missionary societies so organizationally viable. Charles Sellers, *The Market Revolution: Jacksonian America, 1815–1846* (New York: Oxford University Press, 1991), 216. Victor B. Howard, *Conscience and Slavery: The Evangelistic Calvinist Domestic Missions, 1837–1861* (Kent, Ohio: Kent State University Press, 1990), 5.

13. Howard, *Conscience and Slavery,* 29. Ahlstrom, *A Religious History of the American People,* 465.

14. Victor Howard describes how the abolitionist question drove New Schoolers and Congregationalists apart from their joint benevolent programs formed under the Plan of Union. Howard, *Conscience and Slavery,* xii. Lyman Beecher's uneasiness with abolitionism is well known. During the 1836 meeting of the General Assembly he fought conservative attempts to gag all debate on the slavery question but later proved equally quick to disparage the efforts of abolitionists. His advice to abolitionist Theodore Dwight Weld to "pray much, say little, be humble and wait" fairly characterizes one strain of New School reluctance on the matter. It seems that increasingly he too associated abolitionism with New School revivalism and took pains to distance himself from both. See the discussion in Barnes, *The Antislavery Impulse,* 94–96. The advice given to Weld is in Lyman Beecher to Weld, October 8, 1834, *Letters of Theodore Dwight Weld, Angelina Grimke Weld, and Sarah Grimke, 1822–1844* (Gloucester, Mass.: Peter Smith, 1965), Gilbert H. Barnes and Dwight L. Dumond, eds., 173. Charles Grandison Finney's ambivalence toward antislavery agitation is evident in his 1835 "lectures" delivered from the Chatham Street Chapel in New York City. These were later excerpted in newspapers throughout the North, including the *(Hudson) Ohio Observer,* beginning March 26, 1835, and continuing through June. The material quoted here can be found in the June 25, 1835, issue.

15. Fletcher, *A History of Oberlin College,* 75.

16. "Memorial to the General Assembly," April 5, 1836, Records of the Portage Presbytery, Western Reserve Historical Society (WRHS).

17. In 1834 abolitionist students rebelled against the board of trustees at Cincinnati's Lane Seminary over the question of antislavery agitation. The leader of the students was Weld, a Finney protégé who became perhaps the single most effective abolitionist speaker in the North during the 1830s. Many of Weld's fellow students, the so-called Lane "rebels," accepted an invitation from Oberlin College founder John J. Shipherd to enroll in what was becoming a citadel of evangelical Calvinism in the West, Oberlin College. For a brief but clear discussion of the subject, see James Brewer Stewart, *Holy Warriors: The Abolitionists and American Slavery* (New York: Hill and Wang, 1976), 56–59. Howard, "The Anti-Slavery Movement in the Presbyterian Church," 15. The Lorain Presbytery adopted an antislavery memorial in March 1837 for the upcoming General Assembly. See Records of the Lorain Presbytery, February–March 1837, WRHS.

18. Quoted material from the Memorial of the 1837 General Assembly of the Presbyterian Church, excerpted in the *(New Haven) Religious Intelligencer,* June 1837. The stated reason given by the General Assembly for abrogating the Plan of Union was the "confusion and irregularity" that the "unnatural and unconstitutional system of union" brought on the church. Arguments that suggest that slavery had as much or more to do with the conflict include Howard, "The Anti-Slavery Movement in the Presbyterian Church," Staiger, "Abolitionism and the Presbyterian Schism," and Moore, "Robert J. Breckinridge and the Slavery Aspect of the Presbyterian Schism of 1837." In effect, the General Assembly's maneuver dealt a double blow to the Plan of Union because not only was the Plan itself abrogated, but the four synods formed under it, including the Western Reserve Synod, were also exscinded.

19. George Marsden suggests that delegates from the exscinded Plan of Union synods were

confused and at a loss to act upon the General Assembly's decision, but there is little to indicate this in the statements issued by the local Presbyteries. Instead, they simply joined the New School General Assembly that convened the following year. See, for example, Records of the Portage Presbytery, July 25, 1837. Records of the Lorain Presbytery, February 6 and September 20, 1838, WRHS.

20. For a discussion of the antimasonic political appeal, see Paul Goodman, *Towards a Christian Republic: Antimasonry and the Great Transition in New England, 1826–1836* (New York: Oxford University Press, 1988).

21. Regarding antimasonic politics in the Western Reserve, see Chris Padgett, "Abolitionists of All Classes: Political Culture and Antislavery Community in Ashtabula County, Ohio, 1800–1850" (Ph.D. diss., University of California, Davis, 1993), 55–99.

22. *(Ashtabula) Ohio Luminary,* December 10, 1828. In a letter written to the antimasonic organ in Portage County, "Evangelos" offered the "professors of Christianity in Portage County" a stark choice: one might choose to be a Freemason, that is a "tool of a dark and intriguing institution," or, conversely, to stand free of its reach as "a member of a Christian community . . . a citizen of a free and enlightened republic." *(Ravenna) Ohio Star,* April 28, 1830.

23. *Ohio Star,* January 6 and April 28, 1830.

24. For news of election returns, see *Ohio Star,* October 21, 1830. Days before the election, the Antimasonic Central Committee of Portage County defended its congressional candidate Jonathan Sloane against the charge of hypocrisy for running on the antimasonic ticket while privately disparaging the local Presbyterian church establishment: "To most of our citizens it is known, that although Mr. Sloane is not a communicant of the Presbyterian church, yet he every year pays more than any other citizen of Ravenna, for the support of a clergyman of that denomination." *Ohio Star,* October 14, 1830.

25. A good example of a politicking preacher is the Rev. Giles Hooker Cowles, a longtime leader in the Grand River Presbytery, who proclaimed himself a "conscientious Anti-Mason" in a circular that appeared in local papers prior to an election. See *Ashtabula Sentinel,* November 9, 1832.

26. According to one local historian of Hudson, the rate of persistence for the largest taxpayers typically exceeded that for the total population during the first quarter century, which suggests that the propertied—those who arrived early and secured tenure on the land—maintained a more lasting presence in Township. See Michael Allen McManis, "Range Ten, Town Four: A Social History of Hudson, Ohio, 1799–1840" (Ph.D. diss., 1976), 113, 120, and tables A and B. David Hudson was also Justice of the Peace for the first quarter century. Waite, *Western Reserve University,* 41–42.

27. McManis, "Range Ten, Town Four," 123, 135.

28. *Ohio Star,* June 26 and August 4, 1830. Portage County pioneer and church founder Heman Oviatt was a delegate to the county antimasonic convention in 1830 as reported in the September 16, 1830, *Ohio Star.*

29. *Ohio Star,* August 4, 1830. Antimasonry remained a potent third-party force in Western Reserve politics until 1834–35 when political and ecclesiastical boundaries were redrawn. Much

of the antimasonic electoral machinery was consolidated in the rise of the Whig party, while the growing antislavery crusade caused an ecclesiastical shake-up that further split the Plan of Union establishment.

30. Antimasons were among those who introduced antislavery to the Western Reserve. Two years before the arrival of Garrisonian abolitionism, antimasonic papers were agitating the subject: "There is, however, a dark side to the picture of our country's destiny, which however painful to behold, a just and prudent people should not utterly disregard. In the bosom of this free republic, whose bill of rights declares that 'all men are born free and equal,' two millions of our fellow beings are groaning, in bonds of involuntary servitude. . . . In their behalf, no general sympathy has been awakened—nor does our government seem to regard slavery as a progressive and growing evil. . . ." *Ohio Star,* January 6, 1830. The transition from antimasonry to Whig politics and antislavery reform is discussed in Padgett, "Abolitionists of All Classes," 82–99. Warren Isham's name first appeared in the records of the Portage Presbytery as a licentiate from the Hamp[din Congregational] Association of Massachusetts. Records of the Portage Presbytery, April 6, 1830.

31. Because its development had been nurtured by a circle of Yale-trained Congregationalist ministers on the reserve, the college earned local flattery as the "Yale of the West." Hatcher, *The Western Reserve,* 174. For the connections between the Presbyteries and Western Reserve College's founding, see Frederick Clayton Waite, *Western Reserve University: The Hudson Era* (Cleveland: Western Reserve University Press, 1943), 33–48 passim, and Grace Goulder Izant, *Hudson's Heritage* (Kent, Ohio: Kent State University Press, 1985), 146. The names of the college's various founders can be found in Izant, *Hudson's Heritage.* See also the Records of the Portage Presbytery, December 8, 1818. Hudson and Oviatt were original members of Hudson's Congregational church, while Owen Brown joined upon his arrival three years later in 1805. Elizur Wright was the father of Elizur Wright Jr., a leader in Benevolent Empire causes on the Reserve. See David French, "Elizur Wright Jr., and the Emergence of Anti-Colonization Sentiments on the Connecticut Western Reserve," *Ohio History* 85 (winter 1976): 49–66.

32. Regarding efforts to distribute religious literature and the promotion of a tract society in Portage County, see Records of Portage Presbytery, September 7, 1824, April 3, 1827, and September 8, 1829. Regarding Wright's request to preach, see records for January 14, 1829.

33. For a more detailed discussion of abolitionism's introduction in Hudson, see French, "Elizur Wright Jr., and the Emergence of Anti-Colonization Sentiments on the Connecticut Western Reserve."

34. The Plan of Union old guard was angry with abolitionist Beriah Green for siphoning off students and faculty from Hudson's Congregational church by requiring attendance at the college chapel where he presided as chaplain. His abolitionist sermons beginning in November only further incensed them. See Milton C. Sernet, *Abolition's Axe: Beriah Green, Oneida Institute, and the Black Freedom Struggle* (Syracuse, N.Y.: Syracuse University Press, 1986), 23–25, and Izant, *Hudson's Heritage,* 158.

35. Elizur Wright Jr., to Theodore Dwight Weld, December 7, 1832, in Gilbert H. Barnes and Dwight L. Dumond, eds., *Letters of Theodore Dwight Weld, Angelina Grimké Weld, and Sarah*

Grimké, 1822–1844 (Gloucester, Mass.: Peter Smith, 1965), and Elizur Wright Jr., *The Sin of Slavery, and its Remedy; containing some reflections on the moral influence of African Colonization* (New York, 1833), 17, 21.

36. Elizur Wright believed that "a number of ministers have become alarmed and have prevailed upon our Editor [Isham] (apparently by the weighty threat of throwing up their subscriptions) to close his columns against the communications signed E[lizur] W[right] and indeed against everything on the subject." Elizur Wright Jr. to Theodore Dwight Weld, December 7, 1832, *Weld-Grimké Letters*. Regarding the trustees' influence over the *Observer*, see Elizur Wright Jr. and Beriah Green to Theodore Dwight Weld, February 1833, *Weld-Grimké Letters*. The conflict at Western Reserve College prompted Plan of Union stalwarts to examine again their reform commitments. Some, like David Hudson, were content to see the college fall into peaceful obscurity. Others were not so easily reconciled. College trustee Elizur Wright Sr., father of the abolitionist, bided time in the old church, while fellow trustee Owen Brown resigned his position on the board and put aside three decades of membership in Hudson's First Congregational Church to organize a new proabolition Free Congregational Church. Known as the "seceder" church, this body was formed in 1834 and ministered to by sympathetic clergy from Oberlin College in neighboring Lorain County. Oberlinites, including college president Asa Mahan, took turns preaching at the fledgling church. Owen Brown was the father of the abolitionist John Brown. Izant, *Hudson's Heritage*, 159.

37. James H. Fairchild, *Oberlin: The Colony and the College, 1833–1883* (Oberlin, Ohio, 1883), 20. Fletcher, *A History of Oberlin*, 74.

38. Excerpted from the original Oberlin Covenant, and Shipherd's pastoral epistle to the people of Oberlin, reprinted in Fairchild, *Oberlin: The Colony and the College*, 26, 27, 59. Regarding Oberlin as exemplar of the new evangelical culture, see Paul Goodman, "The Manual Labor Movement and the Origins of Abolitionism," *Journal of the Early Republic* 13 (fall 1993), 355–88.

39. The Oberlin Church was formed in September 1834.

40. Fletcher, *History of Oberlin*, 220. Records of the Portage Presbytery, April 7, 1835.

41. Fairchild, *Oberlin*, 75. With the Oberlin Church as its nucleus, the General Association of the Western Reserve was sometimes referred to as the Oberlin Association. Although he was no less an abolitionist, faculty member Henry Cowles begged off from joining his brother John in leaving the presbytery. Apparently Henry Cowles and others, such as Finney himself, resisted joining the new association for fear of offending longtime friends in the presbyteries. Within a decade both men severed their Presbyterian connections to join the Oberlin Association. Western Reserve College, on the other hand, remained loyal to the Plan of Union. Fletcher, *History of Oberlin*, 220.

42. Fletcher, *History of Oberlin*, 254–55.

43. Records of the Portage Presbytery, April 5, 1836. Fletcher, *History of Oberlin*, 220, 254–55. Churches did not always formally request dismissal from their ecclesiastical connections. In February 1837, the Lorain Presbytery resolved to check on a number of churches "which are reported to have left the presbytery." Records of the Lorain Presbytery, February 8, 1837. Com-

paring the numbers of churches reporting to the presbyteries year after year gives some idea of the attrition rate. In the Portage Presbytery, for example, twenty-seven churches were listed in the 1835 records, twenty-four in 1837, twenty-two in 1838, and twenty in 1839.

44. Records of the Lorain Presbytery, February 5, 1839.

45. Fairchild, *Oberlin,* 84–85, 90–91.

46. According to one Oberlin historian, the lines were drawn as follows: orthodox Calvinism, Plan of Union conservatism, distrust of revivalism, and Western Reserve College were arrayed on one side; perfectionism, Congregationalism, enthusiasm for reform, and Oberlin were on the other. Fletcher, *History of Oberlin,* 225–26. In August of 1839 the Lorain County Presbytery reported a protest from two of its members against inviting an individual from the Lorain County Association, "not from personal considerations, but simply from the fact of his ecclesiastical connection." It was well known, according to the protest, that the association does "not admit into their connection those whom we regard as unsound in the faith [and] that their influence upon our churches is very unfavorable." Records of the Lorain Presbytery, August 27, 1839.

47. Fairchild, *Oberlin,* 134. Victor Howard notes that Oberlinites and New Schoolers were pushed apart on joint benevolent programs because the latter, who might have otherwise have been sympathetic to Oberlin-led causes, had to mollify conservatives within their presbyteries. Howard, *Conscience and Slavery,* xii. George Marsden suggests that this is why New Schoolers became less, rather than more, aggressive on such reform issues as slavery after the schism of 1837: "The aggressive phalanx that had marched in the front ranks of American evangelical Protestantism, now thrown on the defensive, was forced to become distinctly Presbyterian. Instead of asserting its rights, it had to defend its constitutionality and prove its orthodoxy." Marsden, *The Evangelical Mind,* 87.

48. Notice of the Grand River Congregational Association can be found in the *Ashtabula (Ohio) Sentinel,* January 12, 1850. Fletcher, *A History of Oberlin College,* 229.

"To Rend the Body of Christ"

Proslavery Ideology and Religious Schism

from a Mississippi Perspective

RANDY J. SPARKS

 The sectional division of the Baptist and Methodist churches in 1844 and 1845 marked a turning point in the history of American religion with important implications for political developments as well. John G. Jones, a prominent Mississippi Methodist minister, recalled the mood among his religious brethren as the schism approached: "The mind of the Church was filled with this unprecedented disaster. To this writer it was the darkest day he had ever seen. . . . It is a fearful thing to rend the body of Christ. . . ."[1] His graphic and gruesome image of bodily mutilation seems almost a foreboding of the terrible bloodshed to come as sectionalism followed its fearful course. Historians have viewed the religious schisms primarily as a prologue to secession, but that tendency has obscured the roots of the schisms and other implications of the divisions, which must also be seen as the culmination of processes long underway in southern religious life.[2]

The schisms cannot be understood without an examination of the development of evangelicalism in the South and particularly the changing nature of the evangelical churches as they moved from sects to denominations. Tensions emerged in the South, as elsewhere in the nation, between localistic religious traditions characteristic of religious sects and the authority and hierarchy associated with the rise of denominations. The transformation from sects to denominations marked a major shift in the history of evangelicalism, a shift with profound effects on evangelical theology, the status of the clergy, the nature of worship, and the role of blacks and women within the churches.

Out of these contradictory impulses came two camps: evangelical traditionalists who attempted to hold fast to the rituals and practices associated with the early churches, and modernists who were more ecumenical and committed to a broad, national religious vision.[3] Through the organization of colleges and seminaries, missionary and benevolent associations, tract societies, Sunday schools, temperance societies, and larger denominational institutions, modernists brought southern evangelicals into the national benevolent empire and made them a part of a vast religious communications network stretching across the nation.[4] The modernists were one group of southerners strategically placed to play a key role in cross-sectional alliances, but at the same time they were caught up in a struggle with localists. Paradoxically, the modernists emerged from that struggle with a slave-based ideology that ultimately subverted their ecumenical commitment to the national benevolent empire and led to the sectional religious schisms.

In marked contrast to the social revolt mounted by evangelical sects in the eighteenth and early nineteenth centuries, modernist leaders of the denominational movement offered a vision of both domestic and social harmony to a region divided by class and race, and their equation of evangelical virtue with a slaveholding republic led to an alliance with the planter elite. Propelled by powerful revivals, the evangelical churches experienced remarkable growth in the early national period. Mississippi Methodists, for example, had only 132 white members and 72 black members in 1805, but by 1827 they had 8,773 white members and 2,724 black members. Impressive growth continued in the decades after 1830, and evangelical membership, wealth, and influence grew at a remarkable rate. Their expansion reflected the dramatic economic and demographic changes underway after 1830 when the state's population more than doubled from 1830 to 1840 and grew almost as rapidly between 1840 and 1850. By 1840 the state had a black majority and was the largest cotton producer in the South. Despite occasional economic downturns, the "Flush Times" of the antebellum era brought prosperity to the state's plantation economy. This dependance on national and international markets created tensions between planters who were committed to the expansion of the Cotton Kingdom and small farmers who were torn between self-sufficiency and greater involvement in the market economy. Cleavages developed between the plantation belts concentrated along the river systems and areas in the southern Piney Woods and the northeastern hill counties isolated from transportation networks and unfit for plantation agriculture. This economic divergence led to sectional animosities that persisted throughout the antebellum period. The phenomenal growth in evangelical wealth and membership mirrored this economic expansion that marked the end of the evangelical "protest stage" and set in motion the move from small sects to major denominations.[5]

With that dramatic expansion, authority within the institutions was exercised increasingly from the top down rather than from the bottom up, and the need for greater institutional organization was accompanied by a growth in denominational authority. Edmund S. Morgan observed a similar phenomenon, with similar results, among New England Puritans:

> Historically the magnification of the minister's office has often gone hand-in-hand with a comprehensive policy of church membership, while a limited membership, emphasizing purity, has been associated with a restriction of clerical authority. Where laymen form a church by freely entered agreement and then create a minister, that minister is likely to direct himself toward serving those who chose him. Though he and they may recognize an obligation to the rest of the world, it is likely to remain secondary and undefined. But as ministers become independent of the laity, they tend to magnify the importance of their own role in the process of redemption and to feel a keener obligation to the unconverted.[6]

Hierarchical structures were already in place among Methodists where authority at the national level was exercised by the general conference presided over by the bishops and in the Presbyterian church, which was governed by a national synod. The Baptists followed suit in 1814 by creating the national Baptist Triennial Convention to organize foreign and domestic missions. Modernists also led in the creation of a variety of denominational and cross-denominational religious, reform, and educational organizations to further spread their message.[7]

The development of denominational institutions brought serious conflicts to the three major evangelical groups—the Methodist Episcopal, Baptist, and Presbyterian churches. Evangelical traditionalists mounted a fierce resistance to the modernists, a dispute that resulted in major denominational splits. In a typical statement of the traditionalist position, one Methodist preacher argued that, "The great cry for 'means and money,' during these last few years to build Colleges, establish Seminaries, erect fine houses for public worship, to support the publishing fund, & c. & c., has raised the suspicions of some of our warmest friends. . . . I am opposed, and ever shall be, to these *Divinity Schools—these Preacher Manufactures.*" In 1839 an elderly Baptist—a member of the first church of that denomination in Mississippi—lashed out at the modernists: "the enemy began to make inroads upon us by sending young theologians from the Academies as missionaries . . . and the poor old Regulars [traditional Baptists] . . . with unsuspecting simplicity, received them into their arms. . . . Then it was that they began to vomit out their heterodoxical [*sic*] sentiments . . . [and] the Missionary System with all its multifarious train, were pressed upon the churches." Congregations outside the towns and plantation districts bristled at modernists' attempts to enhance their power through denominational bodies and resisted attempts to alter traditional practices that often gave more authority to congregations than to ministers. In their view, missionary societies and other national benevolent organizations were part of a scheme by northern and eastern ministers to spread their influence across the nation, a view with substantial basis in fact. For example, historian David T. Bailey found that in the Old Southwest eastern-born ministers held 65 percent of the positions of status in churches during the period from 1815 to 1829.[8]

The transformations were not limited only to denominational structure, but were carried down into the congregations themselves where the traditional evangelical emphasis on lay involvement and authority began to change. In the early New Testament churches no distinction existed between the minister and the laity. The gift of evangelism was only one of many different gifts bestowed upon the faithful, all of whom should use their gifts in the Lord's work. Early evangelical churches functioned in this way; preachers were men much like the members except that they publicly exercised their gift of evangelism. All members, regardless of race, gender, or status, had equally important gifts, and ministry was the work of the entire congregation. In the process of institutionalization, the laity became spectators, a change with a disproportionate effect on women and blacks who were barred from filling church offices but had participated actively in the lay-oriented services.

Evangelical traditionalists attempted to hold fast to this concept of a congregational ministry. Traditionalists among the Methodists, for example, deplored the decline in class meetings and bands that focused on lay leadership and participation, and they charged that modernist ministers refused to conduct the meetings. In traditional practice, the class leader had considerable influence and was regarded as a "sub-minister." Bands—meetings of small groups of the faithful without a minister's presence—also emphasized and encouraged lay independence. The decline of bands meant that "the people look to their preachers as their spiritual leaders. . . ." Similar changes occurred among Baptists and Presbyterians. Modernist Missionary Baptist churches abandoned the intimate foot-washing ceremonies popular among early Baptists, and by the 1840s the festal Presbyterian communion season was a thing of the past. Separate seating by gender, common in early evangelical churches, gave way in town churches to rented family pews, and simple log churches were replaced by costly structures often built in the latest Gothic style. Many of the same churches further segregated blacks by erecting partitions to divide the races or by holding separate services for them.[9]

The fierce debates over church structure, the authority and status of ministers, government policy, and the dangers of the market splintered the Presbyterian, Baptist, and Methodist churches and gave rise to separate traditionalist movements. The Presbyterian church split during the Great Revival over educational requirements for ministers, doctrinal orthodoxy, and synodical authority. The Cumberland Presbyterian Church, organized in Kentucky in 1801, favored lower educational requirements and weaker hierarchical control. The Cumberland Presbyterians, most numerous in less prosperous rural areas of northern Mississippi, became the fourth-largest denomination in the state. The Mississippi Baptist State Convention, organized in 1822 on missionary principles, faced strong opposition from antimissionary traditionalists (sometimes called Hard-Shell or Primitive Baptists) who succeeded in destroying the convention in 1829. It was reorganized in 1836 but once again led to divisions. Traditionalist congregations began organizing their own local Primitive Baptist associations in 1839, but they refused to create larger, statewide bodies and severely limited their associations' authority. The Methodist church faced a similar challenge from the Methodist Protestant church, which was formally organized in 1830 after battles erupted in the 1827 annual conference over the hierarchical episcopal structure of the church, the role of the laity, and the status of the clergy. Like the Primitive Baptists, the Methodist Protestant church attracted most of its members in the southeastern Piney Woods region and the nonplantation areas in the northern part of the state.[10]

As Edmund Morgan suggested, once ministers began to free themselves from lay control, they tended to emphasize a more comprehensive policy of church membership and to focus their attention outward to the wider world. The ambitious modernist ministers worked to professionalize the ministry and thereby elevate their position within the churches and within society. They also sought to reshape American society through a remarkable network of denominational and cross-denominational organizations, educational institutions, and a religious press. Through such efforts they created impressive national "spiritual economies," as Jon Butler called them, that surpassed any other corporate structures of the period. Many of these men were seminary graduates, anxious to assume an elite position in the rapidly expanding professional society emerging across the United States in the early national period. These educated ministers were concentrated in towns and plantation regions in the South where they enjoyed a surprisingly affluent lifestyle that set them apart from their rural brethren and from the early evangelical ministers who often suffered great personal and economic hardships. A recent study of southern town ministers showed that their wealth was four times that of the average American and more than twice as much as their counterparts in northern cities. In Mississippi this group was represented by such men as the Rev. Charles K. Marshall, a college-educated northerner who migrated south in the 1830s and became the Methodist minister in Vicksburg. He married the daughter of the city's founder Newitt Vick and through her acquired an estate valued at $102,000. Indeed, the phenomenon of ministers marrying the daughters of the planter elite was common enough to arouse criticism in the state press.[11]

Unlike many southerners, these successful, well-educated modernists did not feel threatened by the market revolution and the more competitive economic system that accompanied it. They were aware of the necessity for personal control, discipline, and drive the new social order demanded. They advocated the creation of educational institutions and large organizations, such as benevolent, temperance, and tract societies, to replace the personal ties more characteristic of the early evangelicals and their retreat from the world and its temptations. By the 1820s and 1830s the state's evangelical denominational bodies began to establish seminaries or other institutions of higher learning. Such endeavors were costly, and ministers sought the largesse of the planter elite who sometimes sent their children to the schools. Elite patronage led ministers who taught in the schools to boast that their students came "from the most respectable families." Religious institutions were a part of the modernists' attempt to reform the world outside their churches; as one Presbyterian minister explained at an 1838 address delivered at Oakland College, "Unless sound and wholesome moral principles pervade and control the community, the nation must inevitably work its own ruin. . . ." The modernists also furthered education through the Sunday school movement, which was well underway in the state by the 1830s, and through the distribution of scriptures. As early as 1815 a group of Mississippi ministers established the Amite and Florida Bible Society, and by 1830 a Presbyterian minister opened a branch of the American Bible Society in Natchez. Modernists also joined enthusiastically in the national temperance movement and encouraged churches to establish branches. The Presbyterian synod of Mississippi and South Alabama hailed "the present efforts in favor of total abstinence from ardent spirits as among the happiest of our times . . . ," while the Baptist State Convention called on "every patriotic citizen, every one who is fond of good order in society" to support temperance.[12]

Traditionalists, on the other hand, vigorously opposed such efforts to spread the Gospel. They protested "against Missionary, Tract, Sunday School, and Temperance Societies—not because we are opposed to the spread of the gospel, but because our Lord has not commanded any such thing. About Sunday Schools and Temperance societies, we shall say nothing more than we consider them a part of the trumpery of 'Mystery Babylon the Great.'" Traditionalists further accused modernist ministers of using the benevolent institutions as a means of feathering their own nests. As one group of Mississippi Primitive Baptists charged, "This making a trade of religion is a shocking evil. We find tract societies established; charitable institutions set on foot; new plans devised to meliorate our condition; new buildings erected; new laws devised; new improvements suggested; and when we follow them up and see them organized, we shall find the pious, humane, and totally disinterested projectors filling the lucrative places of presidents, scribes, agents, clerks, printers, &c.—a son here, a brother there, and religion is made to answer the purpose of private gain. . . ." The emphasis on missionary work raised theological differences among Baptists in particular. Traditional Baptists held firm to their Calvinist heritage and saw missionary activities as evidence of Arminianism, but even among Baptists doctrinal disputes were secondary to issues of congregational independence and denominational authority.[13]

Traditionalists cited examples from Asia, Africa, and India where missionaries worked hand in hand with colonial governments to force conversions from unwilling natives, and warned that because "the United States . . . refuse to the missionaries the use of the rattan, whip or cow-hide, which have proved to be such powerful auxiliaries among the ruder tribes of men. . . . therefore they preach and practice such things as are best calculated to . . . draw large congregations together; and initiate large numbers into their churches." With large congregations mobilized as voters, modernists would then use the power of the state to further their ambitions. Traditionalists warned that "they [modernists] are fast tending to a law religion, and leading to a union (or what is still worse, if possible, a collusion,) between church and State."[14]

As such fears suggest, antagonisms between modernists and traditionalists naturally carried over into the political sphere. Modernists favored government support for their reform efforts and regulation of ethics and morals, a position that led many of them into the Whig Party. Traditionalists, suspicious of wealth and hierarchy, intensely localistic, and dedicated to egalitarianism, were more often drawn to the Democratic Party. While the motives for individual political allegiance are difficult to unravel, some traditionalists found a close connection between their religious and political views. In the words of a Primitive Baptist preacher: "some persons may think it strange that nearly all the Old School Baptists are State Rights Republicans. But if their form of government and *strict* construction principles were duly considered, it would appear strange that any of them should be otherwise." In keeping with Whig policy, modernists led in efforts to enact temperance legislation, and in 1839 the Whig majority in the state legislature succeeded in passing such a bill. Modernists successfully lobbied the legislature to enact "blue laws" requiring a proper observation of the Sabbath and outlawing gambling and dueling, and they also sought state support for their educational activities. In 1842 the Methodist church petitioned for state incorporation of Centenary College. The act passed both houses of the legislature, but Gov. Tilghman M. Tucker, a Jacksonian Democrat, vetoed it. The governor and his allies, including evangelical traditionalists, saw denominational colleges as antirepublican institutions favorable to a particular class and a violation of the separation of church and state.[15]

Modernists' support for reform movements went beyond the state level, and they became active in national benevolent organizations as well. One of the most popular causes among them was the American Colonization Society. Prominent evangelical ministers joined with members of the planter elite to form a Mississippi chapter of the society in 1831. State denominational bodies expressed their support, churches opened their doors to the society's agents, and the religious press promoted its work. By 1840 Mississippians had donated more than $100,000 to the cause, and the state chapter established its own separate colony in Liberia called "Mississippi in Africa," which was settled overwhelmingly by former slaves freed by sympathetic masters.[16]

Like their involvement in other benevolent enterprises, Mississippi evangelicals' support for the colonization society rested on a shared national consensus; in this case, a common belief growing out of the highest ideals of the Revolutionary era that slavery was unjust and should ultimately be abolished. Methodist minister John G. Jones, a Mississippi native from a slaveholding family, wrote that before the 1830s most evangelicals in the state agreed that slavery "was a great social, political, and moral evil, which, while it had to be endured for the present, ought as soon as possible to be removed." In the early years of the evangelical revolt, some members and even some denominational bodies had been fierce opponents of the institution and demanded that their members free their slaves immediately, but they quickly realized that such a strong stand would doom them in the South.[17]

The basically conservative agenda of the colonization society enabled evangelicals to wring their hands over the injustices of slavery, to support gradual, voluntary plans for emancipation, and to encourage members to free and transport their slaves, without completely alienating slaveholders. Their support for voluntary measures to end slavery brought them closer in line with the national view as it existed before the rise of radical abolitionism and did little to hamper their dramatic expansion in the South.

Modernist ministers actively led the effort to expand evangelical influence to the planter elite. Through the religious press, one of the most powerful weapons in their hands, they championed the growing power and influence of the denominational bodies, called for higher educational requirements for ministers, and urged evangelicals to reach out to the elite. In an 1837 article, the editor of the state Baptist newspaper wrote that it was time for evangelicals to go beyond the "mud-walled cottage" and "ascend the steps of the royal palace, and enter the princely mansion. . . ." [18] The efforts of modernist ministers to extend evangelical influence to the slaveholding elite paid handsome dividends. The two groups worked together on such costly efforts as the colonization society, denominational colleges and other benevolent enterprises, and the construction of handsome new churches and parsonages. Of course, as an additional bonus modernist ministers watched their salaries and their status rise accordingly.

Increasingly after the 1830s evangelicalism gained adherents among the planter elite, and even among the nonconverted, its precepts wrought a transformation in the idealized concept of the planter. In Susan Dabney Smedes' fond recollection of her father, the aristocratic planter Thomas Dabney, she noted that "[h]e was always a strong believer in the doctrines of Christianity, and had great reverence for religion. But he was not a religious man." Even though he was not a church member, he generously supported the evangelical churches in his area, opened his home, Burleigh, to their ministers, and was a liberal contributor to benevolent causes. She wrote, "he did the deeds of a Christian." After the 1830s the spread of evangelicalism transformed the ideal of southern gentility, and even the wealthiest planters like Dabney, the owner of four thousand acres and about five hundred slaves, felt its influence. [19]

The departure of large numbers of traditionalists from the denominational bodies left these institutions firmly in the control of evangelical modernists who were now free to pursue an alliance with the planter elite. As modernists battled traditionalists they honed their hierarchical, corporate vision of the church and carried it over into their idealized vision of a southern slaveholding society. The chief stumbling block in the alliance between modernists and the planter elite was the earlier evangelical opposition to slavery that was one part of their broader challenge to elite culture. By the 1830s, however, significant changes were underway. As evangelicals moved up the social ladder themselves and attracted more members from the slaveholding ranks, they abandoned their protests against elite culture, a process that modernist ministers encouraged as they called on their brethren to enter the princely mansions. But planter suspicions about the evangelical position on slavery lingered. John G. Jones recorded a conversation he had with a "wealthy planter" who asked "if the Methodist preachers were not generally antislavery men." To which Jones responded, "that in the North we presumed they were, but that we of the South looked upon slavery as a civil institution. . . ." Another planter, Edward Randolph, a member of the prominent Virginia family who moved to a plantation near Columbus, Mississippi, experienced conversion in 1832, but he hesitated to join the Methodist church because of "that enquiry in the discipline 'what shall be done to . . . Slavery?'" Jones' reply to the doubtful planter marks one early evangelical response to the slavery issue; slavery was a civil institution, not a religious one, and therefore beyond the scope of the church's mission.[20]

For modernists, often slaveholders themselves, such an ambiguous response did not go far enough either to allay their own misgivings over slavery or to attract planter support. During the late 1820s and 1830s, therefore, elite clergymen quite consciously began to develop a biblical defense of the institution. The proslavery vision that modernist minsters articulated was not simply a response to northern attacks but also a natural outgrowth of a well-established, carefully considered, class-conscious religious vision. Proslavery became a part of the southern manifestation of the national perfectionist impulse, an effort to "modernize" the institution and also to reconcile it with Christian republicanism. The first published biblical defense of slavery in the Old Southwest came from the pen of James Smylie, a prominent Presbyterian minister and educator and one of the largest slaveholders in Amite County, Mississippi. In the 1820s the scholarly Smylie began searching the scriptures for references to slavery and prepared a sermon outlining his proslavery findings. When he first preached his sermon, it "gave great offense, not only to the church but also to his brethren in the ministry, who seriously urged him to preach that sermon no more." His departure from evangelical tradition was too extreme, and he made few converts until abolitionist attacks on the institution became more intense. After the abolitionist presbytery of Chillicothe, Ohio, sent a provocative letter to the Mississippi presbytery, Smylie used his sermon as the basis of a response. When the skittish presbytery refused to endorse it, he had it printed privately, and it quickly gained regional and even national attention. Smylie feared that because of his views he would "be kicked out of the synagogue of Presbyterians, Methodists, Baptists & episcopalians," but by the mid-1830s the climate had shifted, and his pamphlet gained a more receptive audience than he anticipated.[21]

The centerpiece of Smylie's argument was his focus on the household as the cornerstone of southern society—a conservative social vision shared by proslavery authors before and after him. The household represented the first link in a chain of governance that reined in the rampant individualism associated with industrial capitalism in the northeast by creating a modern, hierarchical slave society based on mutual responsibilities and social cohesion.[22] These households were governed by independent white males whose leadership in this republican society extended beyond the family to religious institutions and the civil government. The proslavery ideology was a modernist master stroke that linked religion, family, slavery, and republicanism in a way that maximized the power of male heads of households throughout southern society. It further justified a hierarchical church structure that enhanced their own authority, made them the chief defenders of the now sacred institution of slavery, and, even more than that, made them the judges of the paternalistic slave system and the planters' Christian duties. Once formulated, modernists used their publications, their colleges, and their pulpits to spread their proslavery message across the region where it found a willing and receptive audience among southern slaveholders and firmly cemented the alliance between the modernists and the planter elite.

So successful was the proslavery ideology and so complete was the "great reaction" that set in across the region after the 1830s that virtually no organization in the region dared to oppose slavery. Although traditionalists differed with modernists on almost every issue, on the issue of slavery they stood shoulder to shoulder. Indeed, some traditionalists argued, not without merit, that "the abolition spirit crossed the Atlantic in the same vessel with the missionary spirit. . . ." As early as 1831 Mississippi politician John A. Quitman, a northern native, made the same connection with abolition and benevolent organizations. On a visit to New York City he described the headquarters of various benevolent societies as "splendid edifices" staffed by directors "salaried liberally out of contributions wrung from pious and frugal persons in the South; and these officials, like the majority of their theologians and divines, are inimical to our institutions, and use our money to defame and damage us!" Even northern traditionalists shared that view. In 1850, for example, New York Primitive Baptists assured southerners, saying that "we do not know an Old School Baptist on earth that is an abolitionist. . . . It is our firm belief that the various branches of anti-christ, and the newly invented religious institutions of the nineteenth century have been the principal agents in sowing the seeds of discord between the sister states of our great Republic." In the traditionalist view, abolitionism could be seen as yet another example of the pernicious influence of the benevolent empire and the perfectionist impulse. By and large traditionalists North and South held to the view that slavery was a civil institution beyond their purview.[23]

Even though traditionalists expressed support for slavery, they were not among the prominent clerical defenders of the peculiar institution. Larry Tise's extensive research into the backgrounds of proslavery ministers reveals that in almost every conceivable way, they fit the profile of the modernist clergyman; more than two-thirds of them had seminary training and came from the ranks of the modernist evangelical denominations, they frequently married women from a higher socioeconomic class and entered the ranks of the planters, they were concentrated at the top of denominational hierarchies, often taught or presided over seminaries or church colleges, and often edited religious newspapers. In addition, they actively supported benevolent organizations. Tise maintains that their involvement in the benevolent empire made them more "attuned to national concerns" than other southerners and more in line with national thought.[24]

The educated, elite, ecumenical modernists were the group in southern society most likely to forge and maintain a national allegiance with like-minded northern brethren equally committed to the causes of the benevolent empire. From the Revolution until the 1830s, such an alliance existed, and promoters of national benevolence extolled it as a means of cementing American society.[25] But as radical abolitionism grew in the North and spread through northern churches, southern clergymen began forging an ever-closer alliance with the planter elite and developing a theology and social philosophy that put the northern and southern clergymen on a collision course. Once modernists embraced proslavery there was essentially no constituency in southern churches for national religious organizations because the intensely localistic traditionalists fiercely opposed such denominational bodies.

One of the underpinnings of the national denominational bodies had been the shared legacy of the Revolution. The emerging proslavery ideology, however, destroyed the common national interpretation of the founding documents. Methodist proslavery advocate Rev. Thomas Thornton, president of Centenary College in Clinton, Mississippi, charged that abolitionists "fly to the declaration of our national independence, and by a flagrant perversion of the true intent and meaning of the spirit of that instrument, as well as the language itself, endeavor to persuade and delude men from the Bible and its instructions." Such proslavery writers as Thornton questioned whether the natural rights outlined in the Declaration existed at all. "We know that much is said, and much too has been written about 'inalienable rights,'" Thornton said, "all which seem to us absurd. . . . Take then . . . a people and place them on an equality in every respect, with the most refined, the civilized and the virtuous. Who does not see that it would be to plunge one or the other into scenes of violence and bloodshed? . . ." Such doctrines were clearly incompatible with the stable, hierarchical society proslavery modernists envisioned. Thornton warned that "[a]n abolitionist is not only an enthusiast and a fanatic, but he is also a disorganizer . . . pledged for upturning the institutions of society . . . men are to be thrown back into a state of insubordination and disorder, under the vain show of *equality,* founded on the *abstract* principles of *moral, civil, and natural rights.*"[26]

Another foundation of the denominational institutions, the national benevolent empire, also collapsed as the former allies moved into hostile camps. An exchange between the noted philanthropist-turned-abolitionist Gerrit Smith and the Rev. William Winans, one of Mississippi's most prominent Methodist ministers, reveals the fault lines as they opened between the two groups. Winans solicited a contribution from northerners, including Smith, for the construction of a new chapel in New Orleans, the sort of philanthropic enterprise that had previously garnered widespread national support from Smith and other wealthy northerners. Smith, who had worked with Winans in support of the American Colonization Society, responded to the Mississippian's private missive with a hostile letter in the abolitionist press that read in part:

It grieves me to know that there are some good men at the north who continue their contributions towards sustaining the religion of the south. In a spirit of misguided fraternal and Christian feeling they yield to solicitations for aid to build southern houses of worship, and endow professorships in southern theological seminaries. They know not what they do. . . . I should be gratified in having my white brethren of the south suppose I cherish towards them a generous and brotherly spirit as strong as that which gained me their goodwill in the days of my colonization delusion, my conscience nevertheless, will not permit me to comply with your request.

Understandably stung by Smith's vehemence, Winans responded in the southern press; "I do not consider myself a sufficiently competent judge, in matters of courtesy, to *decide* upon the propriety, in that respect, of answering a *private* letter in the columns of a public journal. But . . . I cannot reconcile your course in this matter to my views of the consideration which is due from man to man." The national benevolent empire splintered into sectional camps as a result of such hostility, and southerners established their own Bible, tract, and missionary societies.[27]

Winans lamented the demise of the combined efforts of northerners and southerners to ameliorate slavery through the colonization society:

> the whole influence exerted by the abolitionists upon the condition and prospects of slaves, is evil and *only* evil. Its effect is to rivet the fetters of slavery. . . . The burdens of the slave were sensibly lessened by the measures adopted by you and your philanthropic coadjutors in that *noblest* of human enterprises; and the shackles of many hundreds of slaves were thrown off, and those of thousands of others manifestly loosened by the eloquence of your judicious pleadings in behalf of humanity: but alas! you saw proper to change the one of *pleading* for that of *denunciation;* and in a moment, your influence changes sides. . . . it tends to perpetuate the bondage of the black man, by disgusting the white man against every measure which tends, no matter how remotely, to . . . his emancipation.[28]

Until the 1840s, support for the colonization society represented the position of the national General Conference of the Methodist Church on the slavery issue. As late as 1840 the majority of northern and southern delegates rejected abolition in favor of colonization, but beginning in the 1830s the issue of slavery disrupted conference proceedings. Winans reported from the 1840 meeting of the conference that "[a]bolitionism, proper, hardly shewed its face" and "when it did venture to do so, it was promptly frowned away by a very large majority of *Northern* delegates." The colonization society collapsed in Mississippi around 1840 as it did across the South, and others joined Winans in blaming northern abolitionists for its failure. This moment marked the end of the colonization consensus that had prevented slavery from becoming a heated issue for the national denominational bodies.[29]

With the collapse of the colonization consensus, more and more northern evangelicals joined the ranks of the abolitionists or at least were forced to move further in that direction to forestall divisions in the North. The Presbyterian church felt the strain in the 1830s as controversy intensified between the more liberal New School and the Old School conservatives, a dispute that culminated in the schism of 1837 when the New School liberals were driven from the fold. While abolitionism was not the only issue that divided the two, most southern synods endorsed the action in large part because of the abolitionists in the New School ranks. The Mississippi synod, in a notice written in part by Smylie, reported that "[t]he Synod has good reason for believing, that an overwhelming majority of the seceding body, and of those of the North who adhere to it, are hostile to one at least of the domestic institutions of the

South." By dividing along theological lines, the Presbyterians managed to avoid a sectional schism until the eve of the Civil War, though in 1844 the Mississippi synod reported that they could no longer rely on the Board of Domestic Missions in Philadelphia.[30]

Among the Methodists and Baptists, however, the debate over slavery followed a different course. As the 1844 Methodist general conference approached, the central issue was the election of a slaveholding bishop, though the issue changed abruptly when news spread that Bishop James O. Andrew of Georgia had become a slave owner through marriage. Southerners were outraged by abolitionists' demands that Andrew be forced to resign his office. When the conference met in Baltimore in the spring of 1844, Winans quickly emerged as a vocal spokesman for the southern position. Some of his contemporaries believed that he might have risen to the high office himself had he not been a slaveholder, a perception that may have added to his impassioned outbursts. His comments provide a revealing glimpse into modernist ministers' thoughts as the showdown over slavery approached. In a voice that "cracked like thunder" he warned northern delegates: "If you pass this action . . . you will . . . cut us off from all connection with masters and servants, and will leave us no option[,] God is my witness that I speak with all sincerity of purpose toward you[,] but to be disconnected with your body. . . . We have no will, no choice in this thing. It comes upon us as destiny; it comes with overwhelming force, and all we can do is to submit to it."[31] Given the developments in southern religion in the preceding decades, Winans' warning that he and his southern brethren could not afford to be cut off from masters is hardly surprising. The entire modernist edifice in the South depended on the alliance with the planter elite. Indeed, the many ties between the two contributed to the evolution of a shared class ideology that modernists simply could not challenge. As Winans said, southerners had no choice, and the unity of the Methodist Episcopal church was destroyed as southerners withdrew to create the Methodist Episcopal church, South, a course that the Mississippi Conference approved unanimously.[32]

Events followed a similar course among the Baptists when northern abolitionists demanded that slaveholders not be allowed to serve as missionaries. The showdown also came in 1844 when the Baptist Acting Board of Foreign Missions ruled that they would not appoint a slaveholding missionary. Some southerners, including the Mississippi Baptist Convention, wanted to delay a division until after the triennial convention met, but the more radical Georgia and Virginia state conventions called for a Southern Baptist Convention, which gathered in May 1845 to formalize a division. When the Mississippi

State Convention assembled to consider separation, a minority of the delegates issued a report "of rather whitewashing order, making it appear that the northerners were not altogether as bad as they might be, but . . . no such spirit of tolerance pervaded that body; they were southerners, they were willing to define their position, take a bold stand, and let the northern abolitionists pursue their own course." One minister said "that the South Baptists would act like men, and stand up to their responsibilities." The Mississippi Convention dissolved its connection with the triennial convention and the American Baptist Home Mission Society.[33]

Many Mississippi preachers and church members were troubled by the schisms and fearful for the future; Methodist preacher Henry Harris noted that the separation "was a sore trial to many members of our Conference." But the rapid growth in the churches after the divisions restored their confidence and seemed to give divine sanction to the separations. In the words of a group of southern Methodists, "their hearts and hands have been strengthened mightily[,] the seal of Heaven's approbation has been set upon their course—the gracious work of the Lord has been gloriously revived—thousands have been brought to the knowledge of salvation, and Ethiopia with glad heart is stretching out her hands unto God." Certainly the rapid growth in the churches among members of both races seemed to justify such optimism. The Methodist membership in the state grew from 2,235 in 1818 to about 61,000 by 1860. In 1836 there were 107 Baptists churches, 92 preachers, and almost 5,000 members; their numbers had grown to 596 churches, 305 preachers, and 41,500 members by 1860. Presbyterian membership grew from just more than six hundred in 1830 to more than seven thousand by 1861. All told, the three major denominations had nearly 110,000 members out of a total state population of 791,000. When southerners withdrew from national denominational bodies one justification they frequently cited was that masters would not allow them to minister to slaves if they remained, and once the divisions took place they redoubled their efforts to spread the Gospel to blacks. Their success was impressive. For example, between 1830 and 1860 Methodists in the state established more than 70 colored missions, and black membership in one Methodist conference grew from 1,587 in 1837 to 12,684 in 1860.[34]

In the decades between the schisms and the Civil War, biblical proslavery permeated southern culture. As the dramatic growth in membership suggests, evangelical modernists gained a wider and wider audience as the antebellum period progressed. In terms of membership, wealth, and influence they continued to outpace the traditionalists, though the debates between the factions continued unabated. The sectional divisions also gave modernists complete control over their own impressive religious apparatus that included colleges and seminaries; newspapers and periodicals; tract, publication, and missionary societies; all now marshaled to further spread their "triumphant ideology" to an eager audience.[35] The proslavery ideology lay at the heart of the schisms of the 1840s, but the splits were not simply a response to abolitionism. Rather, the divisions must be understood as part and parcel of broader developments in southern church life, particularly the struggle between evangelical modernists and traditionalists. Modernists abandoned the doctrine of the equality of all believers, which contributed to the egalitarian impulse in early evangelical churches and replaced it with a hierarchical vision of the church that meshed with a similar social vision. As evangelicals grew from sects to denominations and advanced in wealth and social status, modernists expressed the collective worldview of the southern master class, a view that put them on a collision course with their northern brethren. Their vision became the orthodox one in the antebellum years and increasingly set the South at odds with the rest of the nation. Their vision of a southern slaveholding Zion was a potent one that southern whites proved willing to defend at terrible costs.

NOTES

I would like to thank W. Fitzhugh Brundage, Amy Thompson McCandless, and Jane H. and William H. Pease for commenting on earlier drafts of this essay.

1. Jones, *A Complete History of Methodism As Connected with the Mississippi Conference . . . ,* 2 vols. (1887; Baton Rouge: Louisiana State University Press, 1966), 2:500–501.

2. Evangelicalism is a convenient term, but a difficult one to define. In broad terms evangelicals have been identified as those Christians who emphasize conversion, activism, and biblicalism, but almost from the beginning of the movement its implications for social organization were nearly as significant as theology. See D. W. Bebbington, *Evangelicalism in Modern Britain: A History from the 1730s to the 1980s* (London, Eng.: Routledge, 1989), 2–17; Robert K. Johnston, "American Evangelicalism: An Extended Family," in *The Variety of American Evangelicalism,* Donald W. Dayton and Robert K. Johnston, eds., (Knoxville: University of Tennessee Press, 1991), 261–62; Donald G. Mathews, *Religion in the Old South* (Chicago: University of Chicago Press, 1977), 11–15. The most thorough examination of the religious schisms and one that treats them as a prolog to Civil War is C. C. Goen, *Broken Churches, Broken Nation: Denominational Schisms and the Coming of the Civil War* (Macon, Ga.: Mercer University Press, 1985).

3. I explore the distinctions between modernists and traditionalists more fully in *On Jordan's Stormy Banks: Evangelicalism in Mississippi, 1773–1876* (Athens: University of Georgia Press, 1994). The term "modernist" as I employ it is not intended to suggest a connection with the artistic movement that began in the late nineteenth century and extended roughly to 1945, nor

do I develop specific links between evangelical modernists and the idea of modernity that is used to describe that complex and radical transformation of Western society and economics from 1500 to 1800 (though some connections exist). I have used these terms because to some extent they best represent the ways in which members of these groups saw themselves. Traditionalists traced their heritage back to the early Christian church and defined themselves as the legitimate heirs of their eighteenth-century evangelical forebearers. Modernists, on the other hand, looked favorably upon most of the changes connected with the Market Revolution, embraced the transformation of evangelicalism from sects to denominations, saw themselves as a part of the emerging professional classes, and supported economic modernization that came to include attempts to "modernize" the slave system.

4. Nathan O. Hatch, *The Democratization of American Christianity* (New Haven, Conn.: Yale University Press, 1989), 125–33, 141–46; Jon Butler, *Awash in a Sea of Faith: Christianizing the American People* (Cambridge, Mass.: Harvard University Press, 1990), 257–88; Charles Sellers, *The Market Revolution: Jacksonian America, 1815–1846* (New York: Oxford University Press, 1991), 212–17, 232, 237, 265, 308, 310, 369–70, 385, 390, 402.

5. John G. Jones, *Concise History of the Introduction of Protestantism into Mississippi and the Southwest* (St. Louis, Mo.: P. M. Pinckard, 1866), 102, 110; Henry G. Hawkins, *Methodism in Natchez* (Jackson, Miss.: Hawkins Foundation, 1937), 188. The growth among the Baptists was just as impressive. See "Comparative Statement of the Churches composing the Mississippi Baptist Association, from 1807 to 1847 inclusive," in Mississippi Baptist Association, *A Republication of the Minutes of the Mississippi Baptist Association . . .* (New Orleans: The Association, 1849). Similar growth occurred across the nation. See Hatch, *Democratization*, 3; Butler, *Awash in a Sea of Faith*, 268, 270–88. Anthropologist Mary Douglas noted that in revolutionary religious movements the protest stage usually ends after two or three generations when the growth of the sect demands greater organization and coherence. Douglas, *Natural Symbols: Explorations in Cosmology* (New York: Pantheon Books, 1973), 40–41; John Hebron Moore, *The Emergence of the Cotton Kingdom in the Old Southwest, 1770–1860* (Baton Rouge: Louisiana State University Press, 1988), 16, 28; Joseph G. Baldwin, *The Flush Times of Alabama and Mississippi: A Series of Sketches* (New York: D. Appleton, 1854); Sparks, *On Jordan's Stormy Banks*, 14, 110–11; Allan Kulikoff, *The Agrarian Origins of American Capitalism* (Charlottesville: University of Virginia Press, 1992), 16–17, 21–24, 43–47, 69–77, 112–32, 142–51; Michael Zuckerman, "Holy Wars, Civil Wars: Religion and Economics in Nineteenth–Century America," *Prospects* 16 (1992): 205–40.

6. Morgan, *Visible Saints: The History of a Puritan Idea* (New York: New York University Press, 1963), 143. H. Richard Niebuhr also described an almost inevitable process of "institutionalization and secularization" in new religious movements throughout the history of Christianity, a process well underway among American evangelicals by the 1840s. Niebuhr, *The Kingdom of God in America* (1937; reprint, Middletown, Conn.: Wesleyan University Press, 1988), 164–84.

7. Jones, *Concise History of Methodism*, 102, 110; Walter Brownlow Posey, *The Baptist Church in the Lower Mississippi Valley, 1776–1845* (Lexington: University of Kentucky Press, 1957), 34–36, 73; Gordon A. Cotton, *Of Primitive Faith and Order: A History of the Mississippi Primitive Baptist Church, 1780–1974* (Raymond, Miss.: Keith Press, 1974), 18–27; Jesse Laney Boyd, *A*

Popular History of the Baptists in Mississippi (Jackson, Miss.: Baptist Press, 1930), 54; Mathews, *Religion in the Old South*, 52–54, 125–26.

8. *Western Methodist*, August 22, 1834 (first quotation); September 5, 1834; October 17, 1834; Griffin, *History of the Primitive Baptists of Mississippi*, 75–76 (second quotation); Bertram Wyatt-Brown, "The Antimission Movement in the Jacksonian South: A Study in Regional Folk Culture," *Journal of Southern History* 36 (November 1970): 510; T. Scott Miyakawa, *Protestants and Pioneers: Individualism and Conformity on the American Frontier* (Chicago: University of Chicago Press, 1964), 146; David T. Bailey, *Shadow on the Church: Southwestern Evangelical Religion and the Issue of Slavery, 1783–1860* (Ithaca, N.Y.: Cornell University Press, 1985), 133, 198–99.

9. *Western Methodist*, January 31; June 13, 1834 (first quotation), July 11, 1834 (second quotation). See Sparks, *On Jordan's Stormy Banks*, chap. 6.

10. Percy L. Rainwater, "Conquistadors, Missionaries, and Missions," *Journal of Mississippi History* 27 (April 1965): 140–41; Samuel S. Hill, ed., *Encyclopedia of Religion in the South* (Macon, Ga.: Mercer University Press, 1984), 486–87; Griffin, *History of the Primitive Baptists*, 172–78; Cotton, *Of Primitive Faith and Order*, 18–27; Wyatt-Brown, "Antimission Movement," 502–3, 510, 515; David Edwin Harrell Jr., "The Evolution of Plain-Folk Religion in the South, 1835–1920," in *Varieties of Southern Religious Experience*, Samuel S. Hill, ed. (Baton Rouge: Louisiana State University Press, 1988), 24–30; Ancel Henry Bassett, *A Concise History of the Methodist Protestant Church* . . . (Baltimore, Md.: William McCracken Jr., 1887), 38, 148–50; William Lee Hamrick, *The Mississippi Conference of the Methodist Protestant Church* (Jackson, Miss.: Hawkins Foundation, 1957), 22–30, Miyakawa, *Protestants and Pioneers*, 88–98.

11. Butler, *Awash in a Sea of Faith*, 273; Sellers, *Market Revolution*, 215–17. The average wealth of southern urban ministers was $10,177 compared to $4,376 for the same group in the North. See E. Brooks Holifield, "The Penurious Preacher? Nineteenth-Century Clerical Wealth: North and South," *Journal of the American Academy of Religion* 58 (spring 1990): 17–36; Holifield, *The Gentlemen Theologians: American Theology in Southern Culture, 1795–1860* (Durham, N.C.: Duke University Press, 1978), 24–49. Undated biographical sketch, Charles Kimball Marshall Papers (Mississippi Department of Archives and History). In Natchez, the Presbyterian minister Perry Chase had an estate valued at $65,000 and the Methodist minister W. G. Millsaps held property worth $45,000. James, *Antebellum Natchez*, 245, 247. Liberty (Miss.) *Advocate*, March 28, 1839; Mathews, *Religion in the Old South*, 126–27. On professionalization, see Donald M. Scott, *From Office to Profession: The New England Ministry, 1750–1850* (Philadelphia: University of Pennsylvania Press, 1978) and Samuel Haber, *The Quest for Authority and Honor in the American Professions, 1750–1900* (Chicago: University of Chicago Press, 1991).

12. Margaret DesChamps Moore, "Protestantism in the Mississippi Territory," *Journal of Mississippi History* 29 (August 1967): 367 (first quotation); S. G. Winchester, *The Religion of the Bible, The Only Preservation of our Civil Institutions* . . . (Natchez, La.: n.p., 1838), 7 (first quotation); Synod of Mississippi and South Alabama, *Extract from the Records of the Synod of Mississippi and South Alabama, From 1820 to 1835* (Jackson, Miss.: The Synod, 1880), 16, 22, 118, 129 (second quotation); Columbus First Methodist Church Records (Special Collections, Mississippi State University, Starkville, Miss.), 1837, 1851; *South-Western Religious Luminary*, September 1836;

Sparks, "Mississippi's Apostle of Slavery: James Smylie and the Biblical Defense of Slavery," *Journal of Mississippi History* (May 1989): 92; Richard A. McLemore, *A History of Mississippi Baptists, 1780–1970* (Jackson, Miss., 1971), 128 (third quotation), 159; Tommy W. Rogers, "T. C. Thornton: A Methodist Educator of Antebellum Mississippi," *Journal of Mississippi History* 44 (May 1982): 136–47; Gene Ramsey Miller, *A History of North Mississippi Methodism, 1820–1900* (Nashville, Tenn.: Parthenon Press, 1966), 49–50; Jones, *Complete History*, 2:195. An 1832 document entitled "How Oakland College was established," which lists subscriptions to raise money for the Presbyterian College, reads like a who's who of prominent planters in southwestern Mississippi, including the wealthy Stephen Duncan who pledged three thousand dollars to the institution. See Rev. W. L. Montgomery to Rev. George Potts, January 28, 1832, in Claiborne Papers (Mississippi Department of Archives and History, Jackson, Miss.). Sellers, *Market Revolution*, 279–81; Daniel Walker Howe, "The Evangelical Movement and Political Culture in the North During the Second Party System," *Journal of American History* 77 (March 1991): 1216–39; James Oakes, *Slavery and Freedom: An Interpretation of the Old South* (New York: Alfred A. Knopf, 1990), 121–36; Harry L. Watson, *Liberty and Power: The Politics of Jacksonian America* (New York: Hill and Wang, 1990). On the Sunday school movement, see Anne Boylan, *Sunday Schools: The Formation of an American Institution, 1790–1880* (New Haven, Conn.: Yale University Press, 1988). Mississippi evangelicals were encouraged in these activities by such men as James A. Ranaldson, a native of Massachusetts who came to the state as a missionary from the Baptist Board of Foreign Missions. He spearheaded the push for higher education for Baptists ministers through the Mississippi Baptist Education Society, organized Mission Societies, and became a prominent leader in the state convention. Boyd, *A Popular History*, 54; Posey, *The Baptist Church*, 34–36, 73; Bailey, *Shadow on the Church*, 202–28.

13. Griffin, *History of the Primitive Baptists*, 64–65 (final quotation), 177 (first quotation); Mathews, *Religion in the Old South*, 125–29.

14. Griffin, *History of the Primitive Baptists*, 34–67 (first quotation on p. 58), 177, 207 (second quotation); Mathews, *Religion in the Old South*, 125–29; Wyatt-Brown, "Antimission Movement," 501–29.

15. The temperance bill proved to be unenforceable and it was repealed in 1842. McLemore, *History of Mississippi Baptists*, 128, 159; Edwin A. Miles, *Jacksonian Democracy in Mississippi* (New York: Da Capo Press, 1970), 146–47, 164–65; John Hebron Moore, "Local and State Governments of Antebellum Mississippi," *Journal of Mississippi History* 44 (May 1982): 127–28; Newton Haskin James, "Josiah Hinds: Versatile Pioneer of the Old Southwest," *Journal of Mississippi History* 2 (January 1940): 25; Ronald P. Formisano, *The Birth of Mass Political Parties, Michigan, 1827–1861* (Princeton, N.J.: Princeton University Press, 1971), 102–16; Lawrence Frederick Kohl, *The Politics of Individualism: Parties and the American Character in the Jacksonian Era* (New York: Oxford University Press, 1989); Watson, *Liberty and Power*, 51–55; Griffin, *History of the Primitive Baptists*, 261 (quotation).

16. Norwood Allen Kerr, "The Mississippi Colonization Society (1831–1860)," *Journal of Mississippi History* 43 (February 1981): 1–30; Charles S. Sydnor, *Slavery in Mississippi* (New York: American Historical Association, 1933), 203–8; Jones, *Complete History of Methodism*, 2: 39–33, 79, 148, 389, 535; *South-Western Religious Luminary*, January 1838; Dwight L. Dumond,

ed., *Letters of James Gillespie Birney, 1831–1857*, 2 vols. (Gloucester, Mass.: P. Smith, 1966), 1: 65–66, 70; Sparks, *On Jordan's Stormy Banks*, 71–75.

17. Jones, *Concise History*, 240 (quotation). In a similar vein, Timothy Flint described slavery as "a chronic moral evil, the growth of ages, . . . Leave us to ourselves, or point out the way we can heal this great malady, not at once but in a regimen of years. The evil must go off as it came on, by a slow and gradual method. . . ." Flint, *Recollections*, 343. On evangelical opposition to slavery, see Donald Mathews, *Slavery and Methodism: A Chapter in American Morality, 1780–1845* (Princeton, N.J.: Princeton University Press, 1965) and James D. Essig, *The Bonds of Wickedness: American Evangelicals Against Slavery, 1770–1808* (Philadelphia: Temple University Press, 1982); Larry E. Tise, *Proslavery: A History of the Defense of Slavery in America, 1701–1840* (Athens: University of Georgia Press, 1987), 303–7; George M. Fredrickson, *The Black Image in the White Mind: The Debate on Afro-American Character and Destiny, 1817–1914* (New York: Harper, 1971), 43.

18. Handsome Gothic churches arose in such wealthy cotton towns as Columbus, Natchez, and Port Gibson. The Port Gibson Presbyterian Church cost $40,000, and in Natchez the Presbyterian manse cost $16,000. A Natchez millionaire built a fine home called the "Parsonage" for the Methodist minister there. Sparks, *On Jordan's Stormy Banks*, 100, 103. See also Christopher H. Owen, "By Design: The Social Meaning of Methodist Church Architecture in Nineteenth-Century Georgia," *Georgia Historical Quarterly* 75 (summer 1991): 221–53.

19. Bertram Wyatt-Brown, *Southern Honor: Ethics and Behavior in the Old South* (New York: Oxford University Press, 1982), 102–14; Susan Dabney Smedes, *Memorials of a Southern Planter*, Fletcher M. Green, ed. (1887; reprint, New York: Alfred A. Knopf, 1965), xii, 152–53.

20. Jones, *Complete History*, 499 (first and second quotations); Edward Randolph to "Dear Brother," July 6, 1844 (third quotation; Randolph Papers, Special Collections, Mississippi State University). On the spread of evangelicalism to the planter elite see Mathews, *Religion in the Old South*, 81–83, 156–57; Jan Lewis, *The Pursuit of Happiness: Family Values in Jefferson's Virginia* (Cambridge, Eng.: Cambridge University Press, 1983), chap. 2, and James Oakes, *The Ruling Race: A History of American Slaveholders* (New York: Alfred A. Knopf, 1982), chap. 4.

21. Sparks, "Mississippi's Apostle of Slavery," 89–99 (first quotation on p. 98, second quotation on p. 99); Bailey, *Shadow on the Church*, 216, 222, 227, 232; Tise, *Proslavery*, 174–75, 298–99, 328–30; Jack P. Maddex Jr., "'The Southern Apostasy' Revisited: The Significance of Proslavery Christianity," *Marxist Perspectives* 7 (fall 1979): 132–41; William W. Freehling, "James Henley Thornwell's Mysterious Antislavery Moment," *Journal of Southern History* 57 (August 1991): 393–94; Bertram Wyatt-Brown, "Modernizing Southern Slavery: The Proslavery Argument Reinterpreted," in *Region, Race, and Reconstruction: Essays in Honor of C. Vann Woodward*, J. Morgan Kousser and James M. McPherson, eds. (New York: Oxford University Press, 1982), 27–49.

22. As Larry Tise has demonstrated, the basic outlines of the proslavery ideology remained remarkably consistent over time. Tise, *Proslavery*, 122–23, 328–30. On households, see Elizabeth Fox-Genovese, *Within the Plantation Household: Black and White Women of the Old South* (Chapel Hill: University of North Carolina Press, 1988), 53–70; Stephanie McCurry, "The Two Faces of Republicanism: Gender and Proslavery Politics in Antebellum South Carolina," *Journal of*

American History 78 (March 1992): 1246–47; McCurry, "The Politics of Yeoman Households in South Carolina," in *Divided Houses: Gender and the Civil War*, Catherine Clinton and Nina Silber, eds. (New York: Oxford University Press, 1992), 25–28.

23. Griffin, *History of the Primitive Baptists*, 260–61 (first and fourth quotations); Robert E. May, *John A. Quitman: Old South Crusader* (Baton Rouge: Louisiana State University Press, 1985), 47 (second and third quotations); Fredrickson, *Black Image*, 29–30.

24. Tise, *Proslavery*, 144–46, 149–50, 153, 163, 173–79, 291–93 (quotation on p. 292).

25. Sellers, *The Market Revolution*, 213–14.

26. Thornton, *An Inquiry into the History of Slavery . . .* (Washington, D.C.: W. M. Morrison, 1841), 86 (first quotation), 66 (second quotation), 177 (third quotation). Other proslavery authors saw similar threats to social stability. See Richard Carwardine, "Evangelicals, Politics, and the Coming of the American Civil War: A Transatlantic Perspective," in *Evangelicalism: Comparative Studies of Popular Protestantism in North America, the British Isles, and Beyond, 1700–1900*, Mark A. Noll, David W. Bebbington, and George A. Rawlyk, eds. (New York: Oxford University Press, 1994), 209.

27. *Liberty (Miss.) Advocate*, March 31, 1838 (quotation); *The Baptist* (Nashville, Tenn.), August 1, 1837; Goen, *Broken Churches*, 107. Winans's marriage to Martha DuBose in 1815 brought him land and eight slaves. He also managed his mother-in-law's plantation and slaves. See Winans's Autobiography, 120–22 (Winans Papers, Cain Archives, Millsaps College, Jackson, Miss.). Smith had a similar exchange with Smylie. See Smith, *Letters of Gerrit Smith to Rev. James Smylie of the State of Mississippi* (New York: R. G. Williams, 1837).

28. *Liberty (Miss.) Advocate*, March 31, 1838.

29. Ray Holder, ed., "On Slavery: Selected Letters of Parson Winans, 1820–1844," *Journal of Mississippi History* 46 (November 1984): 346 (quotation); Sydnor, *Slavery in Mississippi*, 215–17; Franklin L. Riley, ed., "A Contribution to the History of the Colonization Movement in Mississippi," *Publications of the Mississippi Historical Society* 9 (1906): 396–99; J. Gales to William Winans, February 15, 1839 (Winans Papers). In Donald Mathews' view, "there was no denomination more closely connected with colonization than the Methodist Episcopal Church." Mathews, *Slavery and Methodism*, 88–211 (quotation on p. 109); Methodist Episcopal Church, South, *History of the Organization of the Methodist Episcopal Church, South . . .* (Nashville, Tenn.: Southwestern Christian Advocate, 1845), 3.

30. Synod of Mississippi and South Alabama, *Extracts from the Records*, 117 (quotations), 169; Mathews, *Religion in the Old South*, 163–64; Elwyn A. Smith, "The Role of the South in the Presbyterian Schism of 1837–1838," *Church History* 29 (1960): 44–63; Walter Brownlow Posey, *Frontier Mission: A History of Religion West of the Southern Appalachians to 1861* (Lexington: University of Kentucky Press, 1966), 372–73.

31. Winans Scrapbook (first quotation, Winans Papers); Methodist Episcopal Church, South, *History of the Organization*, 20 (second quotation); Mathews, *Methodism and Slavery*, 163–64, 212–45; John R. McKivigan, *The War against Proslavery Religion: Abolitionism and the Northern Churches, 1830–1865* (Ithaca, N.Y.: Cornell University Press, 1984), 84–90; Jones, *Complete History*, 2:135; Posey, *Frontier Mission*, 352–63.

32. Methodist Episcopal Church, South, *History of the Organization*, 135–36; Winans Journal,

December 16–20, 1844 (Winans Papers). On August 1, 1844, Methodists met at the Columbus Methodist Episcopal Church to consider the plan of separation. They approved a resolution in support of division that echoed Winans' words; they expressed regret over the separation but noted that it was "necessary to our very existence as a church in the South." (Columbus First Methodist Church Records, Special Collections, Mitchell Memorial Library, Mississippi State University, Starkville, Miss.).

33. *Carrollton Mississippi Democrat*, July 9, 1845 (quotations); McLemore, *History of Mississippi Baptists*, 140–42, 156; Mathews, *Religion in the Old South*, 162–63; *Proceedings of the Ninth Annual Meeting of the Convention of the Baptist Denomination of the State of Mississippi . . . 1845* (Jackson, Miss.: n.p., 1845), 24; Posey, *Frontier Mission*, 363–72; William Wright Barnes, *The Southern Baptist Convention, 1845–1953* (Nashville, Tenn.: Broadman Press, 1954), 12–32.

34. As one Methodist preacher wrote, "At first I much deplored a division of our Church; but facts have convinced me that it was providentially designed. . . ." Thomas O. Summers, ed., *Autobiography of the Rev. Joseph Travis . . .* (Nashville, Tenn.: E. Stevenson and F. A. Owen, 1855), 185; Rev. Henry J. Harris Autobiography (Cain Archives), 60 (first quotation); Methodist Episcopal Church, South, *History of the Organization*, 254 (second quotation); Edward Randolph to "the Preacher in Charge and members of the M.E. Church in Columbus," [1844]; Same to "Dear Brother," July 6, 1844; Same to Rev. G. P. Sparks, June 28, 1845; Same to same, July 16, 1845; W. B. Jones, *Methodism in the Mississippi Conference* (Jackson, Miss.: Hawkins Foundation, 1957), 174–78; Methodist Episcopal Church, South, *Minutes of the Annual Conferences . . . 1845–1851* (Richmond, Va.: John Early, 1846–53), 31, 402, 412, 415; Mississippi Baptist State Convention, "Second Annual Report of the Mississippi Baptist State Convention"; Hill, ed., *Encyclopedia of Religion in the South*, 486–87; Ernest Trice Thompson, *Presbyterians in the South: Volume One: 1607–1861* (Richmond, Va.: John Knox Press, 1963), 175, 433. The state was divided into the Mississippi, Alabama, and Memphis Methodist conferences. The figures come from the Mississippi conference. Hawkins, *Methodism in Natchez*, 188. Baptist State Convention, *Proceedings of the Sixth Anniversary of the Convention of the Baptist Denomination of the State of Mississippi . . . 1842* (Natchez, La.: The Convention, 1842), 20; Jones, *Complete History*, 2:346., 484–85; n.a., *Biographical and Historical Memoirs of Mississippi*, 2 vols. (Spartanburg, S.C.: n.p., 1978), 2:371. On the growth of biracial churches, see John B. Boles, ed., *Masters and Slaves in the House of the Lord: Race and Religion in the American South, 1740–1870* (Lexington: University of Kentucky Press, 1988).

35. Eugene D. Genovese, *The World the Slaveholders Made: Two Essays in Interpretation* (New York: Vintage Books, 1969), 147 (quotation); Elizabeth Fox-Genovese and Eugene D. Genovese, "The Divine Sanction of Social Order: Religious Foundations of the Southern Slaveholders' World View," *Journal of the American Academy of Religion* 55 (summer 1987): 211, 219–20, 225–29; Maddex, "Southern Apostasy," 137, 139–40. By 1858, for example, the Mississippi Methodist Conference supported eight colleges, and in 1855 established its own Book and Tract Society at Vicksburg. See *Biographical and Historical Memoirs*, 2:365.

The Restructuring of Southern Religion

Slavery, Denominations, and the

Clerical Profession in Virginia

BETH BARTON SCHWEIGER

 On a March day in 1852, Rev. Noah Baldwin recorded his doubts about a deed he had accomplished the day before. "Yesterday, (although I have had some scruples in regard to slavery) I purchased a black man named James Martin at 735 dollars. I hope that he will be a good boy, and that neither of us will have cause to regret our relation in this world, nor that which is to come. Had it not been for the desire this man had, that I should purchase him I should not have done it. For this reason, as Slavery is in our midst I was induced to buy him. Pray the Lord to grant, that it may be for mine and his good."[1]

Noah and Nancy McMillan Baldwin were twelve years married and living in the mountains of southwest Virginia when they bought James Martin. At thirty-five, Baldwin had been preaching for the duration of his marriage in a church he described as a "feeble band, numbering at the aggregate 14, most of whom are in the country and all of us in moderate circumstances, so far as *worldly goods* is concerned."[2]

Baldwin's labors in the hard antimission territory of southwest Virginia bore little resemblance to the work of Jeremiah Jeter, fifteen years his senior. In the year Baldwin purchased his first slave, Jeter took the pulpit of Grace Street Baptist Church in Richmond. The son of an overseer, by his own account Jeter grew up determined never to own a slave. In 1828, however, he acquired slaves from his second wife, a planter's daughter from Virginia's Northern Neck. Uncomfortable with what he claimed was the sheer impracticality of manumission, he finally found an argument that put his mind at ease, published in a proslavery tract. Thornton Stringfellow, a fellow Virginia Baptist minister, argued that the Scriptures not only allowed slavery but sanctioned it. Convinced, Jeter became an enthusiastic advocate of the mission to the slaves.[3]

The contrasts between the lives of these two preachers suggest how slavery entangled Christian belief and practice in both the mountains of the southwest and the parlors of Richmond in antebellum Virginia. As their accounts show, not all pastors became slaveholders for the same reasons. Historians have written a host of studies that examine proslavery Christianity and its place in late antebellum southern thought. Yet these focus on proslavery Christianity as an ideology that allowed southerners, Christian or not, to sanctify slavery.[4]

This chapter turns from the ideological focus of this literature to explore the social consequences of proslavery Christianity for pastors and their churches. In particular, it focuses on Methodists and Baptists in Virginia. Proslavery Christianity did more than offer theological support for slavery and an ideological rationale for the southern way of life. It also marked a turning point in nineteenth-century religious practice. The chief consequence of proslavery Christianity for southern churches—denominational schism—wrought deep changes in the ways that southern Protestants experienced church life. In particular, it changed the way that pastors conceived of their own professional identity and their task. The denominational schisms of the 1840s ushered in a decade and a half of unprecedented denominational growth in both the North and the South. Southern Methodist and Baptist clergy built denominational bureaucracies that wielded wealth and easy access to public debates over slavery. The prominence of these institutions permanently altered the clergy's thinking about the proper relationship of religion to society, and hence, their own roles. Jeremiah Jeter's view that Christian slavery wrought social benefits prevailed, and it pushed the church into a place of unprecedented prominence in the public landscape of the Old South.

During the early nineteenth century, the local congregation dominated religious life in Virginia. The drama of conversion and calling unfolded in the context of a tightly knit Christian community. Converted side-by-side with fiery revival preaching, the sons and daughters of planters and merchants linked their spiritual fortunes with the children of yeomen and slaves. The congregations they created, like the revivals themselves, breached the customary social boundaries of nineteenth-century life. The chief criteria for membership in these communities was the conversion experience rather than wealth and honor.[5]

Those young men who suspected the call to preach usually recognized it from the very day of their repentance or soon after. "I saw myself instantaneously a guilty and justly condemned sinner," Noah Baldwin wrote of his conversion in 1838 at the age of twenty-one. "Soon after this my mind was seriously impressed with the belief that it was my duty to preach Jesus Christ to sinners." Convention dictated that the appropriate response to such an impression be fear, humility, and even denial. "The man who entertains just views of the Christian ministry shrinks from its responsibilities," Jeremiah Jeter observed in 1840. Like many others, young Baldwin initially shrank from the responsibility of the call. Overtaken by spiritual depression, however, he determined to preach and found immediate peace of mind. This pattern, common among Protestants since the Reformation, underscored that becoming a preacher in antebellum Virginia remained less a choice than a duty, less a profession than an office.[6]

Yet, if the call involved intense and private spiritual matters, the decision to become a preacher had both public and temporal consequences. No man could take the pulpit without the invitation of the Christian community. In rural Virginia, the church called a pastor just as surely as God himself did. If the young man himself judged the validity of his inward inclination to preach, the community judged the outward signs of his calling, such qualities as prudence, tactfulness, and the ability to teach. As one preacher explained to his son, "of the one *you* must be the judge—of the other—the *church*."[7]

The first test of an aspiring minister's call came among his own people. Church leaders invited a promising young convert to the pulpit to "exhort" after the sermon, where he faced friends and family in the pews and the peculiar "embarrassments," one pastor remembered, "which usually attend the preaching of the Gospel among the people where we have been reared, and who are familiar with our past lives as sinners." Other tests of the call to preach included Sunday school teaching and visitation. If he satisfactorily performed these duties, the young candidate began a period of apprenticeship to an elder pastor. Under the intense scrutiny of both elder pastors and laity, he gradually took on increasing responsibility, including that of occasional preaching.[8]

The process of grooming a young man for the pulpit highlighted the intimate relations and local context of preaching in antebellum Virginia. Clerical authority—although in theory rooted in the call to preach—in practice derived also from a man's position in a particular community of believers, and their consent to his calling. A man became a pastor because his congregation knew him and because he demonstrated his piety and preaching skills among them. Congregations understood their minister's authority as one called out from among them, not as one set above them. This was particularly true for Baptists, who often spent their entire career in a single community.

Localism dominated other aspects of religious life as well before the mid-1840s in Virginia. Denominations remained small and limited in purpose. The astonishing rise in church membership in the early nineteenth century did not result in the growth of denominational enterprises. The majority of pastors worked in hard and isolated places where denominational issues and fund-raising took a minor role in their day-to-day work. A few managed the time and expense to travel to annual denominational meetings; most did not even do that. Yet both Methodists and Baptists faced serious dissent even from the limited growth of organized religious work during this period.

The modesty of denominational goals was particularly evident among Baptists, who traditionally stood firmly for the autonomy of congregations. The Virginia General Association, organized in 1822, was a loosely organized coalition of small groups of pastors and laity devoted to such causes as foreign and home missions that were funded by small contributions from societies scattered across the state. Baptist leaders purposely left their statewide organization weak and did not pretend to represent the interests of Baptists across the state. When the Virginia General Association met for the first time in 1823, just fifteen men, representing seven of the state's twenty associations, assembled.

The small amounts of money these organizations raised further underscored their modest purposes and their small influence. Baptists collected less than $250 from churches across the state in 1823. By 1841, just fourteen of the thirty district associations in the state sent representatives to the general association meeting, and monies collected amounted to less than five thousand dollars. Even the Methodists, who were better organized than the Baptists, raised just five thousand dollars from more than thirty thousand members for their statewide work by 1845.[9]

During the 1830s and 1840s, the controversy over slavery began to threaten this world of local control among southern Protestants. Proslavery Christianity and its consequent schisms broke down much of the provincialism in southern religion by the eve of the Civil War. The distant rumble of abolitionism became a roar by the 1840s that pastors even in the most remote areas of the state ignored at their peril. Although religious leaders shunned outright association of religion with politics, by the 1850s the implications of religious belief stretched far wider than the salvation of individual souls. In the view of denominational leaders, the politicization of religion did not necessarily follow religion's sharp turn into public culture.

By the mid-1840s, southern pastors had convinced themselves and most of those in their congregations of the Christian character of slavery. If few southern Methodists or Baptists openly challenged slavery, however, the increasingly strident tone of their dispute with their northern brethren did not allow the issue to rest. Tensions over slavery mounted, forcing regional schisms in both denominations.[10]

The dispute had particular relevance to Virginia pastors. Although Virginia lay outside of the Cotton Belt, on the eve of the Civil War, it counted more slaves than any other state, and almost 40 percent of the South's free blacks. Half the counties in the Piedmont and Tidewater regions counted 50 percent or more of their population enslaved. Instead of cotton, the state's field slaves cultivated primarily tobacco and wheat. Others fished, mined, and worked in the iron foundries and manufacturing establishments of Richmond. Regardless of where they lived, Virginians encountered slaves in a variety of settings in the course of a single day's work.[11]

Like other white Virginians, pastors who could afford to own slaves likely did so. Measured by the numbers of slaves they owned, Methodist and Baptist pastors were hardly a social elite. Instead, they held slaves at the same rate as other free Virginians. In 1850, two-thirds of all Methodist and Baptist pastors did not own any slaves, a figure that matched that of the free population at large. And of the one-third who did own slaves, the size of their holdings apparently matched that of other free Virginians almost exactly.[12]

If Virginia's pastors were representative in terms of slaveholdings, however, as a group they wielded a disproportionate influence in national and regional denominational affairs. Virginians took a leading role in both the schism and the administration of the newly created southern denominations. Virginia Baptists called the meeting that decided the issue, made up more than 10 percent of its delegates, and contributed a vice president and secretary to the convention. Virginia Methodist leaders also played a key role in the decisive general conference of 1844. William A. Smith, a Virginia pastor and professor at Randolph-Macon College, was one of the most ardent defenders of proslavery Christianity, and his thinking influenced southern Methodism's "declaration of independence" from its northern connections.[13]

The small band of town and city clergy who led both the Methodist and Baptist denominations in Virginia welcomed the new notoriety that the controversy over slavery lent to religion. They had long strained against the provincialism and simplicity associated with their traditions. The denominational schisms of the mid-1840s provided pastors hungry for professional status an unprecedented opportunity for visibility in southern public affairs.

The writings of a Virginia Baptist pastor named Thornton Stringfellow illustrate the ways in which the proslavery argument altered the stance of some pastors toward public affairs. In 1841, Stringfellow published a defense of slavery entitled "A Brief Examination of Scripture Testimony on the Institution of Slavery"—the tract that would convince Jeremiah Jeter that slavery was a necessary and benevolent institution. As the title suggests, in it Stringfellow examined slavery in both the Old and New Testaments, and established a precedent for the institution from a long list of scriptural passages. It became one of the most influential proslavery tracts of the day. He followed this tract with another piece, published in 1860, which moved away from the sufficiency of a biblical precedent for establishing the legitimacy of slavery. The 1860 tract was entitled "Slavery: Its Origin, Nature and History, Its Relations to Society, To Government, and to True Religion, to Human Happiness and Divine Glory Considered in the Light of Bible Teachings, Moral Justice, and Political Wisdom." The difference in the titles suggests more than a change in Stringfellow's own views on the subject; it suggests his play for an audience beyond those in church pews. Here, the Bible was no longer the sole authority on slavery. Stringfellow sought not only to show that slavery was a biblical institution, but he also claimed by his title that slavery was both morally and politically expedient. Although a preacher, Stringfellow now claimed an authority over those who would not be satisfied with a Christian slavery, but those who yearned for a morally and politically expedient slavery as well. Punctuating this reach for new authority was Stringfellow's addition of the title "D.D.," an honorary degree, to his name on the title page of the 1860 tract.[14]

Stringfellow's tract illustrates how proslavery arguments converged with the ambitions of pastors. Denominations provided an indispensable platform from which pastors could assert their authority beyond the church door. The dispute over slavery unmistakably cast denominations as public institutions in antebellum America. It erupted in the context of denominational work; denominational bodies worked to resolve it, and its resolution spawned new denominations. The leaders of denominations on both sides found their own positions enhanced considerably because of their participation in the debate.

Hence, the new southern denominations provided a powerful context in which southern pastors could work out their ambitions for their own careers and their churches. After 1845, they began in earnest to build a religious bureaucracy that rivaled the efficiency, wealth, and size of that of their northern peers. Through appeals to wealthy patrons and church members alike, denominational coffers swelled severalfold in the decade and a half before the Civil War.

In Virginia, growing denominational wealth mirrored that of the state and region. The dominance of American cotton in the world market during the

1850s spread wealth throughout the South, benefitting even areas like Virginia that were outside of the Cotton Belt. In the 1850s, Virginia was the largest, richest, and most populous state in the region. It counted the largest slave population as well as the greatest share of regional manufacturing and urban centers. Encouraged by the construction of hundreds of miles of new railroads during the 1850s, the state economy moved increasingly toward manufacturing. Iron production, for example, increased almost 200 percent in that decade. Agriculture, too, became increasingly mechanized. These developments accommodated rather than excluded slave labor as increasing numbers of Virginia slaves worked in urban and manufacturing settings. By 1861, Virginia produced almost one-third of all goods manufactured in the South and counted 20 percent of the region's railroads.[15]

As beneficiaries of this strong economy, Baptist and Methodist churches surged forward during the 1850s. Where Virginia population increased by 12 percent, Methodist membership grew at more than double that rate, by 27 percent. The number of Methodist churches increased by more than one-third, while the number of Baptist churches grew by one-fifth in the decade.[16]

Gains in church wealth, however, surpassed even membership growth. Between 1850 and 1860, the value of property held by Virginia Methodists more than doubled, while Baptist property values increased by 80 percent. These contrasted to growth rates of 58 percent in the Presbyterian and 65 percent in the Episcopal churches. Where all of these denominations began the decade holding property of roughly the same value, by 1860 Methodists and Baptists held more than twice the amount of property of the other two denominations combined. On the eve of the Civil War, Virginia Regular Baptist and Methodist clergymen were the stewards of $2.9 million worth of property.[17]

Like gains in property, contributions to benevolent causes leaped forward after 1845. By 1861, both churches saw a fivefold increase in donations for denominational work. By 1859, southern Baptists had raised 62 percent more money for domestic and foreign missions than they had raised in thirty-three years before their separation from the North. Total monies raised by the Methodist Virginia Conference grew tenfold between 1845 and 1860. Much of this money came from small donations by individuals. Significantly, northern church societies saw a similar rise in giving for charitable purposes during the 1850s.[18]

If growth in property values signaled the efforts of individual congregations to build better church buildings, growth in contributions for denominational benevolence measured a shift in Methodists' and Baptists' understanding of the relation between religion and society. Denominations were created to undertake benevolent works too large for individual congregations, such as foreign and domestic missions, and education. By consciously expanding the work of denominations, Methodists and Baptists moved sharply away from old ideas of maintaining purity from society toward the goal of influencing it. Denominations were public institutions, and their resolutions, publications, and societies worked aggressively for social consensus in the South of the 1850s.

As defined by nineteenth-century Protestants, religious benevolence was the "interpretation and promulgation of God's goodness." It included all work done in the name of Christ, including evangelism, foreign missions, Sunday schools, and religious education in denominational academies and colleges. By the 1840s, many Virginia pastors came to view slavery itself as a work of Christian benevolence because it offered an opportunity to evangelize slaves. Religious benevolence, however, embraced far more than attempts to encourage individual conversions. It also stressed the social benefits of religious belief, arguing that Christianity benefitted earthly society even as it fitted people for a life in eternity.[19]

Religious benevolence took different forms in the antebellum North and South. Measured against the standard of northern benevolence, southerners practiced a less vigorous, and less successful, form. Yet such a view misconstrues the nature of belief in the antebellum South. In reality, education was the chief benevolent activity of religion in the antebellum South. Southern churches devoted much time and attention to teaching children and adults alike to read and write. In a region with no public schools, churches and ministers shouldered the principle burden of schooling, and this work absorbed much of the "reform" sentiment entertained by northern churches that had the luxury of public schools to teach basic literacy. In addition, slavery monopolized the attention of many religiously minded southern reformers and left many pastors and members with the conviction that the mission to the slaves was the chief, and most useful, benevolent work of their day. Plantation slavery also hindered the growth of towns and cities, depriving the reform-minded of urban social networks and making benevolent societies less visible and viable than those in the North. Southerners also largely ignored the millennialism that drove much northern interest in such work. They did not routinely counter abolitionists' charges that slavery delayed the coming of the Kingdom of God with their own claim that slavery would usher in the millennium. Virginia divines were far more skeptical of apocalyptical predictions than many of their northern peers—and far less interested in them. Their rare comments about the future focused on the imprudence of predicting the time of Christ's return.[20]

By contrasting southern religious benevolence to that of the North, however, historians have underestimated its importance to religious culture of the late antebellum period. Southerners' abiding interest in individual salvation has fueled arguments that proslavery Christianity privatized religious belief and practice in the region. Southerners were largely convinced, in the words of one student of the region, that "religion should put people right with God . . . not tamper with society." This overriding concern with salvation of individuals has been called the central theme of southern religious history.[21]

This view neglects to take into account the clergy's determined, and successful, expansion of denominations during the 1840s and 1850s. When the works as well as the words of southern divines are taken into account, it is clear that denominational growth in the late antebellum South was driven largely by the clergy's vision of them as instruments of social consensus. Southern benevolence, unlike that of the North, remained firmly rooted in a denominational context. Where northerners favored interdenominational organizations for a number of benevolent projects, southerners worked not as Christians nor even as Protestants, but as Baptists or Methodists.[22]

The rise of southern denominations during the 1850s not only emphasized southerners' interest in religion as a tool of social consensus, it also redefined the role of the clergy. The schisms of the mid-1840s, as well as the growing importance of proslavery Christianity to the social and cultural life of the South, coincided with the appearance of a generation of pastors who were keen to establish the professional credentials of the ministry. During the 1850s, a particularly large number of young men entered the ministry. Their careers reached into the 1890s, and their experiences shaped the clerical profession for the second half of the nineteenth century.[23]

Denominational work lay at the heart of these young pastors' perceptions of the professional ministry. The leading pastors of the day were a small group of men, primarily from cities and towns, who wielded an influence far greater than their numbers. With few exceptions, they married the interests of the profession with those of the denomination and encouraged their younger peers to devote themselves to denominational causes. Professional prestige and merit increasingly flowed from connections with denominational projects and leadership. On the eve of the Civil War, advancement into the top ranks of the profession was not based solely on a man's talent in the pulpit or as a pastor to his local congregation; instead, his participation in denominational affairs began to determine his professional fate.

The city-based character of denominational leadership had roots as old as the century. If the majority of pastors lived and worked in rural Virginia, the rare pastor who made his way to the city found a different context for his ministry. Antebellum Virginia was the most urban of the southern states. Although just 9 percent of the state's population lived in towns or cities in 1850, they were centers of commerce, culture, and education. They attracted people who were eager to cast aside rural simplicity and take up the more sophisticated tastes of urban life.[24]

Accordingly, congregations in Virginia cities and towns wielded a disproportionate influence in church affairs across the state. Their members—including many merchants and professionals—gave generously to religious causes and became leaders in state denominational affairs. Not only were city congregations wealthier, more city dwellers belonged to churches than their rural counterparts. The Protestant denominations of the slave South, then, were institutions rooted in towns and cities.

The sense of influence and prosperity in city congregations accrued to their pastors. City and town pastors rarely preached to congregations they had known since youth. Many came there from the countryside, lured by the association of the city with success and sophistication. "I imagine to myself that you have become quite a great preacher," Jeremiah Jeter wrote to a friend in Richmond in 1827. "Situated in the metropolis of the state, in the foundation of polite knowledge, having intelligent companions, recourse to many books, everything to make you diligent in studying, you have improved, I expect, considerably."[25]

Town life was informed by a consciousness of social position that differed markedly from that of the countryside, and as E. Brooks Holifield has observed, "the social ladder leaned heavily against the church house door." Town professionals—lawyers, doctors, teachers, and editors—wielded an economic influence that made them particularly sensitive to social standing. This was especially true for urban Baptists and Methodists, who openly spurned their tradition of "plain-folk" religion. James B. Taylor arrived in Richmond from rural Virginia in 1826 to take the helm of Second Baptist Church. Just twenty-two years old, he was self-educated and believed earnestly in self-improvement. Along with preaching the Gospel, he eagerly complied with the request of many in his congregation, themselves newly arrived from the country, to teach them to read. In a few short years, he purchased an expensive

Richmond home and published two books, and in 1855, he received an honorary doctorate.[26]

Cut off from the culture of husbandry that shaped the rural pastor's experience, city pastors identified their own work with that of professionals and merchants and measured their success against the hard standards of Episcopal and Presbyterian clergymen who often disdained them. Cities, however, yielded to their hopes of social elevation. Honor came to them there far more easily than in the planter-dominated countryside. By the 1840s, urban Baptists and Methodists raised elegant church buildings that rivaled the best of their Episcopal and Presbyterian rivals. The most tangible sign of their success was their own salaries, which were sometimes ten times that of their rural peers. Urban Methodists and Baptists were not as wealthy as their Episcopal and Presbyterian peers, but their average wealth across the South exceeded nine thousand dollars. Such men were hardly marginal participants in southern town life.[27]

From their pulpits and the pages of religious publications, these town and city pastors defined the ideals of the fledgling clerical profession. In contrast to their rural counterparts, city pastors rooted their sense of calling in the affirmation of their peers, in their position as leaders of the statewide church, rather than solely in the approval of their congregations. They successfully argued that the urban model of the ministry, devoted to denominational benevolence, should define their profession. Where rural Methodist and Baptist pastors often farmed or taught school, well-paid urban pastors could afford to forego other sources of income to take up full-time work. During the 1840s, city pastors began to appeal to their peers across Virginia to enter into full-time pastoral work. They objected to pastors working at another vocation during the week, arguing that the "heavy responsibilities" of pastors—such as "benevolent efforts" like committee and board meetings, Sunday schools, and speaking engagements—should compel pastors to take up full-time work.[28]

The schisms of the 1840s, played out in the context of growing sectional feeling and the new public importance of clerical leadership, assured the triumph of these men and their ideas in denominational leadership. The new southern denominations centralized authority in the hands of a small group of men who claimed to represent the views of pastors and churchgoers across the region. This marked a sharp departure from past practice, particularly for southern Baptists. The Southern Baptist Convention, organized in 1845, centralized authority in to an unprecedented degree. Leaders later argued that the new importance of these denominational bodies did not fundamentally alter former practice because they left several controls over their authority in place.

But the small size of the group who directed the separation from northern churches suggested otherwise. Just 293 church leaders attended the Augusta meeting that created the Southern Baptist Convention, and by the last day of the meeting, during which several important issues were decided, only one hundred delegates remained. The small group of leaders in Augusta were confident that their views represented those of southern Baptists as a group. The influence of the convention, then, was greater than ever after 1845.[29] Developments on the state level echoed those of the region. After 1845 Virginia Baptists increasingly focused on the administration of their statewide general association, culminating in its reorganization in 1855. Formerly a loose coalition of separate and largely autonomous boards, the Virginia General Association became a more centralized body under the oversight of a small group of state leaders.

After 1845, these denominational leaders worked not only as Methodists or Baptists, but also as southerners. The schisms between northern and southern Methodists and Baptists plunged religious matters into a regional context. During the 1840s and 1850s, and for many years after, sectionalism entangled the language of religion. Clearly, church leaders of the 1840s and 1850s were concerned with matters far wider than the salvation of souls.

Proslavery Christianity provided a brilliant opportunity for denominational leaders to claim a place in public debate. As historians have shown, this was a sophisticated theological argument that focused on the social benefits of Christian belief. It invited pastors to read the Bible as a text of social economy as well as spiritual revelation.[30] In the context of the national debate over slavery, southern denominational leaders took the public relevance of religious benevolence for granted. They argued boldly that converting slaves would preserve and improve the social and civil order. By 1860, they routinely set forth the secular and religious benefits of slavery on equal terms.

Southern pastors did not commit themselves to slavery as it was but rather to slavery as it could be. Abolitionists made them painfully aware of the institution's flaws. If slavery was sanctioned by God, it was also tainted by sin. As practiced in antebellum Virginia, slavery clearly was not necessarily Christian. Master and slave alike, but particularly slaves, needed to be brought into the Christian fold. The only cure for the abuse of the master-slave relationship, pastors argued, was true religion. "The Gospel is the only remedy for the evils of slavery," thundered Rev. William A. Smith of Virginia.[31]

Denouncing the "evils of slavery," as Smith called them, propelled pastors into a new position. By pleading with masters and slaves to mend their ways, they consciously extended their writings, lectures, and sermons to address non-Christians as well as Christians. Both, they argued, were bound by the Bible. "I am not aware that . . . the failure to profess Christianity free[s] any one from the duty of being a Christian," Smith told his students at Randolph-Macon College.[32] By setting forth standards of conduct for masters and slaves, such pastors as Smith proclaimed not only their interest in the behavior of non-Christians but their authority over them as well.

Proslavery Christianity, no less than abolitionism, was concerned with changing nineteenth-century American society with the Christian message. If abolitionists and proslavery theologians disagreed fundamentally over the message of the Bible, both used it as the basis of their vision to change the world. In their arguments in support of slavery, and for its reform, Virginia pastors boldly asserted their leadership in affairs outside of the church. "The design of the Gospel ministry is not to build up an earthly empire . . . it is to renovate the world," a Baptist association exhorted its membership in 1844. "The Pulpit is the grand instrument of civilization . . . Christianity purifies, enlightens, refines." Yet another pastor argued that the "hundreds of preachers and clergymen of Virginia . . . have the talents and all the requisite powers to effect any great moral revolution."[33]

As leaders of denominations with thousands of members that had taken an irreversible position on slavery, pastors stepped outside of their customary roles as leaders of a congregation. They not only proclaimed salvation from the world but also worked to "reform mankind" and to effect "moral revolution" in the world. Where earlier pastors had set up a rigid boundary between the church and the world and built their authority on its defense, late antebellum pastors clambered over this barrier to lecture non-Christians on the universality of Christian values in issues ranging from the treatment of slaves to sabbatarianism to drinking.

In spite of their interest in public culture, pastors continued to insist that they despised politics. They had long stressed the incompatibility of religion and partisan politics, characterizing politicians and their "dirty work" as unworthy rivals in a contest for the hearts and minds of the people. "The only inquiry is not 'what must I do to be saved' but who, think you, will be president?'" a Baptist noted with disgust at the height of the 1844 contest between Henry Clay and James K. Polk. In an 1855 letter, Rev. Daniel Witt gave full expression to his loathing of politics. "Have you any religion now amongst your people?" he wrote. "The hurricane of political excitement has blasted everything of the sort in these parts. . . . I took no part in the recent election; I have been so disgusted with the preaching politicians and the politicating preachers that I eschewed the whole thing."[34]

Pastors were particularly sensitive to charges that they were merely "politicating preachers." As a Baptist writer put it, ministers who engaged in politics had "come down from a great work to mingle in the heats of passion and debate." The contentious sectarian disputes of their day framed doctrinal disputes as uncompromising battles over absolute truth, which often resulted in the destruction of congregations, friendships, and even family relations. In appealing for harmony, pastors characterized these disputes with political metaphors, complaining of "party prejudices" among ministers. Hence, they separated politics from the public interest, and placed their work squarely in the latter category.[35]

Denominations reshaped the daily work and professional identity of southern pastors in a variety of ways. The pastors' attention was pulled away from the local congregation and toward the regional denomination. The role of the congregation in testing the call of the minister waned. The esteem of a pastor's peers, rather than the convictions of his congregation, became more important to his entry into the ministry. Denominations tied professional credentials more closely to the role of administrator and fund-raiser than that of preacher and pastor. Successful pastors—those rewarded with lucrative pulpits—were committed to, and successful at, enlisting their congregations to contribute money and time to denominational projects. In some cases, pastors even began to view congregations as sources of funds for these projects.

The professional ethos created during the late antebellum years was based on education, organization, and efficiency, all traits valued by urban professionals of the day and necessary to their style of business. Denominations were bureaucracies, and their massive growth in this period reflected the clergy's interest in applying the methods of business to the work of religion. Both Methodists and Baptists increasingly relied on a regional network of denominational committees, rather than individual congregations, to lead works of religious benevolence. In doing so, they moved toward a corporate model of religious work and away from the focus on individual salvation that drove the revivals of the early antebellum period. Denominations organized and linked like-minded people to accomplish works of benevolence across the state and region. What better and more efficient way could there be, they argued, to spread the spiritual and social benefits of Christian faith? They shrugged off the objections of dissenters and seized every opportunity to promote the denomination as the chief agent of religious benevolence. They tirelessly used the religious press, as well as their pulpits, to appeal for donations to this work. Late antebellum southern religious benevolence was less the effort of individuals, or even congregations, than it was the work of denominations.[36]

Even after the growth of denominations began during the 1840s, most Virginia Methodist and Baptist pastors continued to work in small congregations at daily tasks that had defined their calling for hundreds of years. Some dissented from the denominational model of religious life. Among Baptists, particularly, benevolence was a controversial issue, sparking decades of bitter disputes between missionary, or Regular Baptists, and antimissionary Baptists.

Noah Baldwin, living out his career in the antimission stronghold of southwestern Virginia, spent his life in the center of this intense, and sometimes violent, dispute. Although he shared some doctrinal views with his opponents, he differed sharply with them over the value of "connectional work." Antimissionists declared Sunday schools, mission, and educational societies to be extrabiblical and therefore unacceptable, while missionary leaders argued they were the natural activity of the redeemed. "Preached on the subject of industry in business," Baldwin reported in his diary in 1852. "My object was to stimulate to system in business, so that something might be accumulated and given to the cause of benevolence." [37]

Pastors like Baldwin considered the missionary message so important that they were willing to suffer the loss of their jobs, and even physical persecution, for its cause. He himself narrowly missed being tarred and feathered. Some characterized their differences with antimission Baptists as those of enemies on the battlefield. Such fervent commitment was rooted deeply in religious feeling. But something else informed it as well. Baldwin belittled antimission Baptists as backward and unsophisticated. By contrast, Baldwin and his peers viewed themselves and their message of organization, benevolence, and education as progressive religion. [38]

Baldwin's progressive religion largely prevailed among pastors in the mainstream Methodist and Baptist churches after the schisms of the 1840s. Nevertheless, the fault lines between those who advocated "progressive religion" and those who spurned it cut across the antebellum South in several ways. Most clearly, it tended to divide urban and rural religious culture. Less sharp were the divisions between those who linked religion and respectability—the vast southern middling classes and those who aspired to them—and those who spurned the anxiety that such aspirations entailed. Baldwin's determined preaching on the value of "system in business" clearly revealed his own bias. His commitment to progressive religion was a testimony of its appeal even in places far removed from urban denominational conventions.

Noah Baldwin and Jeremiah Jeter represented two different social worlds of the nineteenth-century South. Yet, they shared a vision of religion and their profession. Unlike the rough-hewn pastors of the early part of the century, they fancied themselves professional men who were in a position to use religious benevolence to elevate those beneath them socially. Baldwin and Jeter were committed to a vision of denominational growth and professional status in the Old South that would fit the requirements of the New South far better than that of the Old.

After the Civil War, both continued to be ardent defenders of denominational work. The vision of religion as an instrument of social consensus and improvement seemed more needful than ever in the postwar South. Jeter "preached" his message from the pages of the influential *Religious Herald,* one of the flagship newspapers of the Baptist South, and died an honored pastor in his adopted city of Richmond. Baldwin, whose house was burned to the ground during the war, continued the hard work of a little-known preacher in the mountains of the southwest. Not long before his death, he recorded his weariness in the pages of the diary he had kept for more than forty years. "I now confess humbly before my maker that if I had my life to live over and were left to make to myself the choice of a profession, I never would choose the *office and responsibilities* of a pastor," the seventy-seven-year-old man wrote.[39] Divided as Baldwin and Jeter were by social distance, denominational religion linked their professional and personal interests. Their lives suggest that religion, as much as slavery, bound together the many Souths of the nineteenth century.

NOTES

1. Martin was not the only slave Baldwin acquired. In the late summer of 1865, he recorded the departure of the last of several slaves. Noah Carlton Baldwin diary, 9 March 1852, 25 August 1865, Virginia Baptist Historical Society (VBHS).

2. Baldwin diary, 28 October 1853, VBHS.

3. Drew Gilpin Faust, "Evangelicalism and the Meaning of the Proslavery Argument: The Reverend Thornton Stringfellow of Virginia," *Virginia Magazine of History and Biography* 85 (January 1977): 3–17. For Jeter, see Jeremiah Bell Jeter, *Recollections of a Long Life* (Richmond, Va.: The Religious Herald, 1891); William E. Hatcher, *Life of J. B. Jeter, D.D.* (Baltimore: H. M. Wharton, 1887); Anne C. Loveland, *Southern Evangelicals and the Social Order, 1800–1860* (Baton Rouge: Louisiana State University Press, 1980), 1–6.

4. Mitchell Snay, *Gospel of Disunion: Religion and Separatism in the Antebellum South* (New York: Cambridge University Press, 1993); Donald G. Mathews, *Religion in the Old South* (Chicago: University of Chicago Press, 1977); Loveland, *Southern Evangelicals and the Social Order,* 186–218; Drew Gilpin Faust, ed., *The Ideology of Slavery: Proslavery Thought in the Antebellum South, 1830–1860* (Baton Rouge: Louisiana State University Press, 1981); and Faust, "The Pe-

culiar South Revisited," in *Interpreting Southern History: Historiographical Essays in Honor of Sanford W. Higginbotham,* John B. Boles and Evelyn Thomas Nolen, eds. (Baton Rouge: Louisiana State University Press, 1987), especially 101–7.

5. On Christian community, see Greg Schneider, "The Ritual of Happy Dying among Early American Methodists," *Church History* 56 (September 1987): 348–63; Mathews, *Religion in the Old South;* Loveland, *Southern Evangelicals and the Social Order.* Among the studies that note the unusually diverse constituency of antebellum revivals are Frank L. Owsley, *Plain Folk of the Old South* (Baton Rouge: Louisiana State University Press, 1949; reprint, 1982), 98–102 (page numbers refer to the reprint); Jean E. Friedman, *The Enclosed Garden: Women and Community in the Evangelical South, 1830–1900* (Chapel Hill: University of North Carolina Press, 1985), 3–4; James Oakes, *The Ruling Race: A History of American Slaveholders* (New York: Alfred A. Knopf, 1983; Vintage Books, 1983), 97–98. Donald Mathews has emphasized that congregations were created out of revivals. "The Second Great Awakening As Organizing Process, 1780–1830: An Hypothesis," *American Quarterly* 21 (spring 1969): 23–43.

6. Noah Carlton Baldwin diary, introduction, VBHS; Jeter quote, *Religious Herald* 16 July 1840, p. 1; Sidney E. Mead, "The Rise of the Evangelical Conception of the Ministry in America," in *The Ministry in Historical Perspective,* H. Richard Niebuhr and Daniel D. Williams, eds. (New York: Harper and Brothers, 1956).

7. Robert Ryland to "My Dear Willie," 31 August 1854, VBHS.

8. Edgar Pritchett, born in 1828, in John J. Lafferty, *Sketches of the Virginia Conference* (Richmond, Va.: Christian Advocate Office, 1880), 116. On the congregations' role in the preacher's calling, see Loveland, *Southern Evangelicals and the Social Order,* 23; Randy J. Sparks, *On Jordan's Stormy Banks: Evangelicalism in Mississippi, 1773–1876* (Athens: University of Georgia Press, 1994), chap. 2.

9. On Baptist giving in Virginia, see Garnett Ryland, *The Baptists of Virginia, 1699–1926* (Richmond: Whittet & Shepperson, 1955), chaps. 11 and 15. For Methodist figures, see *Minutes, Virginia Annual Conference of 1875* (Richmond, Va.: Fergusson & Son, 1876), app. 1.

10. On Baptists, see Robert A. Baker, *The Southern Baptist Convention and Its People, 1607–1972* (Nashville: Broadman Press, 1974); William W. Barnes, *The Southern Baptist Convention, 1845–1953* (Nashville: Broadman Press, 1954); Garnett Ryland, *The Baptists of Virginia, 1699–1926* (Richmond, Va.: Whittet & Shepperson, 1955). On Methodists, see Sydney Ahlstrom, *A Religious History of the American People* (1972; reprint, New York: Image Books, 1975) and William Warren Sweet, *Virginia Methodism: A History* (Richmond, Va.: Whittet & Shepperson, 1955). For an account of Baptist accommodation to slavery, see Richard R. Beeman, *The Evolution of the Southern Backcountry: A Case Study of Lunenburg County, Virginia, 1746–1832* (Philadelphia: University of Pennsylvania Press, 1984), 189–91. On the transition from antislavery to proslavery sentiment, see Donald G. Mathews, *Slavery and Methodism: A Chapter in American Morality, 1780–1845* (Princeton: Princeton University Press, 1965); Mathews, *Religion in the Old South;* Loveland, *Southern Evangelicals and the Social Order.*

11. During the 1840s and 1850s, Virginia's slave population grew at a rate of about 4 percent. Twenty-five of the 43 Piedmont counties (58 percent) counted more than half of their population as slaves in 1850, while 12 out of 26 Tidewater counties (46 percent) did so. By 1860, Virginia

counted about 500,000 slaves. On the number of free blacks in Virginia, Dan Carter, *When the War Was Over: The Failure of Self-Reconstruction in the South, 1865–1867* (Baton Rouge: Louisiana State University Press, 1985), 149. On the diversity of Virginia slavery, see Gregg L. Michel, "From Slavery to Freedom: Hickory Hill, 1850–80" and John C. Willis, "From the Dictates of Pride to the Paths of Righteousness: Slave Honor and Christianity in Antebellum Virginia," in *The Edge of the South: Life in Nineteenth-Century Virginia,* Edward L. Ayers and John C. Willis, eds. (Charlottesville: University Press of Virginia, 1991). On free blacks in Virginia, see John T. O'Brien, "Factory, Church, and Community: Blacks in Antebellum Richmond," *Journal of Southern History* 44 (November 1978): 509–36; Luther P. Jackson, "Religious Development of the Negro in Virginia from 1760 to 1860," *Journal of Negro History* 26 (April 1931): 168–239.

12. This data was culled from a reading of the manuscript slave schedules for Virginia from the 1850 U.S. Census. From 283 pastors in my antebellum sample, the resident counties for 60 were not found, and 16 slaves were known to have lived out of state at the time. I searched for 207 names in the manuscript census, and identified 79, or 38 percent, as slaveholders. The total sample for the nineteenth century included 800 men. Beth Barton Schweiger, "The Transformation of Southern Religion: Clergy and Congregations in Virginia, 1830–1895" (Ph.D. diss., University of Virginia, 1994). Other historians have implied that slaveholding among clergy exceeded that of the free population at large. William Warren Sweet, *Virginia Methodism: A History* (Richmond, Va.: Whittet & Shepperson, 1955), 245; Ahlstrom, *Religious History,* 2:107.

13. Sweet, *Virginia Methodism,* 213–26.

14. Stringfellow, *A Brief Examination of Scripture Testimony on the Institution of Slavery* (Richmond, Va.: Office of the Religious Herald, 1841); Stringfellow, *Slavery: Its Origin, Nature, and History* (Alexandria: Virginia Sentinel Office, 1860); Faust, "Evangelicalism and the Meaning of the Proslavery Argument."

15. Gavin Wright, *The Political Economy of the Cotton South: Households, Markets, and Wealth in the Nineteenth Century* (New York: W. W. Norton, 1978); Kathleen Bruce, *Virginia Iron Manufacture in the Slave Era* (New York: Century Company, 1930), chap. 8; James M. McPherson, *Battle Cry of Freedom: The American Civil War* (1988; reprint, London: Penguin Books, 1990), 91–103; James I. Robertson Jr., *Civil War Virginia: Battleground for a Nation* (Charlottesville: University Press of Virginia, 1991), 15–16.

16. CHURCHES IN VIRGINIA, PERCENT INCREASE 1850–1860

	Number of Churches	Accommodations†	Property Value
Baptists	21	20	80
Methodists	37	35	123
Episcopal	9	−15	65
Presbyterian	22	13	58

† Number of seats in all churches

The census did not distinguish between Regular or Antimission Baptists, northern or southern Methodists, or Old and New School Presbyterians. Source: U.S. Bureau of the Census, 1850 and 1860.

17. AVERAGE VALUES AND SEATS PER CHURCH IN VIRGINIA, PERCENT INCREASE, 1850–1860

	Church Values†	Seats Per Church #
Baptist	49%	27%
Methodist	63	0
Episcopal	52	−22
Presbyterian	31	−6

† Total church property divided by number of churches
# Total accommodations divided by number of churches
Source: U.S. Bureau of the Census, 1850 and 1860.

18. Between 1845 and 1860, giving for foreign missions increased from $4,300 to $20,338 in the Methodist Virginia Conference. Conference collections increased from $851 to $8,033 for the same period. Baptist giving for the General Association increased five times from $3,120 in 1851 to $15,607 in 1860. For southern Baptist giving, see Baker, *Southern Baptist Convention,* 202; for Virginia Methodists, *Minutes,* Virginia Annual Conference, 1875 (Richmond, Va.: Fergusson & Son, 1876), app. 1, n.p.; for Virginia Baptists, *Minutes,* Proceedings of the Annual Meeting of the General Association of Virginia (Richmond, Va.: H. K. Ellyson, 1851), 1851 and 1860. Among northern Methodists, monies collected for missions, Sunday schools, and tract societies grew from $113,000 in 1850 to $264,900 in 1860. William McGuire King, "Denominational Modernization and Religious Identity: The Case of the Methodist Episcopal Church," *Methodist History* 20 (June 1982): 75–89.

19. Definition of nineteenth-century religious benevolence is from Faust, "Evangelicalism and the Meaning of the Proslavery Argument," 9.

20. Jack Maddex has argued that proslavery millennialism "transcended denominational boundaries" even beyond the Presbyterians he has studied. Virginia Methodists and Baptists, however, never clearly articulated a position on the millennium. Anne Loveland has stressed the lack of preoccupation with millennial themes in her study of the southern antebellum clergy. Maddex, "Proslavery Millennialism: Social Eschatology in Antebellum Southern Calvinism," *American Quarterly* 31 (1979): 46–62; Loveland, *Southern Evangelicals and the Social Order,* 162. For a different view, see Eugene D. Genovese, *The Slaveholders' Dilemma: Freedom and Progress in Southern Conservative Thought, 1820–1860* (Columbia: University of South Carolina Press, 1992). For examples of Virginia clergy's thoughts on the millennium, see Edward Baptist, "A Sermon on the Millennium," *Religious Herald,* 1 May 1844, p. 1; "A Sermon Preached Before the Strawberry Association at it Last Session," *Religious Herald,* 31 January and 7 February 1856, p. 1. On millennialism in the antebellum North, see James H. Moorhead, *American Apocalypse: Yankee Protestants and the Civil War, 1860–1869* (New Haven: Yale University Press, 1978), 1–22; Ernest Lee Tuveson, *Redeemer Nation: The Idea of America's Millennial Role* (Chicago: University of Chicago Press, 1968).

21. Edward L. Ayers, *Vengeance and Justice: Crime and Punishment in the Nineteenth-Century American South* (New York: Oxford University Press, 1984), 57. For an excellent correction, see John W. Quist, "Slaveholding Operatives of the Benevolent Empire: Bible, Tract, and Sunday

School Societies in Antebellum Tuscaloosa County, Alabama," *Journal of Southern History* 62 (August 1996): 481–526.

22. John W. Kuykendall, *"Southern Enterprize": The Work of National Evangelical Societies in the Antebellum South* (Westport, Ct: Greenwood Press, 1982), 66–99. On Protestant ecumenicism in the antebellum North, see Daniel Walker Howe, "The Evangelical Movement and Political Culture in the North During the Second Party System," *The Journal of American History* 77 (March 1991): 1216–39.

23. Growth in the number of Virginia Methodist pastors more than doubled gains in church membership during the same decade. *Minutes,* Virginia Annual Conference of 1875 (Richmond, Va.: Fergusson & Sons, 1876), app. 1, n.p.

24. David R. Goldfield, *Urban Growth in the Age of Sectionalism: Virginia, 1847–1861* (Baton Rouge: Louisiana State University Press, 1977); Kathleen Bruce, *Virginia Iron Manufacture in the Slave Era* (New York: Century Company, 1931), chap. 7.

25. Jeremiah Jeter to James B. Taylor, 30 March 1827, in George Taylor, *Life and Times of James B. Taylor* (Philadelphia: Bible and Publication Society, 1872), 60, quoted in E. Brooks Holifield, *The Gentlemen Theologians: American Theology in Southern Culture, 1795–1860* (Durham, N.C.: Duke University Press, 1978), 5.

26. George B. Taylor, *The Life and Times of James B. Taylor* (Philadelphia: Bible and Publication Society, 1872); George Braxton Taylor, *The Life and Letters of George Boardman Taylor, D.D.* (Lynchburg, Va.: J. P. Bell, 1908); Holifield, *Gentlemen Theologians,* 5–6. For social ladder quote, *Gentleman Theologians,* 12.

27. In 1844, for example, a prominent Richmond congregation paid its pastor $1,000 annually. Floyd S. Bennett, *Church on Shockoe Hill: A History of Centenary Methodist Church in Richmond, Virginia, 1810–1960* (Richmond, Va.: Whittet & Shepperson, 1962), 28, 41, 50. Holifield has argued that southern preachers were on average more wealthy than their northern counterparts. "The Penurious Preacher? Nineteenth-Century Clerical Wealth: North and South," *Journal of the American Academy of Religion* (spring 1990): 17–36.

28. Robert Ryland, Jeremiah Jeter, and James Boardman Taylor, "To The Baptist Churches of Virginia," *Religious Herald,* 6 January 1842, p. 1.

29. Baker, *Southern Baptist Convention,* 174–75. Despite southern denominations' consensus on slavery, it is notable that they did not organize an interdenominational mission to the slaves. Characteristically, they decided that this work of benevolence, like many others, would remain within the confines of the denomination.

30. As theologian James Henley Thornwell argued, if southerners "array the Bible against our social economy, then our social economy must fall." Quote is from Thornwell, "Religious Instruction of the Black Population," *Southern Presbyterian Review* 5 (January 1852): 380–94, quoted in William W. Freehling, "James Henley Thornwell's Mysterious Antislavery Moment," *Journal of Southern History* 57 (August 1991): 383–406. On political economy, see William A. Smith, D.D., *Lectures on the Philosophy and Practice of Slavery* (Nashville: Stevenson and Evans, 1856).

31. Smith, *Lectures on the Philosophy and Practice of Slavery,* v.

32. Ibid., 320–21.

33. Daniel Walker Howe has stressed the connection between evangelicalism and modernization in the nineteenth century. Ronald G. Walters, among others, has pointed to the Christian utopian impulse shared by northern abolitionists and southern proslavery theologians. Howe, "The Evangelical Movement and Political Culture in the North During the Second Party System." Walters, *The Antislavery Appeal: American Abolitionism after 1830* (1978; reprint, New York: W. W. Norton, 1984), 148. On renovating the world, see "Circular Letter of the Beulah Baptist Association," *Religious Herald,* 1 February 1844, p. 1. On moral revolution, see untitled article by "Philo-Gulielmus," *Religious Herald,* 7 May 1846, p. 1. See also an anonymous article entitled "The Power and Responsibilities," *Religious Herald,* 18 August 1842, p. 1.

34. On Clay and Polk, see "Politics Against Godliness," *Religious Herald,* 26 September 1844, p. 1; Daniel Witt to R. Gwathmey, Esq., 4 July 1855, quoted in Jeremiah B. Jeter, *The Life of Rev. Daniel Witt, D.D.* (Richmond, Va.: J. T. Ellyson, 1875), 198. See also letter of R. McD., 4 November 1852, *Religious Herald,* p. 1, in which the author argues that "political excitement is detrimental to the interests of religion."

35. The state constitution barred ministers from the state legislature, and the convention decreed religious schools could not receive state charters. Nevertheless, whenever Virginians yearned for particularly virtuous politicians, or for an approach that transcended partisanship, they turned to pastors. Methodist bishop John Early was no doubt flattered by a petition from the people of Cumberland County to run for Congress in 1851, but he characteristically declined. A Richmond Methodist congregation found "it inexpedient for a minister of the Gospel to make public speeches on the subject of party politics." "Impropriety of Ministers Meddling With Politics," 23 July 1840, *Religious Herald,* p. 1. For "party prejudice," see James A. Riddick to William Gray, 5 January 1858, William Gray Papers, VHS. On Early, see letter of 1851 to John Early, quoted in "Remarks of J. Rives Childs on the Occasion of the Presentation of the Papers of Bishop John Early to Randolph-Macon College," 23 October 1930, R–M; for Richmond church, Stewards' Book, Centenary Methodist Church, Richmond, 18 October 1852, VSL.

36. In 1852, for example, Virginia Baptists called for $10,000 in the next year solely "for the purpose of enlarging the operations of the Association." "Ten Thousand Dollars," *Religious Herald,* 15 July 1852, p. 2.

37. Baldwin diary, introduction, p. 4; 23 March 1852; 5 April 1852, VBHS.

38. Discord between missionary and antimissionary Baptists dated to eighteenth-century disputes between Separates and Regulars. By 1840, formal schism had created essentially two Baptists sects, the Missionary or Regular Baptists and the Antimission, or Primitive, Baptists. See Bertram Wyatt-Brown, "The Antimission Movement in the Jacksonian South: A Study in Regional Folk Culture," *Journal of Southern History* (1970): 501–29; Garnett Ryland, *The Baptists of Virginia, 1699–1926* (Richmond, Va.: Whittet & Shepperson, 1955), 243–62; Donald G. Mathews, "Antimission Movement," and Chester Raymond Young, "Primitive Baptists," in *Encyclopedia of Religion in the South,* Samuel S. Hill, ed. (Macon, Ga.: Mercer University Press, 1985), 37–8, 612–13. On revivals of 1821, see Jeter, *Recollections,* 41. Quote is from Young, "Primitive Baptists." On sectarian differences as warfare, see B. Hardwick, "Can Mission and Anti-Mission Churches Unite Consistently?" *Religious Herald,* 4 March 1858, p. 1.

39. Baldwin diary, 2 December 1894, VBHS.

"Religion Has Something . . . to Do with Politics"

Southern Evangelicals and the

North, 1845–1860

EDWARD R. CROWTHER

 Historians have offered a variety of explanations of how the religious beliefs of northerners and southerners contributed to secession and the Civil War. Some focus on the common religious values of northerners and southerners in a quest to find divisive sentiments that crossed sectarian lines but confined themselves either to the slave states or the free states. Outstanding monographs elucidate connections between Protestantism and antebellum political culture and show that many northerners and southerners brought a disparaging evangelical rhetoric to the political process. Other historians have emphasized that religious denominations were organizations with deep sectional roots, arguing that the religious secession by southern evangelicals from national evangelical bodies from 1837 through 1845 "exposed the deep moral chasm" between North and South, "contributing" to the political secession of 1860 and 1861. In both views of antebellum religion, relationships between northern and southern denominations after the denominational schisms received short shrift, in part because historians do not study nonevents. Because evangelical denominations did not endorse political candidates and offered only moral criticisms of public issues of the day from 1845 until Lincoln's election in 1860, presumably denominational happenings between those years mattered less than the moral struggles over slavery that provoked religious schism before 1845 and sectional schism in 1860 and 1861. A close reading of the record indicates that northern and southern evangelical denominations did involve themselves in the important secular matters of their day and that their religious discourse not only had implications for the political arena but also affirmed important sectional values, especially around the issues of abolitionism and anti-abolitionism. Antebellum southerners did see a link between religious and political values.[1]

Certainly William Hill, an itinerant Baptist minister in South Carolina, perceived a connection between the pulpit and politics, between moral issues and secular events. Writing in his diary in the spring of 1847, he observed that "[t]his day the Congress of the United States adjourns. What are to be the results of these states God only knows and time will only partially make known. War [with Mexico] is sweeping off its hundreds of our choice young men. Division distracts our national councils. The Abolition mania threatens disunion of our government. May God avert these impending clouds."[2] He believed that Providence controlled human history and that the sectional dispute over the status of slavery in territories acquired from Mexico posed a threat to the Union.

A central aspect in Hill's lamentations involved his assessment of abolitionists, whose diatribes and political activities seemed to him to be poised like a rapier to rend the Union in twain. Hill and his fellow southern evangelicals believed that abolitionism sprang from an unorthodox and antibiblical moral source, that it prevented renewed relations with northern evangelical denominations, and that it represented a real spirit of hypocrisy. During the 1850s, southern evangelicals gradually lost the capacity to distinguish between the terms abolitionist and northerner and, erroneously according to the historical record, made these words synonyms. Most critically, among southern evangelicals, antiabolitionism became a rhetorical and intellectual bridge binding together distinctive, and often disparate, southern regions and attitudes about slavery. Widespread southern antiabolitionism helped create the illusion of a solid South on the eve of Civil War, one that was able to effect secession, temporary political union, and to pursue independence under the belief "*deo vindice.*"[3]

By 1850, southern evangelicals classified abolitionism as a form of "modernism," a term that southern evangelicals used to describe the new speculation on the nature and veracity of the Scriptures, as well as the methods and implications of post-Baconian science. One vexing example of modernism involved the "higher criticism" of Scripture, which had originated in schools of theology in Europe. This new criticism of the Bible called into question traditional beliefs that Moses had written the Pentateuch, the first five books of the Old Testament, and that the miracles described in the sacred text had actually occurred. Some new theologians even debated the reality of a historic Jesus, a line of inquiry that undermined the fundamental concepts of Christianity and salvation itself. Theologians who embraced the higher criticism marched in step with geologists who argued that the Ussherite Chronology, which averred that God created the earth in 4004 B.C., was inaccurate. The earth, its flora, its fauna, had evolved slowly, over tens of thousands of years. The literal words of the Bible—that God created the living world in six days— did not dissuade the higher critics and the new scientists.[4]

The arguments of these modern interpreters of Scripture and nature did not convince southern evangelicals. That no archaeologist had found human remains distributed in the oldest stratum of animal remains only proved that many life forms had perished during the nearly thousand-year-long life of Adam, the first man. It did not prove that they existed before Adam, save by one day. No gradual creation occurred. Rather, said G. B. Hendrickson, *"In the beginning God created the heavens and the earth.* In this sublime announcement, we have the overthrow of all the absurd theories that have perplexed the speculative minds of all ages. . . . The Bible contains more important historical information than can be found elsewhere, but this information is conveyed in a style of simple, unaffected elegance and rugged grandeur that has never been equaled." In short, the biblical story of creation was the truth. Alternative creation hypotheses were mere speculative fancy.[5]

Southern evangelicals believed that anyone who questioned the Genesis account of creation might also take issue with other biblical admonitions. The same speculative spirit that denied biblical literalism might challenge the social, economic, and political relationships in the antebellum United States, which southerners argued had scriptural warrant. Indeed, the motive to question the sacred text or the institutions the text affirmed sprang from a spirit of human apostasy. God, for reasons that he alone understood, allowed many things to exist, such as war, famine, pestilence, death, and human slavery. Christians had the duty to obey God, not to question Jehovah's revealed political economy. For a person to question human institutions reflected a vain attempt to become "more merciful than God himself . . . affecting a philanthropy more pure and all embracing than that of Jesus Christ." The wave of reform sweeping over the northern states—including "socialism," feminism, and abolitionism, like the scientific and critical methods of "modernism"— fashioned the forbidden fruits of the belief that humanity had grown beyond the need for revelation and, now, considered itself better equipped by its own reason to reshape and perfect the world that God had formed in the beginning. An infidel and naive conception of human nature had yielded an unfounded belief in the perfectibility of humankind, a concept that now threatened to make the United States into an unchristian republic.[6]

Southerners formed the perception that abolitionism rooted itself in infidel soil long before 1850, but as southerners observed the northern flirtation with higher criticism, which followed its amorous relationship with natural and romantic religion, southerners made anew and strengthened their mental connection between abolitionism and disregard for the Bible. Antislavery pronouncements and policies of northern evangelicals had fractured three evangelical denominations along sectional lines. Continued antislavery dicta from northern denominations clouded any attempt to reunite the evangelical denominations across sectional lines. In abortive reconciliation attempts and quests to establish diplomatic ties between northern and southern evangelicals, northerners argued that southerners were evil because they tolerated slavery. Southerners argued that northerners were evil because northern abolitionism was contrary to the Bible.[7]

The odyssey of the Methodist Episcopal church and the Methodist Episcopal church, South, offers one powerful example of the continuing moral fracas over slavery and abolitionism to poison intersectional relations. After their denominational schism, northern and southern Methodists continued to hurl moral epithets at one another even as they moved to carry out the Plan of Separation, which formally divided the church along sectional lines, and to create normal intersectional denominational relations. The powerful moral views pitting northern against southern Methodists contributed to rhetorical sectionalism. Indeed, northern and southern Methodists expressed more intersectional hostility over the abortive attempts to implement the Plan of Separation than they had ever uttered in fraternal sentiment before their denominational schism in 1844. By terms of the Plan of Separation, northern and southern Methodists agreed to divide their corporate assets equitably. Common properties included a book concern and the Charter Fund, a pension system for indigent ministers, ministerial widows, and orphans. In addition, the plan allowed individual congregations along the slave state–free state border to choose to affiliate with either northern or southern Methodists in those cases where a border congregation disagreed with the sectional affiliation selected by the annual conference (the state-level Methodist governing body), which directed the border church. If the Kentucky Annual Conference adhered to the Methodist Episcopal church, South, congregations along the Ohio River could dissent by aligning themselves with the annual conferences of Illinois, Indiana, or Ohio. Chaos resulted and created conditions that allowed Methodists in one section to charge Methodists in the other with encroachment. The courts finally had to divide much of the disputed property and territory.[8]

In the years after the separation, annual conferences in the free states for-mally expressed anger that the general conference (the quadrennial national assembly of Methodists) had agreed to the Plan of Separation with the heinous slaveholders and schismatics of the South. According to these northern Meth-odists, Bishop Andrew and his supporters had violated Methodism's neutrality on slavery—and any claim to Methodist property—by insisting that Andrew be allowed to own slaves and to continue to serve as a bishop. Many annual conferences refused to endorse the Plan of Separation, despite the fact that the general conference of 1844, which drafted the plan, contained a majority of northerners, who were no friends of slavery. After numerous northern annual conferences requested the plan's nullification, the 1848 general conference re-scinded it on the grounds that the 1844 general conference had lacked the proper constitutional authority to disburse the assets in question. Northern Methodists, opined the 1848 general conference, retained the sole possession of the book concern and the Charter Fund. The general conference also re-fused to consider normalizing relations with southern Methodists until the latter folk surrendered any claim to the pension fund or colportage enterprise. The conference did not even formally acknowledge the presence of Lovick Pierce, who came to the meeting with an offer of renewed fraternal relations from the Methodist Episcopal church, South.[9]

This northern Methodist conduct outraged southern Methodists, who ex-pressed their disgust with extreme vituperation. Southern spokesmen charged northern Methodists with both unconstitutional and unscriptural conduct. Simply motivated by the peculiarly Yankee lust for "lucre," southerners as-serted, the northern Methodists had refused to disburse pension monies to aged southern ministers, ministerial widows, and orphans since the schism occurred. One southern editor advocated fighting fire with fire and urged the seizure of northern Methodist property in the border states as ransom until northerners implemented the Plan of Separation. Ultimately southern Meth-odists opted for the courts over violence and filed suit to obtain their portion of the disputed property. Methodist mediators settled the first case out of court. In the second case, southern Methodists won on appeal before the Su-preme Court. Northern Methodists did not accept the appellate decision with grace and blasted the Supreme Court as a tool of the "slaveocracy," just as abolitionists would after the court ruled in *Dred Scott v. Sandford*. This north-ern behavior made an inviting target for southern Methodist editors who charged that northern Methodists were unfair and evil individuals who tried to have their own way at all costs. Whenever they lost, Yankee Methodists criticized the rules.[10]

The issue of the sectional affiliation of border churches also led to the judicial bar, following heated and repeated accusations of jurisdictional and territorial violations perpetrated by both free state and slave state Methodists. Kentucky, Missouri, and western Virginia provided the sometimes-violent battleground. One of the most celebrated cases involved the Methodist church in Maysville, Kentucky. It stood within the confines of the Kentucky Annual Conference. That body chose to affiliate with the Methodist Episcopal church, South, a decision that pleased many of Maysville's Methodists. But John Armstrong did not number himself among the satisfied. Because he had contributed most of the money used to build the meetinghouse in Maysville, he sued to prevent slaveholding southern Methodists from using what he considered his personal property. Initially the court played Solomon and divided the use of the building between northern and southern adhering Methodists, allowing each faction access on alternate weeks. On appeal, the southerners won total control of the building. Of course, not all disputes went to court. Southern Methodists in Parkersburg, Virginia, had no desire to permit a judge to decide the fate of their meetinghouse, which was legally the property of the Ohio Annual Conference, a staunch affiliate of northern, antislavery Methodism. The southerners simply seized the edifice and put to flight the northern minister.[11]

Recrimination and combat over implementing the Plan of Separation beginning in 1848 destroyed a temporary but remarkable spirit of forbearance and peace among Methodists immediately following the schism. The "Pastoral Address on Relations with Northern Methodists" at the first General Conference of the Methodist Episcopal Church, South, assumed an extraordinarily charitable tone and attributed the insults southerners had received prior to the schism to a few "individuals and small sections of the Church, North" and not to all northern Methodists or northerners in general. Methodists, north and south, still remained "united in the great love of God among men." Some southern Methodists even wanted to rejoin the two branches of American Episcopal Methodism into one united denomination as soon as it was possible to do so.[12]

This spirit of reconciliation and compromise collapsed under the weight of emotional charges and counter-charges that extremists hurled at each other during the settlement of the property dispute. Henry Biddleman Bascom, a shining star of southern Methodist oratory, said that Yankee Methodists had abandoned the true goal of converting the lost for the false god of abolitionism because of their unwillingness to give slaveholding Methodists property that was due them. In their words, deeds, and attitudes, northern Methodists no longer distinguished themselves from William Lloyd Garrison, Theodore Dwight Weld, Lewis Tappan, and the rest of the immediate abolitionists. Given the immediate abolitionists' assessment of the lack of abolitionist zeal by northern Methodists, Garrison might have found Bascom's comment amusing. But other southerners shared Bascom's attitude. Northern Methodism, warned a Methodist editor in Tennessee, would have to yield its self-righteousness, or else discussion of eventual reunion was no more than a "fruitless expenditure of pen and ink" that could not benefit the South in any way. A Methodist editor from Charleston said that the question of honor alone made any ecclesiastical restoration impossible and cited the insulting abrogation of the Plan of Separation and the refusal of northern Methodists to consider the offer of fraternal relations extended by Lovick Pierce in 1848 to justify the southern intransigence. In addition, northern parsons repeatedly invaded southern territory in order to organize antislavery congregations in the slaveholding states. No scrupulous southern Methodist could endure such affronts without a loss of regard for his erstwhile northern colleagues. Besides, a reunion with avowed abolitionists would inevitably stain southern Methodism with residues of emancipationism. A large number of northern Methodists supported the personal liberty laws passed in northern states in defiance of the Fugitive Slave Act of 1850. Northern Methodist editors expressed approval of the sentiment of mobs that prevented the return south of runaway slaves whom federal marshals had captured. To entertain reunion with northern Methodists, concluded the Charleston editor, "brings doctrines of incendiary tendency to our very homes" because northern Methodists were abolitionists, pure and simple.[13]

Southern Methodists found some of their former colleagues' behaviors especially hypocritical and potentially threatening. Northern Methodists had supposedly considered slaveholding such an evil that, in 1844, they had demanded the resignation of Bishop James Osgood Andrew, a southern bishop and a slaveholder as a result of his marriage. Slave ownership, alleged the northerners, served as a severe "impediment" to the performing of his official duties. Because Andrew refused to manumit his slaves and other southern Methodists had supported him, the Methodist church had divided. It outraged southerners to learn that within the confines of northern Methodist churches after the schism, some four thousand individual Methodists still owned slaves. With tongue in cheek, W. C. Dandy of Maysville, Kentucky, publicized the marriage of a parson in the Ohio Annual Conference to a slaveholding Kentucky widow—a circumstance remarkably similar to Andrew's—"for the information of the guardians of the ministry, North." Southern

Methodists became increasingly agitated by stories of northern, antislavery Methodist annual conferences that allowed slaveholding Methodists in the upper South to remain in good fellowship with what southerners now considered an officially abolitionist denomination. To southerners it seemed that the northern churches preferred maintaining a high number of members to upholding their own standards of behavioral purity. According to one southern writer, the northern dichotomy between belief and action meant either "that they are *insincere* in their denunciations of the South; or . . . that they intend to make inroads upon the South, and over the head of civil law extirpate the evil of slavery." Such immediate abolitionists as Orange Scott and La Roy Sunderland shared the southerners' vituperation at this alleged northern Methodist "hypocrisy," but southern Methodists could not see a distinction between mainstream Methodist behavior and attitudes and that of immediate abolitionists.[14]

Southern Methodists considered the conduct of northern Methodists duplicitous and untrustworthy. Whereas southern Methodists had once discussed the possibility for ecclesiastical reunion with the North, they now described their former northern colleagues as infidels and enemies. In the process of harangue, a growing number of southern Methodists began to call for further action to purge southern Methodism of any taint of abolitionism. These leaders focused on section nine of the *Book of Discipline,* which spoke teleologically of ending the "great evil" of slavery, a phrase that was not only a relic of southern Methodist ties to northern Methodism but also a reflection of the nuances in southern Methodists' views about slavery. Older Methodist leaders, such as William Winans and William Capers, still believed that to practice slavery solely for financial gain was, in fact, a great evil that the church ought to oppose. They still hoped, too, for the right conditions under which slavery might be ended. Thus they opposed deleting the section, even though they believed that southern evangelical masters did not necessarily practice an abusive variety of slavery and that immediate abolitionism constituted folly and bordered on infidelity. Winans argued that no real reason to delete the ninth section existed. State laws made manumission difficult so the offensive section was *defacto* inoperative. As a result of opposition from Capers and Winans at the General Conference of the Methodist Episcopal Church, South, in 1851, the first attempt to repeal the ninth section failed. Undaunted, the South Carolina Annual Conference, whose attitude about slavery's future tended to perpetualism, printed its own version of the *Book of Discipline*— without the noxious ninth section. The desire for sectional unity among southern Methodists, continued negative reaction to the personal liberty laws, the publication of *Uncle Tom's Cabin,* and the diminution and death of the Jeffersonian generation of Methodist leaders produced a solid bloc of southern Methodist delegates who deleted the ninth section at the general conference of 1854.[15]

Only one other antislavery section remained in the *Book of Discipline,* a general rule against the "buying and selling of men, women, and children with an intention to enslave them." It had long provided a target for proslavery Methodists. Yet to expunge it without some grounds other than expediency would leave them open to charges that they were swapping the foundations of the faith for prospects for profit. Opponents of the general rule would have to show that the proviso did not now and was never intended to apply to existing master-slave relations in the southern United States. One writer who attempted this task noted that John Wesley, for all his documented antislavery sentiment, had never issued an ecclesiastical rule on slavery, an institution he, in fact, regarded as purely a civil concern. According to the *Nashville Christian Advocate,* American Methodists had formulated the rule against buying and selling slaves in 1788, not in order to interfere with southern slavery, but to show their approbation of the new republic's decision to end the African slave trade in 1808. Because the rule was authored by Thomas Cooke and Francis Asbury, and not by John Wesley, the *Christian Advocate* opined that the rule was not an essential feature of Methodism. Besides, the term "to enslave" referred to the reduction in status from a free person to a bondsperson and, therefore, could never be properly construed to apply to someone who was already a slave. The antislavery legacy in Methodism reflected only opposition to the further extension of the slave trade, which was historically associated with carnage and brutality that no Christian could condone. The tradition, alleged the columnist, did not in any way affect the conduct of existing slavery.[16]

Sharing this view, the Alabama Annual Conference voted in 1856 to petition the next General Conference of the Methodist Episcopal Church, South, to expunge the buying-and-selling rule. The conference, which met in Nashville in 1858, voted 1,160 to 311 in favor of the Alabama petition. Only delegations from Kentucky, Missouri, and Tennessee opposed removal outright. Arkansas' delegates split: seventeen in favor and sixteen against. Most of those in the minority cited constitutional issues and the fear of giving *defacto* sanction to the reopening of the slave trade as their reasons for opposing the Alabama petition. Lovick Pierce, a Georgian, reminded the reluctant minority that civil law treated the international slave trade as piracy, and these were laws that Methodists, according to the *Book of Discipline*'s section of Christian citizenship, had bound themselves to support.[17]

Rather than solve intersectional relations among Methodists, the denominational schism had produced a Plan of Separation whose implementation had charred what remained of good will between northern and southern Methodists. Sectional recrimination had furthered southern Methodist opposition to abolitionism. And the growing estrangement from northern Methodists and northerners in general resulted within the crucible of purely ecclesiastical affairs. No other southern evangelical denomination endured quite as stormy a separation with its northern colleagues, but both southern Baptists and southern Presbyterians found that their ecclesiastical relations with the North continually ran aground on the shoal of abolitionism.

Each Baptist state denomination in the fifteen slaveholding states had seceded from the national American Baptist Missionary Union (Triennial Convention) and the American Baptist Home Mission Society (ABHMS). Essentially missionary alliances, these voluntary associations had fractured over the question of whether a slaveholder could serve as a missionary. These intersectional missionary enterprises had no property to be divided between northern and southern Baptists. In this one essential way, southern Baptists differed from their Methodist counterparts. Otherwise, once the schism occurred, attempts to find strategies to avoid intersectional discussion over slavery gave way to northern Baptist state convention and associational resolutions denouncing slaveholding and affirming the decisions of the triennial convention and the ABHMS not to appoint slaveholders to the mission fields and southern denunciations of these northern resolutions. Baptists in the South made certain regional adjustments to their newly minted sectional church similar in significance to southern Methodism's adaptations. First, when the Southern Baptist Convention formed in 1845, its membership was made up of congregations instead of individual believers, a denominational polity that mirrored the states'-rights theory of the federal Union. The triennial convention had been composed of individual Baptists. Secondly, Baptists devoted a great deal of energy to developing their own educational and proselytizing materials. They believed that catechisms and theological treatises produced in the North came laced with assumptions conducive to abolitionism.[18]

As Baptists in the South gradually had discerned a need for a trained ministry and developed educational institutions to fulfill it, they initially utilized books and educational treatises written by northerners. One found a course in moral philosophy a standard component of ministerial education. Its instructors generally selected Francis Wayland, *Elements of Moral Science,* as the text. But Wayland was a president of Brown University and, during the years of schism between northern and southern Baptists, had argued in a highly publicized debate with South Carolinian Richard Fuller that the Bible commanded abolitionism and that it did not permit slavery.[19] His basic notions about biblical interpretation and authority also offended southern Baptists. He believed that "the scriptures . . . contain all that God has been pleased to reveal to us by language." He asserted that God also communicated with humanity "by conscience" and through natural revelation and that these latter two sources of religious truth were not necessarily inferior to the Bible. Few southern evangelicals endorsed any revelation apart from the Bible as authoritative. Thus, in 1860 John Leadley Dagg published a southern text to protect southern ministerial students from Wayland's unorthodox views. Entitled *Elements of Moral Science,* it affirmed the supremacy of the literal words of the Bible as the complete and superior revelation of Jehovah to humanity. Dagg and the Baptists were not alone in the concern over the proper relationship among the Bible, the conscience, and morals. Methodist educator R. H. Rivers produced *Elements of Moral Philosophy* in 1859, to protect young Methodist ministers from unsound religious teachings.[20]

Southern Baptists joined with Dixie's Presbyterians in protecting the South from allegedly unorthodox tracts and pamphlets printed by the American Tract Society, an ecumenical and intersectional group that published evangelical catechetical literature. Both groups began to censor tract society literature that, in the process of calling upon sinners to repent, seemed to sensitive southern readers to espouse free labor and implicitly criticize slavery. Both Presbyterians and Baptists began to print their own materials and essentially eliminated their association with the American Tract Society. Whether a text was proslavery or antislavery was in the eye of the beholder during the antebellum period, and ironically, immediate abolitionists also censured the American Tract Society for failing to publish material that condemned slavery.[21]

Presbyterians exhibited the most complex intersectional behavior because their denominational schism did not strictly follow sectional lines. In 1837 Presbyterians had divided themselves into Old School and New School factions, not into northern and southern denominations. Southern Old Schoolers had supported the expulsion of New Schoolers because the New Schoolers were considered to be doctrinally corrupt and their ranks tainted with abolitionists. But especially in Tennessee and Kentucky, one could find many southern New Schoolers. Their adherence to the New School in no way constituted a ratification of liberal theology or immediate abolitionism. Rather, they believed that the Old School had acted unconstitutionally in removing the northern New Schoolers. During the 1850s the southern New Schoolers grew increasingly irritated at the direction of theological liberalism and overt espousal of antislavery and abolitionism taken by northern New Schoolers, and in 1857, the southern New School Presbyterians severed ties with their northern brethren.[22]

Presbyterian Old Schoolers in the North and the South believed that they had solved their abolitionist dilemma by ridding the denomination of abolitionists. Until the outbreak of Civil War, southern and northern Old Schoolers maintained a denominational tie. But during the 1840s and 1850s a few northern Old Schoolers supported cleansing the denomination of slavery. They had to be reminded that "[t]he Church of Christ is a spiritual body, whose jurisdiction extends to the religious faith, and moral conduct of her members. She cannot legislate where Christ has not legislated, nor make the terms of membership which he has not made. . . . Since Christ and his inspired Apostles did not make the holding of slaves a bar to communion, we, as a part of Christ, have no authority to do so." Even in the organizational bonds of a conservative denomination, southern Presbyterians and their northern allies faced challenges from antislavery Presbyterians to issue a ruling against slavery.[23]

In each of the denominational schisms and the difficult intersectional relations that followed, southern evangelicals reacted to abolitionism as a biblically unsound and socially ruinous notion that should not be tolerated. Antiabolitionism served as a cord to bind southern evangelicals together in a region that had different notions about the future of slavery. As historian William W. Freehling has argued most recently, the antebellum South was no monolith committed to the perpetual existence of slavery. Especially in the upper South, conditional termination of slavery, through expatriation or gradually diffusing it away to the lower South or far West, remained one vital part of the southern agenda on the future of slavery. What linked southerners together on the slavery question were certain themes. First, southerners themselves, and not northerners, should determine what had to be done about slavery. Second, most southerners, as instructed by evangelical teaching about slavery, argued that slaveholding per se did not violate biblical teaching. This notion allowed slaveholding perpetualists in South Carolina and conditional terminators in the upper South to coexist, albeit nervously, while the future of slaveholding worked itself out. Finally, where nearly all southerners—even those dissenters who opposed slavery—could agree, immediate abolitionism itself was sinful.[24]

As a result of the lack of consensus about whether and why to extend slavery, the southern political posture on the major sectional issues of the day resembles a tapestry. Southern evangelical denominations refrained from taking strong stands on these issues to avoid alienating the political sentiments of communicants. Evangelical churches, after all, solicited support for a higher cause than did the party leaders. During the complex debates over the status of slavery in territories acquired as a result of the Mexican War or in the Louisiana Purchase, evangelicals followed a consistent course. First, they espoused maintaining the Union. James Henley Thornwell, the "Calhoun of the Southern Church," wrote, "The prospect of disunion is one that I cannot contemplate without horror." Not only might it result in warfare, but in an age ripe with "socialism, communism, and a rabid mobocracy" it seemed folly to attempt to form a new government. Southern religious editors reminded their southern readers to strive for "the most amicable relations with that noble body of men in the Northern states, who amidst storms of obloquy and opposition have steadfastly asserted the constitutional rights of the South and sternly rebuked the wickedness and folly of the fanatics around them."[25]

At the same time, evangelicals attacked segments of northern society, which they lengthened over time to include virtually every northerner, and increasingly gave rhetorical support to contemporary southern society (a way to avoid the question of the termination or the perpetual existence of slavery). Evangelicals even upgraded the stereotypically barbarous sugar planter in Louisiana to benevolent humanitarian. And in practically every written hortatory exercise, southern evangelicals vilified the abolitionist, whom they construed as a godless fool bent upon destroying the Union, southern society, and the word of God.

In denouncing abolitionists, southern evangelical writers especially valued the testimony of blacks themselves, whether from a converted slave or from an African thanking God for the "southern missionary servants to come and make known that salvation to the dark minded inhabitants of Africa." One such tale described the plight of a slave preacher who purchased his freedom and went North, only to discover that the money-grubbing Yankees "charged me like a white man, and treated me like a nigger." A Methodist paper repeated the tale of Mark Bryant, a free black in the South, who willed his property not to any abolitionist group but to *"the missionary society of the Methodist Episcopal Church, South."* The Methodist paper noted that abolitionist harangues made it necessary to tell Bryant's story in the first place, "as a refutation to the charge that the Church, South, shares neither the affection nor the confidence of the colored persons in her midst." Southern evangelical papers delighted in reprinting opinion from the conservative *New York Observer,* a

330 · EDWARD R. CROWTHER

sheet that routinely denounced abolitionists and admitted that blacks were better off as slaves in the South than as free persons in the North. To southerners, it seemed clear that blacks and even honest northerners knew that the abolitionists were mere *"pseudo-philanthropists,"* who interfered in matters beyond their competence.[26]

Southern evangelicals did not simply perceive abolitionists as a threat to slavery or to a literal reading of Scripture. Southern evangelicals understood that the underlying assumptions of immediate abolitionists, especially their notions of human equality, posed a threat to conservative, godly, and republican governance. According to W. J. Sasnett, lower and less-educated classes of people generally manifested "wild fanaticism . . . [and] extravagant, absurd sentiment," thereby weakening any body politic in which they were permitted to participate. Denying black slaves the opportunity to participate in governance preserved the southern political order. In the North, where immigrants and trade-unionists constituted the meanest estate, the unfettered working classes not only jeopardized the continuance of representative government at the state level but also threatened to reduce the federal government to chaos. If sober conservatives failed to arrest the leveling tendencies of the northern "mobocracy," the republic would find itself adrift "on a wild sea of anarchy." In their naive ignorance, the northern underclass appealed to the Declaration of Independence to justify both unbridled democracy and abolitionism: "All men are created equal." To southern evangelicals, such as Presbyterian Frederick A. Ross of Huntsville, Alabama, this self-evident truth was "denied and upset by the Bible, by the natural history of man, and by Providence in every age of the world." William Winans, the Mississippi Methodist, agreed and said that Thomas Jefferson's ideas on the fundamental equality of humankind had yielded "more political evil . . . than from all other causes in the U.S."[27]

Southern evangelicals argued that abolitionism posed other threats to godly Union. First, it encouraged the mixing of politics with the northern pulpit and religious press. The actions and attitudes of a highly visible minority of northern clergymen, such as Henry Ward Beecher, certainly provided southern apologists with easy targets for criticism. He and other ministers had, in fact, encouraged the sending of rifles to Kansas, instead of Bibles, to settle the slavery question there by force. They encouraged their parishioners to resist the Fugitive Slave Law of 1850. Northern religious papers often seemed blatantly partisan, "arraying themselves against what they regard as in the acts of Congress as certain measures favorable . . . to the South." The political conduct on the part of northern churches followed logically their abandonment of biblical theology for overly romantic philosophies, abolitionism, and their surrender to "aspiring, designing demagogues" who uttered philippics to curry their congregation's favor and to facilitate their own advancement. The northern "church, which acts in the squabbles of party platforms is greedy for spoils, and can only excite pity or disgust," declared the *Southern Baptist.* In espousing abolitionism, argued southern evangelicals, the northern pulpit and religions press abandoned true religion for infidel philosophy.[28]

For southern evangelicals to charge northern evangelicals with the exclusive sin of political preaching seems amazing on the surface because southern preachers routinely proclaimed political messages instead of a pure gospel. But southern evangelicals tried to disguise their political ranting as instruction in the Christian duties of citizenship or to bury it deeply in theological defense of slavery. One Mississippi editor, J. T. Freeman, did write that "religion has something—much—everything to do with politics" because the great issues of the day revolved around the question of the moral rectitude of slavery, a discussion that clearly had biblical overtones and, therefore, had rightly become a clerical matter. But Freeman did not directly advocate any specific political action on the part of his readers. In a more humorous vein, William G. "Parson" Brownlow, the fiery evangelical in eastern Tennessee, described a certain reverend Mr. Harrison who "boasted in his pulpit that Jesus Christ was a Southerner, born on Southern soil, and so were his apostles, except Judas, whom he denominated a Northern man." According to Brownlow, Harrison once told his congregation that "he would sooner have a Bible printed and bound in Hell, than one printed and bound North of Mason and Dixon's line." Brownlow's parson may not have uttered strictly political speech, but his monologue had the capacity to incite and certainly had political implications.[29]

To southern evangelicals, abolitionism threatened the Union in a second area—by its encouragement of "treasonous" mob violence associated with antislavery resistance to the Fugitive Slave Act of 1850 and with nativist attacks on Catholic immigrants in northern cities. New England, particularly Boston—the hub of Unitarianism, Transcendentalism, and abolitionism—came to embody the rebellious tendencies that southern evangelicals despised: disregard of both the Bible and the Constitution. Rather than acting like the Apostle Paul and returning the slave Onesimus to his master, Boston mobs had interfered with officers of the court to rescue Fred Wilkins, generally known as Shadrach, in 1851 and Anthony Burns in 1854. In the latter year, nativist riots had erupted against Catholics in Chelsea, Massachusetts. To southern evangelicals, this mass disobedience to civil law had come as a result of northern preachers' abandoning the laws of God, specifically the principles of submission to authority, and the result of the politicians' refusing to abide by the Constitution, claiming a mandate from a higher power. And southern evangelicals did not believe that these sentiments and resulting actions had confined themselves to just a few northerners in one part of the free states. Said the *Nashville Christian Advocate:* "Truly, if these 'despisers of dominion' speak the real sentiments of the Northern people, we have fallen upon evil times." [30]

Abolitionism and its philosophical underpinnings not only caused northerners to misbehave, asserted southern evangelicals, it represented a cancer that eroded northern fidelity to the Constitution and to the Bible. No northerner could produce a single verse of Scripture that mandated masters to manumit their slaves; yet, abolitionists continued to insist that they had found no "single authority for slaveholding by precept or example" in the entire Bible. Southern editors claimed that such demagogic denials of the biblical sanction for slavery were calculated to delude the common citizen in the free states, as "the unlettered Northerner when he reads scripture for himself or hears it read will know that [slavery] is upheld in God's word," unless he is otherwise convinced not to accept what he reads or hears at face value. To Presbyterian Robert Lewis Dabney, who later served as aide-de-camp to Thomas J. "Stonewall" Jackson, abolitionists could not resist the southern strategy—"to push the bible argument continually"—and had no choice but to "assume an anti-Christian position," and quite literally to deny the words of the Bible meant what they said. [31]

Southern evangelicals found abundant evidence convincing them that the North had become more unchristian since it had first espoused emancipation. Many abolitionists had abandoned orthodox teachings concerning the Trinity and had embraced Unitarianism, proving to southern editor Holland Nimmons McTyeire that "the tendency of Abolitionism, or Modern Reform [is] to[ward] Free Thinking and Contempt of the Bible." Some advocates of abolitionism, he noted, also supported the crusade for women's rights, plainly ignoring "what Moses or Paul or any other Biblical writer has said" about the divinely ordered station of the daughters of Eve as subordinate to the sons of Adams. Northern politicians, like William Henry Seward, overturned the celestially dictated rule of law in the name of some "higher law" whenever it was necessary to achieve their mortal designs. "Though many ministers of the gospel are involved in it," said the *Nashville Christian Advocate,* abolitionism "is more closely allied to infidelity than is generally supposed." For the theologically oriented southerner, the dispute between proslavery and abolitionist clergy had eternal consequences. The southerner understood the tensions among abolitionism and its theological underpinnings and southern religious teachings about salvation and Christian duty. Southerners had embraced the notion that the Mosaic code authorized slavery and the belief that Jesus of Nazareth had never condemned slavery. For abolitionists to be correct about the biblical morality of slavery—that humankind had evolved beyond biblical legalism—made Moses totally errant and Jesus less than perfect, transforming the Son of God into a slightly blemished lamb, incapable of "taking away the sins of the world." God, himself, who had issued to Moses the command not to covet or to steal the "manservant" of one's neighbor, had sanctioned the commission of a crime, by forbidding the abolitionists from being true to their own consciences. Hence, abolitionism did not just represent a threat to property but imperiled the moral underpinnings of the worldview of southern evangelicals, which included a belief in the veracity of biblical revelation and eternal salvation for the faithful.[32]

Abolitionists not only denied the revealed word, their antislavery "fanaticism" threatened polite society with "socialism, *teetotalism,* and perfectionism," said Thornwell. "Parson" Brownlow linked abolitionism to "Free Lovers, Free Soilers, . . . Spiritualists, Trance Mediums, Bible Repudiators, and representatives of every crazy *ism* known to the annals of Bedlam." Although both Thornwell and Brownlow wanted to degrade abolitionism in their analyses, they correctly surmised that antislavery and other reform impulses in the North were symptomatic of something more fundamental. The "fanaticism" of the reformers stemmed in part from the need of people to rekindle smoldering emotions nearly consumed in the practice of religion that spoke only of the glories of the world to come in a bland, theological language and that taught acceptance of an immutable status quo. Buoyed with an optimism wrought by a market and an industrial revolution, reformers knew that technology had already enabled humanity to control and transform much of the physical world. Confident in humankind's ability to alter the nature of society, northern reformers refused to accept laissez faire religion. Reform causes also served as a surrogate church. Rather than accepting sin as something both original and lasting or all people as totally depraved, reformers viewed sin as "anything that mitigated against human happiness and welfare." Human behavior, like one's social and economic status, was something that one could improve with human effort.[33]

Rational and orthodox southern evangelicals found such conceptions of sin and human nature far too antinomian. If these ideas overturned biblical authority and thus freed human passions to serve a god of happiness, the southern world would disintegrate. A cosmos lacking definite order frightened southern evangelicals, who believed that God ordered all things. The reality of separate races reflected his will. Abolitionism and its first cousin, Free Love, would lead to racial amalgamation and, ultimately, the deterioration of the races. In debating northerners, southern evangelicals often asked whether abolitionists would permit their own daughters to marry African American men. Clearly the southerners believed that northern abolitionists would not but feared that emancipationists intended such unspeakable calamity to become the fate of southern belles. Given the southern perception that free blacks in the North lived in a degraded condition, southerners believed that abolitionists did not care if slaves were ready for freedom. The abolitionists would free the slave if they could, turning the former bondsmen out in society with no recourse save to steal for a living. In such a scenario, a lawless South would emerge, a land no longer fit for white habitation. Because they believed the motives of the abolitionists sprang from unchristian sources and that antislavery activities held potentially dangerous social and political consequences, the southerners' response to a perceived growth of abolitionist influence in the North seems comprehensible. Abolitionism not only threatened property, it threatened the whole fabric of southern society.[34]

Southern evangelicals believed that abolitionism, if unchecked, would destroy a set of social rituals and everyday interactions in their peculiar biracial society. John Adger, who spent his antebellum ministerial career seeking to make good Presbyterians out of slaves, described the idealized relationship between whites and slaves this way:

> They belong to us. We also belong to them. They are divided out among us and mingled with us, and we with them in a thousand ways. They live with us, eating from the same store-houses, drinking from the same fountains, dwelling in the same enclosures, forming parts of the same families. Our mothers confide us, when infants, to their arms, and sometimes to the very milk of their breasts. . . . See them all around you, in these streets, in all these dwellings; a race distinct from us, brought in God's mysterious providence from a foreign land, and place under our care, and made members of our households. They fill the humblest places in our state and society; they serve us, they give us their strength, yet they are not more truly ours than we are truly theirs.

Because Adger staunchly believed what he wrote, he and his evangelical peers could not construe abolitionists in any other but the most malevolent light.[35]

Southerners typically forbade abolitionists from preaching or teaching in the South, for they believed that any antislavery spokesperson supported "arson, blood, and murder, insurrection and carnage" if such deeds were necessary to free the slaves. The Mississippi Methodist Conference expelled a minister in the Middle Deer Creek Circuit for "holding insurrectionary and seditious opinions and tampering with the slaves." Mobs chased abolitionists out of Auburn, Wetumpka, Troy, and Tuskegee, Alabama. One secular editor in nearby Montgomery chided the Wetumpkans for allowing three emancipationists to flee without corporal chastisement. "Their ringleader should have been hung . . . [and] the others should have been treated to a genteel coat of tar and feathers."[36]

Until the eve of Civil War, evangelicals in fact devoted much of the space in their proslavery polemics to attacks on abolitionists, muting internal moral discussion on difficult and divisive questions of slavery theory and practice, perpetualism versus conditional termination, and Union versus disunion in the process. Evangelicals refused to tolerate outside interference in their domestic affairs by outside busybodies. They loathed the philosophical underpinnings of abolitionist philosophy. They feared a social order with no established means to control African Americans. And they simply hated abolitionists, who not only had not actually freed the slaves, but had, in the minds of southern evangelicals, compelled slaveholders to cling even more tightly to their slaves. Abolitionists' moral harangues had caused southerners to look to the Bible for guidance about slavery in the first place. Robert Lewis Dabney stated this sentiment quite clearly:

> As it is, their unauthorized attempts to strike off the fetters of our slaves have but riveted them on the faster. Does this fact arise from the perversity of our nature? I believe that it does in part. We are less inclined to do that which we know to be our duty because persons, who have no right to interfere, demand it of us. But the change of public opinion in the South [toward antiabolitionism and cautious proslavery] doubtless arose partly from free discussion. We have investigated the subject, and we find emancipation more dangerous than we had before imagined. Who knows but that this uproar of the Abolitionists . . . may have been designed · by Providence as a check upon our imprudent liberality. If we had hastened to give the slave his liberty at once, as I believe public sentiment was tending, we might have done [him] irreparable injury.[37]

Neither the irritation at the abolitionists' attempt to convert southerners to the antislavery cause nor the fear of the social and economic consequences of emancipation, nor even revulsion at the intellectual underpinnings of aboli-

tionism, fully explains the increasingly fanatical southern hatred of abolitionists. Southern constitutional scruples that differed from and sectional insults
inflicted by the abolitionists greatly contributed to, but still do not complete,
the litany of reasons for the manifest southern disdain for abolitionists and an
increasing dislike for the northern society that tolerated them. So much of the
southern bitterness sprang from Dixie's reactions to the hypocrisy, real and
imagined, in northern abolitionism, whose agitators wore cotton shirts while
they excoriated the Cotton Kingdom. The *Biblical Recorder* reprinted from the
North Carolina Standard the following diatribe against northern sanctimony:

> Much of the benevolence of our time is malignant; much of its philanthropy self-
> ish; much of its charity cruel. What a spectacle is presented by the abolitionists of
> our own country! With a self complacent spirit of the pharisee, denouncing whole
> classes and communities of men as brutal and God forsaken, for sustaining a rela-
> tionship co-eval with human history and recognized by the Maker and Redeemer
> of man and His inspired Apostles, while themselves partakers of sin, if sin it be—
> growing fat on the proceeds of slave labor, not merely subsisting on its products
> and clothed in its fabrics—but glorying in the wealth which this system has di-
> rectly supplied.[38]

Still more denunciatory was the jeremiad of Frederick A. Ross, the Presbyterian minister in Huntsville, Alabama. He personally favored a scheme of
compensated emancipation; certainly, he was no perpetualist—but he loathed
Yankee immediatism. About them he intoned:

> Ye men of Boston, New York, London, Paris,—Ye hypocrites—Ye brand me a pi-
> rate, a kidnapper, a murderer, a demon fit only for hell, and yet ye buy my cotton.
> Why don't you throw the cotton into the sea, as your fathers did the tea? Ye Bos-
> ton hypocrites. Ye say, if we had bee in the days of our fathers, we would not have
> been partakers with them in the blood of the slave-trade. Wherefore ye be wit-
> nesses unto yourselves that ye are the children of them who, in fact, kidnapped
> and bought in blood, and sold them in America. For now, ye hypocrites, ye buy
> the bloodstained cotton in quantity so immense, that we have run up the price of
> slaves to be more than a thousand dollars. . . . O ye hypocrites. Ye denounce slav-
> ery; then ye bid it live and not die,—in that ye buy sugar, rice, tobacco, and above
> all, cotton. Ye hypocrites. Ye abuse the devil and then fall down and worship him.—
> Ye hypocrites,—ye New England hypocrites,—ye Old England hypocrites,—ye
> French Revolution hypocrites,—Ye Uncle Tom's Cabin hypocrites,—ye Beecher
> hypocrites,—ye Rhode Island Consocation hypocrites. Oh, your holy twaddle
> stinks in the nostrils of God, and He commands me to lash you with my scorn,
> and His scorn, so long as you gabble about the sin of slavery . . . and buy and spin
> cotton. . . . Ye have, like the French infidels, made reason your goddess, and are

exalting her above the Bible; and in your Unitarianism and neology and all the modes of infidelity, ye are rejecting and crucifying the Son of God!

Ross and his fellow southern evangelicals hated no sin more than abolitionism. So sure was the southern Unionist "Parson" Brownlow that God hated abolitionists too that he believed none of them would ever enter heaven— save "by practicing a gross fraud upon the door-keeper."[39]

By the end of the 1850s, southern evangelicals had chosen their enemies. Anyone or anything that denied their conception of God or their interpretation of the Bible they considered anathema and resisted it. Abolitionists provided the favorite target and allowed southerners to focus their energy on a single external object rather than confront the subtle differences in their notions about the future of slavery and, to a lesser degree, the morality of it as southerners actually practiced it. Southerners united in a fight against abolitionism. But southern evangelicals had always stood strongly against perceived atheism, and they construed their disdain of abolitionism and other evils in northern society as a further exercise of their religion. Only this time, their religious concerns brimmed with political implications. The United States depended upon popular confidence in a federal government to preserve unity. If control of the federal government passed into the hands of individuals (abolitionists) whom southerners considered morally suspect, southern evangelicals would perceive a threat to their religion, their rights, as well as to their property. Continued political Union with northerners might then go the way of shared ecclesiastical bonds.[40]

NOTES

1. The literature on the religion and the Civil War is vast. See Clarence C. Goen, *Broken Churches, Broken Nation: Denominational Schisms and the Coming of the Civil War* (Macon, Ga.: Mercer University Press, 1985), 4 (quote); Richard Carwardine, *Evangelicals and Politics in Antebellum America* (New Haven, Conn.: Yale University Press, 1993); Mitchell Snay, *Gospel of Disunion: Religion and Separatism in the Antebellum South* (New York: Cambridge University Press, 1993).

2. William P. Hill Diary, March 4, 1847, Southern Historical Collection, University of North Carolina, Chapel Hill.

3. Drew Gilpin Faust, *The Creation of Confederate Nationalism: Ideology and Identity in the Civil War South* (Baton Rouge: Louisiana State University Press, 1988), 22–40. Abolitionism and proslavery are slippery terms, mired in the notion of antebellum sectional rhetoric that makes all northerners abolitionists and all southerners proslavery. In reality, immediate abolitionism, which called for freeing slaves right away and allowing them to remain in the United States,

confined itself to small sectors of northern society. Not all southerners, and many northerners, were proslavery, which Larry Edward Tise defines as "favoring the continuance of the institution, or opposed to interference with it." As his research has shown, much proslavery ideology rooted itself in an intersectional conservative ideology and possessed staunch adherents in the northern states through the secession winter of 1860–61. See Tise, *Proslavery: A History of the Defense of Slavery in America, 1701–1840* (Athens: University of Georgia Press, 1987), xv (quote sup.), 204–37, 323–62.

4. "Scripturalism and Rationalism," *Southern Presbyterian Review* 5 (October 1851): 274–75; E. Brooks Holifield, *The Gentlemen Theologians: American Theology in Southern Culture, 1795–1860* (Durham, N.C.: Duke University Press, 1978), 100, 127; John C. Greene, "Science and Religion," in *The Rise of Adventism,* Edwin S. Gaustad, ed. (New York: Harper and Row, 1972), 55–62; Richard T. Hughes, "A Civic Theology for the South: The Case of Benjamin Morgan Palmer," *Journal of Church and State* 24 (August 1983): 458; Walter H. Conser Jr., *God and the Natural World: Religion and Science in Antebellum America* (Columbia: University of South Carolina Press, 1993), 19–21.

5. Quoted material in *Biblical Recorder* (Raleigh, N.C.), April 26, 1851. See generally "Geological Speculation," *Southern Presbyterian Review* 10 (1857–58): 548, 554–55, 562; *Southern Presbyterian* (Columbia, S.C.), November 9, 1854. Southern evangelicals also dismissed theories of polygenesis, which explained the existence of different races of people as a product of multiple creations. Southern evangelicals noted that the Book of Genesis described only one creation, so polygenesis, like other new theories of creation, was antibiblical. See "Types of Mankind," *Southern Presbyterian Review* 9 (October 1855): 251; Charles C. Bishop, "The Pro-Slavery Argument Reconsidered: James Henley Thornwell, Millennial Abolitionist," *South Carolina Historical Magazine* 73 (January 1972): 25.

6. "Scripturalism and Rationalism," 280 (quoted material); *Religious Herald* (Richmond, Va.), November 13, 1851; Richard M. Weaver, "The Older Religiousness in the South," *Sewanee Review* 51 (Spring 1943): 237–38. Eugene D. Genovese makes this point about the moral foundations of southern conservative (proslavery) thinking quite forcefully in *The Southern Tradition: The Achievement and Limitations of American Conservatism* (Cambridge: Harvard University Press, 1994), 32–33.

7. On the northern abandonment of orthodox literalism, see James Turner, *Without God, Without Creed: The Origins of Unbelief in America* (Baltimore: The Johns Hopkins University Press, 1985), 142–50.

8. Carwardine, *Evangelicals and Politics,* 159–66.

9. Frederick A. Norwood, *The Story of American Methodism* (Nashville, Tenn.: Abington Press, 1974), 206–07; Lewis McCarrol Purifoy Jr., "The Methodist Episcopal Church, South, and Slavery, 1844–1865" (Ph. D. diss., University of North Carolina, 1965), 98–99.

10. *Christian Advocate* (Nashville, Tenn.), January 20, April 4, October 15, 1847, May 26, 1848; *Christian Advocate* (New Orleans), June 17, 1854; Charles G. Swaney, *Episcopal Methodism and Slavery, with Sidelights on Ecclesiastical Politics,* reprint ed. (New York: Negro Universities Press, 1968), 172–84.

11. Swaney, *Episcopal Methodism and Slavery,* 163–64; Walter Brownlow Posey, *Frontier Mission: A History of Religion West of the Southern Appalachians to 1861* (Lexington, Ky.: University of Kentucky Press, 1966), 362.

12. *Journal of the General Conference of the Methodist Episcopal Church, South, 1846,* 108.

13. Bascom quoted in Clarence C. Goen, "Regional Religion and North-South Alienation in Antebellum America," *Church History* 52 (March 1983): 31; *Christian Advocate* (Nashville, Tenn.), June 28, 1851; *Southern Christian Advocate* (Charleston, S.C.), July 21, 1851.

14. *Christian Advocate* (Nashville, Tenn.), November 6, 1846 (quotes 1 and 2), June 23, 1848 (quote 3), Milton Bryant Powell, "The Abolitionist Controversy in the Methodist Episcopal Church" (Ph. D. diss., State University of Iowa, 1963), 1. Among the ironies of the southern view of northern Methodists as abolitionists is that northern immediate abolitionists believed northern Methodism should require conversion to abolitionism, which northern Methodist leaders rejected, and might have agreed with the southern critique that northern Methodists cared more for members than for morality. See James Brewer Stewart, *Holy Warriors: The Abolitionists and American Slavery,* reprint ed. (New York: Hill and Wang, 1990), 114; Donald Mathews, *Slavery and Methodism: A Chapter in American Morality, 1780–1845* (Princeton, N.J.: Princeton University Press, 1965), 148–76, and John R. McKivigan, *The War against Proslavery Religion: Abolitionism and the Northern Churches, 1830–1865* (Ithaca, N.Y.: Cornell University Press, 1984), 97–98.

15. *Christian Advocate* (Nashville, Tenn.), July 16, 1848; *Christian Advocate* (New Orleans, La.), February 16, May 24, 1851; *Southern Christian Advocate* (Charleston, S.C.), June 6, 1851; Purifoy, "Methodist Episcopal Church, South, and Slavery," 112.

16. *Christian Advocate* (Nashville, Tenn.), July 16, 1848. Cf. Frank Baker, *From Wesley to Asbury: Studies in Early American Methodism* (Durham, N.C.: Duke University Press, 1976), 152, esp. n. 42. Cf. Christopher H. Owen, "'To Keep the Way Open for Methodism': Georgia Wesleyan Neutrality toward Slavery, 1844–1861," in this volume, 109–33. As a denomination, southern Methodists did not substitute slavery for salvation. Their focus remained on calling sinners to repentence, and they found the abolitionist claims that salvation demanded emancipation lacking explicit scriptural warrant. This view did not mean that southern Methodists necessarily agreed with any extreme proslavery arguments. It only meant that they would not set a standard for emancipation higher than the scriptures demanded, and, as a denomination, they saved their most extreme language to denounce abolitionists rather than to praise slavery.

17. *Journal of the General Conference of the Methodist Episcopal Church, South, 1858,* 443, 445, 448–61.

18. *Southern Baptist* (Charleston, S.C.), January 6, 1844; *Texas Baptist* (Anderson, Tex.), September 23, 1857; *Minutes of the South Carolina Baptist Convention, 1857,* 15–57. Conrad James Engelder, "The Churches and Slavery: A Study of the Attitudes toward Slavery of the Major Protestant Denominations" (Ph. D. diss., University of Michigan, 1964), 78, 81.

19. Deborah Van Broekhoven, "Suffering with Slaveholders: The Limits of Francis Wayland's Antislavery Witness," in this volume, esp. p. 199, shows that Wayland was hardly an antislavery firebrand by the standards of abolitionists. He did not condemn slaveholders or endorse imme-

diate emancipation. Yet he "had long seen chattel slavery as an evil to be eradicated," a position making his entire range of ideas suspect in the sectional cauldron of the 1850s.

20. Francis Wayland, *The Elements of Moral Science,* rev. ed. (Boston, 1841), 147 (quotation); John Leadley Dagg, *The Elements of Moral Science* (New York, 1860), 115–16; E. Brooks Holifield, *The Gentleman Theologians: American Theology in Southern Culture, 1795–1860* (Durham, N.C.: Duke University Press, 1978), 135–36.

21. *Southern Presbyterian* (Charleston, S.C.), May 17, 1856, May 30, 1857; *Texas Baptist* (Anderson, Tex.), September 23, 1857; *Minutes of the South Carolina Baptist Convention, 1857,* 15–57; Clarence C. Goen, *Broken Churches, Broken Nation: Denominational Schisms and the Coming of the Civil War* (Macon, Ga.: Mercer University Press, 1985), 132. The southern evangelical response to northern-based tract societies is a religious counterpart to the call to create "a southern republic of letters," wisely discussed in John McCardell, *The Idea of a Southern Nation: Southern Nationalists and Southern Nationalism* (New York: W. W. Norton, 1979), 141–76. On the American Tract Society, see McKivigan, *War against Proslavery Religion,* 120–23.

22. Ernest Trice Thompson, *Presbyterians in the South, Vol. 1: 1607–1861* (Richmond, Va.: John Knox Press, 1963), 382–83; H. Shelton Smith, *In His Image, But . . . Racism in Southern Religion, 1790–1910* (Durham, N.C.: Duke University Press, 1972), 89; *Minutes of the Presbyterian General Assembly, 1837,* 413–45; C. Bruce Staiger, "Abolitionism and the Presbyterian Schism of 1837–1838," *Mississippi Valley Historical Review* 36 (December 1949): 391–414; Edward R. Crowther, "Southern Protestants, Slavery, and Secession: A Study in Southern Religious Ideology, 1830–1861" (Ph. D. diss., Auburn University, 1986), 129–41.

23. *Minutes of the Presbyterian General Assembly, 1845,* 16–17 (quote); Carwardine, *Evangelicals and Politics,* 166–69.

24. William W. Freehling, *The Road to Disunion: Vol. 1: Secessionists at Bay, 1776–1854* (New York: Oxford University Press, 1990), passim; Freehling, *The Reintegration of American History: Slavery and the Civil War* (New York: Oxford University Press, 1994), 66–67.

25. Thornwell quoted in James Oscar Farmer, *The Metaphysical Confederacy: James Henley Thornwell and the Synthesis of Southern Values* (Macon, Ga.: Mercer University Press, 1986), 247; *Central Presbyterian* (Richmond, Va.), March 29, 1856.

26. Misc. clipping in Robert Burton Anderson Correspondence, 1850–1859, in the Anderson-Thornwell Papers, Southern Historical Collection, University of North Carolina, Chapel Hill (quote 1); *Christian Advocate* (New Orleans, La.), January 10, August 7, 1852 (quote 2); *Christian Advocate* (Nashville, Tenn.), September 1, 1853 (quote 3).

27. W. J. Sasnett, "American Society," *Quarterly Review* 9 (July 1855): 21; Ross quoted in Avery O. Craven, *The Coming of the Civil War,* 2d ed. (Chicago: University of Chicago Press, 1957), 164; Winans quoted in Ray Holder, *William Winans: Methodist Leader in Antebellum Mississippi* (Jackson: University Press of Mississippi, 1977), 195. See also James Henley Thornwell, "Writings on Slavery," Thornwell Papers, Historical Foundation of the Presbyterian and Reformed Churches, Montreat, North Carolina.

28. "Uses and Abuses of the Pulpit," *Quarterly Review* 12 (1858): 356; Sasnett, "American Society," 410–15, 417; *Southern Baptist* (Charleston, S.C.), May 10, December 6, 1854, May 6, 1856; *North Carolina Presbyterian* (Fayetteville, N.C.), December 24, 1859; *Christian Ad-*

vocate (Nashville, Tenn.), October 18, 1850; *Southern Christian Advocate* (Charleston, S.C.), March 24, 1854.

29. Freeman quoted in *Mississippi Baptist* (Jackson, Miss.), May 27, 1858; Brownlow quoted in Walter Brownlow Posey, "The Slavery Question in the Presbyterian Church of the Old Southwest," *Journal of Southern History* 15 (August 1949): 541–42.

30. *Christian Advocate* (Nashville, Tenn.), November 1, 1850 (quote); March 6, 1851; *Southern Presbyterian* (Milledgeville, Ga.), February 20, 27, 1851; *Southern Baptist* (Charleston, S.C.), June 7, 1854.

31. *Southern Presbyterian* (Milledgeville, Ga.), May 20, 1852 (quote 1); *Christian Index* (Macon, Ga.), March 2, 1859; Dabney quoted in Richard T. Hughes, "A Civic Theology for the South: The Case of Benjamin M. Palmer," *Journal of Church and State* 24 (August 1983): 448.

32. *Christian Advocate* (Nashville, Tenn.), June 17, 1851 (quotes), October 20, 1859; *Southern Presbyterian* (Milledgeville, Ga.), February 20, 27, 1851; *Southern Christian Advocate* (Charleston, S.C.), March 15, 1854; *Alabama Baptist* (Marion, Ala.), February 1, August 16, 1845; *Southwestern Baptist* (Tuskegee, Ala.), September 4. 1850.

33. Thornwell quoted in Farmer, *Metaphysical Confederacy,* 218; Brownlow quoted in E. Merton Coulter, *Parson Brownlow: Fighting Parson of the Southern Highlands,* reprint ed. (Knoxville, Tenn.: University of Tennessee Press, 1971), 107; Anne C. Loveland, "Evangelicalism and 'Immediate Abolitionism' in American Anti-Slavery Thought," *Journal of Southern History* 32 (May 1966): 180–81 (final quotation); Ronald G. Walters, *American Reformers, 1815–1860* (New York: Hill and Wang, 1978), 16–17, 36–37, 195–203; Ronald G. Walters, *The Antislavery Appeal: American Abolitionism after 1830,* reprint ed. (New York: W. W. Norton, 1984), 54–65; Paul E. Johnson, *A Shopkeeper's Millennium: Society and Revivals in Rochester, New York, 1815–1837* (New York: Hill and Wang, 1978), 116–35.

34. *Biblical Recorder* (Raleigh. N.C.), April 20, 1860; *Southern Christian Advocate* (Charleston, S.C.), January 28, 1853; Coulter, *Parson Brownlow,* 95.

35. John B. Adger, *My Life and Times, 1810–1899* (Richmond, Va.: Presbyterian Committee of Publications, 1899), 167.

36. Swaney, *Episcopal Methodist and Slavery,* 252 (quote 1); Margaret Burr Deschamps Moore, "Religion in Mississippi in 1860," *Journal of Mississippi History* 22 (October 1960): 233 (quote 2); J. Mills Thornton III, *Politics and Power in a Slave Society: Alabama, 1800–1860* (Baton Rouge: Louisiana State University Press, 1978), 313 (quote 3).

37. Dabney quoted in Farmer, *Thornwell,* 206–07. Southern evangelical intellectual leaders understood all too clearly that their defense of slavery on biblical grounds set standards of high moral conduct for slaveowners and that the slaveowners all too often fell short of these standards. Thus, James Henley Thornwell, whose mind and pen raised southern evangelical proslavery to its most sophisticated height, himself had doubts about the morality of slavery as practiced in the southern states. Freehling, *Reintegration of American History,* 59–81. Baptists in Mississippi struggled with the question of slave literacy and marriage laws. Other southerners, such as Robert L. Toombs and Alexander Stephens, believed the theory of southern slavery was morally defensible, but that there were lapses in practice, which may call for a limitation on slaveholders' rights. See Edward R. Crowther, "Mississippi Baptists, Slavery, and Secession, 1806–1861," *Jour-*

nal of Mississippi History 56 (May 1994): 143–45, and Clarence L. Mohr, On the Threshold of Freedom: Masters and Slaves in Civil War Georgia (Athens: University of Georgia Press, 1986), 240–63.

38. Biblical Recorder (Raleigh, N.C.), May 17, 1860. See also William W. Freehling's synthetic conversations between southern planter and northern traveler. Freehling, Road to Disunion, 1: 15–16. The southern denunciation of abolitionism seethed with anger boiling over to violence.

39. Ross quoted in George C. Whately III, "The Alabama Presbyterian and His Slave, 1830–1864," Alabama Review 12 (January 1960): 41–43; Brownlow quoted in Coulter, Parson Brownlow, 104.

40. This focus on the external threat of abolitionism after 1845 coincides with continued internal development in southern evangelicalism. Southern denominations grew in membership and some embraced benevolent causes tailored to the needs of a slave society. Many ministers began to define their role as a profession, and even Baptist ministers began to "look to denominations, not congregations, as the context for their professional life." See Beth Barton Schweiger, "The Restructuring of Southern Religion: Slavery, Denominations, and the Clerical Profession in Virginia," in this volume, 296–316.

The Sectional Division of the Methodist and

Baptist Denominations as Measures of

Northern Antislavery Sentiment

JOHN R. McKIVIGAN

Few incidents in the history of the antislavery movement are as well known as the sectional schisms of the Methodist Episcopal church in 1844 and of the mission societies of the Baptist denomination in 1845. Historians regularly cite the divisions of these and other denominations in the 1850s as evidence of growing antislavery sentiment in the North as well as proslavery sentiment in the South. Historical accounts rely upon contemporary observers as diverse as Henry Clay, John C. Calhoun, and John Quincy Adams who attributed these denominational dissolutions to a widening divergence between North and South on the moral question of slavery. These accounts maintain that the denominational divisions transformed the northern churches into powerful antislavery exponents well before the Civil War.[1]

Such an interpretation ignores the opinion of the abolitionists, the men and women in the vanguard of the antislavery movement. For example, veteran abolitionist Parker Pillsbury of New Hampshire examined the claims that the postschism northern Methodist Church had taken a clear antislavery position and declared "[g]rosser fraud and falsehood was never told."[2] Other abolitionists similarly complained that the motive of the Baptist separation "was one, not of principle, but of policy," and that northern and southern Baptists still carried on a "cordial fraternization."[3] In sum, the abolitionists offered a two-part critique of the Methodist and Baptist schisms of the 1840s. First, they assessed the causes of the denominational divisions and denied that northern antislavery militancy inside those bodies had been a significant precipitating factor. Second, the abolitionists examined the professions and practices of the northern wings of the churches and charged that neither body had adopted explicit antislavery strictures following the southerners' departure. This chapter will examine the causes and consequences of the Methodist and Baptist schisms and then assess the validity of the abolitionists' disparagement of those events as evidence of advances in northern antislavery sentiment.

The American abolitionist movement arose during the 1830s as a by-product of the upsurge of revivalism popularly know as the Second Great Awakening. Abolitionist principles and objectives led many churchmen to regard social problems, such as slavery, as the products of personal sin. These religiously inspired abolitionists contended that slaveholding was a sin that required immediate and complete repentance in the form of emancipation. The abolitionists' original national organization, the American Anti-Slavery Society, demanded that the churches testify to slavery's inherent sinfulness by barring slave owners from their communion and fellowship. Early abolitionists were confident that once the denominations had adopted such antislavery church disciplines, the slave masters would capitulate to their opponents' superior moral power and voluntarily manumit their slaves.[4]

At the root of the conflict between the abolitionists and the major American denominations were fundamental disagreements concerning the morality of slavery and the churches' responsibility toward the institution. Prior to the emergence of abolitionism, slavery had been judged in terms of its social, political, and economic consequences as well as its ethical implications. Although many denominations made antislavery professions in the immediate post–Revolutionary War era when ideas of natural rights and human liberty were widely accepted, they also expressed concern for the socially disruptive potentials of emancipation. As a result of this ambivalence, the only denominations to enforce antislavery disciplines upon their membership were a few small pietistic sects, such as the Quakers.[5] Highly liturgical denominations, such as the Roman Catholic, Protestant Episcopalian, and Lutheran churches, and strictly Calvinist ones, including the German and Dutch Reformed churches, went to the other extreme and declared slavery a secular matter and therefore an improper subject for ecclesiastical discussion or legislation.[6] Most other churches, including the Methodists and Baptists, initially enacted antislavery disciplines but failed to enforce them. These attempted to placate residual antislavery sentiment by encouraging voluntary programs of amelioration, voluntary manumission, and African colonization that held out only the faintest hope for eventual abolition. Because this last category of denominations were the ones ultimately undergoing sectional schism in mid-century, their early relationship to slavery will be examined in a closer detail.

Originally a movement to reform the colonial-era Anglican church, the Methodist Episcopal church began its life as a separate denomination in the flush of post–Revolutionary War antislavery sentiment. In keeping with the strong expectations of the times, the original Methodist discipline condemned the "buying and selling of men, women, and children" and resolved that members who bought and sold slaves "with no other design than to hold them as slaves . . . shall be expelled." Because of southern complaints about this rule, little effort was taken to enforce it, however. Like their contemporaries many Methodists believed that slavery was progressing rapidly toward its final extinction. Methodism experienced considerable expansion in its first half century, becoming the second largest denomination in the nation. To maintain this rate of growth in the face of changing southern attitudes toward slavery, the Methodists gradually abandoned prohibitions on slave owning. By the 1820s, such a policy was maintained only in the ministry, and there only in states permitting manumission. Methodist leaders feared that a stronger antislavery stand would cause masters to bar the denomination's itinerants from access to their slaves and weaken the church's ability to further projects of amelioration.[7] The Methodists' 1816 general conference made the revealing confession of the church's powerlessness regarding slavery: "little can be done to abolish a system so contrary to the principles of moral justice" and the "evil appears past remedy."[8]

Like the Methodists, the Baptist church had been a small dissenting sect in the colonial era, but their effective evangelical techniques enabled them to grow into the country's largest denomination by the 1830s. The Baptists nevertheless retained traditional opposition to any form of central-governing structure. Therefore the denomination established no official disciplinary position regarding slavery. During and soon after the Revolutionary War, many local associations of Baptist congregations had condemned slavery. In 1808, for example, the New York Baptist Association declared that "the practice of slaveholding ought to be discountenanced as much as possible."[9] Various "Friends of Humanity" associations of Kentucky and midwestern Baptists battled against the introduction of slavery into their locale in the early nineteenth century. The Friends of Humanity association of Illinois Baptist churches resolved to deny "union and communion with all persons holding the doctrine of perpetual, hereditary, involuntary servitude."[10]

By the 1830s, however, the powerful influence of slaveholding members in the denomination and the traditional Baptist hesitancy to involve the church with civil action had quieted nearly all antislavery forces. In addition, bitter disputes in the denomination over questions of mission policy and theology in the early nineteenth century produced a strong sentiment among Baptists against raising another disruptive issue.[11]

Despite the religious community's conservatism on the slavery question, early abolitionists nevertheless envisioned the churches as playing a major role in spreading ethically defined antislavery arguments. In the 1830s, the abolitionists' moral suasion campaign concentrated upon converting the churches and reaching an evangelically oriented audience. Abolitionists lobbied individual church members and denominational assemblies for endorsements of antislavery principles. Abolitionist propaganda endeavored to educate the religious institutions about the ways that their practices sanctioned slavery. While the abolitionists recruited many individual Methodists and Baptists in the 1830s, their early labors bore little fruit in changing the official position of either denomination.[12]

The frustration produced by the churches' repeated rejection of abolitionists' appeals for support led many antislavery militants to reassess their original religiously oriented tactics. Abolitionist followers of the influential William Lloyd Garrison repudiated the nation's churches as hopelessly corrupted by slavery. In the early 1840s, many of the "Garrisonians" began "coming out," or severing all ties with religious institutions, as a dramatic means of protest against the churches' complicity with slavery.[13] When the Garrisonians gained control of the American Anti-Slavery Society in 1840, other abolitionists who retained faith in eventually winning over the churches seceded and regrouped in a new organization, the American and Foreign Anti-Slavery Society (AFASS).[14]

Historians usually minimize the effectiveness of the AFASS because of its inability to finance a large-scale antislavery propaganda campaign. Garrisonian abolitionists accused the AFASS of tempering its criticism of proslavery religious practices in order to placate ministerial fears of disrupting church unity. Both these interpretations overlook the AFASS's valuable assistance to the development of well-organized denominational antislavery movements in the 1840s. For example, the *American and Foreign Anti-Slavery Reporter,* the new society's periodical, gave detailed coverage as well as editorial support to the activities of Methodist and Baptist abolitionists. In addition, these stories were reprinted in sympathetic Liberty Party newspapers, which also applauded the denominational antislavery movements. Other assistance came from the AFASS's practice of hiring lecturing agents to labor primarily among members of their own denomination, such as Methodist Edward Smith and Baptist Charles W. Denison. In turn, leaders of the denominational abolitionist movements, including Baptists Nathaniel Colver and Duncan Dunbar and Methodists Orange Scott and LeRoy Sunderland, served as officers of the American and Foreign Anti-Slavery Society.[15] When efforts by the AFASS and its supporters still failed to produce significant antislavery reforms in either denomination, even these church-oriented abolitionists began to express a preference for a divided church "[u]nless the cause be betrayed for the sake of unscriptural peace and inglorious and unchristian ease."[16]

The abolition campaign in the Methodist Episcopal church moved toward such a dilemma. In the 1830s, Methodist abolitionists led by reverends Orange Scott, LaRoy Sunderland, and George Storrs pushed for enforcement of their churches's long ignored disciplinary condemnation of slavery.[17] Methodist abolitionists held denominational antislavery conventions and founded a permanent national organization, the American Wesleyan Anti-Slavery Society, in October 1840. The new society espoused the abolitionist program of denying religious fellowship to slaveholders and declared its objectives to be "the entire extinction of slavery in the Methodist Episcopal Church in America, and thereby to aid in that great national enterprise . . . its entire extinction in the United States."[18]

Despite financial and propaganda assistance from the non-Garrisonian AFASS, the Methodist abolitionists made little progress. A large majority of delegates at the Methodists' general conference of 1836 publicly resolved that they were "decidedly opposed to modern abolitionism, and wholly disclaim[ed] any right, wish or intentions to interfere in the civil and political relation between master and slave. . . ."[19] Editors of the Methodist press refused to print notices of the activities of the denominational antislavery society. Conservative bishops removed such active abolitionists as Orange Scott and George Storrs from positions of authority in northern conferences.[20]

By the time of the 1840 general conference, abolitionists had made major inroads in annual conferences in New England and upstate New York. The New England Conference under Orange Scott's leadership petitioned the general conference for stronger wording of the "General Rule on Slavery" to make "buying or selling" slaves a disciplinable offense. Not only were Scott's efforts overwhelmingly rejected by the general conference, but, at the same time, the denomination adopted a rule forbidding black members from giving testimony against whites in church proceedings in states where blacks lacked a similar right in civil courts.[21]

With the official machinery of the denomination turned against them, Methodist abolitionists led by Scott began seceding in November 1842 to form a new abolitionized Methodist church. The new "Wesleyan Methodist

Connection" grew within two years to nearly fifteen thousand members in churches from Michigan to New England.[22]

Ironically, the Wesleyans' bolt preceded a similar southern secession from the Methodist Episcopal church by less than two years. Despite their rejection of abolitionism, Methodist church councils continued to pay lip service to their conservative antislavery heritage by endorsements of colonization and by missionary work among the slaves. Although they claimed to be pleased with the departure of the "ruthless spirit" of the abolitionist agitators, conservative northern Methodists took steps to limit defections of antislavery moderates to the Wesleyans. For example, the bishops permitted a number of Methodist antislavery conventions to be held in New England without official harassment. At the same time, editors of several northern Methodist newspapers opened their columns to antislavery articles. The conservatives warned Methodists attracted by the Wesleyans' moral appeals that the church's powerful influence in behalf of amelioration and gradual emancipation would be destroyed if the church adopted undiluted abolitionist doctrines.[23]

The conservatives' conciliatory policy was put to the test at the Methodist General Conference of 1844. Bishop James O. Andrew of Georgia recently had become a slaveholder through inheritance. Andrew wanted to resign his office, but southern militants desired to make this a test of one of the few still respected antislavery rules of the church. Northern conservatives could find no ground for a compromise with southern delegates on this issue. Although 18 northern delegates sided with the South, the conference voted 110 to 68 that Andrew's slaveholding "will greatly embarrass the exercise of his office . . . if not in some places entirely prevent it" and suspended him from his episcopal duties as long as he continued to own slaves.[24] As northern conservatives feared, southerners considered even this mild reproof an acknowledgment by the general conference that a moral stigma was attached to slave owning. Outraged southerners immediately seceded to form the Methodist Episcopal church, South. Efforts to arrange an equitable division of properties failed, and the old and new churches became contentious rivals for the loyalty of congregations in the upper South. At least four thousand slaveholding Methodists from the border states retained their allegiance to local conferences of the northern Methodist Episcopal church.[25]

The Wesleyans apparently were genuinely surprised by the actions of the general conference of 1844 against Bishop Andrew. After careful examination, however, they concluded that the conference's actions had not been guided by genuine antislavery sentiment. The *True Wesleyan*, their principal newspaper, complained that northern Methodists did nothing to exclude the slaveholding ministers and members from the border states who chose not to secede.[26] The Garrisonians' Massachusetts Anti-Slavery Society observed: "the Northern Methodists received their just reward for their wicked attempt to preserve the unity of the Church at the expense of justice and right, in seeing the Church rent in twain by even the feeblest breath of agitation."[27] One political antislavery newspaper aptly summed up the doubts of all abolitionists by observing of the Andrew affair: ". . . what has been gained, for if sound *principle* has not advanced, little has really been gained."[28] All abolitionist factions agreed that their mission among the Methodists had not yet been accomplished.

The relations of the abolitionists to the Baptist schism of 1845 roughly parallel their dealings with the Methodist antislavery developments. A loose confederation of autonomous congregations, the Baptist denomination possessed no central governing structure to establish or enforce an antislavery discipline. Thousands of individual Baptists and their local congregations, however, cooperated in voluntary societies for the support of missions and religious publication ventures. Abolitionist efforts among the Baptists therefore concentrated upon demanding that those societies repudiate all ties with slave owners by refusing their contributions and barring them from any office or appointment. The abolitionists' American Baptist Anti-Slavery Convention, founded in 1840, created a "provisional committee" to collect and distribute funds for missionary activities from those no longer willing to cooperate with slaveholders in the regular societies.[29]

By the early 1840s, abolitionist agitation produced a crisis in the Baptist denomination. In both the Baptist triennial convention that oversaw foreign missions and the American Baptist Home Missionary Society that sponsored domestic missions, conservative northerners had to cope with growing pressure from both abolitionists and southerners. In an attempt to quell southern fears, the mission societies dismissed abolitionists from all leadership posts. For example, a southern and conservative northern coalition in the triennial convention of 1841 successfully blocked abolitionist Elon Galusha's election as a manager for foreign missions. Both societies also issued public circulars affirming their neutrality toward slavery. The conservative northern majority of delegates at the Triennial Convention of 1844 tried to placate both northern and southern militants by resolving that "[i]n cooperating together as members of this Convention in the work of Foreign Missions, we disclaim all sanction, either express or—implied, whether of slavery or antislavery, but as individuals, we are perfectly free, both to express and to promote elsewhere, our own views on these subjects in a Christian manner and spirit."[30]

Apparently dissatisfied with this position of official neutrality, Alabama Baptists in November 1844 wrote the Board of Foreign Missions for a "distinct, explicit, avowal that slaveholders are eligible, and entitled, equally with non-slaveholders, . . . to receive any agency, mission, or other appointment."[31] The board had never received an application from a slave owner for a missionary appointment and complained of being "compelled to answer hypothetical questions." Nonetheless, the board sent the Alabamians that following reply: "If . . . any one should offer himself as a missionary, having slaves, and should insist on retaining them as his property, we could not appoint him. One thing is certain, we can never be a party to any arrangement which would imply approbation of slavery."[32] In an effort to retain southern support, the board reassured slave owners that the society nevertheless still welcomed their membership and contributions. This reply so infuriated southern Baptists that they promptly seceded and launched their own foreign missionary projects.[33]

The American Baptist Home Missionary Society similarly debated the question of supporting slaveholding missionaries. When the name of Georgian slave owner the Rev. James Reeve was presented to the society, its board rejected the appointment on the grounds that his application had been presented as a test case. This action provoked heated debate at the society's anniversary meeting in 1844. The adoption of a resolution, declaring the introduction of "the subjects of slavery or antislavery into this body, is in direct contravention of the whole letter and purpose of the said Constitution, and is, moreover, a most unnecessary agitation of topics with which the Society has no concern, . . ." failed to quell internal sectional tensions.[34] A "select committee" studied the problem and reported back in 1845, advocating the retention of a position of neutrality toward slavery. This report was tabled as unsatisfactory and the society agreed to a sectional division of its resources "upon amicable, honourable, and liberal principles."[35]

The division of the Baptist home missionary effort produced applause from some local associations. The Northern Association of Illinois, for example, officially endorsed the society "in refusing to support slave-holders as missionaries."[36] Conservative northern Baptists, however, vowed to keep their denomination from "the state of bickering and interminable quarreling into which the Methodists have fallen."[37]

The sectional separation of northern and southern Baptists in the denomination's religious publication enterprises never became as complete as occurred in missionary operations. The Baptist General Tract Society and its successor, the American Baptist Publication Society, had never printed an antislavery work. Southerners nevertheless founded their own printing house in 1847, and the American Baptist Publication Society voluntarily withdrew from the slave states. After the missionary societies' schisms, the Baptists' American and Foreign Bible Society managers announced their determination to continue welcoming all Baptists into their organization "on terms of perfect equality." Despite the launching of a Southern Baptist Bible Board in 1851, the American and Foreign Bible Society continued to elect slaveholding officers and to receive substantial contributions from southerners during the entire pre–Civil War period.[38]

The southern secession from the denominational societies produced a divided response from Baptist abolitionists. One faction, led by Nathaniel Colver, pronounced the reorganized northern mission associations practically separated from slavery despite the absence of explicit bars against slaveholders. The American Baptist Anti-Slavery Convention and its "provisional committee" for missions dissolved themselves in 1845, and abolitionists such as Colver remained with the regular benevolent associations.[39] Many other Baptist abolitionists, however, resolved to remain outside the regular denominational mission societies until those bodies' constitutions "have been so defined that their antislavery character shall be distinctly marked."[40] This "come-outer" group launched their own antislavery missionary enterprise that took the name, the American Baptist Free Mission Society.

Non-Baptist abolitionists had difficulty interpreting the Baptists' complicated series of schisms and reorganizations during the mid-1840s. Initially many abolitionists expressed satisfaction over those events but later complained when the reorganized Baptist societies refused to bar slave owners. By 1853, the AFASS concluded that although "many sincere antislavery persons" remained in those mission bodies, "that connection . . . prevents to a great extent the effective development of their anti-slavery tendencies."[41] The Garrisonian AASS also warned that abolitionists who failed to come out of the regular missionary bodies would never bring those societies to an uncompromising antislavery position. Garrisonian and non-Garrisonian abolitionists, however, disagreed regarding the antislavery standards of the American Baptist Free Mission Society. The AFASS endorsed the Free Mission Society as a *bona fide* abolitionist group while the Garrisonians complained that members of the society continued to worship together with nonabolitionist Baptists in their local congregations.[42]

Considerable insight into the dynamics of the Methodist and Baptist sectional schisms can be obtained from carefully examining the abolitionist critique of those events. There is considerable truth to the abolitionist charge that proslavery, not antislavery, forces had taken the final initiative in forcing the church divisions. It was southerners who raised the immediate issues that lead to the schisms, the acceptance of a slaveholding bishop in the Methodist church and the appointment of slaveholding missionaries in the Baptist societies. The abolitionists were not even in a position to lead resistance to those demands as the most active of them had already seceded by the mid-1840s.

This is not to say that more than a decade of agitation by abolitionists in denominational circles had not contributed greatly to causing these schisms. While having failed to convert most northern churchmen to antislavery principles, the abolitionist campaign had helped to rouse the South to an aggressive defense of slavery. The demand for the appointment of slave-owning bishops and missionaries was a form of "loyalty test" posed by southerners to discover how many northerners had been infected by the abolitionist arguments regarding the sinfulness of slaveholding. The abolitionists also contributed to the cause of the denominational schisms by making it more difficult for northern conservatives to compromise with southern demands. The fear of provoking greater desertions to the small abolitionist "comeouter" sects prodded northern conservatives to uphold their churches' long ignored antislavery traditions.[43]

Even conservative northern Methodists and Baptists blamed southern firebrands for forcing the denominations to depart from their neutrality on the question of fellowship with slaveholders. For example, such Baptist conservatives as Wayland, Spencer H. Cone, and John Mason Peck denied that the societies had deviated from their long-standing neutrality toward slavery and instead blamed the breakups upon southern insistence on proslavery policies. The northern delegates at the 1844 Methodist General Conference branded the southern demand for a slaveholding bishop a "dangerous innovation." In attempting to hold border state Methodists in their fellowship, conservative leaders, such as Nathan Bangs, Charles Elliott, and George Peck, declared that the South, not the North, had departed from the traditional Methodist position on slavery.[44]

There is also substantial evidence to support the abolitionists' charge that following the schisms of 1844 and 1845 neither the northern Methodists nor Baptists had adopted an uncompromising antislavery position. Even after the departure of most southern members, the northern wing of each denomination declined to declare slave owning inherently sinful or to subject the practice to church discipline.

When the Methodist Episcopal church gathered in 1848 for the first time since the dramatic 1844 quadrennial conference, several annual conferences presented resolutions asking for a strengthening of the denomination's stand against slaveholding. For example, the Erie Annual Conference sought to amend the Methodists' "General Rule on Slavery" to require dismissal from the church of any member continuing to own slaves where manumission was legally permissible. A coalition of northern conservative and border state delegates, however, blocked this and all other attempts to strengthen church rules against slaveholding at the 1848 as well as the 1852 general conferences.[45]

At the 1856 conference, antislavery annual conferences from New York, Ohio, and Wisconsin managed to get four resolutions to strengthen church discipline against slaveholding considered but none received the required three-fourths approval. The conservative minority even managed to obstruct the publication of the rejected antislavery propositions in the conference's official *Journal.*[46]

A similar state of affairs characterized the northern Baptist position on slavery after 1845. In the American Home Baptist Mission Society, antislavery members pushed for an official prohibition against missionaries either baptizing slaveholders or preaching in churches with slaveholding members. Such a motion was tabled indefinitely in 1848, however, after society officers privately made assurances that they would never appoint a slaveholder as a missionary.[47] The following year, the society issued a report stating that "there is no relation or action of the Society which involves directly or indirectly the countenance and fellowship of Slavery."[48] The American Baptist Missionary Union in 1850 made a similar disclaimer although admitting that slaveholding still was tolerated in its missionary congregations among the western Indians.[49] Despite such claims, both the home and the foreign mission societies expressed their willingness to accept slave owners as members and contributors provided that no demand was made for slaveholding missionaries.

Only years later, did the Baptist societies finally follow up their antislavery professions with actions. The Home Mission Society reduced the number of its missionaries in slaveholding states from fourteen in 1846 to only three in 1850. The Missionary Union finally withdrew its missionaries from the Native American stations after the latter repeated rejected calls to manumit their slaves. The publication and Bible societies, however, adamantly refused to make even minor concessions to their antislavery critics.[50]

Besides the behavior of the mission societies, the practices of individual Baptist congregations and local associations reveal an inconsistent record regarding breaking fellowship with slaveholders. In the years after the Baptists divided in 1845, some northern Baptist associations passed strongly worded antislavery resolutions and ceased fraternizing with slave owners. For example, in 1849, the New Hampshire State Convention voted to "regard American Slavery as an atrocious sin." In 1855, the Massachusetts Baptist Convention denounced slaveholding "an enormous and aggravated evil." [51] The Michigan Baptist State Convention in 1858 declared that "no Society . . . can consistently receive any co-operation from us, if it make any exception in favor of the sin of American Slavery." [52]

In the Midwest and in some eastern cities, however, many Baptist churches continued to welcome southerners to their pulpits and communion tables even during the Civil War. In southern Indiana, for example, the Little Pigeon Association resolved in 1855 that "we wholly disapprobate any interference with the subject of human slavery in such a manner as to interfere with the friendly relations that exist between us and the Associations with whom we correspond." [53] Wayland spoke for most conservative northern Baptists when he denounced church action that automatically treated slaveholders as sinners as "false in principle and unchristian in practice." Some Baptist abolitionists considered these usages so objectionable that they seceded and formed their own churches and associations on uncompromising antislavery principles. [54]

Irrefutable proof of the weakness of northern Methodists' and Baptists' antislavery professions can be seen in the ability of slaveholders to remain unmolested in the religious fellowship of each church until the Civil War. Applying the original religiously inspired standards of their movement, abolitionists denied that the divisions of the Methodists and Baptists had freed the northern members of those churches from complicity with slavery. As a result of the unsatisfactory outcome of the denominational schisms, most abolitionists abandoned the Methodist and Baptist churches by the mid-1840s either to renounce all religious institutions as the Garrisonians did or to create new purified "comeouter" sects, such as the Wesleyan Methodist Connection and the American Baptist Free Mission Society. [55]

Despite the accuracy of the abolitionists' charges, it is nevertheless possible to interpret the church schisms as advances in antislavery sentiment. While rejecting the abolitionist position that slaveholding was inherently sinful, northern Methodists and Baptist church leaders had upheld their denominations' traditional position of regarding slavery as an evil social system that should be gradually extinguished. These northern churchmen could not in good conscience accede to southern demands that the denominations certify the moral rectitude of slaveholding by appointing slave owners as missionaries and bishops. In short, under pressure from the abolitionists and proslavery southerners, northern Methodists and Baptists had abandoned their studied neutrality toward slavery and reaffirmed the long-ignored modest antislavery traditions of their denominations.

Another means of assessing the validity of the abolitionist criticism of the significance of the Baptist and Methodist divisions is a comparison of those churches' relations with slavery with that of other denominations in the mid-1840s. Neither of the supposedly antislavery denominations could approach the standards set by the Quakers, the Freewill Baptists, and the Scottish Presbyterian sects in refusing to sanction slavery by accepting slaveholders as members. Weighed against the official neutrality toward slavery maintained by the liturgical faiths, however, the northern Methodists and Baptists had made undeniably antislavery gestures and statements. The northern Methodists and Baptists were most comparable to the predominantly northern New School Presbyterian, Congregational, and Unitarian denominations in their treatment of the slavery question. Although many individual members of those denominations adopted strong antislavery views, their ruling councils refused to accept the fine points of abolitionist principles on the sinfulness of slave owning and on the church's duty to discipline slaveholding members. By the mid-1840s, northern Methodists and Baptists had joined these last three bodies to create a new mildly antislavery consensus within the northern religious community.[56]

The sectional schism also had important long-range impact on the standing of slavery in the northern churches. Although some southerners remained in fellowship with northern Baptists and Methodists, they were small minorities with limited influence on church policies. This de facto schism helped sharpen sectional polarization and freed northern Methodists and Baptists to speak more aggressively against slavery. For example, during the sectionally divisive political controversies of the late 1840s and 1850s, many northern churchmen made strong public condemnations of slavery. Among Baptists, some local associations and congregations spoke out against governmental policies favoring slavery such as the Fugitive Slave Law of 1850 and the Kansas-Nebraska Act. During the same years, northern Baptist newspapers editorialized on political events with an ever increasing antislavery bias. Even as prominent a conservative spokesman as Francis Wayland joined the moderate antislavery Republican Party.[57]

Among the Methodists, antislavery church members forced open the columns of their denomination's official periodicals by debating the political as well as moral aspects of slavery-related issues. Matthew Simpson's editorials in the Cincinnati-based *Western Christian Advocate,* for example, denounced the Compromise of 1850.[58] Methodist names were prominent on the clerical petitions denouncing the passage of the Kansas-Nebraska Act in 1854. A younger generation of antislavery Methodists, such as Gilbert Haven, became active supporters of the Republicans and their antiextension platform for slavery in the territories.[59]

This politically inspired growth of antislavery feelings, in turn, encouraged a younger generation of churchmen to revive efforts toward strengthening religious antislavery practices in both denominations in the 1850s. Finally when the Civil War irrefutably demonstrated to northerners the moral corruption inherent in a slaveholding society, both denominations took decisive actions to brand slave owning as sin and to campaign for slavery's immediate destruction. In 1860, the Methodist General Conference amended the church discipline to declare the "holding of human beings as chattels" as grounds for expulsion from fellowship. Conservatives, however, destroyed the impact of this action by convincing the general conference to acknowledge the above ruling as merely "advisory." Four years later, the Methodists' rescinded all qualifications on this judgment and also endorsed a federal immediate emancipation program.[60]

The Civil War likewise severed most of the remaining ties between northern and southern Baptists. Southern contributions to northern-based Baptist benevolent associations had been dwindling during the 1850s and nearly disappeared after 1861. By the war's end, both the home and foreign mission societies had endorsed immediate emancipation and begun programs to aid the freedmen. Even local associations that had consistently clung to neutrality regarding slavery finally denounced the institution during the war. The Philadelphia Baptist Association, for example, resolved in 1861 "we confess the sin of human slavery, and earnestly pray for the time when . . . the last vestige of this evil shall be banished from our land."[61]

Although definite progress had taken place in the years since the denominational schisms, there remained serious deficiencies in the northern Methodists' and Baptists' antislavery testimony. Either by their actions or declarations, the northern churches had acknowledged slavery to be an evil system but not inherently sinful. Similar moderate antislavery sentiment had existed in religious circles immediately following the Revolution but had faded within a few decades in the face of slaveholders' resistance to emancipation. By not disciplining slaveholders as they did habitual drunkards, thieves, and adulterers, these religious bodies had sacrificed their most powerful means to attempt to persuade slave owners to manumit their bondspeople. Lacking such an unqualified moral position, the northern Baptists' and Methodists' cautious antislavery professions likewise had a greatly reduced impact on the northern public's toleration of slavery. The inclination of most northern Baptists and Methodists, similar to that of most northern politicians, was to treat slavery as a problem better trusted to southern consciences to solve.

The sentiment of northern religious and political leaders regarding slavery underwent great change in the years following the Methodist and Baptist schisms. However, instead of the churches moving the political system to a stronger antislavery position as the abolitionists had originally envisioned, the reverse had taken place. At best, the large majority of northern churchmen had adopted only a nominal antislavery position before the Civil War, regretting the existence of slavery and hoping for its eventual extinction but refusing to take any precipitous action against an institution so deeply rooted in American social experience. Although such views allowed the northern churches to support the military necessity of a federal emancipation effort during the Civil War, they necessitated no moral commitment on the churches' part to the rights of African Americans. The inadequacy of that position can be seen in the promptness with which the churches joined other northern institutions in abandoning the freedmen during Reconstruction. If the northern churches had adopted an antislavery stand on uncompromising moral grounds at the time of the denominational schisms as the abolitionists had desired, the consciences of the nation might have been sufficiently awakened to the rights of the African Americans to have avoided the tragic racist backlash that followed Reconstruction.

NOTES

1. Examples of such historical accounts are: H. Richard Niebhur, *The Social Sources of Denominationalism* (New York: Holt, 1929), 191–99; Avery Craven, *The Coming of the Civil War* (New York: Scribner, 1942), 201; Chester F. Dunham, *The Attitude of the Northern Clergy toward the South, 1860–1865* (Toledo, Ohio: Gray, 1942), 1–2; Stanley Elkins, *Slavery: A Problem in American Institutional and Intellectual Life* (Chicago: University of Chicago Press, 1959), 184–85; Henry H. Simms, *Emotion at High Tide: Abolition as a Controversial Factor, 1830–1845* (Baltimore: privately printed, 1960), 212; H. Shelton Smith, Robert T. Handy, and Lefferts A. Loetscher, *American Christianity*, vol. 2, *1820–1960* (New York: Scribner, 1963), 178; James G. Randall and David Donald, *The Civil War and Reconstruction*, 2d ed. (Lexington, Mass.: D. C. Heath, 1969), 25–26; Sydney E. Ahlstrom, *A Religious History of the American People* (New Haven, Conn.: Yale University Press, 1972), 657; Donald G. Jones, *The Sectional Crisis and Northern Methodism: A Study in Piety, Political Ethics, and Civil Religion* (Metuchen, N.J.: Scarecrow Press, 1979), 30–33; C. C. Goen, *Broken Churches, Broken Nation: Denominational Schisms and the*

Coming of the Civil War (Macon, Ga.: Mercer University Press, 1985), 1–16; William W. Sweet, "Some Religious Aspects of the Kansas Struggle," *Journal of Religion* 7 (October 1927): 578–81; Liston Pope, "The Negro and Religion in America," in *The Sociology of Religion: An Anthology,* Richard D. Knudten, ed. (New York: Appleton-Century-Croft, 1967), 17–25; Donald G. Mathews, "The Methodist Schism of 1844 and the Polarization of Antislavery Sentiment," *Mid-America* 51 (January 1968): 17–19.

2. Parker Pillsbury, *The Church As It Is; or, The Forlorn Hope of Slavery* (1847; reprint, Concord, N.H.: privately printed, 1885), 46.

3. American and Foreign Anti-Slavery Society, *Thirteenth Annual Report . . . 1853* (New York: The Society, 1853), 97.

4. American Anti-Slavery Society (AASS), *Third Annual Report . . . 1836* (New York, 1836), 29; *Anti-Slavery Record* 3 (October 1837): 113; *Boston Liberator,* 4 October 1834, 1 November 1839, 3 January, 6 March 1840; *New York Emancipator,* 23 April 1836; David B. Davis, "The Emergence of Immediatism in British and American Antislavery Thought," *Mississippi Valley Historical Review* 49 (September 1962): 224; Anne C. Loveland, "Evangelism and "Immediate Emancipation' in American Antislavery Thought," *Journal of Southern History* 32 (May 1966): 181–83, 187.

5. Among the few other pioneer antislavery churches were the Freewill Baptists and the various Scottish Presbyterian sects. See David B. Davis, *The Problem of Slavery in the Age of Revolution* (Ithaca, N.Y.: Cornell University Press, 1975), 42–47, 196–212; Thomas Drake, *Quakers and Slavery in America* (New Haven, Conn.: Yale University Press, 1950), 167–222; Norman A. Baxter, *History of the Freewill Baptists: A Study in New England Separatism* (Rochester, N.Y.: American Baptist Historical Society, 1957), 94–95, 99–101; Andrew E. Murray, *Presbyterians and the Negro—A History* (Philadelphia: Presbyterian Historical Society, 1966), 9–11.

6. To this last group possibly could be added the "Old School" Presbyterian denomination. Lester B. Scherer, *Slavery in the Churches in Early America, 1619–1819* (Grand Rapids, Mich.: William B. Eerdsman, 1975), 126–29, Merton L. Dillon, *The Abolitionists: The Growth of a Dissenting Minority* (DeKalb: Northern Illinois University Press, 1974), 3–12.

7. Donald G. Mathews, *Religion in the Old South* (Chicago: University of Chicago Press, 1977), 66–80; Scherer, *Slavery in the Churches,* 137–41; T. Scott Miyakawa, *Protestants and Pioneers: Individualism and Conformity on the American Frontier* (Chicago: University of Chicago Press, 1964), 174–75, 196–97; Goen, *Broken Churches, Broken Nation,* 79–80; Lewis M. Purifoy, "The Methodist Anti-Slavery Tradition, 1784–1844," *Methodist History* 4 (July 1966): 15–16; Purifoy, "The Southern Methodist Church and the Proslavery Argument," *Journal of Southern History* 32 (December 1966): 325.

8. As quoted in Conrad J. Engelder, "The Churches and Slavery: A Study of the Attitudes toward Slavery of the Major Protestant Denominations" (Ph.D. diss., University of Michigan, 1964), 127.

9. As quoted in Engelder, "Churches and Slavery," 53–61; Goen, *Broken Churches, Broken Nation,* 49–56; Miyawaka, *Protestants and Pioneers,* 150–51.

10. Edward F. Brand, *Illinois Baptists: A History* (Bloomington, Ind.: Pantagraph Printing, 1930), 55.

11. Robert G. Torbet, *A History of the Baptists* (Philadelphia: Judson Press, 1950), 284–86; Merton L. Dillon, "John Mason Peck: A Study of Historical Rationalization," *Journal of the Illinois State Historical Society* 59 (Winter 1957): 390; Engelder, "Churches and Slavery," 57–61.

12. William Goodell, *Slavery and Anti-Slavery: A History of the Great Struggle in Both Hemispheres* (New York: William Harned, 1852), 147–48; Goen, *Broken Churches, Broken Nation,* 78–80, 90–94; Engelder, "Churches and Slavery," 64–71, 118–48.

13. The public's identification of Garrisonianism with comeouterism, anticlericalism, and a variety of heterodox views, however, handicapped their efforts to persuade the churches to adopt abolitionist precepts. Despite its limited effectiveness, the Garrisonians' uncompromising exposure and censure of proslavery religious practices provide the historian with one contemporary standard to measure the antislavery significance of the denominational schisms. *Boston Liberator,* 5 February, 26 March 1847; *New York National Anti-Slavery Standard,* 22 May 1845; Massachusetts Anti-Slavery Society, *Twenty-first Annual Report . . . 1853* (Boston: The Society, 1853), 89; Pennsylvania Anti-Slavery Society, *Thirteenth Annual Report . . . 1850* (Philadelphia, 1850), 45–50; Aileen S. Kraditor, *Means and Ends in American Abolitionism: Garrison and His Critics on Strategy and Tactics, 1834–1860* (New York: Pantheon, 1969), 7–30, 119–22; Lewis Perry, *Radical Abolitionism: Anarchy and the Government of God in Antislavery Thought* (Ithaca, N.Y.: Cornell University Press, 1973), 106–8.

14. A third group of abolitionists, as nearly dissatisfied with the churches as the Garrisonians but not prepared to take the unpopular step of publicly repudiating those institutions, switched their energies from religious to political antislavery action in the late 1830s. These politically oriented abolitionists eventually launched an antislavery political party, the Liberty Party, in 1840. Although the AFASS and the Liberty Party were independent bodies and pursued different antislavery strategies, their memberships overlapped, and the two groups frequently lent support to each other's campaigns. Richard H. Sewell, *Ballots for Freedom: Antislavery Politics in the United States* (New York: Oxford University Press, 1976), 6–25, 20–23, 43–44; James B. Stewart, *Holy Warriors: The Abolitionists and American Slavery* (New York: Hill and Wang, 1976), 81–83, 107–8; Dillon, *The Abolitionists,* 121, 127–28.

15. *American and Foreign Anti-Slavery Society Reporter* 1 (June 1840): 2, 8, 1 (July 1840): 13, 1 (September 1840): 36, 1 (November 1840): 69, 1 (December 1840): 79, 1 (May 1841): 169, 2 (September 1841): 30–31, 2 (June 1842): 56, 2 (January 1843): 119; *Boston Emancipator,* 14 October 1840, 13 May, 7 October, 9 December 1841, 30 June 1842; *Utica (N.Y.) Friend of Man,* 8 April 1840, 20 July, 7, 21, 28 September 1841; Lewis Tappan to William H. Brisbane, 17 December 1842, Lewis Tappan Papers, Manuscripts Division, Library of Congress, Bertram Wyatt-Brown, *Lewis Tappan and the Evangelical War against Slavery* (Cleveland: Press of the Case Western Reserve University, 1969), 198, 248–49.

16. *American and Foreign Anti-Slavery Reporter* 1 (September 1840): 28; also *Anti-Slavery Record* 3 (April 1837): 105, 3 (September 1837): 9–10; *Utica (N.Y.) Friend of Man,* 23 September 1840; *Christian Investigator* 1 (February 1842): n.p.

17. [Methodist Episcopal Church], *Doctrine and Discipline of the Methodist Episcopal Church, 1789,* quoted in Goodell, *Slavery and Anti-Slavery,* 144–50. Also see William Warren Sweet, *Methodism in American History* (1933; n.p., 1961), 237; Mathews, *Slavery and Methodism,* 293.

18. New York *Watchman and Wesleyan Observer,* 10 October 1840; also *American and Foreign Anti-Slavery Reporter* 1 (October 1849): n.p.; *Utica (N.Y.) Friend of Man,* 4 December 1839; Boston *Emancipator,* 14 October 1841; *Cincinnati Herald and Philanthropist,* 27 October 1841.

19. As quoted in Goen, *Broken Churches, Broken Nation,* 80.

20. Lucius C. Matlack, *The Life of Reverend Orange Scott* (New York: Wesleyan Methodist Book Room, 1847), 213; also *Boston Liberator,* 17 July 1840; *Boston Emancipator,* 29 July 1841; Lucius C. Matlack, *Narrative of the Anti-Slavery Experience of a Minister in the Methodist Episcopal Church* (Philadelphia: Merrihew & Thompson, 1845), 22–23; Mathews, *Slavery and Methodism,* 217–18, 229; Engelder, "Churches and Slavery," 132, 141–42.

21. Engelder, "Churches and Slavery," 139–41.

22. *New York True Wesleyan,* 13 January, 20 January, 24 February, 2 March, 25 May 1844; *Utica (N.Y.) Friend of Man,* 26 August 1840, 1 June, 6 July 1841; LaRoy Sunderland to Francis Wright, 2 October 1843, Miscellaneous Manuscripts Collection Manuscripts Division, Library of Congress; Goddell, *Slavery and Anti-Slavery* 490; Smith, *In His Image But,* 107; Goen, *Broken Churches, Broken Nation,* 81–82; J. R. Jacob, "LaRoy Sunderland: The Alienation of an Abolitionist," *Journal of American Studies* 6 (April 1972): 1–9; Chris Padgett, "Hearing the Antislavery Rank-and-File: The Wesleyan Methodist Schism of 1843," *Journal of the Early Republic* 12 (spring 1992): 63–84; Engelder, "Churches and Slavery," 142–43.

23. *Boston Zion's Herald,* 7 December 1842, 25 January 1843; *Cincinnati Western Christian Advocate,* 29 September 1843; *Cuyahoga Falls (Ohio) Christian Witness and Western Reserve Advocate,* 7 September, 28 December 1843, 9 January, 30 April 1844; Lee, *Autobiography,* 251–52; Cameron, *Methodism and Society,* 170–71; Mathews, *Slavery and Methodism,* 233–41, 263.

24. As quoted in Goen, *Broken Churches, Broken Nation,* 83.

25. Hiram Mattison, *The Impending Crisis of 1860: or, The Present Connection of the Methodist Episcopal Church with Slavery, and Our Duty in Regard to It* (New York: Mason Brothers, 1859), 40–42, 114–15; Thomas B. Neely, *American Methodism: Its Divisions and Unification* (New York: Fleming H. Revell, 1915), 69–70; Mathews, *Slavery and Methodism,* 148–64; Goen, *Broken Churches, Broken Nation,* 82–83; Richard J. Carwardine, *Evangelicals and Politics in Antebellum America* (New Haven, Conn.: Yale University Press, 1993), 164–66; Lyons, "Religious Defense of Slavery," 16–17; John N. Norwood, "The Schism in the Methodist Episcopal Church, 1844: A Study of Slavery and Ecclesiastical Politics" (Ph.D. diss., Cornell University, 1915), 130–31; Milton B. Powell, "The Abolitionist Controversy in the Methodist Episcopal Church, 1840–1864" (Ph.D. diss., University of Iowa, 1963), 171–76, 182–89.

26. *New York True Wesleyan,* 4 May, 15 June, 27 July, 3 August 1844; Goodell, *Slavery and Anti-Slavery,* 149–50; Mathews, *Slavery and Methodism,* 269–70.

27. Massachusetts Anti-Slavery Society, *Fourteenth Annual Report . . . 1846* (Boston: The Society, 1846), 68; also *Thirteenth Annual Report . . . 1845,* 52–53; *Boston Liberator,* 21 June 1844, 15 August 1845; Pillsbury, *Church as It Is,* 130.

28. *Hallowell (Maine) Liberty Standard,* n.d., quoted in *New York True Wesleyan,* 29 June, 1844; also Lewis Tappan to William Jay, 14 June 1844, Lewis Tappan Papers, Manuscript Division, Library of Congress; Goodell, *Slavery and Anti-Slavery,* 149–50.

29. *Boston Liberator,* 1 November 1839, 3 January 1840; *Utica (N.Y.) Friend of Man,* 24 August

1841; *Baptist Anti-Slavery Correspondent* 1 (March 1841): 46; *New York Emancipator,* 27 February, 12 March 1840, 9 December 1841, 19 May, 30 June 1842; Andrew T. Foss and Edward Mathews, *Facts for Baptist Churches* (Utica, N.Y.: American Baptist Free Mission Society, 1850), 44–49; Edwin R. Warren, *Free Missionary Principle, or Bible Missions,* 2d ed. (Boston: J. Howe, 1847), 10; Goen, *Broken Churches, Broken Nation,* 90; Engelder, "Churches and Slavery," 64, 67.

30. *American Baptist Memorial* 3 (June 1844): 185; also *Boston Christian Reflector,* 14 May 1844, 25 June 1846; Mary Putnam, *The Baptists and Slavery, 1840–45* (Ann Arbor, Mich.: George Wahr, 1913), 55–59; Engelder, "Churches and Slavery," 70–71.

31. As quoted in Engelder, "Churches and Slavery," 72–73; see also Carwardine, *Evangelicals and Politics,* 169.

32. *Baptist Memorial and Monthly Recorder,* 4 (May 1845): 157; also see Goodell, *Slavery and Anti-Slavery,* 187–88; Mathews, *Religion of the Old South,* 162; Goen, *Broken Churches, Broken Nation,* 95.

33. American Baptist Home Missionary Society, *Thirteenth Annual Report . . . 1845* (New York: The Society, 1845), 7; also *Twelfth Annual Report . . . 1844* (New York: The Society, 1844), 5–6; *American Baptist Memorial* 3 (June 1844): 173–76.

34. American Baptist Home Mission Society, *Minutes . . . 1844,* 5; Carwardine, *Evangelicals and Politics,* 169; Mathews, *Religion in the Old South,* 160–62; Engelder, "Churches and Slavery," 76–77.

35. American Baptist Home Missionary Society, *Thirteenth Annual Report . . . 1845,* 5; *American Baptist Memorial* 3 (June 1844): 173–76; *Boston Christian Reflector,* 8 May 1845; Goodell, *Slavery and Anti-Slavery,* 188–89; Putnam, *Baptists and Slavery,* 38–42, 48–51; Engelder, "Churches and Slavery," 76–78.

36. As quoted in Engelder, "Churches and Slavery," 78.

37. As quoted in Carwardine, *Evangelicals and Politics,* 169.

38. *Utica (N.Y.) Christian Contributor,* 6 December 1848; Foss and Mathews, *Facts for Baptist Churches,* 325–34, 340–44; Putnam, *Baptists and Slavery,* 86–87; Robert A. Baker, *The Southern Baptist Convention and Its People, 1607–1972* (Nashville: Broadman Press, 1974), 197–99, 203, 207; Donald R. Harris, "The Gradual Separation of Southern and Northern Baptists, 1845–1907," *Foundations* 7 (April 1964): 130–31, 139.

39. *Boston Liberator,* 12 May, 16 June 1843, 31 May, 27 September 1844; American Baptist Free Mission Society, *Fourth Annual Report . . . 1847* (Utica, N.Y.: The Society, 1847), 28; Justin A. Smith, *Memoir of Reverend Nathaniel Colver* (Boston: George A. Foxcraft, 1875), 195–200; Warren, *Free Mission Principle,* 11–12; Putnam, *Baptists and Slavery,* 57; Engelder, "Churches and Slavery," 80.

40. *American and Foreign Anti-Slavery Reporter* 2 (July 1845): 42.

41. American and Foreign Anti-Slavery Society, *Thirteenth Annual Report . . . 1853,* 97; *American and Foreign Anti-Slavery Reporter* 2 (September 1844): 5–6, 2 (July 1845): 42; Amos A. Phelps to Lewis Tappan, 2 September 1844, Tappan Papers; Goodell, *Slavery and Anti-Slavery,* 503–8.

42. *Boston Liberator,* 17 May 1844, 15 August 1845; American and Foreign Anti-Slavery Society, *Tenth Annual Report . . . 1850* (New York: The Society, 1850), 60, *Eleventh Annual Report . . . 1851* (New York: The Society, 1851), 73, *Thirteenth Annual Report . . . 1853,* 123; Massachusetts

Anti-Slavery Society, *Fourteenth Annual Report . . . 1846*, 70–71; Stephen S. Foster, *Brotherhood of Thieves; or, A True Picture of the American Church and Clergy* (Boston: Antislavery Office, 1843), 52; Goodell, *Slavery and Anti-Slavery*, 507–08.

43. Lawrence J. Friedman, "'Historical Topics Sometimes Run Dry': The State of Abolitionist Studies," *Historian* 43 (February 1981): 188–91; Mathews, *Slavery and Methodism*, 263–64.

44. *Cincinnati Western Christian Advocate*, 13 September, 4, 11 October 1844; *Boston Christian Watchman*, 14 November 1845, 19 June 1846; *Boston Christian Reflector*, 20 November, 11 December 1845, 2 January, 28 May 1846; *Hartford (Conn.) Christian Secretary*, 5 December 1846; [Methodist Episcopal Church], *Journal of the General Conference of the Methodist Episcopal Church* (New York: Methodist Episcopal Church, 1844), 199–222; George Peck, *Slavery and Episcopacy* (New York: Lane & Tippett, 1845), 111; Mathews, *Slavery and Methodism*, 267–68.

45. Samuel Gregg, *The History of Methodism within the Bounds of the Eire Annual Conference of the Methodist Episcopal Church*, 2 vols. (New York: Nelson and Phillips, 1873), 2:279; *Boston Zion's Herald*, 15 January 1851, 16 January 1856, 5 August 1857, 17 November 1858; *Cincinnati Western Christian Advocate*, 14 April, 22 September, 10 November 1858; *Methodist Quarterly Review* 38 (April 1856): 319, 39 (July 1857): 457–64; William Hosmer, *Slavery and the Church* (Auburn, N.Y.: W. J. Moses, 1853), 36–37, 74–76, 83–84, 98–99, 142; J. Mayland McCarter, *Border Methodism and Border Slavery* (Philadelphia: Collins, 1855), 4–5, 16–18, 87–88; Daniel DeVinne, *The Methodist Episcopal Church and Slavery* (New York: Francis Hart, 1857), 96; Emory S. Bucke, *The History of American Methodism*, 3 vols. (New York: Abingdon Press, 1964), 1:188–89, 199–262, 500–505; Powell, "Abolitionist Controversy in the Methodist Episcopal Church," 171–76, 180–86, 210–19, 226–27, 231–32.

46. Engelder, "Churches and Slavery," 154–55.

47. Engelder, "Churches and Slavery," 79–80.

48. American Baptist Home Mission Society, *Minutes . . . 1849*, 6.

49. *Watchman of the Prairie*, 18 June 1850.

50. American Baptist Home Mission Society, *Annual Report . . . 1852*, 26, 32; *Christian Secretary*, 4 May 1849, 7 June 1850; Harris, "Gradual Separation," 131–33.

51. As quoted in Engelder, "Churches and Slavery," 81.

52. Michigan Baptist State Convention, *Minutes . . . 1858*, 9.

53. John Frank Cady, *The Origin and Development of the Missionary Baptist Church in Indiana* (Franklin, Ind.: Franklin College Press, 1942), 202.

54. *A Review of the Correspondence of Messers. Fulkler and Wayland on the Subject of American Slavery* (Utica, N.Y.: H. H. Cartiss, 1847), 134–35; *Boston Christian Watchman*, 14 November 1845, 19 June 1846; *Cincinnati Cross and Journal*, n.d., quoted in *Boston Christian Reflector*, 26 June 1848; *Hartford (Conn.) Christian Secretary*, 5 December 1845; *Boston Emancipator*, 14 January 1846; American Baptist Free Mission Society, *Annual Report . . . 1857* (Utica, N.Y.: The Society, 1857), 2; Goodell, *Slavery and Anti-Slavery*, 507; Torbet, *History of the Baptists*, 284–86; Justin A. Smith, *A History of the Baptists in the Western States* (Philadelphia: American Baptist Publication Society, 1896), 334–35; Rufus Babcock, *Memoir of John Mason Peck* (Philadelphia: American Baptist Publication Society, 1964), lxvi–lxvii; Harris, "Gradual Separation," 130; Engelder, "Churches and Slavery," 68–69, 81–82.

55. *Boston Liberator,* 15 August 1845; Massachusetts Anti-Slavery Society, *Fourteenth Annual Report . . . 1846,* 69; William Lloyd Garrison to Samuel J. May, 15 August 1845, in Walter M. Merrill and Louis Ruchames, eds., *The Letters of William Lloyd Garrison,* 6 vols. (Cambridge, Mass.: Harvard University Press, 1971–81), 4:3–5; John R. McKivigan, "The Antislavery Comeouter Sects: An Overlooked Abolitionist Strategy," *Civil War History* 26 (June 1980): 142–61.

56. Massachusetts Anti-Slavery Society, *Fourteenth Annual Report . . . 1846,* 72–73; Herman R. Muelder, *Fighters for Freedom: History of Anti-Slavery Activities of Men and Women Associated with Knox College* (New York: Columbia University Press, 1959), 273; Matthew Spinka, ed., *A History of Illinois Congregational and Christian Churches* (Chicago: Congregational and Christian Conference of Illinois, 1944), 147; Irving H. Bartlett, *Wendell Phillips: Brahmin Radical* (Boston: Beacon Press, 1961), 96; Douglas C. Stange, *Patterns of Antislavery Among American Unitarians* (Rutherford, N.J.: Farleigh Dickinson University Press, 1977), 177–90; Samuel C. Pearson, "From Church to Denomination: American Congregationalism in the Nineteenth Century," *Church History* 38 (March 1969): 74.

57. *Boston Christian Watchman,* 8 June 1854; Francis Wayland to "Rev. Dr. Nott," 4 January 1859, Francis Wayland Papers, Brown University Library; Richard H. Watkins, "Baptists of the North and Slavery, 1856–1860," *Foundations* 13 (October–December 1970): 328–29. This argument is made most effectively in Carwardine, *Evangelicals and Politics,* 170.

58. See Carwardine, *Evangelicals and Politics,* 176, 178, 384.

59. *Boston Zion's Herald,* 18 June 1854, 4 March 1857; James Nicols, "Tendency of Current Events in the Moral and Material World," *Methodist Quarterly Review* 34 (January 1852): 82–95; William Gravely, *Gilbert Haven, Methodist Abolitionist: A Study in Race, Religion, and Reform, 1850–1880* (Nashville: Abingdon Press, 1973), 62–63; Carwardine, *Evangelicals and Politics,* 165–66, 234–37, 246–47, 274–76, 298; Victor B. Howard, "The 1856 Election in Ohio: Moral Issues in Politics," *Ohio History* 80 (winter 1971): 24–44; Norton L. Wesley, "The Religious Press and the Compromise of 1850" (Ph.D. diss., University of Illinois, 1959), 56, 156.

60. *New York National Principia,* 16 June 1860, 12 May 1864; *New York Methodist,* 14 July 1864; Luther Lee, *Autobiography of the Reverend Luther Lee* (New York: Phillips & Hunt, 1882), 299, 303, 319; Ralph Morrow, *Northern Methodism and Reconstruction* (East Lansing: Michigan State University Press, 1965), 14–15; Powell, "Abolitionist Controversy in the Methodist Episcopal Church," 226–27; Engelder, "Churches and Slavery," 154–62.

61. As quoted in Engelder, "Churches and Slavery," 88; American Baptist Free Mission Society, *Twenty-first Annual Report . . . 1864* (Utica, N.Y.: The Society, 1864), 3; Harris, "Gradual Separation," 130–44; Powell, "Abolitionist Controversy in the Methodist Episcopal Church," 226–27.

CONTRIBUTORS

JOHN R. MCKIVIGAN is a professor of history at West Virginia University. He is coeditor with John Blassingame of *The Papers of Frederick Douglass* (Yale University Press, five volumes to date). He is the author of numerous scholarly articles and of *The War Against Proslavery Religion: Abolitionism and the Northern Churches, 1830-1865* (Ithaca, N.Y.: Cornell University Press, 1984).

MITCHELL SNAY is the author of *Gospel of Disunion: Religion and Separatism in the Antebellum South* (Cambridge: Cambridge University Press, 1993). He is an associate professor of history at Denison University in Granville, Ohio, and book review editor of the *Journal of the Early Republic*.

DOUGLAS AMBROSE received his Ph.D. from the State University of New York at Binghamton. He is the author of *Henry Hughes and Proslavery Thought in the Old South,* published by Louisiana State University Press in 1996. Ambrose teaches early American and southern history at Hamilton College in Clinton, New York, where he is an assistant professor.

EDWARD R. CROWTHER received his Ph.D. from Auburn University in 1986. His articles and reviews have appeared in a number of publications, including the *Journal of Southern History* and the *Journal of Negro History*. He is Professor of History at Adams State College, Alamosa, Colorado, where he teaches courses in the American Civil War, the American West, and American intellectual history.

HUGH DAVIS received his Ph.D. from Ohio State University in 1969. His *Joshua Leavitt: Evangelical Abolitionist* was published by Louisiana State University Press in 1990. He has also published numerous essays and articles on nineteenth-century reform. Davis is a professor at Southern Connecticut State University, where he teaches courses in nineteenth-century American history.

ROBERT P. FORBES received his Ph.D. from Yale University in 1994. His study of the Missouri Compromise and its aftermath will be published by the University of North Carolina Press. He is a lecturer in history at Yale, where he teaches courses in American cultural, political, and intellectual history.

LAURA MITCHELL received her Ph.D. in American history at Yale University, specializing in nineteenth-century religious and intellectual studies. She is presently an historian with the National Museum of American History at the Smithsonian Institution, where she is working on an exhibition on the history of the Nobel Prize.

CHRISTOPHER H. OWEN received his Ph.D. in history from Emory University in 1991. He is now Assistant Professor of History at Northeastern State University in Tahlequah, Oklahoma, where he teaches courses in southern history and in American social history. He has published several articles and book reviews on the history of southern religion.

CHRIS PADGETT attended the University of California, Davis, where he received his Ph.D. in 1993. He has contributed articles on the abolitionist movement to the *Journal of the Early Republic, Proteus,* and the *American National Biography* project, and he is an assistant professor at Weber State University, where he teaches courses in American and world history.

BETH BARTON SCHWEIGER completed studies at the University of Virginia in 1994. She is the author of *The Conversion of Virginia: Pastors and Their Congregations in the Nineteenth Century,* forthcoming from Oxford University Press.

RANDY J. SPARKS received his Ph.D. in 1989 from Rice University. His book *On Jordan's Stormy Banks: Evangelicalism in Mississippi, 1773–1876* was published in 1994 by the University of Georgia Press. Sparks is an associate professor of history at the College of Charleston where he teaches courses in southern history and the history of religion.

DEBORAH BINGHAM VAN BROEKHOVEN has written articles on Charles Brockden Brown and on women's antislavery activity, including a study on petitioning for *The Abolitionist Sisterhood: Women's Political Culture in Antebellum America* (Jean Fagan Yellin and John C. Van Horne, eds. [Ithaca: Cornell University Press, 1994]). Her book-length study, *Abolitionists Were Female: Rhode Island Women in the Antislavery Network,* is forthcoming from the University of Illinois Press. She is an associate professor of history at Ohio Wesleyan University and is directing a public history project, Grassroots Antislavery Activism in Ohio.

ELIZABETH VARON attended Yale University where she received a Ph.D. in 1993. Her dissertation, "'We Mean to be Counted': White Women and Politics in Antebellum Virginia" is to be published in book form by the University of North Carolina Press. Varon is an assistant professor at Wellesley College, where she teaches courses in U.S. women's history, the Civil War, and southern history.

INDEX

Asbury, Francis, 35, 38, 56–57, 325
Ashtabula, Ohio, 251, 256–57, 265
Ashworth, John, 160
Asia, 279
Atheism, 88, 91
Auburn, Miss., 335
Augusta, Ga., 307
Augusta County, Va., 177–78, 185
Aunt Phillis's Cabin; or, Southern Life As It Is
  (Eastman), 188–89
Austinburg, Ohio, 252

Bacon, Leonard: ABCFM and, 224–25,
  227–28, 231, 238; AHMS and, 232–35;
  American Tract Society and, 235–38,
  245; abolitionists criticize, 228, 237, 239;
  attacks abolitionists, 222–23, 227, 235–
  36; branded as abolitionist, 236, 239; as
  colonizationist, 222–23; as Congregational
  Union president, 234; denominationalism
  and, 232, 234–35, 238; essay on, 221–
  46; Evangelical Alliance and, 227; family
  background of, 222; fugitive slave law
  and, 235; "good slaveholder" concept
  of, 226–27, 229, 231, 235, 238; gradual
  emancipation supported by, 20, 229;
  moderate antislavery views of, 20, 222–25,
  227, 232, 236; New Haven congregation of,
  237; New School Presbyterians criticized
  by, 230, 233–35; nonextensionism and,
  223, 235; opposes proslaveryism, 224–25,
  228, 234, 235–36
Badger, Joseph, 252, 267
Bailey, David T., 99, 276
Bainbridge, Ga., 121
Baldwin, Nancy, 296
Baldwin, Noah: conversion of, 297–98;
  mission controversy and, 310; as
  slaveholder, 296–97, 310–11
Bangs, Nathan, 352
Baptist Church: abolitionists in, 11, 12,
  38–39, 60, 204–5, 208–9, 217, 346–
  47, 349–51, 353–54; in Alabama, 17, 202,
  205–6, 213, 350; amelioration and, 202,
  344; antiabolitionism in, 11, 12, 21, 39–
  40, 208, 349–50, 354; antislavery sentiment
  in, 20, 59, 199–200, 344, 345; benevolent
  movement and, 276, 310, 312, 356;
  Calvinist theology of, 279; colonization
  support in, 172, 197, 202, 344; Columbian

College and, 216; controversies with
  Methodists, 118; decentralized structure
  of, 11, 17, 39–40, 111, 299, 306, 349;
  educational societies of, 275, 310;
  evangelicalism and, 273–95; fellowship
  debate in, 12; Friends of Humanity and,
  345; Fugitive Slave Law (1850) and, 210,
  355; in Georgia, 125, 126, 350; gradual
  emancipation and, 197, 208; in Great
  Britain, 205; governmental structure
  of, 201, 206–7, 211, 274–76, 298, 306,
  326, 342, 345, 349; in Illinois, 345, 350;
  in Indiana, 354; Kansas-Nebraska Act
  and, 210, 211, 355; in Kentucky, 345; in
  Massachusetts, 207, 354; membership of,
  7, 125, 288, 299, 302, 345; in Michigan,
  354; mission controversy divides, 277,
  279, 287–88, 310, 316, 345–46, 353;
  missionary efforts among slaves by, 16,
  341; missionary societies of, 11, 17, 205–
  7, 216, 274, 287–88, 292, 326–27, 343–
  63; in Mississippi, 21, 273–95, 341–42;
  modernist v. traditionalist conflict in, 275–
  76, 277; neutrality toward slavery in, 13,
  110, 349–50, 356; in New York, 208, 345;
  in North Carolina, 59; origins of, 345; in
  Pennsylvania, 356; proslaveryism in, 20, 35,
  60, 160, 190, 195, 198, 199–200, 203, 207–
  9, 213, 215, 282, 296, 350; publication
  societies of, 11, 205, 349, 350–51; racism
  in, 214; "Regulars" in, 275–76, 310, 316;
  relations with government, 111, 117–18;
  sectional schism of, 12, 17, 21–22, 186,
  197, 201, 202, 205, 206, 214, 216, 217, 221,
  222, 273–95, 306–7, 326–27, 343–63;
  "Separates" in, 316; slaves as members,
  180; in the South, 110; in South Carolina,
  199, 205–6, 318, 327; tract society of, 205–
  6, 350–51; views of social order in, 118; in
  Virginia, 21, 35–67, 89, 113, 172, 180, 190,
  195, 296–316. *See also* American Baptist
  Home Mission Society; American Baptist
  Missionary Union (Triennial Convention);
  Brown University; Primitive Baptists
Baptist Foreign Mission Board, 17
Baptist General Tract Society, 350–51
Barclay, John M. G., 163
Barnes, Albert, 92
Barnes, Gilbert H., 6, 83
Bascom, Henry Biddleman, 114–15, 322–23

Beard, Charles A., 3, 24

Beattie, James, 73, 88

Beaufort, S.C., 199

Beecher, Edward, 222, 224–25, 226

Beecher, Henry Ward: abolitionists criticize, 237; Kansas controversy and, 330; moderate antislavery views of, 222, 233, 237

Beecher, Lyman, 253–54, 268

Bender, Thomas, 160

Beneficent Church (Providence), 210

Benevolent movement: and abolitionism, 10, 12–13, 221, 222, 227–28, 231, 236–37, 283–84, 327; antiabolitionism in, 12–13; antimasonry and, 257; Baptists and, 276, 310, 312, 356; benefactors of, 13, 262, 267, 309; colonization linked to, 183–84; conservatives in 13; economics and, 12; education and, 303; evangelicalism, 169–70, 273–74; materialism as obstacle to, 214; Methodists and, 118, 121–24, 311, 314; missions and, 253, 277; modernists and, 277, 278, 284, 289, 319; New York base of, 283; political activism contrasted with, 171, 191; Presbyterians and, 191, 274, 303; slavery issue divides, 274; southern influence in, 11, 13, 189, 303, 306, 309; as subversive to slavery, 176; in West, 262; 309; women in, 20, 170–72, 175, 176, 180, 187–88

Berkeley County, Va., 45

Berlin Wall, 69

Bible, 1, 69–70; abolitionists use, 8, 70–71, 138, 141, 149, 165, 208, 330, 331; blacks and, 23, 204, 226; creation described in, 319; distributed to slaves, 236; distribution of, 351; freemasonry and, 257; fugitive slave issue and, 20, 134–65; Golden Rule in, 136; higher criticism and, 318–20, 327; Abraham Lincoln uses, 138; literalism and, 8, 15, 72, 113, 114, 318–19, 327, 333–34; materialism condemned by, 213; New Testament in, 2, 16, 43, 44, 52, 71, 113, 139, 141, 145–49, 151, 156–58, 163–64, 189, 208, 213, 218, 276, 301, 331, 332–33; Old Testament in, 2, 6, 8, 15–16, 23, 42, 71, 72, 93, 113, 115, 117, 139, 141, 142, 144, 149, 153, 189, 301, 318–19, 322, 332–33, 338; philology and, 140, 161; scientific rationalism and, 318; secession defended

by, 19; slavery attacked by, 72, 149, 162, 165, 200, 208, 308, 327, 332; slavery defended by, 2, 8, 15–16, 42–44, 45, 46–47, 48, 66, 70–71, 75, 76, 92–94, 100, 105, 112, 113, 115, 138, 146, 162, 189, 200, 208, 222, 282, 288, 296, 301, 307–8, 327, 328, 332, 335, 337, 341; slaves' views of, 6; social reform and, 315, 319. *See also* Israelites

Biblical Recorder, 336

Bidwell, William H., 223

Bill of Rights, 79

Birmingham, England, 205

Birney, James Gillespie, 2

Black Belt, 123

Blackford, Mary Berkeley Minor: benevolent activities and, 176; as colonizationist, 174–75, 177, 179–82, 187, 190; family of, 174–75; as slaveholder, 181; supports gradual emancipation, 177, 178, 181–82, 187; *Uncle Tom's Cabin* enjoyed by, 189

Blackford, William, 174, 181

Blacks: as abolitionists, 23, 181; as Methodists, 274, 276, 288; in Massachusetts, 274. *See also* Free blacks; Slaves

Blagden, George W., 224–25

Blakesley, James, 202

Blanchard, Jonathan, 231, 232

Bledsoe, Alfred Taylor, 188

"Bloody shirt," 82

Blue Ridge, 46

Blythe, James, 49

Boardman, Henry, 151

Bode, Frederick, 133

Bowdoin College, 154

Bohemia, 74

Border states: Baptists in, 345; churches in, 12; constitution of, 75; Cumberland Presbyterians in, 276; gradual antislavery sentiment in, 328; manumission in, 15; Methodists in, 114–15, 320–24, 315, 348, 352–53; New School Presbyterians in, 327–28; slavery in, 12, 15, 75, 134, 323, 353

Boring, Isaac, 116

Boston, Mass.: abolitionists in, 176, 182, 188, 208, 211, 260, 331; Baptists of, 207; churches of, 147; fugitive slaves in, 148–49, 152, 331; nativist mobs in, 331–32; Transcendentalists in, 331; Unitarians in, 162, 331

Oakland College (Miss.), 278, 292
Oberlin, Ohio, 263, 271
Oberlin College: abolitionists and, 21, 255, 262; Charles G. Finney at, 254; founding of, 262; manual labor at, 262; perfectionist theology of, 230, 264–65; relationship with Ohio churches, 262–65, 271
Oberlin Evangelist, 264
Ohio: abolitionists in, 21, 263; antimasonry in, 256–57; colonizationism and, 260–63; Congregationalists in, 215, 230, 249–72; Democrats in, 258; Methodists in, 118, 219, 320, 322, 324, 353; Native Americans in, 251; New School Presbyterians in, 249–72; Presbyterians in, 252, 264, 265, 282; slavery controversy in, 21; temperance movement in, 258
Ohio Annual Conference (Methodist), 322, 324
Ohio Observer, 260, 261, 268
Ohio River, 134, 250, 320
Ohio Synod, 265
Ohio Wesleyan University, 219
Old School Presbyterians: antiabolitionism in, 249, 255, 328; Calvinism of, 249, 266; competition with New School by, 234; founding of, 16–17, 249, 286; fugitive slave law and, 141; Plan of Union and, 229; southern support for, 17, 255; toleration of slavery in, 127, 230–31, 243, 327–28, 358
Onesimus, 145–47, 151, 153, 163, 331
Organic sin, 226
Ostrogorski, Mosei, 83
Oswald, 88
Overby, Basil H., 122
Oviatt, Herman, 258, 260, 269, 270
Owen, Christopher, 20, 22
Oxford Movement, 103

Padgett, Chris, 21, 22
Page, Anne R., 174
Palestine, 148
Paley, William, 84, 92, 216
Papacy, 4, 19, 89
Parkersburg, W.V., 322
Parkhurst, John L., 85
Parton, James, 93
Pastoralism, 98

Paternalism, 19, 35–36, 42–44, 50–57, 62, 66, 183, 204, 283
Patriarchal culture, 36, 40, 44–47, 48–50
Patterson, Orlando, 100
Pattillo, Henry, 59
Paul: epistles of, 113, 139, 145, 147–49, 151, 159, 163; views on slavery, 71, 113, 148, 331, 332
Payne, James B., 112
Payne, Joshua, 122
Peck, George, 352
Peck, John Mason, 352
Peggy (slave), 181
Pennsylvania, 72, 87, 151; abolitionists in, 263; Baptists in, 356; colonizationists in, 184–85; fugitive slaves in, 154; Presbyterians in, 267
Pentateuch, 318–19
Perfectionism: abolitionism and, 10, 333; Congregationalists and, 230; New School Presbyterians and, 264; Oberlin College and, 230, 264–65
Perkins, George W., 148–49, 225
Perkins, John, Jr., 106
Personal liberty laws, 323, 325
Peters, Absalom, 232, 233
Pharisees, 149
Phelps, Amos A., 147; attacks ABCFM, 224, 225; Leonard Bacon debates, 226; critical of Congregational Church, 222
Philadelphia, 72, 87, 151, 188; colonizationists in, 184–85; Quakers in, 164
Philadelphia Baptist Association, 356
Philemon, Epistle to, 113, 139, 147–49, 151, 159, 163
Phillips, Wendell, 218
Philology, 140, 143, 147, 161
Piedmont region, 46, 300
Pierce, George F., 112, 116, 121–22, 125; sectionalism and, 122–23; Whig politics of, 123
Pierce, Lovick, 115, 118, 123; opposes reopening of slave trade, 325–26; represents southern Methodists, 321, 323
Pierce, Reddick, 118
Pietist sects, 7, 23, 122; antislavery in, 344; opposition to reformism in, 10–11. *See also* Quakers
Pillsbury, Parker, 236, 343

Snay, Mitchell, 186
Socialism, 319, 320, 333
Solomon, 322
Sons of Temperance, 122
South: as agrarian region, 3; antiabolitionism
  in, 1, 15, 21, 112, 317–42; anti-
  northernism in, 317–18, 331–33;
  antislavery sentiment in, 37, 76; benevolent
  movement and, 11, 13, 189, 303, 306,
  309; class conflict in, 18, 21, 274, 329;
  colonization support in, 15, 20, 77, 172,
  175, 186, 189; economic modernization of,
  18, 278; education in, 115, 199, 201, 202,
  211, 213, 220, 289; English critics of, 189;
  evangelicalism in, 5, 21, 37, 117–18, 125,
  273, 274, 289, 317–42; fictional defense
  of, 188–89; honor of, 17; localism of,
  77; modernization and, 21, 278;
  nonslaveholders in, 20, 119, 126, 130;
  northern condemnation of, 3;
  Presbyterians in, 110, 118; professional
  class of, 305–6; proslaveryism in, 2–3, 7,
  8, 15–16, 17, 22, 37, 70, 227; religion of, 5,
  17; secession and, 15, 19, 21, 111, 122, 123,
  317, 329; sectionalism in, 17, 21, 187; slaves
  in, 6; social order of, 5, 15, 18, 54, 58, 92,
  115, 305–6; suspicion of social reform
  in, 170–71, 191, 329, 332; temperance
  movement in, 122, 124, 191, 333; women's
  status in, 5, 334. See also under individual
  states
South Carolina, 43, 59; abolitionists from,
  180; antiabolitionism in, 198, 318; Baptists
  in, 199, 205–6, 318, 327; churches in, 15,
  16; education in, 66, 91, 93; Federalists in,
  78; Methodists in, 16, 56, 115, 323, 324–
  25; nonslaveholders in, 130; nullification
  and, 260; Presbyterians in, 66, 112–13;
  proslaveryism in, 15, 66, 75, 76, 78, 80, 96,
  112–13, 187–88, 199, 327, 334; secession
  of, 19; slave rebellions in, 76; slaves in, 16,
  56, 191
South Carolina Annual Conference
  (Methodist), 324–25
South Carolina College, 66, 91, 93
Southampton County, Va., 175–76
Southern Aid Society, 234
Southern Argus (Norfolk, Va.), 188
Southern Baptist, 331

Southern Baptist Bible Board, 351
Southern Baptist Convention: American
  Tract Society and, 327; antiabolitionism
  of, 326; benevolence and, 302, 326–27;
  founding of, 17, 287–88, 307, 326;
  governing structure of, 306–7, 326–27;
  membership of, 302; proslaveryism of, 212
Southern Christian Advocate, 115, 117
Southern Churchman (Va.), 172
Southern Lady, The (Scott), 191
Southern nationalism, 17, 189, 211, 220
Southern Presbyterian Review, 66
Southwest, 17, 99
Spain, 74
Sparks, Randy, 21, 22
Sparta, Ga., 112
Spiritualism, 333
St. Clair, Arthur, 251
St. Claire, Augustine, 94
St. Claire, Ophelia, 94
States' rights: Edmund Ruffin and, 189;
  Alexander H. Stephens and, 2; southern
  churches and, 125; viewed as defense of
  slavery, 76–78, 79, 82, 336
Stearns, Jonathan, 152
Stephens, Alexander H., 341
Stewart, Austin, 181
Stone, Thomas, 154–56
Stoneham, Mass., 153
Storrs, Charles, 261
Storrs, George, 347
Storrs, Richard S., 233, 239
Stout, Henry S., 80
Stowe, Calvin, 140, 222, 224
Stowe, Harriet Beecher, 94, 134, 188–89
Strawberry District Association (Va.), 39, 40
Stringfellow, Thornton, 113, 195, 296, 300–
  301
Stuart, Moses, 8; antiabolitionism of,
  141; antislavery opinions of, 152; as
  colonizationists, 164; fugitive slave law
  supported by, 139–44, 148–49; moral
  philosophy and, 140–41; debates
  Unitarians, 140
Stuart dynasty, 124
Sugrue, Michael, 91
Sunday schools, 147, 303; in Mississippi,
  278–79; in Virginia, 187–88, 310
Sunderland, LaRoy, 324, 347